Foreign Affairs

66-15155 (12-20-66)

THE
COMMUNIST
PARTY
APPARATUS

FOUNDATION FOR FOREIGN AFFAIRS SERIES

NUMBER 1:

Globe and Hemisphere: Latin America's Place in the Post-War Foreign Relations of the United States, by J. Fred Rippy

NUMBER 2:

Massive Retaliation: The Policy and Its Critics, by Paul Peeters

NUMBER 3:

Peaceful Coexistence: An Analysis of Soviet Foreign Policy, by Wladyslaw W. Kulski

NUMBER 4:

Germany's Eastern Frontiers: The Problem of the Oder-Neisse Line, by Zolton Michael Szaz, with a foreword by Harold Zink

NUMBER 5:

Strategic Intelligence and the Shape of Tomorrow, by William M. McGovern

NUMBER 6:

The German Opposition to Hitler: An Appraisal, by Hans Rothfels, translated by Lawrence Wilson

NUMBER 7:

Berlin and the Future of Eastern Europe, edited by David S. Collier and Kurt Glaser

NUMBER 8:

From Purge to Coexistence: Essays on Stalin's and Khrushchev's Russia, by David J. Dallin

NUMBER 9:

Western Integration and the Future of Eastern Europe, edited by David S. Collier and Kurt Glaser

NUMBER 10:

Western Policy and Eastern Europe, edited by David S. Collier and Kurt Glaser

NUMBER 11:

The Communist Party Apparatus, by Abdurakhman Avtorkhanov

THE
COMMUNIST
PARTY
APPARATUS

by

Abdurakhman Avtorkhanov

Published in cooperation with
Foundation for Foreign Affairs, Inc.

HENRY REGNERY COMPANY · CHICAGO

FOUNDATION FOR FOREIGN AFFAIRS SERIES, NUMBER 11

The Foundation for Foreign Affairs, 154 East Superior Street, Chicago, Illinois 60611, is a non-profit corporation devoted to the promotion of a wider understanding of international relations—political, economic and cultural. Books in the Foundation for Foreign Affairs Series are published in the interest of public information and debate. They represent the free expression of their authors and do not necessarily indicate the judgment and opinions of the Foundation.

FOREWORD

"Give us an organization of revolutionaries—and we will overturn Russia!"
Lenin, *What Is To Be Done?*, 1902.

"We have conquered Russia. . . . Now we must govern Russia."
Lenin, *The Immediate Tasks of the Soviet Government*, 1918.

"The Russian model reveals to all countries something that is very essential in their near and inevitable future."
Lenin, *Left-Wing Communism, An Infantile Disorder*, 1920.

HISTORY has witnessed three main forms of government: autocracy, oligarchy and democracy. The twentieth century has contributed a new form of rule, heretofore unknown: *partocracy,* which is entitled to take its place alongside the classical forms of rule.

The appearance of this new form of rule is linked to the seizure of state power by the Communists in Russia in 1917. The so-called Western totalitarian regimes arose as a reaction to and as weak imitations of this new phenomenon.

In the Soviet Union there exists a special applied political science dealing with this new form of rule. This science is not only unknown in the West, even in the Soviet Union it is considered an esoteric science and is taught only to the party elite. It has been given a very awkward title, but one that is accurate in its combination of words: "Party Construction." It is taught as a scientific discipline in all Soviet political schools, while in the higher party schools there are even special departments for "Party Construction." The subject of this science, according to the official definition in *Kommunist* (No. 2, 1961) is as follows:

> *Party construction,* a component part of the Leninist doctrine of the party, is the science of the principles of construction, the forms of organization and the rules of the party's internal life, the methods for its direction of organizational and ideological activities, economic, cultural, state and social organizations of the working people.

The present study is devoted to this science and this form of rule. While I have accepted the Soviet definition of the subject matter of this science, I find that it is more accurate and exact to call it "partocracy."

The term partocracy should be understood to mean not only this form of one-party rule unique in the history of state formations but the science and art of this rule as well.

Since I have accepted the Soviet definition of the subject matter, I am adhering to Soviet indications as to the sources of partocracy and the sphere of its competence. Therefore the study begins with a description of Leninist doctrine regarding the party, including ways and means of seizing power, forms of organization and methods of directing this new type of regime. It then goes on to discuss party policy regarding the creation of a new state bureaucracy and traces the process of social transformation of the party. On the basis of these materials it examines the evolution of the party structure as directed in the party statutes. The next section deals with the important but little-understood organization and functioning of the party organs at all levels, from the primary party organizations to the Central Committee of the Communist Party of the Soviet Union. This is followed by an analysis of the ways and means by which the party controls both the state executive organs and the so-called social organizations, such as the soviets, the youth societies and the trade unions. The study closes with an analysis of the party's nationality policy and the relation between Soviet foreign policy and the party's theory of world revolution.

Throughout, the study is historical, so that the reader may compare origins with results, theory with practice. It does not attempt to cover the party's history as a whole, or Communist ideology as such. These are touched upon only to the extent they illuminate the central theme, the organization of the party and its functioning in practice.

The study is based on primary source materials. These include resolutions and decisions of party conferences and congresses, resolutions and decrees of plenary sessions of the party Central Committee, current instructions issued by the Central Committee apparatus and the writings of the founders of bolshevism. All these sources are approached with the critical caution required in making use of sources of any kind, a caution particularly essential in using Communist party sources.

The Soviet Communist party apparatus leads a double life—an outer, official life and an inner, secretive life. It directs the course of the party and the government in a dual manner: on the one hand by published laws and rules based on the CPSU statutes and the Constitution of the U.S.S.R., and on the other by unwritten or at least unpublished laws and rules based on traditional "party apparatus law." The first category consists of formal laws that do not always—in fact, rarely—mean what they say. The second category consists of the real laws, which although not in print or existing only in the form of secret decisions, instructions and regulations of the party Central Committee, nevertheless form the actual basis for the functioning of the Communist party machine. The façade of the party and government apparatus is constructed according to the first type of laws, but the apparatus operates under the second.

The remarkable communist technique of rule; the unique relationship between directing and executing organs; the gradual but unrelenting transfer of state power from official government organs to party organs and the subsequent conversion of the state apparatus into a technical and auxiliary organ serving the party apparatus and making the party bureaucracy the actual ruling force and the government bureaucracy its executive organ; and, most important, the transformation of the party apparatus into a force not only superior to the state but superior to the party itself—none of this is to be found in the written laws of either the state or the party. But it is the essence of unwritten party apparatus law.

Under these circumstances, a study of the technique of bolshevist rule based solely on official party documents can only be incomplete. The student must study not only theory, what the party says about itself, but practice, what the party does. Thus the most important source, though an invisible one, of the present study as a whole is the practice of one-party rule in the U.S.S.R. The analysis and generalization of its unwritten laws and standards, at times elucidated from official party doctrine, at times directly contradicting it, was the most difficult part of the research. Here my first-hand knowledge of the party apparatus gained from working in it has proved indispensable.

The usual study of the organs of party power is limited to an analysis of the functions and functioning of the higher levels of the party and government pyramid. Although the entire party structure is created from the top and these higher levels are the summit, they top a gigantic base composed of elementary power cells. These are the basic elements that gradually grow in complexity and functional importance to make the peak of the pyramid—the Central Committee of the Soviet Communist party and the government. The strength of the communist regime resides, not in the party and government summits, but in its brilliant hierarchical system of power and the use made of that power, resting on the mass base of the party itself and a great network of organizations subordinate to the party. It is this mass base that chiefly distinguishes Soviet partocracy from autocracy or oligarchy. The weakness of the usual oligarchical regime lies in the fact that it not only lacks such a mass base, it relies on the authority of outstanding individuals and not on a permanent structural system. The death of the chief oligarch or the internecine struggle for power among those at the top has in many instances led to a change in the very form of government. Nothing of this kind has as yet resulted from changes in the individuals concerned or from internecine struggle among the leaders in the Kremlin. It may indeed be said that communist dictators come and go, but the communist dictatorship remains. Changes of individuals do not threaten the collapse of communist power, precisely because its solidity and stability do not depend upon an individual, as in the case of a dictatorship, or upon a few individuals, as in the case of an oligarchy, but on a structural system. If dissolution of the system should, however, begin to take place from below, even so great a master of the art of wielding power as Stalin would be unable to hold his throne. For this reason it is important to study the Soviet regime as a structural system of power cells and a hierarchy of party and sub-party organizations, or, to use Leninist terms, to study the apparatus of power in the U.S.S.R. as a unified party machine, in which not only the motor but every separate working part separately and all the transmission belts taken together are important. This was the logic behind the author's decision to analyze the system from the bottom up, that is, from the primary cells of power to its peak in the Kremlin.

A. AVTORKHANOV
Garmisch-Partenkirchen, 1966

Acknowledgements

I acknowledge with gratitude my debt to those whose assistance made this work possible—my school, my students and my colleagues. I am under special obligation to Dr. Stefan T. Possony, who was kind enough to read the entire manuscript and make valuable comments and suggestions. I am particularly proud of the competence of my students, who translated a series of supplements, the last chapters and the appendixes. I am most grateful to the Institute for the Study of the U.S.S.R., Munich, Germany, with which I have been associated for many years, for translating the basic text.

My thanks also to Mary Sanders and my son Tamerlane Kunta for assisting me in putting the footnotes and references into their proper order.

No one but the author, of course, is to be held responsible for the opinions, statements and conclusions drawn in the text. I have read the English text and consider it in general to be a competent translation of my Russian manuscript.

A. AVTORKHANOV
Garmisch-Partenkirchen, 1966

CONTENTS

Chapter I   Lenin's Doctrine of the Party   1

Chapter II   Lenin's Doctrine of the Revolution   19

Chapter III   Lenin's Doctrine of Dictatorship   42

Chapter IV   The Party State—The Party Cadres   58

Chapter V   The Social Transformation of the Communist
                   Party of the Soviet Union   75

Chapter VI   The Evolution of the Party's Statutes   96

Chapter VII   The Party Bureau and the Party Committee   117

Chapter VIII   The District Committee and the Town
                   Committee   133

Chapter IX   The Regional Committee and the Provincial
                   Committee   153

Chapter X   The Central Committees of the Constituent
                   Republics   170

Chapter XI   The Central Committee of the CPSU   192

Chapter XII   The Party and the Government (Soviets)   228

Chapter XIII   The Party and the Trade Unions   239

Chapter XIV   The Komsomol as a Party Tool   250

Chapter XV   The Party's Management of the National
                   Economy   263

Chapter XVI   The Party's Leadership of the Army   290

Chapter XVII   The Party's Direction of the Secret Police   307

Chapter XVIII   The Party and the Nationality Question   318

Chapter XIX   The Party and Foreign Policy   345

Chapter XX   Conclusion: Partocracy   369

Appendixes   377

Notes   391

Index   413

List of Tables

1. Young Specialists Graduating from Institutes for Higher Education, 1933–38 63

2. Increase in Number of Specialists in U.S.S.R., 1926–59..... 65

3. Students Attending Military Schools, 1931–33............ 71

4. Analysis of Party Membership, 1905–32................ 77

5. Analysis of Increase in Party Membership, 1917–21....... 77

6. Class Structure of Prerevolutionary Russia and Modern U.S.S.R. 81

7. Estimate of Working Population of U.S.S.R............. 82

8. Social Composition of New Party Membership in Belorussia.. 87

9. Professions of Party Members, July 1, 1961............. 88

10. Leading Members of Governmental and Party Bureaucracy.. 88

11. Social Status of Recruits to Communist Party of Soviet Union 89

12. Social and Professional Recruits to Ranks of Party in Rural Areas 89

13. Communists' Educational Qualifications, July, 1961........ 90

14. Communist Specialists in National Economy............. 90

15. Distribution of Communists in Various Branches of National Economy, July 1, 1961.............................. 91

16. Distribution of Communists in Rural Areas by Work Categories 91

17. Growth of Party, 1956–61............................ 92

18. Results of 1961 Party Committee Elections............. 113

19. Cells in Soviet Communist Party, 1931................. 122

20. Distribution of Primary Party Organizations in Branches of Economy and Administration, October 1, 1961........... 130

21. Population Statistics of Republics..................... 170

22. National Composition of CPSU, July 1, 1961............ 171

23. Composition of Party Central Committees and Inspection Commissions of Twelve Union Republics................ 174

24. Slav Representation in Party Central Committees of
    Non-Slav Republics 175

25. Functions of Republic Central Committee's Departments.... 183

26. Distribution of Organs of State Administration and Public
    Organizations Among Departments of Central Committee
    of CPSU 201

27. Social and Professional Composition of Personnel of Central
    Committee and Central Inspection Commission of CPSU.... 215

28. Growth in Number of Ministries....................... 264

29. Growth of Military Party Organizations................. 297

30. Percentage of Urban Population in Union Republics....... 323

31. Percentage of Urban Population in Autonomous Republics of
    Russian Republic 324

32. Urban and Rural Populations in Union Republics by Language 324

33. Urban and Rural Populations in Autonomous Republics
    by Language 325

34. Percentage of Persons Employed in National Economy..... 326

35. Percentage of Inhabitants in Rural Areas in Union Republics
    in Intellectual Occupations........................... 326

36. Indigenous Population in Union Republics............... 331

37. Percentage of Russian and Indigenous Populations in
    Autonomous Republics 331

38. Percentage of Russian and Indigenous Populations in
    Autonomous *Oblasts* 332

39. Distribution of Indigenous Population of Union and
    Autonomous Republics, 1959........................ 333

40. Linguistic Russification in Soviet Union Republics......... 335

41. Percentage of Total Indigenous Population of Autonomous
    Republics Using Russian or Another Language as Mother
    Tongue 336

42. Percentage of Nationalities Having No Specific Territory
    Using Russian or Another Language as Mother Tongue..... 336

43. Number of Scientists in Autonomous Republics........... 340

44. Number of Scientists in Autonomous *Oblasts*............. 340

* CHAPTER I *

Lenin's Doctrine of the Party

BOLSHEVISM is not an ideology, it is an organization. Its ideology is Marxism, revised and brought up-to-date as required by the interests of the organization. Bolshevism is not a political party in the usual meaning of the term. The Bolsheviks themselves call it a party, but with the significant reservation that it is a party of a new type. Bolshevism is not a "movement," based on a mosaic of class representation, amorphic organizational principles, an emotional shifting of its masses and an improvised leadership. Bolshevism is a hierarchical organization built from the top down and organized on the basis of a specific body of doctrine precisely developed in theory and applied in practice. The organizational forms of bolshevism are subject to constant change in response to changing conditions of time and place, but its internal structural system remains unaltered. This system is the same today as it was before the Bolsheviks came into power.

Bolshevism was born as a closed hierarchical organization under the conditions existing in the autocratic Russia of the tsars. Bolshevism today is a closed hierarchical organization under the conditions existing in the autocratic Russia of the Bolsheviks.

Conditions of time and of environment fully explain, though they may not justify, the nature of the internal structure of bolshevism. These conditions will be discussed after an examination of the motives and principles of the organization of bolshevism that guided its founder, Lenin.

At the beginning of the twentieth century Russia lagged more than a century behind the West in its internal political development. In spite of the sweeping changes introduced in the 1860's by the Great Reforms of Alexander II—the abolition of serfdom; the reform of the court system, of education and of censorship; and the creation of the *zemstvo*, local self-government organs—the absolute monarchy remained on the whole unshaken. These reforms, resulting in the large-scale onset of the Industrial Revolution, with consequent effects upon the social classes, placed the absolute monarchy in the inescapable dilemma of having to carry the reforms on to their logical conclusion, thus transforming the absolute monarchy into a constitutional monarchy, or limiting their action in order to strengthen the monarchical principle of government. The dynasty chose the second road.

1

It is easy to condemn this choice, but it is important to try to understand it. Russia lacked the necessary conditions for introducing a parliamentary system. The main population of the country, the peasantry, was just emerging from serfdom and was largely illiterate. The Russian bourgeoisie, itself recruited for the most part from the peasantry, directed the economic system effectively but was politically impotent. Even the class that formed the foundation for tsarism, the gentry, was split into two camps, one destined to become a serving bureaucracy with no political ambitions whatever, the other to form an opposition, some of its members as nihilists and some as terrorists. Under these conditions, in an illiterate and immense country, a country lacking in educated classes and without traditions of self-government, a parliamentary monarchy would have been only a façade for an oligarchical government or a transitional step toward another type of personal dictatorship without the legal guarantees existing under the monarchy.

Thus the autocracy lacked a base in society and was maintained only by its organization—a bureaucratic government and a military and police security force—while the social classes that might have been expected to be called upon by history to lead Russia along the "Western path" were too weak, too dispersed and too lacking in ambition.

Under these conditions, Lenin in 1902 wrote his book asking *What Is To Be Done?* to bring down this "superclass" bureaucratic autocracy. In a paraphrase of Archimedes' famous saying, he provided the answer that introduced a new era: "Give us an organization of revolutionaries and we will turn Russia upside down."[1]

Lenin not only provided an answer, he worked out a complete theory of the ways and means of realizing his goal, which may be called a plan for organizing a revolution. The plan will be discussed in detail in a following chapter; it is important at this point to analyze its central kernel—the problem of the party—which for Lenin was the decisive "subjective factor" of the revolution. In *What Is To Be Done?* Lenin for the first time set forth the main organizational principles for creation of the Bolshevist party, as a part of his general plan for organizing a revolution.

Lenin took his point of departure from his main (and undoubtedly anti-Marxist) thesis formulated as early as 1898, namely, that "without a revolutionary theory there cannot be a revolutionary movement."[2] Organization was the alpha and omega of Lenin's plan of revolution. "The proletariat has no other weapon for the struggle for power except organization,"[3] said Lenin, and to this principle he remained true throughout his life.

In spite of his Marxist upbringing Lenin had little interest in Marxism as a scientific theory. He did, however, recognize the need for it as a means to an end, as an ideological weapon for the political purpose of creating his organization of revolutionaries. In this connection Lenin remained true to the dialectic—he passed Marxism, a product of the European mind, through the filter of the specific Russian circumstances, removing from it all that was Utopian and lofty in order to make use of all that was practical and dynamic. In one of his earliest writings, Lenin proposed that there be "worked out [from Marxism] the form of organization most suited to our conditions for spreading social democratism and forging the workers into a political force."[4]

By organization Lenin meant something more than the usual political party, union or league.

In view of the exceptional and decisive importance of this question in connection with the militant arsenal of both historical bolshevism and contemporary communism, it must be examined more closely. Lenin's organization of revolutionaries was not a simple organization but a *system of organizations* with two networks: a *vertical network* made up of the party organizations themselves in a strictly hierarchical order and an equally rigid pattern of subordination; and a *horizontal network* of supplementary organizations, ostensibly nonpartisan but in practice intended to execute the will of the vertical network.

First and above all there must be created a supreme and tightly knit organization of party leaders, what Lenin called an organization of professional revolutionaries. He added:

> Without scores of talented, tested leaders, professionally trained and taught by long schooling, excellently in tune one with another, a consistent struggle of any class whatever is impossible in contemporary society. . . . And I assert that (1) not one revolutionary movement can be consistent without an organization of leaders that is strong and maintains its primacy; (2) the broader the masses spontaneously attracted into the struggle, forming the basis of the movement and participating in it, the more urgent is the necessity in such an organization and the more consistent must be that organization; (3) such an organization must consist chiefly of persons professionally occupying themselves with revolutionary activity; (4) in an autocratic country, the more the composition of such an organization is narrowed down to the participation in it of only such members as occupy themselves professionally with revolutionary activity and have received professional training in the art of struggle with the political police, the more difficult will it be to catch such an organization; and (5) the broader will be the composition of persons both from the working class and from the other classes of society who will have the possibility of participating in the movement and actively working in it.[5]

Under a police regime, then, there must be created an organization of professional revolutionaries whose conspiratorial technique could compete successfully with the similar technique of the political police. This organization must be at the same time an intelligence and counterintelligence organization in the technique of revolutionary work and a "brain trust" and propaganda staff in the general management of the revolutionary underground. Lenin also said:

> Scores of tested revolutionaries professionally *no less trained
> than our police* will centralize all the conspiratorial sides of the
> matter, the preparation of leaflets, the working out of the approxi-
> mate plan, the appointing of a team of directors from each district
> of the city, for each factory quarter, for each educational institu-
> tion, etc.[6]

Lenin rejected as naive and ridiculous the demand that the party
organization be based on the principle of democracy under the conditions existing in a police state. The organization must be constructed
on the strictly conspiratorial principle, with dictatorial direction. Under
the conditions in an autocracy, said Lenin, there can be no democratism,
since democratism

> in the dark recesses of an autocracy, under a regime of gendarmes,
> is only an empty and dangerous game . . . since in fact never did
> any revolutionary organization introduce democracy or can intro-
> duce it. . . . It only makes broad defeats easier for the police. . . .
> The only serious organizational principle for the activity of our
> movement must be: the strictest conspiracy, the most severe selec-
> tion of members, the training of professional revolutionaries.[7]

Party organizations, accordingly, must be headed by leaders appointed
by the party center, not elected by the organizations themselves. The
center is a small group chosen from among the professional revolutionaries themselves; once it is elected it administers freely. It might appear
at first glance that there is nothing original in such a system of organization, that it is the usual type of conspiratorial organization and is illustrated by scores of examples in countries under absolute rule. The plans
and organizations of Babeuf, of Auguste Blanqui, of the Decembrists
and of the Narodniks seemed similar. But the similarity is only superficial. Lenin's planned conspiracy of professional revolutionaries was
basically different from all previous conspiracies: in the first place, as a
system of organization; and in the second, as a hierarchy of mass organizations. The Blanquists and the Narodniks were members of the intelligentsia who aimed at the seizure of power by conspiracy or by acts
of terrorism directed against chiefs of state. Lenin's organization of
professional revolutionaries was the intellectual head, the trained leadership, of the mass organizations of workers, peasants and students
who served as a base for the purpose of seizing power through the
organization of a people's ("proletarian") revolution, either by a single
act, an uprising, or by a long process, a civil war.

In *One Step Forward—Two Steps Back,* written in 1904, in which
he summarized the results of the Second Congress of the Russian Social
Democratic Labor party and answered his opponents, Lenin declared:

> At the Second Congress I noted: one must not think that party
> organizations must consist only of professional revolutionaries;
> we need the most variegated organizations of all types, ranks and

shades, beginning with very narrow and secret and conspiratorial and ending with very broad, free *lose Organizationen*.[8]

Later Lenin wrote:

> The party is the sum of organizations united into one. The party is an organization of the working class, divided into a whole network of all kinds of local and special, central and general, organizations.[9]

In this system of organizations, then, the nucleus of professional revolutionaries is only one of the organizations, but it is the directing, guiding organization, limited in number and restricted in character. It is itself a "party within a party," with the sole difference that it is outside the control of each individual organization and the party as a whole. The organizational structure is built on a strictly hierarchical principle: the nucleus of each superior organization is the directing organ for the next lower one, while the entire network is headed by the supreme authority, the Central Committee, which is at once legislative, judicial and executive. The same hierarchical principle of direction and subordination extends over the horizontal network of organizations "close to the party," or nonpartisan, which are under the control of the party. Lenin ascribed special importance to this principle, of which he said:

> Our party must be a hierarchy, not only of organizations of revolutionaries, but of the mass of workers' organizations.[10]

Thus, according to Lenin's plan, the party is not only a system of organizations but a combination of the most varied elements in a single organizational structure. There are elements of military organization, such as discipline and subordination; of police organization, such as the nucleus of professional revolutionaries; of a fraternal order, such as the special procedure for admission and the secret internal party life; of a punitive organization, such as the special groups of terrorists and "expropriators"; and even of a medieval militant order, as in Stalin's equating the Communist party with an "order of sword-bearers."[11]

Lenin held that the party would owe its strength not to its ideological superiority or the size of its membership but to its degree of organization. Individuals united in an organization could defeat thousands, and in 1902 he expressed this view as an axiom:

> The party is a conscious advance stratum of a class, its vanguard. The strength of this vanguard is ten, a hundred times, greater than its size in numbers. . . . Can the strength of hundreds exceed the strength of a thousand? It can, when the hundred is organized.[12]

Seven years later, in 1909, Lenin again set forth this thesis, in an equally categorical form. In drawing conclusions regarding the Revolution of 1905 he wrote:

> The strength of the working class is organization. Without organization the mass of the proletariat is nothing. Organized it is everything. Being organized is unity of action.[13]

All this does not mean that Lenin underrated the importance of ideology. The party, he said, is created, and the revolution is carried forward, in the name of the building of socialism. Therefore the workers' movement is not simply a revolutionary movement but is also a socialist movement. But Lenin came into conflict with Marx when he propounded the clearly anti-Marxist proposition that the concept of socialism does not emerge from the social conditions of life and the struggle of the working class to build a future, but is the result of theoretical reasoning by the bourgeois radical intelligentsia, which brings the concept of socialism to the working class from without. Lenin wrote:

> We have said that the workers *cannot have* a social-democratic consciousness. This can only be brought in from outside. The history of all countries bears witness that the working class, by its own forces exclusively, is capable of working out only a trade union consciousness, that is, a conviction of the necessity of uniting in unions, of carrying on a struggle with the owners, of securing from the government the publication of these or those laws necessary for the workers. The doctrine of socialism, however, grew out of those philosophic, historical and economic theories that were worked out by representatives of the propertied classes, the intelligentsia. The founders of contemporary scientific socialism, Marx and Engels, themselves belonged by their social position to the bourgeois intelligentsia.[14]

This unorthodox and highly original proposition emerged from a basically voluntaristic plan for organizing a revolution and for organizing socialism. This plan held that it was possible that socialism would not succeed in replacing capitalism, since the working class, of itself, would never arrive at the idea of socialism; but socialism, like the revolution, could and must be organized.

Here Lenin buried without a trace the famous "laws" of Marxist dialectics: if the plan of organization of the revolution constituted silent recognition of the illusory character of the second law of dialectics—the transition of quality to quantity and vice versa—as a law of revolution, the plan of organization of socialism testified to the complete disbelief of Lenin in the third law of dialectics, that is, the law of the negation of negation, from which Marx deduced the replacement of one social and economic system by another, as well. Against Marx's "immanent" laws of the natural-historical process, Lenin set the conscious, organized will of revolutionary creativity, the "will to power." A Nietzschean to the core, Lenin, however, never let himself seem to be an opponent of Marx; he did everything in the name of Marxism.

Lenin's book *What Is to Be Done?*, which furnished well-thought-out theoretical answers to the "damned questions" of the time, was a sensation in the revolutionary underground. It was read, it was debated; some categorically rejected it, others with equal enthusiasm defended it, but it left no one indifferent. Even those against whom it was really directed (it was nominally directed against the "Economists") did not come out openly against Lenin's plan of organization. Its real target was the old leadership of Russian Social Democracy, headed by Plekhanov, Martov, Axelrod and Potresov. Potresov, although he registered his disagreement regarding spontaneity and consciousness, nevertheless spoke of Lenin's plan of organization as "poetry."[15]

Plekhanov was rightly considered, not only one of the most outstanding Marxist theoreticians after Engels, but also the founder of Russian Marxism. Although at his death in 1918 he was an enemy of Lenin, in 1920 Lenin wrote that anyone who had not read everything written by Plekhanov could not regard himself as an educated Marxist. But even Plekhanov did not immediately understand Lenin; at first, like Axelrod, he approved *What Is to Be Done?*, the basic ideas of which had been published in the Social Democratic organ abroad, the newspaper *Iskra* ("The Spark"), of which he was one of the editors. But later, when Lenin's criticism had become sharply partisan, Plekhanov took a neutral point of view. After his break with Lenin in 1903, he undertook to criticize *What Is to Be Done?*, but this, as Lenin himself remarked, was criticism by hindsight, and therefore unconvincing. The same was true of Martov, the founder of menshevism.

In 1903, a year after the appearance of *What Is to Be Done?*, the Second Congress of the Russian Social Democratic Labor party was held, meeting first in Brussels and later in London. The *Iskra* editorial board, consisting of six persons—Plekhanov, Lenin, Martov, Axelrod, Vera Zasulich and Potresov—had until then presented a solid front against the party Right wing made up of Martynov, Akimov and others of the so-called Economists. At this meeting the board split into two groups with differing views on the question of party organization (it is significant that the split was on a question of organization rather than of program); the result was that the party itself split into two blocs, that of the Bolsheviks and that of the Mensheviks. The split occurred over the wording of the first paragraph of the party statutes and became final at the close of the meeting, in the course of elections to the party central organs. The bolshevist bloc was headed by Lenin, supported by the Congress Chairman, Plekhanov. The menshevist bloc was headed by Martov, supported by the other members of the editorial board. The two versions of Article 1, over which the split occurred, were as follows. Martov's version read:

> Everyone accepting its program, supporting the party with material resources and giving it regular personal support under the direction of one of its organizations is considered a member of the Russian Social Democratic Labor party.[16]

Lenin's version read:

> Everyone accepting its program and supporting the party both
> with material resources and by personal participation in one of the
> party organizations is regarded as a member of the party.[17]

The small but fundamental difference between the two versions lay
in Martov's statement that membership was open to anyone who worked
under the direction of the party, while Lenin's provided that party
membership was restricted to persons in one of the party organizations.
Martov would have broadened the party; Lenin had narrowed it. Martov had in mind a thinking party, Lenin a disciplined party. Martov felt
the need for a self-acting party capable of controlling its center, Lenin
for a hierarchical network controlled and directed by an autocratic
center. Martov said at the Congress:

> The broader spread the title of a member of the party the better.
> For me a subversive organization has meaning only to the extent
> to which it reflects the broad Social Democratic party.[18]

Lenin replied:

> We need the most varied organizations of all *kinds, ranks,
> shades,* beginning with extremely narrow and conspiratorial and
> ending with very broad, free, *lose Organizationen.* The essential
> mark of a party organization is its confirmation by the Central
> Committee.[19]

Lenin went even further, calling for mutual guarantees: "Every member of the party," he added, "is responsible for the party, and the party
is responsible for the party member."[20]

In summarizing the work of the Congress, Lenin declared:

> Essentially even in the debates on Article 1 there began to be
> noted the entire position of the opportunists in the organizational
> question: both their defense of a dispersed, not tightly knit party
> organization and their hostility to the idea of building the party
> from above downward.[21]

He reminded his opponents that *Iskra* had approved his plan of party
organization. He wrote:

> The basic ideas on which *Iskra* tried to found the party organiza-
> tions consisted essentially in the following: The first idea, the
> idea of centralism. . . . The first idea must penetrate the entire
> statutes. . . .[22]

The debates on Article 1 were heated and long drawn out. They
occupied several sessions. Akimov reflected the views of the opponents
of Lenin's version when he said that Lenin was trying "to introduce
into our statutes the Arakcheyev system in pure form,"[23] a reference to
Alexander I's ruthless minister. Plekhanov, who remained silent for a

long time and whose view was awaited with great anticipation, made one of the last speeches. He said:

> The more there was said on this subject and the more attentively I have thought of the remarks of the speakers, the more strongly there has formed in me the conviction that right was on the side of Lenin.[24]

In reply to the argument that Lenin's proposal would close the doors of the party to the intelligentsia, Plekhanov cited Engels' remark:

> When you have to do with professors, you have to prepare yourself beforehand for the worst.[25]

Plekhanov did not restrict his support of Lenin to this question alone; he also supported him against an attack by Martynov when the latter, basing his approach on several statements by Marx and Engels, quite justifiably undertook to prove the anti-Marxist nature of Lenin's theory of consciousness and spontaneity and in particular the theory of introducing into the labor movement "socialist consciousness from without."[26]* Plekhanov accused Martynov of taking material out of context and likened him to the censor who said, "Give me the Lord's Prayer and let me take from it one sentence and I will prove to you that the author ought to be hanged."[27]

Nevertheless, this Leninist theory of an active vanguard and a passive proletariat entered the party program developed by *Iskra* and approved with the complete unanimity of Lenin, Martov and Plekhanov. Akimov, in a stroke of genius, foresaw what the statutes and the program would lead to when he declared:

> The struggle to improve the lot of the proletariat is for the party a side issue and interests it only as the situation in which it operates. . . . Accordingly, in this point of the program there has appeared a tendency to separate the party and its interests from the proletariat and its interests. This appeared even more clearly in the section on the tasks of the party. There the concepts of "party" and "proletariat" are completely separated and contrasted, the former as an actively functioning collective person, the latter as a passive environment on which the party acts. Therefore in the proposals of the draft the name of the party figures everywhere as substantive and the name of the proletariat as supplementary (laughter).[28]

The further history of bolshevism shows the profound truth of this prophecy. The names *Bolshevik* and *Menshevik* accordingly fail to reflect correctly the nature of the first split at the Congress. In this

---

*In his brilliant biography of Lenin, Stefan T. Possony shows that Lenin, in a historical irony, borrowed this idea from Kautsky, his main opponent in the Social Democratic movement. *See* S. Possony, *Lenin: The Compulsive Revolutionary* (Chicago: Henry Regnery Company, 1964), p. 61.

basic and fateful dispute as to whether the future "social" party of
Russia should be social-democratic or social-dictatorial, Lenin was in
the minority (a Menshevik) and Martov in the majority (a Bolshevik).
Of the fifty-one votes on Lenin's draft, twenty-three were for it and
twenty-eight against it; on Martov's draft, twenty-eight for and twenty-
two against, with one abstention.[29]

Lenin accepted his defeat in silence, no doubt taking comfort in his
motto "Defeated armies learn well."[30] Having learned at the Congress
how to defeat the enemy, he applied the tactic of weakening its forces
by taking advantage of its internal divisions. This was made easier by
the fact that Martov's majority was not a compact group but consisted
of three different groups of delegates—Martov's own *Iskra* people;
members of the RSDRP abroad and the editorial board of the *Rabochee
Delo* ("Workers' Cause"), who were opposed to the *Iskra* organization;
and delegates of the Jewish Social Union, the *Bund,* who were demanding autonomy within the RSDRP over the objections of Lenin and
Martov. Lenin and his supporters so managed the proceedings that
these last two groups finally walked out of the Congress, making Lenin
the leader of a majority instead of a minority.

The walk-out took place in the course of the elections to the Central
Committee and the editorial board of *Iskra.* The main differences of
opinion arose in connection with the latter. Martov proposed reelection
of the entire editorial board, on the basis that the board had given a
good account of itself, that it had arranged the calling of the Congress
and deserved the support of the party, and that there was no justification for discriminating against any of its members individually. Lenin
argued that the board of six members had, from the editorial point of
view, not justified itself; that it was too large for quick action; and that
the decision should not be based on sentiment. In reality, Lenin's
argument was governed by other factors. The former board had been
divided four to two in favor of Martov, while Lenin had only Plekhanov
on his side. In a board of three Lenin could count on a division of two
to one in his favor.

In order to permit freedom of discussion the members of the editorial board withdrew from the hall. Lenin's efforts to build an organization of professional revolutionaries now bore fruit, for his supporters
backed his proposal with a compact and disciplined majority. When
the editorial board returned to take part in the actual voting, Martov
again warned the assembly that if it were decided to have a three-
member board, he would refuse to serve. Nevertheless, a majority
voted for Lenin's proposal, Plekhanov receiving twenty-three votes,
Martov twenty-two and Lenin twenty.[31] Martov then made what turned
out to be a historic statement:

> Since I have been elected in spite of my declaration that I would
> refuse to be a candidate, I must state that I refuse the honor pro-
> ferred me. . . . I cannot undertake responsibility for the policy

of a group of three persons that, according to the adopted statutes, must exercise a determining influence upon the course of affairs in Russia. I do not wish to be the third in an institution to which the Central Committee will be a mere appendix. . . . In practice the entire party power is being transferred to the hands of two persons, and I value the title of editor too little to agree to be in the position of a third beside them.[32]

Martov's statement meant the onset of a new era in the history of Russian socialism. The RSDRP split into two distinct blocs at the Congress, that of democratic socialism, headed by Martov, and that of "revolutionary socialism," headed by Lenin. The first bloc now began to be called the Mensheviks and the second the Bolsheviks, from the Russian words for "less" and larger," the proportions of votes each had received during the elections to the Central Committee and *Iskra*.

The Central Committee, which, according to its statutes, could co-opt its members, became packed with Lenin's supporters. A party soviet or council was also elected, as a central controlling organ. It consisted of five members, two each from the Central Committee and *Iskra,* and the fifth member, the chairman, being elected by the Congress itself. When Plekhanov was elected to this position, Lenin's victory was complete. However, soon after the Congress Plekhanov fell out with Lenin, having evidently at last begun to be concerned regarding the direction in which his shortsightedness was leading him. An outstanding theorist and brilliant debater, Plekhanov had an organic revulsion against routine everyday party work, for which he thought he had too aristocratic a mind. Lenin, on the other hand, had an equally deep aversion to abstract theorizing, brilliance of expression and resounding phraseology, but was an untiring laborer in the day-to-day work connected with party organization. Plekhanov was a theoretician, Lenin a practitioner, and in this respect they admirably supplemented one another. The union between Plekhanov and Lenin seemed at first to be a perfect marriage of convenience. When Akimov had reminded Plekhanov of the great risk incurred in his political marriage with Lenin, Plekhanov had replied:

> Napoleon had a zeal for divorcing his marshals from their wives; the other marshals gave way to him although they loved their wives. Comrade Akimov is in this respect like Napoleon—he would like at all costs to divorce me from Lenin. But I have more character than Napoleon's marshals; I will not be divorced from Lenin and hope that he does not intend to divorce me.

At this point the minutes note: "Comrade Lenin, laughing, shakes his head in rejection."[33]

But the divorce took place. Under pressure from the mass of ordinary party members and hoping to prevent a definite split, Plekhanov proposed to Lenin that the four former members of the *Iskra* editorial board be recalled. Lenin resigned from the board in protest. There was nothing for Plekhanov to do except to co-opt Martov and the other three former members, who accepted his offer. The result was a new *Iskra,* called by the Bolsheviks the menshevist *Iskra* although it was headed by the bolshevist chairman of the Party Soviet, Plekhanov.

From that moment the RSDRP was in fact split into two parties, and the organizational differences between them gradually developed into tactical and ideological differences.

After the Congress and after the Mensheviks had regained control of *Iskra* and the Party Soviet, but while the Central Committee was still in the hands of the Bolsheviks (Lenin immediately suggested that he be co-opted to it), Lenin published in 1904 a new book, *One Step Forward—Two Steps Back,* in which he defended his plan of organization, arguing that the creation of a unified party was a step forward, while the succession of the Mensheviks to control of the party was two steps back. Lenin declared:

> One step forward, two steps back . . . this takes place both in the life of individuals and in the history of nations, and in the development of parties. It would be criminal cowardice to doubt even for a moment the inevitable, complete triumph of the principles of revolutionary social democracy, proletarian organization and party discipline.[34]

He went on to declare that the difference of opinion between the two blocs during and after the Congress had nothing to do with program or even tactics, but was related to organization. He said:

> The difference comes down, not to program and not to tactical, but only to organizational questions. . . . The position of the new *Iskra* is one of opportunism in organizational questions. . . . In essence already in the quarrels on Article 1 there began to be noted the entire position of the opportunists in regard to the organizational question . . . their hostility to building the party from above down.[35]

He called upon his supporters to wage a bitter and merciless struggle against "opportunists in the question of organization." He wrote:

> In politics sacrifices are not given gratis but are taken from battle.[36]

Lenin equated menshevist opportunism on the question of organization with the opportunism of international social democracy:

> The basic traits of opportunism to which I have pointed (autonomism, gentry or intelligentsia anarchism, lagging behind and Girondism) are observable *mutatis mutandum* (with suitable changes) in all the social democratic parties of the entire world.[37]

The heart of Lenin's plan was given in the words of the man who before the Congress had been considered "Lenin's stick," but who had left him at the Congress—Trotsky. Lenin himself wrote that Trotsky had correctly characterized the party statutes when he had declared:

> Our statutes represent organizational mistrust on the part of the party toward all its parts, that is, control over all local, regional and national organizations.[38]

What was Lenin's view? To this the old Russian revolutionary Vera Zasulich had an answer:

> The party for Lenin is his "plan," his will directing the fulfillment of the plan. It is the idea of Louis XIV, *L'état c'est moi*—the party is I, Lenin.[39]

Martov spoke of Lenin's plan as "the hypertrophy of centralism," while Axelrod characterized it as "a system of autocratic-bureaucratic direction of the party."[40] To these accusations Lenin replied unhesitatingly and, from his point of view, consistently. Yes, he said,

> our party must be *a hierarchy,* not only of organizations of revolutionaries, but of the mass of workers' organizations.[41]

He went even further, saying that he felt flattered when Martov urged the party to start an "uprising against Leninism." All those who had felt themselves badly treated at the Congress, he added,

> were now throwing themselves with sobs into each other's arms and raising the banner of "an uprising against Leninism."

He said:

> Martov has been waiting for the time when he will be as strong as five in order to instigate an uprising against me all alone. Martov is not polemicizing innocently; he wants to destroy his opponent by paying him the highest compliments.[42]

Immediately after the Congress Lenin undertook to carry out his plan of creating a network of local party organizations. In a round-robin letter to his supporters entitled "Letter to a Comrade About Our Organizational Problems," Lenin filled in the details of his plan. He urged that the best comrades in the Social Democratic underground be used, not only in committees, but also in important special activities, such as the operation of printing presses and the distribution of literature, as traveling agitators, in passport offices, as leaders of military groups and as "detachments for combating spies." He issued the following instructions:

> (1) We must convince the workers that the killing of spies, provocators and traitors may, of course, sometimes undoubtedly be necessary. (2) We also need military circles, utilizing persons who have done military service or especially strong and active workers, in case of demonstrations, rescue from prisons, etc.

(3) Along the line of filial departments of the committee there must be organized all kinds of different groups—groups of student and high school youth . . . groups for assisting officials or for transportation, passport printing, conspiratorial quarters groups, groups for keeping an eye on spies, fighting groups, groups for acquiring weapons, groups, for instance, to organize financial enterprises, etc. The entire art of conspiratorial organization must consist in making use of *all* and *everything,* "giving work to all and each," while at the same time retaining the *direction* of the entire movement.[43]

To the objections of party comrades that this too highly centralized organization might be endangered if there should be at the center an incapable individual or even an agent of the political police (a bolshevist deputy to the Fourth State Duma in 1912 turned out to be just such an agent in the Central Committee), Lenin replied by saying that

the principle of election and decentralization, absolutely inadmissible and even harmful in revolutionary work under an autocracy, cannot be a means of combating this.[44]

Lenin regarded work in factories and mills as particularly important, and there too he insisted that the party network be built on the same hierarchical pattern:

Each factory must be our fortress. And for that the factory workers' organization must be as conspiratorial within, as branching without, as every other revolutionary organization. . . . The factory committee must consist of a very small number of revolutionaries, receiving instructions directly from the (next higher) committee. All members of the factory committee must regard themselves as agents of the (next higher) committee, obligated to submit to all its instructions, obligated to observe all the laws and customs of this "army in action" that they have entered, and they do not have the right to leave in time of war without the permission of their superiors.[45]

In a more popular vein, Lenin provided a picture of the kind of centralization of direction he had in mind by comparing the center with a conductor and the party with the orchestra. He wrote:

So that the center can actually conduct the orchestra, it is necessary that it be known exactly who plays when, and which violin, where and how each instrument has been learned and is being learned, who is playing false in which place and why, and who has to be transferred to what place and how in order to correct the discord, etc.[46]

Marx had used the same simile: "The individual violinist conducts himself, the orchestra needs a conductor."[47]

Lenin concluded his remarks on the role of absolute centralization, which he and the Bolsheviks were later to call "democratic centralism," with the important conclusion that

> to conduct the movement there must be the smallest possible number of the most uniform possible groups, with experience as professional revolutionaries. There must participate in the movement the largest possible number of the most varied possible groups and the most varied type of the proletariat (and other classes of the people).[48]

He defined the relation between the center and the party periphery briefly and clearly as "centralization of direction and decentralization of responsibility,"[49] a formula the Bolsheviks observed after they seized power, after the classless society was constructed and even, as they assert, after they had entered the period of full-scale development of communism.

At the height of the struggle between the Bolsheviks and the Mensheviks events took place in Russia that radically altered the conditions of existence and the activities of all political parties. These events began with the demonstration of 140,000 workers on Palace Square in St. Petersburg on Sunday, January 9, 1905. The demonstrators, headed by a priest, Father Gapon, addressed a petition to the Tsar, in which they spoke of the hard life of the Russian worker and called for an eight-hour working day, freedom of press and speech, free labor unions and the calling of an All-Russian Constituent Assembly, demands taken from the program of the RSDRP. In this important hour for Russia the government made the fateful decision to turn weapons against people armed only with ikons, banners and portraits of the Tsar. According to official records 130 persons were killed and several hundred were wounded; Left-wing circles reported that 1,000 were killed and 5,000 were wounded.

News of the firing on the peaceful demonstration evoked throughout the country a tempest of indignation, which was aggravated by the defeat in the war against Japan. The firing on the demonstrators became the spark that set off the first Russian Revolution.

The 1905 Revolution, which changed the absolute monarchy into a limited monarchy with a legislature, freedom for political party activity and limited civil rights, removed much of the reasoning behind Lenin's doctrine of a disciplined party hierarchy. While calling for continued struggle and for training revolutionaries in action, he was forced to revise his doctrine to meet the new conditions. What should be the party structure under a regime with democratic freedoms, that is, in Russia after the Imperial Manifesto of October 17, 1905?

Lenin now for the first time set forth the theory that was from then on to be the guiding principle for all Communist parties operating in democratic countries. The party must have two apparatus, one for legal work and the other for illegal work, or, to use the party jargon, must employ "the combination of legal and illegal work." In practice this means that the party and its separate organizations are each headed by two committees, one a legal committee with its membership at all levels known to all, with its members in parliaments, in trade unions, in local self-governing organs, in overt party institutions, on the editorial boards of the party press and so on. Parallel with it is another committee at each level, with its membership strictly secret and its leadership little known; many of its members are not even known to be party members. Thus if all the known leaders of a Communist party are suddenly arrested and the party itself declared illegal, only individuals have disappeared, not the leadership. The illegal leadership immediately goes into action and at the same time creates a new reserve network of committees.

In his article "On the Reorganization of the Party," written a month after the publication of the 1905 Manifesto, Lenin defined the task of organization:

> Thus, the task is clear: to retain for the time being the conspiratorial apparatus and develop a new, overt one[50]

but

> the new cell must be a less strictly formulated, more "free," "lose" organization.[51]

Lenin did not move an inch from his original doctrine on direction by professional revolutionaries, but he did emphasize the "gigantic significance of succession in the matter of party development,"[52] by which he meant the principle of hierarchical authority.

At the height of the Revolution, in April, 1905, the Russian Social Democrats held their Third Congress, in London. It was attended only by Lenin's supporters; Martov's followers convoked an All-Russian Conference in Geneva. The proceedings of the London Congress provide ample evidence that Lenin had indeed created an organization of professional revolutionaries of the type he had fought for during and after the Second Congress. As presiding officer of the Congress and the generally recognized leader of the Bolsheviks, he saw to it that decisions concerning party organization were in accord with his views on the character and tasks of the party. Among other things, the Congress restored Lenin's version of Article 1 of the statutes, which the Second Congress had rejected.

Even later, when the democratization of the government by the October, 1905, Manifesto seemed to call for a democratization of the party, and Lenin himself recognized the need for "broadening the framework of the party," he declared that it was essential to retain Article 1 for "the discipline and upbringing of *all* members of the party in one of the organizations."[53]

The Revolution of 1905 cut the ground out from under Lenin's radical revolutionary program and introduced a period of conservatism covering the period 1907–11, which was described in the Left-wing press as years of reaction. In order to avoid losing mass support for his bloc, Lenin made temporary peace with the more moderate wing of the RSDRP and brought his group to Stockholm in April, 1906, for the Fourth Congress, known as the "Uniting Congress of the RSDRP," at which the Bolsheviks were represented by 46 of the 112 delegates and the Mensheviks by 62. Defeated at every point in decisions regarding party tactics, and with his followers in a minority in the newly elected party Central Committee, Lenin decided that he would never again unite organically with his opponents in the RSDRP, but would keep his bloc, which now again formed a separate party, as an independent organization. His program consisted in attempting to win over the mass of the lower-level menshevist organizations while carrying on a struggle against those at the top level. As Plekhanov said,

> Lenin wants union like a man wants to unite with a piece of bread: he swallows it.[54]

When the Fifth Congress met in London, in 1907, Lenin was again in control, having won wide support in the lower levels of the RSDRP and gained the votes of the large Polish and Latvian RSDRP delegations.

Even after he was again in control of the party, Lenin was careful to maintain the organizational independence of his bloc. The bolshevist group continued to exist within the party as a tightly organized independent unit, with its own internal discipline, periodical conferences, set of instructions, registration of members and hierarchical system of leadership, subordination and execution. Lenin declared that his bloc was a "tightly bound vanguard of the party."[55]

This brief review of the development of Lenin's views, illuminating the origins of his doctrine—and that of the present party—regarding party organization, may be summarized as follows:

1. The party is built on a hierarchical pattern from the top down.

2. The party is not a single organization but a network of organizations, ranging from a narrow group of professional revolutionaries to broad, "free" organizations.

3. Within each organization there are specialized groups for political activity, military action and supporting services.

4. Central direction is recognized as the main principle in the structure of party organizations, which means that (*a*) the party committee at each level is the highest party authority at that level; (*b*) the members of party committees at any level are not elected but are appointed by higher party committees; (*c*) all district, regional and provincial party committees are directed by the party Central Committee, which in practice is elected, not by the party, but by a meeting of the professional revolutionaries.

5. When the party is forced to exist illegally, the supreme principle

of party organization is the combination of legal work with illegal, meaning the existence of two parallel party apparatus—one legal and overt and the other illegal and secret.

6. The organization made up of the professional revolutionaries (now known as the party *apparatchiks*) within the network of party organizations of all kinds, legal and illegal, is a personification of the party itself; it is the legislative, leading and directing force. It is the "party within a party."

CHAPTER II

Lenin's Doctrine of the Revolution

THE PARTY was not an aim in itself; Lenin needed the party as a weapon for organizing the revolution in Russia, and the revolution as the means for seizing power. Lenin said:

> The question of power is the fundamental question of every revolution.[1]

He regarded power exercised on behalf of the dictatorship of the proletariat as a means of achieving the ultimate aim—the building of communism.

Before analyzing Lenin's teachings on revolution and methods of seizing power, we shall examine briefly the main ideas propounded by Marx on these questions.

In the *Communist Manifesto* Marx and Engels declared:

> The immediate aim of Communists . . . is the conquest of political power. . . . Communists consider it contemptible to conceal their views and intentions. They openly declare that their aims can be attained only by a violent overturning of the entire existing social structure.[2]

At this time Marx supported the concept of organization of revolution, as Lenin did later. However, eleven or twelve years later, in the Preface to his *Critique of Political Economy* published in 1859, he formulated the following general law for all revolutions:

> At a certain stage of its development, the material productive forces of society come into conflict with the existing production relationships. . . . From forms of development of the productive forces these relationships are turned into their chains. Then the epoch of social revolution arrives.[3]

Eight years later, Marx adduced a "natural historical" law for the downfall of capitalism:

> The monopoly of capital is becoming the chains of the means of production, which together with it and because of it has reached its prime. The centralization of the means of production and the socialization of labor are reaching levels under which they are becoming incompatible with their capitalist shell. The latter is

bursting. The end of capitalist private property is at hand. The exploiters are being exploited.[4]

When it was pointed out to Marx that there was a contradiction between, on the one hand, his theory that capitalism was doomed and that the revolution was a "natural historical" inevitability and, on the other hand, that his supporters were making practical efforts to organize such a revolution, he replied that it was true that the destruction of capitalism and the advance of socialism through revolution were inevitable as a result of the "immanent laws" of capitalism, but added:

> Violence is the midwife of every old society when it is pregnant with a new one.[5]

Lenin was a Marxist who declared the midwife herself to be the mother of every revolution and elevated her role to a basic law of communist revolution; he silently discarded the "immanent laws" and returned Marxism to the initial positions formulated in the *Communist Manifesto*.

Such was the origin of Lenin's plan for organizing a revolution, based on two fundamentally anti-Marxist concepts: (1) The proletarian, communist revolution is not the natural and inevitable end of the historical development of bourgeois society—the truth of this fact is proven by the history over the past half-century of the economic and political development of Europe after Marx's formulation of his thesis—but such a revolution can and must be artificially organized. (2) The working class, which, because of its social position Marx considered to be the grave-digger of capitalism and the organizer of the new society of socialism, could never itself be either one or the other if external and, from the class point of view, even hostile forces did not artificially reimplant the ideas of revolution and of socialism.

Applied to Russia, Lenin's plan appeared not only attractive but also the only one possible. According to Marx, the socialist revolution would take place in the more highly developed capitalist countries, and the backward countries would inevitably have to pass through the stage of capitalism before they could enter the path of proletarian revolution. Marx pointed this out directly in the Preface to *Capital*, where he insisted that

> the industrially more developed country shows the less developed country only a picture of its own future. . . . A society cannot skip over the natural phases of development, nor can it replace them by decrees.[6]

According to this theory the proletarian revolution would begin in the highly developed industrial West, not in the backward, peasant East— and certainly not in Russia, where the proletariat was no more than an insignificant island in an ocean of Russian peasants. The reply of Marx and Engels to the question of the Narodniks on whether the peasant commune could form the basis of the development of Russian socialism was, accordingly, yes, it could:

> If the Russian revolution serves as a signal for a proletarian revolution in the West, they will complement each other.[7]

Lenin never openly opposed this Marxist idea, but his entire concept of the proletarian revolution was based on other principles. For him the question was: Is there an infallible means by which it is possible to overthrow the tsarist autocracy? If so, is it possible to use the same means not only to destroy the old regime, but to create a new one? To this question Lenin gave an affirmative answer in his theory on the party.

Marx's idea of a "messianic mission" for the industrial proletariat was based on the belief that the proletariat was the only class in contemporary society that "will lose nothing in a communist revolution but its chains and will gain the whole world."[8] It was also based on his belief that, because of its working conditions and way of life, the proletariat was the only compact class revolutionaries could easily organize to be, in the capable hands of a revolutionary party, the lever of social revolution. However, Marx failed to develop this idea further; following the *Communist Manifesto,* all his subsequent works were increasingly those of a social fatalist, not those of an organizer of revolution. And when Marx excluded England and America from his theory of violent revolution on the grounds that they were democratic countries where the proletariat could come to power by parliamentary means, without revolution, the entire scheme fell to pieces. On one point he remained firm: the revolution would begin in the advanced countries but it could not win in a single country alone, even an advanced one; it would win immediately in a number of countries or it would not win at all—the concept of the permanent revolution.

Lenin began at the point where Marx had left off—and from which he had even retreated. At first he rejected Marx's theory and maintained that the revolution would not necessarily begin in the West but could and probably would begin in the East.

Lenin held that during its imperialist phase of development, capitalism constituted the chain of the world economic and political system. This chain would break, or rather would have to be broken, at its weak link, so that the entire chain would fall apart. The weak link was not the highly developed countries with their democratic state structures and their steady trend toward the relief of social contradictions but consisted of the countries where political, national and cultural oppression was most keenly felt, and where there were sharp social contrasts. Of course, Lenin said, there had to be a certain amount of capitalist development for the emergence of a clearly defined proletarian class through which the revolution would be accomplished. On this basis he produced his own theory of a proletarian revolution and elaborated its tactics and strategy. His theory had no place for Marx's "immanent laws" or for the caprices of spontaneous processes. According to Lenin, the only decisive factors were the skill of the organizer and the "will to power" of the leader. Lenin's own specific contribution to "Marxism" was his theory of the party, of the organization of a revolution and of the principles of the dictatorship of the proletariat. Stalin's classical definition of Leninism was, accordingly, correct:

> Leninism is the theory and tactics of the proletarian revolution in general, the theory and tactics of the dictatorship of the proletariat in particular.[9]

Again, as in the case of the theory regarding the role of the party, the basic idea is correct: organization defeats spontaneity.

Lenin himself was originally convinced that a communist revolution in Russia would be successful only if it were a permanent revolution, that is, if it were supported by a victorious European proletariat. In his first party publication, *Who Are the Friends of the People and How Do They Fight the Social Democrats?* (1894), he had plainly stated that

> the Russian worker, rising to the head of all democratic elements, will overthrow absolutism and lead the Russian proletariat (alongside the proletariat of *all countries*) on the straight road of open political struggle to a triumphant communist revolution.[10]

When Lenin changed his position on this matter several years later he explained the theoretical basis of his departure from the classical Marxist theory of permanent revolution in a number of writings devoted to imperialism. His basic argument was:

> The unevenness of economic and political development is an indisputable law of capitalism. Hence it follows that the victory of socialism is possible originally in a few capitalist countries or even in one separate capitalist country.[11]

To replace Marx's "immanent laws" of the development of capitalism, Lenin claimed to have discovered "immanent laws" of the development of imperialism, according to which wars under imperialism are absolutely inevitable and will be followed by equally inevitable proletarian revolutions. But Lenin deduced these laws, not as a fatalist, but as a voluntarist. The laws of revolution, he said, exist because they have been developed by (1) the people, who do not wish to live in the old way, and (2) the party of Bolsheviks, which heads the struggle. Lenin's conclusions were as follows:

> World capitalism reached—from about the beginning of the twentieth century—the stage of imperialism. Imperialism or the epoch of finance capital is a highly developed capitalist economy when monopolitical unions of capital [acquire] decisive importance. . . . The whole world is already territorially divided among the richest countries, and the economic division of the world between international trusts has begun. Imperialist wars, that is, wars for

domination in the world, for markets, . . . for the smothering of small and weak nationalities, are inevitable in such a state of affairs.[12]

Lenin believed that the consequences of war would be

> horrors, calamities, destruction, outrages, engendered by an imperialist war; all this makes the presently attained stage of the development of capitalism an era of proletarian, socialist revolution.[13]

The other main aspect of his theory was that revolution has to do with the art of *organization*. The above theory regarding imperialism as a source of wars and revolutions accordingly ended in a combination of law and directive:

> As far as objective conditions are concerned, the comprehensive direct training of the proletariat to win political power must be placed on the agenda of the present epoch.[14]

Lenin did not exclude spontaneous revolutions but he did not wish to rely solely on them when planning his tactics. His statements on this subject in an article written in 1901 entitled "Where to Begin?" were prophetic:

> We have been speaking all along about a systematic, planned training, but we have by no means wished to say that the autocracy can fall exclusively by a correct siege or an organized assault. Such a view would be absurdly doctrinaire. On the contrary, it is quite possible and historically far more probable that the autocracy will fall under the pressure of one of the spontaneous outbursts or unforeseen political complications that constantly threaten from all sides. But not a single political party can, without falling into adventurism, build its activities on the basis of such outbursts and complications. . . . The less we rely upon the unexpected, the greater the probabilities that we shall not be taken unawares by any "historical changes."[15]

Lenin maintained that the establishment of a party and the development of a general technique of struggle would not guarantee victory. The next important step to be taken was to develop a doctrine of revolution that would deal with the following matters: (1) the driving forces of the revolution, (2) the foundations of the tactical art of revolution, (3) revolutionary situations, (4) the technique of insurrection and (5) the place of the party in a revolution. In dealing with these problems, Lenin developed an entire doctrine of the methods of communist revolution, which he later applied with great skill. History has caused some revision of Lenin's doctrine, but basically it still serves as guidance for the world communist movement today. The laws of this doctrine are thus not only of historical interest but of current importance as well.

The idea of the driving forces of the revolution concerned the question of which of the social classes or political, national or even religious groups were for one reason or another discontented with the existing regime and could be used in the struggle against tsarism. Lenin phrased this question as follows:

> Every old institution, however strange and rotten it may seem, is supported by the forces of some or other of the ruling classes. And there is only one way to break the resistance of these classes: to find an opening in the society around us and organize for the struggle such forces as can and should by their own social position constitute a force capable of sweeping away the old and creating the new.[16]

According to Marx, in a capitalist society there is only one such force—the proletariat—and Marx based his theory of revolution on the supposition that this class comprised or would comprise the majority of the population in the future. Lenin, who planned for a revolution in a peasant country, believed that a revolution conducted by only one class, the proletariat, would fail. But the working class, the peasants, the liberal bourgeoisie, the oppressed masses of people and even many sectarian religious groups were interested in the struggle with the tsarist autocracy. Because of the wide diversity of possible participants in the forthcoming revolution, Lenin called it not a proletarian revolution but a bourgeois-democratic one, under the "hegemony of the proletariat." The victory of such a revolution would result in the overthrow of the autocracy and the establishment of a democratic republic whose government would include "representatives of the proletariat," that is, Communists.

The revolution would not end at this point, which marked only the first stage and constituted an essential condition for transition to the second stage, that of the proletarian communist revolution. Lenin formulated that the transition was the "development of the bourgeois-democratic revolution into a socialist revolution." He wrote:

> The proletariat must carry the democratic revolution to the end, uniting with itself the mass of the peasants in order to overcome the instability of the bourgeoisie.
> The proletariat must complete the socialist revolution, uniting with itself the mass of semi-proletarian elements of the population in order to break the resistance of the bourgeoisie and paralyze the instability of the peasants.[17]

Or, as he said elsewhere,

> from the democratic revolution we will begin immediately and to the extent of our strength to go over to a socialist revolution.[18]

At this stage the social base of the revolution would become more restricted: the liberal bourgeoisie, who would be quite content with democracy; the peasants, who would benefit from agrarian reforms within the framework of the democratic republic; and all the sectarian religious communities, for whom the atheistic state of the Communists was unacceptable, would all abandon the struggle, leaving only the proletariat, the poorest peasants and the minority peoples.

The latter were the three forces on which communist doctrine would be centered in the second, communist stage. In order to make them the driving forces of the second stage, Lenin had to promise them what he could not give—even if he wished—without betraying the cause of the party and communism. He promised the proletariat not only social reforms, but also dictatorship, although this role had been allotted to the Communist party; to the peasants he promised land confiscated from the landowners, although the party's aim was nationalization of not only the landowners' estates but the land of the peasants as well, in order to establish communes (collective farms); he promised the minority peoples the right of self-determination, including secession from Russia, although the party's aim was the building of communism, not for the Russian people alone, but for all peoples of the world. After his victory Lenin came into conflict with his driving forces, especially the peasants and the minority peoples, who presented their bills for payment, which remained unpaid. He suffered no pangs of conscience when his aim— the seizure of power—had been achieved. "For me," he said, "the practical aim was always important."[19]

Lenin's most important revolutionary discovery for use in the conditions prevailing in Russia came after many long Marxist illusions and ramblings, when he found that the peasant, whom Marx had denounced as reactionary, could be an ally. Prior to this discovery, Lenin had fully shared Marx's view that the peasants were reactionary petty bourgeoisie; in an article entitled "The Tasks of the Russian Social Democrats," written in 1898, he had said:

> The Social Democrats support the progressive social classes against the reactionary ones, the bourgeoisie against the representatives of the privileged and landed estates, *the big bourgeoisie against the reactionary cravings of the petty bourgeoisie.* . . . The petty bourgeoisie is two-faced.[20]

Even at the Second Congress of the RSDRP, Lenin made no special efforts to recruit the peasants as allies of the proletariat. His most radical demand on behalf of the peasants concerned the return to them of the *otrezki,* the small portions of land that had been cut off from the peasant allotments by the landowners at the time of the abolition of serfdom in 1861. There was no question of the confiscation of the landowners' estates. The Revolution of 1905 demonstrated for the first time that it was the peasants who would finally decide the fate of the Russian autocracy; it also showed that a political party that could enlist both the sympathy and the active support of the peasants would find it possible to seize power. He devoted a series of studies to this subject, under the title "The Agrarian Question," which comprised an entire chapter in his doctrine on the organization of a revolution. He eventually concluded that

> the highest principle of a dictatorship is the maintenance of a union
> of proletariat and peasants in order that the proletariat may retain
> a leading role and state power.[21]

How far Lenin deviated from Marxism on the peasant question was shown by his later capitulation to the Social Revolutionary program of socializing land by transferring it to the peasants through peasant committees rather than nationalizing it through transfer to the state. This was in the days when Lenin proclaimed the beginning of the proletarian revolution in Russia, October 25–26, 1917, in the "Decree on Land" adopted by the Second Congress of Soviets.

However, Lenin's capitulation was merely a camouflaged tactic to secure the victory of the communist revolution in an obviously anticommunist country. As early as 1905, in order to appease the dogmatists in his own ranks, he had made a reservation that in no way reflected his own Hamlet-like doubts. He wrote:

> To whom and how should the confiscated lands be given? We
> are not suppressing this question . . . but say: there we will still
> struggle, again struggle, we will struggle in a new field and with
> other allies. . . . At first we will support the peasant to the end, up
> to confiscation, and against the landowner in general, but later . . .
> we will support the proletariat against the peasant in general.[22]

Once the party that would provide sacrificial leadership was organized, the driving forces of the revolution, that is, the classes and groups that would sympathize with and support the revolution, were located; the first-class propaganda apparatus organized and put into operation; and a well-trained machine trained and ready for immediate action in an armed uprising. Would all this be sufficient to start and carry through a revolution and seize power? Lenin said no. All these factors, he maintained, were in essence subjective factors, which influenced and to a considerable degree depended on the subjective will of the revolutionaries. There were also objective factors, which exercised a decisive influence on the outcome of the struggle, such as the general disposition of all the class forces in a given society, the state of the enemy forces, the degree of revolutionary fervor and even the international situation.

A favorable combination of subjective and objective factors, Lenin asserted, would create a revolutionary situation. To start a decisive and final act of revolution, to begin an uprising without a revolutionary situation, would be, according to Lenin, to play at adventurism. A single party's or a single conspiracy's attempt to seize power without a mass base would also be adventurism. He pointed out the difference between his views on the subject and those of Blanqui:

> In order to be successful, an uprising should rely, not on a con-

spiracy, not on a party, but on a progressive class; . . . an uprising should rely on a revolutionary upsurge of the people; and . . . an uprising should rely on a *turning point* in the history of the growing revolution, when the activity of the progressive ranks of the people is greatest, when in the ranks of the enemies and in the ranks of the weak, vacillating, undecided friends of the revolution the *hesitation* is greatest. These are the three conditions in formulating the question of an uprising that distinguish Marxism from Blanquism.[23]

Lenin stated the general laws of revolution in his classical work on revolutionary tactics, *The Infantile Disease of "Leftism" in Communism,* which for communist leaders was what Machiavelli's *The Prince* was for Italian rulers. There are various opinions about the validity of Lenin's laws and about whether there are laws of revolution, but it cannot be denied that his laws reflected his sober attitude, practical outlook and utilitarian purposefulness. Moreover, they are not simply laws but "law-directives" for the actions of world communism. Lenin said:

The basic law of revolution confirmed by all revolutions and especially by all three Russian revolutions in the twentieth century is: for a revolution it is insufficient for the exploited and oppressed masses to realize the impossibility of living in the old way and to demand changes; for a revolution it is essential for the exploiters not to live and govern in the old way. Only when the "lower strata" do not desire the old and when the "upper strata" are unable to live in the old way, only then can a revolution triumph. In other words the truth is: a revolution is impossible without an all-national (involving both exploited and exploiters) crisis.

For a revolution it is essential to ensure first that the majority of workers, or at any rate *the majority of conscious, thinking, politically active workers,* fully understand the necessity of a revolution and are ready to die for it, and second that the ruling classes undergo a government crisis that involves the most backward masses in politics (a hallmark of every real revolution: a rapid tenfold or even hundredfold increase in the number of those capable of political struggle against the government by the hitherto apathetic oppressed masses), weakens the government and makes possible its swift overthrow by the revolutionaries.[24]

Since Lenin completely excluded the possibility of a peaceful transfer of power to the hands of the Communists, he maintained that they must accelerate seizure of power by an uprising as soon as a revolutionary situation had been created. This did not mean that such a situation would always arise without the assistance of the Communists. A revolutionary situation for a communist revolution could be created or fomented by the Communists themselves. The classical and most readily available method, the legal method, was the strike; Lenin spoke of "development of the economic strike into a political one and of the political one into an uprising."[25] However, he added, the forms and methods of struggle can be diverse. All methods and forms of struggle, all means of attaining the aim of the seizure of power, are acceptable in principle. His views on this matter were as follows:

> For the accomplishment of its task a revolutionary class should know how to master *all* forms and methods of social activity. . . . Everyone agrees that the conduct of an army that is not prepared to master all types of weapons, all means and all methods of struggle, would be senseless and criminal. . . . But the same applies to politics as to military affairs. . . . When we have mastered all means of struggle we shall be certain to win.[26]

The general process, then, is that the organized will of the Communists creates a revolutionary situation, which needs only a *casus belli,* that is, some external cause to provoke the outburst, for the revolution itself. A parliamentary crisis or a national crisis such as the Dreyfus Affair in France at the end of the nineteenth century could serve as such a cause. Since causes could be of various kinds and could appear quite unexpectedly, Lenin exhorted Communists to be on the alert. "Politics" he said, "is more like algebra than arithmetic, and even more like advanced than elementary mathematics."[27]

Stalin's views on the outbreak of a revolution are of considerable interest. He wrote:

> How can one define the mood of the moment of revolutionary outburst? When can it be said that the "harvest" has ripened, that the period of preparation has come to an end and that action can begin? (1) When the revolutionary mood of the masses is flowing and overflowing through the territory. . . . (2) When uncertainty and confusion, disintegration and collapse in the enemy's camp have reached the highest point . . . when the neutral elements definitely begin to turn aside from the enemy. When as a result of all this the enemy apparatus of administration together with the apparatus of suppression cease to function, are paralyzed . . . opening the way for the proletariat's right of seizure. . . .[28]

This is exactly what Lenin had said on the subject. What seemed to him important was not only preparedness and capacity for sacrifice but also the degree to which the enemy forces had exhausted themselves in mutual struggle, the degree of competition that the Communist party faced in the workers' movement, the isolation of the Social Democrats from the masses and the degree to which the workers themselves were sympathetic toward the uprising. Before starting the uprising, Lenin considered it necessary to ask:

> Were the historically operative forces of all classes of the society concerned distributed in such a way that a decisive battle had already fully matured, in such a way that (1) all the class forces

hostile to us had fought with each other sufficiently to be weakened by a struggle beyond their capacities; (2) all the wavering, unstable, intermediate elements, that is, the petty bourgeois democracy as distinct from the bourgeoisie, had sufficiently exposed themselves before the people, had sufficiently disgraced themselves by their practical bankruptcy; (3) in the proletariat there had begun . . . a mass mood in favor of supporting the most decisive revolutionary acts. . . . Then the revolution would have matured, then the victory would be ours, if we had correctly studied all the conditions noted above and had correctly chosen the moment, then our victory would be guaranteed.[29]

Lenin attributed especially great, perhaps exclusive, importance to the strength of the influence of Social Democracy on the working class on the eve of the uprising. A successful uprising must be predicated on the ideological and organizational defeat and exposure of the Socialists. He pointed out that

the struggle in Western Europe is far more difficult than the struggle with the Mensheviks. This struggle should be waged mercilessly and should be conducted as we have conducted it, up to the complete disgrace and expulsion from the trade unions of the incorrigible leaders of opportunism. . . . It is not possible to win political power (and there should be no attempt to seize political power) until this struggle has been conducted to a *definite* degree.[30]

Stalin later expressed the same view on the choice of a time for an uprising:

The choice of the moment, as far as the moment for the blow is actually chosen by the party, and not thrust upon it by events, needs two conditions for a favorable decision: (1) "the ripeness of the harvest" and (2) the occurrence of some event hitting one in the eye, a government act, or some spontaneous action of a local character, as an appropriate reason for delivering the blow, for starting the blow, comprehensible to the broad masses.[31]

Stalin even recommended that some sort of general rehearsal of the uprising should be arranged in order to check readiness for the uprising and the determination of the government to defend itself. He said:

Sometimes the party, having done preparatory work for decisive acts, and having accumulated a sufficient quantity of reserves, considers it expedient to perform a trial act, to test the forces of its opponent, to check the military preparedness of its own forces. . . . A "trial of strength" cannot be considered a simple demonstration of the May Day type. . . . It is something between a demonstration and an uprising or a general strike. Under favorable conditions it could develop into the first blow (the choice of a moment), into an uprising (accomplished by our party at the end of October, 1917). . . . Therefore it is more expedient for everyone to conduct a trial of strength when "the harvest has ripened". . . . When making the trial of strength, the party should be ready for everything.[32]

According to Marx the victory of the revolution is guaranteed by the support of the majority of the working class, which also comprises the majority of society. Lenin did not share this point of view. Although he argued that "it is impossible for the vanguard of the proletariat," meaning the Communist party, "to win by itself," he did believe that the vanguard did not necessarily require the support of the majority of the proletariat. Although at one point, in a passage already cited, he said that the victory of the revolution depended upon the support of the majority of the workers, he added, "or, in any case, *the majority of conscious, thinking, politically active workers,"*[33] which of course could mean one-half of the working class or it could mean only one-hundredth. In another equally vague passage Lenin said:

> The art of politics consists in correctly assessing conditions and the moment when the vanguard of the proletariat can successfully seize power, when it can during this, and after this, obtain sufficient support by sufficiently broad masses of the working class and the nonproletarian laboring masses.[34]

Later, Lenin stated more definitely that a well-organized minority could enforce its will on any unorganized majority. This quintessence of Lenin's doctrine of revolution appeared in an article on September 8, 1917, and shortly thereafter, in October of that year, Lenin proved its practical validity. The article, entitled "On Constitutional Illusions," referred to the experience of history and propounded the inevitable victory "of the organized minority if it turns out to be stronger at the decisive moment in the decisive place":

> A revolution differs from the usual state of affairs in a state in that disputable questions of state life are decided directly by the struggle of classes and the struggle of the masses right up to armed struggle. . . . From this basic fact it follows that in revolutionary times it is not sufficient to reveal the "will of the majority"—no, it is necessary to be stronger at the decisive moment in the decisive place, it is necessary to *conquer.* Beginning with the peasant war in Germany in the Middle Ages and continuing with all the big revolutionary movements and epochs up to 1848–71, up to 1905, we see numerous examples of how a more organized, more conscious, better armed *minority* imposes its will on the majority and conquers it.[35]

The October Revolution provided a classic example of such an organized minority in conflict with a weak-willed and unorganized majority that practiced democracy. While making free use of the slogans and ideals of "democracy" in their struggle with the autocracy, Lenin and the Bolsheviks had a strong aversion to any form of democratic administration. When accused of duplicity on this score, Lenin coolly replied,

"What if we do have a somewhat different idea of democracy?"[36] For this reason the question of support for the revolution by the majority of the people, that is, the question of the revolutionary will of the people, was treated in another way. The "organized minority" would not concern itself with organizing the support of the majority of the people until after it had seized power, and even then the gaining of such support would not be a precondition for a "dicatorship of the proletariat." The support of a majority was desirable but not essential. On this point Lenin had no illusions. He merely pointed out that the most important argument against a majority was a *fait accompli* of seizure of power. On the eve of the Revolution he wrote:

> In order to win over a majority of the population to its side the proletariat must first . . . seize power; second, introduce soviet power; . . . third, destroy the influence of the bourgeois and petty-bourgeois conciliators among the majority of the nonproletarian laboring masses.[37]

In a secret letter written a month before the Revolution on behalf of the Bolsheviks' Central Committee, Lenin rejected a demand by his confederates for postponement of action until the majority was in favor of a bolshevist revolution:

> To wait for a "formal" majority is naive: not a single revolution waits for one.[38]

Lenin regarded the conduct of an uprising as a military art, as Marx did. From the time the bolshevist seizure of power by an armed uprising became a matter of urgent importance, that is, from September, 1917, on, Lenin was occupied in studying and passing on to his pupils the tactics and strategy of an armed uprising and the relevant policy, psychology, specific methods, geography, time factors and timing of the first blow. On this subject he also wrote a short theoretical treatise, "Marxism and Uprising: A Letter to the Central Committee," on behalf of the Bolsheviks' Central Committee.[39] The treatise was based on the following argument taken from Engels' "Revolution and Counterrevolution in Germany":

> An uprising is an art in exactly the same way as war. . . . It is subject to certain rules, forgetfulness of which leads to ruin of the party. These rules, being the logical consequence of the nature of the party, of the nature of the conditions with which one has to deal in such a case, are so clear and simple. . . . First, one should never play with an uprising. . . . An uprising is to a great degree equivalent to unknown quantities the value of which can change every day. . . . If the insurgents cannot gather large forces against their opponent they will be routed and destroyed. Second, if the uprising has begun, it is necessary to act with the greatest resoluteness and go over to the attack. . . . Defense is the death of every armed uprising. . . . It is necessary to take the opponent unawares.

> . . . Every day it is necessary to gain new, although small, successes;
> it is necessary to maintain the moral success that gave you the first
> successful movement of insurgents. It is necessary to enlist those
> wavering elements that always go for the stronger and always sup-
> port the more reliable side; it is necessary to force the enemy into
> retreat before it can gather its troops against you; in short, acting
> on the words of the great master of revolutionary tactics, Danton:
> We must dare, and again dare, and forever dare.[40]

These teachings of Lenin were applied in the October Revolution, an
outstanding feature of which was that while aiming at establishment of
a communist partocracy, it disguised itself in the garb of social democracy and democratic freedoms—and this in a country of which Lenin
said in April, 1917:

> At present Russia is the most free, the most progressive country
> in the world.[41]

In order to discover how Lenin's doctrine was applied in the "most
free" country, it is necessary to examine briefly the main stages and
events of the revolution of February, 1917. It should be noted that the
October Revolution was Lenin's revolution and without him would have
been inconceivable.[42] It would have been conceivable without Trotsky[43]
and even more so without Stalin;[44] it would have been conceivable
despite Zinoviev and Kamenev, both of whom voted against an uprising;
but it could not have occurred without Lenin. Here two reservations
should be made: it could not have occurred even under Lenin if, first,
there had not existed in the Russia of the time the democratic freedoms
making possible the destruction of the democracy itself; and, second, if
democratic Russia had cut the Gordian knot by dropping out of World
War I and announcing land reforms, in which case only a narrow circle
of Russian Social Democrat historians would ever have known of
Lenin's existence. Even such a witness as Stalin cynically admitted this
when he said:

> The case of the Mensheviks and Social Revolutionaries who
> *missed power* because of their tactics of endless temporizing on
> questions of *peace* and *land* should also serve as a warning.[45]

Lenin himself said that among other reasons for the Bolsheviks' success
in the October Revolution was the fact that they used slogans about
peace and land.[46]

The February Revolution was not unexpected by Lenin.* Apart from
the fact that Lenin's doctrine of revolution was closely connected with

---

*While it is true that Lenin said in January, 1917 (*Works,* XIX, 357): "We of
the older genration may not live to see the decisive battles of this coming
revolution," in the same article he also said: "The present grave-like stillness in
Europe must not deceive us. Europe is charged with revolution. . . . The coming
years, precisely because of this predatory war, will lead to popular uprisings
under the leadership of the proletariat."

exploitation of war (in Stalin's words, "Leninism is Marxism of the epoch of imperialism and proletarian revolution"), Lenin firmly believed that the war would end in a revolution for Russia. Morevover, he devoted himself and his entire party to the aim of defeating Russia in the war by a revolution at the rear. The slogan that Lenin and the Central Committee used at the very beginning of World War I was "the transformation of the imperialist war into a civil war."[47]

Lenin regarded the defeat of Russia as providing the sole possibility for achieving his aim of seizing power. The Bolsheviks proudly called themselves internationalists-defeatists, and their opponents in the party who worked for a Russian victory imperialists, social patriots and defenders. Only after power had been won did Lenin announce that the Bolsheviks were no longer defeatists but defenders.

Lenin not only expected the Revolution but foresaw the political forces that would come to power as a result of it. In an article on January 31, 1917, entitled "A Revolution in World Politics," Lenin declared that the Tsar would not sign a separate peace treaty with the Kaiser because he knew that after such a peace "a government of Milyukov and Guchkov, if not of Milyukov and Kerensky,"[48] would come to power. When these persons came to power without a separate peace, he said:

> It has turned out to be both and then all three together. . . . Now the main thing is the press and the organization of the workers in a revolutionary S [ocial] D [emocratic] party. . . . Certainly a more revolutionary program . . . and certainly the combination of legal with illegal work.[49]

On March 17, 1917, Lenin outlined the bases of his future tactics:

> Now the next task is the expansion of work among the organized masses; the awakening of new strata in backward, rural, domestic labor; cells in the army for systematic, thorough *Entlarvung* of a new government; and preparations for winning power for soviets of workers' deputies. . . . Not a vestige of confidence in the new government and armed temporizing, armed training . . . for a *higher* stage.[50]

In the first stage of the Revolution Lenin did not count on seizure of power. He was aware, not only of the limitations of his army (by the time of the February Revolution the party had only 23,600 members), but of the hopelessness of a one-party revolution at this stage. Moreover, the political and organizational centers of the party in Russia were destroyed during the war: the bolshevist bloc in the Fourth State Duma, 1912–17, had already been exiled at the beginning of the war, and all the members of the Central Committee and the Russian Bureau of the Central Committee elected at the Prague Conference of Bolsheviks in 1912 had been arrested and exiled. The same fate had overcome the editorial staff of the bolshevist newspaper *Pravda,* headed by Kamenev.

Thus, by the beginning of the February Revolution in Petrograd not a single bolshevist leader remained at large, apart from such middle-level activists as the Secretary of the *Pravda* editorial staff, Molotov, and the members of the local Petrograd Committee of the RSDRP. The role of the Bolsheviks in the February Revolution was, accordingly, negligible, even though on the second day after the Revolution a local group of Bolsheviks in Petrograd issued an appeal (on behalf of the Central Committee of the RSDRP) that was closer to Lenin's point of view than that of the official leadership of the party in Russia.[51]

In March, 1917, the bolshevist leaders, including Kamenev, Rykov, Stalin and Sverdlov, returned from exile. The party Central Committee was reestablished and reconstructed, and began to issue the newspaper *Pravda;* the Central Committee delegated its representatives to the Soviet of Workers' and Soldiers' Deputies, which was organized for the second time during the February Revolution, on February 27, 1917. The Central Committee and the *Pravda* editorial staff announced that party policy regarding the Provisional Government was "pressure on the Provisional Government" with "conditional support" on a one-for-one basis (meaning to the extent the Provisional Government would realize the will of the people, the Bolsheviks would support the government). This policy was far from that of Lenin, for it was directed, not toward "development of a democratic revolution into a socialist one," not toward the preparation of a one-party bolshevist revolution, but toward the legalization and stabilization of a democratic regime. Accordingly, the first war Lenin declared after his return from emigration on April 3, 1917, was against the Russian Bolsheviks and the first revolution he carried out in Russia was against the leadership of his own party.

Lenin outlined his policy and tactics in his "April Theses." Although he did not perplex his enemies (Plekhanov's newspaper *Edinstvo* called the "April Theses" the ravings of a madman), the grave-digger of Russia's democracy shocked his own pupils when he wrote:

> 1. In our attitude to the war, which on Russia's side and under the new government of Lvov and company undoubtedly remains a predatory imperialist one, . . . the slightest concessions to the "revolutionary defensism" are inadmissible. . . .
> 2. The unique quality of the present moment for Russia consists in the transition from the first stage of revolution, which gave power to the bourgeoisie . . . , to its second stage, which should place power in the hands of the proletariat and the poorest strata of the peasantry. . . .
>
> . . . .
>
> 5. Not a parliamentary republic . . . but a republic of soviets of workers, agricultural laborers and peasants' deputies throughout the country, from the bottom up.[52]

On the day after the publication of Lenin's "April Theses" an article in *Pravda* by Kamenev, the head of the Bolsheviks' Central Committee and the chief editor of *Pravda,* declared:

> In yesterday's issue of *Pravda* Comrade Lenin published his "theses." They constitute the *personal* opinion of Comrade Lenin. . . . As far as the general scheme of Comrade Lenin is concerned, it is unacceptable for us insofar as it originates from the recognition of a bourgeois-democratic revolution completed and calculated on the assumption of an immediate transformation of this revolution into a socialist revolution.[53]

In thus dissociating himself from Lenin, Kamenev expressed the point of view of the entire Central Committee and the editorial staff of *Pravda.* Lenin was, of course, treated with respect, but his policy was categorically rejected and declared to be the consequence of "émigré backwardness." Stalin, who was at that time Kamenev's assistant on *Pravda,* expressed himself in the same vein.

In Provisional Government circles there was satisfaction that the "sensible," that is, moderate, policy had triumphed in the Bolshevik party and that Lenin had been isolated. But both Lenin's enemies and his pupils had misjudged him. In less than three weeks Lenin had carried out a revolution in the party. At the All-Russian Conference of Bolsheviks held April 24–29, 1917, his policy was recognized to be that of the entire party and he was accepted as sole leader. The old party leadership capitulated; Stalin was the first to do so; he had given in even before the Conference. A new Central Committee was elected, based on a membership of 79,204. Thereafter, Lenin decided party policy and tactics until, as a result of the bolshevist demonstration against the Provisional Government on July 3 and 4 known as the "July Events," he went underground. This ended the second stage of the Revolution.

If the first stage, from February 27 to April, was conditional support for the Provisional Government, the second stage, from April to the "July Events," was one of no support for the Provisional Government and "All power to the soviets!" Lenin regarded these first two stages as a single period, marked by "peaceful" development of the Revolution. The tactics of this period were intended to create a dual power by placing the soviets in opposition to the Provisional Government, and to provoke a power struggle in which the soviets would win. The assertion that Lenin seriously wished to transfer power to the soviets at a time when they did not acknowledge themselves to be the instrument of the party is mistaken. Even when the Bolsheviks had a majority in the soviets Lenin viewed the slogan "All power to the soviets!" as a tactical weapon only, not as a program. These popular organizations of workers, soldiers and peasants would serve as an outside organization to provide a popular façade for the power toward which he was confidently aiming.

After the "July Events," the "unpeaceful period" of the Russian Revolution began. The July demonstrators, headed by the Bolsheviks, used the slogan "All power to the soviets!"; but in reality the soviets opposed the Bolsheviks and supported the Provisional Government in its successful effort to restore order. The *Pravda* editorial offices were closed down, and Lenin was accused by the Provisional Government of spying for Germany. Kamenev, Trotsky, Lunacharsky and other leading Bolsheviks were arrested, and Lenin and Zinoviev fled to Finland; Stalin was left in freedom, able to walk up and down the Nevsky Prospekt because nobody took him seriously—either as a leader or as an extremist.

Lenin dropped the slogan "All power to the soviets!" and announced a change in party tactics in preparation for an armed uprising. He justified this policy in an article entitled "On Slogans":

> Too often it happens that when history does an about turn, even the progressive parties are unable for a more or less extended time to adapt themselves to the new situation, and repeat slogans that yesterday were correct but today have lost all meaning.[54]

This, said Lenin, applied to use of the slogan "All power to the soviets!" which had been correct from February 27 to July 4 but "has clearly ceased to be true now."[55] During this period, he said, a dual power had existed, a transitional state in which "power was according to voluntary agreement between the soviets and the Provisional Government."[56] According to Lenin the slogan called for the seizure of power by peaceful means. Since the dual power had ended and the Provisional Government had won, "the slogan of transfer of power to the soviets would now sound like quixotism or mockery."[57]

The change of party tactics based on the preparation for an armed uprising found expression in a resolution of the Sixth Party Congress, held in Petrograd at the end of July and the beginning of August, 1917. This resolution stated:

> At the present time peaceful development and painless transfer of power to the soviets have become impossible. . . . The correct slogan at the present time can only be the complete elimination of the dictatorship of the counterrevolutionary bourgeoisie.[58]

The Bolsheviks' prospects, however, seemed slight. It appeared that the new government of Kerensky, which was in power from July 8, 1917, and which enjoyed the support of the democratic section of the army and the people, was finally making democracy secure against the attacks of the Left-wing conspirators. Lenin himself was very pessimistic. He probably regarded his days as numbered when he wrote to Kamenev:

> Comrade Kamenev, July, 1917, *Entre nous*: if I am killed, I request you to publish my notebook: *Marxism on the State*.[59]

The events that not only freed the bolshevist leaders then in prison or underground but brought them to power were the rebellion by General Kornilov directed against the Provisional Government and the Provisional Government's acceptance of aid from the Bolsheviks. The third period of bolshevist tactics in the Revolution lasted only three weeks—from August 25, when Kornilov made his rebellion, to the middle of September. The Bolsheviks, now led by Lenin, took a step apparently returning to the tactics of the first stage, that of conditional support of the Provisional Government. As a masterpiece of political tactics, Lenin's actions at this juncture are worth detailed study. General Kornilov's uprising threatened the existence of Kerensky's government and put the Bolsheviks in the difficult dilemma of having either to support or destroy Kerensky. Kerensky had arrested their leaders, had accused Lenin of espionage and driven him underground, and had closed down the editorial offices of *Pravda,* all acts that Lenin had denounced as a victory for the counterrevolution. For nearly two months Kerensky had been the main target of bolshevist vituperation, and the whipping up of contempt and hatred for him was a constant theme of oral and printed bolshevist propaganda. The majority of the party was against supporting Kerensky; some demanded that both Kerensky and Kornilov be opposed. But no one had dared to suggest the possibility of indirect support of Kerensky. Again Lenin proved that his politics were governed, not by feelings, but by calculation. On August 30, 1917, he wrote a secret letter to the Central Committee defining the new tactics and stating:

> We are going to fight; we, like Kerensky's troops, are fighting Kornilov but we do not support Kerensky, and we expose his weakness. This difference is rather subtle but it is of major importance. . . . What was the change in our tactics that occurred after Kornilov's uprising? It was that we modified the form of our struggle with Kerensky. . . . Without renouncing the task of overthrowing Kerensky, we say: It is necessary to calculate the moment; we are not going to overthrow Kerensky at once, but on the contrary we will now approach the task of the struggle against him, namely, to explain to the people the weakness and vacillations of Kerensky. This has also been done before but now it has become the main thing. . . . Now the main thing is: intensified agitation for our own kind of "partial demands" upon Kerensky: arrest Milyukov, arm the Petrograd workers, legalize the transfer of landed estates to the peasants, introduce workers' control, etc. . . . [Aim] not only at Kerensky, not so much at Kerensky as at the workers, soldiers, and peasants [by emphasizing the] enthralling course of struggle against Kornilov. Enthrall them further, encourage them further to kill generals and officers. . . . It would be untrue to think that we have withdrawn *further* from the task of winning power. No, we have come remarkably near to it, but *not directly,* but from the side. At this moment it

is necessary to agitate not so much directly against Kerensky as indirectly against him, indirectly, that is, demanding active and the most active revolutionary war with Kornilov. The development of this war alone can lead us to power, and in agitation speak less about this, firmly remembering that tomorrow events can place us in power, and then we will not let it loose.[60]

Subsequent events developed in accordance with the program outlined in this letter calling for open struggle with Kornilov and indirect struggle with Kerensky. The Provisional Government overestimated the danger from the Right of restoration of the monarchy and underestimated the real threat from the Left. It accepted Lenin's help and armed his Red Guard, ensuring defeat for Kerensky and victory for Lenin. As Trotsky reported:

> We used the threatened danger in order to arm the workers. . . . Everyone understood that if Kornilov entered a town the first thing he would do would be to cut the throats of the Bolsheviks arrested by Kerensky. . . . Meanwhile the government began to free us. . . . *The army that rose against Kornilov was the future army of the October Revolution.*[61]

Kornilov's defeat considerably heightened the authority and influence of the Bolsheviks in barracks and factories. Party membership increased to 240,000.

The bolshevist leaders now intensified their organizational operations. The Bolsheviks won victories in new elections to city soviets held in Petrograd and Moscow at the beginning of September. Trotsky was elected chairman of the all-powerful Petrograd soviet over the Menshevik Chkheidze, and the Bolshevik Nogin was elected chairman of the Moscow soviet. Lenin reinstated the slogan "All power to the soviets!" He made technical and organizational preparations for the armed overthrow of Kerensky. Two organs for the uprising were formed: the illegal Politburo of the Central Committee, for political leadership of the uprising, created on October 10, and the legal Military Revolutionary Committee of the Petrograd soviet, for military and technical leadership of the uprising, created on October 13.

Kornilov's uprising threw Russia into a nationwide crisis in which, according to Lenin, the upper strata could not rule in the old way and the lower strata did not wish to live in the old way, thus creating a revolutionary situation with all the necessary elements, internal and external, subjective and objective. The inventive Bolsheviks quickly created a *casus belli* by spreading the rumor that Kerensky intended to remove the pro-bolshevist revolutionary garrison from Petrograd and surrender the city to the Germans. This rumor provided the Bolsheviks with an excuse for "defending" the city and "saving" the Revolution, and for creating the Military Revolutionary Committee. At meetings and in their newspapers the Bolsheviks shouted, "Save Petrograd and the

Revolution!" Stalin later explained the aim of these "defensive tactics":

> The Revolution masked its offensive acts with a cover of defense so that it might more easily draw into its orbit the irresolute, vacillating elements. This explains the externally defensive character of the speeches, articles and slogans of this period, which were of a profoundly offensive character in their internal content.[62]

The Military Revolutionary Committee was well disguised; it was headed, not by a Bolshevik, but by a Left Socialist Revolutionary, Lazimir; but its soul and driving force was Trotsky. The real tasks of this legal organ had been defined in Lenin's letter of September 26:

> Without losing a minute, we must organize a headquarters of insurrectionary detachments, distribute our forces, move loyal regiments to the most important points, surround the Aleksandrinka [the Alexandrine Theater, where the "Democratic Assembly" was sitting], take the Petropavlovka [the fortress on the Neva in the center of Petrograd], arrest the General Staff and the government . . . and send to the junkers and wild division detachments capable of perishing, but not of letting the enemy move on the centers of the city. We must mobilize the armed workers, immediately get control of the telephone and telegraph network, place our revolution headquarters at the central telephone station, connect it by telephone with all the factories, all the regiments and all the points of armed struggle.[63]

A Central Committee decree of October 10, written by Lenin, dealing with the implementation of the uprising, stated:

> The Central Committee recognizes that the international situation of the Russian Revolution . ? . and the military situation . . . and the acquirement of a majority . . . in the soviets . . . —all this is put on the agenda by an armed uprising. . . . Thus recognizing that an armed uprising is inevitable and has fully matured, the Central Committee proposes that all party organizations be guided by this and discuss and decide all practical questions from this point of view. . . .[64]

Although Zinoviev and Kamenev voted against the uprising, they were elected to its leading political organ—the Politburo. The Central Committee minutes list the members of the Politburo in order of importance as follows: Lenin, Zinoviev, Kamenev, Trotsky, Stalin, Sokolnikov and Bubnov.[65]

On October 16, 1917, a new and expanded Central Committee was convened, with the participation of leaders of all subordinate central and Petrograd organizations of Bolsheviks. Gathered together were all the eminent political leaders and party organizers. The meeting discussed practical details of the future uprising, the sentiments of the masses, the readiness of various districts, their own forces and those of the enemy, and the location of the enemy forces. The minutes of this meeting were preserved and published, as those of the previous one had been. Analysis shows the meaning of the statement that "an uprising is an art" and the manner in which Lenin's tactical flexibility relied on the skill of his professional revolutionaries. The meeting approved the resolution of the Central Committee of October 10 on the uprising, and decided to place five persons—Sverdlov, Stalin, Uritsky, Dzerzhinsky and Bubnov—on the staff of the Military Revolutionary Committee to strengthen the military and technical leadership during the period of the uprising.[66] The date of the uprising itself was left to be determined by the Politburo.

Even after the adoption of the Central Committee resolutions of October 10 and 16, the majority of the party leaders continued to sabotage their own resolutions. The Politburo stubbornly refused to set a date for the uprising and called for a legal assumption of power through a congress of soviets. This Congress was finally announced for October 25, subject to call by the Presidium of the All-Russian Executive Committee of Soviets, which was still in the hands of the Mensheviks and Left Socialist Revolutionaries.

Lenin was seriously disturbed by the Politburo's temporizing, for he believed that the question of power should be decided, not by voting, not by a "vacillating majority," but by the force and the weapons of the "organized minority." Power, he maintained, should be seized before the opening of the Congress, for if the Bolsheviks were to come to the Congress with power in their hands, the wavering and neutral delegates would come over to their side; the Congress would then be under more firm control and would vote for the soviet power.

As the date set for the opening of the Congress neared, all technical preparations were completed. The local officials of the Military Revolutionary Committee were awaiting Central Committee orders to begin the uprising. All Petrograd was talking of the forthcoming bolshevist uprising; all the newspapers were writing about it. Even the humorless City Duma sent a delegation to Trotsky asking to be informed of the uprising twenty-four hours in advance so that it could take measures "for the maintenance of order." But the Central Committee and the Politburo stubbornly insisted on "legal" assumption of power after the opening of the Congress. Lenin wrote to the Central Committee from his secret flat in Petrograd:

> I am writing on the twenty-fourth and the situation is critical as never before. . . . I am making every effort to convince comrades that now everything hangs on a thread, that there are questions on the agenda that cannot be decided by meetings or by congresses (not even by congresses of soviets), but exclusively by the struggle of armed masses. History does not forgive delay by revolutionaries who could win today (and no doubt will win today), [but] risk the loss of much tomorrow, risk the loss of everything

[by failing to act]. . . . The seizure of power is a matter of an uprising; *its* political aim becomes clear after the seizure. It would
be ruin or a formality to await the wavering voting of October 25.
The people have a right and are obliged to decide such questions
not by voting but by force. The government is vacillating. Whatever happens it must be finished off. Delay in action is equivalent
to death.[67]

On the evening of the same day Lenin, without waiting for a reply, or
perhaps unsure he would get the one he needed, disguised himself as an
ordinary workman and took a streetcar to the Smolny Institute, where
the Bolsheviks' headquarters for the armed uprising, with Trotsky as
head, was situated. He assumed control of the headquarters for the
entire night; in the morning he was dictator of Russia. The era of the
dictatorship of the proletariat had begun.

* CHAPTER III *

Lenin's Doctrine of Dictatorship

ON THE NIGHT of October 24, under Lenin's personal direction and with almost no opposition from the government forces, the Bolsheviks conducted a successful revolution. They took power through the Military Revolutionary Committee, at that time headed by the Bolshevist Podvoisky. At 10:00 A.M. on October 25, Lenin, speaking in the name of the Committee, issued an "Appeal to the Citizens of Russia," in which he said:

> The Provisional Government has been unseated. State power has been transferred to the hands of the organ of the Petrograd Soviet of the Workers' and Soldiers' Deputies—the Military Revolutionary Committee.[1]

At a meeting of the Petrograd soviet, Trotsky, intoxicated less by the triumph of the Revolution than by the brilliance of his own rhetoric, supplemented the dry words of Lenin:

> On behalf of the Military Revolutionary Committee, I announce that the Provisional Government no longer exists. Individual ministers have been put under arrest. Others will be arrested during the coming days and hours. Here we have kept awake during the night. . . . The ordinary citizen has slept without knowing that during this time one government has been replaced by another.[2]

At 10:45 P.M. the Second Congress of Soviets convened.

How correct Lenin had been in urging the Central Committee not to wait for the "vacillating voting" of the Second Congress of Soviets was shown by the composition of the Congress itself. At the First Congress, in June, 1917, the Bolsheviks had controlled only about 10 per cent of the votes. Of the 670 delegates to the Second Congress the Bolsheviks had 300; the Social Revolutionaries 193, including 169 Left Social Revolutionaries; the Mensheviks 68; the United Social Democrats and Internationalists 14; the Polish Socialist party and the Polish Social Democrat party 10; other parties 49. Non-party delegates numbered 36. The Bolsheviks were thus outnumbered by the non-Bolsheviks 370 to 300.[3]

When the Bolsheviks proposed that the Congress sanction the Revolution and approve Lenin's decrees on land, peace and the formation of a

42

Soviet government, the Mensheviks and Right-wing Social Revolutionaries walked out of the Congress in protest, leaving only the Bolsheviks and the Left Social Revolutionaries. As at the Second Party Congress, Lenin now had a majority, and he secured approval of his decrees.

Lenin and the Bolsheviks called the regime established in Russia after the 1917 Revolution a "dictatorship of the proletariat." This term had been used by Marx, who had, however, understood it to mean the democratic rule of a majority of the people over a minority, that is, the rule of the working class over the bourgeoisie, assuming that the proletariat comprised or would comprise the majority of the population of an industrial country. Although Lenin had achieved a "proletarian revolution" in a country where the industrial proletariat comprised an insignificant part of the population, he called his regime a "dictatorship of the proletariat."

Lenin's definition of a dictatorship of the proletariat was as follows:

> The dictatorship of the proletariat . . . means this: only a definite class . . . , the industrial workers, are able to rule the entire mass of the workers.[4]

The 1961 party program asserts:

> The dictatorship of the proletariat is a dictatorship of an overwhelming majority over a minority.[5]

But what percentage of the total population of Russia did the industrial proletariat comprise at the time of the Revolution? The astounding answer is 2.5 per cent![6]

Even in the present-day U.S.S.R., with more than forty years of "dictatorship of the proletariat" and industrialization, the proletariat comprises only 17 per cent, that is, less than one-fifth, of the total population.[7] Even in the highly industrialized United States the proletariat—that is, the blue-collar worker as opposed to the white-collar worker—comprises hardly 20 per cent.[8]

However, the dictatorship of the proletariat is not, strictly speaking, a dictatorship of the *proletariat*. The proletariat, which on Stalin's orders was renamed the working class, in the Soviet states is engaged in the same occupations as its colleagues in the West—manual labor in industrial production. The dictatorship of the proletariat is pure fiction, camouflaging a real force and a real dictatorship, that of the party. It was in this respect that Lenin opened an entire epoch by laying the foundations of the new system of government that I have called partocracy.

Acceptance or rejection of the proletarian revolution and the dictatorship of the proletariat was the main point on which the Social Democrats differed with the Bolsheviks. Lenin and the Bolsheviks zealously argued that the theory of the proletarian revolution and the dictatorship of the proletariat constituted the essence of Marxism. Kautsky and the Social Democrats, also basing their arguments on Marxism, made an equally convincing scholarly refutation of the Bolsheviks' case. How much ink has flowed, how much paper has been wasted in this fruitless quarrel! The problem merits attention here, not as attempt to take one side or another, but as a means of understanding how Lenin interpreted Marx for the purposes of his own doctrine.

Lenin justified all of his theories and each of his acts of political importance by reference to, if not Marx, at least Marxism. Although Lenin revised Marxism from a Left-wing standpoint, whereas Eduard Bernstein revised Marxism from a Right-wing one, his fifty-five volume *Collected Works* contain not one word of criticism of Marx. Lenin spoke of Marx as an incontestable authority, but no one, not even Marx's personal enemies, took such liberties with Marx's political philosophy as Lenin. The reason behind this paradox was that Lenin approached Marxism, not as an academic scholar, but as a pragmatic revolutionary. If Lenin was accused of contradicting or distorting Marxism he calmly replied: "Marxism is not a dogma but a guide to action."

Lenin's philosophical materialism differed from that of Marx. Not being but ideas, he believed, could turn the world upside down. According to Marx, the "basis" determined the "superstructure"; but according to Lenin, the "organized will," even the will of a minority, determines both the "basis" and the "superstructure." If Marx turned Hegel's dialectics upside down in order to make it materialist, Lenin quietly stood "dialectics" on its head and determined actions, not by being, but by mind, with the one difference that according to Hegel mind has an abstract, mystical character—"world mind"—while with Lenin it is of a concrete, creative nature—the mind of the all-powerful party. His favorite saying was an early anti-Marxist statement by Marx himself: "Theory becomes a material force as soon as it controls the masses."[9]

Neither Marx nor Engels wrote a single book or even an article on the dictatorship of the proletariat, although the famous *Short Course in the History of the Communist Party of Bolsheviks* considers this Marx's main teaching.[10] Neither the *Communist Manifesto* nor *Capital* mentions the term. Marx used it in four or five passages in his private correspondence; the Bolsheviks regard two such references as of the utmost importance and cite them repeatedly in justification of their dictatorship. One such reference is in a letter from Marx to the German Socialist Weidemeyer in 1852:

> The class struggle necessarily leads to a dictatorship of the proletariat.[11]

The other is in a letter from Marx to German Socialists about the Gotha program. It reads:

> Between the capitalist and communist societies there lies a period of revolutionary transformation of the first into the second. Corresponding to it is a political transition period, and the government

of this period can be none other than a revolutionary dictatorship of the proletariat.[12]

The main authority on Marxism after Marx and Engels, their pupil Kautsky, regarded these statements about the dictatorship of the proletariat as referring first to a dictatorship of the majority of the people and second to peaceful conquest of political power by the proletariat through gaining a parliamentary majority and using it to form a working-class government, which would carry out a program of social reforms. The only European Social Democrat party program to contain a single word about the dictatorship of the proletariat was that of the RSDRP, which on Lenin's initiative inserted it in the program adopted at the Second Party Congress. There are casual references to it in the writings of the Austrian Socialists, who admitted the possibility of a dictatorship of the proletariat in exceptional circumstances.

Lenin later declared all these parties to be anti-Marxist and reformist, and Kautsky to be the main renegade of Marxism because of his refusal to recognize the proletarian revolution and the dictatorship of the proletariat. All groups in the international and Russian socialist movements that accepted the main principles of the proletarian revolution and the dictatorship of the proletariat united around Lenin and subsequently, in 1919, founded the COMINTERN.

For the new communist movement, in its Russian form of bolshevism, Lenin worked out a new doctrine on the dictatorship, which became a completely independent chapter in the history of Marxism.

What is the essence of Leninism? Stalin replied:

> The basic question in Leninism, its starting point, is . . . the question of the dictatorship of the proletariat, of the conditions of its conquest and the conditions of its consolidation.[13]

It is significant that so authoritative a specialist as Stalin confirms the fact that the theory and tactics of the dictatorship of the proletariat were entirely inventions of Lenin, the essence and basic premise of Leninism.

What is of interest in the present context, however, is not simply the establishment of this fact, which incidentally supports Kautsky's stand in his quarrel with Lenin, but an understanding of what is meant by dictatorship of the proletariat. What is it? What is its real nature? Who are its representatives? Is it the dictatorship of a class or of a party? Is it that of a party oligarchy or of a single person?

The word dictatorship is the most important, while proletariat is a mere adjunct, both grammatically and for purposes of propaganda. This is clear from Lenin's own words. His classical definitions of the communist dictatorship were:

> A scientific interpretation of dictatorship means nothing else but a government unlimited by any laws, and absolutely unhampered by any rules, and relying directly on force[14]

and

> dictatorship means—take this into consideration once and for all,

Constitutional Democrats—an unrestricted government resting on force and not on law.[15]

Further study reveals the existence of an organic link between Lenin's doctrine on the party as a leading force of the Revolution and the dictatorship as a form of state government by the party itself after the Revolution. Just as the one-party revolution was disguised as a proletarian revolution, so the one-party dictatorship was given the somber title of proletarian dictatorship.

Lenin was correct in saying that the Soviet regime originated in bolshevism itself and not in the October Revolution. He said:

> The mechanism of proletarian state power . . . grew out of . . . small, illegal, underground circles over the course of twenty-five years.[16]

Although he came to power under the slogan "All power to the soviets!" and the soviets contained representatives of all three socialist parties—the Social Democrat Bolsheviks, the Social Democrat Mensheviks and the Socialist Revolutionaries—he had no intention of allowing the formation of a "one-type socialist government" including all the socialist parties called for by the group headed by Kamenev. When Lenin, under pressure of the proletariat and its parliament in the form of Kamenev's group (Kamenev was the first chairman of the Soviet "parliament"—the All-Union Central Executive Committee), was forced to enter into negotiations with the Mensheviks and Social Revolutionaries in November, 1917, for the formation of a coalition government, he deliberately dictated unacceptable terms in order to wreck the negotiations. As a matter of tactical principle the Bolsheviks permitted the participation of other parties in their government but only in a subordinate status. It was on this basis that the Left Social Revolutionaries participated from November, 1917, until the conclusion of a separate peace with Germany in March, 1918.

Lenin conceived of the dictatorship of the proletariat as the dictatorship of the Communist party alone. As Stalin said:

> The leader in the system of the dictatorship of the proletariat is one party, the party of the Communists, which does not share and cannot share the leadership with other parties.[17]

Lenin too said:

> A dictatorship of the proletariat is impossible except through the Communist party.[18]

The Twelfth Party Congress, in 1923, gave official sanction to this view, stating that

> a dictatorship of the working class cannot be secured except in the form of a dictatorship of its progressive vanguard, that is, the Communist party.[19]

Power would be exercised, not by the working class, but by the party acting on its behalf—but without a mandate from the proletariat. Two weeks prior to the seizure of power, Lenin declared in an article entitled "Will the Bolsheviks Retain State Power?" that if after the 1905 Revolution Russia had been ruled by 130,000 landowners, after the 1917 Revolution it could be ruled by 240,000 Bolsheviks![20]

To the argument that a proletariat with little culture could not "maintain technical control of the state apparatus" put forward by such Mensheviks as Sukhanov, Lenin replied:

> The proletariat cannot simply master a readymade state machine and put it into motion for its own purposes; the proletariat must demolish it and replace it by a new one . . . put its own new apparatus in its place. This aparatus is the soviets of workers', soldiers' and peasants' deputies.[21]

In speaking of the old state machine to be demolished, Lenin meant the old army, police and government bureaucracy. He quoted Marx's statement that one of the fundamental mistakes of the Paris Commune of 1871 was that it had not demolished the old state machine.

Lenin attributed great importance to the soviets as a form of bolshevist power. On this subject he made so uncompromising a statement that it sounds strange even coming from him. In the article just referred to he declared:

> If the people's creativity in the revolutionary classes had not founded the soviets, the proletarian revolution in Russia would have been a hopeless affair, for with the old apparatus there is no doubt that the proletariat would not be able to retain power and would not be able to create a new apparatus at once.[22]

Ironically, the soviets had been created, not by the Bolsheviks, but by their most hated enemies, the Mensheviks, headed first by Nossar (who used the pseudonym Khrustalov) and then by Trotsky, who had called them into being in St. Petersburg in 1905 and had re-created them in Petrograd in February, 1917. At that time the chairman of the Petrograd soviet was the Menshevik Chkheidze and the chairman of the All-Russian Central Executive Committee of Soviets was the Menshevik Tseretelli. The Bolsheviks' adoption of the system, without which, Lenin said, they could not have secured victory in 1917, was a political usurpation of a foreign idea that had worldwide historical consequences.

The party was founded to carry out a revolution, and it fulfilled its mission. This done, the party had to govern the country. The Bolshevik party, said Lenin, had three tasks:

> The first task was to convince people of the correctness of the party's program and tactics, . . . the second task of our party was the conquest of political power . . . a third task is now being put on the agenda—the organization of an administration for Russia. . . . We have won Russia. . . . Now we must administer Russia.[23]

It was now necessary to transform a party of masters in the art of revolution, and masters in the art of demolishing the state machine, into a party of masters in the art of government, a party of builders of a new social community. Just as Lenin believed that the revolution might or might not occur but could and should be organized, so, after the Revolution and the seizure of power, he believed that socialism might or might not occur but could and should be organized. "Give us an organization of masters in government—and we will remake the nature of humanity," Lenin might have said then, rephrasing his formula on revolution. After the victory of the Revolution, he fought for the organization of government with the same thoroughness with which he had fought for the organization of the party and the organization of revolution.

The belief in a future communist Utopia based on anarchy was placed side by side in remarkable harmony with the conviction that a purposefully organized communist government could subdue the entire world. The merciless destroyer of all governments, the enemy of all law and legality, now devoted all his efforts and abilities to the organization of a centralized and absolutist state machine headed by a close-knit organization of professional masters in the art of government.

Lenin well knew that it was difficult to rule a huge country with only professional masters in government; in some cases it would be expedient, in some impossible, and in others simply not worthwhile. The communist cause could also be served by non-Communists. What was needed was not only an organization of specialists in government but a system of government organization, and, as Lenin said, a system of dictatorship of the proletariat in which the masters in government would act as the leading and directing force.

Analysis of Lenin's doctrine on government organization shows that it was based upon the same methodological principle that organization of the party on its way to government was. The essence of the method is creation of a dual network consisting of a vertical system of government organizations identical with the party itself and a horizontal system of nongovernment organizations, or what is called in Russian *obshchestvennye,* which may best be translated as "social" or "public." The influence, or, as Stalin said, the "tentacles," of the party government system cross the horizontal system of social organization at every level.

The party, Lenin held, could rule the state if it encircled the people materially, technically and politically by agents permanently serving its aims. These agents should for the most part be social organizations, nominally non-party but actually sub-party, which would speak in the name of the people and link the party with the people. Comparing a communist government with a factory, Lenin asserted:

> As the best factory with an excellent motor and first-class machines does not work if the *intermediary mechanism* between the motor and the machines is damaged, so a catastrophe for our

socialist construction is inevitable if it is incorrectly built and the intermediary mechanism between the Communist party and the masses is built incorrectly or works incorrectly.[24]

The intermediary mechanism between the party and the people would consist of the soviets, the *Komsomol* (Young Communist League) and the cooperatives.

Stalin developed this view and commented on it as follows:

> We must speak of the dictatorship of the proletariat from the point of view of its construction, from the point of view of its mechanism, from the point of view of the role and importance of those "gears," "levers" and "controlling forces," the aggregate of which forms the "system of dictatorship of the proletariat.". . . Gears and levers—these are the mass organizations of the party without whose help the realization of a dictatorship is impossible. . . . What are these organizations? . . . The *trade unions,* as mass organizations of the proletariat, linking the party with the class, primarily on the production line; the *soviets,* as mass organizations of workers, linking the party with the latter, primarily on the state line; the *cooperatives,* a mass organization mainly of the peasants [the collective farms are considered an agricultural productive cooperative], linking the party with the peasants primarily on the economic line. . . . The *Union of Youth,* a mass organization of worker and peasant youth called upon to facilitate . . . socialist education of the new generation and the shaping of young reserves; and, finally, the party as the basic directing force in the system of the dictatorship of the proletariat, called to lead all the mass organizations.[25]

Such a system of government has the great advantage for propaganda purposes of making it appear that the mass non-party organizations are the sources of power, each in its own sphere, while in reality they constitute only a façade for the actual source of power—the party dictatorship. Its practical advantage is that the non-party organizations are at the same time channels for expanding the influence, maintaining control and executing the orders of the "masters in power." As Lenin said:

> In general and as a whole there is a nominally non-communist, flexible and comparatively broad, very powerful . . . apparatus, by means of which the party is closely linked with the class and the masses and by means of which, under the party leadership, the dictatorship of the class is realized.[26]

To illustrate what Lenin had in mind, the non-party organizations currently embrace some 75,000,000 trade union members, 28,000,000 adult members of cooperatives and collective farms, 22,000,000 members of the *Komsomol,* 2,000,000 deputies to soviets and 20,000,000 "soviet activists."[27] From the legal point of view these are independent social organizations with their own statutes, but their internal life is strictly regulated by the party and only party members can engage in administrative work. Their decrees duplicate those adopted by the party apparatus at the same level. Nowhere else is the communist philosophy of the "select" and the "crowd" so manifest: even in the non-party organizations the more responsible administrative work is reserved for the select, that is, the Communists. The special party organs, party groups, which are in charge of the non-party organizations, will be discussed later.

The communist methods of administration are, as Lenin taught, always twofold—force and persuasion, punishment and encouragement, elevation and humiliation, the carrot and the stick. Lenin pointed to this dual "method of persuasion based upon force and method of force based upon persuasion," to use the bolshevist phraseology, in the following variant on a definition of dictatorship:

> The dictatorship of the proletariat is a stubborn struggle, a struggle bloody and bloodless, violent and peaceful, military and economic, educational and administrative, against the forces and traditions of the old society.[28]

Stalin said:

> There exist two methods: the method of force and the method of persuasion.[29]

This does not mean that both methods, force and persuasion, are on an equal basis. Regardless of circumstances, the main method is force; persuasion, although acknowledged to be important, is derived from and subordinate to force. It could not be otherwise in a society based on Lenin's definition of a dictatorship as "power resting not on law but on force." Nevertheless, the 1919 party program stated:

> The deprivation of political rights and whatever restriction of freedom there is are necessary only as temporary measures of struggle. . . . To the extent that the possibility of exploitation of man by man disappears, so the necessity of these temporary measures will disappear, and the party will strive for their narrowing and for their complete abolition.[30]

As history has shown, however, the process has taken exactly the opposite direction: the longer the period since the Revolution the wider, deeper and sharper, that is, the more totalitarian, has the dictatorship of the party become. The new party program of 1961, with its main political theses copied in the main from the old 1919 program, replaced the statement just cited with the following declaration:

> The period of developing construction of communism is characterized by the further growth of the role and importance of the Communist party as the leading and directing force of Soviet society.[31]

Accordingly, although Marx and Engels and, after them, Lenin spoke of a gradual "withering away of the state" in the period of socialism and its complete disappearance under communism, the new program has announced a still greater growth of not only the state but also the Communist party; and this despite the fact that the main justifications for the state—the existence of antagonistic classes and the exploitation of man by man—are officially declared to have disappeared in the Soviet Union.

Although the Communists took over from democracy the formula of "universal, direct and secret elections" and even the parliamentary system of representative government in the form of the supreme soviets, they modified it to suit their needs. The 1919 party program stated that

> soviet rule . . . destroys the negative aspects of parliamentarism, especially the division of legislative and executive power.[32]

The separation of powers was replaced by a concentration of powers through a union of the legislative and executive powers in a single organ, the supreme party apparatus.

Up to the present time, however, the party has preferred to rule the country nominally through a parallel apparatus, the soviet or state apparatus. But the top levels of both apparatus—soviet and party— consist of the same persons. As Lenin said:

> As the ruling party we could not help but fuse the soviet "upper strata" with the party "upper strata"—they are fused and will be so.[33]

At the middle and lower levels the soviet apparatus merely repeats the decrees of the parallel party apparatus and sees to it that they are implemented. The state apparatus, like that of the party, uses the combination of force and persuasion described above. Lenin argued that it was impossible to build a soviet state and to govern it only by methods of persuasion, that is, by propaganda and agitation. He even regarded the soviet dictatorship as too weak for the tasks that faced the party:

> Dictatorship is a big word. But big words cannot be thrown to the wind. A dictatorship is an iron government, revolutionarily bold, fast and ruthless. . . . But our government is excessively soft, and quite more like a jelly than iron. . . . The struggle with elemental forces cannot be conducted only by propaganda and agitation, only by the organization of competition, only by the selection of organizers—the struggle must be conducted by *compulsion*.[34]

Lenin regarded every soviet and economic administrator as a dictator in his own field. In reply to the objections of what he called naive idealists that a dictatorship by individual party officials was incompatible with the ideas of soviet democracy as the "highest democracy," he gave an entire lecture on the importance and value of progressive dictators in history, asking:

> Is the appointment of individual persons invested with the un-

limited powers of dictators compatible with the fundamental principles of Soviet rule?

and replying:

> In history the dictatorship of individual persons has very often been the expression of a revolutionary movement, the bearer and conductor of the dictatorship of revolutionary classes; this is witnessed by the incontestable experience of history. . . . There is definitely no contradiction in principle between the soviet democracy and the application of dictatorial power by individual persons.[35]

This was said, not during the Civil War, but in April, 1918.

Lenin gave clear instructions as to how the dictatorship should deal with various "parasites," that is, Russians who preferred to work for themselves rather than for the government. He called for the preparation of "a thousand forms and methods of practical reporting and control" on persons who opposed the dictatorship:

> Variety here is the guarantee of vitality, the assurance of success in the accomplishment of the common single goal—the purging of the Russian land.

He made no class distinctions of those to be purged; the only criterion was their opposition to the regime of forced labor.

In the article cited above, which bears a title still in vogue—"How to Organize Competition"—Lenin further answered his question by pointing to the fact that

> in one place they put in prison scores of rich, a dozen crooks, a half-dozen workers shirking work. In another they set them to cleaning toilets. In a third they furnish them on leaving prison with yellow cards so that the entire people will keep watch on them as dangerous persons pending their correction. In a fourth they shoot on the spot one out of ten guilty of idleness.[36]

Lenin's dictatorship of the proletariat has at its disposal another and perhaps more effective method of control over individuals—economic compulsion, resulting from the state monopoly of production of all kinds. The nationalization of industry and of land placed the entire nation in direct economic dependence on the government. Labor too turned out to have been nationalized. "Whoever does not work shall not eat," says the Marxist formula for the nationalization of labor. Under such conditions labor is by its very nature compulsory. The element of compulsion rests less on the fact that the government dictates where, how and for how long people must work than on the fact that they simply have no choices. In a normal state a person works in order to eat. In the Soviet state a person lives in order to work. Such at least is the official view of the morals of labor.

The party, which has not only absolute political power but also equally absolute economic power over individuals, can direct them even without resorting to administrative repression. The monopoly of the national economy places in the hands of the party a tremendous power in this respect. By use of its economic power alone the party can: (1) destroy some classes and create other "supporting classes" of its own (the new classes, on which the new regime rests); (2) create a new social society in accordance with its prescribed doctrine ("socialism—communism"); (3) determine individual conduct (by economic stimulation or economic deterrence); (4) carry out an uncontrolled and unlimited arming and re-arming of the army; (5) place the national economy of the country at the service of its foreign policy.

What becomes of the dictatorship of the proletariat in the development of a socialist society? Where is its beginning and where is its end? Marx said that the dictatorship of the proletariat is a form of democracy in the period of transition from capitalism to socialism. According to Marx the state (including the dictatorship of the proletariat) is an organ for rule and for the suppression of one class by another. Since under socialism there are in general no hostile classes and therefore no one to suppress, the state will wither away by itself. The era of the dictatorship of the proletariat is the era of this gradual withering away. Engels' classic statement in this regard, cited by Lenin with full agreement, is as follows:

> When there are no social classes that have to be held in subordination . . . when there will be no rule of one class over another . . . then there will be no one to suppress and to hold down, then there will disappear the need for state authority, and social relations will become little by little superfluous and will cease by themselves. In the place of administration by individuals there will be direction by things and management by industrial processes. The state will not change; it will wither away.[37]

Lenin introduced this tenet of Marxism into the party program of 1919, in which he declared that the soviet system itself was leading toward "a gradual drawing of the entire working population into the work of directing the state," and that this trend "leads to the destruction of the state power."[38]

At this point the further history of Lenin's doctrine on the withering away of the state is of interest. In 1933, at the January Plenum of the party Central Committee, Stalin rejected both Engels' thesis and the corresponding point in the party program. He set forth his own shrewd "dialectical" law on the future of the state, proposing that

> the withering away of the state will come not through a weakening of the state power but through its maximum strengthening.[39]

Stalin returned to this question at the Eighteenth Party Congress, in 1939, when he declared:

> We must not apply the general formula of Engels on the future of the socialist state in general to the separate and concrete case of the victory of socialism in one country. . . . We must not demand of the classics of Marxism . . . that they foresee each and every case of the zigzags of history.[40]

He based his revision of Marxism on a citation from Lenin:

> We do not all look upon the theory of Marx as something completed and unshakeable.[41]

He concluded that the state would be retained even under full communism until the "capitalist encirclement" was liquidated. Its maximum strengthening would proceed by creation of

> a well-trained army, well-organized punitive organs, a strong intelligence system.[42]

The 1961 party program adopted this Stalinist doctrine completely in the section on the theory of the state:

> For the complete withering away of the state there is necessary . . . a final solution of the contradiction between capitalism and communism on the international arena in favor of communism.[43]

While at another point the program makes the quite unexpected statement that

> the dictatorship of the proletariat has fulfilled its historic mission and from the point of view of the problems of internal development has ceased to be necessary in the U.S.S.R.[44]

which would seem to indicate that the promise of the program of 1919 regarding the complete cessation of all limitations on freedom when the objective possibility of the exploitation of man by man has disappeared[45] has now become a reality, closer reading of the program makes it clear that this apparently sensational statement is merely another of the verbal tricks in the 1961 program. It is followed soon after by the statement that

> the working class realizes its *directing role* also in the period of developed communist construction[46]

and that, of course, this period

> is characterized by the further *growth of the role and significance of the Communist party.*[47]

Accordingly, the "creative development" of Marxism-Leninism embodied in the Stalinist theory of the state and dictatorship was accepted by the party apparatus and included in its 1961 program. Although they have condemned Stalin for his crimes and rejected various items of his theories as anti-Leninist, neither the party Central Committee, nor Khrushchev, nor the new leadership has criticized Stalin for his main theory—on the state and principles of party dictatorship. On the contrary, only two years after the dethroning of Stalin an official organ of the CPSU declared:

> In militant defense of Leninism and the creative development of the Marxist theory of the state, J. V. Stalin played an outstanding role.[48]

What had in fact occurred was that Stalin had expanded on Lenin's example by removing from the theory on the dictatorship what little Lenin had retained from Utopian Marxism. Stalin not only provided a theoretical statement on dictatorship, he tested in action the main principles of the dictatorship of the party apparatus both over the party and over the country as a whole by gradually liquidating the party and the soviets.

A word must be said at this point on the impact of the NEP (New Economic Policy) on Lenin's theory of the dictatorship. When Lenin witnessed the bankruptcy of his economic doctrine on the possibility of the direct introduction of a "commune" in Russia, he responded intelligently by adopting the NEP of 1921. The NEP also reflected a profound ideological disillusionment. The NEP was an anti-communist act by the communist regime and should logically have ended in a political NEP. The freedom of economic initiative and competition that the people forced upon the party might well have proved to be not only a true prerequisite for a political rebirth of the regime but a fatal precedent for the regime. Lenin called the NEP a breathing space in which to gather strength in preparation for a fresh communist advance. Within a year, at the Eleventh Party Congress, he was saying that the retreat had come to an end and the regrouping of forces for the new attack was beginning.

The Bolsheviks were amazed at the magical force of the NEP. Within two years of the introduction of the NEP, peasant Russia, which in all the years of war communism had preferred to starve rather than sow (since the regime had been seizing all the grain intended for sale), was wallowing in a surplus of grain. The grain problem, which the bolshevist regime has not been able to solve to the present day, was solved by the peasants themselves in two years without plans or party supervisors— and solved so effectively that the party was obliged to find a market for the export of grain.

The Bolsheviks were not only startled but frightened by the unprecedented expansion of the "capitalist" creative powers of the Russian peasantry, which made up 80 per cent of the population of the country. Fearful of the consequences of peasant economic independence of the party, Stalin provided a means of preserving the regime and preventing economic independence of the peasantry by a single blow, which he called a revolution from above. This was the origin of collectivization.

He prepared for the revolution with five years of painstaking preparation of a party and government apparatus to safeguard the regime from internal shocks.

Stalin's intentions regarding collectivization were clear. First, it would nationalize not only the peasant economy but peasant labor; second, it would create through the *kolkhoz* (collective farm) system a means of universal control of the peasantry; third, it would destroy both economically and physically the more dynamic and potentially dangerous part of the peasantry by what Stalin called "liquidation of the *kulaks* [rich peasantry] as a class." These intentions were realized. Although collectivization made agriculture so unprofitable that production is still catastrophically low (Khrushchev himself admitted that it is three or four times lower than in the United States), the state did lose the economic dependence on the peasantry that had resulted from the NEP and made the peasantry dependent on the state. Abolition of the political liberties of the people was reinforced by abolition of their economic liberties. The individual was made totally dependent upon the party state. This was one of Stalin's major accomplishments.

Forced collectivization provoked stubborn resistance in the peasants, with universal but uncoordinated peasant uprisings and mass "women's rebellions"; but by the middle of the thirties the rebellious part of the peasantry population had been crushed, the well-to-do part deported to the Far North and the remaining peasants turned into collective farmers under the watchful eye of the party and the political police, including a new special agricultural political police force known as political departments of machine-tractor stations. The peasants, inveterate rebels against the regime, disappeared as a threat to its safety.

No less important as a means of perfecting the dictatorship was Stalin's liquidation of the autonomous party and the creation of an all-powerful party machine. Lenin was neither a democrat nor a liberal, but he regarded the party congresses and the directing organs elected by them as sovereign. He believed in "collective reason" and the collective leadership of the party. He was often in the minority, sometimes a minority of one, in the Central Committee on particular questions, but the most weighty argument to which he resorted to impose his will on the Central Committee was the threat of resigning.

Stalin had no faith in this manner of dealing. He believed that the founder and leader of bolshevism was being illogical and inconsistent in clinging to this concept of party organization. Direction of a dictatorship could not be democratic, even at the very top. Stalin did not deny that Lenin was guided by good intentions and a sense of justice, limited of course to his party colleagues in the higher party organs with whom he had carried out the Revolution. But good intentions and a sense of justice, even simple loyalty to his own friends and followers, were in Stalin's eyes deplorable preconceptions when the interests of the regime were at stake. He believed that every internal party question had to be regarded

> not from the point of view of justice, but from the point of view of the demands of the political moment, from the point of view of the political necessities in the party at any given moment.[49]

Stalin had no illusions about good intentions. He wrote Maxim Gorky:

> The history of our party teaches that the logic of things is stronger than the logic of human intentions.[50]

Lenin in his political "Testament" bore witness that Stalin was without loyalty even toward the members of his own party and its leadership.[51] Stalin's logic of things indicated that the apparatus must direct the party, not the party its apparatus. Even the nominally higher party organs—the congresses and party committee plenums—must do no more than give expression and official sanction to decisions made by the party machine, and the inner party machine itself must be constructed on the hierarchical pattern that Lenin himself had worked out for the party as a whole.

For the same reason every remnant, nominal or real, of dual power in the state—the soviet power and the party power—must be eliminated. Lenin had been a prisoner of his own propaganda concept that "the soviets are organs of government power." Beginning with the Eighth Party Congress, in 1919, he had repeatedly emphasized the necessity of strengthening the power and prestige of the soviets and on his recommendation the Ninth Party Congress had declared:

> The party organization must in no case set itself the task of replacing the soviets.[52]

From the time Stalin became head of the party machine, he systematically and steadily worked to free himself from this Leninist anachronism by liquidating the nominal dualism of direction. He aimed, not at doing away with the soviets entirely, but at reducing them to fictions while denying them every trace of real directing power. All power must be centered in the party apparatus. This Stalin succeeded in doing by the end of the twenties, when the soviets had lost their power and the indivisible power of the party apparatus was fully established.

It was in this sense and this sense only that the organized process of the withering away of the Soviet state took place along with the other process, the organization of partocracy, as we shall see in the following chapters.

* CHAPTER IV *

The Party State – The Party Cadres

WHAT ARE party cadres? What is the essence of the party's policy with regard to them? Stalin gives the following answer:

> Party cadres are comprised of command personnel, and since our party is in power, they are also the command personnel of the controlling organizations of the machinery of state. Since a correct political line has been evolved . . . the party cadres are becoming a decisive force in the party and the state. . . . Cadres are needed, people are needed, who understand the political line of the party, who regard it as their own personal line, in order to put it into effect, people who are able to be responsible for it, to defend it and to fight for it.[1]

Another official definition states:

> These cadres comprise a basic, permanent staff of trained workers in party, soviet, economic, trade union, *Komsomol* and other organizations, as well as scientific and cultural workers, members of the army and the navy and skilled workers in all branches of the national economy.[2]

There are two essential prerequisites for membership in these cadres: a party membership card and appropriate educational qualifications. Immediately after the Revolution party membership was the decisive factor, but today political reliability is essential in addition to a good party record and suitable professional qualifications. Of two candidates of equal reliability the more talented applicant is chosen.

As we have seen, the creation of cadres of highly qualified professional Communists became the main preoccupation of the party machine from the first days of the Civil War. The Bolsheviks deliberately used "bourgeois specialists" to train the personnel of these cadres, and Lenin declared:

> We must force into our service those whom capitalism has educated to oppose us. We must keep watch over them daily, put workers' commissars in charge of them, and within the framework of our communist organization we must learn from them.[3]

As early as the Eighth Party Congress, the distribution and transfer of these cadres ceased to be a matter for the organs of government. These responsibilities were assigned to the various administrative divisions of Russia. Responsibility for the highest category of workers was assigned to the Central Committee; for the next highest, to the *gubernia* (province) party committee. The *uyezd* (district) committees were responsible for the next lower category; and the lowest category became the responsibility of *volost* (township) party committees.

A resolution of the Eighth Congress (1919) stated:

> The entire distribution of party workers is in the hands of the Central Committee. Its decisions are binding on all. In each *gubernia,* the *gubernia* party committee is in charge of these forces; in the capital cities, the city party committees control them under the guidance of the Central Committee. The Central Committee's task is to conduct a decisive struggle against all manifestations of local preference and separatism in these matters.[4]

The same Congress first formulated one of the main security principles with regard to party cadres. As if obeying Machiavelli's advice to a ruler not to let a commander remain too long in one place, in order to avoid possible separatist conspiracies, the Congress declared:

> The Central Committee is entrusted with the task of *systematically transferring* party workers from one sphere of activity to another and from one region to another.[5]

The main task of the Central Committee had hitherto been the comparatively easy one of providing party and governmental machinery with suitable personnel, but the introduction of the NEP brought a more complex task, that of providing the nationalized economy of the state with new industrial administrators. The phrase "party work" took on a new meaning. Formerly it had implied the conduct of the Civil War, the destruction of the old state and agitation for world revolution. Now party work assumed the more prosaic tasks of factory administration, the repair of houses and the running of public bathhouses. The Tenth Party Congress, in 1921, proclaimed the NEP and simultaneously elucidated the new nature of party work in the following terms:

> The task of the party consists in explaining to every member that now the Russian Communist party is responsible for the economic life of the country, the least skilled and most obscure work is of the highest importance and is responsible party work. . . . The main types of party work at the present time are: the work of collectives in factories, on the railway and in other forms of transport; the execution of various types of work by conscripted labor; work in the fuel supply organizations, in communal dining rooms, barracks, house committees; the repair and proper functioning of public bathhouses; the clearing and repairing of houses; the administration of public gardens, schools and social security institutions, etc.[6]

The Congress ordered each party member (there were then 600,000) to take up this work in his own sphere of activity. The creation of a qualified party apparatus, however, remained an urgent necessity. The Congress ordered that the process be speeded up because only an efficient party machine could ensure the local execution of the Congress' decisions. It proposed investigating the abilities and effectiveness of each Communist with a view to appointing the most able members to positions of authority in both local and central administrations.

The Congress' resolution went on to ordain that every one or two months the local party committees should send from 5 per cent to 10 per cent of their best personnel to the regional committee of the party to take up superior positions there. Similarly, the regional committees were to send from 5 per cent to 10 per cent of their members to take up responsible positions in the *gubernia* organizations; and the latter were to make their most promising members available for posts in the central organization of the party.

A prudent addendum to the resolution declared:

> Members of each committee bear mutual responsibility for each recommendation.[7]

The Fourteenth Party Congress, in 1925, which has become known as the Industrialization Congress, again noted that

> the work of selecting personnel for governmental and economic organizations remains the party's most important task.[8]

This Congress instigated periodical "purges of the governmental apparatus of useless elements," and their replacement by personnel promoted from the lower ranks of the party.[9] From then on purges became the standard means by which new personnel infiltrated all ranks and branches of activity within the party and the state.

New industrial projects and the systematic purge of the economy of its old specialist leaders (especially after the Shakhty Affair in 1928, in which a group of non-communist specialists employed in the industrial center of Shakhty were accused of sabotaging production) made the training of teams of managers and technical specialists, recruited from the ranks of the Communist party and the *Komsomols,* an urgent necessity.

The party had a secure grip on the machinery of government, but not on the national economy, in which workers' commissars and party overseers were still dependent on "bourgeois specialists," many of whom were purged at the time of the Shakhty Affair, for competent advice and technical guidance. By the end of 1927, the entire personnel of the party cadres numbered some 100,000, of whom less than one-fourth of 1 per cent were technical specialists.[10]

In order to provide the industrialization program with specialists and the party's economic organization with competent communist executives, it was necessary to train economic and technical personnel on a national scale. This course was embarked upon at the July Plenum of the Central Committee in 1928, which passed the first party resolution "On Improving the Training of New Specialists." It emphasized that

the training of new specialists is becoming the most important task of the entire party.[11]

The resolution referred to an acute shortage of engineers and technicians, and it revealed that 39 per cent of the technical posts, which should have been occupied by academically qualified engineers and technicians, were held by persons who had only practical experience.

The Plenum ordered a "twofold increase in the proportion of engineering and technical personnel in heavy industry by the end of the Five-Year Plan."[12] In technical institutes serious study was devoted to foreign scientific and technical advances, important foreign specialists were invited to deliver lectures, more teams of young specialists were sent abroad to study and teaching standards were raised by encouraging research both at home and abroad. Many more young scientists were to receive improved postgraduate training.[13]

The Central Committee took special steps to train communist specialists destined to occupy managerial positions in the national economy. To this end the practice of sending communist activists to higher technical institutes was introduced. The resolution stated:

This year no less than one thousand Communists who have already received considerable training in party, soviet and professional work are to be sent to higher technical institutes at state expense. The practice is to be continued in succeeding years.[14]

These one thousand party-sponsored students enjoyed such special material privileges as family apartments and augmented state scholarships, which not even other communist students received.

The Plenum of the Central Committee decided in November, 1929, to double the number of communist activists in higher technical institutes in 1930, and to raise their number to three thousand in 1931. It was also decided to send one thousand communist activists to agricultural institutes in 1930, and to send two thousand in 1931. This practice was extended to the Central Committee of the All-Union Young Communist League, the All-Union Central Council of Trade Unions and the Political Administration of the Army (PUR). The Central Committee of the All-Union Young Communist League was annually to send up to five thousand *Komsomol* activists to institutes of higher education and the Chief Political Administration of the Armed Forces up to three thousand demobilized commanders and Red Army soldiers. The All-Union Central Council of Trade Unions was to send three thousand activists in 1929, and five thousand in 1930, to institutes for higher technical education and agricultural institutes. The Central Committee Plenum proposed that these entrants to institutes for higher education receive supplementary stipends from their sponsors, as had the original thousand students.[15]

At a conference of industrial workers in February, 1931, Stalin criticized the party's management of industry:

> We not infrequently think that management signified merely signing documents. This is a regrettable fact. It reminds one of Shchedrin's pompadours. You will remember how the lady told the young pompadour: "Don't bother your head about science, let others do that, it's none of your affair, your business is to manage and to sign documents." We must acknowledge to our shame that among us Bolsheviks there are not a few such people who conduct their business merely by signing papers.[16]

In this speech Stalin enunciated his famous slogan: "Bolsheviks must master technology."[17] Returning three months later to the problem of the cadres, he proposed to expand their training program, saying:

> We now need three times or even five times the present number of engineers and technicians in industry if we really intend to put our program of socialist industrialization into effect.[18]

At the same time Stalin made an important reservation that clearly reveals the extent to which the Central Committee's policy vis-à-vis the cadres was intended to consolidate its own strength. He said:

> We do not need [just] any managerial and technical resources. We need those managerial and technical resources that are able to comprehend the policy of the working class . . . to assimilate this policy and conscientiously to put it into effect. . . . The working class [i.e., the party apparatus] must create its own technological intelligentsia capable of defending its interests in production as the interests of the ruling class.[19]

Stalin explained why Communists need to have their own intelligentsia by referring to history:

> Not one ruling class has managed to exist without its own intelligentsia.[20]

In 1935 the first recruits were graduated as engineers, and Stalin came up with a new slogan: "The cadres decide everything." Stalin now had his cadres to begin the new purge. He said:

> If we have large and effective cadres in industry, agriculture, transport and the army, the country will be invincibly ours. If we do not have them we shall be lame in both legs.[21]

The slogan "The cadres decide everything" was primarily a political one. It signified that the security of the dictatorship depended on the political reliability of its foremost party, governmental and economic cadres. It was not simply a slogan, it was also a directive that expressed in precise terms the onset of a new stage in the Central Committee's cadre policy. This involved the liquidation of many older party members who had taken part in the Revolution and the Civil War, and their replacement with new ones trained under the direct supervision of the Central Committee. This was the only way Stalin's personal dictatorship could triumph. It was the only way Stalin's party apparatus could finally liquidate the old party and create a new one "in its form and image." The party's plan to create new cadres was completely successful. Nowhere outside the Soviet Union do young people study so enthusiastically. Free tuition, government scholarships and supplementary subsidies provided by various organizations (apart from the special national grants awarded by the local governments of Turkestan and the Caucasus) have created favorable circumstances for study. However, constant checks and cross-checks to eliminate "alien elements" have impinged upon academic life and intimidated students, and many have fallen victim to purges simply because their antecedents were not purely proletarian. At first there was a quota system; of the entrants to institutes of higher education only 35 per cent came from the peasant and administrative strata of society; the remaining 65 per cent were recruited from the working class.[22]

This did not have any appreciable effect on the number of recruits to the cadres. All the institutes of higher education were full and the intelligentsia increased rapidly in number as Table 1, from data published at the Eighteenth Party Congress, shows:[23]

TABLE 1

YOUNG SPECIALISTS GRADUATING FROM INSTITUTES FOR HIGHER EDUCATION
DURING THE YEARS 1933–1938
(in thousands)

SPECIALISTS	1933	1934	1935	1936	1937	1938
Throughout the U.S.S.R. (excluding military specialists)	34.6	49.2	83.7	97.6	104.8	106.7
Engineers: industrial, civil, transport and communications	7.9	18.9	37.2	35.8	34.6	31.3
Agricultural specialists: engineers, agronomists, veterinary surgeons and zoologists	4.8	6.3	8.8	10.4	11.3	10.6
Teachers in intermediate and technical institutes	10.5	7.9	12.5	21.6	31.7	35.7
Doctors, pharmacists and other specialists	8.9	13.6	20.2	23.4	22.2	23.4
Economists and lawyers	2.5	2.5	5.0	6.4	5.0	5.7

Thus, during the six years from 1933 to 1938 the institutes for higher education trained 476,600 young specialists—almost one-half the number of specialists Russia had in 1926. Most of them had had a communist upbringing, and Stalin's party machine also recruited its own cadres from its ranks. These cadres were, in Stalin's opinion, prepared to serve the regime "truly and faithfully."[24]

Relying on these communist cadres, Stalin embarked on his Great Purge of 1936–38. In 1917–20 Lenin had successfully destroyed the old machinery of state, completely liquidating the bourgeois class of civil servants, and Stalin, while maintaining Lenin's governmental machinery, equally thoroughly liquidated Lenin's governmental bureaucracy and replaced it with his new cadres. At the Eighteenth Party Congress, Stalin obliquely but quite eloquently hinted at the extent of the destruction of the old cadres when he said:

> The Central Committee has information that during the period under review more than 500,000 young Bolsheviks have been promoted to managerial posts in the government and the party.[25]

This meant that an equal number of old Bolsheviks had been disposed of in order to leave room for the newcomers. Including the lower strata of the party activists, more than 1,220,000 Communists had been liquidated, according to calculations based on official sources.[26]

At the Eighteenth Party Congress Stalin told delegates that they must

> regard the cadres as the gold reserve of the state and of the party . . . know the cadres, carefully study the virtues and vices of each member of them and ascertain in what job each of them can most usefully serve . . . foster the cadres and help each member to make his way upward.

They must also

> promote new young cadres in a timely and expeditious manner . . . without giving them time to get stale . . . and assign positions to each member of them so that every man feels that he is in the right job and is able to give of his best to the common cause.[27]

Furthermore:

> The cadres must be studied closely and continually in order to keep a check on the activities of each member.[28]

In this way a new party, consisting of professional cadres trained in Stalin's technique of wielding power, was created within the old party. At the same Congress the party's statutes accorded the cadres official status as "activist groups."[29]

The new cadres consisted mainly of technical specialists in charge of plants, factories, mines, crafts, transport and state and collective farms. They have also permeated the administrative machinery of the party, the government and the economy. The personnel of the party are rapidly becoming largely technicians, and technical personnel are being trained to be politically conscious. The party requires that the

cadres accept the official party line and "regard it as their very own."
As Stalin said:

> There is one branch of science that all bolshevist scientists must
> be expert in—that is the Marxist-Leninist science concerning
> society . . . and the victory of communism.[30]

Training in Marxism-Leninism is intended to provide the cadres with
a lifelong supply of "spiritual nourishment." The party school is the
only type of school in the U.S.S.R. from which the pupils never graduate.
It is not merely a place in which to acquire certain information, it is a
political laboratory for the systematic brainwashing of party cadres.
Only those who reach the upper rungs of the political ladder cease to
attend, and then only because they are brainwashing others. The party
has thus created cadres that have no political ambitions but are politically
devoted to it. Although World War II slowed up the cadre training
program, it has since been greatly accelerated. Table 2 illustrates the
increase in the number of specialists during the years 1926–59.[31]

TABLE 2

INCREASE IN THE NUMBER OF SPECIALISTS IN THE U.S.S.R. 1926–59

SPECIALISTS	NUMBER (in thousands)		PROPORTION OF INCREASE
	1926	1959	
Managers of industrial and construction projects, collective farms, administrative institutions and their associated bodies	365	2,223	6.0
Engineers, technicians and agronomists	267	4,683	7.0
Teachers and other cultural and educational workers	486	3,276	7.0
Doctors and medical auxiliaries	199	1,702	8.5
Scientific workers	14	316	23.0

In 1926 2,000,000 persons were engaged in intellectual work; by
1959 the number had risen to 20,000,000. In 1926 there were 168,000
students in institutes of higher education and 181,000 students in technical colleges; by 1959 these figures had increased to 2,200,000 and
1,868,000, respectively. The U.S.S.R. is now faced with a surplus of
cadre personnel. Whereas before World War II it was exceptional for
people who had received secondary education to undertake manual
labor, in 1959 "almost one-third of the manual labor force [had] received secondary or higher education."[32]

This overproduction of cadre personnel brought about the School
Reform of December, 1958, which enabled the party to place obstacles
in the path of candidates for higher education and to be selective in its
choice.

The party machine consists of highly trained theorists whose political reliability has been tested in practice. In addition to the normal training in science or the humanities, these persons have also attended special party schools run either by the Central Committee of the party or by the central committees of the constituent republics.

Senior party officials, the majority of whom are science or arts graduates, are trained in two schools in Moscow, the Higher Party School and the Central Committee's Academy of Social Sciences. In August, 1946, the Central Committee issued a decree "On the Training and Retraining of Leading Party and Soviet Workers." Despite the obvious success of the party's policy in creating and training new cadres, the value of which had been proved by the war, the decree stated:

> The Central Committee is aware that the training and retraining programs for leading party and soviet workers are unsatisfactory.[33]

The decree continued:

> In the matter of training party and soviet workers there is no proper system or order. . . . The party schools that train leading personnel often accept persons who are politically immature and who lack experience in party work. . . . The retraining of leading party and soviet workers is badly organized. Many party and soviet workers have ceased to work systematically to raise the standard of their ideological and theoretical knowledge, and in recent years they have not been required to attend refresher courses, nor is there a set interval of time after which these workers are required to attend such courses. The training of party theoreticians is also unsatisfactory.[34]

The Central Committee took drastic steps to ensure that periodical brainwashing was carried out. It ordered the following categories of personnel to attend nine-month party courses in Moscow: (1) leading party workers—secretaries and departmental heads of regional and provincial committees, members of the central committees of the constituent republics and secretaries of regional committees and of party committees of important cities; (2) leading soviet workers—chairmen, vice-chairmen and departmental heads of regional and provincial and district executive committees, chairmen and deputy chairmen of the councils of ministers of the Union and the autonomous republics and chairmen of the soviets of important cities; and (3) editors and deputy editors of local, regional and national newspapers.[35]

The Central Committee established the Higher Party School, which has a three-year training course with three hundred students per course, and the Academy of Social Sciences. These schools train personnel for jobs in the central organization of the party and on the central committees of the constituent republics, regions and districts; qualified teachers for institutes of higher education; and personnel for research institutes and scientific periodicals.[36]

The Higher Party School offers the following courses: party history; the history of the U.S.S.R.; world history; political economy and historical materialism; logic; the history of international relations and the foreign policy of the U.S.S.R.; economic and political geography; Russian language and literature; foreign languages; the fundamentals of Soviet economy and industrial management; party construction; the fundamentals of Soviet law; and soviet construction.

The Academy of Social Sciences provides the following three-year courses: political economy; the politics and economics of foreign states; political and legal theory; international law; the history of the U.S.S.R.; world history; international relations; party history; dialectical and historical materialism; the history of Russian and Western European philosophy; logic and psychology; literary criticism; and the history of art.[37] Thus, selected workers from the constituent republics undergo training in party schools in courses organized by the parties of the constituent republics.

Since the party machine is the controlling authority for the entire political, economical, cultural and intellectual life of the state, its leading personnel must be highly competent and well versed in political and economic questions. They must know both the techniques of production and the techniques of management. A party worker cannot be merely a specialist in a restricted field of industry or administration. He must be capable of dealing with the diverse situations that face the party, in which he plays a leading role. Since the Great Purge of the thirties, the party has recruited to its ranks young persons qualified in administration, economics and technology, who have enabled it to survive the trying days of World War II. As a Soviet author writes:

> The party makes great demands of its personnel, especially of the members of the party apparatus, which attracts to itself the best people. . . . The party demands wide political vision of its leaders . . . an ability to deal with difficult situations . . . and a knowledge of the way in which the party functions.[38]

If members of the party apparatus prove adept at wielding power, they must be unprincipled political opportunists. They are utterly unlike their forebears, those members of the party who took part in the Revolution and the Civil War. Those men were ideological fanatics; the current generation are fanatics for power. The old revolutionaries achieved power by fighting their enemies in the October Revolution; the new leaders rose to power by destroying the October revolutionaries. The old revolutionaries were strong personalities who had led adventurous lives; the new leaders are stereotyped personalities with a uniform life story. The old revolutionaries argued and thought about issues; their successors merely act on instructions—their one god is Lenin, and his representative on earth is the current party secretary. The old guard are dismissed as fanatics and dreamers, and their successors pose as cynical realists.

The party knows three methods of control: (1) training (which in party terminology is known as *nakachka* (pumping), (2) encouragement and (3) fear.

Training consists of a continual flow of written instructions to local party, soviet and economic organizations, from the central authorities, particularly through its network of official and unofficial instructors. This is reinforced by frequent local visits by party leaders and regular conferences of activists in towns, regions and republics where the decisions of the party authorities and the activities of local organizations are made known. As a rule, the central authorities of the party say what is to be done and the local authorities determine how these decisions are to be put into effect.

The local party authorities must issue the necessary instructions to subordinate party and soviet organizations. Should any difficulties arise in the execution of directives issued by the central organization, the blame is not attached to those who have issued the wrong directives but to the local party authority that has failed to find the proper means of enforcement.

An instance of this occurred during collectivization. Many local party authorities were dismissed on charges of "Leftist excesses," of "distorting the party line," while the Central Committee's executive personnel, who had issued the specific timetable to speed up collectivization, suffered no punishment.

A local party leader is often faced with the dilemma of either putting a decision by the Central Committee into effect and remaining in office and even receiving a state honor, or of failing to do so, thereby risking losing both his job and honors already bestowed on him. He therefore resorts either to repressive measures (which have not always received the sanction of superior authority) or else to such window-dressing methods as reporting that plans have been fulfilled when they have not. Window-dressing as a weapon of self-defense has become such a widespread activity in the U.S.S.R. that in 1961 the Presidium of the Supreme Soviet promulgated a special law against "window-dressers."

Training methods include "exchanges of experiences" between regions, districts and republics. Leaders who have found effective methods of executing plans and tasks allotted by the central authority share their experiences with those who have been less successful.

Many moral and material incentives for workers to turn out good work are provided. They are publicly thanked, testimonials are awarded, the names of highly efficient workers are entered in books of honor, official titles, honors and medals are bestowed, and they are accorded speedy promotion. The highest honor is to be designated a "Hero of the Soviet Union" or a "Hero of Socialist Labor."

No country has ever had as many medals and orders as the Soviet Union now awards. A bulletin issued in Moscow by the Ministry of Defense of the U.S.S.R. in 1958 lists seventy-five different medals and orders that are awarded to Soviet citizens by the Presidium of the Supreme Soviet for military and civilian services. Were a Soviet citizen to be awarded all of them, he would have the dubious privilege of bearing about eleven pounds of metal on his chest. The proliferation of such awards has greatly diminished their prestige. During World War II more than seven million persons received medals and orders; eleven thousand were designated "Heroes of the Soviet Union."[39]

At one time few honors were awarded. During the Civil War only four Red Army commanders received the Order of the Red Banner four times, and these did not include Voroshilov or Budenny. Nowadays the chests of Soviet generals and marshals boast a full complement of medals.

Wide use is made of such material incentives as monetary prizes, bonuses, free holidays at resorts, bolts of material, private automobiles and, more recently, foreign travel.

Officials in government departments and in the party are rewarded for the proper execution of their duties. In addition to high salaries, party workers receive extra payments for their part in the struggle to achieve communism. Capitalist principles are thus utilized to construct communism.

The Damoclean sword of fear is perhaps the most potent weapon in the party leadership's armory, and party cadres are kept in a continual state of fear and tension. Because Communists do not believe in the concept of conscience in the generally accepted meaning of the word, the party leaders resort to fear as a guiding principle in controlling the behavior of their subordinates. It is not conscience but fear of expulsion from the party or of deprivation of liberty that motivates every action of the rank-and-file party worker. One is reminded of Machiavelli's view that fear is a much more effective weapon in the hands of a ruler than love, respect or conscience.

While continuing these methods to control its executive cadres, the party machine does not overlook its principal weapon—the desire for advancement. Through "socialist competition" the party gives its members the opportunity to ascend the ladder of promotion. In this competition distinguished service and devotion to the party produce the best results. Blind, unquestioning devotion to the party is equated with devotion to communism, and it is measured, not in altruistic and grandiloquent pronouncements, but in *poods* of grain, in tons of coal and in the quality of rockets.

A similar policy has been adopted in the Red Army, where the following aims have been pursued: (1) the gradual removal from the Red Army of officers who served in the prerevolutionary old army, (2) the complete removal of Trotskyites and (3) the training of exclusively communist officer cadres, who are loyal to the party machine and have a sound knowledge of modern methods of warfare.

From 1918 to 1920 the Red Army recruited 48,409 officers and

214,000 junior commanders, noncommissioned officers and administrative personnel from the old tsarist army.[40] With their help Lenin and Trotsky rapidly built up the Red Army. Lenin greatly valued their services. In 1919, at the height of the struggle with General Denikin, Lenin said:

> You have heard of a series of brilliant victories by the Red Army. Tens of thousands of old officers and colonels are serving in it. If we had not taken them on and made them serve us, we could not have created the army.[41]

At the end of the Civil War one-third of the Red Army's officers were men who had also served in the tsarist army; they were among the first to be demobilized. By 1928 they comprised only 10.6 per cent of the army's officers.[42]

Despite the measures taken to strengthen the nucleus of communist officers in the army, it grew quite slowly; in 1921 only 20 per cent of the army's officers were Communists; in 1925, 40 per cent; and in 1928, 55.4 per cent.[43]

The military underwent the same purges as did civilian Communists. The first purge of Trotskyites in the army took place in 1923, while Trotsky was still in command of it, by order of the Organizational Bureau (Orgburo) of the Central Committee. The Political Administration of the Revolutionary War Council and a number of military districts were purged of Trotskyites.[44]

During the Great Purge 4.7 per cent of the officer corps were expelled from the party and relieved of their commands. The Purge Commission noted, however, that

> the ideological condition of the army is absolutely sound. This is especially true of the commanders and political personnel.

But the Commission went on to contrast this with the fact that 40 per cent of the army's political staff and 75 per cent of its administrative staff had received no military training.[45]

The general educational standard of the army's commanders was manifestly unsatisfactory. In 1929 their educational qualifications were as follows: 4.5 per cent had received higher education, 57.3 per cent secondary education and 38.2 per cent elementary education.[46] The army needed educated commanders as well as qualified technicians.

The main task of industrialization was to create a military and technological base for communism. All the Soviet five-year plans and the entire economic policy of the party to this day stress that heavy industry is more important than light industry. Heavy industry was called upon to provide the Red Army with high-quality military equipment. As a result of this policy, by 1939 the Red Army had, in comparison with 1930, forty-three times as many tanks; six and one-half times as many aircraft; seven times as much artillery; and five and one-half times as many machine guns. During the same period the tonnage of the Red Navy increased by 130 per cent.[47] It was the task of the party to train for the Red Army highly qualified commanders and technical personnel familiar with the latest developments in military technology.

In 1939 the army was three times larger than it had been in 1930, and the number of military schools, including political and technical ones, had greatly increased. The party sought to bolshevize the army's personnel as well as to introduce new technical developments. Party members formed an ever-increasing proportion of the entrants to military schools, as Table 3 shows.[48]

TABLE 3

STUDENTS ATTENDING MILITARY SCHOOLS 1931–33

TYPE OF SCHOOL	YEAR	PROPORTION OF COMMUNISTS	MEMBERS OF THE ALL-UNION LENIN YOUNG COMMUNIST LEAGUE	NON-MEMBERS
Army	1932	60.3	28.0	11.7
	1933	76.2	18.0	5.8
Navy	1932	34.2	59.8	6.0
	1933	55.0	42.6	2.4
Air Force	1932	71.0	28.8	0.2
	1933	80.5	17.7	1.8
Total	1931	44.1	39.0	16.9
	1932	60.1	28.3	11.6
	1933	76.2	18.2	5.6

The nucleus of party members among the army commanders rose to 67.8 per cent in 1933.

In 1932 six new technical military academies were opened, and existing academies were greatly enlarged. Whereas in 1929 only 30 per cent of the students in military schools were studying engineering subjects, in 1934 the proportion had increased to 70 per cent.[49] The educational qualifications for senior army commanders were also raised; in 1928 only 20 per cent of them had received a higher education, but in 1934 78.9 per cent had.[50]

At this time Konyov, Malinovsky, Grechko, Zhukov, Zakharov, Bagramyan and Eremenko—all later marshals of the Soviet Union— were students at these academies. Even Marshal Budenny and his friend Voroshilov were seated at the desks of the "special faculty" of an academy in order to qualify for official diplomas.

In 1939 the Red Army had fourteen military academies and six special military faculties in civilian institutes of higher education, with an annual intake of twenty thousand students, plus another fifteen thousand correspondence course students. In 1940 two more military academies were opened, along with four new military faculties in civilian institutes.[51] Stalin's purge of 1936–38 liquidated the most distinguished and senior members of the Red Army. The Soviet authors cited above, Colonels D. Voropaev and A. Yovlev, make only passing reference to this bloody period. They state simply:

> Serious difficulties had to be overcome in order to solve the problem of the party cadres. The difficulties were exacerbated by the criminal activities of Yezhov and Beria, who liquidated a considerable number of Soviet military leaders. . . . In 1936–38 not a few experienced commanders and political workers who were devoted to the cause of Soviet power were prosecuted . . . including Marshals Tukhachevsky, Egorov and Blyukher [Blucher], a number of commanders of military districts and heads of central administrative bodies and of institutes for higher education. . . . In 1954–55 they were completely rehabilitated.[52]

Khrushchev's "secret report" to the Twentieth Party Congress provides a more accurate explanation of the origin of the Great Purge. Yezhov used to present to Stalin lists of high members of the party and government who were to be arrested and shot; Stalin would confirm them, and then Yezhov would have them shot. Beria only joined the NKVD toward the end of the purge—in November, 1938. Of this Khrushchev's report declares:

> We are quite right to accuse Yezhov of using base methods in 1937. But this question needs to be answered: Could Yezhov himself decide such matters as the fate of leading party members? No, it would be naive to consider that this was Yezhov's doing alone. It is quite clear that Stalin decided these things. . . . He was the principal prosecutor in all these matters. Stalin not only agreed to all these arrests, he also took the initiative in issuing orders for arrests. . . . Very lamentable consequences, especially at the beginning of the war, followed up Stalin's liquidation . . . of army officers in 1937–41. During these years army officers from company and battalion commanders up to the highest ranking officers were victims of acts of oppression.[53]

Verified statistics show the following survival rates: 2 out of 5 marshals; 2 out of 15 army commanders; 28 out of 58 corps commanders; 85 out of 195 divisional commanders; and 186 out of 406 brigade commanders.[54]

Khrushchev was right when he attributed, in great measure, the Red Army's failures in the first years of the war with Germany to Stalin's liquidation of high-ranking Soviet officers.

In order to make good this loss somehow, and above all to place in command the army leaders who were politically loyal to the party, the Central Committee decided in August, 1939, personally to select 4,000 Communists and draft them into the Red Army. Of these, 2,700 were appointed to ordinary political posts, 1,200 to senior posts and 100 to the topmost army political positions.[55]

In 1940 the Central Committee required all party workers to undergo a military refresher course. On May 7, 1940, in order to make military service attractive to young Communists, the Soviet government introduced the ranks of general and admiral, and on January 7, 1943, gold epaulettes were introduced—in spite of such once-famous slogans as "Death to the generals and admirals" and "Death to the creators of gold epaulettes!"

The war put weapons into the hands of millions of people; at the end of the war the Red Army numbered 11,365,000, and it presented a considerable internal as well as an external threat to the communist regime. The party, quite justifiably, had little faith in the loyalty of Soviet citizens to it, and therefore put into effect three important safety measures: (1) It saturated the army with Communists; in the first year of the war there were about 1,000,000 Communists and 2,000,000 *Komsomols* in the army; by the end of the war there were about 3,325,000 Communists in it, comprising 60 per cent of the total strength of the party. (2) It recruited the top political personnel of the army from experienced party workers—members of war councils, commissars and political instructors, from whose ranks came one-third of the total membership of the Central Committee. (3) It created special punitive detachments of experienced Chekists and party workers called "SMERSH"—"Death to Spies." In addition,

> the Central Committee of the party supervised the transfer and appointment of all military and political personnel of a unit political detachment from the rank of brigade commander and deputy chief upward.[56]

Despite these strict measures, in the very first year of the war about five million Red Army soldiers voluntarily surrendered to the enemy. The communist regime was saved, not by the "wisdom" of the party, but by Hitler's political ineptitude and the disasters Western democracy had suffered.

A radical technological reorientation has taken place in the Soviet army since the end of World War II because of the advent of thermonuclear weapons and intercontinental ballistic missiles. The army is now completely motorized and mechanized. In recent years the military academies have increased their output of engineering and scientific graduates. Official statistics indicate that the ratio of technical command personnel to purely military command personnel is now 1:1–5. The party-*Komsomol* element within the command personnel has increased in size: in 1959 86 per cent of the army and navy officers were Communists and *Komsomol* members,[57] but in 1961 90 per cent.[58]

The army is in the iron grip of the party machine. When Marshal Zhukov found this grip too oppressive, he was immediately dismissed from the government and from the Central Committee. A decree of the

Plenum of the Central Committee held in October, 1957, said of him:

> While Minister of Defense, Zhukov advocated the dangerous and damaging line aimed at restricting the work of the party organizations, political organs and war councils and at liquidating the Central Committee's guidance and surveillance of the army and the navy.

The party reminded all marshals, generals, admirals and other Soviet officers that it, not they, was in ultimate command. The above-quoted decree concerning Zhukov clearly states:

> The main source of our army's and our navy's power lies in the fact that the Communist party is their organizer, guide and educator.[59]

Statistics for 1961 show that more than one-half of the officers of the Soviet army and navy are Communists (not counting *Komsomols*), and 73.7 per cent of these have received higher or secondary education.[60]

Thus new party cadres have been created in every branch of the state administration and in the social and intellectual life of the country.

"Cadres that have mastered the technique of power decide everything"—such was the political philosophy of the new regime. The longevity of the Soviet dictatorship confirms that a correct solution to the problem of self-preservation has been found.

The Communist party has itself undergone a radical social and political metamorphosis. Before examining the evolution of party organizational doctrine as embodied in its statutes, and the power technique of the party machine itself, we shall investigate the way in which the old working-class revolutionary party evolved into a party of "cadres of power," the party of a servile bureaucracy.

CHAPTER V

The Social Transformation of the Communist Party of the Soviet Union

ONE OF the most valuable services Milovan Djilas has rendered has been to attract the attention of research workers to the social structure of communist society. Djilas formed his own conclusions about the "new class," not only by analyzing the communist system, but also from playing a part in a communist administration. He provides a penetrating analysis of the system and substantiates it with evidence obtained at the highest level. Even where his analysis is questionable, the evidence on which it is based is indisputable.

The Soviet Communist party cannot be said to be a party of people holding identical views and sharing the same interests, as its statutes would have us believe. It consists of three clearly differentiated social groups: (1) the party bureaucracy (the leading group), (2) the service or official bureaucracy (the executive group) and (3) groups of manual workers (industrial and collective farm workers).

The Bolshevik party, the "party of the working class," has as its task the achievement of the dictatorship of the proletariat. Lenin attached great importance to the absolute predominance in the party of rank-and-file workers. At the Second Party Congress, in 1903, this gave rise to the famous discussion between Lenin and Martov over the formulation of Article 1 of the party statutes, detailed in Chapter One.[1]

Lenin returned to the question of the social composition of the party at least as many times after the Bolsheviks' victory as he had before the Revolution. During the first Russian Revolution Lenin demanded that

> in the new organizations of the party, for each member coming from the Social Democrat intelligentsia there should be several hundred Social Democrat workers.[2]

While Lenin was reluctant to admit members of the intelligentsia into the party, he was anxious to welcome representatives of the lowest social orders, including even the dregs of society. He wrote:

> The urban and industrial proletariat will inevitably be the nucleus of our party, and we must attract to it, educate and organize everyone without exception: craftsmen, paupers, beggars, servants, vagabonds and prostitutes. . . .[3]

The notion that in establishing the dictatorship of the proletariat the Bolshevik party must consist predominantly of "workers from the bench" was propounded by Lenin in all his speeches dealing with the composition of the party. He knew that the swift growth of the party after the Bolsheviks' victory would be at the expense of those who were most anxious to bring about the Leninist ideal of the dictatorship of the proletariat. Lenin realized that this process of the transformation of the party had begun, and he was powerless to halt it.

He indignantly declared:

> The worst elements are attaching themselves to the ruling party, because it is the ruling one[4]

and:

> We fear an excessive expansion of the party, because careerists and adventurers, who ought to be shot, inevitably seek to attach themselves to a party in office.[5]

At the Eighth Party Congress, in 1919, Lenin proposed a special resolution declaring that

> the party must open wide its doors to the workers and to peasant and worker youth . . . and it must be *very selective* in accepting non-worker and non-peasant elements into its ranks.[6]

A new regulation passed at the Eighth All-Russia Conference of the Russian Communist Party (Bolsheviks) in 1919 required that workers and peasants serve a two-month probationary period on becoming party members, while all other newcomers must serve a six-month period.[7] At the Tenth Party Congress, in 1921, the probationary period for non-workers, including peasants, was extended to one year.[8] At the same time a decree was passed that ushered in a new epoch; it concerned the first purge of the party. A year later, at the Eleventh Congress, the last one Lenin attended, a more radical decree was passed to protect the party from an influx of non-manual workers and peasants. Even workers were to be chosen more carefully. Three categories of candidates for party membership were established: (1) workers (six months' probation as a candidate, three recommendations from persons with a three-year party record and confirmation by the district party committee), (2) peasants (one year's probation, three recommendations from persons with a three year party record and confirmation by the *gubernia* party committee) and (3) non-manual workers (two years' probation, five recommendations from members of five years' standing and confirmation by the *gubernia* party committee).[9]

At the Thirteenth Party Conference (January 14–15, 1924) a decree was passed that not less than 100,000 "bench-workers" be recruited into the party, and that no further "non-proletarian elements" be accepted for the time being.[10] After Lenin's death a new "Leninist summons to workers at the bench" was published that raised the party membership from 446,080 in 1924 to 741,147 in 1925. In May, 1924, the Thirteenth Party Congress ordained that not less than 50 per cent of the party should be "workers at the bench." This was implemented on paper only, as Table 4 shows.[11]

TABLE 4

AN ANALYSIS OF PARTY MEMBERSHIP, 1905–32

| | TOTAL NUMBER OF MEMBERS AND CANDIDATES | PERCENTAGE | | |
YEAR		MANUAL WORKERS	PEASANTS	NON-MANUAL WORKERS
1905 (Jan.)	8,400	61.7	4.7	33.6
1917 (Jan.)	23,600	60.2	7.6	32.2
1917 (Oct.)	240,000	—	—	—
1921 (Mar.)	732,521	—	—	—
1922	401,000	44.4	6.9	48.9
1924	446,080	44.0	28.8	27.2
1925	741,147	57.9	25.3	16.8
1926	1,002,490	58.1	24.6	17.3
1927	1,131,254	56.1	26.3	17.6
1928	1,220,836	57.8	22.3	19.9
1930	1,572,164	65.8(?)	19.7(?)	11.5(?)*
1931	2,066,400	66.9	22.3	11.1
1932	3,172,215	64.5	27.8	7.7

*These are errors in the original party statistics. (*See* the author's *Tekhnologiya Vlasti*, p. 249.)

Table 4 shows the sharp decline in the number of manual workers in proportion to the number of peasants and non-manual workers until special measures were introduced at the Thirteenth Party Congress. It also illustrates a typical Soviet mode of falsification. The years 1918, 1919 and 1920 are omitted; no data about the social composition of the party membership for the years 1917–21 is given. The reason for this omission becomes evident when the data in Table 5, provided by earlier Soviet sources, are interpolated.[12]

TABLE 5

AN ANALYSIS OF THE INCREASE IN PARTY MEMBERSHIP, 1917–21

(in percentages)

YEAR	MANUAL WORKERS	PEASANTS	NON-MANUAL WORKERS	OTHERS	TOTAL
1917	56.5	15.3	21.6	6.1	100
1918	40.1	28.0	25.1	6.8	100
1919	38.3	29.7	24.8	7.3	100
1920	33.2	36.9	22.1	7.8	100
1921	29.7	41.0	26.8	8.5	100

From Table 5 it can be seen that in 1921 only 29.7 per cent of the party's members came from the ranks of the proletariat; the remaining 70.3 per cent were recruited from the petty bourgeoisie (peasants, non-manual workers, artisans, etc.).

Thus party policy was not then, nor is it now, dictated by rank-and-file members. However, the official doctrine that "the Communist party is the vanguard of the proletariat" required that there be a preponderance of workers in it. Hence Lenin's continual concern and the decree of the Thirteenth Congress. The number of workers in the party rose, largely because of an organized recruiting campaign. At the Sixteenth Party Congress, in 1930, Stalin remarked apropos of this that "workers at the bench" were applying for party membership, not individually, but "by the workshop and the factory."[13] Party statistics, however, impute new meanings to the categories manual worker, peasant and non-manual worker—a manual worker is taken to mean not only one who is currently working on the factory floor but anyone who has ever done so. Hence there arose the need to distinguish between manual workers and "workers at the bench." This new distinction makes it evident that the number of manual workers who were members of the party greatly diminished. The percentage of party members who were "workers at the bench" was 18.8 per cent in January, 1924; 40.8 per cent in January, 1925, and January, 1926; and 36.7 per cent in June, 1927.[14] The 1927 figure was despite "Lenin's summons" and two purges of non-manual workers (the higher education institute purge in 1925 and the purge of rural cells in 1926).

Manual workers were also affected by the two subsequent general purges (in 1929–30 and in 1933), especially since, with the beginning of collectivization, the five-year plans and the liquidation of the last remnants of the NEP, the country was plunged into straits of hunger and terror that had no precedent since the Civil War, provoking great dissatisfaction among the worker members of the party.

It was no accident that in 1934 the new party statutes made it more difficult for manual workers to enter the party by lengthening their probation period to one year, while at the same time making it nearly as easy for engineering and technical workers to join as for industrial and agricultural workers. Engineering and technical workers were, in fact, enabled to join the party more easily than peasant and collective farm workers,[15] revealing a new tendency in the regulation of the social composition of the party: the predominance of the manual worker ceased to be a "categorical imperative."

The Seventeenth Congress passed a special resolution that predetermined the composition of what was to be Stalin's party. Its first clause stated:

> In order to prevent further mechanical and indiscriminate acceptances of persons as candidates and members of the party, more

recommendations and sponsors with higher party qualifications will be required. The party must only accept activists who have proved themselves in their work in some social organization, and those who are accepted must be subjected to a rigorous investigation and inquiries must be made of the organization for which the candidate works.[16]

Now the party needed not workers or peasants but "activists" who could survive the most rigorous police investigation. The Union-wide check on party documents and the subsequent "great purge" of Yagoda, Ezhov and Beria were conducted, not from the point of view of what one was yesterday, but of what one might be today or tomorrow.

As a result of this purge approximately 1,220,934 Communists were expelled from the party between 1934 and 1939[17]—almost one-half of the membership of 2,809,786.

Those expelled were replaced by new Communists who had passed the new membership tests, so that by the Eighteenth Congress the party had again increased to 2,476,966 members and candidate members.

The new membership requirements completely ignored origin, profession or type of occupation. The party leaders ceased to be interested in either the backgrounds or abilities of members; the only essential prerequisite for membership was unwavering loyalty to the party machine.

The new requirements were officially formulated in the new statutes of the party promulgated at the Eighteenth Congress, in 1939. The workers lost their former rights, a "single system for workers, peasants and intelligentsia" was instituted[18] and a one-year probationary period for candidates for party membership was established for everyone.[19] In Paragraph 1 of the new statutes party members are required to "observe the strictest party discipline and to put party policy and the decisions of party organs into practice." Among the members' rights listed by the new statutes is the dubious "right of each member to address or question any party committee, right up to the Central Committee."[20]

After the early thirties it is possible to distinguish groupings within the party that are based not on origin but on position and on material and other interests. Political interests ceased to be of importance because they fell entirely within the competence of the party machine. This division into groups is reflected by the terms "party *aktiv*," "soviet *aktiv*," "economic *aktiv*" and *Komsomol aktiv*." The party was horizontally divided into two groups: the activists, who controlled party and state affairs, and the others. But a vertical division within the party is of even greater importance; thus the activist groups do not have equal rights but are subject to a hierarchical system in which the party apparatus forms the highest command group, and the remaining groups command only within the confines of their own spheres of activity. As such they represent subsidiary differentiated groups vis-à-vis the directing and integrating group of the members of the party machine.

Bukharin foresaw just such a change in the structure of the party when he disagreed with Stalin in 1926. He wrote:

> We have in our hands a state and party apparatus, and very often, following the party line, situations arise where we say as if to a military superior. . . "Yes, Comrade Commander" etc. . . . This is a tendency to turn our party into just such a hierarchical system . . . such a tendency exists.[21]

In 1937, Stalin openly declared that the hierarchical structure of the party on a military pattern was not a tendency, but an accomplished fact. Continuing the military metaphor, Stalin stated that the party consisted of three corps: the generals of the party (from 3,000 to 4,000 persons), the "officer corps" (from 30,000 to 40,000) and "noncommissioned officers" (from 100,000 to 150,000).[22] Stalin appears to have regarded all the remaining members (about 2,000,000 Communists) as rank-and-file soldiers incapable of ratiocination.

Two years later the Eighteenth Congress confirmed the rights and privileges of the first two corps within the party in a resolution stating:

> Taking into consideration the special political importance of the party *aktiv* in the life of the party, the constitution will be supplemented by the following point concerning the *aktivs* of city organizations: it is considered essential that in all republics, district and regional centers, without exception, and also in all important industrial centers, the *aktivs* of city party organizations must be called together to discuss very important party and government decisions, and that in large centers, regional as well as city *aktivs* be convened.[23]

In order to assist young Communists to occupy places vacated by old Bolsheviks in the high command and the officer corps, the Congress reduced the party service qualifications for secretaries of district, regional and central committees of national Communist parties from twelve to five years, and for secretaries of city and district committees from ten and seven years, respectively, to three years.[24]

The war brought numerical changes in the party, but it did not alter its vertical and horizontal structure. The postwar period swiftly and finally settled its social, professional and functional character.

Structural changes in the Communist party were prompted by the social upheavals taking place throughout the country, as Table 6 shows.[25]

TABLE 6

CLASS STRUCTURE OF PREREVOLUTIONARY RUSSIA AND THE MODERN U.S.S.R.

CLASSES AND SOCIAL GROUPS (INCLUDING FAMILIES)	PREREVOLUTIONARY RUSSIA		U.S.S.R.	
	1897	1913	1928	1955
Working class, including agricultural workers	14.3	14.8	14.6	44.2
Peasantry				
as a class	68.5	—	—	—
individual peasant farmers	—	66.7	74.9	0.5
collective farm peasants	—	—	2.9	41.2
Bourgeoisie, including rural bourgeoisie and *kulaks*	15.2	16.3	4.6	—
Intelligentsia	2.0	2.2	3.0	14.1
Total	100	100	100	100
Population (in millions)	125.6	139.3	152.3	200.2

Thus, in the U.S.S.R. today the main classes of society are: working class, 44.2 per cent; collective farm workers, 41.2 per cent; and intelligentsia, 14.1 per cent.

In type of profession (physical work) and in source of income (wages) the working class has remained the same as it was before the Revolution; it has only grown quantitatively and qualitatively. It works for the state, and it has lost the legal status it acquired after the Revolution of 1905.

There have, however, been fundamental changes in the life of the peasantry. Its well-being and the size and even source of its income depend not on itself but on the state.

The intelligentsia has become an entirely different class with regard to the size and source of its income and with regard to both its legal position and its social position in Soviet society. It occupies the place the nobility had occupied by heritage and the bourgeoisie had occupied by reason of its economic position. This is not true of all members of the Soviet intelligentsia, of course. The Soviet intelligentsia does not form a homogeneous body. There is the command intelligentsia— the bureaucracy — and the service intelligentsia — technical workers, teachers, doctors, scientists and artists. The former group has occupied the place of the class Soviet statistics about prerevolutionary Russia term the bourgeoisie.

The figure of 16.3 per cent of the population in 1913 as bourgeoisie is utterly false, because this figure included prosperous peasants, who themselves formed 11.4 per cent of the population. If we exclude the latter, the bourgeois landowners class comprised 4.9 per cent of the population of Russia, and of these only 0.2 per cent were landowners.

The emergence of a bureaucracy of specialists in the various branches of governmental, economic, social and cultural life, as distinct from the intelligentsia in general, was a most important new factor in Soviet society. On January 1, 1956, there were 5,553,000 specialists in the U.S.S.R., 33.8 per cent of whom were Communists, with the majority of them engaged in administrative rather than in productive work.

In assessing the social structure of the U.S.S.R. it is important to remember that as well as providing a minority with an opportunity for personal enrichment, the state now also provides the overall majority of workers with their livelihood, as Table 7 shows.[26]

TABLE 7

AN ESTIMATE OF THE WORKING POPULATION OF THE U.S.S.R.

SOURCE OF INCOME AND TYPE OF WORK	WORKING POPULATION IN 1955	
	in millions	in percentages
State economy (salaried)	48.4	56.1
Cooperative enterprises (income as members of *artels*):		
agricultural *artels*	26.0	30.1
craft *artels*	1.8	2.0
Personal subsidiary enterprises (employing members of families)		
collective farm families	6.0	7.0
families of workers and officials	3.7	4.3
Private undertakings	.4	.5
Total	86.3	100

It can be seen that 56.1 per cent of the working population receive their wages from the state, 32.1 per cent from cooperative enterprises and only 11.8 per cent from personal enterprises.[27]

The state employs vast numbers of people, regulates the size and quality of output and controls wage levels. The Communist party is, therefore, able to determine how the national income shall be apportioned; in other words, it sets the standard of living for each Soviet citizen.

Since the state has become the source of his income, the standard of living a Soviet citizen enjoys depends on the place he occupies in the industrial or administrative hierarchy.

As far as Soviet society is concerned, the Marxist-Leninist concept of a class as the "relationship of people to the means of production" is meaningless. Soviet sociologists adhere firmly to this definition, since in law all Soviet citizens have an identical relationship to the means of production whether owned by the state or by collectives. This creates the illusion, advantageous to the regime, that there is no class of exploiters in the U.S.S.R. because there is no private ownership of the means of production. But the citizen's relationship to the means of production cannot be taken as the criterion for deciding to which class of Soviet society he belongs. The sole criterion is his relationship to the organs of administration and distribution. The size of the individual citizen's income depends on the source from which he receives it. The income of a worker, a collective farmer, an engineer or an army officer is standardized and defined; they are hired workers. The income of a member of the bureaucracy is directly proportional to the place he occupies in the social scale or "social stratification" of society. Political authority is the source of his income, and the degree to which he possesses this determines whether he has a luxurious villa or other, less enviable perquisites. The ruling class (the party bureaucracy) is reluctant to share its power with any outsider, and it runs the country through a very highly qualified departmental bureaucracy. The members of its economic, military, police, cultural and ideological organizations are all rewarded according to the same hierarchical principle.

The party bureaucracy and the departmental groups do not constitute a closed class, even though it is much more difficult to enter them than to be expelled from them. Devotion to the regime shapes the bureaucrat's career, but it is the most talented of the loyal men who are chosen for promotion. Devotion to the regime does not mean that communist fanatics are being sought by the authorities; it means devotion to a certain coterie within the party machine and readiness to put the political line of that group into effect.

The privileges and rights of these supporters of the ruling group are assured while those who hold them are of use to the group. These rights are not hereditary; the holder relinquishes them to his successor in office. Nevertheless, children of high party and government officials almost invariably receive higher education, and they often take up careers in their fathers' spheres of activity in the highest strata of Soviet society. Attempts have been made to equalize the wages of the highest officials with those of the ordinary workers, a policy propounded as long ago as Lenin's "April Theses." In September, 1920, the Eleventh All-Russia Party Conference passed the following resolution:

> Responsible communist workers do not have the right to receive personal salary rates, bonuses or overtime payments. A commission must be set up to work out practical measures to eliminate inequalities in the living conditions and incomes of specialists and responsible workers on the one hand and the toiling masses on the other. Inequality violates democracy, adversely affects the party and reduces communist authority.[28]

In March, 1921, the Tenth Party Congress reaffirmed that

> this Congress wholeheartedly supports the policy of equalization in the sphere of material well-being of members of the party.[29]

The party's "asceticism" soon succumbed to the temptations and material inducements embodied in the communist capitalism of the NEP, and the policy of equalization was formally abandoned at the Twelfth Party Conference, held in 1922. Stalin referred to it as a "piece of reactionary petty-bourgeois nonsense," while making the customary reference to Lenin:

> Every Leninist knows, if he is a true Leninist, that a policy of equalization in the matter of day-to-day basic personal needs is nothing but a piece of reactionary petty-bourgeois nonsense worthy of some primitive ascetic sect.[30]

The Twelfth Conference ordained that

> taking cognizance of the fact that the material position of active party workers is at present extremely unsatisfactory, it is deemed necessary immediately to undertake a series of measures to remedy this situation.[31]

At this time there were 15,325 responsible party workers;[32] their salary scales were based on a scale-of-wages decree issued by the government and the All-Union Central Council of Trade Unions. The new wage scale had seventeen grades—the first for apprentices, the second for unskilled workers and the seventeenth for the most highly qualified specialists. Party workers were assigned to the following grades:

Twelfth grade—secretaries of party cells and *volost* committees;

Thirteenth grade—directors of subsections of district party committees;

Fourteenth grade—district party committee instructors, secretaries of *uyezd* committees, secretaries of regional committees of provincial cities and responsible Central Committee workers (investigators, informers, etc.);

Fifteenth grade—directors of subsections of the Central Committee, secretaries of *uyezd* and regional committees in large industrial centers and directors of sections of district committees, regional committees and provincial committees;

Sixteenth grade—deputy directors of Central Committee departments, responsible instructors and members of regional inspection commissions;

Seventeenth grade—members of the Central Committee, directors of Central Committee departments, members of regional bureaus of the Central Committee and secretaries of regional and provincial committees.[33]

The decree stated:

> All the aforementioned comrades must be provided with proper living accommodation (by the executive committees), medical care (by the Ministry of Health) and educational facilities for their children.[34]

A sharp differentiation developed between the various party members, depending on their status: the higher the rank, the higher the standard of living. Rank-and-file members, erstwhile participants in the Revolution and the Civil War, were accorded the same material standards as the ordinary workers, and thus they came into conflict with the privileged party elite. The contrast between the living standards of the ordinary members and the party bureaucrats became a cause for discontent among the people as well as among the lower ranks of the party. This explains why the Thirteenth Party Conference, in January, 1924, declared:

> Negative tendencies include: the considerable disparity in the material well-being of party members, depending on their function.[35]

Consequently, a "party maximum" that laid down the maximum salary a party official might receive was introduced. It ranged from 198 to 250 rubles, depending on geographical situation. In the mid-thirties a new system was introduced that established three categories: (1) district and town party workers; (2) regional and provincial party workers; and (3) workers in the Central Committee of the party.

The living standard of the last two categories cannot be deduced merely from their salary scales. They have many other perquisites, such as a detached house or private apartment in town, as well as a cottage in the country; cars—official and private; domestic servants, including children's nurses, gardeners, hairdressers and chauffeurs; and unlimited expense accounts. The living standard of a party official in the first category is much more modest. He is unable to live on his salary alone. He receives incidental extras in the form of money or gifts in kind to supplement his income. Students in regional party schools receive 170 rubles a month plus 10 rubles for each dependent; the average wage of the industrial worker is about 80 rubles.[36]

The Eighteenth Party Congress, in 1939, declared that

> the Bolshevik party is the leading detachment of the working class, the highest form of class organization . . . in the struggle to achieve the dictatorship of the working class.[37]

But the Nineteenth Congress rejected these words and introduced a new definition of the party: "a militant alliance of persons of the same persuasion—Communists," which rejects the notion of the dictatorship of the working class.[38] After thirty-five years of Communist dictatorship, a rather strange clause appeared in the party's statutes at the Nineteenth Party Congress in 1952:

> Any citizen of the U.S.S.R. who does not exploit the labor of another may become a member of the Communist Party of the Soviet Union.[39]

This proviso would seem to disqualify all senior party officials from party membership, as in the Soviet Union only these senior officials exploit the labor of others; only they have hired servants. The paragraph was deleted from the statutes at the Twenty-second Party Congress in 1961.

The war hindered the party's development as a service bureaucracy. The need to extend the party's social basis reasserted itself for propaganda purposes. The party's political organs conducted a large-scale campaign to recruit new members in the army and the navy. Desire to become a party member became identified with loyalty to the Fatherland. Soldiers in the Red Army asked to join the party so that they could die as Communists. To facilitate this, on September 9, 1941, the Central Committee decreed that military personnel would have to serve only three months as probationary members, and that the method of entry be simplified for them. This led to an artificial increase in the ranks of the party.[40]

The increase in the number of members and candidate members of the Communist party during the war (1941–44) was as follows: 1941, 3,800,000; 1942, 5,149,000; 1944, 5,800,000.[41] The following statistics show the increase in the number of Communists in the Red Army during the war: 1941, 1,300,000 Communists (42.4 per cent of the party's members); 1942, more than 2,000,000 Communists; 1945, 3,500,000 Communists (60 per cent of the party's members and candidate members).[42]

The rapid increase in membership is illustrated by the fact that in the first year of the war the party lost 400,000 members at the front.[43]

Once the war had ended, the party no longer needed to encourage recruitment among rank-and-file Soviet citizens. The Central Committee therefore declared at the Warsaw Conference of the COMINFORM, in 1947, that "the party has no present need to swell its ranks."[44] A year earlier the Central Committee had passed a decree laying down a minimum for recruitment to the party. At the Nineteenth Party Congress, in 1952, it was yet again clearly stated that "the party is strong qualitatively rather than quantitatively."[45]

In other words, once the need to appeal to the nation had passed, the prewar practice of recruiting members on a more exclusive basis, that is, from the service bureaucracy, was resumed.

A decree of the Central Committee dated July 26, 1946, condemned the practice of mass recruitment, stating:

> There have been revealed violations of the Leninist practice of individual selection for party membership, resulting in a deterioration in the quality of candidates accepted.[46]

It went on to say that "only politically prepared leading workers" should be recruited, and that the Central Committee should point out to party organizations the need for a more careful selection of "engineering and technical workers, scientists, agriculturalists and intelligentsia."[47]

Again the party only accepted activists and "leading people," that is, intelligent persons. The rejection rate was therefore quite high; in Moscow it was 22.4 per cent in 1947, and it rose to 46.9 per cent in 1948. As a result, the party almost ceased to grow in size; in 1947 there were more than 6,000,000 Communists, and five years later—in October, 1952—only 880,000 more. This represents an increase of only 160,000 members each year. There are no precise statistics to show which class was most rigorously excluded during this period, but certain trends are evident. For example, during the first half of 1948 the new members recruited by the Moscow party organization were made up of 32 per cent workers and 68 per cent non-workers.[48] This is typical of the situation in the constituent republics of Belorussia and Georgia, as Table 8 shows.[49]

TABLE 8

The Social Composition of the New Party Membership in Belorussia
(in percentages)

Year	Workers and Peasants	Officials and Intelligentsia
1948	18.8	81.2
1949	40.4	59.6
1951	43.9	56.1

Between October, 1952, and January, 1954, officials and intelligentsia in Belorussia comprised 57.4 per cent of the party's recruits[50] and in 1952 in Georgia they comprised 59 per cent.[51]

When referring to "the return to Lenin" at the Twentieth Congress, the party leadership showed that it was not as yet acting on behalf of the proletariat. A Central Committee resolution spoke of the need to "consider incorrect the neglect of certain party organizations to regulate the growth of the party . . . ," and proposed to "strengthen the work of the individual selection of leading persons as candidates for party membership, especially of workers and peasants."[52] The absence of any reference to the "leading members of the Soviet intelligentsia," which the Central Committee's report had mentioned,[53] suggests that the Central Committee felt that the party was not lacking in members drawn from the ranks of the bureaucracy. Moreover, this presentation of the question of regulating the party's composition confirms the fact that the Soviet Communist party has long since ceased to be a working-class party.

It has stood to gain from this, because it has become a party of the state bureaucracy; but it is evidently troubled by the moral loss. Hence the Congress' resolution and the Central Committee's special decision to enlarge the "worker nucleus of the party."[54]

In 1962, for the first time in thirty years, the Central Committee gave information about the professions and nationalities of party members.[55]

Unfortunately, these details refer only to some of the years since Stalin's death (1956–61). In 1956 32 per cent of the party's members were workers, 17.1 per cent were peasants (collective farmers) and 50.9 per cent were non-manual workers.

This means that in 1956, out of a total party membership of 6,760,000 Communists, 3,440,000 were serving in the governmental, party or social bureaucracy.[56]

Workers comprised only 46 per cent of the members of party organizations in industry, and the official statistics do not tell us how many of these actually came from the factory floor. Nevertheless, the measures that were taken to change the social composition of the party did not achieve their goal. In 1961, the "worker nucleus" increased by only 2.5 per cent and the number of peasant members by 0.5 per cent. By 1961 the number of bureaucrat party members had risen to 4,656,-000, as compared with 3,440,000 in 1956.[57]

Table 9 shows how the various professions were represented in the party on July 1, 1961.[58]

TABLE 9

PROFESSIONS OF PARTY MEMBERS, JULY 1, 1961

PROFESSION	NUMBER	PER CENT
Total Non-manual workers	4,656,000	100
Directors of organizations, institutions, enterprises, construction projects, state farms, etc.	474,912	10.2
Agricultural specialists, economists and architects	1,359,552	29.2
Workers in science, education, the health services, literature and the arts	1,001,040	21.5
Workers in trading and food supply	228,144	4.9
Supervisory workers	554,064	11.9
Others, including communications, public works, etc.	1,038,288	22.3

Equally interesting is the grouping of leaders of the governmental and party bureaucracies. The statistics in Table 10 have been abstracted from the 1959 official list of party personnel, which terms them leaders of "social organizations."[59]

TABLE 10

LEADING MEMBERS OF THE GOVERNMENTAL AND PARTY BUREAUCRACY

POSITION	NUMBER
Higher state and party bureaucracy (leading members of administrative organizations)	392,100
Leading officials of industrial and farming enterprises (including collective and state farms)	955,200
Heads and departmental heads of administrative bodies	1,267,500
Heads and departmental heads of trading organizations	334,800
Total	2,949,600

In regulating the social composition of the party, the Central Committee is not only adhering to the principle of increasing the size of the worker nucleus, at the expense of the worker aristocracy, it is also trying to increase the proportion of engineers and technicians who are party members in preference to workers in offices, factories, retail trade, etc. This is borne out by Table 11, which shows the social status of recruits to the party.[60]

TABLE 11

SOCIAL STATUS OF RECRUITS TO THE COMMUNIST PARTY OF THE SOVIET UNION
(in percentages)

OCCUPATION	YEAR	
	1955	1960
Manual workers	30.4	43.1
Collective farm workers	21.3	21.7
Non-manual workers	46.2	34.3
Other specialists	53.6	68.5
Students and others	2.1	0.9
Total number of candidate members	100	100

In the rural areas, the Central Committee recruits the "aristocracy of the collective farms," that is, agricultural specialists as distinct from ordinary farm workers, as Table 12 shows.[61]

TABLE 12

SOCIAL AND PROFESSIONAL RECRUITS TO THE RANKS OF THE PARTY IN RURAL AREAS

OCCUPATION	YEAR	
	1955	1960
Agronomists, veterinarians and other specialists	821	6,597
Tractor drivers, combine operators and other machine operators	13,578	31,976
Workers engaged in stock breeding	12,339	28,302
Agricultural workers and market-garden workers	20,711	32,264

The official communiqué of the Central Committee of the Soviet Communist party reaches the following conclusion:

A characteristic feature of recruitment to the party during recent years has been the ever-increasing influx of engineering and technical specialists from all branches of technology.[62]

Table 13, giving the educational qualifications of members of the Soviet Communist party in July, 1961, illustrates that it is the party of the bureaucratic elite of Soviet society.[63]

TABLE 13

COMMUNISTS' EDUCATIONAL QUALIFICATIONS (JULY, 1961)

EDUCATIONAL QUALIFICATIONS	NUMBER	PER CENT
Total number of members and candidate members of the Soviet Communist party	9,626,740	100
Members who completed higher education	1,283,548	13.3
Members who have not completed higher education	2,852,158	29.6
Specialists in that number	1,792,689	18.6
Members who have not completed secondary education	2,755,652	28.6

Thus almost 43 per cent of the members of the Communist party have received partial or complete secondary higher education. Communist specialists comprised 3,076,200 members of the Soviet Communist party in 1961; in other words, one in three members of the Communist party is a specialist. This naturally led to a sharp increase in the number of Communist specialists occupying leading positions in the national economy, both in industrial enterprises and in the administration, as shown in Table 14.[64]

TABLE 14

COMMUNIST SPECIALISTS IN THE NATIONAL ECONOMY

DATE	TOTAL NUMBER OF SPECIALISTS IN NATIONAL ECONOMY	COMMUNISTS AMONG THEM	
		NUMBER	PER CENT
1928	521,000	6,400	1.2
January, 1941	2,401,000	694,800	20.5
December, 1956	6,257,000	1,744,200	28.0
December, 1960	8,784,000	2,495,200	28.5

Educational qualifications being equal, preference is given to communist candidates for technical and economic posts. It is an unwritten law that the director of an enterprise must be a party member. The chief engineer of a factory is usually a party member. It is therefore not surprising that ambitious engineers and technicians feel obliged to join the party. Table 15 shows the distribution of party members in the various branches of industry in July, 1961.[65]

TABLE 15

THE DISTRIBUTION OF COMMUNISTS IN VARIOUS BRANCHES OF THE
NATIONAL ECONOMY, JULY 1, 1961

BRANCH OF THE ECONOMY	PER CENT
Industry and construction work	33.5
Agriculture and forestry	23.3
Transport and communications	9.2
Material and technical supplies, trade and food industry	5.4
Non-productive industries, including public health, education, culture and science	28.6
Government and party machinery	10.8
Communal administration	2.2

TABLE 16

THE DISTRIBUTION OF COMMUNISTS IN RURAL AREAS BY WORK CATEGORIES

CATEGORY	JANUARY, 1956		JULY, 1961	
	NUMBER	PER CENT	NUMBER	PER CENT
Total of Communists on collective farms	1,400,000	100	1,700,000	100
Agriculture, including specialized fields	896,000	66.7	1,315,800	77.4
Administrative work	504,000	33.3	384,200	22.6

To these must be added another 557,800 Communists who work on state farms (July, 1961).[66]

The temporary decrease in the number of people employed in administrative jobs on collective farms is due to the increase in the size of these farms.

The average length of party membership also shows a sharp decrease. Only 8 per cent have been members longer than twenty-five years; 52 per cent have been members from eleven to twenty-five years; and 40 per cent have been members for less than ten years.[67]

This means that since the death of Stalin 3,886,400 Communists have entered the party, and of the 2,809,000 persons who were members just before the Great Purge, only 777,000 survived—that is, just over one-fourth. The rest—more than 2,000,000 Communists—died from natural causes or as a result of purges.

The increasing youthfulness of party members is also evident elsewhere. At the last Stalinist Party Congress, the Nineteenth, in 1952, 45 per cent of the delegates had been born since the Revolution; at the Twenty-second Congress, in 1961, this proportion had risen to 67 per cent.[68] This reflects the situation in the population as a whole, three-quarters of whom have been born since 1917. In the Soviet Communist party there are 1,898,759 women—one-fifth of the membership.[69]

The trend toward recruiting a greater proportion of younger members to the party and to the party cadres began immediately after the exposure of Stalin at the Twentieth Congress. It was achieved by a sharp increase in the recruitment rate, as Table 17 shows.[70]

TABLE 17

THE GROWTH OF THE PARTY, 1956–61

DATE	TOTAL NUMBER OF COMMUNISTS
January 1, 1956	7,173,521
January 1, 1957	7,494,573
January 1, 1958	7,843,196
January 1, 1959	8,239,131
January 1, 1960	8,708,667
January 1, 1961	9,275,826
October 1, 1961	9,716,005

From these figures it is obvious that in the course of twenty-one months (1960–61) the party increased by almost 1,500,000 members. After the Twentieth Congress it increased by 2,500,000 members. However, the Soviet Communist party does not admit every applicant, but only those from the elite and the more distinguished representatives of the workers and the collective farmers. Khrushchev was quite right when he said:

> If we said: "Let anyone who wishes join the Communist party," we would at once have many million members. But we say: "We do not need this." In order to become a Communist, one must not only understand communism, one must also be an active protagonist of it. And not everybody is capable of this.[71]

Everybody is, however, capable of understanding that, in the conditions prevailing in the Soviet Union, a party ticket is a necessary prerequisite for a career in public life or science and for securing full material and legal privileges.

In 1962, official statistics were published about the national composition of the U.S.S.R. for the first time in thirty years. They confirm what we already know from incidental evidence, namely, that as regards the "coefficient of saturation" by Communists, the Turkestan and Baltic republics remain weak links in the Soviet system; this matter is dealt with further in Chapters Ten and Eighteen.

This examination of the party's social transformation leads an objective observer to conclude that *as the result of a prolonged historical process, the party of the "proletariat" has become the party of the bureaucracy, not only in its interests, but also in its composition.* While no state can dispense with its administrative bureaucracy, the Soviet governmental machine simultaneously performs three functions: those of ruler, employer and distributor; thus it cannot be compared with the bureaucracies of other countries. The present Soviet state truly is, in the words of Marx's definition of the bourgeois state, a manager of the affairs of the Soviet bureaucracy. To state that in the West the state exists for the people and the bureaucracy exists for the state, but in the U.S.S.R. the converse is true—the people exist for the state and the state exists for the bureaucracy—is a simplification, but nonetheless true. It is therefore easy to understand why the theory of the withering away of the state has proved to be Utopian in the Soviet Union. The gradual but swift expansion of both the functions and the sphere of activity of the machinery of state is one of the laws of Soviet socialism, regardless of the fact that from time to time the supreme power now centralizes, now decentralizes, the leading detachments of its bureaucratic army.

The members of the governing bureaucracy are, as we have seen, equals only in the eyes of the people—not in the eyes of the authorities. In this connection there are two sharply defined groups: the group that wields no power (the soviet authority) and the leadership group (the commanding authority). The former group contains representatives of the official bureaucracy, irrespective of rank; the latter group contains representatives of the party bureaucracy. It is the latter group that has the power to legislate.

The party bureaucracy, like the departmental bureaucracy, is organized on hierarchical principles and is concentrated in the secretarial corps of the party. As such it is superior to the committee corps, that is, it is above the controlling *aktiv* of each level.

In order for the party's secretaries to control the members of the party committees, the party's statutes make them independent of the committee members. The secretaries depend only on each other; they are not elected, but they appoint one another. The present electoral system, with its open voting, is a pure formality. The Secretariat of the Central Committee of the Communist party appoints the secretaries of the central committees of the constituent republics. They in turn appoint the secretaries of their provincial committees, who appoint the secretaries of city and district committees. This last group is responsible for appointing the secretaries of the primary party organizations. While these appointments are termed recommendations and confirmations, this does not alter the fact that this hierarchical system has been established by the party's statutes.[72]

The statutes protect the rights and privileges, not only of the party secretaries, but of the entire executive system, from the claims of the rank-and-file members of the party. Another paragraph of the statutes states:

The primary organization of the party cannot decide to exclude a Communist from the party if he is a member of the Central Committee of the party or of the central committee of the republic, provincial, district or city committee.[73]

Having alloted itself such great authority, the party's Secretariat must be well qualified to wield power. And so it is, as the following percentages of personnel who have received complete or partial higher education show: secretaries of rural district committees, 90 per cent; secretaries of urban district committees, 92 per cent; secretaries of provincial, regional and central committees of the constituent republics, 95 per cent. In addition, 60 per cent of the secretaries of the primary organizations of the party have also received either secondary or higher education.[74]

These secretaries possess a wide variety of qualifications; among them are engineers, agronomists, jurists, teachers, etc. Although they have attained positions of prominence because they are Communists, rather than because they are specialists, their skills are good enough for them to be able to organize production and to control its technological processes on behalf of the party.

Relations between the various social groupings within the Soviet Communist party are far from perfect. One can discern three types of conflict here: (1) general conflicts between rank-and-file members and the controlling *aktiv;* (2) specialist and professional conflicts among groups of the controlling *aktiv* (conflicts between party secretaries and committees), or, the same thing, between the party bureaucracy and the departmental bureaucracy; and (3) conflicts between the party and the people. Conflicts in the controlling *aktiv* itself, between the various social groups that comprise it, manifest themselves primarily as conflicts arising from inequality of rights. By law the departmental bureaucracy (Soviet cadres) controls the organs of state administration, but this is only a legal fiction. In actual fact the state administration merely repeats the decisions of the party machine; it merely puts into practice the directives and orders issued by the heads of the corresponding party organ at each level. Thus the state is controlled by two parallel organizations, one of which is small in size but has paramount influence (the party machine), the other, although large in size, of purely technical importance (the machinery of state). This dichotomy of control gives rise to a conflict in interest that persists throughout the entire administrative system. It is resolved at the highest level by uniting the position of first secretary of the party with that of chairman of the government. In 1965 the two positions were separated; the first secretary is now the dominant position. The conflicts between party bureaucracy and departmental bureaucracy are further exacerbated by the fact that there are in the state administrative organs, including the economic administration, specialists, Communists more highly qualified than persons who are members of the party machine. The party machine has also improved in quality and contains a great number of specialists; for example, each local party committee secretariat contains at least two secretaries who are specialists in an appropriate field. The specialists' decisive influence on the running of the country and the party is also evident in the composition of the Presidium of the Central Committee of the Soviet Communist party. Eight of the Presidium's twelve members are qualified engineers. The main source of discontent to the departmental bureaucracy, which controls industrial enterprises, to the economic ministries and to specialist ministries and committees lies in the fact that, although important functions are assigned to them, they lack managerial and executive authority.

The party machine reserves the right to order how things should be done, even to the last technical detail. The resulting constant friction and hidden conflict are a characteristic feature of the day-to-day functioning of the dualistic administrative regime. This struggle between the various groups of the nation's leading personnel is directed at obtaining an equitable share of power for themselves within the framework of the existing system. There is no conflict among them, however, when it comes to defending their privileged position from any possible challenge to it by the rank-and-file members of the party or by the nation at large.

* Chapter VI *

The Evolution of the Party's Statutes

THE STATUTES of the Soviet Communist party consist of a set of rules and statements and a system of standards on the party's structure. They regulate the life of the party and decree how it shall function in other organizations. Whereas the program of the Soviet Communist party defines the immediate and the ultimate aims of the party and the ways in which those aims shall be realized throughout the world, the party's statutes determine the standards of party life and provide its "constitution."

The statutes of the party as approved by the Twenty-second Congress, unlike the new program, did not present any Khrushchevian novelty. They were merely the latest version of the old statutes that codified Bolshevik party practice before the Revolution and have shaped both the party and the state administration since that event. The then Second Secretary of the Central Committee, F. Koslov, correctly declared:

> The fundamental Leninist organizational principles of the structure and function of the party are propounded by the present statutes and they remain unshakeable.[1]

An analysis of the 1961 statutes therefore involves an examination of the fundamentals of Lenin's teachings on the structure of the party and of the evolution of these teachings in the party's statutes. The first part of this theme was studied in Chapter One, and the second part—the history and role of the party's statutes—is dealt with in this chapter.

The party statutes approved by the Second Party Congress were not Leninist in the most important respect: the principles concerning the creation of a central party leadership. Lenin supported monistic centralism in the party's administration, whereby all the central institutions of the party would be subordinate to the supreme center—the Central Committee. The Second Party Congress, however, upheld the principles of "multicentralism" and of the division of powers and established three mutually independent centers: the Central Committee, the Central (press) Organ and the Party Soviet. The Central Committee was a political and organizational center, the Central Organ was an ideological and programing center, and the Party Soviet was the supreme arbiter and coordinator between the other two bodies.

At the Third Congress Lenin reviewed the statutes approved at the Second Congress; the Central Committee subsequently became the sole center of the party. The Central Organ was to be appointed by the Central Committee and the Party Soviet was disbanded. One of the most important statutes concerning the relationship between central and local organizations remained inviolate even in the statutes of the Third Congress, however. This statute, formulated by Lenin, proclaimed:

> All the enactments of the Central Committee are binding on all party organizations.[2]

There were stormy arguments over this question with the *Bund,* the Jewish socialist organization, which demanded political independence for individual action; this protest showed that bolshevism not only denies as a matter of principle the right of independent political thought to its members, it also rejects independent political initiative of local Russian and other national party organizations. This is a logical consequence of the basis of the party's organizational structure—absolute centralism, which the Fourth Congress (in 1906) termed "democratic centralism."

While the statutes of the Third Congress, like those of the Second Congress, say that local organizations are autonomous in the management of local affairs, the autonomous rights of, for example, the Caucasian or Polish Social Democrats were only of the same order as those of the Kursk or Orel Social Democrat organizations.

When the Manifesto of October 17, 1905, proclaimed the fundamental political freedoms (freedom of speech, of conscience and of political association), Lenin was faced with an entirely new situation. How should the party function when these freedoms existed? How ought the illegal party apparatus be reorganized to function as a legal body? What old organizational principles should be retained? Lenin answered these questions at the Fourth Congress, in 1906, with his formula on democratic centralism. According to this, "the electoral principle must be introduced into party organizations from the lowest to the highest,"[3] but with one proviso—that two party machines be created, one for legal and the other for illegal work. The control center was, of course, situated in the illegal organization; the legal sector acted merely as the executive organ for carrying out the decisions of its illegal but dominating partner. Lenin's demand was not included in the statutes of the Fourth Congress, however; despite his efforts, the Menshevik majority successfully demanded the reestablishment of the two legal party centers—the Central Committee and the Central Organ. The statutes spoke of the democratic foundations of the party's structure in the following terms:

> All the party's organizations are built on the principles of democratic centralism.[4]

The formula of democratic socialism was a compromise between the two factions of the Russian Social Democrat Revolutionary party—between bolshevism and menshevism—but with the difference that each faction interpreted the formula in its own and diametrically opposed way.

At the Fifth Party Congress, in 1907, where the Bolsheviks were in the majority, the party's statutes were revised yet again: the Central Committee once more became the sole and supreme organ, and the Central Organ was to be appointed, as under the rules of the Third Congress, by the Central Committee.

This was the last time the statutes were revised before the 1917 Revolution. At the Sixth Party Congress, held in 1917 after the February Revolution, the Bolsheviks returned again to the question of the party's rules. This seemed quite natural, if only because, in Lenin's words, "Russia has become the freest country in the world."[5]

The immediate goal of the party's program, that of overthrowing autocracy and creating a democratic order, had been achieved. All the revolutionary parties, including the Bolsheviks, had achieved unlimited freedom of political action. They now all had the chance to prove by their actions what they understood by the word democracy, especially with regard to the internal organization of their respective parties. However, the review of the party's statutes at the Sixth Congress did not concern itself with democratizing the structure and leadership of the party; instead it further centralized the party and reinforced the absolute authority of its leading members. Three important addenda to the statutes made by the Sixth Congress confirm this view. (1) The now famous opening paragraph, which established that

> a member of the party is any person who subscribes to the party's program, who enters one of its organizations, *who submits to all the ordinances of the party* and who pays his membership dues.[6]

(2) Entry into the party was further restricted by the introduction into its statutes of this new second paragraph:

> New members of the party are accepted by local party organizations on the recommendation of two party members.[7]

(3) There was established a sort of Central Committee within the Central Committee, a sort of *corps d'élite* (not unlike a large Politburo), which in fact usurps the functions of the Central Committee proper and controls it as well as the rest of the party.[8]

The additions to the statutes were only a precise legal formulation of those organizational bases of the party that Lenin had advocated from the time of the Second Party Congress. Before the Revolution Lenin had justified his advocacy of an absolutist party on the grounds that Russia was an absolutist state, but after the party became a legal organization in a democratic Russia, it perpetuated its dualistic nature and maintained both secret (illegal) and public (legal) organizations.

This dualism was of the greatest advantage to the Bolsheviks on their way to power. After the events of July, 1917, the principal bolshevist leaders, as we have seen, were forced to go underground (Lenin and Zinoviev) or were arrested (Kamenev, Trotsky and Lunacharsky), and the old illegal party apparatus successfully undertook the task of preparing for an armed insurrection against Kerensky's government. The secondary leaders of the party, the "nucleus of professional revolutionaries"—Stalin, Sverdlov and Bukharin—reorganized the party machine in preparation for the forthcoming uprising. The Bolsheviks' October coup was successful because both internal and external conditions were propitious; it was also a triumph for the tactical skill and organizational techniques of Leninism.

The Bolsheviks had come to power, and the Russian Communist party became the ruling party. The "true Soviet democracy" had triumphed. What had changed in the organization and structure of the Communist party? The changes in the party statutes after the bolshevist revolution stemmed from the fact that the Bolshevik party had become the sole ruling political party in Russia. The so-called dictatorship of the proletariat was merely the external form of the single-party bolshevist dictatorship. Lenin did not attempt to hide this well-known fact.[9] It was therefore essential legally to confirm the party's ascendancy over the machinery of state and the dictatorship of the central party machine over the party as a whole in the new party statutes. The principal directives to this end were contained in the 1919 program and in the decisions of the Eighth Congress on this question. One of these declared:

> The existence of a single centralized Communist party, having a single Central Committee controlling the entire work of the party throughout the R.S.F.S.R., is essential. All the decisions of the Russian Communist party are unconditionally binding on all sections of the party, irrespective of nationality. The central committees of the Ukrainian, Latvian and Lithuanian Communists enjoy the rights of district committees, and are completely subordinate to the Central Committee of the Russian Communist party.[10]

Acting on the directives of the Seventh Congress, the Eighth Conference of the Russian Communist party (Bolsheviks), held in December, 1919, promulgated the first postrevolutionary statutes of the party, which provided the basis for all future party statutes under Lenin, Stalin and Khrushchev. Its main organizational principles are as follows:

1. "The Central Committee directs the works of the central soviets and the social organizations through the party fractions" (Article 24).

2. The party is constructed on a hierarchical principle; the decisions of lower organizations are confirmed by superior organizations, to whom they are accountable and responsible (Article 18).

3. Just as the Central Committee controls on a national scale, so, too,

do local committees control state or social organizations at their respective levels (Articles 32, 41 and 45).

4. At congresses, in institutions and organizations where there are not less than three party members present, "party fractions" are established (these are now called party groups) to execute the directives and decisions of the party; these fractions or groups are entirely subordinate to the party committee of their particular level (Article 60).

5. "The strictest party discipline is the first duty of all members of all party organizations. The ordinances of party centers must be put into effect swiftly and fully" (Article 50).[11]

Before the Bolsheviks came to power, admission to the party was restricted by conspiratorial considerations. Each new member had to prove his loyalty and usefulness to the party by participating in the activities of one of the party organizations. After they took control the qualifications for membership were made more exacting. The status of candidate member, under which a potential member must serve a probationary period during which the party ascertains his suitability for full membership, was introduced for the first time.

A statute introduced in 1919 established a two-month probationary period for workers and peasants and a six-month period for others; the number of sponsors remained two.[12] Despite the continuing consolidation of the absolutist tendencies in the party, the 1919 statutes retain some features of the old democratic centralism in the internal life of the party, as the following proposals show:

1. Democratic centralism remains the guiding principle of the organizational structure of the party (Article 10).

2. "Within the party the discussion of all difficult questions of party life is completely free until a decision has been made" (Article 50).

3. "All party organizations are autonomous in deciding local problems" (Article 12).

4. Although communist fractions (party groups) are subordinate to the appropriate committee, "in questions affecting their internal life and day-to-day work, the fractions are autonomous" (Article 62).[13]

Thus as socialism approaches, only to be succeeded by communism, these "survivals of democracy" gradually disappear from the party's statutes. Although the formula of democratic centralism and interparty democracy was contained in the Stalinist and even in the present party constitution, it is a terminological anachronism rather than a definition of the true state of affairs.

In accordance with the 1919 statutes, supreme authority rests with the annual party Congress. Between congresses the supreme organ is the Central Committee, consisting of nineteen members and eight candidate members. The Plenum of the Central Committee meets once every two months and consists of the following three groups: the five-man Politburo, which conducts domestic and foreign policy; the Orgburo, which controls organizational policy and the distribution of the leading party cadres; and the Secretariat, which deals with current executive work.

The Politburo and the Orgburo meet periodically without their auxiliary technical personnel. The Secretariat is a continuously active body with a large staff and a multiplicity of departments, subdepartments, and sections; it comprises the Central Committee, which is the highest power in the party and the state. In Lenin's time, however, the Plenum of the Central Committee was still the highest body of the collective leadership, and its decisions were a directive for the Politburo, the Orgburo and the Secretariat.

In August, 1922, the Twelfth Conference of the Russian Bolshevik party introduced new statutes that merely confirmed prevailing practice, whereby democratic centralism discarded one of its principal elements —the right to elect the leaders of party organizations. Henceforth the secretaries of inferior party organizations were to be confirmed (appointed) by superior party organizations, even though they would be formally elected by their party organizations.[14]

In subsequent party statutes, even up to the present time, these new practices acquired the force of law. The Secretariat of the Central Committee of the Soviet Communist party was empowered to appoint the secretaries of the central committees of the constituent republics; the secretariats of the republic central committees were to appoint the secretaries of regional committees and of area committees; and these were to appoint the secretaries of city and district committees, who were to appoint the secretaries of primary party organizations.

During the period when there was opposition within the party— Trotsky's "Leftist opposition" in 1924, the "new opposition" in 1925 of Zinoviev and Kamenev, and the "Rightist opposition" of Bukharin, Rykov and Tomsky in 1929—the party machine acquired absolute power. The roots of Stalin's terrible cult of personality, that is, of the historical birth of Stalinism, lie here. It was Lenin who made the Stalinist epoch possible by making two decisions that were of enormous importance to the party and to the nation. These were (1) the famous Tenth Party Congress' resolution, in 1921, "On the Unity of the Party," and (2) the appointment of Stalin as General Secretary of the Central Committee in 1922.

The Tenth Congress' resolution "On Party Unity," which was written by Lenin, finally set the apparatus of the Central Committee at the head of the party. It was empowered to exclude even members of the Central Committee if they showed any independence of thought in important matters of current policy.[15] Each time he sought to overcome opposition, Stalin invariably referred to this decision of Lenin. In addition, Khrushchev referred to it when he liquidated the opposition of Molotov, Kaganovich, Malenkov and others.

The Fifteenth Congress, in 1927, introduced yet another new point into the party's rules, stating:

> Party members who choose to refuse to answer questions asked by a control commission are liable to immediate expulsion from the party.[16]

Stalin did not content himself with stifling all opposition within the party. The struggle against freedom of opinion within the party assumed the form of periodical purges of potential critics. The organs of government are also subject to these purges, which Stalin and his pupils justify by quoting Lenin's directive that

> only by *checking people* and by checking the way they fulfill their duties can we ensure that work is properly carried out and policies are put into effect.[17]

The Seventeenth Congress, in 1934, empowered the party leadership to carry out periodical purges without the knowledge of the Congress and even without the knowledge of the members of the Plenum of the Central Committee (Article 9).[18]

Even so, the 1934 statutes still speak of democratic centralism within the party and provide a definition of this phrase. Paragraph 18 states:

> The guiding principle of the organizational structure of the party is democratic centralism, which signifies: (1) the freedom to elect all controlling party organs from the highest to the lowest, (2) the periodical calling to account of party organs by their own party organizations, (3) strict party discipline and the submission of the minority to the majority and (4) the absolute supremacy of all decisions by higher authorities on subordinate bodies and on all party members.[19]

This definition has been included in all subsequent editions of the party's statutes. However, of the four points enumerated in it, only the last point reflects the real situation. We have seen that the alleged freedom to choose party secretaries is nonexistent, for they have in fact always been appointed from above. Moreover, the entire personnel of an inferior party organization must be approved by superior authority. A party committee is formally answerable only to its local organization, and a report by a party secretary is usually no more than a directive from the central authority, either to the entire party or to a local organization. The demand for discipline and the submission of the minority to the majority is made on the rank-and-file members, but not on the party apparatus. Stalin provided the first example of the way in which a minority of party officials deal with a majority in the Central Committee, or even in the Presidium, in 1937, when he liquidated 113 of the 128 members and candidate members of the Central Committee who had been elected at the Seventeenth Congress, in 1934. Thus a minority of 15 members of the Central Committee disposed of the majority of that body. In the summer of 1957 Khrushchev provided a second example, when the Presidium of the Central Committee decided by a majority of 7 to 4 to dismiss him from the post of first secretary. Not only did Khrushchev's minority group proceed to unseat Molotov's majority group, they also branded them an "anti-party group." At the Twenty-second Congress Khrushchev sarcastically referred to Molotov's "supposedly arithmetical majority."

As the party machine became more powerful, the party congresses lost their significance as the nominal supreme authority of the party. They were consequently convened with increasing infrequency. Only two annual party congresses were held after Lenin's death—the Thirteenth and the Fourteenth Congresses—and subsequently they have been held at irregular intervals. In 1927 a change was made in the party's statutes by which congresses were to be held biennially instead of annually. At these congresses new elections to the Central Committee were to be held, and at the first Plenum of the Central Committee after each congress, elections to the leading organs of the Central Committee, including the secretary general, were to be held. Each time these reelections brought with them some degree of risk to the party apparatus. In 1934 a new statute ordained that from then on congresses should be held triennially, and this arrangement was confirmed in 1939. Nevertheless, the first party congress to be held after this rule was passed was held fourteen years later! The same thing happened with the sessions of the Plenum of the Central Committee, which were at first held once every two months (1926 statutes) and then three times a year (1939 statutes). But between 1941 and 1952 it met only three times: in January, 1944, February, 1947, and August, 1952.

In 1934 a special paragraph listing the duties of a party member was introduced into the statutes. A party member is under obligation: (1) to observe the strictest discipline and put the party's policy and the decisions of the party organization into practice; (2) to extend his knowledge of Marxism-Leninism and to impart it to nonmembers; and (3) to be a model worker and citizen and an efficient worker in his calling.[20]

Paragraph 40 states that in the future the appointments of new members to regional and republic central committees must be confirmed by the Central Committee of the party.[21] The remaining "autonomous" rights of the Communist parties of the constituent republics were thereby usurped by the Central Committee, which insisted that the republics' Communist parties be empowered to decide local questions *insofar as the settlement of them does not run counter to party decisions.*[22] The clause dealing with the internal autonomy of communist fractions in organizations and institutions was now dropped. The fractions were renamed party groups, and the party cells were renamed primary party organizations.[23]

After the new party statutes were approved, in 1934, a purge began throughout the party and the rest of the nation. In a few years this became known as the Great Purge or the *Yezhovshchina.*

The party statutes approved at the Eighteenth Congress, in 1939, were a triumph for Stalin's monolithic dictatorship; both the party and the soviets subsequently became political fictions, and the party machine and the secret police became the two mainstays of the regime. The changes introduced in these statutes reflected and legalized the position that had developed within the party. The Central Control Commission, which had been set up in 1920 at Lenin's instigation and which was elected by the party Congress, had had the right to superintend the Central Committee and its machinery; but now it became subordinate to the Central Committee. In 1934 the Commission became the Central Committee's Commission for Party Control, although its members were still chosen by the party Congress.

Any semblance of control over the party's leading figure disappeared; Stalin, the lawgiver, also became the judge of his own actions. The introduction of the institution known as the party *aktiv* was an innovation quite in keeping with the cult of personality. The statute that introduced it merely confirmed the long-established practice whereby the party elite (the party cadres) posed as the party and the party machine put its decisions into effect. This elite pretended that its voice was the voice of the party as a whole; it now received the official title of party *aktiv* and it was to meet regularly in various regions and cities.[24]

By the late thirties the long process of social transformation within the party had reached completion. The Soviet Communist party had lost the self-assumed status of the party of the proletariat and had become, as we have seen, the party of the service bureaucracy, the party of the party activists.

The prodigious increase in the number of technologists brought about by the industrialization program; the creation of a whole class of rural bureaucrats as a result of collectivization; the continuous diversification of the administrative machinery of state as a result of the growth of the army of state officials; and, finally, the considerable enlargement of the party and the governmental organizations—all these factors caused an influx of new members into the party. Only one qualification other than proletarian origin was necessary for a successful career during the early years of Soviet rule—a party membership card. Proletarian antecedents are no longer obligatory, but two documents are: a party card and an academic diploma. Those who are academically qualified now seek to join the party in order to obtain a membership card. The party machine needs qualified personnel, and so it has taken appropriate action: in 1939 it abolished the statutes that discriminated against the recruitment of officials and intellectuals to the party and cancelled the peasants' and workers' privileged position as candidate members of the party.[25] In this way a party with an entirely new social composition was created. As the party machine had intended, the party as a whole ceased to be a sovereign political body and became an ever-increasing reservoir of highly qualified officials and executives. Having this reservoir of many millions of trained, disciplined and, above all, well-qualified members, the party authorities are able to keep a check on even the remotest corner of the vast country and control every minor component of the vast governmental machine. Logically enough, another innovation in the 1939 party statutes empowered the primary party organizations to keep check on the activities of industrial enterprises and of agriculture.[26]

Another new provision introduced in 1939, which at first sight seems to contradict what has been said above, ordained that all elections to party organizations should be conducted by secret ballot.[27] But the Central Committee only permitted this right to be exercised in circumstances where the party had become merely an organized bureaucracy, staffed by persons who were docile, attentive to their work and utterly uncritical. These secret elections were a concession to the times, for since 1936 Stalin's Constitution of the U.S.S.R. had been in existence with its "most democratic and secret elections." The "secret" elections within the party were about as secret as the elections to the Soviet "parliament."

Khrushchev was the author of the 1952 party statutes presented at the Nineteenth Congress. Significantly, he omitted the passage that had appeared in the introduction to the previous set of statutes referring to the Communist party as the "leading detachment of the working class of the U.S.S.R." Instead it was stated that

> the Communist Party of the Soviet Union is a voluntary militant union of people of the same views—of Communists; it is an organization of people of the working class, of the working peasantry and of the working intelligentsia.[28]

Other changes further defined and increased the obligations of a member of the party; there were eleven "obligations" and five "rights." The new statutes defined more precisely the method by which secretaries of less important party committees were to be confirmed in their posts by their superiors; they also appointed plenipotentiary representatives of the Central Committee's Party Control Commission to function in all the republics and regions independent of local party committees. The right of controlling primary party organizations was extended to primary organizations in trading enterprises.

Party congresses are now to be held once every four years, and the Plenum of the Central Committee is to meet twice yearly. (The 1939 statutes had stated that a congress should be held triennially and that the Plenum should meet three times a year.)

One paragraph in the new statutes introduced an important new principle; it stated that primary party organizations do not have the right to expel a member of the Central Committee of the Communist party of a constituent republic, or of a province, region, district or city. He can only be expelled by his party committee if the decision is supported by a two-thirds majority of a general meeting of the respective body.[29] This excludes the party elite from the jurisdiction of the local party organization. The party caucus, which perpetually talks about democracy within the party, has arbitrarily established "class courts"— one for the privileged (the party committees), and the other for the rank-and-file members (the primary party organizations).

In 1952 important organizational changes were also made in the top party organizations. The Politburo was transformed into the Presidium, and the Orgburo was disbanded and its functions transferred to the Secretariat of the Central Committee. Khrushchev said hardly anything about the reasons for this change at the Nineteenth Congress. He confined himself to the following statement:

> The draft statutes propose to transform the Politburo into the Presidium of the Central Committee, which will conduct the work of the Central Committee between Plenum meetings. Such a reform is expedient because the name "Presidium" corresponds more closely to the functions that the Politburo actually performs at the present time. Experience has shown that the day-to-day organizational work of the Central Committee can best be concentrated in one body—the Secretariat—and so there is no further place for the continued existence of the Orgburo.[30]

The intention behind this reform was, however, quite clear; it was an attempt to limit Stalin's monopoly of power by creating a college (Presidium) of leading members of the party to take the place of the Politburo, which Stalin had long since liquidated.

After Stalin's death Khrushchev explained to the Twentieth Congress what he himself had thought of the Politburo at the time of the Nineteenth Congress. He said:

> The importance of the Politburo of the Central Committee has been diminished and its work disorganized by the creation within the Politburo of several commissions—the so-called groups of five, six, seven and nine.[31]

These various Politburo commissions consisted largely of persons who were not members of the Politburo; they assumed the powers of the Politburo and their decisions were considered to be decisions of the Politburo even though not confirmed by a meeting of that body. Stalin's pupils wanted to liquidate the Politburo as well as these commissions, in order to regain the political power Stalin had usurped from them. The pupils acted cunningly, but their master outwitted them. At the first Plenum of the Central Committee held after the Nineteenth Congress, Stalin put forward a proposal that the Presidium of the Central Committee be chosen from twenty-five members and eleven candidate members, even though the former Politburo had never contained more than eleven members and three or four candidate members. By introducing this proposal to enlarge the supreme organ of the Central Committee to thirty-six members, Stalin seemed to have gone further than his pupils toward establishing broad collective leadership. In reality he was pursuing two aims: first of all, to outnumber in the new Presidium the old members of the Politburo whom he no longer trusted, and, secondly, to create a practical need for the establishment of a small group within the Presidium to deal with day-to-day work. Stalin called this group the Bureau of the Presidium of the Central Committee of the CPSU. Its composition is unknown, but one thing is certain: it contained only those members of the old Politburo whom Stalin wished to nominate. It was quite understandable that one of the first acts of his heirs and successors was to overthrow the old Presidium and to abolish the Bureau of the Presidium, as an unauthorized body.[32]

A new Presidium was created, consisting of nine of the eleven members of the old Politburo—Pervukhin and Saburov replaced Andreyev and Kosygin—and it was proclaimed an "organ of collective leadership." The Orgburo remaind in abeyance; its functions were assigned to the Secretariat because, declared Khrushchev, ". . . experience has shown the expediency of this decision."[33] He was quite right, because the Orgburo had been the last refuge of democracy at the highest level within the party, where politicians working outside the apparatus of the Central Committee had had a dominant (juridical and "arithmetical") influence on organizational and personnel policy in the nation: all the highest managerial officials in the state as well as in the party had been appointed or removed at the instigation of this body.

The Secretariat of the Central Committee was naturally unhappy about the existence of such a body, even if it only existed on paper. That was why it was abolished after Stalin's death and why it has not been revived.

We have seen how the social metamorphosis that occurred within the party was ultimately reflected in the party's statutes. In 1934 they still referred to it as "the vanguard of the proletariat of the U.S.S.R.," and in 1939 as "the vanguard of the working class of the U.S.S.R." In 1936 Stalin renamed the Soviet proletariat the working class, declaring that there was no proletariat as such in the U.S.S.R.—it only existed in capitalist countries. In 1952 the statutes referred to the party as the vanguard of three social groups: the workers, the peasants and the intelligentsia—but in 1961 they say more simply: "The Soviet Communist party is the vanguard of the Soviet people."[34]

The new program states that

> the state that has arisen as the state of the dictatorship of the proletariat has, in a new and contemporary phase, become a people's state.[35]

Although these definitions are no more than meaningless terminology, they are a documentary acknowledgment of a fact of worldwide importance: the complete victory in the U.S.S.R. of two social phenomena that have no parallel in history—a state bureaucracy and a party bureaucracy.

The bureaucratization of state and party emphasizes rather than diminishes the importance of bolshevism's organizational principles concerning the leadership of the party. The greater the number of members of the intellectual elite of Soviet society who enter the party, the greater the danger that this party will cease to heed the bidding of the party machine, and the more difficult its administrative tasks will consequently become. The new statutes clearly foresee this possibility. Although they are more tolerant in tone than the 1952 statutes (which had appended a threat of expulsion to each "obligation of a party member"), the new statutes do, in fact, encumber the entire party with the heavy fetters of official power, as the first section, "Members of the Party, Their Duties and Rights," shows.

As we have seen, Lenin had originally imposed only three obligations on a party member: acceptance of the program, material support and participation in one of the party organizations. In August, 1917, he added a fourth obligation: obedience to party decrees. These four obligations were included in the 1926 statutes and remained in force for eight years. In 1934 nine more obligations were added, making thirteen in all. The 1939 statutes list fourteen obligations; in 1952 this number was more than doubled; but 1961 broke all records. The bureaucratization of the party is vividly illustrated by the bureaucratization of its statutes. They seek to regiment the lives of members in a way incomprehensible to a person living in the West. No resumé of them can adequately convey the thoroughness, the universal solicitude and the refinement of detail with which the party machine looks after party members. The following is a list of only their day-to-day duties, as listed in Articles 1 and 2 of the 1961 statutes:

A party member must: (1) accept the party's program; (2) accept the party's statutes; (3) actively participate in the building of communism; (4) work in one of the organizations; (5) execute the party's decisions; (6) pay his membership dues; (7) struggle to create the material and technological base for communism; (8) be a model of communist toil; (9) raise productivity; (10) be an enthusiast for everything new; (11) pass on the benefit of his experience to others; (12) master technology; (13) improve his qualifications; (14) look after public property; (15) unswervingly put party decisions into effect; (16) explain party policy to the masses; (17) assist the development of ties with the masses; (18) show sensitivity toward people; (19) answer workers' questions; (20) actively participate in politics; (21) actively participate in administration; (22) set an example in the execution of his social duty; (23) aid the development of communist relations; (24) master Marxism-Leninism; (25) raise his ideological standard; (26) facilitate the development of communist man; (27) fight bourgeois ideology; (28) fight the private property mentality; (29) fight religious prejudices; (30) observe the principles of communist morality; (31) place social interests above personal ones; (32) be an active proponent of the ideas of internationalism; (33) be an active proponent of the ideas of Soviet patriotism; (34) fight nationalism; (35) fight chauvinism; (36) strengthen the friendship of the peoples of the U.S.S.R.; (37) strengthen the ties of the U.S.S.R. with the socialist camp; (38) strengthen the ties with the proletariat of the world; (39) strengthen party unity; (40) protect the party from outsiders; (41) be just toward the party; (42) be vigilant; (43) maintain party and state secrecy; (44) develop criticism and self-criticism; (45) unmask and remedy shortcomings; (46) fight against ostentation; (47) fight against over-confidence; (48) fight against complacency; (49) fight against paro-chialism; (50) fight against the suppression of criticism; (51) fight against all acts detrimental to the party or state; (52) report detrimental acts right to the Central Committee of the CPSU; (53) carry out the policy of selecting cadres on political and professional merits; (54) be an implacable opponent of any violation of cadre policy; (55) maintain party and state discipline; (56) know that the party has one law, one discipline for all; (57) increase the defensive strength of the U.S.S.R.; (58) fight for peace; (59) fight for friendship between nations. That is not all. To these must be added the twenty-six commandments of the "Moral Code for the Builders of Communism" from Paragraph 58.[36] It must be no mean physical feat for a member of the Soviet Communist party to fulfill the grand total of eighty-five obligations!

Members of the Soviet Communist party have rights as well as duties, but these are far less numerous; there are only five of them. A party member has the right: (1) to elect and be elected to party organizations; (2) to discuss freely questions of party policy—"before a decision has been made"; (3) to criticize any Communist; (4) to take part in meet-ings where he is himself under discussion; and (5) to make depositions right up to Central Committee level and to demand an answer.[37] Some of these rights are illusory, for the party's unwritten laws forbid mem-bers to criticize either the Central Committee or the party leaders. The Central Committee is considered to be an infallible body, and thus above criticism.

At the Twenty-second Congress Khrushchev and his friends severely criticized Stalin's violations of Leninist standards of party leadership and announced that they had returned to those standards. There is only one way to check the veracity of this claim: by comparing the fundamental standards of Lenin's party statutes with those embodied in the new statutes. We have already established that Lenin was not in fact a democratic centralist but an absolutist centralist, in matters concerning relations between central and local party organizations, between the party machine and the party itself. Lenin, however, recog-nized the party congresses as the sovereign body, and he considered the party machine at every level to be merely an executive body.

Lenin's standards of party leadership as expressed in his last version of the party statutes, in 1922, may be summarized in the following principles:

1. Party congresses must be held annually, and each year they must

elect the members of all the principal party bodies (Article 20); *they are now held once every four years.*

2. All-Union party conferences of representatives of local organizations must be held annually, between congresses (Article 26); *these have now been abolished.*

3. Meetings of the Plenum of the Central Committee, at which its executive organs (the Politburo, etc.) must give an account of their activities, must be held once every two months (Article 24); *these are now held twice a year, for the Plenum of the Central Committee itself to give an account of itself to the Presidium and the Secretariat.*

4. The Congress must elect an independent supreme court of the party as well as the Central Committee (Article 50); *this Central Control Commission, which must not be confused with the Central Revision Commission—the latter has no political importance—does not now exist.*

5. The Central Committee and the *gubernia* and *oblast* committees must send each other written accounts of their work, the Central Committee once every two months and the others monthly (Articles 27, 36); *now the Central Committee of the CPSU merely "informs" them about its work* (Article 36, 1961 statutes).

6. "All party organizations are autonomous in deciding local matters" (Article 12); *this is now true only 'if these decisions are not contrary to party policy"* (Article 21, 1961 statutes).

7. "The question of excluding *anybody* from the party is decided by a general meeting of the organization to which that person belongs" (Article 4); *now "the question of excluding from the party members, candidate members of the central committees of the Communist parties of a constituent republic, of provincial, regional, district or city party committees and of members of revision commissions is decided at a plenum of the appropriate committee by a two-thirds majority vote of its members"* (Article 11, 1961 statutes).

8. Party groups (fractions) in non-party organizations are "entirely subordinate to the appropriate party organization; in matters touching their internal life and day-to-day work they are autonomous" (Article 62); *now their internal "autonomy" has been abolished.*

9. Lenin's statutes did not discriminate between "active and "passive" party members—between the elite and the masses—when discussing matters of party policy; *the new leadership gave official recognition to the social pyramid within the party.* For the discussion of party decisions and the examination of local matters, five categories of active members have been established. They are, in ascending order of importance: district, city, regional, provincial and republic groups of activists (Article 30, 1961 statutes). The meetings of these activist groups are held in private and only certain officials and so-called leaders of production are admitted by special pass.

As we have seen, the 1961 statutes contain little that is original, for they are taken entirely from the old Stalinist statutes. The only two propositions in them that contain any innovation are those dealing with the collective leadership of the party and the systematic repopulation of the party's controlling organs.

The principle of collective leadership was never mentioned in either Lenin's or Stalin's party statutes. In Lenin's day collective leadership at the highest level—in the Congress, the Plenum of the Central Committee and the Politburo—was taken for granted, while under Stalin it was considered equally indisputable that there should be only one leader— the general secretary of the party. The 1961 statutes mention collective leadership in the Introduction and in Paragraph 28, which states:

> Collective leadership is the highest principle of party leadership. . . . The cult of personality and the violations of democracy within the party that resulted from it cannot be tolerated in the party, for they are incompatible with Leninist principles of party life.[38]

It is noteworthy that the "highest principle" of collective leadership only appeared in the statutes after the post-Stalinist genuine collective leadership had been dispersed.

The Communist Party of the Soviet Union has a hierarchical structure and a monopoly of political power, and thus it cannot eschew leadership by one person. It would be naive and unrealistic to suppose that a dictatorial regime can govern "democratically" and "collectively" for a prolonged period. A collective dictatorship can exist in the form of, say, a directory, but this can only be a temporary arrangement. This happened immediately after Lenin's death, and again in the early post-Stalinist years. Secondly, a directory presupposes the presence in it of more or less equally distinguished politically ambitious politicians. Khrushchev very sensibly immediately invalidated his newly proclaimed "highest principle of party leadership" by appending to it the proviso that "collective leadership does not remove personal responsibility."[39]

The new statutes devote a special paragraph (Article 27) to "democracy within the party," that is, the freedom to discuss questions of party policy.

The paragraph states:

> Free and businesslike discussion of party policy . . . is an inalienable right of the party member and an important principle of democracy within the party. . . . Within the framework of individual organizations or within the party as a whole discussions are possible on difficult or insufficiently clear questions.[40]

This extremely important paragraph is an almost word-for-word recapitulation of part of the 1939 statutes.[41]

This fact speaks for itself. Democracy within the party as proclaimed by Stalin—once the party had been annihilated and dictatorship of the party machine firmly established—was merely an empty propaganda slogan. Even this innocent conjuring with terminology was accompanied by reservations. Thus free discussion is possible if the need for it is recognized by several regional and republic party organizations; if there is no clear majority within the Central Committee; and if the Central Committee wishes to "consult the party."[42] These reservations were taken from the 1939 statutes.[43] In his report the late F. Kozlov laid particular stress on the question of democracy within the party, but he did not say anything new about it. He merely addressed a serious warning to those Communists who interpreted the phrase too literally:

> We cannot allow the whim of any small group of muddled or immature people to involve the party in fruitless discussion, lest individual anti-party elements embark upon actions that might disrupt party unity.[44]

Thus, any party member who seriously contemplates exercising his "inalienable right" to freedom of opinion and discussion risks being classed at best as a muddlehead and at worst as an "anti-party element."

Paragraph 25 of the 1961 statutes introduced a new principle for systematically repopulating the party organizations. It provides that: (1) at each election not less than one-quarter of the Central Committee of the CPSU and its Presidium must be elected for the first time; members of the Presidium do not usually serve more than three terms, that is, twelve consecutive years; (2) at each election not less than one-third of the central committees of the constituent republics and of provincial and regional party committees must be elected for the first time; and (3) one-half the members of area, town and other party committees and of the primary party organizations must be elected for the first time; moreover, the members who come into categories (2) and (3) above cannot serve more than three consecutive terms, that is, a total of six years. Exceptions to this include the central committees of the Ukraine, Belorussia, Kazakhstan and Uzbekistan, where congresses are held once every four years; thus their members can serve up to twelve years consecutively.

The importance of this principle is, as usual, nullified by a proviso; the same paragraph that introduces the principle of systematic rotation of party personnel also contains a demand for the maintenance of the "principle of continuity of leadership." In order to ensure this continuity, the statutes permit

> certain party workers, by virtue of their acknowledged authority, high political, organizational and other qualities to be elected to leading organizations for a more prolonged period

that is, for a virtually unlimited time.[45]

This proviso concerns the members of the Central Committee of the CPSU; another, relating to members of republic, provincial, regional, city and district committees, states:

> A meeting, conference or congress can, bearing in mind political

and professional qualities, elect any worker to a leading organization for a more prolonged period.[46]

The important thing is, *who* defines and ascertains the high authority and the political and professional qualities of these people? The statutes do not tell us, but every party member knows who this supreme arbiter is. At the center it is the apparatus of the Central Committee; locally it is the appropriate local party committee. Officials of the party and of the state who are devoted servants of the party machine do not take the risk of seeking election. Faithful and efficient service to the party guarantees them unlimited tenure in the central or local organizations of the party. What, then, is the point of including the paragraph about systematic rotation of the party's personnel? It covertly provides a legal basis for the Stalinist practice of carrying out *systematic purges of the party and of the state*. The new program envisages extending the application of the personnel rotation principle.[47] According to Kozlov it had been very effectively applied in 1961 (even before it had been approved by the Twenty-second Congress!) during party conference elections to important offices and at congresses held by the Communist parties of the constituent republics. Table 18 illustrates the results of this new-style party purge in the 1961 elections.[48]

TABLE 18

Results of 1961 Party Committee Elections

Committee	Number of Members	Number Removed from Office	Per Cent Removed from Office
District and town committees	280,000	112,000	40.00
Area and regional committees and committees of constituent republics	20,000	9,000	45.00
Central committees of constituent republics	63	32	50.78
Central Committee of the CPSU members	133	67	50.37
Central Committee of the CPSU candidate members	122	65	53.78

The upper ranks of the party show a progressively increasing turnover in personnel, while the party statutes envisage the contrary. This is probably because the new Central Committee wanted to eliminate from the upper and middle ranks of the party the protegés of and the covert sympathizers with the "anti-party group," which was led by Molotov, Kaganovich and Malenkov.

Kozlov's interpretation of the rotation system confirms our conclusion that it is a veritable purge weapon. He said:

> The expediency of such a system of election to party organs is obvious. The leadership must continually receive new blood. . . . At the same time it is essential to relieve the leading organs of the party of people who have been in office too long, who have become convinced that they are indispensable . . . who stubbornly continue to occupy leading positions.[49]

This means that the new paragraph dealing with the rotation of personnel was necessitated not so much by concern for party democracy as by the necessity to legalize systematic purges because party bureaucrats seldom relinquish office of their own free will. Kozlov cited an example, which he probably considered typical, of a secretary of a regional committee in Dagestan, who, in response to a request for his resignation, declared: "Not a single Tsar surrendered his powers voluntarily, and I do not propose to surrender mine without a struggle."[50]

What are the Soviet Communist party's future prospects as the controlling authority within the state? How will the party evolve internally? How is the building of communism affecting the party organization? How far has the Marxist-Leninist doctrine of the withering away of the state been applied to the Soviet Communist party?

We have seen that even before the war Stalin had radically revised the Marxist doctrine of the withering away of the state, when he declared at the Eighteenth Congress that the state would continue to exist under communism until "capitalist encirclement" had been destroyed.[51]

The new program of the Soviet Communist party, which has been evolved from the Stalinist theory, states:

> Historical processes inevitably lead toward the withering away of the state. For the state to wither away completely certain internal conditions are essential—the building of a highly evolved communist society—as well as certain external conditions—the victory and consolidation of socialism in the international arena.[52]

With regard to the ultimate fate of the Communist party, Khrushchev went even further than Stalin. Stalin said:

> With the withering away of the dictatorship of the proletariat the party must also wither away.[53]

But, according to Khrushchev, the party will continue to exist even after the state has withered away. On this proposition Khrushchev based the following thesis of the program:

> The period of the full-scale building of communism is characterized by the further *growth of the role and importance of the Communist party* as the controlling and guiding force of Soviet society.[54]

In ordinary language, this means that the bureaucratic role of the party, its importance as an administrator, supervisor and checker both of people and of the good things of life they produce, will increase to an even greater extent while communism is being built than it did while socialism was being built. This is, of course, contrary to Marxist-Leninist teaching, but it does not contradict the abundant experience of the U.S.S.R. and its satellites: communism can neither be constructed nor continue in existence without the support of an absolute dictatorship. So the theory of the withering away of the state under socialism or communism has proved to be true in only one respect: the official organs of governmental authority in the U.S.S.R.—the soviets—have long since withered away and become the stage properties of authority; real political power has passed to the party, or, more specifically, to the party machine. This machine does not envisage the withering away of its authority, either over the people or over the party as a whole.

Khrushchev and his adherents described to the whole world the monstrous crimes against humanity of the Stalinist system. But the main question—how the Stalinist inquisition became possible—was not answered in the records of the Twentieth and Twenty-second Congresses, nor in Khrushchev's speeches. Politically minded persons cannot accept the party leadership's argument that Stalin's crimes were possible because of the existence of the Stalinist cult of personality. Khrushchev said:

> The new program and statutes restore the Leninist standards of party life and exclude the possibility of a revival of the personality cult.[55]

The statutes themselves declare:

> The Soviet Communist party is building its work on the basis of unswerving adherence to Leninist standards of party life, to the principle of collective leadership and to the all-round development of democracy within the party.[56]

But were not these standards contained in earlier versions of the party's statutes? Stalin himself had written in 1936, in the Constitution of the U.S.S.R., which is still valid:

> Article 127: Citizens of the U.S.S.R. are guaranteed inviolability of personal freedom. No one can be arrested other than by reason of a court order or the sanction of the public prosecutor.[57]

A few weeks after this Constitution was passed the arrest of millions of people throughout the country began. What guarantee is there that Khrushchev's program and statutes will prove a more effective weapon against the arbitrary use of power than Stalin's Constitution was? Molotov was quite right when he asserted that such guarantees do not exist because of the nature of the communist regime. Khrushchev himself quoted this assertion in the following way:

> Molotov has sought to justify what happened during the personality cult period and has predicted that similar acts are possible in the future.[58]

Khrushchev himself obviously had little faith in statutory guarantees when he said:

> There is one thing no paragraph in the party's statutes takes cognizance of—the party's leaders must understand that they must not allow a situation to arise where any one person, even the most worthy authority, can cease to take account of the opinions of those who have elevated him to his position.[59]

Is there any general guarantee against a new period of Stalinism—against a repetition of the arbitrary use of power and mass oppression? Yes, there is. The people must be granted fundamental civil liberties, the police state must be abandoned and the rule of law must be fostered, so that the people are masters of their own fate and not the pawns of "partocracy." The communist system does not permit other guarantees and, indeed, history does not know of any.

The unmasking of Stalin and his crimes at the Twentieth and Twenty-second Congresses did not influence the new statutes. Under Khrushchev the party Congress did not revive the so-called Leninist standards in the party "constitution." On the contrary, in the name of an anti-Stalinist Congress, it legitimized the traditional Stalinist standards embodied in the Stalinist party statutes. The Stalinist doctrine of the ever-growing role of the party apparatus, based on an unwritten law that the apparatus does not exist for the party but the party for the apparatus, has completely triumphed.

Chapters Seven through Eleven examine in detail the structure and working of the party machine at every level—from the party committee of the primary party organization right up to the Central Committee of the Soviet Communist party.

Chapter VII

The Party Bureau and the Party Committee

The following terms have become established in party parlance: "the central party apparatus," "the local party apparatus," "the central party organs" and "the local party organs." If by central party apparatus is meant only the Central Committee of the Soviet Communist party and its organs, then by local party apparatus or local party organs is meant the entire party and administrative hierarchy, in ascending order of importance as follows: party committee or party bureau; district committee; town committee; area committee; regional committee; provincial committee; central committee of a constituent republic.

The primary party bureau or party committee is the most elementary cell of the local party apparatus; its highest superior is the central committee of the constituent republic. We shall therefore begin our analysis of the work of the local party apparatus and of the functions, rights and obligations of each of its stages with its lowest ranking cell—the primary party committee.

The term "cell" was introduced by Lenin before the Revolution; it was officially retained by the Soviet Communist party until the Seventeenth Congress, when the cell was renamed the primary party organization, and its controlling organ, the cell bureau, was termed the "party bureau" or the party committee, depending on how many people were in the organization. The title of the leader of the organization remained as before: the secretary.

Theoretically, all the committees of the party, from the primary party organization to the Central Committee, are executive organs of their respective party organizations and of the party itself. So say the party's statutes. But in reality the party organizations and the party as a whole are the executants of directives; they are the executive organs of their respective committees, or, to be more exact, of their secretariats. An analysis of the relationship between the local party apparatus and the party organization will show this to be so.

What is the party committee? How has it been created? What are its theoretical and actual positions in the life of the primary party organization? What are its rights and its obligations to the district committee?

We have seen that Lenin attached great importance to the creation of primary party organizations—cells at the lowest level—in plants, factories, barracks and schools. Where there was any working-class group, there a party cell or group had to be created. The main organ-

117

izational lesson the Bolsheviks learned from their defeat in the 1905 Revolution was that the already excellent structure of the highest levels of the party needed the support of an equally good party network at the lowest level. On March 19, 1908, the bolshevist newspaper *Proletarian* declared:

> We must set ourselves a new task—in every factory, in every plant and in every workshop we must establish and consolidate, if only on a small scale, strictly Social Democrat party committees and groups. . . . If we manage to emerge from the present period of oppression having created strictly party collectives in all industrial enterprises, we shall win the day.[1]

The 1912 Conference of Bolsheviks in Prague ordered an increase in the work of creating and coordinating a dual network of party cells, both legal and illegal. The Conference indicated the need to pursue the course of "creating illegal Social Democrat cells, surrounded by as complex a network as possible of all manner of legal workers' societies. . . ." In addition, well-prepared party newspapers were to serve as an important link "in the business of establishing organizational ties between illegal cells and between Social Democrat cells in legal societies."[2]

Lenin regarded the revolutionary newspaper, not only as a source of information, but also as a weapon for education and organization. Even when the bolshevist press again began to appear legally in Russia (*Pravda* was first published on May 5, 1912) the Bolsheviks continued to issue illegal publications as a means of communication between illegal and legal party cells.

During World War I mobilization considerably depleted the party cadres in plants and factories, but strengthened them in barracks and in the trenches. The bolshevist centers (two had been selected at the Prague Conference: the Central Committee for overall leadership, to be located abroad, and the Russian Bureau of the Central Committee, for work inside Russia) constantly took care to see that weakened or self-disbanded party cells were immediately reestablished by attracting new blood into the party, mainly at large enterprises in Petrograd and Moscow. These activities of the party apparatus at the lowest level bore fruit during the October Revolution. A Soviet historian of the party has rightly said:

> During the October Revolution the party cells provided a strong central core for the insurgent masses, and only by relying on the mighty strength of the organized workers of the low-level party network was the Bolshevik party able to lead the rebels to victory and to power.[3]

Stalin's colleague L. Kaganovich said the same thing:

> In our Revolution the cells played the extremely important role of direct organizer of the masses in the revolutionary struggle.[4]

Thus the cells played a threefold role in the history of bolshevism before the Revolution: as party agitation and propaganda points at the lowest level, as a communication channel between the party and the working masses and as militant centers ready to act when called on to do so by the superior party center. Although these tasks were laid down in many prerevolutionary party documents, some of which have been cited above, nothing is said in the prerevolutionary party statutes about the cells and their duties. They are first mentioned in the statutes approved at the Eighth All-Russia Conference, held in December, 1919. Paragraph 47 declares:

> *The party cell is the elementary party organization.* The cell must be sanctioned by town or district committees and must have not less than three members.[5]

Paragraph 48 of the 1919 statutes defines the place and function of the cell:

> The cell is an organization that links the workers and the peasant masses with the leading organ of the party in a given locality. It is the function of the cell: (1) to disseminate party slogans and decisions among the masses; (2) to attract new members; (3) to assist the local committee in its organizational and agitation work; and (4) actively to participate in the economic and political life of the country.[6]

For the conduct of day-to-day work a general meeting of the cell was to elect a cell bureau for a three-month term of office. The Twelfth Party Conference, in August, 1922, reiterated these points about the cells, but added that the secretary of a cell must have been a member of the party for at least one year.[7]

In the statutes approved by the Fourteenth Congress two changes were introduced: the cell must not only receive new Communists, it must also educate them; and the bureau of the cell was to be elected for six months instead of three.[8] Thus the cell and its bureau act, not only as representatives of authority, but also as organizers and agitators whose duty is to propagate the "slogans and decisions of the party" among the masses. The cell's most important function within the party is to receive and educate new members in the spirit of discipline and communism. Its most important duty vis-à-vis its superior—the district committee—is to help this body in its organizational and agitation work.

Cells were established in various industries, on state and collective farms and in higher education, rural, domestic and military establishments. They were, in fact, set up everywhere where there were three or more party members.

When communist power was seriously challenged during the Civil War, Communists considered themselves mobilized, and the cells militarized. A decision of the Tenth Congress, in 1921, declared that, in view of the need to defeat the enemy,

the militarization of the party organization had been inevitable.
. . . This found expression . . . in extreme organizational centralism
and in the contraction of the collective organs of the party organization. Party directives became battle orders issued by the leading party institutions, which were carried out to the letter without
any discussion by the rank-and-file members of the party.[9]

After the Civil War and the introduction of the NEP, the party Central Committee decided that it could control the party by the normal
methods of democracy within the party. Hence the decision of the
Tenth Congress to change over from militarization to a workers' democracy within the party:

> The ordinary demands of the moment require a new organiza-
> tional form. A workers' democracy is just such a form. The party
> must be democratized just as resolutely and energetically as it has
> latterly been militarized.[10]

What is a workers' democracy within the party? The Congress'
official definition declares that it is

> an organizational form . . . that guarantees all party members
> active participation in the life of the party, in the discussion of all
> questions, in deciding all these questions and an equally active part
> in building up the party. Democracy prevents the bypassing of
> elective methods, it makes wide use of elections in all institutions
> from the lowest to the highest and it ensures that these institu-
> tions are accountable for their actions and open to inspection.[11]

No such workers' democracy within the party has ever existed in the
Soviet Communist party. The Tenth Congress passed another resolution "On Party Unity," which completely contradicted the above quoted
resolution and gave both local and central party authorities wide repressive powers against those who presumed to hold views that were not
in accord with official policy. This resolution stated:

> The Congress ordains the immediate disbandment, without
> exception, of groups that have been formed to support this or that
> platform and enjoins all organizations strictly to forbid any minor-
> ity projects. Failure to execute this decision of the Congress must
> involve absolute and immediate expulsion from the party. In
> order to maintain strict discipline within the party and to achieve
> the highest degree of unity . . . the Congress empowers the Central
> Committee, in cases where discipline has been violated or minority
> views have been expresssed, to use all disciplinary measures, even
> expulsion from the party. If the offender is a member of the
> Central Committee he must be demoted to candidate status, or in
> extreme cases expelled from the party.[12]

This resolution, written by Lenin, subsequently provided Stalin with
his strongest argument and weapon for achieving a second militarization of the party and also for securing the political and even the physical

annihilation of actual or potential enemies of the dictatorship of the proletariat. It was, in fact, a political cloak for the "dictatorship of the party apparatus."

The second militarization of the party began a year after Stalin became General Secretary of the Central Committee, in April, 1922. It began in the cells when, in 1923, the Twelfth Congress decided to replace the old technical secretaries of the cells with new secretaries, who were put in control as sole leaders of the cell bureau and the party organization as a whole. The resolution introducing this change states that there should be a "replacement of the old cell secretaries who performed technical functions by party organizers capable of leading the party cell."[13]

Beginning with the party cell, the same hierarchical system of party administration that Lenin had worked out for the conditions prevailing in the Russian autocracy before the 1905 Revolution was gradually reestablished. The same administrative class of professional party men was also created, the lowest ranking member of which was the new secretary of the cell. Within the primary organization an unofficial but very real hierarchy exists, headed by the secretary, to whom the bureau is subordinate; the rank-and-file members are subordinate to the bureau. The only addition to the first paragraph of Lenin's party statutes was made at the Sixth Congress, after the February Revolution, and this introduced the word "subordination." A party member had an obligation to "obey party decisions," that is, to obey the decisions of the party machine.[14]

At the Eleventh Congress it was established that "appointment of secretaries of provincial and district committees must be confirmed by higher party authority."[15] This principle has been retained in the party's statutes, and it is applied to the entire party hierarchy, including the secretaries of primary organizations, who are formally elected at party general meetings (even now by secret ballot) but only become secretaries after they have been approved by higher party authorities.

The Thirteenth Congress, in 1924, took a new step toward the bureaucratization of the party when it ordered:

> All work performed by the cells must be imbued with a greater degree of planning. Particular attention must be paid to ensure that all members and candidate members of the party . . . have assimilated the principles of bolshevist iron discipline.[16]

To all appearances, democracy within the party remains in existence and is being extended, because a bureau must now consist not of three but of seven to nine persons, and a district committee must have fifteen to seventeen members.[17]

On March 21, 1931, the Central Committee ordered that party cells in industrial enterprises where there were more than five hundred Communists should be reorganized into three-stage party organizations: a party committee, a workshop cell and a detachment cell. The detachment secretary was to be subordinate to the workshop secretary, who in turn was subordinate to the party committee secretary. The new cell or party committee thus created for itself a complete machine consisting mainly of supernumerary workers, in order to control the masses and to assist in the attainment of production and other targets. Table 19 shows the types of cells in the Soviet Communist party in 1931.[18]

TABLE 19

CELLS IN THE SOVIET COMMUNIST PARTY IN 1931

TYPE OF CELL	PARTY COMMITTEES	REGULATION CELLS	CELLS	CANDIDATE GROUPS	MEMBERSHIP
Workers'	377	10,927			729,898
Transport	189	3,416			211,570
State farm			2,353	120	47,726
Machine-tractor station			274	18	4,536
Collective farm			12,234	2,670	234,510
Rural			12,486	3,021	226,616
Soviet*			8,538		308,407
Higher education institute			957		107,615

*figures incomplete

No statistics are available on the number of military cells in 1931.

The greatest number of Communists (1,000,000) belonged to the industrial cells; in the countryside there were about 500,000 Communists; and in soviets and institutes of higher education there were 415,000 Communists. The preponderantly industrial membership of the party would seem to illustrate the "proletarian" nature of the dictatorship. As we have already seen, the social structure of the party was radically altered at the end of the thirties.

As the number of primary organizations increased, they were split into groups and subgroups. According to the 1934 statutes, in large enterprises, institutes, collective farms, higher education establishments and military units containing more than one hundred Communists, party organizations were to be formed, subject to approval of the appropriate authority, in each workshop, section or subsection. In a large plant, for example, where the primary organization contained more than one hundred Communists, it would follow this pattern: plant party committee, workshop party organization, section party group, brigade party group and team party group. The main prerequisite for the creation of a team party group is the presence of three or more members.

At the head of the party committee stands a bureau of from nine to eleven persons, elected annually by a general meeting of the entire primary organization. The bureau is headed by the party committee's secretary and his deputy, who are paid party workers. The workshop organization is headed by a "party organizer," and the remaining sections are led by "party group organizers." The 1934 statutes ordered that, in addition to its political duties, the primary organization undertake the following economic tasks: (1) mobilize the masses at industrial enterprises, state farms and collective farms to fulfill production plans and the reinforcement of workers' discipline and the development of shock-working (*udarnichestvo*) methods and (2) fight against laxity and the unbusinesslike conduct of affairs.[19]

As we have seen, the 1934 statutes introduced for the first time a paragraph dealing with the individual obligations of each party member. This paragraph stated that the party member must observe the strictest party discipline, put the party's policy and the decisions of the party organs into practice, make unceasing efforts to master the fundamentals of Marxism-Leninism, explain the party's decisions to non-members and as a member of the ruling party be a model of discipline and efficiency in his work.[20]

Before 1939 the primary party organization and its leaders—the secretary and party committee—enjoyed certain limited rights in the field of production. Their principal job was to keep a check on the workers and to help the managerial staff of industrial and farming organizations to fulfill economic plans. The Eighteenth Congress also gave the primary party organizations the right to keep a check on the administration, in a statute declaring:

> To increase the role of primary party organizations in productive enterprises, including state and collective farms and tractor stations, and to make them more responsible for the way these enterprises function, the primary party organizations are given the right to keep a check on the activities of the management.[21]

In practice this meant that the local party apparatus (the party committee, the district committee and the town committee) had the right to keep a direct check even on the activities of the management of concerns of national importance. In this way the central authorities had a twofold check on managerial personnel: governmental control, through the various central agencies (the State Planning Committee, the ministries, etc.) and party control, through the local party organizations.

The Eighteenth Congress replaced the term party committee with the word bureau. Bureaus were established in party organizations with fifteen or more members. Party committees were established in large enterprises and institutes where there were more than five hundred party members and candidate members, but in each case the permission of the Central Committee of the Soviet Communist party had to be obtained first. The Nineteenth Congress retained this statute but decided that there need be only three hundred members and candidate members in a plant before a party committee could be set up.[22]

The statutes of the Twenty-second Congress largely retain the old structure and function of the primary party organizations. Where party organizations consist of fewer than fifteen members, a secretary and a deputy secretary are elected; in an organization with more than fifteen members a bureau is established; and in organizations where there are more than three hundred Communists (in exceptional cases more than one hundred) party committees are established. On collective farms party committees are established when there are more than fifty Communists (by "Communist" is meant member or candidate member of the party).[23] For the creation of party committees only the permission of a regional committee or of the central committee of a constituent republic is now necessary.

In a primary organization having more than fifty members party organizations can be established in workshops, sections, farms or brigades with the permission of the district or town committee. Within these organizations party groups may be set up in brigades, detachments, etc. This method of organization enables the party machine to achieve complete control over the administration as well as over the masses.

Before dealing with the organizational problems that arise in the work of the various branches of the primary party organizations, we shall examine the statutes dealing with the organization of the ruling party organs.

The first of these declares:

> Democratic centralism is the guiding principle in the party's organizational structure.[24]

This principle is of purely theoretical significance. The following procedure is typical of elections to primary party organizations. They are held annually at a special election meeting. Since the 1937 addendum to party statutes, they have been conducted by secret ballot. An official representative of the district or town committee comes to the meeting with a prepared list of candidates for the positions of secretary and part of the bureau. These candidates are presented simply as having been "recommended" by the superior party authority, but the meeting knows that a "recommendation" is a party order that it must execute. The same procedure is repeated at each successive step up the party ladder. This procedure was included in the 1952 party statutes and was confirmed by the Nineteenth Congress.[25]

The numerical composition of the bureau or party committee is determined by the size of the primary party organization; usually from five to eleven persons are elected. Because of their importance, these invariably include the secretary, the chairman of the local trade union committee and the chief executive of the industrial or other enterprise concerned. Until 1937 these three persons comprised a so-called triumvirate and bore collective responsibility for the work of the management, the party organization and the trade union. In 1937 this arrangement was altered in order to strengthen the position and personal responsibility of the chief executive of the enterprise. The rest of the members are recruited from local party activists. Before the ballot the meeting selects a "commission of tabulators" consisting of party members who are not candidates, to count the votes. The successful candidates are those who receive the greatest number of votes, and these must be not less than one-half the votes of all party members present. Candidate members cannot be elected, nor can they have a casting vote. The tabulators publish their results at the meeting and transmit them to the next highest party authority. The newly elected bureau or party committee arranges its own organizational meeting, at which the members elect the secretary, his deputy, the editor of the local paper and the leaders of the various bureau sections. Each bureau member is personally responsible for some aspect of the work at an enterprise, in an institution, on a state or a collective farm, at an educational establishment or in a military unit. The number and type of the sections of a bureau or party committee depend on the size and type of the primary party organization. Before the war the party committee of an industrial organization would have approximately the following sectors: (1) organization instruction sector; (2) cadre sector; (3) culture propaganda sector; and (4) sector for agitation and mass campaigns, etc. A workshop cell would have the following sectors: (1) party recruitment sector, (2) political and technical training sector, (3) mass agitation sector, (4) sector for work among women, (5) sector for checking the part played by Communists in socialist competition and in shock-work methods and (6) sector for assessing and assigning party tasks.[26]

The head of a sector is usually a member of the party committee or bureau, but occasionally a party activist occupies the position. The main purpose of the sectors is to control the lives of those who are not party members, and the strict stratification of party political work helps to make this control more effective.

The 1961 statutes impose even more detailed obligations on the primary organizations, according to which they must

> maintain direct contact with the workers, rally them around the Communist party and organize the masses in putting party policy into practice.

A primary party organization: (1) receives new members; (2) educates Communists in the spirit of devotion to the party cause; (3) organizes the study of Marxist-Leninist theory while rejecting revisionism and dogmatism; (4) concerns itself with advancing the leading role of Communists in society and the state; (5) organizes the execution of all economic plans within its own sphere of activity; (6) conducts political propaganda among the people and educates them in the spirit of communism; (7) by means of criticism and self-criticism fights against bureaucratism, parochialism, cheating the state and breaches of discipline; and (8) assists the area, town and district committees in all their activities, and is accountable to them.[27]

To these have been added the twelve obligations contained in the new program's "Moral Code of a Communist." The primary organizations must strive to ensure that not only Communists but all Soviet citizens fulfill these duties. Because of the nature of the communist political system and its doctrines, it is impossible to carry out such obligations as the fostering of "humane relationships and mutual respect between people: man is to man a friend, comrade and brother." The cost to the Russian people of communist "humanitarianism" since the Revolution is notorious. Nor was the Kremlin's humanitarianism in Hungary in 1956 less costly. The communist dialectic, with its theory of the class struggle, can give no guarantee against a repetition of this in the future, and the inclusion of an old religious precept in the "Moral Code" shows just how elastic the morals of the Kremlin's high priests are. Some of the obligations contradict each other: while the principle of "fraternity" is being urged upon the party member he is told he must show "implacable opposition to the enemies of communism."[28]

Other obligations merely repeat the constant slogans of communism: "Devotion to the cause of communism, love for the socialist Fatherland and the countries of socialism," "conscientious work for the good of society . . . ," "the concern of each member for the preservation and increase of the community's wealth," "high consciousness of social duty . . . ," "collectivism," etc.[29] In a word, everything is in the name of communism, through communism and for communism.

The 1961 statutes extended the range of enterprises and organizations in which primary party organizations have inspection powers. They now inspect the activities of managements in all industrial and trading enterprises, on state and collective farms and in planning organizations, design bureaus and scientific research institutes.[30]

The right to inspect, according to the official interpretation, means: (1) the right to know how work is progressing in an enterprise and to inspect its files and (2) the right to hear progress reports from the head of an enterprise and to make recommendations to him concerning future work.[31]

The primary party organization does not, however, have the right to interfere in operational orders issued by the head of an enterprise. It cannot issue orders to him, nor can it countermand his orders. It cannot appoint or dismiss employees, but the prudent manager generally tries to insure himself against falling foul of the party authorities by seeking the prior approval of the party committee's secretary for his more important commands and his recommendation for the appointment or dismissal of workers. The secretaries of industrial party committees and bureaus are invariably highly trained both politically and technically. Most of them are graduate engineers and technicians. This is quite understandable, because just as great demands are made on them in the fields of technology and of economics as on the director of an enterprise. As the official party handbook says:

> To ensure the correct technical policy at an enterprise these are the duties of a primary party organization: . . . The secretary must know the industry and be abreast of developments in similar enterprises. Only by understanding the technological bases of the technological processes is he fully qualified to direct the party organization, correctly to assess specialists' opinions and to form his own opinion in technical matters.[32]

The main aim of all the party political and organizational work of the secretary of a party committee is the fulfillment and overfulfillment of the enterprise's economic plans:

> Everything that a primary party organization does is ultimately aimed at improving production figures. . . . Under all circumstances, the work of a party organization and, consequently, of its secretary, is judged by practical results.[33]

The party's instructions make these secretaries, from both an organizational and a material point of view, independent of an enterprise's managerial staff; they are the eyes and ears of the party in the enterprise.

Primary party organizations of ministries, state committees, central soviet and economic institutions do not have the right of inspection. They are directly supervised by the party apparatus at their respective levels. This does not mean that these institutions are not subject to the surveillance of the local party committee, however. The local party committee is obliged to keep watch on the activities of every institution and on the behavior of every public servant, whatever his rank. If it notices any deviation from the party line by an institution or its leaders, the party committee must immediately report it to the next highest party organization, as the following statute shows:

> The party organizations of ministries, state committees, economic councils and of other central and local soviet and economic institutions and departments that do not have the duty of checking upon the activities of management must actively encourage further improvement of the working of the apparatus . . . must take steps to strengthen discipline in the state . . . must promptly report to the appropriate party organs any malfunctioning of institutions and of individual workers, irrespective of the posts they occupy.[34]

This means that the party committees or bureaus of primary organizations in district and town soviet and economic institutions and organizations report defects to the district or town committee of the party, while party committees and bureaus in regional institutions and organizations must report them to the regional committees. Party committees in ministry and central departments must similarly report any defects they uncover to the central committees of the Communist parties of the constituent republics or else to the Central Committee of the Soviet Communist party. Failure to report defects or deviations renders the secretaries of primary organizations liable to dismissal and to expulsion from the party. The official instructions to primary organizations in soviet institutions emphasize that

> among the duties of the party organizations of soviet institutions, some of the most important are those of reporting shortcomings in the work of institutions, of noting the shortcomings of individual workers and of reporting the facts together with relevant comments to the appropriate party organ.[35]

The party apparatus obliges local party committees to eliminate defects immediately:

> This does not exclude the possibility, but, on the contrary, it presupposes, that the party organization immediately gives to the higher party organs correct information about the state of affairs in the institution concerned.[36]

The party apparatus requires that the secretary of a party committee in a soviet institution should be not a subordinate worker but a party observer keeping watch over the director of that institution. The head of the institution would, of course, be a Communist, and he would also have been appointed by a superior party authority; but by placing its own direct and paid representative near him, the party apparatus obtains an additional guarantee that any act of disloyalty or abuse will be quickly discovered. The party apparatus takes every precaution to see that the secretary of a party committee is not a close friend of the head of the institution, so that relations between them always remain on a strictly official footing. Therefore the regional committees enjoin district and town committees to ensure that

> at the head of all party organizations in institutions there should stand people *who are independent,* who are capable of steadfastly and consistently following the party line.[37]

Party organizations on collective and state farms work on the same principles as do those in industrial enterprises in towns; they have the right to check on the management and direction of these farms. Moreover, the secretary of a party committee is invariably a member of the administration of the collective farm, and thus has the opportunity to keep a daily check on the work of the farm's chairman. His other function—that of maintaining an overall political check on the ordinary workers on the collective farm—is no less important. The party's instructions make particular mention of the political surveillance duties of the collective farm's party committee:

> A primary party organization is a political organization. It must be in touch with all aspects of life and with the work of the collective. . . . It approaches each task as a political organization should. This means that in assessing the results of any practical work, the party's first consideration must be the *general interests of the party* and it must above all keep a close check on the way in which the party's directives are being executed in its own sector.[38]

The party apparatus has always regarded the possibility that the rural areas might evade its control as the greatest potential danger to the regime. Even in Lenin's celebrated "Testament" it is pointed out that a rift between the peasantry and the proletariat would be the beginning of the end for Soviet power.[39] That is why the party apparatus directs that "in putting any measure into effect, the party organization must strive to reach *every collective farmworker.*"[40] In collective farm primary party organizations, party committees have been set up where there are more than fifty Communists, and in state farms where there are more than one hundred Communists. In these instances party groups of brigades, farms and sections are afforded the rights of primary organizations.

Party organizations in establishments for higher education do not have the right to check up on the activities of the administration, but they have the very important duty of

> training highly qualified specialists educated on the basis of Marxism-Leninism. The primary party organizations in these establishments . . . must deeply penetrate all aspects of the higher education establishment collective, and engage more specifically in their most important task—the ideological and political education of the students. It is their duty to be in close contact with the students, *to know their mood* well and to react quickly to all new phenomena that manifest themselves among the students and the teaching staff.[41]

The party committees in institutes of higher education work in close contact with the inspectors of faculties, who are themselves a type of political commissar or political instructor of students and teachers. These inspectors were first introduced after the unrest among students in the U.S.S.R. during the "thaw" of 1956.

In 1962 new facts about the state of the primary organizations were made public. These show that, after the Twentieth Congress, in 1956, a consolidation of the primary party organizations, together with a consolidation of the collective farms and the merger and reorganization of certain institutions and administrative bodies, took place. As a result, the number of primary party organizations decreased by 55,000.

On the other hand, in some branches of the economy and the administration—construction sites, state farms, cultural institutions, the public
health service, trade, the food industry and communal institutions—
there was an increase in the number of primary organizations. Table 20
shows the distribution of these primary organizations on October 1,
1961.[42]

TABLE 20

THE DISTRIBUTION OF PRIMARY PARTY ORGANIZATIONS IN THE VARIOUS BRANCHES
OF THE ECONOMY AND THE ADMINISTRATION, OCTOBER 1, 1961

BRANCH OF THE ECONOMY OR ADMINISTRATION	NUMBER OF PRIMARY PARTY ORGANIZATIONS	NUMBER HAVING PARTY COMMITTEES
Total number of primary party organizations	296,444	13,220
In industrial enterprises, communications and construction work	75,681	2,057
On collective farms	41,387	5,721
On state farms	9,206	2,718
In institutions, organizations and economic organs	52,501	255
In teaching establishments and scientific, cultural and medical institutions	56,968	347
In trading enterprises	12,594	2

From Table 20 it is evident that the majority of primary party organizations (170,170) have been concentrated in the administrative and
managerial organs, while less than half of them (126,274) are related
to production of goods or food. But this is compensated for by the
fact that the primary party organizations in industry are larger than
those in the administrative organs and by the additional creation of
workshop party organizations (which have increased from 57,000 in
1956 to 187,000 in 1961), 103,800 of which have the same rights as
primary party organizations. Besides this, the number of party groups
has also increased: there were 174,000 in 1961. Thus the whole of
industry is securely under direct communist surveillance and direction.
    Primary party organizations having up to fourteen party members
and candidate members predominate (42.6 per cent), and those containing from fifteen to twenty-five members form 24.3 per cent of the
total. Primary party organizations containing from twenty-six to one
hundred party members or candidate members form another 28.1 per
cent of the total number, and those with more than one hundred members comprise only 5 per cent of the overall total.[43]
    The average number of Communists per primary party organization

in the various branches of industry is as follows: in industrial enterprises, 61; in construction enterprises, 39; on state farms, 74; in scientific institutions, 74; and on collective farms, 34.[44]

The collective farms still contain the smallest proportion of Communists, while the state farms contain an even higher percentage than
industry does. Between 1957 and 1961 a mass mobilization of workers
in institutions and industry for work on state farms took place.

Above all these primary party organizations stands the local élite—
the local party *aktiv*, which consists of 1,800,000 members of the party
committees and bureaus of the primary party organizations. If to them
is added the "party corpus"—from the district committee right up to the
central committees of the constituent republics (a total of 306,000
persons)—the total party *aktiv* consists of more than 2,100,000
persons.[45]

The work of the military primary party organizations, which is extremely important to the party, is dealt with in Chapter Sixteen.

The structure and tasks of the primary party organizations just
examined show their importance as the direct instruments of the
dictatorship among the masses. The regime has achieved its original
ideal: to encompass the entire nation in what Stalin termed the party's
"tentacles." The party has complete political control of the people
and of the state, of the economic and the military bureaucratic machines.
It is clear that the party places at the head of the primary cells—the
party committees—professional party workers who follow the party
line, not out of fear, but for reasons of conscience. The party apparatus
gives them the requisite political authority and a high degree of material
security so that they are independent of the directors of industrial
enterprises or the heads of institutions. The party's instructions state
quite explicitly:

> Complete independence from soviet economic organizations is
> the most important prerequisite for party organizations to be
> able to examine economic questions and uncover deficiencies. The
> party keeps a strict watch to see that the independence of its
> officials is not violated, in order that nothing may deter them from
> self-criticism or criticism. . . . The party workers who enjoy this
> independence are paid out of the party budget, and they are for-
> bidden to accept any form of payment from economic organiza-
> tions. The slightest violation of this independence could lead to
> the party's officials' becoming the prisoners of the economic organs.
> . . . As the Central Committee has repeatedly pointed out, the
> appointment of party workers to fictitious posts or the award of
> premiums from the economic organs to gain their approval con-
> stitutes *bribery* and would mean that the party leaders would
> become subordinate to the economic leaders.[46]

To ensure that party committee secretaries are not "bought" by
directors of industrial enterprises, they are paid by the district or town

committee and are forbidden to accept payment from enterprises or institutions. Industrial enterprises and institutions transfer money for these party workers' salaries to the district or town committee, which in turn hands it to the ultimate recipient. The same salary procedure is also practiced at higher levels of the party's organization.

Chapter VIII

The District Committee and the Town Committee

THE DISTRICT COMMITTEE of the party, in the country, or the town committee of the party, in towns, is the next stage up in the hierarchy of the party's organizational apparatus. Whereas the primary party organizations were established largely on a production and territorial basis, all the party organizations and their executive organs from the district committee up were constructed on administrative and territorial principles. The administrative governmental divisions of the U.S.S.R. correspond to the territorial divisions of the Soviet Communist party: the district executive committee corresponds to the district committee; the town executive committee to the town committee; the area executive committee to the area committee; the regional executive committee to the regional committee; the provincial executive committee to the provincial committee; the council of ministers of a constituent republic to the central committee of the Communist party of the constituent republic; and the Council of Ministers of the U.S.S.R. to the Central Committee of the CPSU. The party committees of rural production managements, which were set up in 1962 and abolished in 1964, were the same as the rural district committees, but were two or three times larger.

The district organ of the party is the most important one in the direct realization of the tasks and aims of the dictatorship. According to 1960 statistics there were 3,501 rural district committees in the U.S.S.R. In 1962, about 1,500 party committees of collective and state farm production managements were established in their place.[1] In 1965, the reestablished district committees numbered 2,432.[2] The village was, and still is, a bottleneck for the Central Committee:

> The Central Committee requires that special attention be paid to the further strengthening of the district committee. . . . The party is anxious that the leaders of district committees and also of executive committees of district soviets should be organizers of the masses who are energetic and full of initiative, people who are well-versed in agriculture.[3]

The main tasks of district party organizations as laid down in the party statutes are: (1) political and organizational work among the people in the spirit of the building of communism; (2) the fulfilling and over-

133

fulfilling of economic plans; (3) the organization of ideological work, the propagation of Marxism-Leninism among the people and in party organizations and leadership of all propaganda and cultural organizations in the district; (4) leadership of local organizations of the soviets, trade unions, *Komsomol,* cooperative and other social organizations through the party groups in them; (5) the selection and deployment of managerial cadres in town and country; (6) the recruitment of a wide circle of workers for work in the party apparatus; (7) leadership of local party institutions (the editorship of newspapers, publishing, libraries, etc.); (8) periodical reporting about their work to the regional committee; and, most important of all, (9) leadership of the primary party organizations.[4]

District committees and town committees are considered the most important detachments in the party apparatus because they have direct control over the primary party organizations, which, in turn, put into effect the highest party directives. The district committees are directly connected with both the processes of production and the worker masses. The district party organizations are actually the sum of the primary party organizations of a given district.

According to the statutes, the highest organ of a district organization is its biennial party conference, whose delegates are elected at meetings of primary party organizations. At these conferences party, economic and cultural questions are discussed and the executive organ of the party organization — the district committee or town committee — is elected by secret ballot.[5]

The elections to the party committee are, however, "organized"; that is, the results are prearranged by higher authority. Elections to the district and town conferences are organized by the district and town committees, and elections to the regional conference are organized by the regional committee. The party apparatus of the appropriate level decides who will be on the new party committee and the next higher party apparatus, whose representatives take part in the elections, determines who will serve at its head. The Central Committee of the CPSU has issued a special instruction "On the Conduct of Elections to Leading Party Organs," which states:

> On the decision of the presidium of the conference [the presidium is appointed by the party apparatus itself and consists mainly of members of the party apparatus] representatives may be called together to make a preliminary selection of candidates for election to the new district or town committee. . . .[6]

Persons who are not members of the organization in question, who do not participate in the conference and who are even quite unknown to local Communists can be nominated as members and leaders of a party committee. They may be party or state officials who have been sent by the central authority to work in the districts.

The members of a district committee are elected from a group of from fifty to sixty members and from ten to fifteen candidate members of the district committee. The district committee holds plenary sessions at least once every three months.[7]

Who are the people chosen by the party? The great majority of them belong to the so-called leading *aktiv* of the district, who are permanent officials of the district. The others are workers and collective farmers elected for the sake of appearances as representatives of the "people" and the "toiling masses," yet even they are not rank-and-file representatives of the people, but worthies in their respective spheres—brigade leaders, collective farm chairmen or bemedaled "Heroes of Socialist Labor."

The first organizational plenum of the district committee, in the presence of all members and candidate members (the latter are there in a purely consultative capacity), is devoted to electing the bureau of the district committee, the secretaries of the district committee, the heads of departments and the editors of local newspapers.[8] The same official and authorized representative of the superior regional committee of the party who has been present at the conference remains to see that the candidates who have been selected by the secretariat of the party regional committee are duly elected. He proposes these "recommended" candidates, and as a rule they are elected; but occasionally they are opposed on political or moral grounds. If a candidate sponsored by the district committee meets strong local opposition, he is replaced by another of the district committee's candidates. It sometimes happens that a recommended candidate fails to get elected even though no prior objection to him has been made. The district committee plenum cannot, however, choose its leaders without the agreement and recommendation of the regional committee, for the secretaries of the district committees are confirmed, that is, are virtually appointed, by the party regional committee. This was plainly stated in the party's old statutes.[9]

The bureau consists of from seven to eleven party members and from three to five candidate members. These invariably include three secretaries of the district committee and the chairman of the district executive committee. The remaining members are elected from such leading responsible workers of the district as the heads of departments of the district committee, the public prosecutor, the head of the committee for state security, the head of a large production concern or a newspaper editor. After the plenum, the bureau is considered to be the ruling organ of the district committee and the first secretary and his deputies are formally accountable to it. It meet weekly under the chairmanship of the first secretary or one of his deputies. These meetings are convened by the secretary, and he is responsible for drawing up the agenda. The bureau has many duties. It organizes, confirms and controls the primary party organizations; regularly hears accounts of the work of these party organizations; and keeps a register of Communists and directs their ideological education—all functions entirely within the party. But it also has state administrative functions; it controls directly (through its departments) or indirectly (through party groups) in town or village: (1) the organs of state power; (2) economic institutions and collective and state farms and (3) social organizations (trade unions, *Komsomol,* cooperative concerns, voluntary societies and sports organizations).

The working rights and administrative principles of the district committee and the town committee are identical; any formal differences are the result of different conditions in town and country, of the economy of a district, or of the administrative and territorial importance of a district (capital district committees, frontier district committees).

Let us now turn to the rural district committee, which consists of cadres qualified in two areas: in general administration and in the conduct of agriculture.

The party committees of production administrations of collective and state farms established in place of the rural district committees by the November, 1962, Plenum of the Central Committee of the CPSU had the following structure: the party committee (sixty members); the bureau (eleven members); the secretary; his first deputy (in charge of the ideological department); his second deputy (in charge of the organizational department); a group of inspector-party organizers (from ten to twelve members) directly subordinate to the first secretary; the head of the office of party education; and several general instructors. The rural district committee's apparatus consists of about twenty responsible workers.[10]

The secretary of a district committee is an agricultural specialist who is in reality the sole master of the enterprise; he runs the place and keeps an eye on everything that is going on in his district. The secretary and his district committee operate in much the same way as military and police administrations do.

In an official Soviet publication entitled *The Rural Regional Committee of the Party,* devoted to the experiences of the working of a rural district party organization during the last years of Stalin's life, the authors describe the district committee:

> Three or four years ago in the Kotovo district committee (Odessa region) it was possible to see this sort of picture. From daybreak all the telephones would ring continually, a line of visitors would form up, streams of couriers emerge from the collective farms. Packets would be stamped "Express, Sowing Campaign" or "Harvesting Campaign." By nine o'clock in the First Secretary's office would gather the Chairman of the district executive committee, Stengach; the head of the district agricultural department, Basiel; and the head agronomist, Sergienko. There would then take place what was jokingly called the "issuing of orders." "You, Comrade Stengach," the district committee Secretary would say, "must today

get started on hoeing between the rows of beet: there's a hitch in the Borshchansk sector—see about it. You, Comrade Basiel, take my car and go to Aleksandrovka: judging by the operations summary they are lagging behind about the fallow. Send the head zootechnician to Liubomirka: if not today, then tomorrow; the new mass farrowing must begin. You, Comrade Sergienko, prepare the operations summary at once for the region. . . ." The routine efficiency campaign has only just started . . . officials have been sent to each of the backward villages. The district committee can be said to be up to its ears in work. It tries to handle even the pettiest matters itself and its officials try to decide every question. One gets the impression that anything sent to the district executive committee immediately gets mislaid. The bungling and red tape of officialdom has killed initiative and reduced the efficiency of district organizations.

The authors go on to relate that, after the Plenum of the Central Committee of the CPSU in September, 1953, at which Khrushchev first announced his plans for agriculture, the district committee adopted a new way of working. Nevertheless, it continued to act on behalf of everybody, to make decisions for everybody and to usurp the functions, not only of the state administration in the person of the district executive committee, but even of the purely agricultural experts.

Meanwhile, according to the Constitution of the U.S.S.R., there are neither district committees nor regional committees, nor even central committees, but there are district executive committees and regional executive committees, which are the organs of governmental authority on the spot. In this instance the district executive committee has all the necessary departments to administer the district: an agriculture department, a finance department, an education department and a local industry department. But all these departments and the district executive committee as a whole are the technical offices of the corresponding departments of the district committee. Even the documents of these offices are null and void in the eyes of the local party *aktiv* if they are not franked with the official stamp of the party district committee.

The authors quoted above write that the collective farm cadres are so accustomed to the powerlessness of the official organs of authority that when the district executive committee wants to show its authority by issuing an order, it is simply ignored:

> The ruling collective farm cadres have not been accustomed to executing the district executive committee's directives to the letter, since when these directives are not ratified by the district committee's seal they are not considered binding.[11]

The replacement of state (soviet) organs by party organs has become an unwritten but invariable rule. Therefore the ordinances of the organs of state authority are ignored if they do not bear the visa of the appropriate party committee. This has led to the simultaneous promulgation of ordinances by the district executive committee and the district committee, by the central committee of a constituent republic and the republic's council of ministers, and by the Central Committee of the CPSU and the Council of Ministers of the U.S.S.R.

According to Page 79 of the Constitution of the R.S.F.S.R., the following are within the competence of the local soviet: (1) control of cultural, political and economic construction in its territory, (2) the development of the local budget, (3) control of the activities of administrative organs subordinate to it, (4) the maintenance of public order, (5) cooperation in strengthening the country's defense potential and (6) the maintenance of law and the preservation of the citizens' rights.

In reality these duties lie within the competence of the local organs of the party. Only after the appropriate party committee has discussed and taken decisions on literally every question—political, economic, cultural, technical, financial and even on matters concerning sports— within the given territory, can there take place the "formulation of party decisions in the soviet."

Thus not only the soviets—as fictitious organs of governmental power —but also the so-called social, cooperative and sports organizations do not have the right to regulate their own affairs, or to appoint or dismiss their own officials without the permission of the local party organ, in this instance the party district committee. This state of affairs is especially resented by collective farmworkers, who, although they are by law the proprietors of the collective farms, are even deprived of the right to elect their own chairmen.

At the Twenty-second Congress a district committee in the Smolensk region that in a short space of time replaced thirty-two collective farm chairmen without informing the collective farmworkers in advance was cited. Criticizing this practice, one of the collective farm chairmen declared at a district party conference:

> The district committee rules the collective farms from a position of strength, wielding the threat of severe penalties and even of expulsion from the party.[12]

If the main economic task of the district committee is to direct and control the collective farms and the workers on them, then its main organizational task is the apportionment of cadres and control of their work. Above all, the present district party apparatus itself—the district committee—is an institution of highly qualified officials. The official publication of the Central Committee of the CPSU writes:

> The party worker is called upon to teach the cadres; that means [he] must be well briefed on current problems. For this they must not only have a good general education but they must also be qualified in technology or agronomy. . . . As far as the further strengthening of the organizational work of the party apparatus is

concerned, this means that it is necessary to strengthen control over the work of all soviet, trade union, *Komsomol* and economic organizations and organs.[13]

Party workers are these qualified leaders.

Here are typical statistics for one of the typical regions of the R.S.F.S.R., the Saratov region: 90.8 per cent of the secretaries of party district committees and town committees and 87.4 per cent of chairmen of the executive committees of this region have received partial or complete higher education; "almost half of them are industrial or agricultural specialists."[14] In the Ukraine 95 per cent of the secretaries of district committees and town committees and chairmen of town district executive committees have received partial or complete higher education, and one-third of the workers in them are industrial or agricultural specialists.[15] In Belorussia 90 per cent of the secretaries of district committees have received higher education,[16] in Tadzhikistan 63.9 per cent,[17] in Azerbaidzhan 82.5 per cent[18] and in Kazakhstan 82 per cent.[19]

Communists serving on district committees are divided into two categories: rank-and-file Communists and "staff workers of the district committee" (also called "leading comrades" or "responsible workers"). The official definition of a staff worker states:

> The list of positions over which the party organ keeps constant observation is generally termed the staff. The staff is a circle of persons who must each be well known to the party committee. The inclusion of a post in the staff list means in practice that appointments to such a post must always be confirmed by the party organ. This condition must be fulfilled both on appointment to, and resignation from, such a position.[20]

Thus the staff workers of party district committees are officials who are appointed, transferred or dismissed only by decision of the bureau of the district committee, or by "permits" issued by its departments. The number of staff appointments depends on the size and the economic importance of the district. A district committee staff always includes the following posts: the secretaries and deputy secretaries of primary party organizations, chairmen of collective farms, chairmen of rural soviets, district executive committee heads of departments (education, health and road departments, the district agronomist, the responsible secretary of the district executive committee, the deputy chairman of the district executive committee, etc.), instructors, propagandists, district committee lecturers, newspaper and printing workers (except the editor-in-chief), district trade union leaders and leaders of *Komsomol*, volunteer and sports organizations. A district committee staff may include persons holding all categories of position, even those that can be done by non-members of the party. For example, in 1954 the Altai provincial committee issued a list of district jobs for which appointments had to be confirmed by the district committee. This list embraced 450 posts, including the following: accountants of the district representative of the Ministry of Supply, fire-brigade captains, instructors of the district department of Central Statistical Administration, secretaries of *Komsomol* organizations, local postmasters, etc.[21]

District workers who are not members of the party's district committee staff are members of the regional committee staff. These include district committee and district executive committee leaders and the regional representatives of republic or all-Union departments or government organs who are working in the district (the district representative of the State Budget Commission, the district prosecutor, the inspector from the State Control Organization, the local manager of the State Bank, trade union leaders, the head of the district inspectorate of the Central Statistical Administration, etc.).

In other words, the officials of the local "autonomous administration" are members of the district committee staff, but the representatives of superior party apparatus and central government organs are appointed from above and form part of the regional committee staff; or, where this does not exist, they form part of the central committee of a constituent republic. Even when such workers are appointed from above, however, there exists an "agreement" with the district committee as to the candidature of persons to be appointed. A district committee, for its part, has the right to recommend the appointment or dismissal of a staff worker of a regional committee who is working in its territory, although it cannot make a unilateral decision on the matter. As can easily be seen from the list of these posts, the superior party and governmental organs exclude from the sphere of direct dependence on the district committee those very officials who carry out the functions of inspection on the spot, which are of vital importance to the central authority.

However, receiving orders from above and subordinating themselves in a legal respect to the superior governmental organs (and through them also to superior party organs), these officials are politically subordinate to the district committee as members of the given party organization. Their political and professional fate depends largely on the district committee. Moreover, the district committee keeps a direct daily watch over the actions of every official in the district, regardless of whether he is a member of the district or of the regional staff.

The district committee can only indirectly, through the appropriate party groups in the soviet, trade union or sports organization, effect legal formulation of appointments, transfers and dismissals of state or public officials on its staff. Only party and *Komsomol* workers can be appointed and removed directly by the district committee. Party decisions on organizational questions and on personnel appointments are made in two ways: (1) the bureau of the district committee passes a resolution concerning the appointment of a responsible official, which, if the appointment has been made in deference to the Soviet line, usually states:

The party group of the presidium of the district executive committee is entrusted with the task of formulating the said decision in accordance with soviet practice.

If the appointment has been made to a trade union, cooperative or sports organization, the same decisions are addressed to the party groups of the particular organizations. (2) Middle-rank officials are appointed without the decision of the district committee bureau, but only on the "permit" of the district committee. The permit states that the district committee recommends the Communist for a post in such and such an institution or organization. The head of the institution then issues an official order for his appointment. The same appointment procedure applies to communist officials in the so-called elective public organizations, as well as at conferences and congresses.

Although party committees predetermine the appointments of "elective" officials, the party group of the organization to which they are appointed must ensure that they are "elected" at a general meeting. What then are party groups and what are their functions? The party's statutes say of them:

(67) At congresses, conferences and meetings convened by soviets, trade unions, cooperatives and other mass workers' organizations, as well as in the elective organs of these organizations where there are not less than three party members present, *party groups* are to be organized. The task of these groups is generally to strengthen the party's influence, to propagate its policy among non-members . . . to check that party and soviet directives are executed. (68) Party groups are subordinate to the appropriate party organs: to the Central Committee of the CPSU, the central committee of the Communist party of a constituent republic, to the provincial committee, regional committee, area committee, city committee or district committee. In all matters party groups are strictly and inflexibly bound by the decisions of the leading party organs.[22]

Party groups in non-party organizations are constantly active institutions in contact with and subordinate to the appropriate party committee. The party committee maintains official contact (directions, instructions and appointments) with the non-party organizations through the leaders of the party groups, who are usually the leaders of these organizations.

Town committees have the same statutes, rights and duties as district committees. The town committees of Moscow, Leningrad and of certain large towns with district subdepartments are exceptions to this rule; their statutes more nearly resemble those of a regional committee, but their position is not analogous. In towns with a district subdepartment, the town committees have nothing to do with the primary party organizations. They are under the supervision of the town district committees. The town committee controls these district committees. There are in the U.S.S.R. 1,682 town committees and 352 town district committees.[23]

The structure of the town committee's apparatus is more complex and wider in scope than that of the rural district committee. It takes into account the special needs of urban life, the character and conditions of urban communal economy and the principal industries located in the town. The task of the party town committee is to ensure that the primary party organizations of the town are led by qualified party members in their task of fulfilling state production plans. The official slogan of its party work has become "Judge the quality of party work by the quantity of output."

The structure of town committees and the number and designation of their departments are frequently changed. Usually a town committee has the following departments: organization department; industry and transportation department; administration, trade and finance department; school department; propaganda and agitation department; department for work among women; and department of culture.

The personnel of district committees and town committees is not large in comparison with their duties and responsibilities; they usually number from thirty to forty persons. They have almost unlimited opportunities for getting activists working outside the party apparatus to undertake party work. The Twenty-second Congress attached particular importance to this. Khrushchev then declared:

> In the party organs there must be ever more commissions, departments, instructors and secretaries of district committees and town committees, working on communal principles.[24]

At the beginning of 1962, there were 48,000 supernumerary instructors, 105,000 supernumerary lecturers and 600,000 members of party commissions controlling the administration of industrial, trading and agricultural enterprises working in the party apparatus.[25]

In the district committees and town committees permanent commissions (commissions to study the latest experiences in industry, construction and agriculture; an ideological commission; a party organization commission; a commission for personal affairs and for recruitment to the party; etc.) whose members are specialists working outside the party apparatus have been established; the majority of these persons are members of committees. These commissions fulfill the role of consultative organs of the party apparatus on a wide variety of economic, administrative, cultural and ideological problems. The permanent commissions have 77,000 communist members. In the district committees and town committees there are supernumerary departments, even departments for industry and transportation, for propaganda, for schools, for party organization and for work among women.[26] Permanent commissions are now being established in regional committees and in the central committees of the constituent republics. In all, about 900,000 Communists work as supernumerary party workers. To these should be added another 2,000,000 Communists who have been chosen to staff the party organs.[27] With such a vast network of supernumerary party workers, the district committees and town committees have under their constant surveillance, control and leadership all spheres of life in district and town and all the primary party organizations.

In the party committees in the Ukraine, for example, an average of from three to twenty supernumerary instructors work in a single committee.[28] In the Soviet Communist party as a whole there is one supernumerary instructor for every five primary party organizations. In many district committees, town committees, regional committees and in the central committees of constituent republics there are permanent efficiency advisory councils (in party offices—libraries), technical and economic advisory councils, etc.

Since 1935 the profession of "party worker" has been officially recognized, and the controlling organ of the party organization has been legally and actually divided into the "party apparatus"—appointed and paid workers of the party organ engaged solely in party work—and the "party committee," whose elected members work mostly outside the party apparatus. The Central Committee of the CPSU is trying to introduce certain correctives, which, however, cannot fundamentally alter this state of affairs. The following official statement clarifies the wishes of the party apparatus:

> The party has never regarded its apparatus merely as persons who are entirely to do party work. The apparatus consists of members of committees, the bureaus of primary party organizations and a large number of elected activists. . . . Party activists' opportunities are truly unlimited, and they must boldly use these opportunities, thereby increasing the strength of the *apparatus tenfold*.[29]

If this assertion is accepted, then the party apparatus consists of the already indicated 2,000,000 Communists elected to various party organs (bureaus, party committees, district committees, town committees, area committees, regional committees, provincial committees and central committees of constituent republics). But the nucleus of the professional party workers comprises only one-quarter of this number—about 500,000 professional party workers, including former secretaries of primary party organizations. The party apparatus workers may be divided into two categories: those who are formally elected (secretaries, heads of departments and editors) and those who are simply appointed (deputy heads of departments, instructors, inspector-specialists, propagandists, lecturers and the administrative personnel of committees).

In the town committees party workers are largely chosen from the industrial sector of the town. Usually there are three secretaries in a town committee: the first secretary, who has overall control; the second secretary, who controls the cadres; and the third secretary, who is concerned with industry, transportation, construction and communications. The third secretary, as a rule, is an engineer. An engineer also heads the industrial department.

The principal functions of the town committee are as follows: (1) the execution of party policy in the town; (2) the control and leadership of non-party institutions and organizations in putting into effect directives of the party and the government; (3) the control and leadership of primary party organizations; (4) general political supervision over the population of the town; (5) the organization of all economic plans and state assignments.

The structure of the party apparatus, the principle of the organization of its departments, the staff of party workers and the creation of an establishment of supernumerary party workers correspond to these functions.

The town committee is formed on the same principles and for the same period of time as the district committee (two years). It consists of from fifty to sixty party members and from ten to fifteen candidate members. The plenum of the town committee elects its bureau of from seven to nine persons, including the three secretaries, who must be confirmed in their posts by the party regional committee.[30]

According to the new regulations, the plenum of the town committee approves and controls the heads of the departments of the town committee; it also appoints the editor of the local newspaper, which is considered to be the organ of the town committee. The departments of the town committee do not have the right to give orders on their own authority. They act only in the the name of and in fulfillment of the enactments of the town committee bureau, on the instructions of its first secretary. They are in twofold subordination: they put into effect the enactments of their own committee and those of the analogous department of the superior committee. If there are contradictions or divergencies between the ordinances of one committee and the directives of a superior department, then the latter are put into effect because they are based on the decisions of a superior committee. However, the superior department does not have the right to alter an incorrect decision of an inferior committee (the bureau of a town committee); it must instead propose the rejection of such a decision at a meeting of its committee (the bureau of the regional committee). The official statement says:

> The department of the party committee conducts practical work in fulfilling party decisions. Relying on the decisions of the bureau of the party committee or on the ordinances of superior party organs, the department provides explanations on practical matters in party work, arranges the fulfillment of individual tasks and instructs the workers in local party organizations.[31]

The town committee realizes its leadership of organizations or institutions either directly, through its own apparatus (departments), or else indirectly, through party groups, acting within them. The staff workers in town committees include a sizable number of the responsible communist officials of the town. In addition, staff officials of the regional committee (officials appointed from the region) and even staff officials of the Central Committee of the CPSU (the heads of important enterprises, high-ranking military officers, etc.) work in the town. The latter, as members of a primary party organization, are nominally but not administratively under the control of the town committee. They are cadres of the Central Committee of the CPSU, which alone has the right to issue orders to them. The staff members of the town committee establish the way in which all responsible posts may be filled; that is, whether they should be filled only by party members or by others appointed by the decision or the permit of the town committee. Should it be necessary to appoint a non-party specialist to an important post, for example, to the directorship of a scientific institute, this appointment is made either by a higher administrative organ or by the town council (the town executive committee) with the concurrence of the party town committee. The number of staff posts in a town district committee or a town committee depends on the size of the town and on the number of enterprises and institutions situated within its boundaries. For example, in 1940 the Sverdlovsk district committee in Moscow had a staff of 800 persons, 425 of whom were members of party cadres (including the secretaries of primary party organizations); the others were officials in enterprises and institutions in the district.[32]

Apart from the three secretaries of the town committee itself, the bureau of the town committee includes one or two heads of departments of the town committee, the chairman of the town executive committee, certain important economic and administrative officials in the town, sometimes a local trade union leader and, in Stalin's day, usually the chief of the local branch of the NKVD (security police). The functions of the bureaus of the district committees, town committees and regional committees are officially described as follows:

> The bureau is the executive organ of the district committee, the town committee, the regional committee, etc. In the intervals between plenary sessions of these committees it controls the entire activities of the party organizations; ensures the practical execution of directives issued by higher party organs; issues instructions on important economic, cultural and party construction work; selects and confirms a definite group of workers; and reviews and decides the personal affairs of Communists.[33]

According to the bureau's constitution, it is an organ for collective leadership. Important matters of principle concerning the work of the party committee and of all local organs of power must be decided at meetings of the bureau. The party apparatus (departments, instructors) prepares the agenda. Before it is submitted to the bureau for discussion and decision, each political, economic, cultural or personal question is carefully studied and investigated by the party apparatus. For this purpose, communist specialists serving on permanent commissions of the party committee—and even outsiders—are called in, if necessary.

As a result of this study, the party apparatus draws up a "draft decision of the bureau," which is circulated in advance to members and candidate members of the bureau. Formerly such a draft was concealed from the organizations and institutions affected by it, but now it is recommended that it be shown to them in advance so that they can give an expert explanation and eliminate any deficiencies pointed out even before the bureau meets.[34] As well as the members and candidate members of the bureau, leading party officials and officials who have been called in to give expert advice have the right to attend bureau meetings. After the relevant problem has been discussed, these experts are required to leave the meeting before a decision is reached. The committee's first secretary formulates the final decision (or supplement to the draft decision) after the matter has been discussed. A decision is then reached by means of a vote. The bureau rarely makes a decision contrary to the wish of the first secretary. If this happens, he has two arguments in reserve: he can either refer the matter to a superior committee, or he can dismiss the matter from discussion and take the appropriate action through the agency of his party apparatus, bypassing the bureau. In the latter case the party apparatus acts entirely in the spirit of the prevailing party doctrine, according to which "the party apparatus is a concentration of the best people in the party, its most experienced, authoritative and well-tried cadres."[35]

This is, in a sense, quite correct. The history of the Soviet Communist party is full of examples of the victory of this apparatus, not only over all opposition, but also over "collective leaderships" and over the whole party because in this apparatus are concentrated the virtuosos of political power.

Between conferences the plenum is considered to be the highest ruling organ of the town committee. It meets every three months. These meetings are conducted by the bureau of the town committee (in practice, by the secretary of the town committee). The plenum discusses questions that have been decided in advance by the town committee and publishes them on its own authority. Theoretically, each member of the plenum has the right to initiate discussions on local and even on general party policy. This right is seldom exercised, lest the proposer be accused of making an "anti-party attack," with all the unpleasant consequences that would entail. Plenary meetings are generally held in secret. Only a limited number of activists receive invitations to attend, but responsible officials of the party apparatus, even though they may not be members of the plenum, attend by virtue of their positions. The exclusive nature of the membership of the plenum and the secrecy in which it is held are explained by the fact that secret letters and directives of the Central Committee of the CPSU, matters that are not to be published in the press nor even made generally known within the party, are disclosed at these meetings.

The extent to which a Communist knows the high policy of the party depends on how far up the political ladder he is. Secret documents are classified, and the Central Committee of the CPSU issues precise instructions on what documents are to be disclosed to each level within the party.

Decisions of the plenum are normally communicated, not only to the party organization, but also directly to state, trade union, cooperative and social organs and to town organizations, for which they are mandatory.

One of the most important functions of the district committees and town committees is the management of the "party economy," which includes the registration, recruitment and expulsion of party members; the distribution and storage of party documents; the system of accountability to higher party organs; and the party's information and statistical services. Fear of spies, which the party constantly fosters, and the synthetic fear of imaginary enemies, who, it is alleged, desire to infiltrate into the party by deceitful means in order to discover its secrets and harm it from within, have led to the establishment within the Soviet Communist party of scrupulous methods of accountancy and cross-checking without precedent in the history of bureaucracy. The sectors of "party statistics" and "individual party cards" in district committees and town committees know more about the party's members than the members themselves. Party regulations became especially exacting in this respect after the famous edict of the Central Committee of the CPSU issued on May 13, 1935, "On the Checking of Party Documents." An edict issued by the Plenum of the Central Committee held in December, 1935, "A Review of the Check on Party Documents," stated:

> All the evidence provided by the check on party documents has shown the extreme importance of the party's order that the more progress we make the more the class enemy resorts to the most ingenious fighting methods, exploiting for this purpose in the first place the time-serving complacency and slackness of certain Communists. Only an absence of bolshevist vigilance can explain the many instances of the gross violation of the party's statutes with regard to the reception of new members. . . . Manifest enemies of the party have contrived to enter its ranks, including even the spies of foreign intelligence services, who have joined in the guise of political emigrants and members of fraternal Communist parties.[36]

The "check of party documents" after Kirov's murder was only a prelude to the unparalleled tragedy that overtook the party itself: the physical annihilation of its basic cadres, which Stalin's former pupils and executives described with such authority at the Twentieth and Twenty-second Party Congresses. The Plenum declared that the management, control and issuing of party documents should be dealt with, not by technical personnel, but by responsible officials of the party apparatus. It proposed that responsible party officials should themselves undertake the business of receiving new members and issuing party documents, stating:

> Only in this way can the secretaries of party, district, town and regional committees really know the members of the party.[37]

From then on it was not the primary party organizations, nor even the appropriate departments of district committees and town committees, but the first secretaries of these committees who were responsible for the usefulness to the regime and the devotion to the party apparatus of each newcomer to the party membership. The decree stated:

> The secretaries of town committees and district committees are personally and directly responsible to the Central Committee of the CPSU (B[olshevik]), to provincial and regional committees and to the central committees of the Communist parties of constituent republics for the proper issuing of party cards and candidates' cards. . . . New party membership and candidate membership cards, as well as registration documents, are issued by the Central Committee of the CPSU(B.) directly to the first secretary of the regional committee, the provincial committee or the central committee of the Communist party of a constituent republic. . . . The secretaries of regional committees, provincial committees and of the central committees of the Communist parties of constituent republics issue the party cards directly to the first secretaries of district committees for distribution to their members.[38]

Another innovation was the issue to each Communist of a registration card bearing the same number as his party card. This new card "tied" the Communist to his own party apparatus, and even now a Communist may not move from one district to another without the special permission of his district committee or town committee.[39] When he moves to a new place, his party registration card follows him through party channels. Were he to move without seeking permission, no local party organization would receive him and his party card would not be recognized. If the member did not return to his former organization within three months, or otherwise legalize his position, he would automatically cease to be a party member. His registration and membership cards would then have to be sent to the Central Committee of the CPSU, together with the reasons for their return.

A single system for registering Communists has been set up in the CPSU. For each member there is a registration card, a record card and a party card, all of which bear the same number, as well as a registration form. Apart from these there are two other cards: a statistical card and an alphabetical card. The main party documents—the party card, the registration card and the record card—are all printed on special paper by the Moscow typography, which also prints currency notes. They are under the supervision of the "sector for the individual party card," which is a section of the Party Organs Department of the Central Committee. Party cards are issued to members personally by the secretary of the district committee or town committee; the registration card remains in the hands of the district committee; and the record card, which is a document confirming the issue of a party card, is sent to the Central Committee of the CPSU. On June 26, 1956, the Central Committee of the CPSU published a new instruction "On the Method of Registering and Issuing Party Cards and Candidates' Cards of the 1954 Type."[40] This instruction in essence preserves the Stalinist method of running the "party economy," as established in 1935. The instruction contained the following points: (1) The basic documents that determine party membership are the party card and the registration and record cards; candidate membership is determined by candidate, registration and record cards. (2) Party documents are signed and issued by first or second secretaries of district committees or town committees and by the heads or deputy heads of political departments of the army after they have been ratified by regional or area committees, or by the central committees of constituent republics, or by political administrative bodies of the army. (3) Party membership and candidate membership documents are sent out by the Central Committee of the CPSU to district committees and town committees and to the central committees of constituent republics on the application and the authority of the first secretary of a party committee. Party document forms are issued to first secretaries of town committees and district committees by the secretaries of regional or provincial committees, or of central committees of constituent republics, on "written request."[41]

Before filling out party documents, each Communist completes a detailed registration form, formulated by the Central Committee of the CPSU. The new norms established in the registration form for social categories of recruits to the party are significant. The instructions state that in determining the social position of accepted candidates for party membership it is essential to be guided by the following considerations:

> (1) Manual workers and peasants, irrespective of whether they are non-manual workers at the time of their candidature, are classed as manual workers or peasants. (2) Non-manual workers and peasants who are engaged in manual work at the time of their candidature are classed as manual workers.[42]

This is obviously a stratagem designed to increase the percentage of "workers" in the party, and party statistics therefore designate as workers persons who, though they were manual workers when they joined the party, have for many years been engaged in non-manual work. The instructions also give a more precise definition of what the term "non-manual worker" means in party statistics:

> The social group of non-manual workers contains administrative, economic, engineering, technical, scientific and teaching, cultural, medical, legal, statistical and production personnel of enterprises, institutions and organizations, as well as the middle, senior and top-level personnel of the Soviet Army and Navy.[43]

The instructions liberally define the concept of native language. A Latvian, Uzbek or Chechen who speaks Russian fluently may state on the registration form that his native language is Russian:

> Under the heading "native language" may be written the language that the Communist speaks fluently and in which he writes, irrespective of nationality.[44]

However, in the sections dealing with the applicant's parents' occupation prior to 1917 (this question is still included in party documents, more than forty-eight years after the Revolution) and with the political personality of the Communist, the wording is severe, searching and detailed. The instructions declare:

> Under the heading "Have you participated in opposition or anti-party groups" it is necessary to indicate specifically when and where the member or candidate member took part in opposition and anti-party groupings.[45]

He must also state whether he has ever been on trial and, if the charge was dismissed, it must be indicated on the record card when and by what organ.[46] Even a member or candidate member who is being readmitted to the party must have the reasons for his previous expulsion entered on his registration documents.[47]

Party cards and registration and record cards are filled out by the Communist, and signed by the secretary of the district committee and the town committee, the head of a political department of the army and a Communist who has received a party card, "in special ink obtained from the Central Committee of the CPSU."[48]

All three documents—the party card or candidate's card, the registration and the record cards—have photographs of the holder affixed to them and

> the seal of the district committee, town committee or political department of the army must be so affixed as to cover part of the photograph. The seal is affixed by a special adhesive obtained from the Central Committee of the CPSU.[49]

The way in which party documents are stored and conserved is so strict as to be laughable, as if the CPSU were a small island surrounded by a sea of spies. The Central Committee of the CPSU sends supplies of party documents to the first secretaries of the regional and provincial committees and the central committees of the constituent republics and to the heads of political administrations or departments "via the dispatch service of the MVD [security police] of the U.S.S.R." The regional and provincial committees and the central committees of the constituent republics address them to the first secretaries of the district committees and town committees "through special channels of the Ministry of Communications of the U.S.S.R." in "the factory packages of GOSNAK [state directory of currency] with lead seals."[50] The secretaries of provincial and regional committees and of the central committees of the constituent republics are responsible to the Central Committee of the CPSU for the documents, and the secretaries of district committees and town committees are responsible for them to the next higher committee. These committees must keep their reserves of party documents in "fireproof shelves under the care of the first secretary."[51]

On March 13, 1957, the Central Committee of the CPSU published new instructions "On the Registration of Members and Candidate Members of the CPSU." They reaffirmed the principles laid down by the Central Committee in 1935 and 1956 and ordained that the basic registration document for the personnel of party organizations was the registration card, which was to have the same number as the party card, and that the district committee was to carry out the personal registration of Communists in the town committees on the basis of these registration cards. These cards were to be kept in the "section for party statistics and the section for the individual party card" of district committees and town committees, "in iron shelves or safes."[52] In the future, the registration of party personnel was to be conducted on the basis of statistical reports received from district and town committees.

In the primary party organizations the registration of Communists is to be conducted according to lists or cards. The main registration duties rest upon the district committees and the town committees. According to the instructions these duties include: (1) the personal registration of Communists in the district or town and the protection of registration cards; (2) the registration of newcomers to the party or of those who have come from other organizations and the removal from the register of members who have left the district or have been expelled; (3) the regular entry of supplementary notes on the registration cards of Communists; (4) the direction and control of registration of Communists in the primary organizations; (5) the supply of systematic "statistical records" concerning the personnel of district and town organizations to regional committees, provincial committees and the central committees of constitutent republics.[53]

A Communist's registration card is a highly confidential personal document. The first part is filled out and signed by the holder, and the second part is filled out by the district committee or the town committee. Only the secretary of the district committee or the town committee has the right to make entries on the second part of the card, and then only in special ink. Even members of the party apparatus can only see their registration cards if they have the permission of the secretary of the district committee or town committee. The instructions also declare:

> With the permission of the secretary of the district committee or town committee registration cards can be used by responsible workers of the district committee or town committee, by secretaries of primary party organizations and by the representatives of higher party organizations.[54]

Such strict secrecy about the registration cards can only be explained by the fact that they contain, in addition to factual information about the activities of party members, secret details of their political and moral qualities that have been collected by the party apparatus and even by the state security organization. Although the instructions state that "*should circumstances require it* members and candidate members may be appraised by the contents of their registration cards,"[55] this section deals with those exceptions when the card is "white" (that is, when it bears no unfavorable remarks) or when it belongs to a high-ranking member of the party apparatus (a secretary of a regional committee, a provincial committee, or the central committee of a constituent republic or a member of the Central Committee of the CPSU) who is above suspicion. This revised registration system is based on the party apparatus' distrust of the members of the party; it is an accurate barometric guide to the variations in the composition of the party, a filter for use in systematic purges and an instrument for intimidating potential opposition within the party.

* CHAPTER IX *

The Regional Committee and the Provincial Committee

THE CENTRAL COMMITTEE of the CPSU formulates high policy, but Russia is actually run by the secretaries of the regional committees. The regional committee is the third step of the party hierarchy ladder, both from the bottom (party committee, district committee, regional committee) and from the top (Central Committee of the CPSU, central committee of a constituent republic, regional committee). The U.S.S.R. is divided into 137 *oblasts* (regions); thus the Soviet Union is administered by 137 regional committee secretaries. Stalin called the secretaries of primary party organizations the noncommissioned officers; the secretaries of district committees and town committees the officers; and the secretaries of regional committees the generals of the party. These "generals" have far greater power over their territories than the prerevolutionary governor-generals ever possessed.

But herein lies a paradox. Each party committee secretary is in himself a powerful person, but collectively these secretaries are of no importance. No matter how insolent, ambitious and arbitrary they are in their own domains, they immediately become docile, servile and obsequious when they are gathered together in Moscow. The present-day party secretary, the leading party *apparatchik,* the prototype of whom the party considers to have been Lenin's "professional revolutionary," is an experienced and highly qualified bureaucrat. But he is a new type of bureaucrat—a political bureaucrat who knows all the details of policy and the economics and techniques of industrial production. The Central Committee teaches its members that

> politics cannot be divorced from production, nor can successful economic work be divorced from political work. Therefore each person working in the party apparatus must, irrespective of his position, have a sound knowledge of economic questions and be an expert in political work.[1]

Especially exacting demands are made of the leader. He must "know a great deal and possess firmness of character and independence,"[2] but he must above all be an organizer and have a thorough knowledge of the party apparatus, because the fate of the party's policy depends on

153

the quality of the work of the party apparatus. That is why the Central Committee points out to its cadres:

> The organization of the work of the apparatus depends on the secretaries of the party committee, primarily on the first secretary. He is required to ensure that all departments and workers act purposefully, directing their efforts at organizing the masses. The proper organization of the work of the apparatus presupposes the efficient allocation of assignments and the exercise of personal responsibility in executing them.[3]

Most of the present leading cadre members in regional committees, provincial committees and central committees of constituent republics entered the party after the Great Purge of 1936–39. At that time, of the 121 first secretaries (104 regional committees, 6 provincial committees and 11 central committees of constituent republics), 118 were shot. The names of the three survivors are well known: Khrushchev, Zhdanov and Beria. By the beginning of 1938, 35 per cent of the members of the primary party committees, 41 per cent of the district committees, 46 per cent of the town committees and 60 per cent of the members of the regional committees, provincial committees and central committees of constituent republics had been replaced.[4] By the beginning of 1939, the leading positions of the regional committees, provincial committees and central committees of constituent republics had been almost completely repopulated. At the same time, the Central Committee maintained its policy of promoting workers from the lowest ranks of the party—activists in the primary party organizations, most of whom were engineers or technical workers, who were thought to be competent technical specialists but devoid of political ambition. Thus by 1939, 54 per cent of the secretaries of the regional committees, provincial committees and central committees of the constituent republics were being recruited from the primary party organization *aktivs,* and 7,250 secretaries of the district committees and town committees came from the same source.[5] The second such influx into the secretarial corps came twenty years later, after the Twenty-first Congress of the CPSU, in 1959.

What is the difference between the province (*krai*) and the region (*oblast*)? The region is one of the four basic administrative units of the U.S.S.R. (region, district, town and village); the province is, according to the official definition, a large administrative unit containing, as a rule, autonomous or administrative regions.[6] There are only six such provinces. All the regional committees of the regions forming a province are directly subordinate to the provincial committee. These are mainly autonomous national regions and areas situated in the outlying parts of the Soviet Union or administrative regions that have been united into a single province to facilitate economic and political administration (e.g., the Kazakh S.S.R.). In matters of party rights there is no difference between the regional committee and the provincial committee.

Nor do they differ in structure. The provincial committee is simply a large regional committee. The party's statutes accord them equal rights and obligations. Because of this, everything said below about the regional committees holds true for the provincial committees. Although according to the Soviet constitution autonomous regions are administratively autonomous, the party statutes in fact rate their regional committees as one stage less important than ordinary party regional committees. Ordinary regional committees are directly subordinate to the Central Committee of the CPSU, but the regional committees of autonomous regions are subordinate to the Central Committee only through the provincial committees.

An autonomous Soviet socialist republic is considered to be the state of a particular nation. Unlike the constituent republics, such a "state" has no national Communist party, but only a party organization with the status of an ordinary party organization of an administrative region. It therefore has no central committee, but is simply the party "regional committee" of that particular autonomous republic. The regional committees of autonomous republics are subordinate, just as administrative regional committees are, directly to the Bureau of the Central Committee of the CPSU for the R.S.F.S.R. Regional committees of autonomous regions and autonomous republics of constituent republics, apart from the R.S.F.S.R., are subordinate to the central committee of the appropriate constituent republic.

The regional party conference, which takes place once every two years, is the supreme authority of the regional party organization. Elections to it are held at district and town conferences, in accordance with procedures laid down by the regional committee. Delegates are elected by secret ballot, but the list of delegates is compiled and agreed upon beforehand by a representative of the regional committee and the presidium of the conference.

The agenda of a regional conference is usually as follows: (1) report by the first secretary of the regional committee; (2) report by the chairman of the regional inspection commission; (3) elections of: (a) the regional committee, (b) the regional inspection commission and (c) delegates to the republic party conference and to the CPSU Congress, if the regional conference takes place in the R.S.F.S.R. immediately prior to the Congress.

The first secretary's report describes: (1) how directives issued by the Central Committee of the party have been carried out in the region and (2) the future tasks of the regional party organization in fulfilling new directives. The reports of the 137 regional party secretaries are so alike, despite their authors' differences in ability, nationality and temperament, as to be virtually indistinguishable in structure and content. The reason for this is quite simple: these reports are constructed according to a pattern supplied by the Central Committee; they vary only with the particular economic characteristics of each region. They are, in fact, more in the nature of directives from the central authority than locally compiled reports. Because they clarify the Central Committee's policy with reference to each particular region, the delegates do not presume to criticize them. Criticism and self-criticism are always directed at individual members of regional committees and at the leaders of local soviet and economic organizations. Such criticism is generally aimed at furthering national rather than local interests. The regional inspection commission's report on the conduct of local affairs and on the budgeting of the various branches of the regional committee organization—the publishing organization, the editorial personnel, the party office, etc.—is a mere formality.

The elections at the regional conference, as at the district conference, are carried out by secret ballot, but members and candidate members are chosen with greater care. The conference decides the numerical size of the regional committee; on an average it numbers from seventy to eighty members, from thirty to forty candidate members and from thirty to forty members of the regional inspection commission. The Central Committee does not examine the list or confirm the appointment of rank-and-file members of the regional committee; it does, however, issue directives that ensure the election of predetermined numbers of members from each of the social, professional, national and age groups. All the prospective members of a regional committee are verified by a department of the leading party organs; they are then discussed by the presidium of the conference under the guidance of the first secretary, and only then are their names entered in the list of candidates. This list is then presented to a session of the conference in order to determine whether any candidate should be withdrawn. Additions to and deletions from the list of candidates are made by open ballot. Next, each candidate is put to the secret vote. A "counting commission" consisting of persons who are not candidates is elected to count the votes. Candidates who have received more than 50 per cent of the votes are considered to have been elected to the regional committee. The former practice of "drawing the line" under the list of candidates so that the number of members of the regional committee should not exceed a permitted maximum has been discontinued; the number of candidates may now exceed the number of vacancies. Delegates to a party congress and members of the regional inspection commission are elected by a similar procedure. At the conference a resolution is passed approving the first secretary's report on the tasks of the regional party organization. It repeats the injunctions of the Central Committee and the tasks outlined by the first secretary.

After the conference has ended, the first organizational plenum of the regional committee takes place; this discusses only matters concerning the elections to the bureau of the regional committee and to the secretariat of the regional committee and the appointment of heads of departments, the chairman of the party commission and the editors of newspapers. These elections and appointments are carried out by open vote, but nobody is actually elected here; the plenum is presented with a list of members of the bureau, and the secretariat, heads of departments, newspaper and periodical editors and the chairman of the party commission, that has already been confirmed by the Central Committee. The responsible representative of the central committee of the republic, or of the Central Committee of the CPSU for the R.S.F.S.R., present communicates to the plenum the Central Committee's "recommendations" for appointments to responsible positions in the regional committee. Until recently such "recommendations" were invariably accepted. Since Stalin's death the communist leaders have returned to Lenin's formulas of "the centralization of leadership" and "the decentralization of responsibility," which, when applied to regional party organizations, means independence in matters of local administration, provided that the general party line is maintained. The party's statutes say of this:

> All party organizations are autonomous in deciding local questions if their decisions do not run counter to party policy.[7]

In 1956–57, in a series of decrees of the Supreme Soviet of the U.S.S.R., measures aimed at decentralizing certain functions of the legislative, judicial, administrative and economic organs and their transfer to local organs (the law "On the Transfer to the Competence of Constituent Republics of Legislative Powers, and the Structure of the Courts of Constituent Republics and the Promulgation of Civil, Criminal and Court Codices," the law for the reorganization of industrial management, etc.) were enacted. This was the juridical side of the matter. In actuality, decentralization meant the handing over to local party organs of greater rights in self-administration and the imposition on them of greater responsibility for the proper functioning of local organs of power. A certain broadening of the administrative and financial rights of regional committees, provincial committees and especially of central committees of constituent republics has taken place.

The regional committee has three spheres of activity: (1) leadership of the inferior party organs (district committees, town committees), (2) leadership of the organs of state administration at its own level, and (3) leadership of the social organizations of the region. The structure of the regional committee corresponds to these three categories. The number and nature of its departments are determined by the administrative characteristics and the character of the economy of the region. The departments that exist in every regional committee are as follows: (1) party organs department; (2) department of propaganda and agitation; (3) industry and transport department; (4) agricultural department; (5) soviet administration department; (6) trade, finance and planning department; (7) schools department; (8) general department; (9) special sector; (10) bureau of party commission; and (11) regional committee affairs department. The titles of these departments describe their functions; the two most important are the party organs department, formerly called the "department of leading party, trade union and *Komsomol* organs," and the department of propaganda and agitation. The first directly instructs, inspects and guides the district committees and town committees. It selects the secretaries of the district committees and town committees and controls their appointment, transfer and dismissal. The party organs department also regulates the social, professional and national composition of the party through the organizational and instructional departments of the district committees and town committees. Since all secret information (registration cards, etc.) concerning Communists is accessible to this department alone, the reports of even its most junior officials have a powerful influence over the appointment and dismissal of officials in all other organizations in the party and the state. The party organs department also controls the trade unions and the *Komsomol*. The party organs department controls the trade unions of a region through the party groups of the presidium of the regional soviet of trade unions, but it has direct control over the regional committee of the *Komsomol* (all the leaders of the *Komsomol* regional committees are members of both the All-Union Leninist Young Communist League and the Communist Party of the Soviet Union).

The department of propaganda and agitation controls all forms of agitation (political study groups, meetings, newspapers, radio, cinema, television, theaters, etc.) and all forms of propaganda (political schools, seminars, lectures, publishing, party offices, libraries, writers' and artists' unions, etc.). According to the official definition, the difference between agitation and propaganda is that agitation is imparting a little political knowledge to a large number of people, and propaganda is imparting a great deal of political knowledge to a few people. The division of functions and objectives between agitation and propaganda is effected on this principle.

The industry and transportation, agricultural, trade, finance and planning and the soviet administration departments as well as the schools department are subsidiary departments. They control all the regional organs of state and cooperative institutions and enterprises and also their personnel. The industry and transportation department has complete control over industrial enterprises and transportation at the local level, but at the republic level it can exercise only political supervision and has no right to intervene in operational or administrative matters. The heads of such undertakings are appointed by ministries of the U.S.S.R. to which they are directly subordinate. The local regional committee is responsible for the fulfillment of the economic plans of all enterprises situated within its territory. The agricultural department of the regional committee directly controls the agricultural production administration of the regional executive committee. It controls the state and collective farms through the appropriate inter-district agricultural production administration units and through the party district committees. The trade, finance and planning department has direct control of regional institutions (the trading department, finance and planning departments of the regional executive committee and the regional consumer cooperation union) and political supervision over the local branch of republic institutions (regional branch offices of state committees). The schools department directly controls the regional executive committee department of the Ministry of Education; it also has direct control over the senior schools of the region, but it controls the secondary and primary schools via the district committees and town committees. The soviet administration department controls and politically supervises the apparatus of the regional executive committee, of the regional military commissariat, of the regional court, of the regional prosecuting magistracy, of the regional office of MOOP (the Ministry of the Protection of Social Order—the security forces and the civil police) and the regional office of the Committee for State Security (the political police). Since the principal officers of the prosecuting magistracy and the state security committee are appointed and removed only by higher authority, the regional committee's supervision and control over them have political, not administrative or functional, importance.

In addition to carrying out the functions already mentioned, the regional committee's departments issue instructions to the corresponding departments of the district committees and the town committees. The general department is a general office for all departments of the regional committee apart from the special sector. All incoming and outgoing correspondence from all party, state and public organizations and institutions of the districts and towns of the region or with other regions passes through this department. It is the regional committee's "curator of printed matter": papers of the regional committee's departments become official only when they have been registered by the general department, have been given a serial number and have been stamped with the regional committee's stamp, which is in the possession of the head of the department.

The department of regional committee affairs controls the regional committee's finances, engages and dismisses technical personnel and is the official representative of the regional committee in dealings with other institutions. It controls the finances of regional committee enterprises (publishing houses, party offices, etc.).

The special sector has a special place in the regional committee apparatus; it is in fact its secret political department, and within the regional committee it is subordinate only to the first secretary. It is also subordinate to the special sector of the central committee of a constituent republic or of the Central Committee of the CPSU. The staff of a special sector is independent of the ordinary regional committee apparatus and consists of the sector chief, his assistants, secretaries, cipher clerks, special typists, a record keeper and a stenographer. The head of the sector is usually appointed by the Central Committee, and the others are chosen locally by the local first secretary and the regional state security chief. Because of the nature of its work very strict regulations control recruitment to the special sector. Through it the Central Committee's special sector conveys orders and information to the regional committee, and local information is transmitted through the same channels to the Central Committee. These sectors have various means of communication at their disposal. Depending on the importance and urgency of the message these range from periodically changing cipher and codes to the special messenger services of the state security organization and the civil police. The location of a regional committee's special sector is usually isolated from the other departments. Only the secretary of the regional committee has the right to enter it. The directives and information of the Central Committee are classified according to varying degrees of secrecy—some documents are revealed only to the first secretary, some to all the secretaries, a third group to the regional committee bureau and a fourth to the plenum of the regional committee and to the regional committee *aktiv*. The regional committees and provincial committees of the R.S.F.S.R. and the central committees of the republics also have permanent facilities for direct telegraph and telephone communication with the central government.

The heads of the regional committee and provincial committee departments are technical specialists: the chief of the industry and transportation department is a qualified engineer; an agronomist or veterinary surgeon heads the agricultural department; the trade, finance and planning department is headed by an economist; etc. There are, of course, exceptions, but only in the case of very experienced party organizers. The regional committee has an equally considerable number of staff workers. In the regional committee, as in the district committees and town committees, a record is kept of all officials in the region who can be appointed, transferred or dismissed only on the decision of (depending on the importance of the post) the bureau or the secretariat of the regional committee or by the permits of its departments. In the region there are also leading officials—staff workers of the central committee of the republic or of the Bureau of the Central Committee of the CPSU of the R.S.F.S.R.—whose fate is not in the hands of the regional committee. These include secretaries of the regional committee, its heads of departments, newspaper editors, public prosecutors, heads of the regional state security committee and others who derive their authority from central agencies.

According to the statutes (Articles 43 and 45), the regional party conference is the highest authority in the regional party organization; in the intervals between conferences this authority belongs to the regional party committee (the plenum of the regional committee); the bureau of the regional committee (from nine to eleven persons) and the secretariat of the regional committee (five persons) are the highest executive organs of the regional committee. The highest organs of the regional party organizations are, therefore, in descending order of importance: the regional party conference, the plenum of the regional committee, the bureau of the regional committee, the secretariat of the regional committee and finally the first secretary of the regional committee. But this is only the constitutional, juridical order of the hierarchy of the regional party organization. The actual order of power is depicted by the same scheme turned upside down; thus the true order of power is the first secretary, the secretariat, the bureau, the plenum and the conference.

The statutes do not indicate the functions of the regional committee bureau; it is a sort of presidium of the Central Committee on a regional scale, i.e., a regional "collective leadership." It includes all five regional committee secretaries, the heads of its main departments (if they are not already regional committee secretaries), the chairman of the presidium of the regional executive committee of soviets, plus the leading economic or administrative officials of the region. (Under Stalin the head of the NKVD was always a member of the bureau, but now this is not always so.) The bureau also has four or five candidate members, most of whom work outside the party apparatus. They attend all meetings and have the right to a deliberative vote. The bureau usually meets weekly in private. Its agenda is drawn up in advance; drafts of future decisions are also distributed in advance to members, as well as to persons and institutions affected by them. The first secretary takes the chair, and the head of the general department keeps the minutes. In addition to personnel matters, the widest variety of questions concerning the political, economic and cultural life of the region are discussed. The first secretary formulates the final decisions, which are approved by a majority of votes.

All the main questions at the bureau have been prepared by the departments of the regional committee and have been sanctioned by the appropriate secretaries of the regional committee, so that the session of the bureau is of a more or less formal nature. Nevertheless, since Stalin's death the Central Committee has been trying to make the bureau an organ of party self-administration in the region. The bureau does not have its own permanent executive machinery. The secretariat of the regional committee must ensure that its decisions are put into effect. The secretariat of the regional committee in fact provides the party and the state administrative machinery of the region. It is theoretically accountable to the bureau and the plenum of the regional committee, but in practice it is accountable only to the Central Committee. Even according to the statutes its rights and functions differ but little from those of the bureau. The statutes state:

Secretariats may be set up for the examination of day-to-day problems and for checking the execution in regional committees, provincial committees and central committees of constituent republics.[8]

From this it is evident that the "day-to-day problems" that face the regional bureau lie within its competence. There is an essential difference in the legal position of the bureau and the secretariat, and also in the position of the first secretary in each organ: the bureau can make political decisions, whereas the secretariat can only make organizational decisions. In the bureau the first secretary is a *primus inter pares,* whereas the first secretary in the secretariat is both theoretically and actually the master.

The duties and competence of each regional committee secretary are precisely defined. The first secretary has general oversight of the bureau, the secretariat and the apparatus of the regional committee, and he is the only person empowered to represent the regional committee before the central committee of the republic or the Central Committee of the CPSU. He cannot, of course, alter the Central Committee's party line, but he can adapt it to suit the conditions of his region. He cannot ignore the Central Committee's directives on certain definite matters, such as the execution of plans, but he can suggest to the Central Committee that they be modified to meet local conditions. This happens quite often, since the first secretary in that way advances not so much the interests of his region as his own career. Repeated failure to fulfill plans means that he will lose his job. Each of the other four secretaries controls his own speciality and one or two departments of the regional committee; together with the heads of these departments, he is responsible to the first secretary for their work. The staff of the departments consists of two types of worker: the permanent professional party worker (department heads and their deputies, sector leaders and instructors) and the supernumerary party worker (mainly instructors, lecturers, propagandists and members of the permanent commissions of the regional committee). According to *Pravda,*[9] in January, 1962, there were more than 320,000 supernumerary party workers in district, town, regional, provincial and republic central committees—80,000 instructors and inspectors, 140,000 lecturers and speakers and 105,000 members of permanent commissions and soviets. In 1961 2,110,000 members were elected to party committees at all levels, constituting 21.5 per cent of the party membership.[10] In Ukrainian party committees there are more than 55,000 supernumerary workers—four times the total number of professional party workers.[11] From this it would appear (somewhat improbably) that there are only 14,000 paid party workers in the Ukraine. Permanent commissions and soviets vary in type according to the economic character of the district, region or republic. The following commissions exist in all committees: commissions for questions of economic construction, commissions for organizational work and supernumerary commissions in district committees and town committees for the preliminary examination of questions concerning "acceptance into the party and the personal affairs of Communists." These commissions only prepare recommendations for party committees to consider; the latter make the actual decisions.

These commissions should not be confused with the special party commission of the regional committee, appointed from the members of the regional committee. The party commission of the regional committee has the same duties within the limits of the region as the Central Committee of the CPSU's Party Commission has on a national scale. According to the statutes it

> keeps a check on the observance of party discipline by members and candidate members of the CPSU, it prosecutes Communists who are guilty of violating the program and the statutes of the party, or who are guilty of failing to maintain party and state discipline, or of violating party morality.[12]

The chairman of the party commission is elected at a plenum of the regional committee; its members are appointed by the bureau of the regional committee. There is also a regional inspection commission, whose members are elected at the regional party conference. Its tasks are to ensure clerical efficiency, the swift passage of business and the observance of budgetary discipline in the technical apparatus of the regional committee. The inspection commission is answerable to the regional party conference and also to the regional committee.

The most important function of the regional committee is to ensure not only the day-to-day political but also the "operational" guidance of district committees and town committees. Political stability among the general population and the execution of all party and state plans in town and country depend on the quality of the leadership and on the organizational capacities of the party town committees and district committees. That is why the Central Committee judges the quality of the regional committee's work by the way district committees and town committees cope with their tasks. The Central Committee affords the regional committees unlimited right of control over town and district organizations—the right of direct organizational interference in their internal affairs, the right to dismiss and appoint their leaders and even the right to dissolve these organizations and their committees if they do not obey the orders of the regional committee. The statutes put all this in rather vague terms:

> The regional, provincial and republic party committees control the area, town and district party organizations, check their activities and systematically listen to the reports of area, town and district party committees.[13]

This leadership of the regional committee goes into action at the district and town conferences, at which new party committees are elected.

Although the statutes talk about democracy within the party and free party elections by secret ballot, the Central Committee obliges the regional committees to keep a check on the elections, to propose the candidates and to nominate the personnel to be appointed to the leading organs of the district committee and the town committee. This was the practice in Stalin's day and it remains so. The Bureau of the Central Committee of the CPSU for the R.S.F.S.R. passed a special decision on this matter on December 3, 1956, declaring:

> Certain regional committees and provincial committees are continuing to allow . . . serious defects and mistakes to occur in choosing, deploying and training cadres, are not carefully investigating before conferences the quality of the leading workers in district and town party organs, have no clear idea about the practical abilities of a number of workers nor about the attitude of Communists to them. As a result, there are occasions at conferences when they do not elect to party committees individual workers recommended by the regional committees of the CPSU. . . . The Bureau of the Central Committee of the CPSU for the R.S.F.S.R. considers that the indicated errors in the conduct of district and town party conferences occur largely because certain regional committees and provincial committees do not in fact control the conduct of those conferences. . . . The secretaries and members of the bureaus of a number of regional committees do not take part in the work of the conferences, thereby imposing the entire responsibility for the way in which they are conducted on the instruction staff of the regional committees.[14]

As a result of this, the Bureau of the Central Committee of the CPSU for the R.S.F.S.R. ordered:

> 1. All regional committees and provincial committees must improve the way in which they manage the conduct of district and town party conferences.
> 2. Regional committees and provincial committees must be more painstaking in their selection of leading cadres in districts and towns, and ensure the election to party committees of the most experienced and suitable workers.
> 3. Regional committees and provincial committees must establish day-to-day control . . . over the conduct of district and town party conferences, and ensure active participation in their work of secretaries, of members of bureaus and of other leading workers in regional and provincial party and soviet organs. . . .
>
> . . . .
>
> 7. The Party Organs Department of the Central Committee of the CPSU for the R.S.F.S.R. must strengthen its surveillance over the conduct of district and town party conferences.[15]

This decree of the Central Committee of the CPSU must be obeyed by all regional committees in organizational matters.

The decree considers the preparation for and conduct of elections to district and town party committees the personal and most important task of secretaries and members of regional committee and provincial committee bureaus. They must ensure the election to district and town committees of previously selected leading officials who have been recommended by regional committees even if unacceptable to the delegates of these conferences. Despite this, the same decree also contains a clause that declares:

> Party committees must pay attention to the need for the strictest observation of democracy within the party at party conferences.[16]

Electoral democracy at district conferences serves only as a cover to give legal force to the elections by the regional committees of leading officials in town and country.

The "elections" to the regional committees and provincial committees are under similar constant surveillance. Regional and provincial conferences are held in the national republics with the participation of secretaries or members of the presidium of the central committee of the republic, and in the R.S.F.S.R. in the presence of members of the Bureau of the Central Committee of the CPSU for the R.S.F.S.R. or its responsible workers. Just before regional conferences the Party Organs Department of the Central Committee of the CPSU for the R.S.F.S.R. presents to the Bureau of the Central Committee of the CPSU for the R.S.F.S.R. a list of leading officials in regional and provincial party committees who must be elected to these committees. The Bureau of the Central Committee issues a decree "recommending" these persons to *regional party conferences* and to the plenums of regional committees as secretaries, heads of departments and members of bureaus. Responsible representatives of the Central Committee, who sit in the presidiums of the conferences and the plenums of the regional committees and provincial committees as representatives and observers for the Central Committee, arrive armed with the appropriate lists. These representatives are equally responsible with the first secretaries of the regional committees and provincial committees to the Central Committee for the success or failure of the conferences and plenums. At regional committee organizational plenums the Central Committee representatives report the Central Committee's recommendations with regard to the appointments to leading positions. These recommendations then become the electoral choice of the plenum. The results of these elections are then referred to the Central Committee for confirmation. If successful candidates have been previously recommended by the Central Committee, their election is automatically confirmed; if they have not been recommended, their candidature is subjected to discussion. Once an official has been confirmed in office by the Central Committee, he needs only its recommendation the next time he seeks election to the same post; subsequent confirmation is dispensed with.

We have seen that documentary communications between the Central Committee, regional committees and provincial committees are used for day-to-day matters and for office routine. For matters of extreme importance there is always a live contact between the Central Committee and the regional committee: in the person of the first secretary of the regional committee on the one hand, and of the responsible instructor of a department or a member of the Bureau of the Central Committee on the other.

Responsible instructors and inspectors of the Central Committee are assigned to definite regions and provinces for purposes of surveillance and instruction. The responsible instructors and inspectors of the Central Committee are a permanent reservoir from which the Central Committee recruits new secretaries for regional committees and provincial committees and departmental heads for the central committees of the republics. Regional committee first secretaries are periodically summoned to Moscow to present progress reports; formerly these reports were submitted to the organizational bureau of the Central Committee, but now they are referred to the Bureau of the Central Committee for the R.S.F.S.R. or to the Secretariat of the Central Committee of the CPSU. The first secretary's report is preceded by an inspection by a special brigade of instructors and inspectors from various departments of the Central Committee that checks the work of all departments of the regional committee. The leader of this brigade also makes a report, mainly on the deficiencies, omissions and errors of the regional committee. After a detailed discussion of both reports, the Central Committee passes a resolution assessing the situation in the region and the work of the regional committee, pointing out defects and giving directions to the regional committee and to the appropriate departments of the Central Committee as to what should be done to eliminate those defects. Reports may also be made on separate, special questions concerning the regional committee's work (ideological questions, questions concerning economic and political campaigns, etc.). If the Central Committee points out failings that also occur in other regions, these are published in the central party press for the information and guidance of all regional committees.

In Stalin's time a type of party worker evolved whose unapproachability, conceit and hauteur increased as he climbed the promotion ladder. Now, since the crisis over the personality cult, such officials have had to adapt their behavior to new conditions. The party unequivocally condemns "workers who, when they ascend the ladder of promotion, begin to put on airs, become 'potentates' and exaggerate their own importance."[17] Since the revelations about Stalin's crimes and the repudiation of the personality cult, the official slogan "Seek the advice of the people in everything" and the party leaders' "pilgrimage to the people" have made another look at the old party protocol and at the behavior of local leaders necessary. The Central Committee of the CPSU and the party press are paying more and more attention to this. The

Central Committee's anthology, *Questions of Party Work,* devotes a special chapter to how a party worker should behave.

This book makes some remarks about the conduct of party secretaries and lays down standards for them to follow. The principal demands of the new protocol are as follows:

Spend time among the people in order to study them.

(1) Accessibility of the leader—this is not a gesture on his part, nor a bid for popularity; it is an essential attribute of leadership, it is one of the unwritten duties of a leader. For the party worker there is no substitute for personal contact with the people. No matter how experienced a leader may be, without constant contact he cannot *know profoundly, nor understand and appreciate, the state of affairs and his duties.*

Spend time among the people in order to direct them.

(2) It is a tradition of our party to educate the workers as organizers among the masses. . . . It stands to reason that, in this respect, certain demands are made of a regional committee secretary, while different demands are made of a district committee secretary. But each party leader must visit enterprises and institutions—that is where the fate of our economic plans is decided. . . .

Receive people in order to know the truth.

(3) In a number of party organs an improper practice has grown up whereby various unjustified measures are devised in order to impede access to their leaders. In some regional committees passes to see Communists have been abolished but those to see secretaries, that is, to see people for whom it is especially important to know the truth, have been retained.

Read correspondence in order to know about complaints.

(4) Party committees receive many letters, and a leader should be familiar with their contents. . . . It not infrequently happens that a worker in the party apparatus, desiring to please his superior, does not trouble him with letters of complaint; in reporting them he tries to tone them down and even conceals part of them from his chief.

Do not insult subordinate workers.

(5) Leaders cannot be tolerated who unpremeditatedly call any worker a loafer or a dunderhead. . . . People are only rude when they know that they can get away with it.

Be tactful.

(6) There are leaders whom one could never accuse of deliberate rudeness, but who are nevertheless tactless . . . who really think that it is not incumbent on them to observe the ordinary conventions of common courtesy . . . this comes out in their behavior, manners and conversation.

Be polite.

(7) Sometimes a leader talks to a visitor without looking up from his desk, and wearing a blank expression. That is tantamount to

saying that the matter the visitor has come about is no concern of his.

Do not overtly insist on having your own way.

(8) At party conferences certain leaders have been criticized because they use certain expressions as orders to emphasize their personal wishes; when addressing "subordinates" one should not say "I object to this," "I am opposed to that," "I absolutely disagree," "I do not want."

Do not vaunt one's own superiority.

(9) A leader must always behave with great tact, simplicity and modesty. However, there are leaders who behave with a marked lack of modesty. They preach rather than talk, and they always stress that they are superior to others. Just such a person will hold a meeting with a number of people present: production managers, engineers, foremen, representatives of design organizations. The leader, obviously ignoring all of them, proceeds to telephone, sometimes to more than one person at a time, about matters that have no relevance to the meeting. Sometimes he even indulges in intimate domestic conversation on the telephone, while the others present are wasting their time.[18]

Such insolent behavior on the part of officials occurs because they are out of touch with the people. Elected by neither the party nor the people, nor accountable to them, appointed by and dependent on higher authority, these officials act in the same way as their superiors do. They serve higher authority. They know too well that popularity is a transient phenomenon but power is a permanent thing. In their hearts they are convinced that authority and the people are poles apart. Their interests do not coincide. It is impossible to serve party and people simultaneously, at least for any length of time. They sacrifice popularity in the name of authority. Their authority does not depend on popularity, but their "popularity" depends on their authority.

The Plenum of the Central Committee of the CPSU held in November, 1962, decreed the reconstruction of the regional party apparatus in order to convert the functional and party-administrative committees into party production committees, that is, economic committees.

No change was made in the party's hierarchical principle. The old administrative ladder was reconstructed on a production principle. The regional and district administrative units were divided into two independent and parallel administrative units: industrial and agricultural.

The decisions of the November, 1962, Plenum state:

1. The administrative organs of the party are to be reorganized from top to bottom, based on the principle of production.

2. As a rule, within the present province or region there are two independent party organizations: (*a*) a provincial or regional party organization containing Communists working in industry, construction work, transportation, teaching establishments and scientific research institutes, planning and design organizations and institu-

tions serving industrial production and (*b*) a second provincial or regional party organization consisting of Communists working on collective and state farms, in agricultural teaching institutions and in scientific research institutions, at enterprises that process agricultural products, at food manufacturing establishments and other organizations connected with agriculture.

3. The provincial and regional party organizations, respectively, must have: (*a*) a provincial or regional committee for industrial production management or (*b*) a provincial or regional committee for agricultural production management.

4. Party district committees for agriculture are to be abolished and in their place committees of collective and state farm production managements are to be set up.

5. Zonal and section committees for management by party organizations of industrial enterprises must be set up on the territory of rural production managements.[19]

Industrial and agricultural regional (and provincial) committees were to be guided in all their actions by the relevant sections of the statutes of the CPSU concerning provincial and regional party organizations, while party committees of collective and state farm production administrations were guided by the sections relating to town committees and district committees. The statutes of the town committees themselves and of the town (industrial) district committees remained as before. The state (soviet) administrative organs in districts, towns, regions and provinces were also reorganized on the same production principles. In regions of the U.S.S.R. where industry and agriculture do not play an important role undivided regional committees continued to exist. In the autonomous regions and republics the regional committees also remained undivided.

In the logical, unitary and time-tested hierarchy of the party leadership there was formed a dualism of power in its most important sectors —the district and the region. This led, despite the official doctrine, to an artificial rift between town and country, between the industrial worker and the peasant. The party was divided into two large sections, each having its own hierarchy: an industrial Communist party and an agricultural Communist party. These two party lines were united in Russia by the Bureau of the Central Committee of the CPSU for the R.S.F.S.R., and in the constituent republics by the presidiums (the secretariats) of the central committees of the Communist parties of the constituent republics. This "production" division of the party adopted by Khrushchev was artificial and, because of the nature of the communist regime, unreal. The reconstruction of the party organs in the "production" districts and regions was discarded by the Central Committee after Khrushchev's downfall in 1964.[20]

In the next chapter we shall examine the structure and functions of the fourth-highest stage of the party hierarchy—the central committees of the Communist parties of the constituent republics.

CHAPTER X

The Central Committees of the Constituent Republics

According to the Soviet Constitution the U.S.S.R. is a federative state formed "on the basis of voluntary association of soviet socialist republics, each of which has equal rights."[1] Table 21 gives details of the populations of the fifteen republics.[2]

TABLE 21

POPULATION STATISTICS OF THE REPUBLICS

REPUBLIC	POPULATION (in thousands)	INDIGENOUS POPULATION (in percentage)
Russian Socialist Federated Soviet Republic	117,534	83.3
Ukrainian S.S.R.	41,869	76.8
Belorussian S.S.R.	8,055	81.1
Uzbek S.S.R.	8,106	62.2
Kazakh S.S.R.	9,310	30.0
Georgian S.S.R.	4,044	64.3
Azerbaidzhan S.S.R.	3,698	67.5
Lithuanian S.S.R.	2,711	79.3
Moldavian S.S.R.	2,885	65.4
Latvian S.S.R.	2,093	62.0
Kirghiz S.S.R.	2,066	40.5
Tadzhik S.S.R.	1,980	53.1
Armenian S.S.R.	1,763	88.0
Turkmenian S.S.R.	1,516	60.9
Estonian S.S.R.	1,197	74.6

Each of these republics, except the R.S.F.S.R., has its own national Communist party led by a central committee. All these parties are considered to be part of a single all-Union Communist party—the Communist Party of the Soviet Union, headed by a single Central Committee.

The Central Committee of the CPSU controls the party organization of the R.S.F.S.R. through its Bureau; this body enjoys the same status as the central committees of the other constituent republics.

Table 22 shows the national composition of the CPSU and the percentage of Communists in the indigenous nationalities of each of the fifteen republics.[3]

TABLE 22

THE NATIONAL COMPOSITION OF THE CPSU (JULY 1, 1961)

	POPULATION (in thousands)	NUMBER OF COMMUNISTS (in thousands)	PERCENTAGE OF COMMUNISTS IN POPULATION
U.S.S.R	208,000	9,626	4.6
Russians	114,100	6,117	5.4
Ukrainians	37,250	1,412	3.7
Belorussians	7,913	287	3.6
Uzbeks	6,000	143	2.3
Kazakhs	3,620	149	4.0
Azerbaidzhanians	2,900	106	3.6
Armenians	2,800	161	5.7
Georgians	2,700	170	6.0
Lithuanians	2,300	43	1.8
Moldavians	2,200	27	1.2
Tadzhiks	1,400	33	2.3
Letts	1,400	34	2.4
Turkmen	1,000	27	2.7
Estonians	990	24	2.4
Kirghiz	970	27	2.7
Other nationalities	27,400	866	3.1

The Georgians (6 per cent), Armenians (5.7 per cent), Russians (5.4 per cent) and Kazakhs (4 per cent) have the four highest percentages of party members. The disproportionately large early growth of the party in the R.S.F.S.R. still persists. In Central Asia and in the Baltic provinces the proportion of Communists in the indigenous nationalities is half or less than half that of the Russian areas; this does not mean, however, that communist power is only half as strong in those areas as it is in the central and Russian areas. The slow growth of the party in the national republics must be regarded, not only as a conscious rebuff to communism, but as evidence of the party's reluctance to open its doors wider to these nationalities.

The Bolsheviks have never taken seriously the concept of the "sovereignty" of their national minorities, since it has never been their intention to allow the latter to be genuinely self-governing. They have, however, succeeded in developing a form of pseudo-sovereignty that is unique in history. This pseudo-sovereignty has on paper all the external trappings of true sovereignty, permitting the national republics to have their own parliaments and governments and the right to formulate foreign policy, to possess armed forces and even to secede from the Soviet

Union. In actual practice, however, all this is fiction. It is true that the citizens of the national republics are in the eyes of the law equal to the citizens of Russia; from a psychological point of view this parity of legal status represents a considerable advantage for the Soviet form of pseudo-sovereignty, because absence of legal discrimination against the national minorities is accepted by the outside world as evidence that they are not discriminated against in any form. The "constitutions" of the republics, which contain provisions for parliaments, presidents, ministers, and even for conduct of foreign policy, are often taken at their face value, and it is forgotten that the Soviet Constitution itself is only a specious disguise for a centralist, one-party absolutism. As Lenin once said:

> We must know and remember that the whole Constitution of Soviet Russia in law and in practice is based upon the fact that the party corrects, prescribes and builds everything according to one single principle.[4]

Up to the beginning of the thirties the republics of the Soviet Union did enjoy some degree of administrative freedom through both party and government organs, although this did not amount to sovereignty. After the establishment of Stalin's personal dictatorship, absolute centralism was carried to extremes and the degree of autonomy that had existed vanished. Every question regarding administration had to be submitted to Moscow for decision. After Stalin's death some decentralization took place, and the power of the local party apparatus in the Union republics was increased. Other changes of a liberal nature in Soviet nationality policy also took place, and the expanded rights were embodied in a series of decrees passed in Moscow in 1957. This did not, however, fundamentally change the status of the non-Russian republics, whose sovereignty remains fictitious. There is, for example, no difference whatsoever between the power to initiate and enact legislation vested in a Union republic such as Turkmenistan and that vested in an ordinary Russian administrative or territorial unit such as Orel *oblast*. The central committee of Turkmenistan has no more rights than the Orel *oblast* party committee; indeed, the CPSU statutes place together in one and the same paragraph the rights of central committees in the Union republics and of Russian *oblast* committees. The same applies to the supreme soviet and council of ministers of Turkmenistan. The sole difference is that in Turkmenistan laws enacted in Moscow are formally approved by the appropriate organs, whereas this duplication is not carried out by party or soviet organs at the *oblast* level, which simply conform to the R.S.F.S.R. laws.

Some of the Soviet Union republics in practice have more legal rights than others, although according to the Constitution all are equal. This legal inequality arises from a number of national and political factors in the history of the national republics. The R.S.F.S.R. enjoys a more privileged position than any of the other republics. The degree of internal autonomy permitted the non-Russian republics by the Soviet leaders is determined by (1) the nature of annexation (by arms or by peaceful means) to Russia of a given nation and the nature of their relations in the past, (2) the degree to which communist ideology has struck root in a given nation and (3) the percentage of Communist party members among the indigenous population, and the extent to which the latter is susceptible to nationalism.

On this basis the Soviet national republics may be divided into two types. One consists of those that are "self-governing" in the sense that the administration is in the hands of indigenous Communists, with use of the native language at all levels and Russian used only as a *lingua franca* and confined mostly to the apex of the administrative apparatus. The second type comprises the "governed" republics, in which the government at all levels above the rural is largely in the hands of non-indigenous cadres, with Russian the predominant state language in the urban areas and the native language on a par with Russian only in the countryside.

The positions in the party apparatus of the governed republics that are generally held by non-indigenous (usually Russian) personnel are as follows: (1) the second secretary of the central committee of a republic; (2) the first deputy heads of central committee departments (where an alien is not the head); (3) the head of the special section of the central committee; (4) the first deputy chairman of the committee of the party commission (where an alien is not the chairman); (5) the second secretaries of *oblast* committees (where the first secretary is not an alien); (6) the first secretaries of city committees and the second secretaries of district committees; (7) the secretaries of party organizations of ministries; and (8) the secretaries of primary party organizations in large factories and state farms.

In the government apparatus the positions that are generally held by non-indigenous (usually Russian) personnel are: (1) the first deputy chairman of the presidium of the supreme soviet of a republic and the first deputy chairmen of *oblast* executive committees and chairmen of city committees; (2) the first deputy chairman of the council of ministers; (3) the chairman of the KGB (Committee for State Security) and *oblast* and *raion* commissioners of that committee; (4) the chairmen of the national economic council and of GOSPLAN (the state planning organ); (5) the first deputy ministers (where the minister is not an alien); (6) the first deputy heads of the supreme court and the procurator's office in the republic; the chief of criminal investigation; (7) the commanders of garrisons; and (8) the directors of key factories and of organs controlling communications.

In the light of the above list it is possible to divide the Union republics of the U.S.S.R. into five that are run by their own nationals (the Ukraine, Belorussia, Armenia, Georgia and Azerbaidzhan), and nine that are largely governed by aliens (Uzbekistan, Kazakhstan, Tadzhikistan, Turkmenistan, Lithuania, Estonia, Latvia, Kirghizia and Moldavia). All the autonomous Soviet republics are governed republics.

All the self-governing non-Russian republics except Azerbaidzhan were originally drawn toward Russia through fear that they would find themselves under the domination of stronger neighbors professing a different religion. Azerbaidzhan does not entirely fit into the self-governing category; the central party and government apparatus uses mainly the Russian language, and the number of non-Azerbaidzhanians in the administration, particularly in the capital, Baku, is high. This is understandable, for the greater part of the Russian population of Baku has lived there for generations; their representation in the state administrative apparatus roughly corresponds to their numerical strength.

The Central Asian and Baltic republics and Moldavia have the lowest percentage of native Communist party members in their populations, and they may thus be termed the most "ideologically underdeveloped" areas in the Soviet Union.[5]

Under present party policy, however, it is no longer the number of indigenous party members in the administrative apparatus of a given republic that is taken as the yardstick of the degree of party control, but the degree of "internationalization" that has taken place. In this respect Kazakhstan has become exemplary in the eyes of the Soviet leaders, since it has the most mixed population of any Soviet republic. The corollary of this policy is that attempts by indigenous party leaders in the non-Russian republics to fill as many posts as possible with their own countrymen are condemned as a manifestation of "local nationalism." Table 23 shows the composition of the party central committees and inspection commissions of twelve Union republics.[6]

TABLE 23

COMPOSITION OF THE PARTY CENTRAL COMMITTEES AND INSPECTION COMMISSIONS
OF TWELVE UNION REPUBLICS

REPUBLIC	TOTAL NUMBER OF MEMBERS	NUMBER OF INDIGENOUS MEMBERS	PERCENTAGE OF TOTAL
Moldavia	159	44	27.6
Kazakhstan*	244	105	43.0
Kirghizia	177	98	55.0
Latvia	213	137	64.0
Estonia	172	119	69.2
Uzbekistan*	282	198	70.0
Turkmenistan	186	133	72.0
Lithuania	210	152	72.4
Tadzhikistan	244	179	73.4
Azerbaidzhan	288	183	80.3
Georgia	225	214	95.2
Armenia	163	162	96.5

*Data for Kazakhstan and Uzbekistan are for 1961; for all other republics, 1963–64.

Data on the degree of internationalization that has already taken place in the non-self-governing republics are rarely disclosed by the party Central Committee in Moscow, but available information on the personnel holding senior posts at republic, town and district levels makes it possible to determine which posts have been "internationalized" in the case of middle-grade party *apparatchiks* and government officials. The only thing that is known for certain is that in order to qualify for appointment these officials must know Russian but need not have a knowledge of the local language. Data on the composition of the party apparatus in Uzbekistan, Tadzhikistan, Turkmenistan and Kirghizia (which comprise Soviet Turkestan) is pertinent. In 1929 throughout Turkestan there were 335 Turkestanis and 2,932 Russians and Ukrainians holding top posts. Twenty years later the ratio was the same, with 486 Turkestanis and 3,675 Russians and Ukrainians. With the exception of Tadzhikistan and two *oblasts* in Kirghiza, 85 out of 150 *oblast* party secretaries were aliens, and of the 13 members of the bureau of the Frunze *oblast* committee only four were Kirghiz.[7] In 1945, 4 out of 5 ministers were Uzbeks; in 1957, 3 out of 5. But every minister had a Russian deputy. At top party level the pattern was reversed; in 1958 in nine district party committees all the second secretaries were Russians.[8] Official Soviet data on Kirghizia for 1964 show that only 648 (47 per cent) of party central committee workers were Kirghiz; all the rest were aliens, including 509 Russians. Of six *oblast* committee secretaries, only two were Kirghiz.[9]

Data for the Ukraine and Belorussia more or less correspond to those for Georgia and Armenia in Table 23. Russia does not have its own Communist party.

The number of Slavs holding positions in the highest party organs in most of the non-Slav republics is far in excess of their numerical strength among the local population, as Table 24 shows.[10]

TABLE 24

SLAV REPRESENTATION IN THE PARTY CENTRAL COMMITTEES OF THE
NON-SLAV REPUBLICS

REPUBLIC	PERCENTAGE OF SLAVS IN THE CENTRAL COMMITTEE	PERCENTAGE OF SLAVS IN TOTAL POPULATION
Moldavia	72.4	27.3
Kazakhstan	57.0	52.4
Kirghizia	45.0	37.0
Latvia	36.0	33.8
Estonia	30.8	22.5
Uzbekistan	30.0	14.5
Turkmenistan	28.0	18.7
Lithuania	27.6	18.8
Tadzhikistan	26.4	14.7
Azerbaidzhan	19.7	14.3
Georgia	4.8	11.5
Armenia	3.5	3.5

Only in the three self-governing republics of Azerbaidzhan, Georgia
and Armenia is the ratio nearly balanced. Paradoxically enough, the
situation in these three republics, and in those others where Slav representation in the party and government apparatus is disproportionately
strong, tends to give rise to nationalist sentiments. The self-governing
republics are more vocal in their claims for running their own internal
affairs and there is more independent spirit, which encourages aspirations to genuine national sovereignty. In those republics where the
process of denationalization is taking place and the native population
is becoming the minority (as in Kazakhstan and Kirghizia), resentment
against the alien element is strong. This nationalist spirit is to be found
mainly among the intelligentsia and is regarded by Moscow as dangerous. The situation in these Central Asian republics is aggravated by
the fact that the tense relationship between the first party secretaries,
who are natives, and the second secretaries, who are invariably Russians,
and between ministers and their first deputies amounts almost to racial
hostility. Although nominally holding the reins of power, the first
secretaries and ministers are in practice the subordinates of their Russian
deputies, whom they resent as the watchdogs of Moscow. There is
therefore increasing criticism of this form of discrimination and also of
the unjustly low share of the national income received by the Central
Asian republics.

In recent years there have been several cases of conflict between local
officials and those appointed from Moscow. Each time the second secretaries and first deputy ministers have retained their posts, while their
native-born chiefs have been removed on various grounds, principally
those of pursuing nationalist aims and filling posts with members of
their own race. Those removed in this way were: Yusupov, Niyazov,
Kamalov and Mirza Akhmedov (Uzbekistan); Shayakhmetov, Tashenev,
Daugenov (Kazakhstan); Kulatov and Razzakov (Kirghizia); Babeuf
(Turkmenistan); Uldzhabaev (Tadzhikistan) and Mustafaev (Azerbaidzhan). There is no organized nationalist opposition in these republics,
but the signs of resistance to Moscow's denationalization policies on
the part of top party officials have caused the Soviet leaders to revive
party and government organs for the closer surveillance of the Central
Asian and Transcaucasian republics. This is a return to the practice
in the early years of Soviet rule of maintaining special branches of the
party Central Committee on the spot to control the apparatus in these
republics.

What are the structure and functions of the central committees of
constituent republics, and how far do their autonomous powers really
extend?

The central committee of the Communist party of a constituent
republic is the penultimate stage in the ascent to the summit of the
party hierarchy. It is directly subordinate to the Central Committee of
the CPSU. In the constituent republics that have been divided into

regions (Ukraine, Belorussia, Kazakhstan and Uzbekistan), the central committees control district and town party organizations via the party regional committees. Where there are no regional divisions, they control them directly. The rights and functions of the republic central committees derive from the rights and jurisdictions of the constituent republics. What the Constitution of the U.S.S.R. refers to as the "sovereign rights" of the constituent republics are actually the rights and functions of the central committees of these republics. They are laid down in detail in the republics' constitutions in accordance with a set juridical pattern. A study of one of these constitutions therefore provides a complete picture of the structure of all of them. According to Article 19 of its constitution the sovereign rights of the government of the Kirghiz S.S.R. include the following rights:

(1) to determine the constitution of the Kirghiz S.S.R.; (2) to form new regions; (3) to form new districts, towns, rural and settlement soviets and to determine their boundaries; (4) to promulgate legislation for the Kirghiz S.S.R.; (5) to maintain public order and protect citizens' rights; (6) to draw up the national economic plan and the state budget of the republic and to see that it is implemented; (7) to form economic administrative districts; (8) to ensure the implementation of local budgets of districts and towns which are directly subordinate to republic organs, as well as of the regions of the Kirghiz S.S.R.; (9) to fix and collect state and local taxes in accordance with the laws of the U.S.S.R.; (10) to manage insurance and savings organizations; (11) to manage banks and industrial, agricultural and trading enterprises and organizations within the republic, and also to control local and republic industry and construction work; (12) to supervise affairs and management of federal enterprises; (13) to organize the use of land and of mineral, forest and water resources; (14) to control living accommodations and public works; (15) to control road construction, transportation and communications; (16) to promulgate legislation concerning work conditions; (17) to be responsible for public health; (18) to run the social security service; (19) to have charge of primary, secondary and higher education; (20) to control cultural and scientific organizations and institutions; (21) to promote physical culture and sport; (22) to promulgate legislation concerning the composition and procedure of courts of law and the civil and criminal codices; (23) to grant Kirghiz citizenship; (24) to grant amnesty to and to pardon citizens convicted by Kirghiz courts; (25) to legislate on marriage and family matters; (26) to have diplomatic relations with foreign countries; and (27) to determine the composition of the military forces of the Kirghiz S.S.R.[11]

These sovereign rights may be divided into three categories:

(1) *Formal rights.*—These are formally embodied in laws, orders and ordinances published on the authority of the central party powers.

(2) *Fictitious rights.*—These exist on paper but cannot be effectively exercised; for example, rights concerning defense and foreign affairs, or

the one on page fifteen of the constitution, which states that the Kirghiz S.S.R. has the right voluntarily to withdraw from the U.S.S.R.[12]

(3) *Effective rights.*—These are the rights of the administration of the territory. These effective rights are enjoyed by the administration of the Kirghiz S.S.R. to the same extent and in the same way as any Russian region. The difference lies only in the outward formulation: while the Russian region is considered merely an administrative unit and its administrative organs the executive organs of the central power, Kirghizia is considered a sovereign state within the U.S.S.R. with all the trappings of a real state and the stage properties of sovereignty— its constitution, parliament (supreme soviet), government (council of ministers)—and even with the right to conduct its own foreign policy and to set up its own national army.

A constituent republic does not, however, have the same rights in all branches of administration. According to the constitution in each constituent republic there are two types of ministries (administration): (1) Union-republic ministries and (2) republic ministries. To the first type belong the ministries of health, foreign affairs, culture, defense, communications, agriculture, finance and several state security industrial ministries (of these, the ministries of foreign affairs and defense are fictitious). Over these ministries there exists a twofold authority—a central one, from the corresponding ministry of the U.S.S.R., and a local one.

The second type of ministry includes those of road transportation and highways, waterways, education (except for higher education, which is controlled directly from Moscow), social security, construction and trade.[13] The constituent republic has sovereign control of these, subject to the general laws of the U.S.S.R. and the routine directives of the departmental committees of the Council of Ministers of the U.S.S.R.

The organs of state power and state administration (supreme soviet, council of ministers) of the constituent republic exercise their sovereign rights of administrative management, duplicating the laws of the central power, only on the initiative, decision and under the supervision of the central committee of the Communist party of the constituent republic. The rights, obligations and functions of the central committee of the Communist party of the constituent republic derive from its place in the party hierarchy, and not from any alleged sovereignty of the republic itself. The power of the central committee of the constituent republic differs from that of the regional committee or even the district committee, not by reason of its scope, but because it is higher up the party ladder.

Therefore the party statutes, when they speak of the obligations of the central committees of republics, regional committees, town committees and district committees, bracket them together and distinguish between them only by their position in the party hierarchy. This emphasizes the fact that their common obligations are based on common rights enjoyed by each of the party organs within its own territorial limits. The statutes declare:

> Republic, provincial, regional, area, town and district organizations and their committees must be guided in their work by the program and the statutes of the CPSU, must carry out within the limits of republic, province, area, town or district all work to put policy into practice, and organize the execution of directives issued by the Central Committee of the CPSU.[14]

Here the difference between party organization (the highest party power in a given territory) and the party committee (the executive power) is consciously ignored, thereby legalizing the independence of the party organs from their party organizations. Therefore, too, the plenary powers that the statutes give these organizations "to put into effect the policies of the party" and to organize "the execution of directives issued by the Central Committee of the CPSU" are powers given to the party committee, or, more precisely, to the party apparatus of that committee. Paragraph 42 of the statutes defines the powers, obligations and directives of the Central Committee of the CPSU to party organizations and to their organs without, as we have seen, differentiating between party organizations at various levels. The tasks and obligations of all the local party organs have been dealt with in detail in Chapters Eight and Nine; only those tasks of the central committees of constituent republics that arise specifically from the nominal "autonomy" of the republics themselves will be dealt with here. They are: (1) to ensure close political supervision by the party apparatus over the indigenous population; (2) to communize the people by creating what the Stalinist formula termed "a culture, national in form, socialist in content"; (3) to create local cadres, "national in form and Muscovite in content"; (4) to cultivate the formal attributes of a national state as a façade to conceal Moscow's party and state absolutism.

In every other respect, the tasks and obligations of the central committees of the republics are identical with those of the regional committees and provincial committees of the ordinary Russian provinces.

The central committee of a republic controls all inferior party organizations and their committees. But in party and legal status it occupies the same position as the ordinary provincial committees or even regional committees of the Russian regions. The similarity of their status vis-à-vis the lowest party organizations is emphasized by the statutes, which state:

> The regional committee, the provincial committee, the central committee of the Communist party of the constituent republic control the area, town and district party organizations, check on their activities and systematically listen to area, town and district committee reports.[15]

If, however, the constituent republic has subdivisions, its central committee no longer directly controls the town and district organizations;

it controls the subdivision committees and only through these are its directives and instructions communicated to the town committees and district committees. In their turn, such subdivision committees are not directly linked with the Central Committee of the CPSU; they receive directives via their own central committee, to which they are subordinate. The same thing is true of the subdivision committees of the autonomous republics and regions in constituent republics. This is officially formulated in Paragraph 47 of the statutes:

> Party organizations in autonomous republics, and also in autonomous and other regions *that form part of provinces* and of constituent republics, work under the leadership of provincial committees of the central committee of constituent republics.[16]

Since a new and intermediate stratum below the central committee of a republic has appeared, nothing has formally changed with respect to party rights. On the other hand, the real position of the republic central committee has changed from the party apparatus point of view. (By party right is meant according to the statutes and by party apparatus right is meant the unwritten but overriding right of party apparatus.)

First secretaries of central committees of republics with subdivisions are in direct contact with the first and second secretaries of the Central Committee of the CPSU, to whom they are personally accountable. They are members of the Central Committee of the CPSU, and they attend the Plenum of the Central Committee of the CPSU. Their high position in the party hierarchy is advantageous to the central committees they head and to the "sovereignty" of the constituent republics those committees run.

The central committees of republics are recruited on the same principles as the lower-ranking party committees. The party congress is considered the highest organ of the Communist party of a constituent republic. A congress is held every other year. Republics that have subdivisions (the Ukraine, Belorussia, Kazakhstan and Uzbekistan) hold congresses every four years.[17]

The republic central committee determines the composition of the representation at a congress. Delegates are elected by each subdivision (where these exist), or at town and district conferences (where there is no subdivision). The central committee does not appoint delegates by name, but presents each lower organization with a list that states how many delegates it is to elect and from which social or professional group they must come. These quotas must be adhered to at the elections to the party congress. The congress agenda and the reports to it are discussed beforehand and are first confirmed by the presidium of the central committee and then at a plenum of the republic's central committee. The agendas of all congresses are standardized just as those of less important party conferences are; they have the following pattern: (1) the central committee's report; (2) the inspection commission's report; (3) elections to the central committee and inspection commission; (4) elections of delegates to the Congress of the CPSU. Sometimes economic or cultural questions currently concerning the republic are included in the agenda for discussion and decision.

Plenipotentiary representatives of the Secretariat of the Central Committee of the CPSU are invariably present at these congresses. These usually include heads of Central Committee departments and their deputies and responsible instructors, but rarely the secretaries themselves. Just as the representatives of the republic central committee attend regional party conferences with a prepared list of the future leaders of the regional committee, so the representatives of the Central Committee of the CPSU bring a list of the leaders of the republic's central committee—presidium members, secretariat, heads of departments, newspaper and periodical editors and chairmen of the party commission and the inspection commission. This list is examined at a meeting of the Secretariat of the Central Committee of the CPSU and is accepted as the recommended list.

The republic central committee, consisting of from 160 to 260 members and from 40 to 50 candidate members, is elected by secret ballot; an inspection commission of from 30 to 50 members is also elected. On each occasion the congress itself decides the numerical size of each of the party organs. At the first organizational plenum of the republic central committee after the representative of the Central Committee of the CPSU has communicated its recommendations, members and candidate members are elected.

The presidium of the republic central committee (from nine to eleven members and from four to five candidate members); members of the secretariat (five members), including the first secretary; the heads of the central committee's departments; the editors of central committee newspapers and periodicals; and the chairman of the party commission are appointed (the presidium appoints the party commission). At the same time a plenum of the inspection commission is held at which its chairman, deputy chairman and secretary are elected.

After the plenum of the republic central committee, the Secretariat of the Central Committee of the CPSU again examines the list of elected leaders of the central committee of the republic and finally confirms it.

All republic central committee secretaries are members of the republic presidium, except in the Ukraine. The chairmen of the republic council of ministers and presidium of the republic's supreme soviet are always members of the republic central committee presidium. The remainder are chosen from leading economic, administrative, trade union and military personnel.

Any party member can be elected to the republic central committee presidium, but to be elected a member of a republic central committee secretariat (and also a member of a regional committee secretariat) it is necessary to have been a party member for at least five years. It is not difficult to see why. The presidium of the central committee is, according to the constitution, the second highest organ after the plenum of the central committee; in reality it is an organ that sets the seal of legality on decisions that have already been taken by the republic secretariat of the central committee, just as at regional level the secretariat itself is an advisory organ to the first secretary of the republic central committee. This in no way diminishes the role the secretariat's members play, because the secretariat is the permanent controlling, guiding and supervisory party government of its republic. The secretariat is, in theory, answerable to the presidium and the plenum of the republic central committee, but in practice it is answerable only to the Secretariat of the Central Committee of the CPSU.

The secretariat of a republic central committee has a staff of professional and part-time party workers. It is constructed on the same principles as the regional committee or the provincial committee. The size of its staff, the number of its departments and the professional qualifications of its workers depend on the size, importance and economic character of the republic. For example, in 1961, at the organizational plenum of the Lithuanian central committee nine departments were set up; at the organizational plenum of the Armenian central committee ten departments were established; while Azerbaidzhan and Uzbekistan each formed twelve departments, including a "central committee sector" and an administrative department for central committee affairs.

The following departments exist in the central committees of all the constituent republics: (1) party organs department; (2) ideological department; (3) industry and transportation department; (4) construction department; (5) agricultural department; (6) science, culture and training institutions department; (7) administrative organs department; (8) trade, finance and planning departments; (9) central committee sector; (10) party commission; (11) administration of affairs of republic central committee; and (12) general department.

These departments directly control three networks: (1) the network of the corresponding departments in regional committees, town committees and district committees; (2) the ministries, state committees, agencies of the constituent republic and branches of central agencies in the given republic; and (3) republic social, sports and voluntary organizations (both directly and through the party groups).

Table 25 shows the institutions and organizations of the central committees of the constituent republics.[18]

TABLE 25

THE FUNCTIONS OF A REPUBLIC CENTRAL COMMITTEE'S DEPARTMENTS

NAME OF DEPARTMENT	WHERE IT ALLOCATES CADRES, CONTROLS AND INSPECTS
Party organs department	(1) regional committees, town committees and district committees

(2) trade unions and *Komsomol*

(3) sanctioning the appointment of leading cadres of central committee departments, regional, town and district committees

Department of propaganda and agitation

(1) corresponding departments of regional committees, town committees and district committees

(2) printed and oral party propaganda in the republic

(3) organs of administrative propaganda (supreme soviet, ministries)

(4) propaganda organs and social organizations (trade unions, *Komsomol,* etc.)

(5) unions of writers, artists, composers

Industry and transportation department

(1) corresponding departments of regional committees, town committees and district committees

(2) Union-republic ministries, ministry of local industry, ministry of communal economy, road transportation ministry

(3) republic rail, water and air transportation administration

Construction department

(1) corresponding departments of regional committees

(2) republic state committee for architectural and constructional affairs, ministry of construction

(3) state and collective farm constructional organizations

Agricultural department

(1) corresponding departments of regional committees and district committees

(2) ministry of agriculture

(3) branches of central agricultural agencies

(4) ministry of production and food manufacture

Department of science, culture and training institutions

(1) ministry of education, ministry of culture, ministry of health, ministry of social security, state scientific and technical committee of the republic

(2) academy of sciences of the republic

Department of administrative organs

(1) corresponding departments of regional committees and town committees

(2) committee of state security, state supervision commission, ministry of foreign affairs, supreme court procuracy, ministry of justice'

(3) apparatus of supreme soviet and republic council of ministers and MOOP

Department of trade, finance and planning organs	(1) corresponding departments of regional committees, town committees and district committees
	(2) state planning commission, ministry of trade, ministries of finance, of republic central statistical administration
	(3) republic council of cooperative system
Central committee sector department	(1) special sectors of (regional committees) town committees and district committees
	(2) secret information service of the republic central committee
	(3) communications with the special sector of the Central Committee of the CPSU
Department of central committee administration	administration of the budget of party economic enterprises and the technical apparatus of the republic central committee
Party commission department	(1) the party commissions of regional committees
	(2) the decisions of regional committees, town committees and district committees on personal matters (expulsions from the party, etc.)
General department	general office of the central committee

As in the regional committees, each central committee department is divided into subdepartments—into various sectors, depending on which branches of the state and party administration it embraces. The number of sectors in a department exactly corresponds to the number of branches concerned with its work. All the republic central committees have the same apparatus structure, but the number of staff workers in each depends on the scope of its work. The structure, the staff and the budget are determined by the Central Committee of the CPSU.

The constituent republics are ostensibly sovereign states within the Soviet "federation," but their Communist parties are not vouchsafed even a semblance of autonomy. The old Leninist principle of absolutist centralism in the organizational structure of the party is rigidly upheld. As early as 1919 the Eighth Congress reiterated this principle:

> The Eighth Congress of the Russian Communist party decrees: the existence of a *single* centralized Communist party with a single Central Committee leading the entire work of the party is essential. . . . All the decisions of the Russian Communist party and its leading institutions are unequivocally binding on all sections of the party, irrespective of their national composition. The central committees of the Ukrainian, Latvian and Lithuanian Communists enjoy the rights of regional committees of the party and are completely subordinate to the Central Committee of the Russian Communist party.[19]

The republics have developed and continue to function on this principle. In Stalin's day complete centralization was carried to the point of absurdity, as we shall see.

The rejection of the Stalinist cult had its effect even on the party apparatus. As we have seen, the partial decentralization of the administrative organs after Stalin's death, which in party parlance was termed "an expansion of the rights of the constituent republics," was in reality a widening of the rights and functions of the republic central committees. This was effected by the following decrees of the CPSU:

1. The decree of the Central Committee "On the Method of Reviewing Certain Organizational and Party Questions" (August, 1955). This gave regional committees, provincial committees and republic central committees the right (a) to transfer similar jobs in the party organs from one organization to another within the limit of the permitted establishments and (b) to determine the expenditure on each item of the party budget, except for the wages fund, within the limits of that budget. It also empowered district committees and town committees to issue new party cards to Communists who have forfeited them (formerly only regional committees and republic central committees had this right).[20]

2. The decree of May 21, 1957, "On Released Secretaries of Primary Party Organizations." This permitted regional committees, provincial committees and central committees (a) to establish posts in primary party organizations for secretaries who have been released from other work within the limits of the approved party budget and establishment, provided that the Central Committee of the CPSU is informed of this, and (b) to make up from party funds the salary of a secretary of a primary party organization who has not been released from production work.[21] Both these decisions eloquently illustrate what elementary rights were withheld previously from the republic central committees in the conduct of their internal affairs.

3. The decree of August 2, 1957, "On Conferring on Central Committees of Communist Parties of Constituent Republics the Right to Decide Certain Party Organization, Budget and Financial Questions." This decree proved even more important for the expansion of republic central committees' rights; it gave the central committees the following rights:

A. (1) To confirm the establishment of town committees, district committees and other party institutions within their jurisdiction; (2) to disband old and to set up new town committees and district committees; (3) to fix town committees' and district committees' salary scales, within the limits of the wages fund; (4) to alter the establishments of regional committees and republic central committees, provided they do not affect the party structure and the establishment of party workers in the republic.

B. (1) To form new and to disband existing districts and also to set up district centers; (2) to transform workers' settlements into towns; (3) to place towns under the authority of a district, region or republic (these decisions must always be communicated to the Central Committee of the CPSU and to the Presidium of the Supreme Soviet of the U.S.S.R.).

C. (1) To commence or to stop publication of district and town newspapers and also departmental newspapers and journals; (2) to approve the structure and establishments of republic and regional newspapers and journals within the usual establishment and salary scale limits; (3) to confirm the industrial and financial plan of republic central committee publishing houses; (4) to determine the amount of radio broadcasting.

D. (1) To set up or to disband offices of political enlightenment and evening universities of Marxism-Leninism; (2) to run refresher courses for party workers and propagandists.

E. (1) To confirm schemes and approve estimates for the construction of buildings for party organs and for institutions under their jurisdiction, subject to regulations laid down by the Central Committee of the CPSU; (2) to approve plans and estimates for residential accommodation (for party workers).[22]

4. The decree of September 30, 1958, "On the Further Extension of the Rights of Central Committees of Communist Parties of Constituent Republics, Provincial Committees, Regional Committees, Town Committees, District Committees and Primary Party Organizations in Deciding Party Organization and Finance and Budgetary Questions." The most significant points of this decree were: (a) With the concurrence of party organs departments and the administration of the Central Committee of the CPSU, the central committees of constituent republics have the right to confirm and to alter the structure of individual town committees and district committees within the limits of existing establishments and salary scales. (b) The republic central committees are permitted to grant party committees in enterprises and institutions having a membership of more than one thousand the rights of a district committee in questions affecting the personal affairs of Communists, to conduct the registration of members and candidate members and to accept them into the CPSU. (c) Instead of the monthly account of members' subscriptions, the republic central committees, provincial committees and regional committees must account to the Central Committee of the CPSU every three months. (d) The republic central committees, provincial committees and the regional committees are permitted to decide whether it is necessary to obtain the minutes of meetings of bureaus, of plenary sessions of town committees and district committees and of meetings of the party *aktiv* (formerly this was an essential part of the supervision of local party organs). (e) Republic central committees have the right to translate into their national language the texts of secret decrees and letters of the Central Committee of the CPSU sent to town committees, district committees and to primary party organizations, "having ensured the strict observance of the approved

method of storing and returning these documents." (*f*) Regional committees, provincial committees and republic central committees are permitted to establish posts in party committees for supernumerary inspectors.[23]

We have seen with what great care the apparatus of the regional committee is selected and what exacting demands are made of its officials. Even greater care is exercised in recruiting personnel for the apparatus of a republic central committee and in creating for its departments highly qualified cadres of specialists in organizational and propaganda work and in industrial and agricultural work.

The personnel of a republic central committee apparatus are selected and appointed by the relevant departments of the Central Committee of the CPSU. Except in the Ukraine and Armenia, local national cadres are invariably employed, together with cadres from Moscow. In all the other constituent republics the first secretaries of the central committees are nationals, while the second secretaries are Russians. The chairmen of governments are nationals, while their first deputies are Russians. The chairmen of supreme soviets are generally nationals, but their first deputies are Russians. Herein is the complete triumph of Soviet "national autonomy"—national in form, but centralist in essence. The second secretaries are the real masters, appointed by Moscow as its inspectors, its eyes watching the local nationals in order to prevent them from manifesting any symptoms of "bourgeois nationalism." The second secretaries and the first deputy chairmen are directly answerable, not to the central committee of the republic to which they have been assigned, but to the Secretariat of the Central Committee of the CPSU, for the precise and unswerving pursuance of the party line in the republic. To enable them to keep a check on the entire machinery of the party and the state, party and soviet organizations conduct their business in two languages—Russian and the local language. All meetings of the secretariat and of the presidium of central committees of republics are conducted entirely in Russian. A local Communist who does not know Russian cannot work in the party apparatus. The relative importance of the first and second secretaries in the presidium and secretariat of the republic central committee is similarly reversed. The first secretary presides over the presidium of the republic central committee, while the second secretary presides over the secretariat. Since the role of the secretariat—as the real conducting and leading organ—is the same throughout the party system, the second secretary predetermines at a meeting of the secretariat all the main questions that are formally within the competence of the presidium of the republic central committee. The Central Committee of the CPSU always makes sure that second secretaries and first deputy chairmen from Moscow do not enter the intimate circle of local national leaders; nor does it let them stay in one republic for very long. The centralized distribution of party cadres and their systematic transfer from place to place prevents the development of separatist or nationalist tendencies and renders most unlikely the default of the party satraps as a result of their coming to terms with local officials. These principles are not a product of the Stalinist cult; they are Leninist principles that were accepted as long ago as the Eighth Congress in 1919. A resolution of that Congress stated on this score:

> The whole business of distributing party cadres is in the hands of the Central Committee. Its decisions are binding on everyone. . . . The Central Committee of the party is entrusted with the task of conducting the most decisive struggle against the *exercise of local interests* and *separatism* in these questions. The Central Committee must *systematically move* party workers from one branch to another, from one district to another, with a view to achieving the most profitable use of them.[24]

Similar advice was proffered by Machiavelli to his Prince!

Surveillance and control of the central committees of constituent republics by the Central Committee of the CPSU is effected not only through a centralized cadre policy, not only through the offices of "second secretaries" and "first deputies," but also through its own apparatus. The Central Committee of the CPSU reinforces the supervision of local nationals by the second secretaries by keeping a continual close watch over these same second secretaries. This surveillance and direct control of the republic central committees is achieved by (1) *leadership:* (*a*) the secretaries of the Central Committee of the CPSU; (*b*) branch departments of the Central Committee of the CPSU over corresponding departments of republic central committees; and (2) *inspection:* (*a*) Ideological Commission of the Central Committee of the CPSU; (*b*) Commission for Organization and Party Questions of the Central Committee of the CPSU; and (*c*) Party Commission of the Central Committee. In addition, each secretary of a republic central committee is personally responsible to the first secretary of the CPSU for the state of work of his department. Formerly a "National Commission of the Central Committee" existed in the Central Committee of the CPSU. This was a consultative organ of the Central Committee's Orgburo for the affairs of the national republics—the Caucasus, Turkestan and the autonomous regions and republics of the Russian Federation. The apparatus of the Central Committee of the CPSU itself has been reorganized on national and territorial principles. There now exist two parallel apparatus of the Central Committee of the CPSU: (1) the Central Committee apparatus for the constituent republics and (2) the Central Committee of the CPSU apparatus for the Russian republics—the Bureau of the Central Committee of the CPSU for the R.S.F.S.R.

In all departments of the Central Committee there are specialist-inspectors for the constituent republics, among whom are also representatives of the nationalities of the constituent republics, working mainly as instructors or experts on national questions.

Although the central committees of constituent republics theoretically enjoy equal rights, as we have seen, in practice they are far from equal. It would be ridiculous to say that the R.S.F.S.R. and Kirghizia, or the Ukraine and Estonia, have equal rights. The rights of the party appa-- ratus of a constituent republic stem not only from the formal, "con- stitutional" rights of that republic, but also from the *actual inequality* of the republics. Large republics have *relatively* considerable party aparatus rights; small republics have few rights. But in both large and small republics the main principle of bolshevist government remains inviolate: the party's statutes allow the establishment of only one center; to whom and to what extent its functions are delegated, that same center decides.

The decision of the November, 1962, Plenum of the Central Com- mittee of the CPSU effected changes in the structure of the apparatus of the central committees of constituent republics. Each republic cen- tral committee had the following leading organs: (1) bureau for indus- trial leadership, (2) bureau for agricultural leadership, (3) secretariat of the central committee and (4) a presidium of the central committee of the republic (formerly the bureau of the central committee) "for deciding questions affecting the whole republic and for coordinating the activities of branch bureaus."[25] It was stated at the Plenum that the branch bureaus of the central committee enjoy a high decree of auton- omy in their work. Taking the Ukraine as an example, the departments of the central committee were distributed among the bureaus as follows: to the industrial bureau of the central committee were subordinate: (1) the department of heavy industry, (2) the department of machine construction, (3) the department of transportation and communications, (4) the department for light industry and the food industry and (5) the department for construction and urban economy. The following departments were subordinate both to the industrial and to the agri- cultural bureaus: (1) the party organs department, (2) the ideological department and (3) the department of trade and finance organs. The following departments were directly subordinate to the secretariat of the central committee: (1) the department of science and art, (2) the de- partment of administrative organs, (3) the party commission and (4) the administration department.[26] Also directly subordinate to the secre- tariat were, of course, such departments and organs of the central com- mittee as the special sector of the central committee, the committee for party and state inspection and the council of ministers of the constituent republic. In the central committee of the Communist party in the Latvian S.S.R. the bureaus and the presidium had the following com- position:

   1. *The personnel of the industrial bureau of the central committee.*— (*a*) bureau chairman (secretary of the central committee); (*b*) his deputy; (*c*) first secretary of Riga town committee; (*d*) first secretary of Liepay town committee; (*e*) head of industrial and transportation department of the central committee; (*f*) chairman of the republic's *sovnarkhoz;* (*g*) head of construction department of the central com-

mittee; (*h*) deputy chairman of the republic's council of ministers; and (*i*) chairman of fishing industry management board.

2. *The personnel of the agricultural bureau of the central committee.* —(*a*) chairman of the bureau (secretary of the central committee); (*b*) deputy chairman; (*c*) head of agricultural department of the central committee; (*d*) chairman of "agricultural technology" section; (*e*) deputy chairman of council of ministers—minister for production and manufacture of agricultural products; and (*f*) deputy chairman of the republic's *sovnarkhoz*.

3. *The personnel of the presidium of the central committee.*—(*a*) first secretary of the central committee; (*b*) second secretary of the central committee; (*c*) a secretary of the central committee (chairman of the committee for party and state inspection); (*d*) a secretary of the central committee (chairman of the agricultural bureau); (*e*) chairman of the presidium of the supreme soviet; (*f*) chairman of the council of ministers; (*g*) commander-in-chief of the Baltic military district; and (*h*) head of department of party organs.

4. *Candidate members of the presidium.*—(*a*) chairman of the council of trade unions and (*b*) secretary of the central committee of republic *Komsomol.*[27]

From an analysis of the personnel of the leading organs of republic central committees it is obvious that, as before, the secretariat of the central committee remained the real leader of the central committee— the bureaus of the central committee were headed by the central committee secretaries themselves and the presidium of the central committee consisted largely of the same people. There had been, nevertheless, an important innovation: those organs of central committees that dealt with economic matters contained leading economic specialists in addition to party apparatus workers. The party bureaucracy had been obliged to share its power with the economic bureaucracy, and this led to even greater technocratization of the party apparatus and to the broadening of the social basis of the dictatorship.

In the Turkestan and Caucasian republics, the Central Committee of the CPSU has decided to return to the administrative pattern of the first years of Soviet power, when in Turkestan and the Caucasus the Bolsheviks placed associate central committees directly appointed by Moscow at the head of the national party organizations. In Turkestan they were called first the Muslim Bureau of the Central Committee of the Russian Communist party (Bolshevik), then the Turkestan and finally the Central Asian Bureau of the Central Committee of the Russian Communist party (Bolshevik). In the Caucasus they were called the Caucasian Bureau of the Central Committee of the Russian Communist party (Bolshevik). Their task was to ensure the forcible execution of sovietization and bolshevization. Appointed from Moscow and independent of local organizations, these organs of the Central Committee of the party resolved all local problems in the way Moscow required. As Turkestan and the Caucasus developed their own communist cadres, the party Central Committee disbanded these associate committees. When the present Constitution of the U.S.S.R. came into force, in 1936, constituent republics were created in Turkestan and in the Caucasus, and the Central Asian Bureau and the Trans-Caucasian provincial committee were abolished. At the head of each national Communist party was placed a "national" central committee, which was in direct contact with, and directly subordinate to, the party Central Committee in Moscow.

This continued to be so until November, 1962. The November Plenum then decided that the time had come when it was necessary to return to the principle of associate administration in the national republics. A Central Asian Bureau of the Central Committee of the CPSU was established, to which the central committees of the Communist parties of the Uzbek S.S.R., the Turkmenian S.S.R., the Tadzhik S.S.R. and the Kirghiz S.S.R. are directly subordinate. The chairman of the Central Asian Bureau is appointed by the Presidium (the Secretariat) of the Central Committee of the CPSU; he does not belong to the local nationality.

The members of the bureau are the first secretaries of the central committees of these republics and the four leaders of the reestablished economic filial organizations—the chairman of the Central Asian *sovnarkhoz,* the head of the principal administration for irrigation and state farms, the head of the Central Asian administration for cotton production and the manager of the Central Asian construction office. The members of the bureau are appointed by the same Presidium (Secretariat) of the Central Committee of the CPSU. For Trans-Caucasia the Trans-Caucasian Bureau of the Central Committee of the CPSU has been established, on the same principles. The Central Committee of the CPSU has thereby retreated from its 1957 reforms for "expanding the rights of the constituent republics." Although there has been no official communique about the liquidation of these bureaus for Central Asia and the Caucasus, it appears that after Khrushchev's overthrow they were in fact eliminated.

Khrushchev proclaimed the ascendancy of economics over politics, but in fact his main aim was the same as Stalin's was: to have absolute totalitarian surveillance and control over the people. In this, Khrushchev went even further than Stalin: *he supplemented surveillance at home with surveillance at work.* Khrushchev described the ultimate goal of his organizational policy in the following frank words:

> We have ten million party members, twenty million *Komsomol* members, sixty-six million trade unionists. If we set all these forces in motion and used them for *inspection* purposes, then not a single mosquito would fly past unnoticed.[28]

In Chapter Eleven we shall examine the development and functioning of the Central Committee of the CPSU, which Stalin termed the "supreme party Areopagus."

CHAPTER XI

The Central Committee of the CPSU

THE CENTRAL COMMITTEE of the CPSU is at the summit of the party apparatus pyramid. We shall now examine the organization and structure of the highest organs of the party, compare their theoretical with their actual position and, since their present correlationship is the result of a long historical process, analyze their historical development.

The highest organs of the party are, in descending order of importance: (1) the Congress of the CPSU, (2) the Plenum of the Central Committee, (3) the Presidium of the Central Committee and (4) the Secretariat of the Central Committee.

The Congress of the CPSU

The statutes of 1961 state:

> The party Congress is the supreme organ of the Communist Party of the Soviet Union. Congresses are convened at least once every four years. The convening of a congress and the agenda are announced not less than six weeks in advance. Extraordinary congresses are convened by the Central Committee of the party on the initiative or the demand of not less than one-third of the party's members, as represented at the preceding congress. The Congress is valid if not less than one-half of the party membership is represented at it. The representation is determined by the Central Committee.[1]

The Congress, according to the statutes, is authorized to: (1) hear and confirm the reports of the Central Committee, of the Central Inspection Committee and of other central organizations; (2) review, modify and approve the program and the statutes of the party; (3) determine the party line on questions of domestic and foreign policy and examine and decide the most important questions of communist construction; (4) elect the Central Committee and the Central Inspection Committee.[2] The Stalinist party statutes contained the same clauses.

If the Congress really had these rights, it would indeed be the highest organ of the party. While during Lenin's lifetime and for a few years after his death the congresses really played the role of the highest legislative organ of the party, they have subsequently played a purely propagandist role. The highest party apparatus does, however, time its biggest and most sensational decisions to coincide with a congress in order to receive the moral support of the entire party.

The usurpation of the supreme power of the congresses has proceeded gradually; it progressed simultaneously with the prolonged process of establishing the dictatorship, first of the party bureaucracy and then of Stalin alone, in the years of struggle among the Stalinist party apparatus men on the one hand and the "Left," "new" and "Right" oppositions on the other. According to the statutes congresses must be held annually, but the Fourteenth Congress, in 1925, was the last annual one. Subsequently, as the party apparatus became more important, the congresses were held less often. The Congress in those days heard the reports of the Central Committee apparatus and criticized, directed and gave new directives. The most important point was that each year elections to the highest organs took place in an atmosphere of more or less genuine democracy within the party. Even the general secretary had to be annually reelected at a plenum of the Central Committee that had itself been newly elected at the Congress. Old revolutionaries, people of principle and conviction, participated in each congress and were elected to the Central Committee; thus each time both the general secretary and the party bureaucracy itself took the risk of losing power.

Having triumphed over the opposition, Stalin began to circumvent the party's statutes. He failed to summon the Congress at the proper intervals; the next Congress—the Fifteenth Congress—was convened only after two years—in 1927. At this congress the united Trotsky-Zinoviev opposition bloc was finally liquidated, its leaders expelled from the party and the statutes amended so that the Congress was to be held once every two years.[3] Even this must have seemed too frequent to the party apparatus, for the next congress was held three years later, in 1930, despite the explicit requirement of the statutes that a congress be "summoned not less than once every two years."[4] The Seventeenth Congress was held in 1934, and Stalin legitimized this frequency when he recorded: "Regular congresses must be held not less than once every three years."[5]

The apparatus of the Central Committee lost all interest in the supreme organ. During the Great Purge (1936–39) the Central Committee apparatus annihilated about one-half of the party membership without summoning a congress. This made it plain to the whole country that party congresses, as the supreme organ, had become a fiction. It was not surprising that the Eighteenth Congress was convened not after three years but after five, and the Nineteenth Congress was not held until fourteen years later. Thus the party Congress ceased to be the supreme political organ. The failure to hold congresses regularly was not the only, perhaps not even the principal, violation of democracy within the party. The most important violation was that under Stalin—and even now—the party congresses are *organized* rather than convened. The apparatus of the Central Committee of the CPSU prepares, organ-

izes and conducts them as it sees fit. No improvisation, no initiative
from below and no free elections to the Congress are permitted. The
apparatus of the Central Committee decides exactly when a congress
shall be summoned, it draws up the agenda and it decides the exact
composition of the delegate body. The delegates are elected according to a procedure defined by the Central Committee at regional and
provincial conferences and at congresses of the Communist parties of
constituent republics. But before delegates are entered as candidates,
the Central Committee apparatus and the central organs of the political
police subject them to the most stringent screening, not simply to
establish their reliability as Communists (which would be done by local
party organs), but also to ascertain their devotion and reliability vis-à-
vis the Central Committee and its leaders. Only persons who have
passed these tests arrive at the Kremlin as Congress delegates.

The Plenum of the Central Committee

The Plenum of the Central Committee is a periodically summoned
meeting of all members and candidate members of the Central Committee (members have a casting vote, and candidate members have a
deliberative vote). Like the party Congress, the Plenum has had varied
importance at different periods in the party's history. There was a time
when it was the "collective leadership," and there was a time when it
was of no importance at all. Experts are divided as to the role it plays
at the present time. Some think it to be the highest organ of the party
after the Congress; others consider it to be merely an imposing façade
concealing the real location of power in the party—the apparatus of the
Central Committee.

The party statutes passed by the Sixth Congress, in July–August,
1917, said of the Central Committee:

> (13) The Central Committee is elected at the annual Congress.
> A small team of Central Committee personnel undertakes the day-
> to-day business of the Central Committee. Plenary meetings of the
> Central Committee are held not less than once every two months.
> The Central Committee represents the party in relations with other
> parties and institutions, organizes various party institutions and
> conducts its activities.[6]

The statutes passed at the Eighth Congress, in December, 1919,
state:

> The Central Committee is elected, consisting of nineteen mem-
> bers (and twelve candidate members) .... The Central Committee
> represents the party in relations with other parties and institutions,
> organizes various party institutions, conducts its activities, appoints
> the editors of central press organs, the workers under its control,
> organizes and conducts enterprises that are of importance to the
> entire party, deploys the forces and resources of the party .... The

Central Committee directs the work of the central soviet and social organizations via the party fractions. The Central Committee holds not less than one plenary session every two months on previously appointed days.[7]

The statutes passed at the Twelfth Congress, in August, 1922, repeated the above, except that they ordered that the number of members of the Central Committee must be decided each time by the Congress itself.[8]

In the statutes passed at the Fourteenth Congress, in 1925, the functions of the Central Committee were more precisely defined:

> The number of persons to be elected to the Central Committee is to be determined by the Congress . . . . Between congresses the Central Committee conducts all party work . . . . The Central Committee directs the work of the central soviet and social organizations through the party fractions . . . . The Central Committee regularly informs the party organizations about its work.[9]

The same formula was included in the 1934 statutes and confirmed by the Seventeenth Congress, with the following addendum:

> In order to strengthen the bolshevist leadership and its political work, the Central Committee has the right to set up political departments and to apportion Central Committee party organizers in the backward sectors of socialist construction.[10]

The plenary sessions of the Central Committe subsequently took place, not once every two months, but once every four months.[11]

In the 1939 and the 1952 party statutes the rights of the Central Committee were the same as in the 1925 statutes, but the period between plenary sessions of the Central Committee was lengthened. The Plenum is now held twice a year.

The latest statutes (Twenty-second Congress, 1961) state of the Central Committee:

> (35) In the intervals between congresses the Central Committee of the CPSU directs all the activities of the party, of local party organs, selects and deploys leading cadres, directs the work of central state and social organizations of the workers via the party groups in them, creates various organs, institutions and enterprises of the party and directs their activities, appoints the editors of central newspapers and periodicals, disburses the resources of the party budget and supervises its execution. The Central Committee represents the CPSU in relations with other parties.
> (36) The Central Committee of the CPSU regularly informs party organizations about its work . . . holds not less than one plenary session every six months.[12]

Speaking of the Central Committee, the authors of the Stalinist and especially of the post-Stalin statutes deliberately confuse these two completely different functions—the Central Committee as a between-Congress law-promulgating college elected by a congress (the Plenum of the Central Committee) and the Central Committee as the secretariat or even as the executive apparatus of Central Committee officials. This makes it automatically possible to transfer to the executive-technical apparatus the rights and functions that the statutes assign only to the Plenum of the Central Committee. In the same way as it has dealt with the party Congress, the Central Committee apparatus has begun to ignore the plenary sessions of the Central Committee.

Thus, despite the statutes' requirement that a plenum of the Central Committee be held not less than once every six months, after the Eighteenth Congress the first Plenum was held two years later (February, 1941), the second two years after that (January, 1944), the third three years later (February, 1947) and the fifth five years later (August, 1952).[13]

Khrushchev told how at the beginning of the war between Germany and the Soviet Union, a plenum of the Central Committee was held in Moscow to discuss the situation and make decisions, but its members had to disperse because Stalin did not want it to meet. Since Stalin's death plenary sessions of the Central Committee have been held at the proper intervals. In Stalin's day these sessions were held in secret and only a brief official communique and the resolutions passed were published after they adjourned. Nowadays both public and secret plenary sessions are held. Under Stalin plenary sessions were attended only by members and candidate members of the Central Committee plus a very narrow circle of high-ranking officials holding "invitation cards." Nowadays plenary sessions are held with hundreds of non-members of the Plenum present, and even non-members of the party make speeches. Stalin never directed a plenary session in person, preferring to transfer this role to his assistants, and only very occasionally would he reply personally or interrupt a speaker. But Khrushchev introduced the new "democratic" style plenum, which he conducted personally; he proffered sharp rejoinders and cross-examined high-ranking officials in a style worthy of an attorney.

The plenary sessions of the Central Committee are convened by decree and the agenda is drawn up by the Presidium of the Central Committee. All questions to be discussed and confirmed by it are discussed and decided in advance by the Presidium. These questions are prepared and predetermined by the Secretariat of the Central Committee of the CPSU. However, the apparatus attaches great importance to the Central Committee Plenum as a propaganda device. The Central Committee prefers that the most important decisions of both domestic and foreign policy should appear to be made by the Plenum. Most important of all, the Presidium and the Secretariat of the Central Committee formerly gave accounts of their work at the sessions, but now the Plenum is called to account by the Presidium and the Secretariat.

The Presidium of the Central Committee

The statutes say of the Presidium:

> The Central Committee of the CPSU elects a presidium to conduct the work of the Central Committee between plenary sessions.[14]

In other words, the Presidium is the highest organ of the party after the Congress and the Plenum of the Central Committee.

The Presidium (Politburo) played the role of a second close-knit "collective leadership" in Lenin's time, for a short time after his death and also in the years immediately following Stalin's death; but during the years of Stalin's dictatorship it played no part at all.

Prior to 1952 the Plenum of the Central Committee had elected three executive organs: the Politburo (1917), the Orgburo (1919) and the Secretariat (1919). The Politburo and the Orgburo were colleges whose members (except for one or two Central Committee secretaries) worked outside the Central Committee apparatus in governmental or public positions. They only met at sessions, usually once or twice a week. The third organ, the Secretariat of the Central Committee, was and is the permanent business organ of the Central Committee. In rights and functions it is the least important of the three. The 1919 statutes give the following definition of their functions:

> (25) The Central Committee forms the Politburo for political work, the Orgburo (from five to seven persons) for general supervision of organizational work, and for day-to-day work of an organizational and executive character it forms the Secretariat, consisting of three members of the Central Committee working permanently in the Central Committee.[15]

In 1919 these organs included the following persons: *Politburo*: Lenin, Trotsky, Stalin, Kamenev, Krestinsky; candidate members: Bukharin, Zinoviev, Kalinin; *Orgburo*: Krestinsky, Stalin, Byeloborodov, Serebryakov, Stasova; *Secretariat*: Krestinsky, Serebryakov, Stasova.[16]

Although the Politburo continued to exist, Stalin was able to bypass it and, by utilizing various combinations of the apparatus, to make it ineffective. His favorite method of doing this was to set up various commissions of the Politburo having the rights of the Politburo itself but not consisting of all its members.

At the Twentieth Congress Khrushchev declared:

> The importance of the Politburo of the Central Committee was diminished and its work disorganized by the setting up of various commissions within it—the so-called groups of five, of six, of seven and of nine. For example, the Politburo resolution of October 3, 1946: "Stalin's proposal: (1) Politburo Commission for

foreign affairs (the 'six') must in the future, in addition to foreign affairs, also deal with questions of internal construction and domestic policy. (2) The 'six' co-opts Comrade Voznesensky and will in the future be called the 'seven.' "[17]

If the commission acts as a directive organ in dealing with questions of both domestic and foreign policy, then the Politburo becomes superfluous. Khrushchev went on:

> What card-trick terminology! It is clear that the setting up within the Politburo of such commissions . . . violated the principle of collective leadership. The result was that certain members of the Politburo were deprived of the opportunity to examine very important matters of state.[18]

At the organizational plenum of the Central Committee after the Nineteenth Congress, in 1952, the Politburo was replaced by the Presidium. In this way the old members of the Politburo thought to get rid of the Stalinist "commissions," which had so deftly usurped their power. But Stalin outmaneuvered them. He agreed to the setting up of the Presidium of the Central Committee, but proposed that it be a large "democratic" presidium including new blood instead of the narrow Politburo of older people. Khrushchev interpreted Stalin's intention thus:

> Stalin evidently intended to do away with all the old members of the Politburo. He often said that members of the Politburo must be replaced by new people. His proposal after the Nineteenth Congress to set up a twenty-five-man presidium was aimed at getting rid of all the old members and introducing into it less experienced people who owed everything to Stalin.[19]

The proposal was, of course, accepted by the Central Committee Plenum, which had been enlarged to 125 members and 111 candidate members. Stalin achieved more than this because, at his suggestion, a "Bureau of the Presidium" was set up, which was to be a "presidium within the Presidium." It was probably created in order to bypass certain of the old members of the Politburo, of whom Khrushchev spoke. The Bureau of the Presidium was disbanded two days after Stalin's death, on the grounds that it was unconstitutional.[20] The composition of the Bureau of the Presidium is as yet uncertain. One English writer deduces from indirect evidence that it consisted largely of former members of the old Politburo.[21]

The Presidium of the Central Committee of the CPSU, as elected after the Twenty-second Congress, consists of twelve members and five candidate members. Eight of the twelve members and three of the five candidate members are professional workers in the party apparatus; the rest are workers in the governmental apparatus, but they no longer include the minister for war or the minister of foreign affairs. The Presidium of the Central Committee does not have an official chairman. Its meetings are presided over either by the first secretary or by the other members in turn. Its minutes are signed by the first secretary and, according to Khrushchev, meetings take place weekly. In addition to the members and candidate members, Central Committee secretaries and persons specially invited to discuss particular questions may attend these meetings. In Lenin's time members of the Central Committee had the right to attend meetings of the Politburo and the Orgburo and to exercise a deliberative vote. These rights have been withdrawn, and the minutes of Central Committee Presidium meetings are no longer distributed to local party organs.

The Secretariat of the Central Committee

According to the statutes, the Secretariat of the Central Committee is the fourth highest party organ, ranking after the Congress, the Plenum and the Presidium. They state that the Central Committee of the CPSU chooses a secretariat "for the direction of day-to-day work, mainly for choosing cadres and for organizing the control of work done." Here the party legislators have obviously minimized the actual role and deliberately concealed the real position of the Secretariat in the party power hierarchy. The Congress, Plenum and Presidium exercise their prerogatives insofar as the Secretariat permits. Of these three organs only the Secretariat exercises its constitutional rights. Congresses, plenary sessions and the Presidium of the Central Committee itself are party platforms of various dimensions; the Secretariat is the sovereign power in the party. The essential difference between party apparatus right and party constitutional right is illustrated by the fact that while the powers of the Congress, of the Plenum and of the Presidium are based on the statutes, the power of the Secretariat is based on the party and the state apparatus. This also explains the fact that the head of the Secretariat always wins in any great crisis among the party leadership: Stalin triumphed after Lenin's death, Malenkov was victorious after Stalin's death (a short-lived success because of his personal character) and Khrushchev was successful when, on June 18, 1957, after the Presidium of the Central Committee had ordered his removal, he made use of the Secretariat to destroy and disperse the Presidium, declaring it to be an "anti-party group." Moreover, the Secretariat compelled the Plenum of the Central Committee to sanction this decision. Thus the Secretariat, not the Plenum or the Presidium, has gradually become the highest organ of the party. Although the various statutes name the Central Committee as the highest party organ between congresses, in reality the Secretariat of the Central Committee occupies this position.

The Secretariat of the Central Committee is only the head, the leader;

the apparatus of the Central Committee is the body of every party building and is the machinery of power. It consists of departments and subdepartments, which together cover all spheres of state, economic, cultural and public life of the country. Until the Seventeenth Congress (1934) only functional departments existed in the Central Committee. The Seventeenth Congress abandoned this system and introduced throughout the party machine, including the Central Committee, the system of consolidated production departments. A resolution of the Congress explained:

> In each production department all the work for the given branch of industry is to be concentrated: party organization bureau, the distributing and training of cadres, mass agitation work, production propaganda, control of the execution of party decisions by Soviet economic organs and party organizations.[22]

The following departments of the Central Committee were established: (1) Agricultural Department; (2) Industrial Department; (3) Transportation Department; (4) Planning, Finance and Trade Department; (5) Political and Administrative Department; (6) Department of Leading Party Organs; (7) Department of Culture and Propaganda; and (8) the Institute of Marx-Engels-Lenin, and two sectors: the administration sector and the special sector.[23]

Five years later, at the Eighteenth Congress (1939), the system of functional departments was revived in the party apparatus, including the Central Committee, leaving only the agricultural and schools departments. The main reason for this was to concentrate all the cadres of party and state in one department. For this purpose the Chief Administration for Cadres was established; similar cadre departments were also set up at local levels. One of the Central Committee secretaries was placed at the head of cadre administration, and at local level one of the local committee secretaries was appointed. The Congress' resolution stated:

> Experience has shown that the splitting up of the selection of cadres according to the various production departments of the party apparatus has delayed the solution of the problem of selecting and allocating cadres. This task demands that all cadre work be directed by a single center concentrated in a single apparatus.[24]

After the war the mixed functional branch system was established, with a certain degree of specialization of the branch departments. The 1952 statutes and the latest statutes (those of 1961) do not indicate the number or the names of the Central Committee departments or local committees; some have even been made secret departments. But data published by the Soviet press have made it possible to establish that the departments shown in Table 26 exist in the present-day Central Committee.[25]

TABLE 26

DISTRIBUTION OF ORGANS OF STATE ADMINISTRATION AND PUBLIC ORGANIZATIONS
AMONG THE DEPARTMENTS OF THE CENTRAL COMMITTEE OF THE CPSU

DEPARTMENT OF THE CENTRAL COMMITTEE OF THE CPSU	FUNCTIONS	SUBORDINATE STATE OR PUBLIC ORGANS
Party Organs Department	(a) selection of workers for apparatus of the Central Committee of the CPSU (b) registration, selection and allocation of workers in regional committees, provincial committees and central committees of constituent republics (c) leadership and allocation of trade union and *Komsomol* cadres (d) sanctioning appointments to military, secret police and diplomatic cadres (e) sanctioning appointments of leading workers in the U.S.S.R., constituent and autonomous republics	(a) regional committees, provincial committees and central committees of constituent republics (b) All-Union Central Council of Trade Unions, central committees of trade unions (c) Central Committee of All-Union Leninist Young Communist League (d) Advanced Party School of the Central Committee of the CPSU (e) *Party Life*
Department of Propaganda and Agitation	(a) registration, training and allocation of professional propaganda cadres (b) ensuring propagation of Marxism-Leninism in all spheres of party, state and public life (c) leadership of propaganda and agitation apparatus in party, state and public organizations	(a) departments of propaganda and agitation in regional committees, provincial committees and central committees of constituent republics (b) mass agitation and propaganda departments in trade unions and *Komsomol* (c) mass propaganda departments of ministries, committees and departments (d) central newspapers (*Pravda, Izvestia, Trud, Komsomol Pravda,* etc.) periodicals (*Communist, Questions of Philosophy, Questions of History,* etc.) (e) State Committee for

		Press, Radio and Television Broadcasting (f) State Committee for Cultural Links with Foreign Countries (g) unions of writers, artists and musicians (h) the Central Committee of the CPSU's Academy of Social Sciences (i) institutes of social sciences of the Academy of Science of the U.S.S.R. (j) the Central Committee of the CPSU's Institute of Marxism-Leninism and other ideological institutes
Agricultural Department	(a) registration and allocation of agricultural cadres (b) issue of instructions to agricultural departments of regional committees, provincial committees and central committees of constituent republics (c) control and inspection of state agricultural organs	(a) Ministry of Agriculture of the U.S.S.R. (b) republic committees of agriculture (c) the Lenin Academy of Agriculture (d) *Soyuzselkhoztekhnika* (the All-Union Combine) (e) the State Committee for Grain Purchase
Department of Science, Higher Education Institutes and Schools	(a) registration and allocation of scientific and school cadres (b) control and supervision of scientific and scholastic institutes (c) issuing of instructions to similar departments in regional committees, provincial committees and central committees of constituent republics	(a) Academy of Sciences of the U.S.S.R. (b) Ministry of Higher and Secondary Specialist Education (c) State Committee for Professional and Technical Education (d) State Committee for the Coordination of Science and Techniques
Department of Culture	(a) registration and allocation of culture cadres (b) supervision and control of cultural educational institutes of state and public organizations	(a) Ministry of Culture of the U.S.S.R. (b) theaters, cinemas and concert platforms
Department of Heavy Industry	(a) registration and allocation of cadres (b) inspection and control	(a) ministries for heavy industry (b) Ministry for Geology

	of administrative organs of heavy industry	and the Conservation of Mineral Resources (c) Ministry of Energy and Electrification (d) corresponding departments of GOSPLAN
Department of Light Industry	(a) registration and allocation of cadres (b) inspection and control of administrative organs of light industry	(a) departments of light industry of GOSPLAN (b) ministries of light industry and food industry
Department for Machine Construction	(a) registration and allocation of cadres (b) inspection and control of machine tool industry	(a) Ministry for Automation and Machine Construction (b) Ministry for Radio and Electronics (c) Ministry for Electronics Technology (d) corresponding department of GOSPLAN
Department of Defense Industry	(a) registration and allocation of cadres (b) inspection and control of administrative organs of defense industry	(a) Ministry for Defense Technology (b) Ministry for Aviation Technology (c) State Committee for Exploitation of Atomic Energy (d) corresponding departments of GOSPLAN (e) Ministry of Medium Heavy Machine Construction (the production of atomic weapons)
Department of Chemical Industry	(a) registration and allocation of cadres (b) inspection and control of administrative organs of chemical industry	(a) Ministry for Chemistry (b) corresponding departments of GOSPLAN
Department for the Fuel Industry	(a) registration and allocation of cadres (b) inspection and control of administrative organs of fuel industry	(a) Ministry for Fuel Industry (b) corresponding departments of GOSPLAN

Department for Construction	(a) registration and allocation of cadres (b) inspection and control of administrative organs of construction industry	(a) State Committee for Construction (b) Ministry for Construction of Electric Power Stations (c) Ministry for Transportation Construction (d) corresponding departments of GOSPLAN
Transportation Department	(a) registration and allocation of transportation cadres (b) inspection and control of administrative organs of transportation and communications industry	(a) Ministry of Communications (b) Naval Ministry (c) Ministry of Ways of Communication (d) corresponding departments of GOSPLAN
Department of Trade, Finance and Planning Organs	(a) registration and allocation of cadres (b) inspection and control of administrative organs for trade, finance and planning	(a) Ministry for External Trade of the U.S.S.R. (b) State Committee for External Economic Links (c) ministries for inland trade of constituent republics (d) Ministry of Finance of the U.S.S.R. (e) GOSPLAN of the U.S.S.R. (f) Central Statistical Board (g) the State Bank (h) the Bank for Financing Capital Investments (i) committees for wages and labor (j) Consumer Cooperative Organization of the U.S.S.R.
Administration Department	(a) registration and allocation of cadres (b) inspection of administration organs (the administration department of the Central Committee only inspects these organs; the corresponding secretaries of the Central Committee of the CPSU have direct control over them)	(a) Committee for State Security of the U.S.S.R. (b) Supreme Court of the U.S.S.R. (c) Procuracy of the U.S.S.R. (d) Soviet armed forces (e) Committee for the People's Control (f) MOOP
Foreign Department	(a) registration and allocation of international cadres	(a) Ministry of Foreign Affairs

	of the CPSU (b) communications and controlling contacts with foreign Communist parties	(b) foreign Communist parties in non-communist countries (c) worldwide communist trade union movement (d) "fighters for peace" (e) worldwide communist youth movement (the "festivals") (f) periodical *Problems of Peace and Socialism*
Department for Socialist (bloc) Countries	communications and contacts with Communist parties	Communist parties of the "people's democracies" of Europe and Asia
Department of Security	guard and security for members of the Central Committee and the government	(a) security service of the Central Committee (b) defense forces of the Kremlin
Chief Political Administration of Soviet Army and Navy	(a) registration and allocation of political cadres in army and navy (b) party and political leadership of the armed forces	(a) Soviet Army and Navy (b) Political Administration of Forces of the Committee for State Security and MOOP (c) party organization of armed forces
Special Sector	(a) secret registration and secret affairs of leading cadres (b) direction of personal secretariat of first secretary of the Central Committee	system of special sectors of regional committees, provincial committees and central committees of constituent republics
Party Commission of the Central Committee	(a) party court for violation of party statutes and program (b) supreme appeal court for party punishment and expulsion	all party members except members of the Central Committee of the CPSU and members of the Central Inspection Commission
General Department	general office of the Central Committee of the CPSU	correspondence and affairs of the Secretariat of the Central Committee of the CPSU
Administration of the Central Committee of the CPSU	conduct of administrative and economic affairs of the Central Committee of the CPSU	(a) technical apparatus of the Central Committee of the CPSU (b) budget of the Central Committee (c) Central Committee enterprises (publishing, printing secret documents, bulletins, etc.)

To these departments of the Central Committee of the CPSU must be added the departments of the Central Committee of the CPSU for the R.S.F.S.R. They are: (1) Party Organs Department; (2) Department of Propaganda and Agitation; (3) Science, Schools and Culture Department; (4) Agricultural Department; (5) Industry and Transportation Department; (6) Administrative and Trade and Finance Organs Department.

Some ministries that have only a formal relationship with one of the departments of the Central Committee are, in reality, under that department's supervision. Their policy is directed and their topmost cadres appointed by the first secretary of the Central Committee of the CPSU himself. These include the following ministries: the Ministry of Defense, the Ministry of Foreign Affairs and the Committee for State Security. (At various times there have been special secretaries of the Central Committee for supervising the NKVD and the State Security Committee —Yezhov, Kuznetsov, Kirichenko and Shelepin.)

The Party Organs Department is the most important of all the departments of the Central Committee of the CPSU. This department has had several different designations—the organization department, the cadre department, the cadre administration—but its functions have never changed: the selection and allocation of the topmost cadres of party and state. In a conversation with an Italian communist delegation led by the Deputy Secretary General of the Italian Communist party, Longo,[26] the Deputy Head of the Party Organs Department, Yakovlev, characterized the functions of the department as those of the leading department of the Central Committee. The Party Organs Department deals with the registration of leading cadres and appoints all the cadres for leading positions in the party apparatus (regional committees, provincial committees and central committees of constituent republics), in the state apparatus (regional executive committees, provincial executive committees, councils of ministers and supreme soviets of the republics), trade unions (the All-Union Central Council of Trade Unions and central committees of republic trade unions), the *Komsomol* (Central Committee of the All-Union Young Communist League) and other social organizations. The Party Organs Department sees to the appointment and removal of all cadres and even of members of the apparatus of the Central Committee of the CPSU. The cadres chosen and appointed at the wish of other departments of the Central Committee of the CPSU are appointed with the *concurrence and the sanction* of the Party Organs Department. This department has four functional sectors: (1) the sector for organization and constitutional questions, (2) the sector for membership personnel and the single party ticket, (3) the sector for party cadres and (4) the sector for trade unions, *Komsomol* and soviet organs. In addition there are four territorial sectors, probably: (1) the Ukraine sector, (2) the Belorussia and Baltic province sector, (3) the Central Asia and Kazakhstan sector and (4) the Caucasus sector.

The Department of Propaganda and Agitation is also very important. In the Soviet budget three items of expenditure are kept a strict secret. These are expenditures on the armed forces, on the political police and on propaganda. It is impossible to find out the size of the gigantic direct and indirect expenditure on propaganda. It is only possible to estimate the size of the army of propagandists, which is divided into three corps. The first corps is a constantly active group of professional propagandists belonging to the party apparatus, numbering about 500,000 persons. The second corps is an intermittently active group of so-called supernumerary propagandists, numbering about 2,000,000 persons (these form the committee corps at all levels). The third corps consists of the staff propagandists in institutions, enterprises and public organizations (part of the soviet, the trade union and the *Komsomol aktiv*), numbering about 500,000 persons. The propaganda apparatus itself has two networks: (1) the vertical network for propaganda (the propaganda apparatus of the party committees), in which the leading propaganda cadres of the party are concentrated, and (2) the horizontal network for propaganda (institutions, enterprises and public organizations), which is a subsidiary network for political and particularly for industrial propaganda.

The Communist party is an ideocratic party; it does not tolerate deviations from orthodoxy in its ranks or coexistence with other ideologies in its society. Therefore, once they gain power, Communists begin by liquidating what they had furiously defended when they were in opposition—they abolish democratic liberties and establish supervision over the way their citizens think. Such intolerance of others' views and ideological systems is, however, more than evidence of a morbid fanaticism for upholding the purity of their own ideology. This ideology is regarded as an instrument of policy for achieving the seizure of power before revolution and as an instrument for retaining and reinforcing their grip on power after revolution. Ideology becomes an instrument for organizing the struggle for power. In his first work, *Who Are the Friends of the People* (1894), Lenin described his attitude to ideological questions in the words of the contemporary German Marxist leader, W. Liebknecht: "Studieren, Propagandieren, Organisieren"[27]—to study in order to propagandize, and to propagandize in order to organize. Lenin attached particular importance to printed propaganda. In *Where to Begin* (1901) he expounded the fundamentals of communist doctrine concerning the role of the press. Lenin demanded that the press "arouse in all strata of the people who are even to the slightest degree politically conscious, a passion for making *political accusations*,"[28] as a preliminary condition for the organization of collective dissatisfaction with the existing order. Lenin asserted:

> It is unthinkable in present-day Europe that a movement that lacks a political [press] organ merits the name political. Without it our task of concentrating all the elements of political discontent and protest and of fertilizing the revolutionary movement of the proletariat with them is absolutely impossible.[29]

Thus Lenin came to his famous thesis concerning the role of the newspaper:

> The newspaper is not only a collective propagandist and collective agitator, it is also a collective organizer.[30]

The first generation of Bolsheviks were masters of propaganda and agitation. This was of particular importance in the Revolution of 1917 and in the subsequent Civil War. It was also acknowledged by the Bolsheviks' enemies. In one of his books Lenin quotes a tribute to the skill of bolshevist propaganda in the White newspaper *Russia* of November 29, 1919, which stated:

> It seems that there is no sphere of life, no event, phenomenon or movement that cannot be used to influence the minds of one's supporters or one's enemies. The bolshevist leaders have applied all their gifts and efforts to propaganda and agitation, as well as enlisting the remarkable talents of writers, poets, actors, musicians, singers, artists and sculptors. . . . Streets, fences, walls, the corners of houses, the windows of shops and trams, railway stations in every town are plastered with all manner of Soviet newspapers, with issues of special wall newspapers, with placards, slogans, etc. To give the enemy his due and not to belittle his strength, every line of the newspapers is permeated with the same propagandist tone, is full of vigor and inspiration, the placards are colorful, they are pithy and clever, the summonses are fervent, the slogans and quotations are polished and striking.[31]

Almost five decades have passed since then, and the former social dynamism of Soviet propaganda has been dissipated by communist reality. But militant propaganda provides the basic content of Soviet intellectual life. Now it captures, not by enthusiasm or quality, but by an organized and massive encirclement of the Soviet citizen by a gigantic army of propagandists, beginning literally in the cradle and lasting to his death. The propagandists' opportunities have multiplied enormously. In 1960 Soviet propaganda had 62,700,000 radio receivers at its disposal. More than 100 television stations are in operation, as well as more than 200 low-power television booster stations.[32] The number of periodicals, notes and bulletins has reached 3,761 editions (3,600 titles), with 27,502 issues per year, and a total of 46,368,000 copies per issue in 56 languages, including 13 foreign languages. In 1960, 9,544 different newspaper editions were published, with 940,450 issues per year and a total of 68,600,000 copies per issue (*Pravda,* 6,300,000 copies per issue; *Izvestia,* 2,600,000 copies per issue; *Komsomol Pravda,* 3,400,000 copies per issue; *Pioneer Pravda,* 3,900,000 copies per issue; *Trud,* 1,300,000 copies per issue). Newspapers are published in 66 languages of the peoples of the U.S.S.R.[33] In addition there is an enormous output of books devoted entirely to propaganda. In 1960, 11,130 political and social books were published, totaling 169,900,000 copies in 96 languages (including 38 foreign languages).[34]

The Central Committee considers the foremost tasks of contemporary propaganda to be: (1) the creation of a new Soviet man and (2) the mobilization of the people to fulfill economic plans. A special decree of the Central Committee of the CPSU of January 9, 1960, said of the first task:

> The creation of a new man with communist traits in his character, with communist habits and morals, the liquidation of the survivals of capitalism in people's consciousness is now one of the main practical tasks.[35]

The third generation of Bolsheviks now rules the country; yet after almost half a century of intensive work by the highly evolved communist ideological machine, the "new man with communist traits" has not yet arrived on the scene. The Central Committee's admission is very important, since it suggests that although it is possible to create new political administration systems, it is not possible to create new "political people." The former Secretary of the Central Committee of the CPSU, L. Ilichev, described propaganda's second task in the following words:

> Are there scales on which it is possible to weigh the fruits of ideological work? There are, and this is not a paradox. They are the scales on which we weigh our daily bread, our cotton, steel, pig iron, meat, butter, coal, oil and other material assets. It is axiomatic that a direct and mutual link exists between higher production and good ideological education work.[36]

This assertion expressed the pragmatic philosophy of the party's ideological leadership very well.

The size of the Central Committee's staff is always changing; it has increased in the same way as the parallel state bureaucracy has grown. Under Sverdlov in 1919 it consisted of only 20 to 30 responsible workers; by December 1, 1929, it had grown to 534 persons; it now has about 1,300–1,500. The senior ranks of the Central Committee apparatus alone provide most of the personnel who in practice rule and run both the party and the state. Estimating that the Central Committee has twenty-five departments, with five sectors (or subdepartments) and twenty branch inspectors in each department, it is possible to deduce the approximate size of the overall contingent of leading workers in the

Central Committee of the party. Taking into account the categories of responsibility, it will look like this:

First category — 25 departments × 1 head		=	25 persons
25 departments × 3 deputies		=	75 persons
	Total		100 persons
Second category — 125 sectors × 1		=	125 persons
125 sectors × 3 deputies		=	375 persons
	Total		500 persons
Third category — integral instructors/inspectors		=	500 persons
branch instructors		=	250 persons
	Total		750 persons

Responsible workers in the Central Committee = 1,350 persons

At the head of these departments stands the Secretariat of the Central Committee (from five to nine persons); each of the secretaries except the first secretary has the oversight of several similar departments. The main functions of the Secretariat are concerned with the day-to-day work of the Central Committee, the cadres and inspection—making it the sole real power in the party.

Under the communist regime whoever controls the cadres controls the state. In view of their exceptional importance, matters affecting the cadres (the appointment, movement and removal of responsible leaders and officers of party and state) were at first dealt with by a special organ chosen by the Plenum of the Central Committee—the Orgburo. At first only one member of the Central Committee apparatus was a member of the Orgburo—the first secretary of the Central Committee. Later two more secretaries were added. The rest of its members (from seven to nine members plus from three to four candidate members) were elected from responsible leaders of the state working outside the Central Committee. It was Lenin's intention that this composition should ensure an impartial and objective selection of workers, based on their practical and political qualities. From the mid-thirties the Orgburo, like the Politburo, existed only on paper. Although Orgburo meetings were convened, it was only in order to vote on decisions that had already been made, and sometimes even acted on, by the Central Committee Secretariat. Therefore the decision of the Nineteenth Congress to liquidate the Orgburo and transfer its functions to the Secretariat simply gave official confirmation to the real position.

The selection, appointment and dismissal of cadres are effected according to carefully defined practice. At each stage of the party ladder there exists a ready-made hierarchy or staffing pattern, by which responsible workers are divided into categories according to rank.

The highest party cadres are divided according to the following order:

1. *Responsible workers of the establishment of the Plenum of the Central Committee*

(a) members and candidate members of the Presidium of the Central Committee;

(b) members of the Central Committee Secretariat;

(c) chairman of the Party Inspection Committee;

(d) first secretary of the Central Committee.

They can be appointed, transferred or dismissed only by the Plenum of the Central Committee.

2. *Responsible workers of the establishment of the Secretariat of the Central Committee*

(a) heads of Central Committee departments and their deputies; heads of sectors and their deputies; Central Committee instructors;

(b) editors of central press organs of party and government;

(c) ministers; their deputies; members of colleges of ministries; heads of principal administrations; leaders, deputies and members of colleges (committees); heads of departments and deputy heads of central agencies (committees);

(d) the entire apparatus of responsible workers of the ministry of foreign affairs; ambassadors; counselors; military attachés; trade representatives;

(e) secretaries of area, regional and provincial committees; secretaries of central committees of constituent republics; heads of departments of these committees; secretaries of the capital town committees of Moscow and Leningrad; chief editors of their press organs; chairmen of councils of ministers and presidiums of supreme soviets of constituent republics;

(f) chairman, deputies and members of the Supreme Court of the U.S.S.R.; prosecutor general of the U.S.S.R.; his deputies; prosecutors of republics and regions; leaders of the State Security Committee up to and including regional leaders;

(g) personnel of the Presidium of the Supreme Soviet of the U.S.S.R. (except the chairman, who is a regular member of the Plenum and Presidium of the Central Committee); chairmen and their deputies of constituent republic soviets and of the Council of Nationalities of the Supreme Soviet of the U.S.S.R.; chairmen and deputies of Supreme Soviet commissions; heads of departments and their deputies in the apparatus (the secretariat and administrative offices) of the Presidium of the Supreme Soviet;

(h) military personnel up to and including the rank of divisional commanders; the heads of divisional political departments;

(i) chairmen of *sovnarkhozy;* their deputies and administration chiefs;

(j) leaders and their assistants (heads of departments and deputies) of the All-Union Central Executive Committee of Trade Unions, All-Union Leninist Young Communist League, sports organizations and social organizations (Committee for Peace, Societies of Friendship, etc.);

(k) leaders of creative workers' organizations (Union of Soviet Writers, Union of Soviet Composers, etc.); leaders of their publishing organs;

(l) leaders of central scientific institutes; leaders of the Institute of Marxism-Leninism; leaders, teachers and students of the highest party schools (Academy of Social Sciences of the Central Committee of the CPSU, the Highest Party School of the Central Committee of the CPSU; leaders and teachers of party schools of the central committees of constituent republics).

3. *Responsible workers of the establishment of departments of the Central Committee*

(a) the secretaries of the capitals' district committees; heads of departments of capitals' town committees; responsible workers of central scientific institutes, of party research institutes and their editorial boards; heads of departments of regional committees, provincial committees and central committees of constituent republics;

(b) leaders of republic enterprises (if they are not on the Secretariat establishment); directors of trusts;

(c) responsible workers of central governmental organs having the rank of controller, auditor, inspector; the middle ranks of the diplomatic and secret police services.

For appointing, transferring or dismissing workers in the first two categories the decision of the Plenum and the Secretariat is needed. The appointment of workers in the third category requires the "permit" of the appropriate department of the Central Committee; they can be removed or transferred by the written direction or the oral agreement of these same departments. Thus the Secretariat, which was created "to conduct day-to-day business and, mainly, to select cadres and act as an organization for the control of work done," in fact directs the whole army of officials. This makes it the supreme power within the state. The members of the Central Committee Presidium, the members of the Central Committee Plenum and delegates to party congresses pass through the filter of this all-powerful Secretariat. Only after they are chosen and recommended by the Secretariat does the Central Committee admit them, and on the Secretariat's directive they may be thrown out. If one talks of dictatorship in the U.S.S.R., then one should speak, not of the dictatorship of the proletariat, but of the dictatorship of the Secretariat! That is one facet of the Secretariat's daily round; besides this it has to wield daily authority over all the organs of the state and over the so-called social organizations. It does this in two ways: directly, via the departments of the Central Committee of the ministries and the agencies; and indirectly, via party groups in the formally elected congresses, conferences, consultations, institutes and organizations (the Supreme Soviet, trade unions, unions of writers, artists, composers, etc.).

The 1961 statutes state:

> Party groups are subordinate to the corresponding party organs: to the Central Committee of the CPSU, to the Central Committee of the Communist party of a constituent republic, to the provincial committee, the regional committee, the area committee, the town committee and the district committee. In all questions party groups are obliged strictly and undeviatingly to be guided by the decisions of the leading party organs.[37]

Thus party groups are the indirect organs of power of the Secretariat and the departments of the Central Committee in all organizations outside the party. The Central Committee and its departments invest their powers in these groups, so that in all questions they can be "strictly and unswervingly guided by the decisions of the leading party organs," that is, by the apparatus. The party apparatus wants to secure the strict observance of Soviet legality and of "Soviet democracy" in these "elective" organs. The Supreme Soviet of the U.S.S.R. provides an example of this. To endow this "legislative" body with the authority of common consent and to make it a supreme authority, the party apparatus includes in it both Communists and non-party members (approximately in the proportion of four to one), and it presents directives to it, not as orders, but as "recommendations" and "proposals." This is also done indirectly through communist deputies of the Supreme Soviet who form the party group. Before the beginning of each meeting of the Supreme Soviet, the party group holds a private meeting at which the members are informed of decisions that have been reached by the Central Committee on all the questions in the agenda of the forthcoming session.

According to the party statutes, the party group does not have the right either to discuss or to reject decisions (made, of course, without reference to it) that have been made by the Secretariat or the Presidium of the Central Committee. The party group is obliged to approve these decisions, to proclaim them as being its own decisions, to defend them when they are discussed in the Presidium of the Supreme Soviet (which also has its own party group) and in the Council of Ministers of the U.S.S.R. (which does not have a party group, for all the ministers are party members; even though according to the Constitution of the U.S.S.R. a non-party member can be a minister, this has never happened anywhere in the Soviet Union). The acceptance of decisions is guaranteed not only by an organized majority of communist deputies obedient and submissive to the party apparatus, but also by careful selection (also by the party apparatus) of the non-party deputies, who are simply extras.

It is now clear that neither the Constitution of the U.S.S.R. nor the party statutes reveal the real sources of supreme power in the state and the party. The articles in each of them dealing with the supreme legislative organs of the state and of the party, respectively, are meaningless fiction. The supreme state power is situated outside the organs of state; it is in the party organs. Here too, the power pyramid is not constructed as the party statutes suggest, that is, with the Congress at the summit, then the Plenum, the Presidium, the Secretariat and finally the first secretary. The real state of affairs is quite the reverse. The first secretary is in fact at the apex of the pyramid of power in the party and the state, irrespective of whether he occupies the position of head of the government or head of the state. The personal power of the first secretary of the Central Committee has far outstripped his constitutional rights, as the following words of Lenin at the Ninth Congress (1920) show:

> It must first be emphasized, in order to avoid misunderstandings, that only decisions of the Central Committee made collectively in the Orgburo or the Politburo, or at a plenum, may be acted upon by the secretary of the Central Committee of the party. Otherwise the work of the Central Committee cannot be properly conducted.[38]

When the Stalin cult was being denounced, these words of Lenin were frequently quoted in the party press. But Khrushchev showed that although Stalin was dead, the first secretary of the party was not, when he declared in a conversation with writers:

> The resolve we have shown toward the hesitant and the deluded was not to everyone's taste. One may ask what right we have to bring up and decide questions. To this we must answer: the right of leadership.[39]

The Central Committee elected at the Twenty-second Congress differs considerably from that elected at the Twentieth Congress. Its membership has been considerably enlarged; it now consists of 175 members (instead of 133) and 155 candidate members (instead of 122). The Central Revisory Commission has 65 members, as before.

Only 37 per cent of the present Central Committee belonged to the Committee elected at the Twentieth Congress. Khrushchev introduced a majority of new members. The composition of the personnel of the leading organs of the CPSU reflects the social mosaic of the upper strata of Soviet society and the social and professional composition of the communist ruling class.

The relative sizes of the various social groups of the Central Committee are shown in Table 27.[40]

TABLE 27

SOCIAL AND PROFESSIONAL COMPOSITION OF THE PERSONNEL OF THE
CENTRAL COMMITTEE AND THE CENTRAL INSPECTION COMMISSION OF THE CPSU

SOCIAL GROUP	MEMBERS OF THE CENTRAL COMMITTEE	CANDIDATE MEMBERS OF THE CENTRAL COMMITTEE	MEMBERS OF THE CENTRAL INSPECTION COMMISSION	MEMBERS AND CANDIDATE MEMBERS OF THE CENTRAL COMMITTEE AND THE CENTRAL INSPECTION COMMISSION	PERCENTAGE OF OVERALL NUMBER
Party bureaucracy	89	67	30	186	47.1
State bureaucracy	57	54	21	132	33.4
Military bureaucracy	15	17	3	35	8.9
Cultural bureaucracy	4	6	4	14	3.5
Economic bureaucracy	3	4	3	10	2.5
Trade union bureaucracy	4	1	3	8	2.0
Secret police bureaucracy	—	1	—	1	0.3
Worker-peasant group	3	2	1	6	1.5
Indeterminate	—	3	—	3	0.8
Total	175	155	65	395	100

From Table 27 the following points are evident:

1. The party bureaucracy is, in both quality and quantity, the "leading and directing force" in the organs of the Central Committee. About 51 per cent of the members of the Central Committee are professional party workers (89 out of 175), and they form 47.1 per cent of the Central Committee and the Central Inspection Commission.

2. Next comes the governmental bureaucracy—33.4 per cent of the overall number. Together with the party bureaucracy it comprises 80.5 per cent of the total.

3. Since the Twentieth Congress the military bureau has more than doubled its representation in the Central Committee and the Central Inspection Commission (8.9 per cent). The Stalinist marshals Zhukov and Vasilevsky (besides Voroshilov and Bulganin) have been removed from the Central Committee, and marshals who served under Khrushchev's political command during the war have replaced them.

4. The number of cultural representatives, especially writers, in the

Central Committee and the Central Inspection Commission has increased almost threefold, and for the first time a few scientists have been included.

5. The low percentage of economic workers engaged directly in material production (2.5 per cent) is in sharp contrast to the size and importance of the economic bureaucracy in the country.

6. Very few trade-union bureaucrats are included, despite the new program's emphasis on the growing role of the trade unions in the construction of communism and despite the numerical preponderance of the trade unions over all other "social" organizations in the U.S.S.R.

7. For the first time in Soviet history there is not a single professional member of the secret police on the Central Committee. The titular head of the Committee for State Security is included, but only as a candidate member. (After Khrushchev, he was included as a member.)

8. For the first time in forty years several representatives of the people —manual workers and peasants—have been admitted to membership of the Central Committee and the Central Inspection Commission. They form 1.5 per cent of the personnel, and their role is purely decorative.

The new Presidium of the Central Committee (as of January, 1966) has twelve members, five of whom belonged to Stalin's Central Committee before the war. Eight of the twelve are engineers. Five of the Secretariat's nine members are engineers and the remaining four are ideological experts. In the Presidium and Secretariat of the Central Committee there was only one former manual worker—Khrushchev himself—and now there are none.

The main decisions on questions of domestic and foreign policy and on organization (party organization and the cadres) in the highest organs of the Central Committee of the CPSU are made only after the questions have been thoroughly studied and prepared by: (1) experts, (2) special commissions of the Central Committee (these may be either temporary or permanent), (3) the departments of the Central Committee and (4) the secretariat of the first secretary of the Central Committee.

The Central Committee experts are either staff workers (workers of appropriate departments of the Central Committee and of the secretariat of the first secretary of the Central Committee) or temporary workers who normally work outside the Central Committee and who have been asked to supply information or express an opinion on the question under discussion. The latter may include specialists who are not party members. The practice of setting up commissions (of members and non-members of the Central Committee) to study and prepare recommendations on certain questions is the most frequent and best-tested method of work of the Central Committee. In almost every branch of the Central Committee's work permanent or temporary commissions have been set up by the Politburo. As Khrushchev told the Twentieth Congress, Stalin had even begun to replace the Politburo itself by commissions, allocating to them the right to make final decisions (although they only gave recommendations for Politburo decisions). These commissions have now resumed their advisory status. It is difficult to say exactly what permanent commissions of the Central Committee now exist (apart from the two that were set up at the November, 1962, Plenum of the Central Committee of the CPSU—the Ideological Commission of the Central Committee and the Commission for Party and Organizational Questions). Judging by past experience it may be assumed that there exist at least another two commissions, namely, the Foreign Policy Commission of the Central Committee and the Defense (military) Commission of the Central Committee. Both of these commissions used to meet under Stalin's chairmanship.

The departments of the Central Committee not only control the corresponding departments of inferior party organs, they directly control the ministries of the U.S.S.R. and the central agencies. They are therefore the real ministries of the U.S.S.R. The departments of the Central Committee together with the ministries under their control prepare drafts of decisions for the highest organs of the Central Committee. The Central Committee departments are the main channel for the preparation of decisions. The head of a Central Committee department is usually (though not necessarily) a member or candidate member of that committee. In addition each of the Central Committee secretaries (except the first secretary) has the general supervision of two, three or more departments and, consequently, through these departments the Central Committee controls also the corresponding state organs (ministries).

After a question of policy or economic or personal affairs has been studied by experts and by the Central Committee departments and commissions, it reaches the secretariat of the first secretary with the appropriate recommendation in the form of a "draft decision" of one or other of the leading organs of the Central Committee. The first secretary's personal advisers and experts again study the matter thoroughly and report their conclusions to him. If he decides that the question has been studied sufficiently and agrees with the recommendation (together with any additions or alterations his own secretariat may have made), he then sends it to one of the following: (1) the Secretariat of the Central Committee, (2) the Presidium of the Central Committee, or (3) the Plenum of the Central Committee (as a rule via the Presidium of the Central Committee; but if the first secretary proves to be in the minority in the Central Committee, he can summon a plenum and appeal to it).

The question is then discussed at a meeting of one of these bodies, whose participants have received the "draft decisions" in advance. The meeting is also attended by persons reporting on the business under discussion (the reporter must be a leading member of the relevant department of the Central Committee or the secretary of the Central Committee responsible for the work of that department) and by the relevant experts. The non-members of the body are present while their question is being discussed, but if they are not responsible party apparatus workers they withdraw before a decision is reached. A decision is made by a simple majority vote. Decisions on state affairs and on admission to the highest party organs acquire the force of law only after they have passed through the appropriate state organs of power—through the Council of Ministers of the U.S.S.R. or the Supreme Soviet of the U.S.S.R., depending on the nature and importance of the matter and on the formal requirements of the Constitution of the U.S.S.R. Such is the normal method of deciding a question in the U.S.S.R.; but unilateral decisions are also made by the first secretary with the backing of his personal apparatus. Stalin acted in this way after the Seventeenth Congress in 1934, and it is probable that Khrushchev did the same on occasion. One cannot say this about Brezhnev, however.

The decision of the November, 1962, Plenum of the Central Committee of the CPSU to reorganize the party organs also affected the Central Committee's apparatus. Three economic bureaus of the Central Committee were set up, in which the supreme directive power of the Central Committee on economic questions was concentrated. These bureaus were: (1) the Bureau for Industry and Construction, (2) the Bureau for Chemical and Light Industries and (3) the Bureau for Agriculture. The corresponding economic departments of the central committees of constituent republics were subordinate to them, and their leaders were members of the appropriate bureau. A most important innovation here is that the Secretariat of the Central Committee, which directly controlled these bureaus, decided to share its economic power with the top economic bureaucracy. Representatives of the economic bureaucracy were supposed to participate, not only in working out the general economic policy of the party, but also in drawing up day-to-day directives. To implement this, leaders of the main central economic agencies, committees and ministries were admitted to the bureaus of the Central Committee. Members of the bureaus were appointed by the Secretariat and confirmed by the Presidium of the Central Committee.

One of the Central Committee secretaries was a chairman of each bureau, and he was confirmed by the Plenum of the Central Committee. On the same principle, that of combining party apparatus workers with high functionaries from outside the party, two Central Committee commissions have been set up: the Commission for Organizational and Party Questions and the Ideological Commission. Both are led by secretaries of the Central Committee. Unlike the economic bureaus, these commissions do not have executive and administrative authority. They are only supervisory and subsidiary advisory organs to work out recommendations for the solution of organizational and ideological problems.*

---

*The November, 1964, Central Committee resolution retained these two commissions but abolished the branch bureaus.

Another decision of the November, 1962, Plenum established a special network for party inspection—the Committee for Party and State Inspection of the Central Committee of the CPSU and the Council of Ministers of the U.S.S.R., with similar committees in the central committees of constituent republics, in the Bureau of the Central Committee of the CPSU for the R.S.F.S.R. and their representatives in provinces and regions. The chairmen of the committees are confirmed by the plenum of the appropriate central committee and, on the soviet side, by the presidium of the appropriate supreme soviet.

The members of the Committee for Party and State Inspection are appointed by the Secretariat and confirmed by the Presidium. They include the head of the Department of Administrative Organs of the Central Committee of the CPSU and representatives of the Supreme Court, of the Procuracy of the U.S.S.R., of the State Security Committee and also of the so-called social organizations—the All-Union Central Council of Trade Unions, the All-Union Leninist Young Communist League, etc. The chairman of the committee is both a secretary of the Central Committee of the CPSU and deputy chairman of the Council of Ministers of the U.S.S.R.

The November Plenum stated that the committee's main task is to assist the Central Committee and the Soviet government

> in the organization of systematic checking of the way in which directives of party and government are executed in the further *improvement of the leadership* of communist construction, in the maintenance of party and state discipline and of socialist legality.[41]

In giving his reasons for setting up a new central agency for party and state inspection, Khrushchev said:

> We must return to Lenin's advice, while taking into account present-day conditions, and create organs for party and state inspection from the highest to the lowest level.[42]

Khrushchev accused Stalin of abandoning at the Seventeenth Congress Lenin's unitary system of party and state inspection and of establishing separate party and state inspection organizations. He said that, contrary to Lenin's principle, Stalin did not want to allow the representatives of the people to participate in the inspection of the work of soviet and party institutions. An analysis of Khrushchev's proposals and of the November Plenum's decrees shows, however, that they were not so anxious to heed Lenin's advice as they were to return to Stalin's *practice*. Lenin's idea of creating party inspection—of a highest party court—would have led to the existence *alongside the Central Committee* and *independent of the Central Committee* of a supreme party inspection organ elected by the party Congress for: (1) the inspection of the Central Committee apparatus, leaders and officials; (2) the inspection of the rest of the party apparatus; and (3) the inspection of the activities at all levels of all economic, soviet, administrative, trade union and

Komsomol organizations. The Tenth Congress, in 1921, set up just such an inspection organ,[43] the Central Inspection Commission of the Party (CIC). According to the party statutes, a definite number of members of the presidium of this commission were to be present as observers at meetings of the Politburo and Orgburo of the Central Committee with the right to a deliberative vote, just as representatives of the Central Committee were at meetings of the presidium of the CIC.

At the Twelfth Congress (1923) on Lenin's instigation the organs for state inspection (Workers' and Peasants' Inspection—WPI) and for party inspection (CIC) were united.[44]

This inspection organ was disbanded by Stalin at the Seventeenth Congress in order to ensure his complete personal dictatorship. A party inspection organ was set up in its place, appointed by and directly subordinate to the Central Committee—the Central Committee's Commission for Party Inspection (CPI). A similar government-soviet inspection organ was established under the name Commission for Soviet Inspection (CSI). The difference between Stalin and Lenin was not that Stalin separated party and state inspection, but that *Stalin liquidated the supreme party court, which was independent of the Central Committee apparatus.*

The reestablished party court—the Committee for Party and State Inspection—can inspect everyone except officials and leaders of the apparatus of the Central Committee and of the Council of Ministers. It is the instrument the highest level of the party bureaucracy uses to inspect the rest of the party and the state bureaucracies.

More than that, it is an expression of the organized distrust in the apparatus of the Central Committee of the CPSU of the officials of the party and state apparatus in regions, provinces and constituent republics. That is why it has been established on the same principles as those on which Stalin's inspection system was built. Its inspectors are not elected but appointed from above, and they are completely independent of the rank-and-file membership of the party and of the people. As Khrushchev pointed out, the new inspectorate has a more prosaic task:

> The inspection organs have the important task of unmasking window-dressing, localism, corruption, waste, embezzlement of state property, etc. These things, unfortunately, are widespread. State funds are squandered on bribes, living accommodations are improperly allocated, plots of land are granted, pensions awarded, places are obtained in institutes of higher education and even diplomas are awarded illegally.[45]

Another old ailment of the Soviet system, which even Stalin could not cure, has also become prevalent—that is, the massive embezzlement by leading state officials of "socialist" property. Embezzlement cases involving 56,000,000 rubles came before the courts in the first half of 1962.[46]

In connection with the creation of a party control center, republic, *krai* (provincial) and *oblast* (regional) committees of the Committee for Party and State Inspection have been established, including 1,057 town and *raion* (district) committees, 348 committees for industrial production zones, and 1,643 committees for state and collective farms. By 1963, 193,000 groups and 323,000 posts had also been established in factories, state and collective farms, trading organizations, public institutions, schools, etc. More than 3,000,000 persons were participating in the work of these groups and posts.[47]

In December, 1965, the Committee for Party and State Inspection was renamed the People's Inspection Committee, but the apparatus was not changed.

Very little has been published regarding the sources of income for the maintenance of the immense party machine and its manifold activities. The Soviet Communist party has a single centralized budget and a single list of regular appointments in the party apparatus, from the Central Committee secretaries down to and including the secretaries of primary party organizations.

The sources of the party income are: (1) subsidies from the state budget of the U.S.S.R., which are listed under "social and cultural expenditure"; (2) monthly party members' dues in the form of a fixed percentage of their salaries (according to Paragraph 7 of the party statutes, from 0.5 to 3 per cent of their monthly earnings); (3) incomes from party enterprises, mainly party publishing firms such as that of *Pravda;* and profits from publications of the Institute of Marxism-Leninism, such as the works of Marx, Engels, and Lenin, and official party publications.

As the only state party in the country, the Communist party apparatus performs highly important state functions and accordingly enjoys state financial support for the performance of these functions. Nevertheless, the Central Committee carefully conceals from the party and the people the fact that state subsidies are received, and no information is provided as to their extent. The party statutes mention only two sources of income—members' dues and the income from party enterprises. Subsidies from the state are disguised as "other income." The relevant paragraph of the statutes states:

> The financial resources of the party and its organizations are derived from members' dues, returns from enterprises and other income.[48]

Expenditures in the party budget are mainly for the maintenance of local party apparatus, with the party apparatus of district committees, town committees, and area committees making up 87.8 per cent of the total; the apparatus of *oblast* committees, *krai* committees and the central committees of the Union republics accounted for the remaining 12.2 per cent.[49] The maintenance costs of the apparatus of the party Central Committee constituted 6 per cent of the total in 1956.[50] After the Twentieth Party Congress this item increased considerably because of the creation of a parallel party Central Committee apparatus for the R.S.F.S.R. A similar increase occurred in the case of the regional apparatus as a result of the creation of the double network of parallel industrial and agricultural regional and provincial party committees after the November, 1962, Plenum of the party Central Committee.

Expenditures for the party Central Committee apparatus not only cover the cost of maintaining its employees, which does not constitute a large sum, they involve the much larger expense of maintaining the Central Committee higher party schools, providing refresher courses for higher- and middle-grade propagandists and maintaining an entire network of party educational organizations, the cost of which in 1952 constituted about 20 per cent of total expenditures for the apparatus. The Central Committee budget covers the costs of two higher party schools—the Central Committee Academy of Social Sciences (formerly the Institute of Red Professors) and the Central Committee Higher Party School—and also a World Higher Party School for foreign Communists providing two-year "Lenin courses," which have been attended by many leaders of foreign Communist parties both before and after the war. The Central Committee also provides regular refresher courses for secretaries of regional committees, provincial committees, and the central committees of the Union republics. In 1952 the number of persons attending these schools totaled 35,000. During the five years preceding 1952, 400,000 higher and middle grade propagandists attended refresher courses.[51] The sources of income and the expenditures for the unpublished operations of the party are completely hidden from view.

The supreme auditing organ of the party for financial affairs is the Central Inspection Commission. In order to invest it with authority and independence, it is elected at party congresses. Its members cannot be members of the Central Committee. The Central Inspection Commission is legally empowered by the party to control the entire Central Committee financial machinery and also that of the apparatus of the Central Committee Secretariat. The party statutes adopted at the Fourteenth Party Congress, in 1925, give the following description of the functions of the Central Inspection Commission:

> The Central Inspection Commission inspects: (1) the speed and accuracy of the conduct of business in the central organs of the party and orderliness in the apparatus of the Secretariat of the party Central Committee and (2) the funds and enterprises of the Secretariat of the party Central Committee.[52]

The statement that the Central Inspection Commission "inspects the orderliness of the apparatus of the Secretariat of the Central Committee" has been deleted from both the Stalin era and the post-Stalin era party statutes. Although the new statutes preserve the right of the Central Inspection Commission to inspect the funds and "conduct of business in the central organs of the party," this right is only nominal. The Central Inspection Commission limits its activities to preparation of a statement of the accounts of the Central Committee on the basis of a financial report furnished by the Management Board of the Central Committee, that is, without the relevant documentation and information on income and expenditures. Inspection of the "conduct of business" in the Central Committee involves preparing another statement on the costs of office administration on the basis of data covering the entire Central Committee and listing the number of papers received and sent out and the number of complaints and appeals sent to the Central Committee and their results. The management aspect of meetings of the Secretariat and the Presidium of the Central Committee, and of the personal secretariat of the first secretary of the Central Committee, has been removed from the auditing competence of the Central Inspection Commission. It is, therefore, not surprising that the reports of the commission at party congresses are only formal. The commission has no power over the local auditing network. The local auditing commissions are not subordinate to the Central Inspection Commission but to the relevant party committees whose accounts they audit!

Although the role of the Central Inspection Commission as an organ for auditing the apparatus of the party Central Committee is negligible, this does not mean that the members of the commission are negligible. On the contrary, the Central Inspection Commission has a very imporant political and recording role in the Kremlin court etiquette. In this hierarchy the members of the Central Inspection Commission come after the members and candidate members of the Central Committee and before ministers and marshals who are not members of higher party organs. The members of the Central Inspection Commission participate in plenums of the Central Committee and receive its reports for information on a courtesy basis (they have no official right in this regard, but the Central Committee apparatus invites them to Central Committee plenums, where they have an advisory vote). The main significance of the Central Inspection Commission lies in the fact that it is a reserve from which future members and candidate members of the party Central Committee are recruited.

On October 14, 1964, the Secretariat of the Central Committee, with the concurrence of the Central Committee Presidium, took advantage of Khrushchev's absence from the Kremlin (he was on vacation along the Black Sea) to carry out a coup to overthrow him. Although the official communique stated that Khrushchev was relieved of his duties on his own request (because of advanced age and poor health),[53] he was, in fact, overthrown by a well-organized conspiracy. Khrushchev's duties were divided between Brezhnev (First Secretary of the party Central Committee) and Kosygin (Chairman of the Council of Ministers). The 1964 "October Revolution" against Khrushchev may be compared to the unmasking and condemnation of Stalin, for which Khrushchev himself was largely responsible. In both cases there was a rebellion against arbitrary, one-man rule and a tendency toward dictatorship by a group of persons, or "collective leadership," as it is called in party jargon (leaving aside the question of whether such "collective leadership" is capable of existing for any length of time). While the unmasking of Stalin demonstrated that the "gods" of communism can be sinners and even criminals, Khrushchev's overthrow created a precedent of worldwide historical importance by proving that even in a communist state a dictator can be toppled as the result of a high-level plot.

The first attempt to remove Khrushchev was in June, 1957. Although Khrushchev had legally—that is, according to the party statutes—been dismissed by a 7–4 vote of the Presidium of the party Central Committee, he settled the matter in his favor by simply disregarding the vote and branding those who had voted against him as an "anti-party group" that constituted nothing more than "an arithmetical majority."

Why did that coup fail and the recent one succeed? The answer to this question is to be found in the nature of the forces involved in both instances. The first coup was carried out by the Central Committee Presidium, which has only moral authority (although according to the party statutes it constitutes the highest party organ between plenary sessions of the Central Committee); the second was engineered by the Central Committee Secretariat, which has the party, state, military and police apparatus behind it. The Presidium is merely a weekly gathering, a "little party parliament," a "talking shop," while the Secretariat is the permanently active sole repository of supreme power, even though from the juridical standpoint it is subordinate to the Presidium. The Secretariat, which in 1957 saved Khrushchev by its counterrevolution against the "anti-party group," was in the end also responsible for his overthrow.

Khrushchev was the victim of his own campaign against the personality cult: the victim, that is, of the forces he had unleashed at the Twentieth Party Congress. At the same time he was condemning Stalin's personality cult, he was methodically and energetically setting about building up his own and turning himself into an all-powerful dictator such as Stalin had been. By concentrating party and governmental power in his hands and becoming Supreme Commander of the Armed Forces, Khrushchev had achieved in five years what Stalin had taken decades to accomplish. In the end Khrushchev's word was just as much law as Stalin's had been. The party functionaries in control of the party and the state feared for the stability of their positions just as they had under Stalin. No one, from a *raion* committee secretary to a Central Committee Presidium member, was safe from Khrushchev's irrational outbursts. Even such close associates and Central Committee secretaries as Kirichenko, Aristov, Belyayev, Ignatov, Mukhitdinov and Furtseva, who had kept him in the position of First Secretary of the party Central Committee, were cast aside once Khrushchev felt that he was sitting sufficiently firmly in the saddle. The anti-Stalinist Central Committee elected at the Twentieth Party Congress lost over 60 per cent of its members at the Twenty-second Congress. Almost all *oblast, krai* and republic central committee secretaries were replaced, and ministers came and went in rapid succession. Under the pretext of "promoting young forces," Khrushchev carried out a systematic purge in the party and state apparatus.

Although Khrushchev's purges were bloodless and did not involve the use of mass preventive terror, as Stalin's had done, they were none-theless purges and created bitterness and dissatisfaction among the old elite, who incited the rank-and-file party members against Khrushchev. While Khrushchev grew in moral stature in the eyes of the party and the people by refraining from using Stalin's bloody methods—even against the Molotov group in 1957—he may also have lost politically by doing so, since it is quite possible that if he had physically liquidated this group he would still be in power. The greatest risk the new "revo-lutionaries" ran was of being pensioned off as Molotov was.

The motives of the new men in the Kremlin in deposing their former tutor and leader were formulated in the following allusion to Khrushchev that appeared in the October 17, 1964, issue of *Pravda:*

> The party of Lenin is an enemy of subjectivism and inertia in communist construction. Wild planning, premature conclusions, hasty, unrealistic decisions and actions, boasting and blather, over-preoccupation with administration, unwillingness to take account of the fruits of science and practical experience . . . are alien to it. Communist construction does not allow bureaucratic methods, one-man decisions. . . . Only on the basis of the Leninist principle of collective leadership can the growing creative initiative of the party be guided and led. . . . In carrying out its general line the party has consistently and uncompromisingly opposed the ideology and practice of the personality cult and continues to do so. . . . Here's to new successes of the party and people in implementing the decisions of the Twentieth, Twenty-first and Twenty-second con-gresses and the program of the Communist Party of the Soviet Union!

From the above, it is clear that the new leaders are not opposed to Khrushchev's policies but to methods and "subjectivism."[54]

Thus the main, decisive reason for Khrushchev's removal was that he had liquidated this "collective leadership" and turned the party Secretariat, Presidium and Central Committee into mere advisory bodies. Khrushchev's inconsistency in domestic policy, his bureau-cratic urge to reorganize the administrative organs of party and state constantly and his endless planning experiments in agriculture and industry had resulted in chaos and uncertainty.

The situation as regards foreign policy was little better. Khrushchev, although no advocate of war, was the kind of "fighter for peace" who might have easily provoked a war. An impulsive, unstable man of "premature conclusions" and "hasty decisions," he appeared even to top party functionaries a dangerous dictator exercising sole control over a gigantic nuclear arsenal.

Khrushchev's departure will not affect the Kremlin's present foreign policy of "peaceful coexistence"—made necessary by the advent of thermonuclear weapons—which has always been interpreted by Soviet leaders and Soviet ideologists as a tactical course and not a program, a means to an end and not an end in itself, a compulsory pause in the march toward world communist revolution and not genuine peaceful coexistence. It is often forgotten that the principal author of the "revisionist conception" of certain Leninist principles presented at the Twentieth Party Congress, namely, that wars are not inevitable, that coexistence is an objective necessity, that communism will triumph over capitalism in the course of peaceful economic competition and that Communists can choose between peaceful and non-peaceful means of coming to power in non-communist countries according to circumstances, was the ideological apparatus of the party Central Committee headed by Suslov, who was also the author of the new party program in which this concept was incorporated. Suslov provided the theoretical basis for all the new theses at the Twentieth and Twenty-second congresses. Certainly, Khrushchev proclaimed them, but this was only to give the impression that he personally was the "continuator" of the teachings of Marx and Lenin. Indeed, it would be naive to suppose that Khrushchev, unversed in theory, could have formulated the new theses, let alone have written the new party program. At the same time, Khrushchev's adventurism and his habit of alternately blowing hot and cold made a consistent and purposeful Soviet foreign policy impossible.

It is therefore clear that it is a mistake to regard Khrushchev as a "progressive" and a "revisionist" in contrast to the hardened "dogmatist" Suslov. Khrushchev's departure will have no radical effect on party policy as laid down in the resolutions adopted at the Twentieth and Twenty-second congresses or on the ideological differences between Moscow and Peking. This was to a certain extent confirmed by a lengthy editorial in the November 1, 1964, issue of *Pravda,* which reiterated the principal theses concerning foreign and domestic policy in the party program and called the program "a torch lighting the way into the future." Although the new Soviet party leaders are already showing a more flexible and conciliatory attitude toward Peking in an attempt to end the ideological warfare within the world communist movement, this will not affect the party's basic purpose of achieving hegemony in the communist world movement and looking after the state interests of the U.S.S.R.

As for Soviet diplomacy, the party's foreign policy instrument, this will no longer be governed by the whims of a single man but by a group of realists. Soviet foreign and domestic policy is now in the hands of the managers and the engineers. This means that there will be less phrase-mongering and more concrete action, fewer threats but more deeds. A more systematic siege of the Free World and a more systematic infiltration of communist ideas into the developing countries have begun.

It must be stressed that Khrushchev's overthrow does not simply mean the replacement of the party First Secretary and the Chairman of the Council of Ministers and a separation of party power from state power; it means an attempt to put an end to one-man dictatorship once and for all and to return to collective dictatorship. The principle of collective dictatorship, or "collective leadership," was first proclaimed by Stalin himself at the Fourteenth Party Congress, in 1924, after Lenin's death, in the following words:

> The party cannot be led from outside the collective. It is stupid to think so after Ilich's death. . . . Collective leadership—that is what we need now.[55]

The principle was proclaimed for the second time on March 14, 1953, just over one week after Stalin's death, by Malenkov, who was forced to do so by his colleagues in the Presidium of the party Central Committee after they had removed him from the post of party first secretary. On this occasion, the "collective leadership" was abolished in three stages: by Beria's execution in June, 1953; by Malenkov's removal from the post of chairman of the Council of Ministers in February, 1955; and by the expulsion of the Molotov group from the Central Committee Presidium in June, 1957.

The third "collective leadership" has now come to power, not in the wake of a dictator's death, but over his political corpse, as the result of a brilliantly engineered and executed plot. Inasmuch as this plot was directed mainly at abolishing Khrushchev's one-man dictatorship as such and thus at introducing "internal party democracy," if only at the highest level, Khrushchev's overthrow must be regarded as the first step toward extending this "internal party democracy" to all levels. This would mean no less than a complete rejection of any kind of dictatorship of the party apparatus within the party.

The Soviet Communist party now has 11,500,000 members, roughly one-half of whom are intellectual workers. It can no longer be ruled by Stalin's terrorist methods or by Khrushchev's primitive demagoguery. It is becoming rational, critical and demanding. This development calls for restoring the party's authority over its functionaries and granting more freedom inside the party. Of course, the party has a long way to go before reaching this stage, but the general tendency cannot be denied. In other words, it can be said that the present "collective leadership" is temporary; it is the preparatory stage in either the establishment of a new one-man dictatorship or the democratization of the entire party. The power struggle within the party will, in the end, revolve around this dilemma.

The following chapters will examine the manner in which the party apparatus controls the state and social organizations.

* CHAPTER XII *

The Party and the Government (Soviets)

GREAT revolutions are invariably accompanied by noble utterances and ambitious promises, but their instigators never set about the task of creating a new order with the enthusiasm and maniacal zeal with which they destroy the old order. The transition from great words to great deeds, from negative criticism to positive proposals, from destruction to construction, has always proved a difficult and sometimes even impossible task for the great revolutionaries of the world. Because of this, some of them have recoiled from the newly emergent order and others have deliberately abandoned it. It has been said of those revolutions that they have eaten their own children. Lenin was an unrivalled master of simultaneous destruction and creation. He was not held in thrall by slogans. After he had utterly destroyed the old machinery of state, he proceeded to construct his own machinery of state out of his own material.

The soviets provided a ready-made organization for wielding power, and the immediate task was to imbue them with the spirit of communism. Although Lenin had said that the 240,000 members of his party could easily cope with the task of administering Russia, practice proved that people called upon to destroy are unable to create. Moreover, barely one-half of these 240,000 were more or less literate. Almost the entire colossal bureaucratic apparatus of the country either overtly or covertly sabotaged the work of the new political authority. It was even rumored that prerevolutionary ministerial officials had refused to show "secret" state documents to their new bolshevist masters because they thought their tenure of office would be short! The Bolsheviks gave them short shrift, and the officials' action was declared to be sabotage and a crime against the state. To deal with this situation the CHEKA (All-Russian Extraordinary Commission for Struggle Against Counterrevolution, Sabotage and Speculation) was created.

Communist power is the art of ruling people, things and the process of labor. From this threefold definition arose the need for the gradual conversion of the party of professional revolutionaries and wreckers into a party of rulers in which ideocrats (for politics), bureaucrats (for administration) and technocrats (for production) must be represented in approximately equal numbers. This was an unprecedented and extraordinary task for fanatics of destruction. The history of the Communist

Party of the Soviet Union from the first years after the seizure of power is largely the history of this great transition. Lenin merely laid its foundations when he defined the party's foremost task as that of administering the new state. The party had to learn how to rule the people in the name of the people. Although Lenin's famous slogan "Every cook (female!) must learn how to run the state" only superficially touched on the problem of the structure of the new state, it undoubtedly reflected the belief that it would be easier to appear to rule by consent through the people's own "representatives" than to rule as an open dictatorship. He emphasized the popular character of the state and the proletarian or peasant origin of the majority of its official legislative body—constituted by the All-Russian Central Executive Committee, the Central Executive Committee and the Supreme Soviet.* The titles of its institutions and organizations (the "worker state," "the worker-peasant government," "the worker-peasant Red Army," "people's commissars," etc.) sought to conceal the fact that the source and strength of real power was the party.

At first it was only necessary to destroy the old state apparatus and to improvise a new administration with the aid of a vast army of commissars. But the governmental apparatus needed practical experts and technical executives, which the party could not as yet provide. As early as 1923 Lenin wrote:

> Things are so bad in our state apparatus that we must first think very seriously how to deal with its defects.[1]

He allocated the task of devising measures to remedy this situation, not to the cooks, but to the party:

> We must at all costs set ourselves the task of renovating our apparatus of state: we must study, study and study again.[2]

By this he meant not merely political theory but the practical training of Communists in practical state administration. He suggested that a study be made of the art and science of administration, of bourgeois experiences in administration in Germany and England and of the writing and publishing of textbooks on the construction of the state and on administrative techniques. He also proposed to send young people abroad to gain administrative skill. In a word, now that the party had learned how to effect a successful revolution it must cap the victory by learning how to administer the state.

Special stress was laid on the importance of young people as the party's most dependable weapon and reserve force. Lenin hoped that they would progress from the stinging slogans and resounding declarations of revolutionary romanticism to the prosaic life of construction and creative training. He reminded the younger generation that it was

---

*The term "soviet" has two meanings for the Communists: (1) an organ of state power and form of government; (2) an organization for mass participation by people of the "working classes."

not enough to vanquish the bourgeoisie, it was also necessary to master the bourgeois science of domination over both society and nature. In a speech at the Third *Komsomol* Congress, in 1920, Lenin said:

> It is only possible to become a Communist when you have enriched your mind with a knowledge of all those riches that man has developed.[3]

On the basis of Lenin's directives and the experience gained in the first decade of rule, a definitive new doctrine of power was worked out, under the name "party construction." Party construction was the doctrine or science, not only of the principles of the structure, the forms and the methods of the bureaucracy's direction of the party, but also of the structure, the forms and the methods of the party's direction of the state. This twofold doctrine, with its two spheres of action, the party and the state, required the creation of an organizational structure of communist power with two apparatus, a party apparatus and a state apparatus. That this apparent dualism of power is an illusion becomes immediately clear if attention is drawn, not to the nominal Constitution of the U.S.S.R., but to the actual constitution of the party apparatus. The state apparatus at each level, from the rural soviet to the Council of Ministers of the U.S.S.R., is merely a technical executive organ of the party apparatus. Its territorial administrative units, its structure, and its subdivisions correspond to the administrative status and structure of the party apparatus at each level. The legislative, supervisory and managerial power is concentrated in the party apparatus and the executive and technical power in the state apparatus. The nominal legal organs of state power in the U.S.S.R. are in reality functional, derivative organs that derive their authority from the leading organs of the party apparatus.

The Constitution of the U.S.S.R. maintains that the sovereign power is vested in the organs of government:

> *Article 3.*—All power in the U.S.S.R. belongs to the workers in town and country in the person of the soviets of workers' deputies.
>
> . . . .
>
> *Article 30.*—The Supreme Soviet of the U.S.S.R. is the highest organ of power in the state.
>
> . . . .
>
> *Article 57.*—The supreme soviet of a constituent republic is the highest organ of power in that republic.
>
> . . . .
>
> *Article 89.*—The supreme soviet of an autonomous republic is the highest organ of power in that republic.
>
> . . . .
>
> *Article 94.*—The soviets of workers' deputies are the organs of state power in provinces, regions, autonomous regions, areas, districts, towns and villages.[4]

That is, all power, from top to bottom, is vested in soviets of workers' deputies elected "by secret ballot on the basis of universal, equal and direct suffrage."[5] Although this might seem to refute what has been said about the location of the center of legislative power in the U.S.S.R., closer examination of the machinery of the Soviet state, of election practice and the legislative activities of the soviets reveals that the true holder of legislative power hides behind a welter of democratic terminology and exploits the soviets as pseudoparliamentary bodies for its own political convenience. The actual practice of communist rule directly contravenes the provisions quoted above. According to Leninist doctrine, the prerogatives of legislative power rest solely in the party Central Committee; the state, together with its apparatus, is only a weapon in the party's hands for putting its will and its aims into effect.

Lenin laid down principles on the relationship between the party's legislative power and the technical role of the organs of state. He declared:

> Not a single important political or organizational question may be decided by a state institution in our republic without *the guiding directions* of the party Central Committee.[6]

Lenin was true to himself when, without any diplomatic evasions or propagandist embellishments, he stated bluntly that the party itself represented the Soviet state:

> The state is only a weapon of the proletariat in the class struggle. A special cudgel, *rien de plus*.[7]

Both the state and its highest organs, then, are only a cudgel in the hands of the real legislator, the party apparatus. This extremely important principle of the Leninist doctrine of power is expressed officially, in slightly disguised form, in Article 126 of the Constitution of the U.S.S.R., which states:

> Citizens of the U.S.S.R. are guaranteed the right of banding together in social organizations: trade unions, cooperative associations, youth organizations, sports and defense organizations, cultural, technical and scientific societies, while the *most active and conscious* citizens . . . voluntarily join together in the Communist Party of the Soviet Union, which is the leading detachment . . . and represents the guiding nucleus of all workers' organizations, both social and governmental.[8]

The Communist Party of the Soviet Union is, accordingly, an organization above all social and state organizations and the "guiding nucleus" of the state and its supreme legislative organs. It is simultaneously legislature, judiciary and executive. The regime's official term "soviet democracy" means rule by the Communist party. The party rules through four professional cadre groups: (1) the cadre organization of party *apparatchiks* (the party bureaucracy), (2) the soviet administrative bureaucracy (service bureaucracy), (3) the economic bureaucracy (the technocracy) and (4) the social and cultural bureaucracy (culture, sport, the unions of writers, artists and composers, voluntary societies, etc.).

The party bureaucracy is the main group; the remaining three are auxiliary groups, not only in relation to the technical assignment of functions, but also to the rights of each of the groups in the party's bureaucracy. The latter three groups work within the state apparatus or in social organizations, and so receive directives and instructions from the first group, which controls their work. Moreover, their representatives are appointed, transferred and removed by the first group, which is the party apparatus acting in the name of the entire party. In order to get a clear picture of the relationships between these groups within the party and of the relationship between the party bureaucracy and the state apparatus as a whole, it is necessary to examine both the written Constitution of the U.S.S.R. and the unwritten constitutional practice of the party. We shall first examine how the soviets are created and who belongs to them, and then how and in what degree they exercise legislative power and administrative functions.

According to the Constitution, the rural soviet is the elementary cell of state power in the countryside; in the city the city soviet fulfills this function. The highest national organ of state power is the Supreme Soviet of the U.S.S.R. Each soviet also elects its own executive organ, the executive committee. The hierarchy of organs of state and executive power is as follows, in ascending order of importance:

Organs of State Power	*Organs of Executive Power*
Rural soviet	Rural executive committee
Raion (district) soviet	*Raion* executive committee
City soviet	City executive committee
Oblast (regional) soviet	*Oblast* executive committee
Krai (provincial) soviet	*Krai* executive committee
Supreme soviet	Council of ministers of the republic
(of an autonomous or a constituent republic)	
Supreme Soviet of the U.S.S.R.	Council of Ministers of the U.S.S.R.

Members of rural, city, *raion, oblast* and *krai* soviets are elected for two years; those of the supreme soviets of autonomous and constituent republics and members of the Supreme Soviet of the U.S.S.R. are elected for four years. The nominal election procedure is the same as that in parliamentary democracies, except that each locality or each electoral district nominates only one candidate on behalf of the "bloc of Communists and non-members of the party." No rival candidate, not even a Communist, is permitted. Before the start of an election campaign, the party apparatus at each level draws up a list of future deputies. If elections to the Supreme Soviet of the U.S.S.R. are imminent, the Secretariat of the Central Committee of the CPSU draws up for lower party organs a list giving the proportion of representatives from each social group that must be represented at the forthcoming Supreme Soviet. Detailed instructions are given as to how many deputies must be party members and how many non-members; what percentage must consist of representatives of the party and the soviet bureaucracy, industrial administrators, military personnel, workers in science, culture, the health service, representatives of arts, of manual labor (industrial and farm workers), representatives of the main nationalities (in the case of the national republics) and finally what percentage must be women. The average age of the future deputies is also controlled. Local party organs (regional committees, provincial committees and central committees of republics) are at liberty to fill out these lists with the names of candidates they intend to nominate as deputies to the Supreme Soviet of the U.S.S.R. (except those candidates the party Central Committee itself nominates from among representatives of the central bureaucracy for election by the given republic or region). After this the lists of candidate deputies, after repeated checking and screening, are sent from all the republics and regions to the Central Election Commission, consisting of representatives of the party Central Committee, the All-Union Central Trade Union Council, the Central Committee of the Young Communist League and other social organizations. In effect, they are returned to the Secretariat of the party Central Committee for screening by its own apparatus in the case of party members and by the State Security Committee in the case of non-members of the party. The names of those who pass this screening are published in central and local newspapers and announced at election meetings as candidate deputies.

The U.S.S.R. is composed of 15 constituent republics, 20 autonomous republics, 8 autonomous *oblasts,* and 10 national areas (*okrugs*), in all, 53 political subdivisions.

The Supreme Soviet of the U.S.S.R. consists of two houses—the Soviet of the Union, with 1 deputy for each 300,000 electors, and the Soviet of Nationalities, with 1 deputy per national area (*okrug*), 5 from each autonomous region (*oblast*), 11 from each autonomous republic, and 25 from each constituent republic. The two houses have equal standing. The Soviet of the Union protects the general interests of the state, the Soviet of Nationalities the interests of national minorities. The Supreme Soviet of the U.S.S.R. contains representatives of about 60 nationalities and peoples. In 1946, of the 1,339 deputies 682 were in the Soviet of the Union and 675 in the Soviet of Nationalities. The two soviets included 1,030 members of the higher administrative bureaucracy and of the intelligentsia, 102 workers and 217 peasants.[9] The workers and peasants are such in name only, being members of the "worker-peasant aristocracy"—skilled workmen, foremen and collective farm chairmen. Of the 1,339 deputies, 254 (19 per cent) are non-members of the party. About 25 per cent of the deputies are women. In 1962 the Supreme Soviet included 1,443 deputies, 791 in the Soviet of the Union and 652 in the Soviet of Nationalities, as follows:[10]

1. *Party and state bureaucracy*

Leaders of party apparatus	259
Leaders of soviet apparatus	192
Collective farm chairmen	99
Military personnel	62
Chairmen of state economic enterprises (*sovnarkhozy*)	44
Heads of industrial undertakings	31
Directors of state farms and of experimental enterprises	18
Trade union leaders	12
Young Communist League leaders	7
Leaders of other social organizations	3
Total	727

(50.4 per cent of the total)

2. *Intelligentsia and worker-peasant aristocracy*

Skilled workers and foremen	98
Specialists and foremen at collective and state farms	55
Heads of higher education and academic institutes	51
Health service and education workers	49
Artistic workers	47
Engineering and technical workers	14
Total	314

(21.8 per cent of the total)

3. *Manual labor group*

Male and female industrial workers	189
Male and female collective farm workers	162
Male and female workers on state farms and in state experimental enterprises	51
Total	402

(27.8 per cent of the total number of deputies)

In 1962 the number of deputies who were non-members of the party rose to about 24 per cent of the total.[11]

The increase of the proportion of industrial and agricultural workers and of non-members of the party in the present Supreme Soviet as compared with the Stalinist Supreme Soviet has altered neither the character nor the function of the soviet organs as the executive organs of the party apparatus. On the proposal of the plenipotentiary representative of the party Central Committee, the Supreme Soviet elects at the first session its "collective president"— the Presidium of the Supreme Soviet of the U.S.S.R.—and its executive organ—the Council of Ministers of the U.S.S.R. The laws that the party Central Committee has decided to pass at the sessions of the Supreme Soviet pass first through the party group of the Supreme Soviet and are then proposed in its name for "discussion" by the entire Supreme Soviet.

The entire subordinate network of the supreme soviets of the constituent and autonomous republics, as well as of the provincial, regional, town, district and rural soviets, is organized in a similar fashion. The bases of representation vary, depending on the "status" of the soviet and on the size of the population it represents. For example, for the Supreme Soviet of the R.S.F.S.R. there is one deputy per 150,000 inhabitants; for a rural soviet of the R.S.F.S.R. one deputy per 100 inhabitants; but in a town soviet, one deputy to not less than 350 persons.[12] Local soviets create their own executive committees, which are administrative organs covering all branches of life. Similarly, provincial, regional, district and town executive committees have various departments for such fields as industry, trading, finance, education, roads, internal affairs, culture, etc. Over all these departments is the presidium of the provincial, regional, district or town executive committee, consisting of a chairman, deputies, a secretary and members. Party groups are also set up within the soviet and the presidium, through which the party apparatus at each particular level directs both these soviets and their executive organs.

The soviets play a dual role in the state: as executive and technical administrative organs of the party apparatus and as pseudo-organs of state power. The latter role is no less important than the former; the soviets thus not only create the illusion of overall popularly elected power, but are the legal organs for executing the orders and decisions of a narrow circle of party apparatus workers among the broad masses of the population. Deputies by the mere fact of their election to the Supreme Soviet or to local soviets become active promoters of party policy. In this respect a deputy, whether a party member or not, plays no role at all (all active Soviet citizens, members and non-members of the party alike, are considered to be Bolsheviks). The number of non-party member deputies is progressively larger in the lower ranks of the soviet hierarchy. Even in the supreme soviets of constituent republics 30 per cent or more of the deputies are not party members. In 1959 the proportion of non-members of the party was as follows: Uzbekistan, 26.8 per cent; Kazakhstan, 31.3 per cent; Ukraine, 31.7 per cent; and Russia, 32.6 per cent. Together with the communist deputies, these non-party deputies form the vast army of the legislative corps. In January, 1959, there were 1,800,000 deputies in local soviets, in addition to 750,000 activists working in the permanent commissions of local soviets.[13] The "soviet apparatus," which consists of more than 2,500,000 persons, exists as a fictitious legislator; yet as a network of executive administrative organs it is an essential supplement to the party apparatus. The apparatus of soviets also includes very important organs of administration, such as the secret police, the army, the organs of economic administration and the foreign policy apparatus, as well as the judicial and law enforcement organizations.

The position and functions of the courts and the procuracy as envisaged in the Soviet Constitution differ from their actual positions. For example, the Constitution of the U.S.S.R. says that "judges are independent and are subject only to the law"[14] and that

> the supreme supervision of the precise execution of the laws by all ministries and subordinate institutions as well as by individual officials and by citizens of the U.S.S.R. rests on the public prosecutor of the U.S.S.R.[15]

In reality every legal decision is made with the ultimate concurrence of the supreme political authority of the day, no matter what laws formally exist. The party is that authority. The role played by the "independent" judges and prosecutors during Stalin's time is all too well remembered, and their real position remains unchanged. They are dependent on those who appoint and dismiss them, that is, on the organs of various levels of the party apparatus. Officially the Soviet judicial system consists of people's district or local courts elected for three years by popular election. Regional and provincial courts are elected by the corresponding soviets for five years, and the supreme courts of autonomous and constituent republics by the appropriate supreme soviet for a similar period.[16] One very important fundamental element of this election procedure, which is mentioned neither in Soviet laws nor in commentaries on them, is that non-members of the party cannot be appointed as judges but can act only as "people's assessors," while the party organ at the appropriate level—the bureau of the party committee or the administration department of the party committee—has the right to appoint and remove members of courts. The same party organ has the unwritten, but invariably exercised, right to give judges oral instructions for action in particular criminal cases if the case in any way concerns the interests of the party committee. Since the Soviet judicial system is not under any centralized state control or hierarchy, the apparatus of the judicial organ at each level receives its directions from the corresponding soviet, which in practice means from the administration department of the *oblast* committee, the *krai* committee or a constituent republic central committee.

The procuracy is in a somewhat different position. The procurator general of the U.S.S.R. is appointed by the Supreme Soviet of the U.S.S.R. for a period of seven years, and the procurators of constituent and autonomous republics, *krais* and *oblasts,* by the procurator general for five years. Area, city and *raion* procurators are appointed by the procurator of the constituent republic, subject to confirmation by the procurator general.[17] The underlying idea of the system is clear: it is intended to ensure unity and uniformity in the execution of the general line of the dictatorship in all parts of the U.S.S.R., and to prevent separatism on the part of either the national republics or individual

organs of the state administration. Lenin himself emphasized the importance of this aspect of the procuracy's functions when he said:

> The procurator has the right and the duty to do only one thing:
> to ensure the establishment of a really uniform understanding of
> the law throughout the republic, regardless of any local differences
> and despite all local influences.[18]

The task of a procurator is, accordingly, to be a vigilant central party
organ for maintaining surveillance over the deeds and misdeeds of local
organs of state administration. Although the procurator has no administrative power, he is required to protect against illegal acts by the
state organs of administration and to be on the lookout for any illegal
acts, even of the organs of the state security organization. The security
organs are always protected by their "special position," although a "special procurator" exists to deal with State Security Committee affairs.
Each procurator of a *raion, krai* or republic is appointed and may be
dismissed with the concurrence of the appropriate party organ. The
day-to-day party management and party control of the procurator's
staff is carried out by the same administration department of the given
party committee. Nevertheless, the role of the procurator's organs as
informers and vigilantes on the lookout for violations of party directives
and of laws based on them is very important. Since the central party
leadership places great value on this aspect of the procuratorial network's
service, it does not always take the side of the party organs in conflicts
between a procurator and local party organs.

With regard to the interrelationships and allocation of functions
between the party apparatus and the government apparatus, the central
party leadership seeks to ensure the appearance that party organs do
not usurp those of the soviet organs. Decisions of party congresses and
conferences have the same aim; this is mentioned in the party statutes.
The Ninth Congress, in 1920, noted:

> The party organization must in no instance set itself the task of
> replacing the soviets. . . . All work of party organizations in this
> sphere must be conducted through the corresponding soviet
> organs.[19]

A resolution of the Eleventh Party Congress, in 1922, stated it even
more explicitly:

> The changeover, which has begun since the Civil War, to eco-
> nomic construction is turning local soviets, which during the Civil
> War played the role of agitation and mobilization centers, into the
> practical leaders of local economic life. . . . While retaining [and]
> preserving for itself the overall leadership and direction of the
> entire policy of the Soviet state, the party must make a very much
> clearer demarcation between its day-to-day work and the work of
> the soviet organs, between its own apparatus and the apparatus
> of the soviets.[20]

The 1961 statutes again emphasized this point.[21]

Nevertheless, these decisions and constitutional rules have failed to change the character of administration, under which the party apparatus plays the leading legislative role and the soviet apparatus the auxiliary executive role. A similar relationship exists between party law and state law, the latter being a function of the former. This is recognized by the leading authorities of Soviet "legal science" in statements that directives of party organs have "the force of practical decision, the force of law."[22] This was openly declared by the founder of the Soviet state, Lenin, when he said:

> We must know and remember that the entire legal and practical constitution of Soviet Russia is built on the fact that the party amends, appoints and constructs according to one symbol.[23]

Such is the true role of the soviets and of the soviet administrative apparatus.

* Chapter XIII *

The Party and the Trade Unions

As WE HAVE SEEN, an exclusive permanent organization of leaders resting on the party rank and file, and a rank-and-file Bolshevik party resting on widespread organizations subordinate to the party, constituted Lenin's organization on the road to power. The party's work after it came to power was based on the same model. At the top of the CPSU is the permanent organization of party apparatus workers, a relatively small group because the number of posts in the party administrative apparatus is kept to a minimum; even the CPSU, though it is called a great mass party, is in fact limited in number by the theory that it is the vanguard of the nation. On the other hand, the so-called social organizations subordinate to the party are limited only by the size of the population. Ideally, according to the doctrine of social organizations, every individual in the population is involved in a social organization of one type or another, including soviets of various kinds; trade unions; cooperatives, including collective farms; the Young Communist League; the Young Pioneers; and various unions of representatives of the liberal professions, such as the Writers' Union, the Composers' Union, the Artists' Union, the colleges of advocates, cultural, scientific and sports societies and unions created for international propaganda objectives (the Union of War Veterans, the Union of Soviet Women, the Union of Youth Organizations, etc.). Thus, in practice, not only the entire adult population of the country but also a large proportion of the younger generation is under the surveillance of one or other of the organizations supervised by the party. The main reasons for creating such organizations are: (1) to assure effective supervision and leadership of people of all social classes; (2) to involve these classes in various forms of "communist education" appropriate to the particular intellectual level, profession and age; and (3) to make each organization an instrument of communist power in its own particular sphere.

How is this policy put into practice among the members of the working class? The place of the trade unions in bolshevist doctrine provides a classic example of how bolshevism refuses to permit a rival power to exist in its own sphere of action, whether in the worker movement before the seizure of power or in the Soviet "proletarian" state after the seizure of power. Trade unions were first formed in Russia during the

239

period 1905–7. At that time a fierce struggle developed between Bolsheviks and Mensheviks over the questions of the social character of the
trade unions and their position in the struggle against the autocracy.
The Mensheviks' views were in essence similar to those held by the
Socialist parties of Western Europe; they saw the function of the trade
unions to be defending the social, legal and economic interests of the
workers. The Bolsheviks, on the other hand, under their doctrine of the
nature of political power, held that all working-class organizations, such
as social, cultural or sports organizations, must serve in the party's
struggle to gain political power. A bolshevist resolution submitted to the
party Central Committee in November, 1905, says of the trade unions:

> We acknowledge the vast importance of the trade unions for the
> practical education of the working class in the struggle with capi-
> talism [and] for the cause of the political liberation of the people.
> . . . We resolve that party organizations make systematic use of
> existing and new trade unions with a view to spreading socialist
> agitation and propaganda. The overt presence of the Social Demo-
> crats in the unions and conspiratorial organizational work must
> supplement each other . . . in order to exert the dominant influence
> in each nation.[1]

A resolution submitted by the Bolsheviks to the "unifying" Fourth
Party Congress, in 1906, declared:

> The party must strive by all means to educate workers who
> participate in the trade unions in the spirit of the wide under-
> standing of the class struggle and of the socialist tasks of the prole-
> tariat, in order by its activities to conquer the real leading role in
> such unions.[2]

The Fifth Party Congress, at which the Bolsheviks had an overwhelming
majority, adopted a resolution by Lenin that demanded "acceptance by
the trade unions of the party's ideological leadership."[3] The Bolsheviks,
it was believed, had to be everywhere, not only in the trade unions, but
also in all of their branch organizations and in even the most innocuous
workers' society. The purpose for which the workers had banded themselves together was of no consequence, but it was highly important to
take possession of the organization from within. A resolution of the
party Central Committee in February, 1908, stated:

> Concerning legal societies, such as the Society for Mutual Aid,
> the Society for Teetotalism, etc., it is essential that there be formed
> in them close-knit groups of Social Democrats to conduct party
> work.

Another resolution, adopted by a bolshevist conference in December,
1908, declared that "legal and illegal trade unions, clubs and the various
workers' educational societies . . . must be the pivot" of party political
work.[4]

The February Revolution in 1917 gave new life to the trade unions, which then had about 1,500,000 members. The Bolsheviks, who regarded the factory committees as the fortresses of a future armed insurrection, made great efforts to secure control over them. The Sixth Congress, in August, 1917, devoted special attention to bolshevist work in the trade unions. The problem of preparations for insurrection involved clarification of the role to be played by the trade unions, and the Congress resolved that

> the trade unions, as fighting organizations of the working class, are vitally concerned in the successful outcome of the revolution and must be in close contact with the political party of the proletariat in order to achieve this end.[5]

In the October, 1917, Revolution the Bolsheviks viewed the trade unions as a legal form of workers' organization for carrying on the illegal work of the Bolsheviks aimed at overthrowing the old regime. They were merely an instrument for, in the first place, educating workers in the spirit of the bolshevist program, and, in the second, for using this organized mass in the struggle to seize political power.

After the Bolsheviks seized power, the trade unions continued to exist, but with somewhat different functions. Whereas formerly they had served as an instrument for achieving the seizure of power, they now served as a means for bolstering that power. Lest the trade unions gain the false impression that they were the proletarian dictator in whose name power was seized, the party officially declared them to be affiliated with and subordinate to the party. This subordination was effected through so-called communist blocs in the trade unions. It was not easily accomplished. The trade unions, while giving full support to the general policy of the Soviet government, when it came to matters concerning the administration of the nationalized industries held the viewpoint expressed by the well-known bolshevist slogan "Factories and plants to the workers!" From this the Soviet trade union leaders (also Communists) drew the conclusion that henceforth the management of factories and plants would pass into the hands of persons directly chosen by the workers. The Russian workers felt so strongly on this matter that in order to ensure their support in the Civil War, the Bolshevik party included in its program of 1919 the following patently un-bolshevist statement concerning the role of the trade unions:

> Being already, in accordance with the laws of the Soviet republic and with established practice, participants in all local and central organs of industrial administration, the trade unions must achieve the actual concentration in their own hands of the entire administration of the entire national economy.[6]

A year later, at the Ninth Party Congress, after their victory in the Civil War, the Bolsheviks explained that the statement dealing with trade unions in their program meant that under a Soviet regime the tasks of the trade unions lie mainly in the sphere of economic and educational organization. They must carry out these tasks, not as a self-sufficient, organizationally isolated force, but as one of the basic *apparatus of the Soviet state,* led by the Communist party[7]

and that

as communist consciousness develops, the trade unions . . . must gradually change into auxiliary organs of the proletarian state.[8]

The trade unions would, accordingly, not control the management of industry and agriculture, but would be controlled by it—under the overall leadership of the party, of course.

This retreat from the party program by Lenin encountered serious organized resistance on the part of a number of leading party members, a resistance that crystallized in the "Workers' Opposition" of Shlyapnikov, Medvedev, Kollontay and others. The main point of their platform was:

The organization and the administration of the national economy belongs to an All-Russia Congress of Producers, united in production trade unions, which choose the central organ that directs the entire national economy of the republic.[9]

This demand, based on the 1919 program, was submitted by the Workers' Opposition at the Tenth Congress, in 1921. Lenin fiercely attacked the Workers' Opposition on the grounds that its demand threatened "subordination of the party to non-party chaos"[10] by a rebirth of the Utopian and anti-party provision in the old program and in tactics of the party under the old slogan "Factories and plants to the workers!" He also regarded the demand as a threat to the communist regime itself. It is therefore quite understandable why Lenin proposed that

the Congress of the Russian Communist party sees in the views of the aforementioned group of persons a prodigious political error and a direct *political threat to the maintenance of power.*[11]

The Congress declared the ideas and demands of the Workers' Opposition to be an "anarchist-syndicalist deviation" and ordered that recognition be given to the need for waging an unswerving and systematic struggle against these ideas and to the fact that the propagation of these ideas was incompatible with membership in the Russian Communist party.[12]

At the end of 1919, and even before the Workers' Opposition episode, the communist group in the presidium of the Central Trade Union Council had issued orders that a hierarchy of party organizations be created in the trade unions, to consist of the existing communist blocs and headed by the communist bloc in the Central Trade Union Council. A decree by this bloc, headed by Tomsky, Lutovinov and others, submitted to the party Central Committee for ratification stated:

> All blocs of all-Russian production associations now in existence or about to be reestablished must be directly subordinate to the communist blocs of the All-Russian Central Trade Union Council.[13]

Lenin also opposed this proposal as a potential cause of disintegration of political power within the party. Not only did the party Central Committee firmly reject the demand, the Tenth Party Congress passed a special resolution subordinating the bloc to the party Central Committee and the blocs of local trade union associations to local party committees.[14]

In December, 1919, Lenin prudently added a new section to the party statutes, "On Party Blocs in Institutions and Organizations Outside the Party," which contained the following two provisions:

> 1. In all non-party congresses, conventions, institutions and organizations (in soviets, executive committees, trade unions, communes, etc.) where there are not less than three party members, party groups are to be formed whose task it is to do everything possible to strengthen the party's influence, to put its policies into effect in all extra-party organizations, and to carry out party control of the work of such institutions and organizations.
>
> 2. The groups are completely subordinate to the party. In all questions where legally binding decisions have been already made by the appropriate party organization, the groups are obliged strictly and undeviatingly to adhere to these decisions. The party committee has the right to admit new members to the group and to expel existing members.[15]

The effect of these provisions is that in a non-party organ nominally selected by popular election, the communist blocs (now known as party groups) are merely functional cells of the party apparatus. The right of the party committee to appoint or dismiss any member of the group clearly reduces to a fiction the rights of the soviets, trade unions and other nominally "non-party organizations." This does not mean that the organizations themselves are fictitious. It means that their true function is to serve as the party's instruments for imposing its policies on the mass of non-members. Thus the trade unions became defenders of the interests of the Soviet state rather than of the Soviet proletariat.

To enable the trade unions to carry out the function assigned them by the party, the state has conceded to them some of its own functions and administrative rights, such as the right to control employment, the right to supervise the operations of labor supply organs, etc. The entire state social insurance budget, which in 1960 amounted to seventy billion rubles, has been handed over to the trade unions,[16] and the trade-union leadership uses these funds to finance its own projects (pensions, grants, health resorts, sanatoriums, children's institutes) as well as to maintain its own gigantic bureaucratic and propaganda apparatus. The trade-union bureaucracy, like the industrial and agricultural bureaucracy, provides many of the most secure positions for the Soviet elite. Large sums are spent on the maintenance of the trade-union *aktiv,* that is, the Soviet worker aristocracy, through whom the trade union and the party leaders maintain contact with the masses. The trade unions have their own rest homes, sanatoriums and resorts, but the widespread impression that almost every Soviet worker has the right to a free annual vacation is mere propaganda. In 1960, 3,800,000 of the 56,000,000 trade-union members—only 6 per cent of the total—spent their vacations at trade-union rest homes and sanatoriums. Recipients of free holidays are chosen, not on medical grounds, but on "merit," that is, on the number of awards they have received, on their production records and on the positions they occupy in the trade-union bureaucracy's hierarchy. On the other hand, "spiritual nourishment," which is subsidized out of the social insurance budget, is available to all members of the trade union. In 1960 trade-union members had at their disposal for the purposes of "communist education" 15,500 clubs; 122,000 reading rooms; 29,000 libraries containing over 167,500,000 books; 20,000 cinemas; and 6,000,000 amateur arts groups.[17]

Although Lenin said that

> from members of trade unions in a proletarian state one should only require understanding of comradely discipline . . . and help with regard to Soviet power

and that

> the trade unions must be the closest and unfailing collaborator with the power of the state . . . which the Communist party controls[18]

he nevertheless greatly valued the role of the trade unions as an intermediary between the party and the working masses. He fully recognized that the trade unions could only successfully fulfill such a task if they protected not only the interests of the employer—the state—but also those of the workers themselves. According to Lenin, this *"contradictory situation"* requires *"special tact,* the ability to approach the masses in a special way."[19] He also believed that if the party were to ignore the trade unions' extremely important roles as intermediary and promoter of party influence among the masses, the result would be:

> Just as the best factory with an excellent engine and first-class machinery will be useless if there is a defect in the transmission system from engine to machine, so too catastrophe will be inevitable for our socialist construction if the transmission system from the Communist party to the masses—the trade unions—is wrongly constructed or does not function properly.[20]

Since Stalin's death this transmission mechanism has become even more important, and the new party program emphasizes this fact. The organization of the trade unions is so constructed as to enable them to fulfill the following tasks with maximum efficiency: (1) their basic political task as an instrument of party policy and an organ of "communist education" (Lenin: "Trade unions are the school of communism"); (2) their basic production task as an auxiliary organ of the state apparatus for maintaining labor discipline, raising productivity and ensuring the fulfillment and overfulfillment of production plans; and (3) serving simultaneously as a reservoir from which to recruit part of the administrative and economic bureaucracy (Lenin: "The trade unions are a school of administration"). Accordingly, the "collective agreements" concluded with the state administration on behalf of the workers give first consideration to defending the interests of the state and of state enterprises, while the workers' interests are of secondary importance.[21]

Soviet trade unions are organized on an industrial rather than on a craft basis. Membership is nominally voluntary, but is virtually obligatory for all paid workers in public enterprises and in state and party institutes (party bureaucrats belong to the Cultural Workers' Union!). Members of the armed forces and students do not belong to unions. Each industry has a trade-union organization in each administrative division of the U.S.S.R. The structural pattern of the trade-union organs is similar to that of the party, as follows: factory or works trade-union committee, *raion* trade-union committee, *oblast* or *krai* trade-union committee, central trade-union committee of a republic, Central Trade-Union Committee of the U.S.S.R. From the region up, the branch trade unions are united under a common leadership in the form of "trade-union councils": regional trade-union council, provincial trade-union council, republic trade-union council, All-Russia Central Trade-Union Council.

The members of trade-union committees and councils are elected at conferences (in *raion,* city, *oblast* and *krai*) and at congresses (in republics and for the U.S.S.R. as a whole) from lists of candidates approved by the corresponding party committee and presented by the party groups. Members and non-members of the party are in almost equal proportions, at lower levels, but the higher the trade-union organ (e.g., the directorate or presidium), the greater the proportion of party members elected, until at the top level (the Presidium of the Central Trade-Union Committee of the U.S.S.R. and the Presidium of the All-Russian Central Trade-Union Council) there are no non-members at all. In trade-union committees and councils the Communists band together into a separate party group, headed by the leader of the local trade-union organization. The party group receives directives concerning trade-union policy from a higher trade-union committee and directives concerning political matters from the party committee at its own level. The departments of the party organs of the party committee direct the work of the party groups and supervise assignments among the group members.

Industrialization has brought about a radical change in the social structure of the population. Whereas in 1913, 82 per cent lived in the country and only 18 per cent in urban areas, according to the 1959 census only 52 per cent of the population are living in the country and 48 per cent in the cities.[22] Corresponding changes have taken place in the proportion of rural to urban workers, and in the nature of employment. In 1959, the 99,130,000 persons employed, not counting dependents, comprised 47.5 per cent of the total population of 208,827,000. Of these, 62,961,000 (30.2 per cent of the working population) were urban laborers and office workers; 32,280,000 (15.5 per cent of the working population) were collective farm workers; 3,623,000 (1.7 per cent of the working population) were in the army; and 266,000 (0.1 per cent of the working population) were independent peasants or rural craft workers.[23] Of the total, 20,459,000 (20.7 per cent of the working population) were engaged in intellectual work.[24] The general cultural level of the population has also risen. According to the 1897 census, 26.3 per cent of the population between nine and forty-four years of age were literate; by 1926, 56.6 per cent were literate; and by 1959, 98.2 per cent.[25] The number with secondary or higher education has also risen. In 1959, 13,400,000 persons had received a partial higher education or had complete specialist secondary education, and 45,300,000 had completed a secondary or seven-year school course.[26]

These changes were reflected in the social and professional composition and educational level of the worker class. According to Soviet data, before the Revolution no member of the working class had completed a secondary education; in 1926 only 1.5 per cent had; and by 1939 the percentage had risen to 4.3 per cent. In 1959, 39 per cent of the urban workers and 21 per cent of the collective farm workers had received at least a secondary and in many cases a higher education.[27] (Whereas in 1926 there were 168,000 students in higher schools and 181,000 students in technical schools, in 1959 2,200,000 students were attending higher schools and 1,868,000 were attending technical schools).[28] There was a colossal increase in the number of persons engaged in intellectual work, rising from 2,500,00 intellectuals (specialists and civil servants) in 1926 to more than 20,000,000 in 1959.

These figures provide a basis for estimating the production and professional composition of the Soviet trade unions. Since all workers and officials are, as a rule, trade-union members, of the 62,000,000 state employees, 42,000,000 are industrial workers (in production trade unions) and 20,000,000 are non-manual workers (in institutional trade unions).

The breakdown of intellectual workers is as follows (in thousands):

engineering and technical workers	4,205.9
agronomists, zoologists, veterinary workers and forestry workers	477.2
medical workers (from doctors to nurses)	1,702.5
teachers and scientific workers	2,835.8
workers in literature and the printing industry	104.1
cultural and enlightenment workers (i.e., professional propagandists)	462.3
workers in the arts	190.6
legal personnel	78.7
communications workers	476.4
workers in trade, the manufacturing industries and supply (excluding leaders)	1,933.4
planning, accounting and control commission workers	3,501.9
office workers	535.9
workers in communal enterprises and public services	277.1
agents and filing clerks	146.0

To these must be added the 2,946,600 members of the leading party and state bureaucracy.[29]

The October Revolution was made possible, not only through the organizational skill of the Bolsheviks, but also by the triumph of demagogy over reason. A typical example of bolshevist demagogy was the slogan advocating equal wages for the higher bureaucracy and the workers. In the "April Theses" Lenin wrote:

> The payment of all officials when selected or when changed shall not at any time be higher than the average wage of a good worker.[30]

He repeated this principle in his book *Revolution and the State,* where he called for "aligning the payment of all salaried persons in the state with the level of the worker."[31] After the Bolsheviks' seizure of power this plan was revealed to be utter fantasy. It cannot, of course, be asserted that the Bolsheviks made no effort to keep their promise of "egalitarian communism," especially where the wages of senior communist officials were concerned. In 1918 Lenin censured the managing body of government affairs for raising his own salary. At the Eleventh Party Conference and the Tenth and Eleventh Party Congresses it was stressed that responsible communist workers should not receive salaries higher than those of the rank-and-file members or higher than the average worker's wage. Eventually a "party maximum" for officials' salaries was established. But the system broke down in practice. The introduction of the NEP and the subsequent currency reform, which established a firm exchange rate for the ruble, crushed all manifestations of egalitarian communism. First to fall was the wage structure, where the old capitalist principle of wage differentiation, not only between officials and workers but also between various types of workers, was completely rehabilitated. The All-Russian Central Trade-Union Council worked out a table of wage scales for workers and engineering and technical workers in industry on the following lines:[32]

WAGE SCALE CATEGORIES

	Unskilled Workers				Skilled Workers			
Category	1	2	3	4	5	6	7	8	9
Coefficient	1	1.2	1.5	1.8	2.2	2.5	2.8	3.1	3.5

	Specialists							
	Junior				Senior			
Category	10	11	12	13	14	15	16	17
Coefficient	4.2	4.6	5	5.5	6.2	6.7	7.2	8

The skilled worker accordingly began to receive 3.5 times more, and the engineer 8 times more, than the ordinary worker. As time went on, the disparity increased, bringing with it a process of social differentiation in Soviet society on a new basis. In place of the liquidated ruling classes, a new dominant class began to emerge, proletarian in origin but petty bourgeois in its outlook and way of life. But it was not until 1934, at the Seventeenth Party Congress, that Stalin gave the new ruling class the right to live "in a bourgeois manner," despite Lenin's theory of asceticism; he justified his action by quoting Lenin. At the same time, the party maximum wage was abolished and no limit set on the incomes of the higher party bureaucracy. Manual workers' wages were determined in accordance with the wage scales, wage tables and wage qualification handbooks, while the wages of non-manual workers were to be determined by their position grades and fixed salary scales.

In the U.S.S.R. 75 per cent of the workers are paid on a piecework basis, supplemented by "periodical payments." Engineering and technological workers and officials are paid monthly. The present basic rule of the wage structure is that labor productivity must rise at a greater rate than wages, but in the honeymoon years of the Soviet regime it was held that the raising of real wages of the workers was a condition of and a guarantee for the growth of labor productivity. According to GOSPLAN figures for the period from October, 1922, to January, 1924, the average gross daily output per worker in the fourteen most important nationalized industries increased by 23 per cent, while the average weekly earnings of the worker rose by 90 per cent. This type of correlation between growth of output and growth of wages was then abandoned as incorrect. A decision of the August, 1924, Plenum of the Central Committee stated:

> This swifter growth of wages was hitherto unavoidable and was in general legitimate . . . . However, the long-continued correlation of growth of wages and of productivity threatens the interests

of industry and of the state. The development of industry, the power of the state, the possibility of a prolonged period of growth in wages themselves and their fixation at current levels demands the reverse relationship—a large growth of gross output . . . . The growth of labor productivity must overtake the growth of wages.[33]

When Soviet economists write about labor productivity in the U.S.S.R. and in the Free World, they apply two different criteria. They claim that in the U.S.S.R. increases in labor productivity result from "economy of time, by which a smaller quantity of work acquires the ability to create a greater quantity of material benefits."[34] Under capitalism, on the other hand, an increase in labor productivity results from raising the norm of exploitation of the working class, in accordance with Marx's theory of surplus value. But if Marx's theory is applied to the Soviet economy, it is clear that the Soviet economic system is a state capitalist monopoly ideally suited to the utmost exploitation of the workers. It is ideally suited for this purpose because it is not only a state monopoly of the means of production but also a state monopoly of the labor market, both in industry and in agriculture. Wage norms and workday quotas are not established by the free play of prices or by freely negotiated agreements between the interested parties, they are set by unilateral administrative actions on the part of the state, in spite of such nominal rules as "collective agreements," the collective farm statutes, etc.

In 1951 it was reported that under Stalin's five-year plans the increase in industrial production due to increased labor productivity was 51 per cent in the first five-year plan period, 79 per cent in the second, 69 per cent in the fourth and 68 per cent in the fifth; it was estimated that labor productivity would increase by 80 per cent by 1960.[35]

To what extent have wages actually increased? From 1913 to 1956, according to official figures, average annual labor productivity increased ninefold, but wages increased only 4.8 times, which is in accord with the Soviet rule that the growth of productivity must outstrip that of wages. Although the post-Stalin policy on labor and wages has provided a considerable raise in the workers' living standards, especially for the lower-paid workers, it has remained unchanged on this fundamental question. On March 24, 1962, a special party Central Committee decree dealing with the work of the party organization in the Tashkent *combinat* emphasized that

the Central Committee of the CPSU considers it quite improper that the tempos of wage growth in the combinat in 1961 have overtaken the tempos of labor productivity growth.[36]

While the issuing of such a decree by any government or party in the West would have provoked a storm of protest from the trade unions, in the Soviet Union the trade-union leaders themselves shared in initiating the decree. The Soviet workers did not react by striking, because in the Soviet "workers' " state, strikes are forbidden by law.

CHAPTER XIV

The *Komsomol* as a Party Tool

ACCORDING to the *Komsomol* (Young Communist League) statutes,

> The All-Union Leninist Young Communist League is an independent social organization that unites in its ranks the broad masses of leading Soviet youth. It works under the leadership of the Communist Party of the Soviet Union.[1]

The *Komsomol* accepts as members persons between the ages of fourteen and twenty-eight, on the recommendation of two *Komsomol* members or one party member.[2] The recommendation is only a formality, however, since as a rule new members have to be actively recruited.

The party statutes say of the role of the *Komsomol* in the party apparatus that

> it is an active assistant and reserve of the party. The *Komsomol* assists the party in bringing up young people in the spirit of communism. . . .[3]

The *Komsomol* accordingly has the following tasks: (1) serving as a party reserve from which to recruit new party members, (2) working "as an assistant to the party" in putting party directives into effect and (3) being a school for the "communist upbringing of young people." The *Komsomol* apparatus is designed to carry out these tasks.

The leading *Komsomol* organs bear names similar to those of the party organs, and their organizational structure is also similar to that of the party. Its highest organ is the All-Union Congress of the *Komsomol,* which meets once every four years. It elects a central committee whose plenum elects a bureau to direct the overall work of the *Komsomol,* and a secretariat to conduct day-to-day organizational and executive activity. Members of the central committee plenum and of the other leading *Komsomol* organs are also members of the party, and have been approved in advance by the Secretariat of the party Central Committee. The lower *Komsomol* committees, similarly organized, are the central committees of each republic; *krai* and *oblast* committees; city and *raion* committees; bureau and *Komsomol* committees of the primary organizations.

The party committees at each level appoint and remove the members of these committees, although there are formal elections. The party statutes establish the right of the party to leadership and supervision of the *Komsomol*:

> The *Komsomol* works under the leadership of the CPSU. The work of local *Komsomol* organizations is directed and supervised by the corresponding republic, *krai, oblast, okrug,* city, and *raion* party organizations.[4]

Sections of party organs have direct control over the *Komsomol* apparatus. The first secretary of the *Komsomol* committee at each level is also a member of the party committee at that level.

In order to see how the party apparatus has gradually converted the old revolutionary *Komsomol* into an instrument for extending and strengthening its power over Soviet youth, it is necessary to examine briefly the various stages in the history of the *Komsomol*.

Any revolution is an explosion of youth, with young people in the forefront irrespective of the political plans of its leaders. Such was the revolution of October, 1917. Its military organizers in Petrograd were people under thirty and its foremost political leaders were about thirty; only Lenin was over forty.

The same was true of the Civil War, which followed the Revolution. The old and the new Russia confronted each other, both physically and in their views. The White Army leaders were former tsarist generals, old men of sixty or more, but the Red Army was commanded by former lieutenants, second lieutenants and noncommissioned officers, and in many cases young persons from civilian life. Marshal Tukhachevsky commanded an army when he was twenty-five, and a front (against Denikin and later Pilsudski) when he was twenty-seven. Army Commander First Class Fedko commanded an army and a front when he was twenty-one! The regiments and divisions of the victorious Red Army were commanded by individuals of *Komsomol* age. What was the "military secret" of this victory?

The secret was youth. The temerity of youth, the desire for adventure, the thirst for action and the readiness to sacrifice oneself in the cause of high abstract ideals—such are the attributes of revolutionary youth in general and such were the attributes of the *Komsomol* youth of the period of the Revolution and Civil War. These qualities of youth, skillfully exploited by the efficient bolshevist propaganda machine, wrought what the Bolsheviks themselves subsequently called "revolutionary wonders." During the Civil War years such notices on *Komsomol* buildings as "District committee closed: members have gone to the front" were common. *Komsomol* members left the cities and went to the front in large numbers to fight "the bourgeoisie" and to gain power for the workers, "for the Third International." They went from the villages to fight "the landowners," "for land, for freedom and for a good future." *Komsomol* committees proclaimed the mobilization of their followers from the age of fifteen upward. These were genuine volunteers, because the *Komsomol* mobilized only persons not subject to military service.

The Second *Komsomol* Congress announced its first mobilization as follows:

> For the defense of the republic and to serve the front and rear of the Red Army, members from the age of sixteen upward are to be mobilized.[5]

The famous *Komsomol* writer Ostrovsky, author of *How The Steel Was Tempered,* wrote that "together with the *Komsomol* membership card we received a gun and two hundred rounds."[6] Any who refused to go to the front simply returned their *Komsomol* cards. Few refused, and those who did were subjected to a social boycott and publicly proclaimed to be cowards and deserters from the Revolution. In the areas in the vicinity of the front, all *Komsomol* members joined, and *Komsomol* organizations in the rear sent up to 30 per cent of their members, while many non-members also applied to join. One such application read:

> We are still youngsters, some of us are fifteen, some sixteen and some seventeen, but the flame of struggle against these White parasites has burst out among us and we are prepared to set out at once for the battle.[7]

The old Bolsheviks were delighted at the success of their propaganda among the *Komsomols*. Kirov said:

> And those of us who were then at the front remember what an important, I would say exceptional, part the *Komsomol* then played. It must be said, Comrades, that we Bolsheviks are people who can fight with no thought for our own safety, and we have more than once looked with "envy" at the heroes whom the *Komsomol* gave us at that time.[8]

The Bolshevik party was the only political party in Russia that from the very beginning, in the first Russian Revolution, conducted work among young workers, soldiers and students, in order to take them under its wing, from both a political and an organizational point of view. In the eyes of the Bolsheviks there was no such thing as a neutral nonpolitical youth organization. Lenin wrote at the time:

> Young students and more especially young workers will decide the outcome of this struggle.[9]

A youth organization must have the same aim as the party itself. On the eve of the October Revolution, at the Sixth Party Congress, in August, 1917, the question of youth movements was discussed. Bukharin gave a speech on the role of youth in preparations for an armed bolshevist uprising. The resolution passed after his speech pointed out that, once the "direct struggle for socialism" had begun, the party must devote the "maximum attention" to the creation of bolshevist revolutionary youth leagues.[10]

However, the Bolsheviks did not succeed in creating a centralized communist youth organization until a year later, in October, 1918. Prior to this, various revolutionary youth organizations had existed, some of which were in sympathy with the Mensheviks, the Social Revolutionaries, the anarchists or the "neutrals." The various titles of these organizations illustrate their sympathies: Socialist Union of Worker Youth, Union of Worker Youth—the Third International, Peasant Socialist Youth Union, Union of Peasant Youth—the Third International, Union of Youth, New Student, Awakening, etc. Not one of the youth unions, even those under bolshevist tutelage, wished to be called "communist," despite the fact that from the beginning of 1918 the Bolsheviks had been calling themselves not Socialists but Communists.

The Russian *Komsomol* was founded at the First Congress of Worker and Peasant Youth, which took place in Moscow October 29–November 4, 1918. At the congress 176 delegates from the youth organizations under the leadership of the Bolshevik party were present, while from the non-bolshevist unions only persons who were considered to be sympathetic to the Bolsheviks were invited. In answer to the question "Which party do you belong to or sympathize with?" eighty-eight said that they were Communists, forty-five that they were "non-party members" (which at the time meant anti-Communists), thirty-eight replied that they were "sympathetic" to the Soviet regime, three to the Social Democrats, one was a Social Revolutionary and one an "anarchist-individualist."[11]

The congress failed to agree on a title for the new youth league. Six voted against calling it the Russian Communist Youth League and seventeen abstained. On the other hand, it was unanimously decided that the new league should be independent of the Bolshevik party organization.[12]

Shortly afterward, this decision was annulled by the party Central Committee. In August, 1919, the party Central Committee and the apparatus of the *Komsomol* Central Committee, which it controlled, issued a joint decree stating:

> The Central Committee of the Russian *Komsomol* is directly subordinate to the Central Committee of the Russian Communist party. Local organizations of the league are to work under the supervision of local committees.[13]

It took some time to put the decree into effect. Some members of the *Komsomol* Central Committee vigorously and persistently opposed liquidation of the independent youth organization. Among them were such leading *Komsomol* workers as Dunaevsky, Polifem and Yakovlev. When this group became convinced that it was impossible to save the independence of the *Komsomol*, they tried to organize a new Union of

Councils of Worker Youth, and to set up special youth sections in the trade unions to defend the interests of the "toiling youth of Russia."[14]

The views of Dunaevsky's group were condemned in a decree of the party Central Committee in September, 1920, and the group was accused of anti-party activities and "youth syndicalism." The members of the group were removed from their posts in the *Komsomol* Central Committee, and Dunaevsky, the leader of the group, was expelled from the party. However, this did not put an end to opposition in the Youth League. Just before its Third Congress, in 1920, the League called more insistently than ever for the independence of youth organizations and protested against making the *Komsomol* into a bureaucratic appendage of the party.

Certain nationalist communist opposition movements were also emerging within the League. The most numerous and politically influential was the Ukrainian opposition movement in the *Komsomol*. It was led by the Donbas *Komsomol*, which put forward two demands: that the Ukrainian *Komsomol* be independent of the League and that the *Komsomol* be independent of the party. Just as in the party itself, the fate of each opposition group was determined by the party apparatus. Some members were expelled from the party and from the *Komsomol*, others were dismissed from their work, and others were deported to remote districts.

The victory of the party apparatus over the *Komsomol* killed the feature that had made the *Komsomol* important: its internal dynamism. This caused a loss of faith in communist ideals; as a result many members left the *Komsomol* and former revolutionaries became well-meaning nobodies. Many lost interest in politics. Drunkenness and hooliganism increased, and a feeling of pessimism prevailed until it became "Yeseninism," after the poet Yesinin. The *Komsomol* crisis of the twenties is reflected in the statistics of *Komsomol* growth during those years:[15]

Year	Number of members
1918	22,000
1919	90,000
1920	400,000
1921	400,000
1922	247,000
1923	284,000

As the figures show, after the Civil War ended in triumph for the Communists the membership stopped growing, and a year later, in 1922, about one-third of the members left the movement.

The former party of revolutionaries, having obtained power and annihilated the old ruling classes, now began to turn itself into the new ruling class. The civil liberties granted by the February Revolution were now completely suppressed. The party whose banners had once proclaimed the broadest political freedoms, social equality and an implacable opposition to all forms of tyranny and arbitrary rule had undertaken to rule the country, not on the basis of general, let alone "proletarian," consent, but simply as it saw fit in the sole interests of the Communist party. The sailors of the Baltic fleet, whom Lenin had called the pride of the Revolution and who had actually entrusted him with power, now rose against him during the Kronstadt uprising in 1921. Communists and *Komsomol* members were among the insurgents. The uprising was not directed against a Soviet regime, for its slogan was "For soviets without Communists." The uprising was suppressed with great savagery, and the NEP was introduced. These events had a further depressing effect on the morale of the once revolutionary *Komsomol*.

During the years of discussion within the party, the thinking section of the *Komsomol* invariably took the part of the opposition movements. This first happened during Trotsky's "Left opposition" in 1923–24. Trotsky was the first important figure in the party to divine that the secret of Stalin's organizational plan was to place the apparatus above the party. Trotsky believed that only the younger members of the party could end the dictatorship of the apparatus over the party, hence his slogan: "The young people are the truest barometer of the party." He had great faith in the students. "The young people who are studying," wrote Trotsky,

> are recruited from all strata of Soviet society, and their variety reflects all our plusses and minuses. We would be fools if we were not to listen most attentively to their views . . . and it is a very bad thing that overzealous members of the party apparatus regard them with contempt. They are our test and our replacement, and tomorrow will be theirs.[16]

Trotsky's campaign against the party apparatus achieved considerable favor among the younger generation, especially the students. A party discussion in Moscow in December, 1923, and January, 1924, of seventy-two party cells in the higher education establishments, indicated that thirty-two (2,790 persons) supported the Central Committee and forty (6,594 persons) supported Trotsky.[17] The situation was approximately the same elsewhere and might have proved disastrous for the Central Committee apparatus if the party and the *Komsomol* had known that Lenin's "Political Testament," locked in the Central Committee safe, demanded the immediate dismissal of Stalin as General Secretary of the Central Committee, for "rudeness, disloyalty and capriciousness."

Such were the political factors that brought about increasing ideological dissension, organizational weakening and psychological crises in the ranks of the Young Communist League. Taking advantage of Lenin's absence during a serious illness, the Thirteenth Party Conference condemned Trotsky and the younger members of the party, and in response to the behavior of student members of the party ordered that "all non-proletarian elements be refused admission to the party,"[18] a rule which, in practice, excluded students. Soon after this the persecution of students who had voted for Trotsky began. Many were expelled from their institutions, regardless of services rendered during the Civil War. At the same time, attempts were made to make the *Komsomol* organization appear imposing, revolutionary and international in character. For this purpose, at its Fourth Congress, in 1924, the *Komsomol* added Lenin's name to its title to make it the "All-Russian Leninist Young Communist League." At its Seventh Congress, in March, 1926, the word "Russian" was replaced by "Union," thus giving the League its present title.

The "new opposition" of Kamenev and Zinoviev in 1925 was another opposition movement within the party in which the *Komsomol* participated. The principal center of opposition in both the party and the *Komsomol* was in Leningrad. Having used Zinoviev's group to condemn Trotsky and his young supporters, Stalin now prepared to liquidate this second "enemy," Zinoviev. At the Fourteenth Party Congress Zinoviev read a report opposing Stalin and his apparatus, using the accusations that Trotsky had leveled against Stalin. Zinoviev and Kamenev were supported by the entire Leningrad *Komsomol* organization, which also made its own accusations against the Stalinist apparatus of the party Central Committee and against the *Komsomol* Central Committee. Their accusations spoke of a "degeneration of the *Komsomol*," of the *Komsomol's* surrender of "October positions," of the need to establish "equal rights for party and *Komsomol*." It is interesting that Nikolaev, who was later to murder Politburo member Kirov, was among the few members of the Leningrad *Komsomol* who remained faithful to Stalin.

Again the opposition was quickly crushed. All the members of the Leningrad *Komsomol* committee were dismissed, and at the time of Nikolaev's trial in 1935 they were shot. This marked the end of the *Komsomol* as a revolutionary and *political* organization. The second stage in its history coincided with the rise of Stalin as sole dictator. The *Komsomol* no longer had anything to do with politics, which was now reserved to the party, or, more particularly, to its apparatus. The *Komsomol* was assigned the role of "reserve of the party, assistant to the party," an instrument in the hands of the party apparatus for the spiritual subjugation of Soviet youth. The *Komsomol* was henceforth to concentrate on the utilitarian tasks of acting as executor of party economic decisions and as a school for bringing up young people in communism.

The drama of industrialization, exploits on the labor front, heroic deeds in the development of new regions—these are the activities the party now preaches for the *Komsomol*. The party apparatus cultivates "socialist" toil as a "thing of honor, a thing of glory, a thing of valor and heroism" (Stalin). All this is, of course, done in the name of the construction of socialism. At the same time, the younger generation is called upon to undertake a campaign for science. The slogan Lenin proclaimed at the Third *Komsomol* Congress, "Study, study and study again," is one of the most frequently heard battle cries. The network of technical schools is spreading and the number of students and of grants is increasing. In all new enterprises, such as new construction projects, the development of new regions, the construction of new cities, school teaching, "cultural expeditions" into the countryside for the liquidation of illiteracy among the peasants and "shock work and competition" to fulfill study or production norms, the *Komsomol* finds opportunities for applying its energies. The Bolsheviks have succeeded in imbuing some young *Komsomol* members with a sense of the drama of the "new construction" and the "heroics of toil." The Stakhanovite movement was not merely a forced system of sweat labor, and it was no accident that it was started in honor of International Youth Day in the youth sector of the Central Irmino mine in the Donbas.

The figures below show the growth of the *Komsomol* during its forty years of existence.

Year	Number of Members
1918	22,000
1919	90,000
1920	400,000
1921	400,000
1922	247,000
1923	284,000
1924	406,000
1925	520,000
1926	890,000
1927	1,055,000
1928	2,000,000
1931	3,000,000
1936	4,000,000
1949	9,300,000
1954	18,825,000
1958	18,000,000
1961	19,000,000
1964	22,000,000

During the early five-year plans the *Komsomol* mobilized its members for the construction of new factories in the Urals and Siberia, for forestry work in the north, for work in the Donbas mines, for developing the far eastern areas. The *Komsomol* built the city of Komsomolsk-on-Amur and the subway in Moscow. Even where the Stalinist regime was most hated—in the countryside—the *Komsomol* produced its heroes (Maria Demchenko, Pasha Angelina and Konstantin Borin). The "campaign for science" was also successful: during the first and second five-year plans the *Komsomol* membership had 118,000 engineers and

technical workers, 69,000 agricultural specialists, 800 doctors and
91,000 teachers.[19]   In 1958 there were 500,000 engineers and technicians in the *Komsomol*. Of the *Komsomol* apparatus *aktiv*, 97 per
cent had received secondary or higher education.[20]

During Stalin's struggle against the opposition and in the early five-
year plans, N. Chaplin, A. Milchakov and A. Kosarev successively held
the post of general secretary of the *Komsomol*. Together with their assistants they turned the *Komsomol* into a willing agent of the party apparatus and a "school for reservists" from which the party recruited its
most faithful new functionaries, persons who were willing to act in
unquestioning obedience to its will.

Kosarev and his *Komsomol* Central Committee greatly assisted Stalin
in this respect. The party laid on the shoulders of the young people
the burden of all new enterprises, all the "great construction projects
of socialism," the Stakhanovite movement, the "culture" campaign and
the campaign for collectivization. In the years 1929–30 *Komsomol*
members established five thousand collective farms, and 93 per cent
of the rural *Komsomol* members lived on collective farms.[21] Kosarev
and his friends sincerely and fanatically helped Stalin to involve the
Komsomol in the "building of socialism." Stalin valued Kosarev's work,
and at the Seventeenth Party Congress, in 1934, Kosarev was not only
elected a member of the party Central Committee but was also made
a member of the Orgburo.

But Stalin was difficult to please. In November, 1938, a special
plenum of the Central Committee of the Young Communist League was
convened. Stalin conducted it personally. During the session its entire
Secretariat and Bureau, including Kosarev, were arrested as enemies
of the people. An official source reports that under Stalin's leadership
the Plenum "drove out the traitors and renegades who had infiltrated
into the *Komsomol*."[22] They were not only driven out, they were im-
prisoned in the basement of the NKVD as "spies, wreckers and terrorists." The "Kosarev group case" included the following secretaries of
the Central Committee of the Young Communist League: Lukyanov,
Gorshenin, Feinberg, Vershkov, Vasilieva and others. The former
Komsomol general secretaries Chaplin and Milchakov and the leaders
of the Communist Youth International, Shatskin, Chemodanov, Lominadze and others, were also arrested. At the Twentieth Party Congress
Khrushchev revealed that Kosarev and his colleagues had been shot
after prolonged physical torture.[23]

At the Thirteenth Congress of the Young Communist League, Shelepin officially rehabilitated Kosarev and his group:

> When speaking about education, it is impossible to forget the
> damage done by the cult of personality . . . . A heavy loss was
> inflicted on the *Komsomol* when the so-called Kosarev case was
> fabricated. It has now been established that it was completely
> without foundation in fact.[24]

The *Komsomol* purge was not confined to the central organization. In all the constituent and autonomous republics, *oblasts* and *krais,* all the leading *Komsomol* members were arrested. A typical charge was "the preparation of terrorist acts against the party leaders and the government," based on the accusation that the former *Komsomol* worker Nikolaev had murdered Kirov. Among the thousands of *Komsomol* leaders arrested there were, of course, no Nikolaevs, but Stalin no doubt regarded every *Komsomol* activist as a potential terrorist.

The complete annihilation of the *Komsomol's* leadership at both local and national levels marked the end of the second phase in the history of the movement. The collapse of the *Komsomol* apparatus and its replacement by completely new and inexperienced but even more loyal young people was accompanied by a profound psychological crisis among the rank-and-file members, particularly students.

The first months of World War II showed how greatly Stalin's system was hated by the younger generation. The Red Army, almost 70 per cent of which consisted of *Komsomol* members and Communists, was well armed (the German General Guderian stated that the Soviet tanks were larger and better than his own), but its leaders had been removed by Stalin's purges and it had no will to fight in defense of Stalin's power. Millions of Red Army men began to abandon their weapons, to cross over to the enemy or to retreat deep into the country without offering any serious resistance. In three or four months the German Army had reached the outskirts of Moscow, and in 1942 they occupied the Northern Caucasus and reached the Volga. It was Hitler's shortsighted policy of murder and starvation in the occupied territories rather than Stalin's wisdom that provoked the Russian people to turn so savagely on the German forces. Once again the main burden and the main losses were borne by the younger generation. Soviet propaganda made extremely skillful use of the gross political blunders the Germans made in their conduct of the war. Ilya Ehrenburg wrote that "in Germany only the dogs and unborn children are innocent." Soviet propaganda laid special emphasis on personal successes of Soviet terrorists and partisans in the enemy rear and of Soviet snipers at the front:

> Sniper Smolyakov in his short life fired 126 bullets and killed 125 Fascists, *Komsomol* member Ludmilla Pavlyuchenko annihilated 309 Hitlerites, sniper *Komsomol* member Nina Onilova with her "Maximilian" annihilated more than 2,000 enemy soldiers.[25]

Stalin's propaganda achieved its aim, and Soviet youth proved that it could fight if it was obliged to do so by a foreign "liberator."

As in the Civil War, *Komsomol* members were sent to the most dangerous sectors of the front. But the NKVD also used the *Komsomol* to organize terrorist, diversionist, wrecking, spying and partisan groups in the German rear.

> Young people formed 60 per cent of the partisan detachments. During the first two years of the Fatherland War alone, partisans

killed 300,000 of Hitler's troops, blew up or burned 895 stores, destroyed 3,263 road and railway bridges. . . . By September, 1943, more than 1,300 *Komsomol* diversionist groups were operating against enemy lines of communications.[26]

The NKVD and the Soviet government assigned such groups to perform acts of provocation. A diversionist group in the Nikolaev region "distributed leaflets and *disrupted agricultural work,*" and another member of the "Young Guard" (described by the writer Fadeyev in the novel with that title) in Krasnodon saw to it that the "members of the Young Guard *burned grain, drove off cattle* and set fire to the labor exchange."[27] The *Komsomol's* exploits, both purely military in defense of the Fatherland and purely criminal against their own people, were highly valued by the government. More than 3,500,000 *Komsomol* members were awarded orders or medals. Of eleven thousand "Heroes of the Soviet Union," seven thousand were former *Komsomol* members. Of the *Komsomol* members who worked in the German rear, ninety-nine received the title "Hero of the Soviet Union," and fifty thousand were awarded orders or medals.[28] In 1945 the *Komsomol* as a whole was awarded the Order of Lenin for the third time for its services during the war.

The victory of the U.S.S.R. over Germany was a victory of the Stalinist system over the peoples of the U.S.S.R. and of Eastern Europe. Very soon after the victory Stalin began preparations for another great purge, involving a campaign against "cosmopolitans" and "cringers," the disgrace of prominent Soviet army leaders, the "Leningrad Case," the "Kremlin doctors' case" and purges in the people's democracies.

The period after Stalin's death was one of great expectations and hopes. For the first time in twenty years, young people, especially student members of the *Komsomol,* showed a noticeable interest in power politics. After the denunciation of Stalin at the Twentieth Party Congress, this interest in politics began to assume active forms. Young people in the *Komsomol* regarded the denunciation of Stalin as the beginning of a new era in the country's history, the beginning of the liberalization in political and intellectual life. *Komsomol* writers at once produced the first critical, "seditious" works — Dudintsev's *Not by Bread Alone,* Evtushenko's *Winter Station,* Granin's *Special Opinion,* etc. Young writers and critics in books and in literary criticism began to demand greater creative freedom, and some even openly repudiated the notorious "socialist realism" as the sole creative method in Soviet literature. For the first time in thirty or thirty-six years people began, without the sanction of the party apparatus, to speak the plain truth to each other and to call a spade a spade.

The intellectual ferment among writers after Stalin's death was temporarily halted by the eclipse of the editorial staff of the periodical *Novy Mir* ("New World") and the public condemnation of many writers, but it was renewed after the Twentieth Party Congress. In many publications communist writers indulged in partly covert, partly overt criticism directed less at Stalin's personality than at the Stalinist regime. In the main philosophical journal, *Questions of Philosophy,* the critics B. Nazarov and O. Gridnev advanced the slogan "A little less leadership and a little more action."[29] Their central theme was that literature cannot exist without creative freedom. They based their argument on the assertion that

> the higher man's cultural level is, the stronger in him is the aspiration to appraise everything for himself, and the more vigorously he will defend his right to judge everything for himself.[30]

But immediately afterward, during the insurrection in Hungary in which writers played so large a part, the party press began a new campaign against possible "heretics" among Soviet writers.

For the first time in the history of the Stalin regime there took place a political activization of the student population, going far beyond the legal framework of ordinary Soviet "criticism and self-criticism." It was an utterly new phenomenon, quite new to the Soviet scene but common in prerevolutionary Russia, when the words "student" and "revolutionary" were almost synonymous. The newspaper *Komsomol Pravda* declared:

> There is now no ground to complain about the lack of discussion among young people, especially among *students.* Many discussions are being held on the most varied topics. . . . However, one cannot do other than take exception to some of the discussions that have been held *lately* in a number of our institutes of higher education, some of which have been of an extremely frank and even hypercritical nature. . . . At such discussions it has been possible to hear *demagogic* utterances, which try *directly to belittle* the indisputable achievements of our socialist culture. Often—and in our view this is the worst thing about them—such utterances are couched in resounding *ultrarevolutionary* phraseology calculated to astound the hearer by its "boldness" and to provoke applause.[31]

Similar and sometimes even more critical articles have appeared in newspapers in the Baltic states, Leningrad, the Ukraine, etc.

In the end, the periodical *Kommunist* devoted a special editorial to Soviet students, emphasizing (1) the need to strengthen the struggle with bourgeois and petty bourgeois ideology, "which is penetrating into our country via the radio, the press, etc."; (2) "the need to hold discussions with the entire body of students to *reveal* that the incorrect speeches that have been made have no foundation in fact"; (3) "the impossibility of taking a liberal attitude to those who do not try to understand obscure questions but *deliberately* introduce confusion and disorganization"; and (4) the need to combat the liberal attitude toward those in higher educational institutes who "forget that collective farmers and workers are paying for their training. . . . Party organizations must try to ensure that a *firm hand* makes itself felt in every academic institution."[32]

According to Shelepin, the Kremlin considered that its basic task in youth work was to educate young people to strive "for the romance of revolution, for heroic deeds."[33] It was necessary to restore in youth a faith in communism and to spur it on to new exertions and exploits:

> All the many and varied means of ideological influence must be directed to educating the young builders of communist society.[34]

These means, it may be said, are considerable. In the U.S.S.R. 133 *Komsomol* and 20 Pioneer newspapers are published, as well as 44 periodicals for young people. In 1958 a single issue of such publications totalled about 14,000,000 copies. They are published in 26 different languages of the Soviet Union. The "Young Guard" *Komsomol* publishing house issues hundreds of books, propaganda, political tracts and literature, numbering in all over 20,000,000 copies a year.[35] The *Komsomol* central newspaper *Komsomol Pravda* publishes 3,000,000 copies. (In prerevolutionary Russia the total daily output of all newspapers was 3,500,000 copies.) Besides this, propaganda is spread among young people via the 58,000 cinemas, the 31,000,000 radios and loudspeakers, the 400,000 libraries and the rapidly expanding network of television stations.[36]

The vast combined propaganda machinery endlessly—day in and day out, year after year—presses upon youth a single idea: that it is necessary to make sacrifices in the name of socialism in the U.S.S.R. today and in the name of world communism tomorrow. Self-sacrifice, obedience and action are the three qualities the party apparatus seeks to foster in young people, and for this purpose the party has worked out to the last detail a special science called "communist upbringing." Everything that appeals to young people everywhere—sports, travel, games, music, painting, dancing and even love—is exploited. The party bureaucracy as the ruling class teaches its children, who are to succeed it, what has hitherto been termed the prejudices of "bourgeois-aristocratic culture." Shelepin has declared that the central and local committees of the Young Communist League must

> more actively imbue young people with good taste, teach them properly to assess what is beautiful and what is ugly, to pay attention to externals, to deportment and manners. . . . We must devise a good marriage ceremony . . . perhaps it would be worthwhile to wear wedding rings. . . .[37]

Nevertheless, young people in the U.S.S.R. have lived, and still live, a double life: one life in the *Komsomol*—obedient, dutiful, watchful and communist—and another life at home, where no human activity is barred, not even rock and roll or the twist. Lenin was right when he said:

> "According to Marx the most impregnable fortress is the human skull."[38]

CHAPTER XV

The Party's Management
Of the National Economy

THE PARTY directs and controls the economy of the U.S.S.R. through the following channels: (1) special state supervisory organs—GOS-PLAN (State Planning Commission), the Committee for Peoples Control, GOSBANK (State Bank), the Ministry of Finance and various committees of the Council of Ministers of the U.S.S.R.; (2) the primary party organizations; and (3) the economic departments of the party committee at each level. The methods differ in the two main branches of the economy, industry and agriculture. They also depend on the structure of the respective organs of economic management, their status and their permanent staffs.

Industry

In the U.S.S.R. all branches of industry are state owned, but they vary in importance and status depending on whether they are all-Union, republic, or local.

Industry was not immediately nationalized after the Revolution. Three weeks after the Bolsheviks came to power they announced, on November 27, 1917, the introduction of "worker control" of production. The "workers' controllers" were political commissars appointed by the party to supervise the owners of industrial enterprises. Their directives and decisions had the force of "revolutionary law" and were binding on the owners as well as on the workers. On December 14, 1917, the Supreme Soviet of National Economy (VSNKH), consisting of representatives of the people's commissariats and of the All-Russian Council for Worker Control, was created. It was the first communist organ for the nationwide economic direction of all industry, finance, trade and even agriculture. When on January 30, 1918, a government decree nationalized large enterprises, the Supreme Soviet of National Economy became the organ for operational as well as general management of nationalized enterprises, through a system of "principal directorates" and trusts. The Fourteenth Party Congress, in 1925, announced the industrialization of the country, on a course giving priority to the development of heavy and military industry over light industry and food. This doctrine still holds forth today. In 1932 the Supreme Soviet of National Economy was divided into three people's commissariats, for heavy industry, light

industry and forestry. The further development of existing industry, the
appearance of new branches of industry, the continual centralization of
administration and Stalin's mania for breaking down the operational
management of the economy into small units led to a situation in which,
by 1947, fifty of the fifty-nine ministries of the U.S.S.R. were concerned
with economic affairs, as shown in Table 28.[1]

TABLE 28
GROWTH IN NUMBER OF MINISTRIES

MINISTRIES	1917	1918	1924	1936	1947
Ministries of the U.S.S.R.					
Administrative and political			4	5	6
Economic			6	12	50
Social and cultural				1	3
Total			10	18	59
Ministries of constituent republics					
Administrative and political	6	6	3	2	5
Economic	7	6	5	8	18
Social and cultural	1	6	3	4	5
Total	14	18	11	14	28

Stalin consistently followed a policy of absolutist centralization, not
only in the spheres of administration and politics, but also in the management of the national economy. He achieved coordination by centralized planning through GOSPLAN. After Stalin's death, the party
Central Committee restored order by reducing the number of ministries
to twenty-five, including sixteen economic ministries, and in 1957 it
reorganized industrial administration by abolishing the economic ministries and creating councils of national economy (*sovnarkhozy*) in each
economic administrative region. This decentralization of industrial
administration was accompanied by decentralization of a number of
other administrative and political ministries. Although it was advertised
as an expansion of the rights of the constituent republics, in reality it
increased the range of the responsibilities and the supervisory rights of
the party central committees of the constituent republics. After the
Supreme Soviet ratified the reorganization on May 10, 1957, industry
and construction were to be administered on a regional basis. The
boundaries of the regions were defined by the supreme soviets of the
constituent republics in accordance with decisions of the party central
committees of the republics, and the council of ministers of the constituent republic concerned created a council of national economy for each
region. In January, 1959, sixty-eight such councils were created in the
R.S.F.S.R., including one in each autonomous republic, eleven in the
Ukraine, six in Uzbekistan, nine in Kazakhstan and one in each of the
remaining constituent republics. They took over all the enterprises of
the former all-Union and constituent republic economic ministries, as
well as some local industrial enterprises.

It soon became clear that the economic system of the U.S.S.R. was so highly integrated and the regions so dependent on each other for raw materials and technical cooperation that efficiency demanded a centralized administrative system. Under pressure from the local organs of power, the economic councils began to allocate national resources to satisfy "local objectives," in a manifestation of what was called *mestnichestvo* (localism). As a result, the party Central Committee considerably restricted the decentralization of industry. A republic council of national economy was created in each constituent republic to provide a single economic administration superior to the local councils, and the smaller economic regions were consolidated, nineteen regions, each in charge of several councils, being created in the U.S.S.R. These economic regions disregard the administrative boundaries of the constituent republics; the four Central Asian republics—Uzbekistan, Turkmenistan, Tadzhikistan and Kirghizia—constitute a single economic region, as do the three Caucasian constituent republics of Azerbaidzhan, Armenia and Georgia.

The party apparatus has allocated leadership and political supervision of the economy in the following manner. It has retained political leadership for itself, via the hierarchical network of economic sections of party committees at all levels, from the U.S.S.R. Central Committee to the district committee. Economic sections of the Central Committee select personnel, issue directives and direct the day-to-day political work of the U.S.S.R. GOSPLAN, State Economic Council and state economic committees of the Council of Ministers and of "coordination and planning councils" of the newly enlarged economic regions. In the constituent republics the economic sections of the party central committees act in a similar capacity, giving political guidance to the local organizations of the GOSPLAN and the councils of national economy of the administrative regions in their own territories. The *oblast* and *raion* committees have the right to exercise political supervision over enterprises and trusts of Union or republic importance on their territory, and they have the right to intervene in the operation of local industrial enterprises. Therefore, with respect to the Council of National Economy and its subsidiary enterprises, the economic sections of regional committees and district committees are party informants and controllers. They do not, however, have the right to interfere directly in internal administrative and operational matters, as the party Central Committee entrusts the administrative and operational leadership of the local councils of national economy to the corresponding council of the constituent republic. This council was subordinate politically to the economic sections of the party central committee of the constituent republic, administratively to the council of ministers of the constituent republic, and from a planning and operational point of view to U.S.S.R. GOSPLAN for current planning and to the State Economic Council of the U.S.S.R. for long-range planning. There was an organizational weakness at the topmost level because of the lack of an effective single supreme council.

The party apparatus has also established a series of supplementary supervisory and inspection bodies for industry, sometimes parallel, sometimes complementary, to each other. "Ruble control" is vested in the State Bank and the Ministry of Finance, the control of labor and wages in the State Committee for Labor and Wages of the Council of Ministers of the U.S.S.R., the control of social problems and social security in the trade unions, the control by the secret political police in special sections of the economic administration of the Committee for State Security of the U.S.S.R. and the Committee for Peoples Control of the U.S.S.R. and direct political control in the primary party organizations.

This last form of party control is highly important. As noted in Chapter Seven, the party statutes give the primary party organizations the right to control the work of the administrations of (1) production and trading enterprises, (2) design organizations and industrial scientific research institutes and (3) collective and state farms.

The primary party organizations of ministries, state committees and other administrative organs of soviets do not have control rights but are required to inform the appropriate party organizations of the shortcomings of officials and heads of institutions "irrespective of the positions they occupy."[2] On June 26, 1959, the party Central Committee published a special decree providing for the formation in primary party organizations of party "commissions for the control of the administration's activities" in production and trading enterprises. The tasks of these commissions, it stated, included

> control of the prompt and high-quality execution of plans and tasks in deliveries to other economic regions, for the defense industry, to control the quality of products, to ensure the application of new techniques and technological information, to encourage mechanization and automation. Control commissions were set up in trading enterprises to ensure a continued abundance of goods and to see that the rules of soviet trading are observed.[3]

As a result, the following production and trading party commissions were set up:

Production.—(1) commissions to control the execution of state orders and cooperative deliveries to other enterprises and state collective farms; (2) commissions to control the execution of special deliveries and export deliveries; (3) commissions to control the quality of manufactured goods; (4) commissions to control the lowering of costs and improvements in the quality of construction work; (5) commissions to control the rational use of transport resources; and (6) commissions to control the spread of new techniques.

Trade.—(1) commissions to ensure an uninterrupted abundance of goods; (2) commissions to ensure the observance of the rules of soviet trade; (3) commissions to supervise the reduction of expenses in turn-over and manufacture.

If local manufacturing conditions require, the local party committee can create other commissions as well. The commissions work under the party committees, party bureaus and secretaries of primary party organizations. After investigation of an organization, a party control commission reports the results to the appropriate party bureau or party committee that created the commission, to the party meeting and to the industrial or agricultural authorities. If the latter fail to take action to eliminate deficiencies discovered by the commission, the party committee (or party meeting) has the right to prosecute the person responsible. If this does not have the desired effect, the party committee (or party bureau)

> applies for assistance to *raion,* city, *oblast* or republic party and soviet organizations, to the councils of national economy of the economic administrative region.[4]

This complex network of commissions places a director under the strict supervision of the party organization. It is quite natural that he will try to escape their eye, either by exploiting his own position of authority or by simply ignoring the commissions. Foreseeing such a possibility, the party Central Committee has noted:

> The central committees of the Communist parties of constituent republics, *krai* committees, *oblast* committees, city committees and *raion* committees must help primary party organizations to control the work of enterprises . . . . Leaders of economic councils, enterprises and other soviet and economic organizations must speedily examine the statements of primary party organizations and commissions without delay.[5]

Moreover, the party Central Committee has given primary party organizations the right to refer to it directly, over the heads of local party authorities, if their control rights are ignored:

> If the indicated leading organs do not act on information supplied by a primary party organization, the latter can inform the Central Committee of the CPSU and the Council of Ministers of the U.S.S.R. about this.[6]

Members of party control commissions are elected for one year, as are members of the party committee (or party bureau), at party general meetings, and may be reelected at ordinary general party meetings. In military enterprises and in "special enterprises" (those of a highly secret character), the party commissions consist only of Communists working in that sector and authorized by the state security organization to undertake secret work.[7]

The multiple control of the Soviet planned economy system has one plus and many minuses. The plus consists of the fact that the apparatus is controlled from top to bottom by the country's economic administration through the various control organs, each for its own branch or sphere. The system enables the party apparatus to obtain a complete picture of the general situation, so that it can effectively direct the economic administration and the actual manufacturing processes.

Of the many minuses perhaps the most important is the extensive proliferation of the economic bureaucracy and especially of the control bureaucracy. Such an all-pervading, importunate and detailed control impels the leaders of industry to struggle for self-preservation rather than to promote the best interests of production. They must at all costs fulfill and overfulfill the state plans, even if the quality of output suffers. The same control bodies, and the innumerable regulations they issue, stifle the initiative of the director and undermine his authority as the sole person in charge of a concern. One of the directors of a leading Moscow factory, a deputy to the Supreme Soviet of the U.S.S.R., A. Gromov, complains:

> In present-day industrial plants the need not infrequently occurs for an immediate alteration to be made in a manufacturing process [or] for staff, particularly engineers, to be transferred from one section to another. The present system of staff registration by the finance organs ties the director hand and foot. We are unable to transfer even one person from one section to another, even if such a transfer is urgently necessary.[8]

Fear of being called to account by control authorities obliges the director to obey regulations even if they hinder the progress of work.

The bureaucratic system itself crushes and hampers initiative. An example of this, cited in *Pravda* on May 10, 1954, describing the organization of the Ministry of Construction, quite vividly characterizes the gigantic bureaucratic system of the entire Soviet economy, despite the partial decentralization that has taken place. The Ministry had 514 administrations, sections and sectors, and in the thirteen months ending in January, 1954, it had received or dispatched 1,500,000 documents, that is, 5,000 documents daily. At the same time, the Ministry had sent daily to its enterprises up to 2,350 circulars and letters containing instructions.[9] The party leadership is complete and efficient insofar as political and bureaucratic control over people in industry is concerned, but this does not mean that the Soviet economic system functions efficiently.

The system of councils of national economy did not improve this situation. Thus less than a year after the deposition of Khrushchev, the Central Committee of the CPSU in plenary session (September, 1965) and the Supreme Soviet of the U.S.S.R. (October, 1965) revised all the reforms Khrushchev had instituted concerning the decentralization of industrial administration and decided to return to centralized management as it had existed under Stalin, on the basis of branches of industry. Twenty-two all-Union ministries, twenty-five republic ministries and fourteen functional and branch state committees to the Council of Ministers of the U.S.S.R. were formed. Of these, all of the all-Union ministries and twenty of the republic ministries are industrial. Five republic ministries and ten state committees are political-administrative or social-cultural departments. In all, sixty-one ministries and state committees make up the Council of Ministers (in 1947 there were fifty-nine). To this must be added about ten deputy chairmen of the Council of Ministers; two first deputy chairmen and fourteen prime ministers of the Councils of Ministers of Union republics included in the composition of the Council of Ministers of the U.S.S.R. because of their positions; and the chairman of the Council of Ministers of the U.S.S.R.

Thus the Soviet government consists of eighty-eight cabinet members. Since such an unwieldy cabinet is impractical for regular and rapid operational work, a smaller "inner cabinet," called the Presidium of the Council of Ministers of the U.S.S.R. (interestingly enough, such a cabinet is not provided for in the Soviet Constitution), was formed. This smaller cabinet includes thirteen persons (the chairman himself, his two first deputies and ten ordinary deputies).

Before analyzing the substance of the new reforms, it is necessary to consider briefly the dogmas prevailing up to now in Soviet economics. These dogmas were derived from Marxist-Leninist economic theory. The official Soviet "political economy of socialism" states that none of the capitalistic economic categories is applicable to the Soviet economy. However, even in Stalin's time some Soviet economists began to speak of the existence of objective laws of development in the Soviet economy analogous to the laws of the capitalist economy.

The first economic discussion on this topic, organized by the Central Committee of the CPSU, took place during Stalin's time, in November, 1951, in connection with the preparation of a new textbook on the "political economy of socialism." On the eve of the Nineteenth Party Congress (September, 1952), Stalin himself joined the discussion by publishing his famous *Economic Problems of Socialism in the U.S.S.R.* Some of the Soviet economists at the meeting proposed the fundamental principles of "stimulation" that underlie the present Soviet economic reforms. Stalin said that some Soviet economists mechanically transferred to the Soviet economy concepts taken out of Marx's *Capital*. Stalin wrote:

> Marx analyzed capitalism in order to explain the source of capitalist exploitation, surplus value. . . . It is therefore understandable that in this Marx used concepts fully corresponding to capitalistic relationships. But it is more than strange to use these concepts now.[10]

Stalin decisively rejected the concept of profit for the Soviet economy, saying, "The goal of capitalist production is the extraction of profits . . . the goal of socialist production is not profit. . . ."[11]

Stalin did not need just any profitable economy, but an economy that even if unprofitable would be under the absolute control of the party. There was no place in Stalin's policy for the slightest manifestation of spontaneity, that is, objective freedom. According to Stalin, it was not the spontaneous force of economic laws, even economic laws of socialism, but the conscious will of the dictatorship that directed the Soviet economy. Stalin was the voluntaristic teacher of the voluntarist Khrushchev. Stalin even denied the significance of the law of value as a regulator of Soviet production; according to him, the price of a Soviet commodity was not determined by its cost of production plus a certain profit margin, but by the arbitrary decision of GOSPLAN! Stalin maintained a course aimed, in accordance with Marxist-Leninist dogmas, at the complete elimination of the commodity economy and the establishment of so-called direct product exchange between city and country. He wrote: "Commercial relationships are incompatible with the prospective transition from socialism to communism."[12]

In these matters there were no differences in principle between Stalin and Khrushchev. In fact, it was Stalin who restrained Khrushchev from a premature transformation of the collective farm villages into *agrogorods,* i.e., cities in the country. And it was Khrushchev who cut down even those private plots Stalin had permitted the collective farmers to have. It was Khrushchev who issued a series of laws against "parasites." Khrushchev strove for the same ends in economic policy that Stalin had: gradual elimination of commercial relations based on cash payments in the country, accelerated liquidation of the *kolkhoz* market by a reduction or seizure of the private plots of the collective farmers and restriction of private livestock raising. The same goals were served by the Khrushchevian laws prohibiting workers on state farms and city workers and employees to have milk cows or pigs in their private possession. Therefore, Khrushchev's reforms in industry and agriculture involved the administrative methods but not the social principles of the system. The difficulties in the Soviet economy, however, are not in the sphere of management, but in the very nature of the economic system itself. They are not temporary difficulties arising from external circumstances, as Kosygin indicated at the Plenum of the Central Committee in September, 1965. They are specific, organic defects inherent in the Soviet economic system, which is based on compulsion.

This system, although very successful with the military industry, could not be effective in the development of the economy as a whole because Stalin's dogma of the primacy and priority of the development of heavy industry over light had legalized a permanent disproportion within industry and between industry and agriculture. But since under Stalin there was compulsory labor as well as a compulsory system of management, all the leading elements were in some sort of contact with each other. When Stalin's heir decided to do away with one leading element of Stalin's "socialism"—compulsory labor, not only the "mobile concentration camps" (which were shifted from one corner of the country to another for "urgent projects"), but also the "voluntary-compulsory" labor at enterprises and on collective farms (Stalin's "labor laws" of 1940, which prohibited workers from leaving an enterprise, transferring from one enterprise to another or being late for work under penalty of imprisonment; the law of minimum "work days" *(trudoden)* on collective farms; the law denying internal passports to collective farmers; etc. were repealed)—the whole "socialist system of operating the economy" began to totter; its internal malady began to be manifested on the surface. The Khrushchevian reforms were the first attempt to cure this malady by localizing its external manifestations (decentralizing the ailment) but leaving untouched the Stalinist system of operating the economy.

After eight years it became clear that Khrushchev had only intensified the course of the disease, causing more chaos in his efforts to heal it. The new leaders in the Kremlin found themselves facing a dilemma: should they return to the orthodox Stalinist system of management with forced labor or admit the bankruptcy of that system and take the *first tentative* step on the path to the "capitalization of communism," i.e., the incorporation of capitalistic features in the communist economy?

The Kremlin leaders chose the second way. Formally the impression is created that the old Stalinist form of centralization is being restored. But the Soviet leaders are right in saying that this is not at all a return to the past. Behind the façade of the administrative reforms of management one must see their deep *social-economic significance*. Behind the subjective intentions of the Soviet leaders one must see the objective logic of the paths of further development of the Soviet economy. The Soviet leaders want to preserve the system of socialism, but in such a way that it functions like a capitalist system, that is, profitably. This is the first time that the Soviet leaders have admitted the failings of Stalin's economic policy with regard to the proportional development of all parts of the national economy. Kosygin said at a plenum of the Central Committee:

> For a long time we have not had the proper proportion between the development of agriculture and the development of industry. . . . An incorrect relationship was formed between the development of industry in Group A (heavy industry) and industry in Group B (light industry). For many years now industry in Group B has been lagging in its development . . . the backwardness in agriculture and industry in Group B has caused the known disproportion between production of consumer goods and production of the means of production. This could not help showing up in the rate of growth of the real income of the population on the level of material incentives. The central problem is the elimination of this backwardness. . . .[13]

A short time ago such a statement would have been considered a grave sin against the "party line." Khrushchev's main accusation in the overthrow of Malenkov was that Malenkov had violated the dogma of the "primacy of heavy industry" over light.

Kosygin not only admitted the errors in the dogma, he proposed—and the Plenum of the Central Committee passed—a resolution on the introduction into the Soviet economy of methods that up to now have been considered the "cursed law" of capitalism. The substance of these methods was the *restriction* of the sphere of action of the state plan and the expansion of the sphere of action of the laws of the market. This point is formulated in the resolution of the Plenum of the Central Committee as follows:

> To recognize the necessity to eliminate superfluous regulation of the activities of enterprises, to reduce the number of plan indicators set from above, to furnish enterprises with the necessary means for the development and improvement of production, to improve the utilization of such important economic levers as *profit, price, bonus and credit*.[14]

Formerly it was thought that if an enterprise had fulfilled its task for "total output" then it had also fulfilled its production plan. Now plan fulfillment is to be judged, not by how much is produced, but by how much is *realized* (sold). Kosygin noted:

> Fulfilling the task for realization of output will require the enterprise to pay more attention to quality. . . . If the task for realization of output has as its goal to link the enterprise more closely with the consumer, the indicator for profitability will serve as the best means for the orientation of the enterprise toward raising the effectiveness of production. . . . In this not only the amount and growth of profit is important but the level of profitability, that is, the amount of profit received for each ruble of the production funds (capital investment).[15]

This is exactly the philosophy of Western individual capitalism, transplanted in the soil of Soviet collective state capitalism.

Commenting on Kosygin's remarks, the Deputy Chairman of the State Committee for Labor and Wages, B. Sukharevski, admitted a fact that had previously been hidden from the people: that 50 per cent of Soviet industrial enterprises operate at a loss. He wrote:

> The interests of stimulation demand that part of the income be divided between society [the state] and the enterprise. What kind of income are we talking about? Primarily, net income which in the enterprise is mainly realized in the form of profit. At present only about 5 per cent of profit goes to the funds of the enterprise. Approximately half of all industrial enterprises do not have their own fund.[16]

Even in enterprises that operate profitably, various incentive payments and bonuses from the enterprise fund do not amount to more than 2 per cent a year. Such a situation does not give the personnel of an enterprise an interest in the growth of its profitability. The new system of creating funds out of profits at enterprises and distributing them among the workers of the enterprise (supplemental to the base pay) is supposed to stimulate both quality of output and profitability. The essence of the new system is that the employees of the enterprise in a way participate in the profits of their enterprise. This is also a capitalistic idea. But the amount of profit left to the enterprise depends on the value of the production funds (capital); thus payment for capital, i.e., interest, is introduced. Kosygin even said that in time this "interest" would replace the turnover tax (the indirect tax the population pays for consumer goods). It should be pointed out that to this day the turnover tax serves as the main source for the subsidization of unprofitable enterprises.

The new, previously unheard of tasks assigned Soviet industrial enterprises called for corresponding rights. These rights have been granted. The Central Committee and the Council of Ministers of the U.S.S.R. passed the "Decree Concerning the Socialist Enterprise." Kosygin described the nature and extent of the new rights thus:

> At the present time, four indicators concerning labor are set for the firms—the productivity of labor, the number of employees, the average wage and the wage fund. Of the above listed indicators, it is proposed to set only one—the wage fund.[17]

In the future, said Kosygin, it will be possible to do away with planning the wage fund too. He added:

> The rights of the enterprise to make use of operating capital, depreciation allowances and also income realized from the sale of surplus equipment and other items of value are being expanded. Housing constructed out of the funds of the enterprise will all be distributed among the employees of that enterprise. The rights of the enterprise to utilize the savings achieved in the wage fund during the whole year are being expanded. The enterprise independently, without registering with financial organs, will confirm the structure and size of its personnel complement and also the budget for administrative expenditures. The initiative and independence of the enterprises in solving many other questions is being expanded.[18]

The following indicators will still be planned from above and set for the enterprises: (1) volume of realized output; (2) basic assortment of output; (3) wage fund; (4) total profit and rate of return; and (5) payments into the budget from profits of the enterprise or payments for the production funds (interest) and allocations from the state budget to enterprises.

In addition, the central government organs will plan and confirm the volume of centralized capital investment, the entry into operation of new productive capacity, the goals for the introduction of new technology and the indicators for material-technical supply. The introduction of a "state certificate of quality of production" is planned (this measure is solely designed to raise the competitiveness of Soviet industrial products in developing countries, where up to now they have been losing out to better-quality Western products).

The new reforms, although they constitute a certain amount of progress in stimulating the development of the Soviet economy, market relationships and the labor market, are still inconsistent. The inconsistency is manifest, not only in the preservation of bureaucratic centralized planning, but also in its "perfection" as stressed in the decision of the Plenum of the Central Committee (bureaucratic planning in reality is not a "scientific method" at all but that same notorious "voluntarism" of Stalin that Khrushchev also inherited). The inconsistency reveals itself in the emphasis on and the legalization of the simultaneous expansion of the rights of local enterprises, Union republics, all-Union ministries and the U.S.S.R. GOSPLAN.

Elementary logic indicates that the rights of subordinate organs may be expanded and guaranteed only by narrowing and limiting the rights of higher commanding organs. However, on this question the Soviet leaders think in terms of "dialectic logic." They decree the simultaneous expansion of the rights of both subordinate and commanding organs. The passage concerning this topic in the resolution of the Plenum of the Central Committee states that the new reforms

> combine unified state planning with cost accounting for the enterprises, centralized administration (of industry) by branches with wide republic and local economic initiative, the principle of "one-man management" with a strengthening of the role of the production collectives.[19]

L. Brezhnev, First Secretary of the Central Committee of the CPSU, gave substance to this thesis as follows:

> The problem of properly combining centralism with rights, initiative and responsibilities on the local level is a problem of the first order, and a problem of immense political implications. Under the new system, centralism and democracy in the management of industry will be harmonized very well. In particular, this harmony finds expression not only in the creation of Union-republic ministries and economic combines in a number of branches of industry but also in the broadening of the rights of the Union republics on questions of planning, capital construction, financing, labor, and wages.[20]

As an interpretation of what Brezhnev said, K. Mazurov, First Deputy Chairman of the U.S.S.R. Council of Ministers, declared in the Central Committee's and government's report to a session of the U.S.S.R Supreme Soviet that the governments of the Union republics will decide independently the following questions:

(1) the redistribution, within certain limits, of capital investment among separate industrial construction works in the republics;

(2) the establishment of construction-installation works using non-centralized sources of financing;

(3) the confirmation of title lists for the heaviest industrial construction works;

(4) the confirmation of title lists for the construction of administrative and public buildings, clubs, theaters and halls of culture; and

(5) the confirmation of draft plans drawn up by U.S.S.R. ministries for all enterprises located on the territory of the republics, as well as schemes for the creation of new enterprises of all-Union significance; proposals will be submitted to the U.S.S.R. government.[21]

However, Brezhnev, speaking at a plenum of the Central Committee, pointed out the limits of this "independence" of the Union republics:

> Here before the Plenum one must assert with all firmness that the ministries and the ministers personally must bear full responsibility before the party and the state for the work of the branch of economy which they head. . . . In order to successfully resolve the problems set before them, the ministries must be the supreme authority in their branches.[22]

What sort of role will the party play in these new conditions? Kosygin gave a complete answer to this question in his report:

> From the very essence of the proposed measures it follows that party direction and control of the economy is being increased still more. The responsibility of the Union-republic central committees of the party and of the territory and region party committees for genuine scientific management of industry is growing significantly, free from any influence of either localism or departmentalism. . . . Especially being increased at the present time is the responsibility of the territory and region committees of the party for management of industry. Without substituting for economic organs, and giving up their petty interference in management functions, the party committees *from top to bottom* are being called upon to use their own inherent resources and methods. . . . Along with the broadening of the rights of enterprises and the increase of their independence, the role of party organizations in production is also being enlarged.[23]

To this same end, Brezhnev too voiced an appeal for "steadfastly adhering to the line of strengthening the role of the party."[24]

The aims of Kosygin and Brezhnev were written into a resolution of a Central Committee plenum and were thus transformed into law. The resolution emphasizes that the new reforms

> raise still higher the role of party organizations of the republics, territories, regions, cities, districts, enterprises, ministries and departments in the struggle for securing for the economy a high rate of growth and increase their responsibility for the work of the enterprise and economic organs.[25]

This is indeed true. Every broadening of the rights of local party organs (city, district, region and territory committees) is a broadening of the rights and authority of the central committees of the party in these republics, as is every broadening of the rights of the Union republics. The central party apparatus, as in the time of the Khrushchev reforms, is delegating part of its rights and responsibilities to local party committees with the intention of broadening these rights and responsibilities if the reforms turn out to be successful and of taking them back if they fail. All this is contained in Lenin's formula "Centralization of leadership; decentralization of responsibility."

In his report Kosygin entered into polemics with the Western press, predicting allegations by the West about "a crisis in the Soviet economy," "a bourgeoisie regeneration," "a replacement of the planning principle by the spontaneous mechanism of market regulation."[26] To such conclusions about the new reforms Kosygin replied in advance: "Vain hopes! They would like to have their wishes taken for realities."[27]

However, not only the Western experts but also the Chinese communist orthodoxists in Peking reached the same conclusions regarding the new Soviet reforms. The following is *Pravda's* report on the reaction of Peking to the decisions of the March Plenum of the Central Committee on agriculture and the September Plenum on industry:

> In the central organ of the Chinese Communist party there is a verbose editorial article entitled "A Rebuff to the Profuse Talk of the CPSU Leadership about Unity of Action." The policy of the CPSU, which is aimed at the building of a communist society, is being labeled a policy of the bourgeoisie regeneration of the Soviet people. . . . The decisions of the March Plenum of the Central Committee of the CPSU are interpreted in the following way: "The new leadership of the CPSU is accelerating the development of capitalism in the countryside. It is developing private enterprise, increasing the size of private plots of land, raising the number of privately owned cattle, expanding a free market, and is encouraging free trade." The decisions of the September Plenum of the Central Committee are characterized in the article as "the restoration of capitalism in the U.S.S.R."[28]

Professor Ye. Liberman, one of the high priests of the present reforms, replied to both the bourgeoisie experts and the Chinese communist critics in a *Pravda* article entitled "The Plan, Direct Relationships and Profitableness." In the article Professor Liberman modestly denies not only his own authorship of the ideas of the new reforms but also their authorship by academicians V. Nemchinov, V. Trapeznikov and L. Leont'ev. He attributes the new ideas to none other than Lenin himself, saying:

> Even a slightly educated person knows very well that the principles of financial accountability and profitability are *Leninist principles of management* to which the Soviet economy has conformed since 1921.[29]

As a matter of fact, "even a slightly educated person" knows very well that in 1921 the first market categories were introduced into the Soviet economy by the granting of private and state capitalism (concessions, rents) within defined limits, with the state preserving the "commanding heights of the economy" (heavy industry, transport, banks, land). But these "Leninist principles" are known by another name, which Professor Liberman has avoided—the NEP. To assert, however, that the Soviet economy is conforming to the Leninist principles of 1921, i.e., to the principles of the NEP, means either to ignore the existence in the history of Soviet Russia of a person like Stalin or to utter sheer nonsense, intended just for the "slightly educated." Even the famous "financial accountability," which Stalin too permitted, was and has remained ever since, according to the testimony of Kosygin, a mere "formality."[30]

Professor Liberman goes further. By attempting to substantiate the new reforms scientifically, he turns upside down not only the economic doctrine of Marx but also what has since come to be known as the "political economy of socialism." For almost five decades the Soviet people have been taught that the drive for maximum profits is the meaning and motive power of capitalist development. It is indeed also the basic law of capitalism. On the other hand, the idea of profits and gains has been organically alien to socialism. The basic law of socialism is described as the desire for the maximum satisfaction of the vital needs of the people. Now, however, Professor Liberman disputes capitalism's right to a monopoly on the profit motive. Here is his interesting reasoning:

> Profit has existed for thousands of years. . . . But just on this basis alone the apologists of capitalism should not ascribe to themselves a monopoly in the use of profit.* To be sure, profit historically will not remain an invariable category, just as commodity production is not altogether a rigid system of production. It is therefore not at all surprising that socialism, while developing a systematically planned system of commodity production, at the same time is creating and using profit as its own special economic category.[31]

Professor Liberman nevertheless thinks that profit under socialism is essentially different from profit under capitalism in that the former is not simply profit, but "socialist profit." He writes:

> Many superficial reviewers in the West speak ironically of the term "socialist profit." In their view the essential nature of profit does not change with the addition of the adjective "socialist." They do not understand that this "adjective" was created by the greatest of all revolutions in the history of mankind.[32]

---

*It is noted that the first such "apologist of capitalism" was Karl Marx himself, who wrote: "The permanent objective of capitalist production consists of producing maximum surplus value with the minimum outlay of capital." (*Capital*, IY, chap. ii, 552 [1957].)

Of course, even these "superficial observers" would have nothing against this "adjective" if the Soviet professors were consistent in their use of it; they are always saying "socialist profits," "socialist prices," "socialist capital investment," but why then cannot they say "socialist capitalism"?

What is the general conclusion to be drawn from all this? What sort of perspectives are there for the development of Soviet industry in the light of the new reforms? The present reforms, in contradistinction to the Khrushchev reforms, are not merely *institutional*. They do not merely represent another shuffle of bureaucrats in the hierarchy of economic management, nor are they a simple return to Stalinist centralization. The new reforms introduce a *new element* into the social system of the Soviet economy. Practical experience has convinced the new leaders in the Kremlin that many of the spontaneous laws of Soviet economy are stronger than party decrees. The decisions of the September Plenum of the Central Committee of the CPSU are a partial capitulation to these spontaneous laws.

This capitulation is taking place under the slogan "For the scientific method of approach." (Note that it is not for the Marxist but the "scientific" method of approach.) The party commentators on the decisions of the September Plenum of the Central Committee say openly that, wherever Marxist ideology contradicts the facts of life, the party prefers to give up such ideology. Following is an appropriate passage from the commentary in the organ of the Central Committee of the CPSU:

> The party is not afraid to take a second look at its point of view on this or that question if the necessity of this is prompted by the realities of life, by changing conditions. . . . Scientific integrity shows itself not just in defending to the end correct conclusions but also in having the courage to give up mistaken or antiquated conclusions and theses. . . . The party sees its obligation in listening attentively to the pulsations of life . . . and when necessary to make corrections in its policy. If some policy leads to a contradiction with life, the party cannot hide it and give the appearance that everything is going well. In place of an antiquated policy or a policy that has not proved itself, the party must work up a new policy which corresponds more fully to the objective needs of society. . . .[33]

The official journal of the party has stated that

> passing like a red thread through all the plenums of the Central Committee since October, 1964 [when Khrushchev was overthrown], is the idea that the management of the economy must be built on a *scientific basis,* taking into account and skillfully using the objective laws of social development. The scientific method of approach to the management of the economy presupposes the *correct use* of such categories as commodities, money, prices, profit and credit.[34]

Such reasoning testifies to the new leaders' serious intentions and their realistic approach. Their arguments are typical not of dogmatists but of accountants, engineers and managers. Nevertheless, the decisions of the September Plenum of the Central Committee are only the first step, which will be successful only if it is followed by the second and decisive step: a genuine return to the NEP of Lenin, in the city as well as in the countryside. This must include such measures as transferring the land to the peasants after disbandment of the Stalinist *kolkhozy*; allowing free private initiative in the production of consumer goods on the scale that existed during the NEP; raising the real wages of workers in such a manner that they will seek work rather than avoid it (the phenomenon of the "parasites"); limiting the effect of the "foreign trade monopoly" law, especially in regard to consumer goods; and, finally, introducing gold-backing of the ruble, making it a fully convertible currency.

If all these things were done, would the communist dictatorship cease to exist? The answer is no. Exactly these measures existed during the NEP with a communist dictatorship. And that dictatorship was by far more popular with the people than the present one.

Agriculture

Throughout the entire history of the collective farm system, agriculture has been the party's Achilles' heel. A history of all the party and soviet decisions and administrative acts dealing with the need to organize effective direction and control of the peasantry would fill many books.

One of the Bolsheviks' first decrees after the October Revolution—the Decree on Land—was copied entirely from the program of the Social Revolutionaries, that is, from the peasant party, which the Bolsheviks called a "bourgeois-*kulak*" party. The substance of the decree was, in Lenin's words, that the "land must be handed over to the peasants."[35] He went on to say:

> Here are heard voices saying that this decree was drawn up by the Social Revolutionaries. So be it. It is a matter of indifference who compiled it, but, as a democratic government, we cannot evade the commands of the ordinary people, even though we do not agree with them. . . . Whether it is in the spirit of our program or of the Social Revolutionary program is beside the point. The point is that the peasantry should receive a firm assurance that there will be no more landowners in the countryside, and let the peasants them-selves decide all these questions, let them arrange their own lives.[36]

The supreme control over execution of the land reform was to be effected by a special organ of the new Soviet government—the People's Commissariat for Agriculture.

However, this obviously unbolshevist decree was only a tactical maneuver intended to rally peasant support for the Bolsheviks. The actual bolshevist agrarian program called for nationalization of the land.

The Civil War, which began soon afterward, enabled the Bolsheviks to nationalize the land without fanfare and without a new decree, and even to attempt to introduce a system of "communes" in peasant Russia. This was done by proclamation of "war communism," under which everything—trade, industry and peasant labor—was considered to have been nationalized. In the countryside "produce levies" were imposed, which Lenin said were intended "to confiscate all surpluses, to establish a compulsory state monopoly."[37] The peasants responded by reducing the size of the areas under grain cultivation and slaughtering their cattle. Trade came to a stop. A threat of prolonged famine hung over the whole country.

The policy of war communism was not only prompted by the demands of the Civil War, as Soviet historians have always maintained; it was also a first experiment in the forced introduction of communes. Lenin himself said later:

> Practice has shown that these experiments have also played a negative role when people who have gone into the country with the best intentions and desires to organize communes, collectives, have been incapable of discerning . . . that *past attempts at collective enterprises only provide an example of how not to run a farming unit.*[38]

The NEP, proclaimed at the Tenth Party Congress in 1921, replaced the "produce levies" with a reasonable "produce tax," proclaimed freedom to trade and recognized the right to engage in private enterprise within certain limits in both city and country. The short-lived golden age of Soviet capitalism lasted from 1921 to 1928, and it was the only period in which communist Russia had an abundance of agricultural produce. It was so successful in fact that Lenin called a halt at the Eleventh Party Congress, in April, 1922. He declared that the retreat had ended and that the party would regroup its forces for a new advance under the slogan "Who—whom?"—who would beat whom in competition, the NEP or socialism.

The NEP was so successful that two years after its introduction the Soviet government had accumulated such large grain reserves that the Twelfth Party Congress, in April, 1923, issued a decree requiring the government to arrange for the export of the surplus:

> It is necessary to provide for the export of peasant grain surpluses that cannot be used within the country. In order to satisfy this urgent need of the peasant economy, the government must make it possible for peasant wheat to be sold abroad without hindrance.[39]

And a year later, in January, 1924, the Thirteenth Party Conference stated that the urban and industrial population of the U.S.S.R. is not a sufficient market for peasant output. Peasant grain may rise in price as a result of its conquering foreign markets. Having ascertained the urgent need to export agricultural products, the party last year took this circumstance into account.[40]

The grain surpluses lasted only as long as the peasants, under the NEP, dealt with only two institutions—the land section of the government Central Executive Committee for land affairs and the finance section for taxation. When the party intervened in the peasants' affairs the picture changed drastically. This took place when Stalin reintroduced a type of war commission in the country areas in the form of forced collectivization. The NEP was abandoned, although to this day no party decision or government decree has officially ratified the action. Nor have the Soviet laws concerning land and its free use, which had, in Stalin's words, "to be set aside during the period of complete collectivization," been repealed.[41] Stalin, without a decision by a party congress or even by the Central Committee, publicly spoke for the first time of "complete collectivization" on December 27, 1929. He announced that the party was about to reverse its peasant policy, to carry out complete collectivization and to liquidate the *kulaks* as a class. On January 5, 1930, his proposals were ratified by the party Central Committee in a decree "On the Rates of Collectivization," which called for complete collectivization throughout the Soviet Union by the fall of 1931, or by the spring of 1932 at the latest.[42]

This is not the place to describe the cost of putting Stalin's plan into effect or the sacrifices the Bolsheviks exacted in the process. The party organization that resulted is, however, of importance to our general theme.

The collectivization of agriculture brought with it numerous institutions and organizations for directing and controlling the collective farms. These included: (1) the rural party cell, (2) the rural soviet, (3) the *raion* land section, (4) the *raion* planning commission, (5) the *raion* executive committee, (6) the commission on harvest productivity, (7) the collective administration, (8) the machine-tractor station and (9) the *raion* party committee. Each of these organs had powers of direction and control within its own sphere. In addition a permanent organ consisting of responsible members of the party *raion* and *oblast* committees, who issued orders to the collective farms on their personal initiative during such special campaigns as those for sowing, harvesting and grain collection, was also created.

These were by no means the party's only agencies for directing and controlling the collective farms; they constituted merely the first rung of a long bureaucratic ladder stretching from the village to Moscow. The Communists apparently believed that, having inundated the countryside with bureaucrats (Khrushchev complained that there were seven men behind every plow), they had really solved the grain problem! Less than a year after the commencement of collectivization, the Fourteenth Party Congress, in July, 1930, noted that the party had "successfully solved the grain problem,"[43] and every succeeding party Congress has declared that the problem has at last been solved. It was said again by Malenkov at the Nineteenth Party Congress, in 1952; but ten years later, at the March, 1962, Plenum of the Party Central Committee, Khrushchev said that Malenkov had been lying.

In January, 1933, Stalin made a serious attempt to solve the agricultural problem by bureaucratic and police methods. He declared:

> The party must take the direction of the collective farms into its own hands. The party must go into all the details of collective farm life and collective farm management.[44]

Political sections were created in the machine-tractor stations and on state farms. "Political sections" was a stereotyped term concealing a network of skilled political police masquerading as agricultural specialists, exercising special powers and directly appointed by the party Central Committee. The January, 1933, Plenum of the Central Committee issued the following decree:

> Political sections are to be organized in all machine-tractor stations, consisting of the head of the station, his two deputies and a *Komsomol* assistant. The chief of the political section has complete authority over party and *Komsomol* organizations in the machine-tractor station and on the collective farms it serves. . . . The chiefs of machine-tractor station political sections are to be appointed by the party Central Committee.[45]

It is significant that the chiefs of political sections were placed in charge of not only the collective farms but also the party district committees.

In all, 3,368 machine-tractor station political sections were created, and 2,021 political sections on state farms.

The November, 1934, Central Committee Plenum decided to abolish the political sections on the grounds that they had fulfilled their purpose. The decree in question stated that

> the seventeen thousand workers in machine-tractor station political sections and the eight thousand workers in political sections of state farms, who were carefully hand-picked by the party Central Committee, have accomplished their gigantic task in two years.[46]

The "gigantic task" referred to had consisted in completely breaking the peasants' resistance to the collective farms. The political section apparatus was to be merged with the party district committees, in which agricultural sections were to be created. At the same time the Plenum provided that the secretaries of district committees and the deputy directors of machine-tractor station political sections were to be appointed and removed by the party Central Committee.[47]

The party has subsequently returned many times to the problem of the political and organizational direction of agriculture. Numerous reorganizations and mergers have taken place in existing agricultural organizations, and many supplementary organizations have been created from time to time to reinforce the organs of the Ministry of Agriculture—known before the war as the Collective Farm Center and afterward as the Council for Collective Farm Affairs of the Council of Ministers of the U.S.S.R. However, these many reorganizations have not succeeded in removing agricultural production from its permanent state of crisis. At the Twentieth Party Congress Khrushchev placed the entire blame on Stalin:

> Stalin knew the country and agriculture only from films. These films presented an overoptimistic picture of agriculture. Many films depicted collective farm life as one in which tables groaned under the weight of turkeys and geese. It is obvious that Stalin thought this really was so.[48]

At the beginning of 1953, Stalin, according to Khrushchev, had proposed to impose a tax of 40,000,000,000 rubles on the peasants, although the collective farms were being paid only 26,000,000,000 rubles for the entire amount of agricultural produce supplied to the state.[49]

The first important decision of the "collective leadership" after Stalin's death was one concerning agriculture. At the September, 1953, Plenum of the party Central Committee, Khrushchev read a report on "Measures for the Further Development of Agriculture in the U.S.S.R." From this report the nation learned for the first time that, while industrial production had risen by 230 per cent between 1940 and 1952, the gross output of agriculture had risen by only 10 per cent.[50] In view of the fact that between 1926 and 1952 the urban population trebled while the total population of the country grew by 40,000,000, it is obvious that collective farm production failed to grow in proportion during this period and that cattle production even declined. According to Khrushchev's figures on the eve of collectivization in 1928 there were 66,980,000 head of cattle, but thirteen years later—in 1941—there were only 54,500,000 head of cattle, or 12,300,000 fewer, and in 1953 there were 56,600,000 cattle, that is, 10,200,000 fewer than in 1928.[51] Such were the results of collectivization and party direction of collective farming.

The same Plenum passed measures designed to rescue agriculture from this impasse by appealing to the "personal material interest" of the collective farm workers. Khrushchev justified the new policy by a direct reference to Lenin:

> V. I. Lenin pointed out that for the transition to communism a considerable number of years would be required, and that during this transitional period the economy must build . . . on personal interest, on personal involvement, on economic considerations.[52]

But Khrushchev neglected to add that Lenin had used this statement to introduce the NEP.

The impasse in Soviet agriculture cannot be explained by backwardness in agricultural techniques. At the end of 1958 there were about 1,700,000 tractors, 700,000 trucks, 500,000 combine harvesters and 120,000 silo combines available.[53]

The decisions of the September, 1953, Plenum of the party Central Committee and subsequent decisions introduced many changes into the administration of Soviet agriculture. Collective farms were given considerable authority to plan and conduct their own affairs, and bureaucratic pressure from above was eased. In 1957 the machine-tractor stations were disbanded, their equipment was handed over to the collective farms and a network of technical repair stations was established.

But again these changes proved to be temporary. The most radical change in the administration of agriculture since the formation of the political sections was effected by a decree of the March, 1962, Plenum of the party Central Committee, which virtually reestablished the entire party political and administrative apparatus for control of agriculture. In his report to the Plenum Khrushchev made the remarkable statement that

> an organ that could manage Soviet agriculture, can engage in the organization of production and deliveries . . . such an administrative organ does not exist. Nor has it existed during the years of Soviet power. Agriculture was and still is *badly managed*.[54]

Under the 1962 administrative organization of agriculture two parallel administrative apparatus were created, one a soviet (government) system for administration and production and the other a party system for political leadership and control. Both existed at stages ranging from the inter-*raion* level to an all-Union center. The Council of Ministers of the U.S.S.R. joined the party Central Committee in approving the organization in a decree dated March 22, 1962.

The structure and duties of the administrations were as follows:

1. *The territorial collective and state farm administrations* combined several of the former administrative *raions* (in the R.S.F.S.R. an average of ten *raions* each and in the Ukraine three *raions* each). Their duties were: (*a*) to organize and control the carrying out of party and government decisions on agriculture and on the production and delivery of agricultural products; (*b*) to direct production and delivery organizations, and to ensure the fulfillment of production plans and state purchases by collective and state farms; (*c*) to plan accounting and bookkeeping, and to examine production and finance plans and the annual accounts of collective and state farms.

2. Within the administrations a system of *party organizers* was set up (with groups of inspectors) for *oblast, krai* and constituent republic

central committees. Party organizers were political commissars who were to oversee not only the administration but also all the party *raion* committees of the regions within the particular administrative area. Although they were nominally regarded as "*oblast* committee party organizers," they were appointed or removed by the CPSU Central Committee, the Bureau for the R.S.F.S.R. or by the party central committee of the republic for the other constituent republics.

3. Each administration was headed by a *council,* which consisted of the following officials: the chairman (also head of the administration); the members, including the party organizers, the *Komsomol* organizers, the first secretaries of the *raion* committees and the chairmen of the *raion* executive committees, and the head of the agricultural technology department (*selkhoztekhnik*). The decisions of the council were binding on the administration. The members of the council were confirmed in office by the *oblast* committee, the *krai* committee, the central committee of the republic and the appropriate executive committees or republic councils of ministers.

4. Oblast *and* krai *administrations for the production and collection of agricultural produce* were also created.

A party political apparatus to provide leadership and control was created, in the form of a network of committees for agriculture. Their structure and responsibilities were as follows:

1. The regional or provincial committees for agriculture, whose membership consisted of a chairman (the first secretary of the party *oblast* committee or *krai* committee), the first deputy chairman of the *oblast* executive committee (ex officio the chief of the *oblast* or *krai* administration for production and supply, and in the autonomous republics the minister of production and supply), the head of the agricultural section of the *oblast* or *krai* party committee, the chairman of the agricultural technology department and the head of the *oblast* or *krai* experimental station. Their duties were: (*a*) to supervise the fulfillment of party and government agricultural plans and to carry out control duties and (*b*) to be responsible for the status of agriculture.

2. The committee for agriculture of the constituent republics, whose membership consisted of a chairman (the first secretary of the party central committee of the constituent republic), a vice-chairman (the deputy chairman of the council of ministers of the constituent republic, ex officio minister of production and supply), the head of the agricultural section of the central committee, the chairman of the agricultural technology department, the minister of agriculture, the deputy chairman for agriculture of GOSPLAN, the chairman of the committee for hydrographic enterprises. Their duties were (*a*) to supervise the fulfillment of party and government decisions and (*b*) to be responsible for agriculture.

3. The All-Union Committee for Agriculture, whose membership

consisted of a chairman (the deputy chairman of the Council of Ministers of the U.S.S.R.), the head of the agricultural section of the Central Committee of the CPSU for the constituent republics, the chairman of the State Committee for Supply for the U.S.S.R., the Minister of Agriculture, the Chairman of the All-Union *selkhoztekhnika,* the deputy chairman of GOSPLAN for the U.S.S.R. and the deputy chairman of the State Economic Council for the U.S.S.R. Its duties were: (*a*) to plan the production and supply of agricultural products; (*b*) to examine production plans, apportion material and technical resources earmarked for agriculture and examine plans for capital investment and construction in agriculture; (*c*) to control the execution by industry of agricultural orders; (*d*) to direct long-range planning; (*e*) to apportion cadres of specialists in agriculture; and (*f*) to discuss scientific and technical problems in agriculture.[55]

At each level (apart from the all-Union level) a committee for agriculture, headed by a first secretary of a party committee, was the immediate directing and controlling organ for all party, soviet and agricultural organs on all questions concerning the production and supply of agricultural products. A remarkable feature of the system was the fact that the apparatus of collective and state farm administrations was not continued up to the all-Union level. Accordingly, the Committee for Agriculture acted as an all-Union organ for the direction of agricultural production, since the new law limited the Ministry of Agriculture of the U.S.S.R. to dealing with agricultural research and experimental stations.

Khrushchev declared that the two measures of the March Plenum— the creation of a dual apparatus for agricultural administration and for agricultural technology, and the replacement of rotation cultivation by intensive farming—would result in a steep rise in agricultural productivity. He accordingly appeared to be charging the repeated failures of Soviet agriculture to the type of bureaucracy and the technical methods employed in farming. But the real cause of the trouble lay in the *social aspects* of the collective and state farm system.

Khrushchev's denial of the existence of a state of crisis in Soviet agriculture was unconvincing in view of the facts he cited. He declared at the Plenum that production fell short of the goals set in the Five-Year Plan for 1961: grain production was short 1,000,000,000 poods* (8,400,000,000 instead of 9,400,000,000), meat production 3,000,000 tons (8,800,000 instead of 11,800,000) and milk production 16,000,000 tons (62,500,000 tons as against 78,400,000).[56]

The future holds even greater problems. The Seven-Year Plan ending in 1965 called for production of 12,000,000,000 poods of grain annually by the end of the period, and the Twenty-Year Plan proposed by the 1961 party program called for an annual grain output by 1980 of

*One pood equals 16.38 kilograms.

18,000,000,000 to 19,000,000,000 poods. Not even Soviet economists believe these plans can be achieved.

In November, 1962, a special plenum of the party Central Committee was held, to consider "the development of the economy of the U.S.S.R. and the reconstruction of the party's direction of the national economy." The Plenum declared:

> In our time the party is not only required to be able to supply a proper slogan, but, with its knowledge of affairs, it must give positive directions on the everyday problems of production, the development of industry, agriculture and all branches of the economy.[57]

It went on to point out that to achieve this end it was necessary to base the structure of the leading party organs from the lowest to the highest on the system of production.[58] It then decided to reconstruct the party organs and to revise the system of economic decentralization adopted in 1957. In the sphere of economic administration the Plenum decided: (1) to enlarge the councils of national economy (in the R.S.F.S.R., for example, by increasing their number from twenty-five to sixty-eight); (2) to set up a single economic operations center for the entire U.S.S.R.; (3) to set up state committees of the Council of Ministers of the U.S.S.R. for each branch of the economy, for the operational direction of technical policy; and (4) to recognize the U.S.S.R. GOSPLAN as the organ for long-range planning.

Later the Supreme Economic Council of the U.S.S.R. was created, as the supreme directive and administrative organ. To it are subordinated the Council of National Economy, the U.S.S.R. GOSPLAN and the state committees. The twenty-seven or more economic ministries and departments of Stalin's day are now replaced by a single gigantic bureaucratic economic body with numerous departments enjoying the rights of the former administrations and ministries. The role of the national economic councils will be reduced to that of the old Soviet *combinats*. The U.S.S.R. National Economic Council will direct their current production planning and will have operational direction of the national economic councils, while the state branch committees of the Council of Ministers of the U.S.S.R. (of which there are twenty-four) will determine the technical policies of national economic council undertakings.[59] By reverting to this old policy of centralization, the Central Committee Plenum also emphasized that "the national economic councils should be endowed with broad rights," and that there should be worked out a new "law concerning socialist enterprise, bearing in mind the further expansion of the director's rights."[60]

Elective "production committees" of workers and officials have been set up in industrial enterprises, but their rights are only advisory.

The structure of the party organs in the R.S.F.S.R. was set up as follows (in descending order):

1. *Industry.*—(*a*) Presidium, Secretariat of the CPSU Central Committee; (*b*) Industrial Bureau of the Central Committee; (*c*) Bureau of the CPSU Central Committee for the R.S.F.S.R.; (*d*) Bureau of the CPSU Central Committee for the R.S.F.S.R. for Industry; (*e*) *oblast* committees (*krai* committees) for industry; (*f*) city committees, industrial district committees, industrial-production party committees (of zones and groups); (*g*) primary party organizations in industry.

2. *Agriculture.*—(*a*) Presidium, Secretariat of the CPSU Central Committee; (*b*) Agricultural Bureau of the Central Committee; (*c*) Bureau of the CPSU Central Committee for the R.S.F.S.R.; (*d*) Bureau of the CPSU Central Committee for the R.S.F.S.R. for Agriculture; (*e*) *oblast* committees (*krai* committees) for agriculture; (*f*) party committees for production collective and state farm administrations; (*g*) primary party organizations in agriculture.

In the constituent republics the structure was:

1. *Industry.*—(*a*) Presidium, Secretariat of the CPSU Central Committee; (*b*) Bureau of the Central Committee for Industry; (*c*) party central committee of constituent republic (presidium, secretariat); (*d*) bureau of the central committee of the republic for industry; (*e*) *oblast* committees for industry; (*f*) city committees, industrial district committees and industrial-production party committees (of zones and groups); (*g*) primary party organizations in industry.

2. *Agriculture.*—(*a*) Presidium, Secretariat of the CPSU Central Committee; (*b*) Bureau of the Central Committee for Agriculture; (*c*) party central committee of constituent republic (presidium, secretariat); (*d*) bureau of the central committee of the republic for agriculture; (*e*) regional committees for agriculture; (*f*) party committees for production collective and state farm administrations; (*g*) primary party organizations in agriculture.

In accordance with this new structure for the party organs, *raion* and *oblast* soviet state organs were reorganized on the production principle.

It should not be assumed that the Khrushchev reform was a liberalization of party control. As *Pravda* declared:

> Party committees are called upon to direct not territory, but the reality of people who do not simply live on a particular territory but are engaged in a particular activity . . . . The party organs were and still are organs for political and organizational direction.[61]

This is true. The party organs were and remain primarily organs of political dictatorship, and it is only as such that they are also organs of economic dictatorship.

The two plenums of the Central Committee following Khrushchev's overthrow were primarily devoted to the problems in agriculture. The November, 1964, Plenum reestablished the old system of a single party organization and abolished the Khrushchevian division of the party into industrial and agricultural organizations. The party committee of the

Kolkhoz-Sovkhoz Production Administration became, as in Stalin's time, the district committee. The production administrations were also abolished.[62] The March, 1965, Plenum, following Brezhnev's speech on economic problems in agriculture, declared that all the measures of Khrushchev and the Central Committee to raise the level of agricultural productivity in the period 1959–64 had been in vain. It was explained that instead of a growth of 70 per cent in agricultural production (as provided for in the Seven-Year Plan) the actual growth was only 10 per cent. The Plenum passed a resolution for the investment of 71,000,-000,000 rubles (approximately 72,000,000,000 American dollars at the official Soviet rate of exchange) over the next five years for raising agricultural production. It was also declared that past *kolkhoz* debts be written off, that purchase prices of *kolkhoz* products by the state be raised and that a series of material concessions be granted: allowing possession of more privately owned livestock and of private farm plots, granting credits to construct collective farm buildings and allowing the collective farmers to obtain fodder from the *kolkhoz* general fund for their own use.[63] The March Plenum thus decided to raise the general level of the so-called personal material incentives of the collective farmers.

The reason for the permanent underproduction crisis in Soviet agriculture is not, however, backward technology, but the social system itself, that is, the organization of people on collective farms. While this system exists the crisis in agriculture will remain unresolved.

* CHAPTER XVI *

The Party's Leadership of the Army

CERTAIN sections of the Soviet state, such as the army and the political police, require a special type of organization and special forms of party leadership. Both these institutions, the two main pillars of the regime, are by their nature centralized administrative organs. In them the party leadership considers even the slightest semblance of "inner-party democracy" impermissible. The party has completely centralized direction, and the members of the centralized organs are appointed, not elected.

Since a military dictatorship relies directly on the army, special measures to prevent the army from disobeying orders are unnecessary. It is a quite different matter when a political dictatorship relies on civilian support: in that case it can only be secure and stable if the army is a reliable administrative tool. No political dictatorship in history, including the National Socialist dictatorship, has found an effective means of creating such a tool. Only the Bolsheviks have created a highly organized party political apparatus superior to the command apparatus at all levels of the military hierarchy.

The first official act of Soviet rule and of the Communist party in creating such an apparatus was a decree of April 6, 1918, introducing a system of military commissars in the Red Army. This was done five months after the seizure of power and six weeks after the creation of the Red Army. The experience of five months in power had shown the Communists that the stability of the "dictatorship of the proletariat" and its continued existence depended on the behavior of the army, and that the behavior of the army depended on the establishment of effective party control over its commanders. By birth and upbringing the higher command personnel of the Russian army were of anti-communist origin. Since the party could not immediately replace them with its own cadres, it was necessary to prevent a possible betrayal of the communist cause by the army's commanders. It was also necessary to turn the army itself, including its old bourgeois aristocratic personnel, into a weapon of the communist dictatorship. A resolution of the Eighth Party Congress, in 1919, on the "Military Question," formulated this bolshevist aim with complete clarity. It stated:

> The revolutionary character of the army is determined above all by the character of the Soviet regime, which creates this army,

which sets its tasks and thus converts it into *its own weapon*. On the other hand, the adaptation of this weapon to the Soviet regime is achieved . . . by the organization of commissars and communist cells and, finally, by general party and soviet leadership of the life and being of the army.[1]

The resolution also outlined the main practical tasks of the party in the matter of strengthening party control of the army:

(1) To continue the employment of military specialists in command and administrative posts, to establish over them constant centralized party political control via commissars, to dismiss those who prove to be politically and technically useless. (2) To organize a system for attesting command personnel and impose on commissars the tasks of periodically compiling such attestations. (3) To recruit new commanders from members of the proletariat and the semi-proletariat.[2]

The military commissars had political control and even prosecution rights and functions in addition to the same command rights as military commanders. The resolution gave to commissars alone "the right to impose disciplinary penalties (including the right to arrest people) and the right to commit persons for trial."[3] The authority of the military commissars was further strengthened by the fact that the "special sections" of the army and of the fronts were directly subordinate to the commissars.[4] Thus the military commissar system was a system of political control on behalf of the regime, a leader of the army's party political apparatus on behalf of the party Central Committee and a punitive organ of the CHEKA. It was completely effective. It first created the Red Army and then made it an efficient and reliable weapon for the communist dictatorship. Lenin was quite right when he observed: "Without the military commissar we would not have a Red Army."[5]

In April, 1918, the All-Russian Bureau of Military Commissars was set up and in September, 1918, the Revolutionary War Council (Soviet) of the Republic was created, together with military war councils of the army and of the fronts, which assumed control over political leadership of both military commanders and commissars.

At first, party organizations in the army had elective organs in the form of regimental, divisional and army party committees. The Central Committee, however, soon noted that the elected party committees did not always feel obligated to obey the directives and orders of the civilian party organs—the Central Committee and its representatives in army units in the person of the recently created political sectors— and on December 5, 1918, the Central Committee issued a decree disbanding all party committees in the army and setting up a large network of political departments as party organs, appointed by the Central Committee itself.[6] The political sectors were both party and state organs, subordinate locally to the military commissars and at the top to the All-Russsian Bureau of Military Commissars. The Eighth Party Congress did away with this bureau and replaced it with a central political section of the Revolutionary War Council of the Republic. In May, 1919, the political section of the Revolutionary War Council was transformed into the Political Administration of the Republic, headed by a member of the party Central Committee.[7] This organization, now called the Principal Political Administration, began to direct all political and party work in the army, with the rights of a section of the party Central Committee. As long as there were political commissars, it effected its direction through them.

The scheme of organization of the commissars was as follows (in descending order of importance): (1) Revolutionary War Council of the Republic, (2) Revolutionary War Council of the Front (army group) or Army (or *raion*), (3) corps commissar, (4) divisional commissar, (5) brigade commissar, (6) regimental commissar, (7) battalion commissar, (8) company political instructor.

By a decree of the Central Executive Committee and the Council of People's Commissars dated September 22, 1935, a military-party hierarchy was officially established in the army by the introduction of the following political titles: (1) junior political instructor, (2) political instructor, (3) senior political instructor, (4) battalion commissar, (5) senior battalion commissar, (6) regimental commissar, (7) brigade commissar, (8) divisional commissar, (9) corps commissar, (10) army commissar Grade II, (11) army commissar Grade I.

The military commissars directed the political sections at their own level. The system of military commissars, introduced as a temporary expedient until the Red Army could create its own command personnel, became a permanent administrative organ of the party Central Committee over the army. A decree issued after the end of the Civil War, at the Tenth Party Congress, in 1921, declared that it was necessary

> to preserve the political apparatus of the Red Army in the form in which it has developed during the three years of war, to improve and strengthen its organization, to strengthen its ties with local party organizations, while preserving its complete independence.[8]

This decision was taken because of the impending threat of Red Bonapartism; some Red Army officers, heroes of the Civil War, had not only begun to treat military commissars with little respect but had criticized the party's general policy. On the other hand, among the commissar and political section personnel, opposition developed to the strict tutelage of Communists from the Central Committee who had spent the entire Civil War well behind the lines and who were now reaping the fruits of victory.

The military commissars and political sections had justified their existence, but peace time conditions required that they be headed by new people. Hence the Tenth Party Congress' decision that through the Political Administration of the Workers' and Peasants' Red Army and its political sections, the party Central Committee must effect the large-scale renewal of commissar personnel and of the personnel of the army's political organs, with a view to revitalizing them by the introduction of new workers and by transferring old ones to other positions in the army.[9]

For this purpose the next Congress (the Eleventh, in 1922) ordered the number of Communists in the army's political apparatus to be increased by mobilizing Communists born in the years 1899, 1900 and 1901.[10] The Congress also confirmed an important resolution of the Eleventh Party Conference:

> The party is faced with the urgent task of turning the barracks into an institution parallel to the party schools.[11]

Compulsory "communist education" was thus introduced into the army.

Once commissars and newly trained "Red commanders" began to be appointed to positions of command in the army, the question again arose as to whether the office of commissar should be abolished. The existence of the communist commissar alongside and over the communist commander was regarded with disfavor by the latter. The Revolutionary War Council defined the difference in positions of commissar and commander by remarking:

> If a regimental commander is the head of a regiment, then the commissar must be the father and spirit of the regiment.[12]

A regimental commander who, like the commissar, was a Communist, and had perhaps been a commissar himself, knew perfectly well that the commissar had been attached because he himself was regarded as politically untrustworthy. The recognition by the party Central Committee of the bad effect upon the morale of the entire command personnel led to a constant vacillation of the party and government on the question of abolishing the office of military commissar, as is shown by the following series of party and government acts alternately abolishing and reviving the system. (1) On March 2, 1925, commanders were given sole command and military commissars abolished. The post of commander's political section assistant was created. (This order was not issued to units commanded by non-members of the party.) (2) On May 16, 1937, the post of military commissar was reintroduced. (3) On August 12, 1940, military commissars were abolished and the post of deputy commander for political affairs was introduced. (4) On June 6, 1941, military commissars were reintroduced. (5) On October 9, 1942, military commissars were abolished and deputy commanders for political affairs were reintroduced.

All political workers in the army were given military ranks and insignia similar to those of the command personnel: junior lieutenant, lieutenant, captain, major, lieutenant-colonel, colonel, major-general, lieutenant-general, colonel-general, army general, and marshal of the Soviet Union. The commander became the sole head, while the former commissar became his deputy for political affairs, with equal or lower rank. Although discrimination of the commanders was officially abolished, in reality it continued to exist. The deputy commander for political affairs was the real commander of the unit. As a result of the system, the ranks held by political commanders do not necessarily have any relation to their bearers' importance. In connection with the first decision to introduce sole command in the army, a letter from the party Central Committee dated March 6, 1925, emphasized that

> with the establishment of sole command, the role of the political sections as the organs of the party in the army becomes much more important.[13]

The leading role of the political organs in the army was first formulated as a party rule in the party statutes adopted at the Fourteenth Party Congress:

> The general leadership of the party work in the Red Army and the Red Fleet is effected by the Political Administration of the Workers' and Peasants' Red Army as the military section of the Central Committee. The Political Administration of the Workers' and Peasants' Red Army conducts its work via political sections appointed by it (fronts, military districts, fleets, armies, divisions), military commanders and party commissions elected at army conferences.[14]

This formula for party political work in the army was retained, with variations, in subsequent party statutes. Those of 1961 stated:

> The direction of party work in the armed forces is effected by the CPSU Central Committee via the Main Political Administration of the Soviet Army and Navy, which functions with the powers of a department of the Central Committee of the CPSU.[15]

The Central Committee directs and controls the army through: (1) the network of the Main Political Administration (the political sections), (2) military councils, (3) special sections and (4) military party organizations.

The hierarchy of political sections is of the same pattern as the military hierarchy: Main Political Administration; political administration of each branch of the services (Political Administration of Land Forces, Political Administration of the Navy, Political Administration of the Air Force, Political Administration of Anti-Aircraft Defense, Political Administration of Rocket Force and Political Administration of Internal [Political] Troops); political administrations of military areas; political sections of corps and political sections of divisions; and regimental political deputy commanders, battalion political deputy commanders and company political deputy commanders. The Bureau of the Main Political Administration is the "collective leadership" at the head of the Political Administration, which, in addition to the chief of the Political Administration, apparently includes the chief of the political administrations of each branch of the services and the secretary of the party Central Committee in charge of the armed forces.[16]

The sections in the Main Political Administration and also in the political administration of each branch of the services are as follows: (1) agitation and propaganda section; (2) party organization section, which directs military, party and *Komsomol* organizations; (3) organizational and instructor section, which directs the political sections; (4) culture and education section; (5) information section, which directs the collection of secret political information about the political morale of the army; (6) cadre sector, which trains, appoints and dismisses all cadres of political officers; and (7) administrative and economic section.[17]

The political administrations of the military districts have been organized on the same principle.

The Main Political Administration acts independently of the minister of defense and parallel to his command apparatus. The minister of defense is responsible for the administrative direction and military training of the troops. The head of the Main Political Administration is responsible for both this and for the political reliability of the army. Directives and instructions of the Main Political Administration have the force of law for the army, while orders from the cabinet ministers are either based on directives of the Main Political Administration or bear the signatures of the heads of both organizations. Moreover, the political organs are not only the party's directing authority but have also been assigned administrative powers. The same structure exists at the lower command levels. An official publication of the Ministry of Defense states:

> Directives and instructions of political organs on questions of organization and conduct of party political work in the forces are binding on political organs at lower levels and also on the commanders and chiefs at those levels. *The political organs fulfill not only the functions of party organs but also the functions of a military-political (administrative) apparatus.* The heads of political sections in military units, being party leaders, are at the same time deputies of the commanders of these units for political affairs. *As the direct heads of all the personnel they have administrative powers* appropriate to their service ranks.[18]

In other words, the head of the political section is not only the political head of the unit, he is also the direct head of all the personnel of the unit, even though he has the modest title of "deputy commander for political affairs."

After Marshal Zhukov's disgrace, when he was accused of wishing to free the army from the tutelage of the party, the political sections and the military councils, party control organs in the army greatly increased their activities. The Principal Political Administration of the Ministry of Defense was removed from the Ministry of Defense and was renamed the Main Administration of the Soviet Army and Navy. Once again new statutes and instructions were devised for regulating the work of political organs, military councils and party military organizations. The party Central Committee's "Recommendations" of October 30, 1957, concerning the work of political organs, stated that they

> must undeviatingly put party policy into effect, and daily educate the personnel of the army and navy in the ideas of Marxism-Leninism. Political organs, as organs of the party, must influence all aspects of the life and activities of the army, and permeate everything.[19]

The work of political organs, including their direction and control of the army, is based on an information and intelligence service strategically placed in all units. They have two channels of information—a network of secret agents of the special sections (military political police) and their own network of party informers. The official leadership says of the importance of party information:

> Well-placed information services enable the political organs to be always abreast of events, to take timely action regarding deficiencies in the work of officer personnel and of party and *Komsomol* organizations. The party information service must be high-principled, objective, truthful . . . in order correctly to determine the political morale of personnel.[20]

Just as the leaders of civilian party organizations are experts in the industries of their *raion,* city or *oblast,* so too must the leaders of army political organs be military experts. In the army, political workers are politically superior to their commanders, and in military matters they must be their equals. The official leadership puts special emphasis on this point:

> It is most important that political workers be militarily well trained if they are to be able to carry out their political duties successfully in the armed forces. They must have the ability to understand questions of organization and method in the conduct of military training and the exploitation of the military technology and weapons of their own branch of the forces.[21]

Such expertise enables the political organs to control the army's military activities and to carry out periodical assignments of commanders to political work and political workers to command positions, without violating the organizational principle of the political organs and their system of control.

The political apparatus of a regiment or ship is considered to be the most important link in the system of party direction and control of the army and the navy. The political apparatus of a regiment or ship is headed by a deputy commander for political affairs. In addition, the apparatus personnel includes the secretary of the party bureau, the propaganda worker, the head of the club and the secretary of the *Komsomol*. The powers and duties of the deputy commander are laid down in the military regulations. He is the direct head of all personnel. While he is technically subordinate to his commander, his real superior is the head of the political unit of which his section forms a part. He continuously informs the political section of the political morale of his own unit, especially among the officers and the commander. He organizes the political and military training of his unit, controls supplies and directs the work of party and *Komsomol* organizations. He directs the battalion political deputy commanders and ensures that political work is carried out among the families of military personnel. He also organizes links with civilian party organizations of the area.

As we have seen, party organizations in the army were at first set up on the pattern of army organizations—by regiment, division, corps and district. It soon became clear that this military hierarchy, when transferred to the party, involved a potential danger of "separatism" of military party organizations from the central party leadership—the party Central Committee. The latter therefore decreed that army and division party committees be disbanded and their functions handed over to political sections appointed by the Central Committee itself. According to a Central Committee instruction issued in December, 1919, the company party cell (the party organization of the company) was to be the basic party unit in the army. In time, party organizations began to be set up at regimental level and in military institutes, but only as primary party organizations. This does not, however, mean that the Central Committee has restricted the growth of the party in the army. On the contrary, it has always regarded the barracks as a "school of communist education" for young Soviet citizens and as a reserve from which to fill the party ranks, as the growth of the party in the army shows.

Table 29 shows the growth of military party organizations.[22]

TABLE 29

GROWTH OF MILITARY PARTY ORGANIZATIONS

YEAR	NUMBER OF COMMUNISTS	PERCENTAGE OF TOTAL PARTY MEMBERSHIP
October, 1918	35,000	12.0
February, 1919	122,000	39.0
August, 1920	300,000	65.0
End of 1941	1,300,000	42.4
End of 1942	2,000,000	54.3
End of 1945	3,500,000	60.0
End of 1961	900,000(estimate)	9.0

From Table 29 it is apparent that during the periods when the regime was in greatest danger—in the Civil War (1920) and in World War II (1945)—the party greatly increased its nucleus in the army. In 1920, 65 per cent of the party's members were in the army, and 60 per cent were in the army in 1945. (In 1920, 300,000 of the total of 5,000,000 Red Army men were Communists.)[23] In 1945, there were 3,500,000 Communists in the Red Army of 11,365,000.[24]

Primary party organizations are created in regiments, in separate units (battalion, division, company, squadron), on board ships and also in all military institutes and training establishments where there are three or more party members. To conduct day-to-day business where there are fifteen or more members, a bureau of eleven or more persons is chosen by secret ballot. The bureau elects a secretary and one or two deputy secretaries by open ballot. In a party organization where there are fewer than fifteen members, only a secretary is elected. In a regiment where there are more than seventy-five Communists, a party committee having the rights of a *raion* committee is elected. In such a case, battalion party organizations have the rights of primary party organizations and company party organizations have the rights of a shop organization. Party committees are also set up in the administrations of military districts, of military groups, in fleets and in central military directorates, where there were formerly political sections.

The party statutes define the general tasks of military party organizations as follows:

> Party organizations of the Soviet Army are directed in their activities by the program and the statutes of the party, and work on the basis of instructions that have been confirmed by the Central Committee. They ensure the putting into effect of party policy in the armed forces, rally their personnel around the Communist party and educate the military in the spirit of Marxism-Leninism. They educate the fighters in the spirit of devotion to the Fatherland, reinforce discipline, mobilize personnel to fulfill tasks in political and military training, the mastering of new techniques and weapons and the impeccable execution of their military duty, of orders and directives issued by their commanders. Party organizations and political organs of the Soviet Army maintain a close link with local (civilian) party committees and systematically inform them about political work in military units; the secretaries of military party organizations and the leaders of political organs participate in the work of local party committees.[25]

Army primary party organizations have the right to admit new members and candidate members to the party, to examine the personal affairs of members and to expel them from the party. At monthly general meetings a wide range of questions is discussed, from general party policy (the unqualified approval and elucidation of this policy) to specific questions concerning military life, including the discussion of measures to execute the orders of the minister of defense and of the head of the Main Political Administration. A special Central Committee instruction defines the tasks of the bureaus of army primary party organizations as follows:

> The bureau is enjoined: (1) to put into practice decrees of the supreme party organs and decisions of general meetings of organizations, and to check that they are carried out by every Communist; (2) to direct the party organizations of subsections; (3) to work individually with Communists, to control the way in which they carry out their duties, to educate them ideologically and to assign party missions to them; (4) to see that Communists make outstanding progress in military and political training and that they fulfill all the requirements of military regulations; (5) to educate new members of the party politically; (6) to direct *Komsomol* organizations; (7) to make periodical reports to the party organization on the carrying out of the decisions of party meetings and the fulfillment of work plans.[26]

This work is carried out by the party committees, bureaus and secretaries of party organizations in army units and sub-units under the direct leadership of the deputy political commander's apparatus, and through it the leadership of the next higher political section. The deputy commander is not answerable either for his work or for his behavior to the unit party organization, which does not have the right of control over the section commander but can inform higher authority about shortcomings in his work or submit such shortcomings to "criticism and self-criticism" at a general meeting. Once every three or four months unit political sections convene meetings of the military *aktiv,* whose membership includes commanders, political workers, members of party committees and bureaus, secretaries of party organizations, party organizers, members of party commissions, propaganda workers, etc. At these meetings, decisions of the party Central Committee and directives of the Main Political Administration are made known, and guidelines are established for the execution and fulfillment of these decisions.

Superior to party committees of units or bureaus of primary party organizations of sub-units are the party commissions. These exist at three levels—division, corps and military district. They are elective "collegiate organs" of the political sections of military groups and of political administrations of military districts, fleets and flotillas. They are elected at military party conferences, to which they are formally accountable.

Questions concerning admission to the party, the personal affairs of Communists and *Komsomol* members and the hearing of appeals against expulsion from the party or *Komsomol* by military party organizations all come within the competence of the party commission. Its decisions have the force of law after they have been ratified by the head of the political section or by the head of the political directorate.[27] Thus the most important function of *raion* and city committees—the acceptance or rejection of applications for party membership—is in theory effected in the army by the party commission, but in reality is done by the head of the political section acting alone. Co-opted party commissions were set up in December, 1919, and became elective organs in 1921. The Tenth Party Congress allowed them to become elective organs provided the necessary guarantees as to their obedience were forthcoming.[28] Such a guarantee took the form of the subordination of the elected "collegiate leadership" to a party general appointed from above.

In addition to the party and political organs of the Main Political Administration system, there is in the Soviet armed forces yet a third set of directing and controlling party and state organs—the military councils.[29] The most important of these are the military district councils. Until Marshal Zhukov was removed as Minister of Defense, the military district councils were only advisory organs to the commanders of military districts.[30] After Zhukov's dismissal, they became the highest *political command boards of the military districts.* An official Soviet handbook defines their present role as follows:

> The military council is a collegiate organ for the leadership and direction of the armed forces, which has been set up in military districts, fleets and flotillas and in armies of the armed forces of the U.S.S.R.[31]

The military district council directs military and political training and administrative and mobilization work. Its members include the commander of the military district, as chairman; the head of the district political administration; and a member of the military council, as a representative of the party Central Committee. The former "military commissar" was the prototype for this last member, and he is in fact the supreme party controller of both the military and the political leaders of the district—the district commander and the head of the district political administration. Orders and commands of the commander and the head of the political administration do not have the force of law unless they have been signed by the third member of the military council. This was so during the war and has become so again. Each branch of the armed services has its own military council.[32]

The Supreme Military Council of the U.S.S.R. is above all the armed forces of the U.S.S.R. as a military and political collective leadership. Finally, there is yet another ever-present and unobtrusive, all-powerful but secret, organ of party control over the army—the secret political police. Their spy network is of seemingly modest proportions, but is in fact all-seeing. Its members are scornfully referred to in police slang as *seksots* (secret informers). The State Security Committee has a special administration for the surveillance of the army, called the Main Administration of Special Sections. In the military districts, corps, divisions and the fleet, the organs of the political police are officially called special sections or counterintelligence sections. They have only business contacts with commanders, political organs and military councils, and they are not subordinate or accountable to any of these. Through their secret network of agents they study the political morale of all military personnel, primarily, of course, of command and political personnel. Systematic reports by specially entrusted members of special sections in military units and by heads of special sections in divisions and corps are collated in the administrations of special sections of the military districts. From these they are sent to the State Security Committee of the U.S.S.R. The State Security Committee's Main Administration for Special Sections filters all the district reports and selects everything that typifies the salient features of the political morale of the entire army. The bulletins compiled in this manner are sent to the Secretariat of the Central Committee of the CPSU. Together with other bulletins (included in *The Internal Situation in the U.S.S.R.*) also compiled by the State Security Committee, concerning the political morale of the civilian population, these reports are intended to reproduce without falsification or embellishment the real political temper of the army and the peoples of the U.S.S.R. For a one-party dictatorship, which has no opportunity to sound the mood of the nation through the usual channels of public opinion—parliament, a free press, opposition parties, etc.—the official channels of the political police are of great importance because they are the sole source of accurate information.

Thus the military party organizations control the command personnel; the political organs control the party organizations and the command personnel; a member of the military council controls the command personnel, the party organizations and the political organs; and all of these are controlled by the secret network of special sections.

To persons who have not lived under a dictatorship such a complex and interwoven system of control seems preposterous. But such a system of control of the army is an obvious necessity in a communist state. It affords a maximum guarantee to the one-party regime against the only considerable threat to its existence—a possible insurrection in the army.

The Central Committee of the CPSU exploits this guarantee with considerable skill.

The history of the Red Army from the day of its inception to the present prompts the conclusion that of the three pillars of the Soviet regime—the party, the secret police and the Red Army—the first two have ruled the country, while the last has merely been ruled.

After World War II the army's role in the system of the regime began to change. At first the change was only psychological and not structural. The course and the outcome of the war were decided, not by the party or the police, but by the army and its generals. The nominal party representatives (members of military councils) and the police (heads of special departments) under the commanders were in fact subsidiary forces; they were engaged only in propaganda work or surveillance and did not exercise command. The Soviet Army's capture of Berlin struck

Stalin not only as a triumph but also as a warning that such an army could also take Moscow. Hence the preventive, albeit bloodless, purge of the military high command following the war. Its victims were the group of military commanders headed by Marshal Zhukov, including Marshals Novikov, Vershinin, Bogdanov, Voronov and others. In Stalin's logic, the Kremlin doctors' affair was ultimately intended to serve as the finishing touch in the elimination of the more politically ambitious marshals and generals after the fashion of the Great Purge of 1937–39. Stalin decided to place at the head of the armed forces only military specialists he was certain had no aspirations for power. Such trustworthy people included, among others, Vasilevsky, Shtemenko, Kuznetsov, Artemiev and Govorov.

Stalin's death forestalled an extensive new purge and implemented the involvement of the army generals in the political intrigues taking place at the summit of the Soviet leadership. One of the first acts of the post-Stalin leadership was the immediate rehabilitation of the Zhukov group. Since that time, the army has played an active role in the internal party struggle for power among Stalin's heirs. Its role has been particularly significant in such cases as the removal and elimination of Beria and his police force, the exposure of Stalin's crimes against the military cadres, the removal of Malenkov (as a result of which Zhukov became a minister of defense) and the liquidation of the collective leadership led by Malenkov and Molotov (as a result of which Zhukov became a member of the Presidium of the Central Committee of the CPSU).

Khrushchev created a precedent in the history of the communist dictatorship by bringing military elements into the political struggle in the Kremlin, an act that would have been impossible under Lenin. Even Stalin, who continually resorted to the most improbable combinations of forces in the power struggle, had cautiously avoided involving the army general staff in this struggle. He knew well from history that the bayonets constituting the power behind the throne of a dictator can easily be turned against him. For the same reason, Zhukov believed that the power he had won for Khrushchev was in fact to be jointly held by the party and the army. This meant that the party organs in the army were to play only an auxiliary role as they had done during the war, and that a commander and not a political commissar was to be master of the situation.

Grasping the danger of the situation in time, Khrushchev, in October, 1957, sent Zhukov to Yugoslavia and in his absence removed him from his post as Minister of Defense and from the Presidium of the Central Committee. This unprecedented method of displacing a minister attested to the fact that Khrushchev and his followers were not certain that they could effect the removal of an army minister in the usual manner. However, the ill-fated Khrushchev, in acting this way, had no idea that this precedent would become a part of the system. He had even less reason to believe that the army would arrogate to itself the right to participate in determining the general party line, particularly matters of defense or foreign policy. Having replaced the Bonapartist Zhukov with the political time-server Malinovsky, and having removed from the military leadership such ambitious marshals as Sokolovsky, Zakharov, Golikov and later, in all likelihood, Chuykov as well, Khrushchev thought that he had re-created the situation that had existed in the army under Stalin.

This was, of course, a fatal error on his part. In the first place, Stalin himself was of the opinion that the Soviet general staff had to be thoroughly purged in order to restore it to its former condition; and in the second place, Khrushchev was not Stalin. Though the Soviet marshals had not had a great excess of affection for Stalin, they nevertheless had feared him and had been prepared to reckon with his military capabilities and stern, resolute character, about which they have written so extensively in connection with the twentieth anniversary of the Soviet victory in Germany. Thirdly, Khrushchev had created a precedent, not only insofar as military interference in politics was concerned, but also with respect to the party civilian leaders' practice of appealing to the same military personnel in the event of reshuffles in the Kremlin.

This last circumstance played the decisive role in Khrushchev's career. He undertook extraordinary measures of an organizational nature in an attempt to subordinate the entire armed forces to his personal control and thus prevent the military and party elites from exploiting the army for the purpose of effecting a revolution. He introduced the rank of supreme commander of the armed forces, hitherto unknown in peacetime, in order to award it to himself. However, having sensed that he had reached an impasse in his plans for improving agriculture and raising the standard of living, Khrushchev decided to implement a policy of stricter economy in the army. He adopted a new nuclear ballistic missile strategy, with the announced intention of reducing Soviet naval and infantry forces and using the resources and people thus freed for employment in agriculture and industry. Military personnel who objected were removed from their posts. While reiterating the ideas of Marshal Sokolovsky and General Cherednichenko and not denying the importance of the new weapons systems and the necessity of correspondingly new strategic concepts, they subjected Khrushchev's policy of economy to what was, for the military, effective if mild criticism.[33] What finally exhausted the patience of the military was probably a decree of the Presidium of the Central Committee and the Council of Ministers drafted by Khrushchev. The essence of the decree, published in the October 2, 1964, issue of *Pravda*, ten days before Khrushchev's overthrow, is contained in the following excerpt:

> In working out the long-range plan for the near future, N. S. Khrushchev emphasized, it is necessary to be guided by the idea that the primary task of this plan is to further raise the standard of living of the people. While during the period of the first five-year

plans and the postwar years we laid primary emphasis on developing heavy industry as the basis of raising the economy of the entire
country and strengthening its defense capability, now that we possess powerful industries and have a good defense posture the party
sees as its task the ensuring of more rapid development of branches
of the economy that produce consumer goods.

Khrushchev himself, relying on the military for support, had ousted
Malenkov in 1955 precisely because the latter had suggested abandoning
the old dogma of the primacy of heavy industry in favor of a drastic
increase in consumer goods. It is impossible to convince the military of
any country of the need to produce more butter than guns, and this is
particularly true of Soviet marshals. To make matters worse, Khrushchev undertook a too obvious policy of discrimination with respect to
highly placed military cadres, promoting some and ignoring others for
purely personal reasons. Promotions in rank and position and praise
in the history books went mainly to those military persons who had
served on fronts where Khrushchev had been a member of the military
council. In failing to take into consideration not only the Secretariat
and the Presidium of the Central Committee but also the army, Khrushchev closed the circle of dissatisfied individuals.

Khrushchev's pupils from the Central Committee Secretariat are again
bringing the army into play, and there is now no doubt that the army
played an active part in the revolution of October, 1964. This conclusion is based not only on a general political analysis of the events
preceding Khrushchev's fall, but also on a great many direct and cir-
sumstantial indications following it. The most important of these are
the following:

1. The Stalinist dogma of the primacy of military industry has been
reinstated. At first the new Soviet leaders, quite understandably, were
very cautious in this regard. Three weeks after Khrushchev's removal,
Brezhnev declared: "The development of heavy industry must be subordinated to the demands of continually rearming the entire national
economy, to the needs of defense, as well as to the needs of quickening
the pace of agriculture and light food industries."[34] In December, 1964,
at a session of the U.S.S.R. Supreme Soviet, Kosygin let it be understood that the new leaders had annulled the resolution of the Central
Committe Presidium and the U.S.S.R. Council of Ministers of October 1,
1964, concerning the abolition of the primacy of heavy industry, including military industry. He declared that the party and the government
had decided "to strengthen the economic and defense posture of the
country on the basis of the development of heavy industry."[35] The
country's economic development plan for 1965 was formulated accordingly: the goal for planned economic growth over 1964 for "production
of the means of production" (Group A) was set at 8.2 per cent, and for
"production of consumer goods" (Group B) at 7.2 per cent. In 1966
the proportion between these branches will remain almost the same;

the 1966 plan provides for a growth of Group A industry by 6.9 per cent and Group B by 6.0 per cent. The military share of the budget has been increased to 13,430,000,000 rubles.[36] However, no one knows the real size of the purely military budget and the extent of expenditures on the military industry. Exactly how much would go to strictly military industry is unknown.

2. Chief of General Staff Marshal Zakharov, who once repudiated Khrushchev's military and strategic concepts, including his "subjective," "unqualified" interference in military affairs, has returned to duty. After his reinstatement Zakharov wrote an article on the tasks and the rights of the military. This article was undoubtedly approved by the Central Committee and was recommended for the political schools. In it Zakharov spoke out against interference in military affairs as practiced by Stalin and Khrushchev, particularly interference that ignored the opinions "of outstanding military theorists and practitioners. . . . The more complex the tasks to be solved, the greater their scope, the more skilled must be the leadership."[37] Speaking of military organs, he set forth an operational thesis, counter to all previous practice, under which the party *apparatchiks* would exercise centralized leadership over army institutions and personnel selection:

> Enormous responsibility rests on the officers, generals, admirals and marshals of these institutions. They work out the plans for military training of all branches of the armed forces and arms of the service, *submit concrete recommendations and directives on matters relating to their organizational structure, training, indoctrination, and the deployment and utilization of cadres, etc.*[38]

The functions indicated above had hitherto been considered the unchallengeable prerogatives of the apparatus of the party Central Committee.

3. The policy of economy at the expense of the military budget has been admitted to be an error and the declaration of the new leadership in December, 1964, that the military budget would be reduced has been contradicted. Kosygin did, however, attempt to justify the new leadership's capitulation to the demands of the army by saying that "to economize on defense in the present situation would mean to go against the interests of the Soviet state."[39]

4. Civilians in the secret police and the army have received promotions in the party. Shelepin, who managed and in conjunction with others still manages party relations with the army, has been promoted to membership in the Central Committee Presidium; Ustinov, the aging head of the military industry, has been appointed a secretary of the Central Committee and a candidate member of the Central Committee Presidium; Yepishev, the head of the Main Political Administration of the army and navy, has been raised to the rank of member of the Central Committee; Semichastny, the head of the KGB, to whom domestic troops of MOOP are operationally subordinate, has been

promoted from candidate member to full member of the Central Committee.

5. Zhukov has been partially rehabilitated. This should be viewed not only as criticism of Khrushchev but also as the new leadership's admission of the correctness of Zhukov's views on the relative competence of and the boundaries between the military leadership and the party leadership at the summit and between the commanders and the "deputy political workers" below. For the first time the army has secured rehabilitation of officers who were executed, not by Stalin, but by Lenin (for example, Corps Commander Dumenko), on charges of conspiring against the Soviet regime.

In short, in the eyes of the army the present party apparatus lacks its former prestige. Its leaders are not Lenin and Stalin, nor even Malenkov and Khrushchev. During the war Khrushchev's heirs were either deputy political officers or did not smell gunpowder at all.

With due reservation regarding the danger of overestimating the army's place in the Soviet regime, the following conclusions may be considered indisputable. The Soviet generals are no longer the object of politics but now make politics themselves. From the instrument of policy it was under Lenin and Stalin, the army has become a political force. Although the army is now in a position to influence policy in the country, it does not claim for itself more than the right to the limited degree of domestic military and political autonomy to which even Zhukov at one time aspired. How the army will conduct itself in future decisions on important domestic and, more especially, foreign problems cannot be predicted with certainty. But one thing is clear: henceforth these decisions can be reached only with the army's participation. For the first time in the history of the dictatorship there is appearing in the former monolith of party absolutism a clear partition of power, with the military machine beginning to act as an opposition to the party machine. The Achilles' heel of the Soviet regime is no longer the division of the Soviet state into party (Brezhnev) and government (Kosygin), but the increasingly evident division between civil and military power.

CHAPTER XVII

The Party's Direction of the Secret Police

IN SPEAKING of the communist regime it is essential to make a clear differentiation between the regime itself and its functional organs of administration. The secret political police, like all other organs of the administration, is a specialized unit of a larger police regime. Its professional function—as political watchdog and physical inquisitor—has made it notorious as an evil genius and superforce in the Soviet state. It is, however, only a professional weapon of universal Chekism. It is the police personification of the entire communist regime. In a book published during Stalin's lifetime, this author wrote:

> The Stalinist regime is held together, not by the organization of soviets, not by party idealism, not by the power of the Politburo, not by Stalin's personality, but by the organization and technical skill of the Soviet political police force, in which Stalin himself plays the role of first policeman. . . . To say that the NKVD is the state secret police conveys very little. . . . To say that the NKVD is a "state within a state" is to underestimate its importance, for the very posing of the question allows for the presence of two forces: that of the normal state and that of the supernormal NKVD, while there is but one force, universal Chekism: state Chekism and party Chekism, collective Chekism and individual Chekism; Chekism in the sphere of theory and daily action; Chekism from top to bottom of the social scale.[1]

Even after the death of Stalin, the execution of Beria and the other heads of the Soviet secret police and the denunciation of Stalin, communist power remained based in the secret police. The annihilation of old Chekists and the attacks on Stalinist practices only strengthened the CHEKA system, since all its crimes were ascribed to persons and not to the system.

The material apparatus of communist power consists of several elements, including the Soviet secret political police, the gendarmerie troops (called the Troops of the Committee for State Security), the army, the Main Political Administration and its network, the special sections in the armed forces, the courts, the procuracy, the prisons, the concentration camps and, finally, over them all, the "leading and directing force"—the Communist party.

Some of these organs (the courts and the procuracy) nominally act on the basis of written laws; others (the political police, the gendarmerie and the political organs) on the basis of exclusive rights and unwritten laws, the extent and nature of which are determined by the party first secretary.

To say that there is in the Soviet system a division of spheres of action between the political police and the party, or competition between them, is an oversimplification. The party owes its long life to the political police, while the police owe their privileges and exceptional rights to the party. Between them there is only a technical division of functions such as exists between the members of a single organism: the party is the brains of the regime, the police its soul—but it is a soul that at times obviously affords protection to its brain. The present regime in the Soviet Union could exist as a one-party dictatorship even without the party (as it did under Stalin), but it could not exist without the police. Lenin was right when he said of the CHEKA: "Without this institution the workers' [soviet] regime could not exist."[2]

The Soviet police does not limit itself to physical suppression of actual or potential enemies of the regime. It enters all spheres of human association and thought and promotes the ideals of party consciousness and "vigilance." Physical terror is, of course, a terrible thing; but it is possible, if not to avoid it, at least to gauge it physically by degrees: prison, penal servitude or death; but to measure the scale and the depth of the horrors of spiritual terror would require the combined imaginations of a Shakespeare and a Dostoevsky.

The bolshevist political police was born with the 1917 Revolution. The organ in whose name power was seized—the Military Revolutionary Committee—handed power over to the official Soviet government, the Council of People's Commissars after the latter was created; but on October 26, 1917, it continued to act as a political police force. A decree of the Soviet government dated October 30, 1917, declared the Military Revolutionary Committee to be an organ of police surveillance assigned to execute instructions of the Council of People's Commissars, preserve "revolutionary order" and conduct the struggle against counter-revolution.[3]

On October 28 the Soviet government published a decree abolishing freedom of the press in Russia (on October 26, the day after the coup d'état, the Constitutional Democratic newspaper *Rech* ["Speech"], the *Den* ["Day"] and the *Birzhebye vedomosti* ["Stock Exchange Gazette"] had been suppressed). On December 7 and 20, 1917, the All-Russian Extraordinary Commission for the Suppression of Counterrevolution, Sabotage and Speculation (CHEKA) replaced the Military Revolutionary Committee. The party Central Committee subsequently indicated that the creation of a special political police of this type was required by a party that could not retain power by the usual methods of propaganda and agitation. A Central Committee decree of February 28, 1919, stated:

> The need for an organ for merciless retribution is recognized throughout the party.[4]

The CHEKA was the only organ of Soviet power to have unlimited special rights. Old professional revolutionaries, such as Dzerzhinsky, Menzhinsky, Latsis and Peters, were chosen to serve on it, and in 1919 Stalin joined the CHEKA as a Central Committee observer. The first Chairman of the CHEKA, the Old Bolshevik and Russified Pole Felix Edmundovich Dzerzhinsky, who had spent many years in penal servitude, declared somewhat sentimentally that "a Chekist has a warm heart, a cold mind and clean hands."[5]

Within a few weeks all Russia was covered by a close network of "extraordinary commissions." By the first half of 1918, 40 *gubernia* and 365 *uyezd* extraordinary commissions were created.[6] On February 21, 1918, a decree of the Council of People's Commissars gave legal force to the "extraordinary rights" of the extraordinary commissions and demanded that "speculators, burglars, hooligans and counterrevolutionary agitators be shot on the scene of the crime."

Lenin regarded this weapon of arbitrary mass terror as both a means of annihilating the actual enemies of the communist regime and as a warning to any who might be tempted to oppose it in the future. He said:

> This rabble must be dealt with in such a way that everyone will remember its fate for years to come.[7]

Just how successfully the commissions worked is shown by the official records of the Moscow CHEKA alone. Between December, 1918, and November, 1920, it destroyed fifty-nine counterrevolutionary organizations, including twenty-two White Guard, twelve Right-wing Social Revolutionary, fourteen Left-wing Social Revolutionary, three Menshevist, one Anarchist, five Underground Anarchist and two "maximalist" organizations.[8]

The "clean hands of the Chekist" of which Dzerzhinsky spoke were not idle. Whereas under the tsars between 1821 and 1906, 997 criminals had been executed (mainly regicides, patricides and triple murderers) more than 1,000,000 persons were shot between 1917 and 1923, under the CHEKA. In one and one-half days the Chekists executed more persons than had been executed in eighty-five years in tsarist Russia.[9]

Since the number of arrests grew faster than the number of those shot, Dzerzhinsky suggested in 1919 that Soviet concentration camps be organized. His reasoning, presented at a meeting of the CHEKA on February 19, 1919, was as follows:

> Little use is being made of the labor of persons under arrest, and so I propose . . . these concentration camps to utilize the labor of those who have been arrested . . . for those who cannot work without a certain degree of compulsion. Or, if we take soviet institutions, here too a punishment for a remiss attitude to work, for negligence, for tardiness, etc. must be applied. We can also apply this measure to our own workers.[10]

This proposal inaugurated an entirely new epoch in the U.S.S.R.—the concentration camp era. Within a month of Dzerzhinsky's speech the Soviet Parliament issued a decree on "forced labor," which was to be carried out by the CHEKA. A "Central Camp Directorate" under the MVD was established in Moscow. The CHEKA organs worked under the leadership and control of the party committees. In 1918 "control boards" were set up in local CHEKA units, consisting of one representative of the CHEKA and two representatives of the party committee at the same level. The party Central Committee stated:

> CHEKA units have been set up, exist and function only as the direct organs of the party, in accordance with its directives and under its control.[11]

Lenin demanded the direct participation of all Communists in the work of the CHEKA organs, declaring that "a good Communist is at the same time a good Chekist."[12]

Soon the master of the "naked sword of the proletariat" (as Stalin called the CHEKA), the terrible chief of the Soviet supreme inquisition, Dzerzhinsky, expressed deep compassion for the children whose fathers he had pitilessly executed. He proposed to the Soviet government the creation of an All-Russia Children's Commission of the CHEKA to care for orphaned children, with himself as chairman. His motives were weighty, if somewhat strange:

> I think that our apparatus is one of those that works with extreme precision. Its branches are everywhere and people respect them. They are held in awe.[13]

His recommendation was adopted.

On February 6, 1922, the CHEKA was renamed the GPU (State Political Administration). Its rights were reduced, but only outwardly and only temporarily. Political sections of executive committees were set up as GPU organs, as well as of central executive committees in the autonomous republics. A special government decree defined the GPU's tasks as follows: (1) to suppress counterrevolution and banditry, (2) to fight spying, (3) to protect means of communication, (4) to afford political protection to frontiers, (5) to prevent frontier crossing and trafficking in contraband and (6) to execute special government assignments "to protect the revolutionary order."[14]

The formation of the Union of Soviet Socialist Republics, in December, 1922, led to the formation of a centralized political police—the OGPU (United State Political Administration) of the Council of People's Commissars of the U.S.S.R. In the constituent republics OGPU administrations were set up to act as affiliated branches. The OGPU's tasks were: (1) to direct the GPU's of constituent republics and the special sections of the military districts under their jurisdiction, as well as transport organs of the GPU on railways and waterways; (2) to direct and administer the special sections of fronts and armies; (3) to organize defense of the U.S.S.R. frontiers; and (4) to direct operational work at the all-Union level, that is, to direct the management and organization of political spying both within the country and abroad.

In July, 1934, the OGPU was renamed the NKVD (People's Commissariat for Internal Affairs). This title became the symbol of an inquisition without precedent even in Soviet history. At first the people hoped that the change of name would be followed by a less oppressive regime, particularly because the judicial board of the OGPU was officially abolished, although it soon reappeared under the innocent new title "Special Council." The number of tasks assigned to the NKVD increased ominously. A government decree stated that these tasks were: (1) to secure "revolutionary order" and the security of the state; (2) to protect socialist property; (3) to maintain population statistics (registration of births, deaths, marriages, and divorces); (4) to guard the frontiers; (5) to operate the concentration camps; (6) to administer escort troops; (7) to administer paved and unpaved roads and automobile transport; (8) to administer government survey and cartographic work; (9) to administer forest conservation; (10) to administer resettlement schemes and (11) to administer the control of weights and measures, etc.[15]

It soon became clear that the expansion in the NKVD's responsibilities gave the Soviet secret police legal authority to interfere in everything, including family life.

In February, 1941, the NKVD was divided into two independent police organs—the NKVD (police troops) and the People's Commissariat for State Security (the secret police)—but they were reunited in July, 1941, at the beginning of the war. In April, 1943, the NKVD was again divided into these two commissariats, renamed the MGB (Ministry for State Security) and the MVD (Ministry for Internal Affairs).

The secret police organs in the constituent republics, although according to the Constitution ministries of the republics, are not subordinate to the republics. Regarding this unusual state of affairs in Soviet democracy the official statement is as follows:

A characteristic feature of the status of rights of the MVD of the U.S.S.R. and the MGB of the U.S.S.R. is that, unlike other constituent republic ministries, the local organs of these ministries do not have a dual allegiance.[16]

In other words, the political police organs in constituent republics are not only not subordinate to the local supreme soviets, they are not even subordinate to the supreme party organs—the central committees of their republics' Communist parties.

On the day after Stalin's death (March 5, 1953) the MVD and the MGB were again reunited, and a single MVD of the U.S.S.R. was created, headed by Beria. In March, 1954, the MVD was again divided, with considerable changes in the internal organization of the police system. The State Security Service was separated from the MVD (actually the secret police) and organized as a new institution entitled the KGB (Committee for State Security) of the Council of Ministers of the U.S.S.R. A decree of the Presidium of the Supreme Soviet of the U.S.S.R. on this new reorganization appeared in the press, but it gave no indication of the range of duties, obligations and rights of the KGB. There was probably no need to do so, for the basic tasks of the secret police have remained the same from 1917 to the present day. Names have changed, heads have fallen (of the seven chiefs of the secret police before and after the war, one died by his own hand, one was poisoned and five were shot), but the system has remained inviolate. Moreover, Soviet commentators think along the same lines. The book *Soviet Administrative Law,* published in 1959, states:

> It is a duty of the KGB of the U.S.S.R. to take the necessary measures to ensure the security of the state by exposing and bringing to trial spies, diversionists, terrorists, traitors to the Fatherland and other agents of foreign intelligence service . . . to reveal crimes against the state and to conduct the preliminary investigation of them.[17]

In the constituent and autonomous republics, KGB administrations have been created, formally under the local councils of ministers. In constituent republics having *oblasts,* the *oblast* executive committees have *oblast* KGB administrations. The Ministry of Internal Affairs of the U.S.S.R. has been liquidated, and its armed forces and frontier troops have been transferred to the new KGB of the U.S.S.R. Ministries for the protection of social order (MOOP) have been created in constituent and autonomous republics, with limited functions of maintaining public order through the police troops, etc. Officially the local MOOP units have a dual allegiance—to the local authority (the council of ministers of the constituent or autonomous republic) and to their higher authority, the KGB of the U.S.S.R., but in actuality the latter has operational control when needed. The sole basic change that distinguishes the present secret police from Stalin's secret police is that something similar to a political "collective leadership" in the form of committees has been set up above the organs of the secret police at both national and local level. Since the creation of committees of state security was prompted by the need to revive Leninist principles of leadership and Dzerzhinsky's method of operation, the "collective leadership" was only a revival of the old practice of party control over the police through permanent representatives of the party apparatus at every level of the KGB. Accordingly the system of local KGB's has by no means involved dual allegiance to local soviet and party organs and to the central authority, the KGB of the U.S.S.R. The right of party central committees of the constituent republics and party *oblast* committees to control secret police organs is limited to party surveillance; it does not include the right to intervene in operations or administration.

Neither the party central committees of the constituent republics nor their supreme soviets nor the *oblast* committees nor the *oblast* executive committees can issue decisions or laws binding on local KGB units. Nor can they appoint or dismiss KGB chairmen, heads of regional administrations or even district representatives of the KGB. While according to the Constitution the appointment and dismissal of chairmen of local KGB's are effected by decrees of the supreme soviets of the constituent or autonomous republics, in actuality their appointment and dismissal are effected by two departments of the Central Committee of the CPSU —the Party Organs Department and the Administrative Department, through the KGB of the U.S.S.R.

The work of party organizations in the KGB system is similarly arranged. They do not have the right of control, but they can initiate action. The party statutes' requirement obliging party members and primary party organizations "promptly to report to the appropriate party organs shortcomings in the work of institutions and also of individual workers, irrespective of the posts they occupy," refers to these organizations.[18] The party organizations of the KGB are not subordinate vertically, like all other primary party organizations (except the army), they are subordinate to the corresponding party *raion* and city committees. Exceptions include party organizations in the armed forces of the KGB of the U.S.S.R., where, as in the army, there exists a system of political administration organs (political sections) to which they are subordinate. The primary party organizations of KGB organs are in a special position with regard to participation in the "production" work of their institutions. Primary party organizations of the KGB not only do not have the right to control the work of their institutions, they also do not have the right to know the nature of such institutions. Members of a collective of a party organization know only the secrets of a service sector individually. This is quite understandable, for at meetings of KGB party organizations generals and boilermakers, investigators and cooks, cabinet ministers and charwomen sit side by side. After all, the party is the "party of the whole Soviet people"! Therefore the tasks of primary party organizations of KGB organs are confined to the narrow limits of questions of ideology, discipline and the personal affairs of Communists. As in ordinary civilian organizations, the Chekists conduct systematic brainwashing in carrying out their work. Cynics believing in no dogma at all, the Chekists also conscientiously and with a great show of zeal study the dead language of Marxism-Leninism, which they learn by heart in order to reach the predetermined conclusion that police vigilance is the supreme task of Chekist work. (The evolution that has taken place in the doctrine of vigilance since Stalin's death is characteristic: in the 1950 edition of *Soviet Administrative Law,* the chapter on the NKVD states: "Vigilance is the duty of every Soviet citizen."[19] In the 1959 edition of this work, this passage has been altered to: "Vigilance is the duty of each worker, in whatever sector he may be."[20]

With respect to personal matters—admission to or exclusion from the party, or the imposition of party penalties—the primary party organizations of KGB organs act in meticulous accordance with the party statutes; but here too there is one vital deviation from the usual party norms: workers in the KGB apparatus are forbidden to recommend candidates for party membership.* Therefore even KGB workers entering the party cannot be recommended by their own party colleagues but must seek the recommendation of party members who have known them in their previous employment or in school.

The leadership of the entire system of KGB organs is centralized in the Secretariat of the Central Committee of the CPSU. The Administrative Department and the Party Organs Department of the party Central Committee engage in the allocation of Chekist cadres at all levels, and the first secretary himself directs the apparatus of the KGB of the U.S.S.R. In the central committees of the republics and in *oblast* and *krai* committees there are also administrative sections, which, in strict accord with instructions of the party Central Committee, maintain party control only over local KGB organs. In the republics, one of the central committee secretaries, generally a member of the local state security committee, oversees the party line in the KGB's work. In turn the KGB chairman is a member of the local party committee, in order to ensure that close contact in the work between the party committee and the state security committee is maintained.

The party organizations for the special sections work in especially close contact with the KGB organs. The KGB has a network of official residents in all institutions, organizations and enterprises, known as "heads of special sections," who engage in political and operational work in their own institutes (to prevent counterrevolution, anti-Soviet propaganda, spying, "wrecking," etc.). They are not accountable to the party organization in their work, but the party organization is obliged to cooperate with them, not only in their official activities, but also in their secret work.

The question of creating in the party itself a secret agency of the organs of the Soviet secret police had been long debated. Although Lenin said that every Communist must be a Chekist, the recruiting of secret agents from within the party was forbidden. With the appearance

---

*Information provided by V. P. Artemiev, a former NKVD colonel.

of opposition elements within the party, Stalin not only removed this prohibition, he also created, in competition with the NKVD, a network in the party of police organs in the form of the Special Section of the party Central Committee and the special sections of the republic party central committees, *oblast* committees and *krai* committees. The NKVD organs also received permission to recruit Communists as *seksots* (secret informers). This was done in various ways—by locating "ideological *seksots,*" or hiring them, or recruiting Communists whose political or social past was shaky or who had become caught in the Chekists' net through some misdeed.

Stalin's logic in creating a dual network of secret police in the party worked well, for the party remained the only organization in the Soviet state outside the control of the secret police. If any danger threatened Stalin and his regime it could come only from the party, especially from its topmost ranks.

An enormous literature exists dealing with the methods and scope of the Soviet secret police in Stalin's time. Much has been written about the Great Purge, in particular about those who helped carry it out and the methods they employed. The authoritative account is contained in Khrushchev's historic report on the personality cult to the closed session of the Twentieth Party Congress. For understandable reasons, Khrushchev did not state the total number of the victims of the *Yezhovshchina* but confined himself to the conclusion that

> the number of arrests on charges of counterrevolutionary crimes was more than ten times greater in 1937 than it was in 1936.[21]

The data cited by Khrushchev on the execution of party leaders and the methods employed in the purge are astounding. Khrushchev declared:

> It has been established that of 139 members and candidate members of the Central Committee elected at the Seventeenth Party Congress, 98, that is, 70 per cent, were arrested and shot. . . . This fate befell not only members of the Central Committee but also the majority of the delegates at the Seventeenth Congress— 1,108 of the 1,958 delegates were arrested.[22]

Concerning the methods used, including trumped-up charges against leading party cadres, Khrushchev declared:

> The NKVD undertook to employ the criminal method of preparing lists of people whose trials came within the jurisdiction of military tribunals. Their sentences were decided in advance. Yezhov usually sent the lists to Stalin personally, and he would approve the proposed punishments. In 1937 and 1938, 383 such lists were sent to Stalin, containing the names of thousands of party, soviet, *Komsomol,* military and economic workers. He approved these lists.[23]

What Khrushchev had reported to the secret session of the Twentieth

Congress as Stalin's personal crimes, he described at the Twenty-second Party Congress, at a session open to the world, as the collective crimes of the supreme organ of the party—the entire Stalinist Politburo. Khrushchev's new companions (Shelepin, Serdyuk, Podgorny, Polyansky, Shvernik and Rodionov) also cited numerous facts and documents in this connection.

Despite the 1936 Constitution, between 1936 and 1938, without orders or sanction from public prosecutors, Stalin's government arrested up to five million Soviet citizens, hundreds of thousands of whom were shot "according to lists," not only in the capital, but throughout the country, after being sentenced by regional and republic "NKVD *troikas*" (consisting of the NKVD chief, the public prosecutor and the secretary of the party *oblast* committee or the secretary of the central committee of a constituent republic Communist party).

What guarantee is there that Brezhnev's new Constitution will prove a more effective weapon against the arbitrary use of power than Stalin's Constitution was? The only effective guarantee against a repetition would be to grant basic civil liberties and to establish a regime based on law. The cardinal contradiction in the Kremlin's action on condemning Stalin lay in that, while doing so, it was forced to administer the country in a Stalinist manner. Stalin was powerful, not because of his personality cult, but because of his system. The Stalin cult has been unmasked, but the Stalinist system continues to exist.

The death of Stalin, the shooting of Beria and his closest associates and the denunciation of Stalin and Stalinist crimes dealt heavy blows to the prestige of the NKVD.

The new Central Committee leadership, in the course of diminishing the "consequences of the cult of personality," not only put the KGB organs under party control, it considerably reduced its exclusive rights. In September, 1953, the Special Council (the non-judicial tribunal of the secret police) was abolished. In 1956 two highly important government decrees were promulgated concerning the Ministry of Internal Affairs and the concentration camps. They were not published, but an official party journal summarized them as follows:

> 1. The administration of the MVD and the administrations of the militia are reorganized into single administrations of internal affairs of the executive committees.

(Subsequently the MVD of the U.S.S.R. was abolished and only the MVD's of constituent and autonomous republics were retained—these were later renamed the MOOP.)

> 2. The continued existence of corrective labor camps is recognized to be inexpedient, and it has been decided to reorganize them as corrective labor colonies . . . . To strengthen the control over the activities of corrective labor institutions of executive committees of local soviets, observer commissions have been established con-

sisting of representatives of soviet, trade union and *Komsomol* organizations.[24]

The party bureaucracy has brought the political police back under its control, disposed of its old leaders, reorganized its internal structure and placed bureaucratic controllers from the party apparatus in all its important detachments. This does not mean that the Soviet state has ceased to be a police state, but it does indicate that the police force has ceased to be all-powerful.

CHAPTER XVIII

The Party and the Nationality Question

ON THE EVE of the Sixteenth Congress of the Soviet Communist party, in 1930, the author, at that time an enthusiastic young supporter of Lenin's nationality policy, wrote the following in an article in *Pravda* entitled "For the Implementation of Party Directives on the Nationality Question":

> Neither our achievements to date nor the present pace of our cultural and economic construction in the national minority regions ensure the fulfillment of the entirely clear and practical directives of the Tenth and Twelfth Party Congresses (1921 and 1923) either during this five-year plan or during successive ones. It is necessary to undertake now, in the period of reconstruction, the task of practical elimination of the actual inequality of the nationalities. . . . It must not be asserted that the proletarian revolution will not do anything that is economically inexpedient at a given time.[1]

Already the Soviet leaders were, in fact, beginning to betray openly the principles proclaimed at the Tenth Party Congress, which had been laid down as follows:

> The policy of tsarism consisted in destroying among the non-Russian peoples the rudiments of any statehood, in mutilating their culture, in restricting their language and in Russifying them. . . . It is the party's task to help the toiling masses in the non-Russian nations to overtake Central Russia, which has forged ahead, and (1) to develop and strengthen among themselves forms of the Soviet system corresponding to their national way of life; (2) to develop and strengthen a functional national language, courts, administrative and economic organs, and governmental bodies composed of members of the indigenous population; (3) to develop among themselves a press, schools and a theater . . . in their native language.[2]

In actual practice, the common attitude toward the Soviet non-Russian nationalities was one of "Great Russian chauvinism," which was attacked at the Twelfth Party Congress in 1923:

> The situation in a number of national republics (the Ukraine, Belorussia, Azerbaidzhan, Turkestan) is complicated by the fact

that a large section of the working class belongs to the Great Russian nationality. Ties between the working class and the peasantry are hindered chiefly by remnants of Great Russian chauvinism to be found in both party and soviet organs. In these conditions, talk about the superiority of Russian culture to that of more backward peoples (Ukrainians, Azerbaidzhanians, Uzbeks, Kirghiz, etc.) is none other than an attempt to consolidate the supremacy of the Great Russian nationality.[3]

Such party self-criticism was made at recurring intervals, but did not bring an improvement in the situation. Even today the non-Russian peoples of the Soviet Union continue to be subjected to economic and cultural Russification.

This policy is being carried out under the slogan of the "internationalization" of Union and autonomous republics, which, since the Great Russians are numerically predominant in the Soviet Union, in practice means Russification. This chapter will attempt to define the nature and extent of this process; to give a comparative analysis of the development of the Soviet Great Russian heartland or "metropolis" and of the peripheral non-Russian regions; and to show in which direction the "new stage in the development of national relations in the U.S.S.R." proclaimed in the 1961 Soviet party program is likely to lead. Each of these subjects will be treated from the political, economic and cultural angles.

It must be stated at the outset that a direct comparison between Soviet colonialism, that is, treatment of the non-Russian national minorities, and "classic" Western colonialism is invalid. There are important differences between the two systems.

Soviet colonialism is ideocratic and supraracial in nature; this lends it a dynamic foreign to the Western form, which amounted merely to economic exploitation. The foremost objective of Soviet colonialism is political and ideological control. In Western colonial empires the indigenous population did not enjoy the legal rights of the people of the metropolis and was discriminated against, but retained its national identity. The Russian Communists, on the other hand, eliminating this national identity, sought a solution to the nationality problem through full integration of non-Russian peoples with the Russians, through both assimilation (an organic process) and Russification (an artificial process). This was only the ultimate goal, however; at first, in order to win the support of the nationalities, the Russian Communists did not seek to destroy their identity. This was a temporary and forced concession to the nationalist movements that developed after the 1917 Revolution. The Bolsheviks, although more extreme centralists than the Russian tsars had ever been in their colonial policy, recognized that the great failure of tsarist imperialism had been discrimination against the languages and culture of the non-Russian minorities. Therefore they proclaimed cultural autonomy for the nationalities and their right to secede from the new Soviet state—a purely tactical concession that the Communists had no intention of honoring.

This communist policy appealed to the non-Russian peoples and was a decisive factor in the Bolsheviks' eventual victory over the White counterrevolutionaries. Although Stalin exaggerated the role of the non-Russian nations in this victory, he was not far from the truth when he wrote:

> The Revolution in Russia would not have triumphed and Denikin and Kolchak would not have been defeated if the Russian proletariat had not had behind it the sympathy and support of the oppressed peoples of the erstwhile Russian Empire.[4]

Indeed, the general strategic aims of the communist revolution, and not any new moral philosophy about freedom and equality for colonial nations, explain Soviet nationality policy. Lenin and his disciples made it clear that the national and colonial question was for them a matter of tactics and a derivative part of the larger strategic aim of setting up the "dictatorship of the proletariat."[5] Soviet nationality policy has been shaped by (1) the need to entrench the regime, (2) the long-range domestic goal of preparing conditions within the Soviet Union for the creation of a single communist nation and (3) the long-range goal in foreign policy of establishing worldwide communist rule. During the initial stage of "national demarcation" it was not, however, these goals that were stressed, but the need to accelerate the economic and cultural development of the non-Russian nations in order to transform them into modern industrial states with sovereign rights equal to those of the Great Russian nation. Party officials during the twenties were ordered not to adopt stereotyped communist tactics when dealing with the non-Russian nations, but to modify these tactics in accordance with varying local conditions. The policy of the tsars was condemned as reactionary, colonial and imperialist, and the struggle of the non-Russian nations against the autocracy was praised as a progressive struggle for national liberation. Any former or current advancement of strictly Russian interests was regarded as the product of "great-power chauvinism" and declared the principal enemy of party nationality policy. Local nationalism was considered a lesser evil and a natural reaction to great-power chauvinism. This stage of bolshevist policy ended at the beginning of the thirties.[6]

The second stage brought a virtual reversal. Local nationalism became regarded as the principal danger, and the policy of *korenizatsiya* (appointment of indigenous cadres to party and government posts in the non-Russian republics) was abandoned in Tataria, Turkestan, the Caucasus, the Ukraine and Belorussia.[7] Even the aggressive foreign policy of Imperial Russia in the Caucasus and Turkestan was rehabilitated, on the grounds that its results were progressive, while the national liberation movements of the subjugated nations against tsarism were proclaimed reactionary. The Russian people were described as the elder brother of the Soviet national minorities; this new line coincided with the stimulation of purely Russian patriotic feeling, which reached a crescendo during and after World War II. In his famous toast at a Kremlin victory banquet on May 24, 1945, Stalin referred to the Russians as the "leading nation" in the Soviet Union,[8] and in the post-war Zhdanov period, Russian precedence in all fields of science and discovery was claimed. Stalin's successors have, however, abandoned the dogma of "Russian precedence," preferring to attribute such achievements as the Sputnik to the communist system and not to the Russian genius, for fear that encouragement of Russian nationalism would conflict with the ideology and practice of communism. The third stage in the Kremlin nationality policy, which is now in progress, is marked by an acceleration of the internationalization of the non-Russian Soviet republics, as laid down in the 1961 party program, which speaks of the "growing together" of the nations of the Soviet Union and the "achievement of their complete unity."[9]

All this is part of the objective laid down by the Soviet party program of 1961, which states that in the course of the next twenty years the Soviet national minorities will begin to merge, or, in other words, to lose their national identity. The program stated:

> Large-scale communist construction signifies a new stage in the development of nationality relations in the U.S.S.R. characterized by a further rapprochement of nations and the achievement of their complete unity. . . . Borders between Soviet republics within the confines of the U.S.S.R. are increasingly losing their significance.[10]

And an authoritative party journal adds:

> Alterations and more precise definitions with respect to borders and forms of national and state organization are probable.[11]

Among the methods by which the new party program proposes to hasten the process of ultimate dissolution of the nationalities as ethnic and state entities, the most effective is held to be intensification of the mass migration policy, which has already reduced the indigenous populations of Kazakhstan and Kirghizia to minorities in their own countries and is hastening the internationalization of the Union republics.

The party program notes:

> The Russian language has become the common language for international intercourse and for collaboration among all peoples of the U.S.S.R. . . . The increasing scale of communist construction demands constant interchange of cadres among the nations.[12]

And the journal of the U.S.S.R. Soviet Academy of Sciences Law Institute states explicitly:

> At the present time the problem of mutual relations between the nationalities of the U.S.S.R. has a purely and directly com-

munist purpose—the achievement of all-round unity among Soviet nations, with the final prospect of complete coalescence. Therefore, whereas formerly the degree of federalization, the nature of the national state system and the juridical maintenance of national and state borders meant a guarantee of national freedom, now in essence they have no such meaning. Already one can say with confidence that in this respect national statehood and the federal system have on the whole fulfilled their historic mission.[13]

The journal goes even further, with a frankness rare in Soviet publications, revealing the Soviet formula for creating one single nation in the U.S.S.R. It is stated outright that the policy of assimilation is "denationalization":

> In fact, mutual assimilation of nations denationalizes national and territorial autonomy and even Union republics, in this respect, too, bringing Soviet society closer to the point at which a complete political and legal merger of nations will become a matter of the foreseeable future.[14]

Available data indicate that this assertion is a logical interpretation of the new party program and also an authentic statement of the true purpose of the current policy of internationalization of the economies, cultures and territories of the national republics.

What have been the effects of this policy? As early as 1927 the directives of the Fifteenth Party Congress for the First Five-Year Plan abandoned the aim of building up the industrial potential of each national republic and ordered instead the forced development of heavy industry, mainly on the territory of the R.S.F.S.R.[15] Subsequent capital investments were made in industry in the national republics, not for the benefit of the latter, but because of the effectiveness of such investment from the point of view of the state as a whole.

The economic policy of the Soviet Communist party toward the "national," i.e., non-Russian, republics of the Soviet Union has two main aims. One is to make every national republic into a specialized part of the total economic structure of the U.S.S.R. (Official Soviet slogans for this program call for "specialization" of production, "cooperation," and "division of labor" with other republics.) The other is to integrate the native inhabitants and those who have moved in from other parts of the Soviet Union, by means of large-scale organized resettlement. (The government's slogan for this policy is "internationalization" of the national republics.)

In the face of this program of economic centralization, the national republics affected have been, and are, quite helpless to press for the creation of independent national economies of their own. A prominent Soviet economist has made this quite clear:

> It is, of course, inexpedient to create more or less fully developed industrial complexes in the smaller republics, which are

developing as integral parts of the basic economic regions of the country.[16]

As a result of this long-standing economic policy the national republics have not been allowed to create independently operating national economies; they have had to develop separate branches of a national Soviet economy whose ulterior purpose is to prohibit them from existing as economic units outside the Soviet empire.

One highly important result of the Soviet policy of internationalization of the national republics has been to divide each national republic into two parts—a *national* rural area and an *international* urban area. All new cities and workers' settlements and all important industrial areas in the national republics are being populated with people of other nationalities coming in from outside the particular republic.

Despite a declared policy of internationalization of industry, the industrialization of the national republics lags significantly behind that of the Russian metropolis. The uneven development and the considerable industrial lag in the national republics as compared with the R.S.F.S.R. is reflected in official Soviet data on population figures for urban and rural areas in the Union republics and the autonomous republics of the R.S.F.S.R. in Tables 30 and 31.[17]

TABLE 30

PERCENTAGE OF URBAN POPULATION IN UNION REPUBLICS

REPUBLIC	PERCENTAGE
R.S.F.S.R.	52
Armenia	50
Azerbaidzhan	48
Ukraine	46
Turkmenistan	46
Kazakhstan	44
Georgia	42
Lithuania	39
Kirghizia	34
Uzbekistan	34
Tadzhikistan	33
Belorussia	31
Moldavia	22

As Table 30 shows, of the twelve non-Russian republics listed, five (Moldavia, Belorussia, Tadzhikistan, Kirghizia and Uzbekistan) have less than 35 per cent urban population, six have less than 50 per cent, and only Armenia has reached 50 per cent. (Latvia and Estonia are omitted, as large numbers of Russians lived in both countries before their annexation by the Soviet Union and the proportion of their urban

population [56 per cent] is in both cases higher than even that of the
R.S.F.S.R.)[18]

TABLE 31

PERCENTAGE OF URBAN POPULATION IN AUTONOMOUS REPUBLICS OF THE
RUSSIAN REPUBLIC

REPUBLIC	PERCENTAGE
R.S.F.S.R.	52
Yakut	49
Udmurt	44
Tatar	42
Chechen-Ingush	41
Buryat	41
Bashkir	38
Kabardin-Balkar	38
Daghestan	30
Mari	28
Chuvash	24
Kalmyk	21

For both the Union republics and the autonomous republics the
figures are for the entire population, both native and non-native. The
native population by itself is still basically agricultural in a majority
of the Union republics and in all of the autonomous republics, as shown
by Table 32.[19]

TABLE 32

URBAN AND RURAL POPULATIONS IN UNION REPUBLICS BY LANGUAGE

POPULATION	TOTAL NATIVE POPULATION	URBAN POPULATION	PERCENTAGE OF URBAN POPULATION
Russians	124,119,000	73,487,000	59.1
Armenians	2,510,000	1,333,000	53.1
Estonians	953,000	439,000	48.1
Latvians	1,360,000	636,000	47.0
Ukrainians	33,225,000	11,469,000	43.5
Georgians	2,765,000	1,017,000	36.8
Lithuanians	2,287,000	795,000	34.8
Azerbaidzhanians	2,198,000	1,004,000	33.7
Turkmen	997,000	250,000	25.0
Belorussians	6,952,000	1,673,000	24.1
Kazakhs	3,580,000	846,000	23.6
Tadzhiks	1,459,000	319,000	21.9
Uzbeks	6,007,000	1,286,000	21.2
Moldavians	2,287,000	230,000	10.8
Kirghiz	965,000	104,000	10.7

Only two native populations, the Russians and the Armenians, make up more than 50 per cent of the urban population, while three national groups make up from 40 per cent to 50 per cent, three from 25 per cent to 40 per cent, one 25 per cent, four less than 25 per cent and two only about 11 per cent.

The same low proportion of native urban population is found in the autonomous republics, as can be seen in Table 33.[20]

TABLE 33

URBAN AND RURAL POPULATIONS IN AUTONOMOUS REPUBLICS BY LANGUAGE

POPULATION	TOTAL NATIVE POPULATION	URBAN POPULATION	PERCENTAGE OF URBAN POPULATION
Tatars	4,946,000	2,095,000	42.4
Ossetians	368,000	118,000	32.1
Abkhazians	62,000	16,000	25.8
Chechen-Ingush	519,000	131,000	25.2
Komi	259,000	65,000	25.1
Bashkirs	617,000	144,000	23.3
Karelians	119,000	27,000	22.7
Karakalpaks	168,000	34,000	20.3
Mordvinians	1,004,000	195,000	19.4
Daghestanis	918,000	163,000	17.1
Udmurts	557,000	97,000	17.4
Yakuts	242,000	38,000	15.7
Chuvash	1,335,000	206,000	15.4
Buryats	240,000	35,000	14.6
Kabardians	227,000	30,000	13.2
Komi-Permyaks	126,000	13,000	10.3
Maris	480.000	45,000	9.4

As Table 33 shows, in three of the seventeen autonomous republics, natives make up less than 25 per cent of the urban population; in five, less than 20 per cent; and in four, less than 15 per cent.

The denationalization of the non-Russian republics, both Union and autonomous, is a striking testimony to the extent to which the Kremlin has failed to pursue in its own empire the kind of "anticolonial" policy it has urged on others. In reality, it has maintained within its borders a number of communist republics as underdeveloped as the developing countries of Asia and Africa.

The proudly proclaimed policy of the internationalization of the populations of the non-Russian republics serves both to promote the primary aim of imperial control and denationalization and to mask the actual party policy of creating Russian cities in the national republics. Moreover, internationalization is called an achievement of the republics themselves.

Additional information on the general industrial backwardness and uneven industrial development of the national republics may be obtained from data on the number of persons employed in the national economy. Table 34 gives the percentages of those employed in some branch of the national economy in the U.S.S.R. as a whole and in selected non-Russian republics in 1959.[21]

TABLE 34

PERCENTAGE OF PERSONS EMPLOYED IN THE NATIONAL ECONOMY

AREA	PERCENTAGE
U.S.S.R.	27.0
Kirghizia	19.5
Turkmenistan	19.2
Azerbaidzhan	19.0
Uzbekistan	17.2
Tadzhikistan	14.5
Moldavia	14.4

There is also a definite contrast between the R.S.F.S.R. and the Union republics with regard to the portion of the population in intellectual occupations. Since the urban population in the Union republics has, in the main, been "internationalized," the data in Table 35 are given for the rural population only.[22]

TABLE 35

PERCENTAGE OF INHABITANTS IN RURAL AREAS IN THE UNION REPUBLICS
IN INTELLECTUAL OCCUPATIONS

UNION REPUBLIC	PERCENTAGE
R.S.F.S.R.	13.6
Kirghizia	12.5
Estonia	12.4
Georgia	11.9
Armenia	10.5
Latvia	10.3
Uzbekistan	9.8
Azerbaidzhan	9.6
Ukraine	9.2
Turkmenistan	8.8
Tadzhikistan	8.8
Belorussia	8.0
Lithuania	7.4
Moldavia	6.5

As Table 35 indicates, all the Union republics cited above have fewer people engaged in intellectual work than the R.S.F.S.R. Eight republics have almost one-third fewer. The fact that backward Kirghizia, with nearly as many people in the rural areas engaged in intellectual work as in the R.S.F.S.R. and Kazakhstan (not shown above, but with 16.3 per cent), even surpasses the R.S.F.S.R. is to be explained by the fact that in Kirghizia 60 per cent, and in Kazakhstan 70 per cent, of the population is made up of immigrants from other areas.

In allocating productive resources and new capital investments, Soviet authorities are not guided by the interests of the national republics composing the U.S.S.R.; they aim solely at the maximum economic and military might of the Soviet state. Official party propaganda, especially in the developing countries, maintains that Soviet economic plans always give preference to the developing of the national republics. Both the facts already given and those contained in the latest Seven-Year Plan refute this Soviet contention.

Under that plan, of the total capital investment for 1959–65 of 1,488,000,000,000 rubles planned, capital investment in the R.S.F.S.R. amounted to 8,120 rubles per capita as against an average of 5,073 in the other thirteen republics, not including Kazakhstan. No allowance was made for the degree of backwardness or stage of development of the various republics, and there was no attempt to distribute resources in proportion to need. In Kazakhstan, where the native population is only 30 per cent of the total, planned capital investment amounted to 12,527 rubles per capita, while in several of the most backward republics, where the majority of the inhabitants are of the indigenous nationality, the corresponding figure was less than 5,000 rubles (Belorussia, Tadzhikistan and Moldavia).[23]

Such obvious discrimination in the financing of the Soviet economy has led to serious discontent among the leaders of the Union republics; some of them have complained of unjust treatment on the part of Moscow. The reaction of the central authorities to such complaints is reflected in a statement by former party Central Committee Secretary L. Ilichev:

> Survivals of nationalism are very much alive. . . . They may be seen in the attempts of individual workers to "garner" more of some needed or unneeded appropriation for "their own" republic or region at the expense of overall state interests.[24]

Where do the profits from industrial enterprises located in the Union republics go, and what happens to the income realized from their natural resources? The answer to these questions is found in the Soviet manual of financial law:[25]

> Cash profit goes into the budget depending on the type of subordination of the enterprise: that from enterprises of Union subordination goes into the Union budget, that from enterprises of

republic subordination to the republic budget and that from enterprises of local subordination to the local budget.

Under this principle, the entire revenue from heavy industry and from the exploitation of natural resources in the national republics goes into the central fund in Moscow. As far as the turnover tax is concerned (and this represents the greater part of net income), this too goes into the central fund in Moscow.[26]

The Soviet press often reports a sharp increase in the state budgets of the Union republics. The Soviet author cited above states that the budgets of the Union republics rose from 24.1 per cent of the total state budget of the U.S.S.R. in 1940 to 55.7 per cent in 1962.[27] Closer examination shows that the apparent increase is deceptive. Before the reorganization of industrial administration, finances and capital investments in enterprises at Union level in the Union republics were handled directly through the central budget in Moscow. Since the transfer of these enterprises to nominal control by the national republics, all financial operations for these enterprises are nominally handled through the state budgets of the national republics. This is what the Soviet author has in mind when he declares that the growth of the budgets in the republics

is conditioned by measures in the reorganization of industrial control and construction and by the related transfer of an absolute majority of enterprises

to the Union republics.[28]

It is clear that as far as the economic development of the national republics is concerned, the party rules, not in accordance with its solemn declarations made in the past or with the decisions of the recent Tenth and Twelfth Congresses for the Preferential Economic Development of Backward Non-Russian Peoples, but on the basis of the economic effectiveness of capital investment and military considerations in the regions selected for industrialization.

The industrialization of the U.S.S.R. has led not to a narrowing but to a widening of the differences in economic development between Russia proper and the national republics and between the different national republics themselves. As a result, many of the Union republics may truly be termed "underdeveloped countries." These republics are Kazakhstan, Kirghizia, Belorussia, Tadzhikistan, Turkmenistan, Uzbekistan and almost all of the autonomous republics, where the economies are not allowed to rise above the level of supplying raw materials and semifinished products.

The subservience of the Union republics of the U.S.S.R. to the central authorities is most apparent in the budgetary sphere. The hallmark of a sovereign state is its ability to draw up and allocate its own budget, impose taxes and control expenditure, even when it is part of a federal system. Under the Soviet budgetary system, however, the Union republics have to abide by the financial and general economic policy laid down in Moscow. The new party program states explicitly that the central planning organs

> assure the pursuit of a uniform state policy in technical progress, capital investment, distribution of production forces, labor payment and prices and the creation of a single system of accounting and statistical computation.[29]

This does not leave much in the hands of the Union republics. Under the Soviet system there is a single centralized budget, which includes the Union budget and the so-called state budgets of the fifteen republics. Prior to 1957 these state budgets were drawn up and ratified in Moscow and had to be complied with unquestioningly. Under the laws of 1957, however, which extended the rights of the Union republics to some degree, the council of ministers of each republic is entitled to discuss the draft budget, which is then forwarded to the U.S.S.R. Council of Ministers and ratified by the Supreme Soviet in Moscow. Those sections of the budget relating to the various republics also come before the supreme soviets of the latter for ratification.

The financial organs at republic level thus remain branches of the central authority invested with no more than administrative and executive functions. Even after their expansion, in 1957, the prerogatives of the Union republics in budgetary affairs remain meager; councils of ministers are entitled to: (1) make proposals for capital investment by their ministries and to ratify an estimated expenditure of up to five million rubles for investment in industries of Union-republic importance; (2) fix the number of personnel in the government apparatus, within the limits of the wage fund allotted to them; (3) allocate expenditure and revenue, as laid down by the central authorities and (4) increase allotments for repair of housing, schools and hospitals—but here again only so long as the general budgetary provisions fixed in Moscow are not infringed.[30]

Nor can the Union republics be said to benefit fully from the industrialization taking place on their territory (even though the national economic councils [*sovnarkhozy*] are subordinate to the republic councils of ministers), since deductions from the resultant profit go to the central finance organs, to be incorporated into the total Soviet state revenue. The same applies to the proceeds of the turnover tax levied on goods sold within a given republic, which represents the major part of the net income from such sales.[31]

The Soviet press makes frequent references to the sharp increase in the Union-republic budgets over recent years.[32] On closer inspection, however, this increase proves to be illusory.[33]

The Union republics were, however, quick to make the most of the degree of decentralization that took place during the Khrushchev regime. This led to attempts to secure some measure of autarchy, arousing a sharp reaction from the central authorities. The Central Committee organ *Kommunist* has summarized Moscow's attitude in four points: (1) "the interests of the Soviet people as a whole must be given strict priority" in the national republics; (2) "the economic foundations of each republic rest on state socialist property, which does not belong to any one nation but to the whole Soviet people"; (3) "a fetish for national sovereignty and a narrow interpretation of national interests can only cause harm"; (4) "resources must be invested in those places where the state can obtain maximum economic effect with minimum expenditure."[34]

The second method by which the Soviet leaders are pursuing their policy of denationalizing the non-Russian areas is of a demographic nature: mass migration of labor. The party is convinced that its program of resettlement of the labor force will play a decisive role in the eventual dissolution of the ethnic homogeneity of these areas, thus solving the whole nationality question.

The new party program speaks of "constant exchange of cadres between nations," but in practice it is a one-sided exchange, since thirteen of the fifteen Union republics have populations varying between 1,000,000 and 6,000,000, whereas Russia has a population of 117,-000,000 and the Ukraine 42,000,000. Russian, Ukrainian and, to a lesser extent, Belorussian manpower is being directed to industrial development areas in the non-Slav republics, particularly those in Central Asia and, to a lesser degree, in the Caucasus, on an allegedly voluntary basis. Thus what is taking place in these areas is not so much Russification as Slav colonization. This migration program has been stepped up since the adoption of the 1959–65 Seven-Year Plan, and therefore the last Soviet census, in 1959, does not accurately reflect the present situation. An authoritative Soviet journal states:

> In the process of socialist construction there is a clear tendency, in the republics that were most backward before the Revolution, toward a decrease in the proportion of indigenous nationalities. Simultaneously, the proportion of representatives of other peoples in the population of the national republics and *oblasts* is steadily increasing. Whereas in 1926 only 5 per cent of the total number of Russians in the U.S.S.R. lived outside the R.S.F.S.R., in 1959 the figure had already reached 14.2 per cent.[35]

Table 36 gives the percentages of indigenous population in the Union republics.[36]

As Table 36 indicates, in two Union republics, Kazakhstan and Kirghizia, the indigenous population is actually a minority (30 per cent and 40.5 per cent of the population, respectively). As national republics, therefore, they exist in name only. The nonindigenous population in seven of these republics ranges from 33 per cent to 47 per cent.

The exceptionally intensified "internationalization" process is even more vividly illustrated in the autonomous republics and the autonomous

TABLE 36

INDIGENOUS POPULATION IN THE UNION REPUBLICS

REPUBLIC	PERCENTAGE
Russia	83.3
Armenia	88.0
Belorussia	81.1
Lithuania	79.3
Ukraine	76.8
Estonia	74.6
Azerbaidzhan	67.5
Moldavia	65.4
Georgia	64.3
Uzbekistan	62.2
Latvia	62.0
Turkmenistan	60.9
Tadzhikistan	53.1
Kirghizia	40.5
Kazakhstan	30.0

oblasts. Tables 37 and 38 show the correlation of Russian to indigenous population in these areas.[37]

From Tables 37 and 38 it is apparent that the autonomous republics and *oblasts* have already been denationalized to such an extent that they are virtually Russian areas. The satisfaction with which the central authorities view this process is indicated in the following statement in an official Soviet source:

> Now not only republics, but also towns and *raions* and the labor force at thousands and thousands of factories, construction sites,

TABLE 37

PERCENTAGE OF RUSSIAN AND INDIGENOUS POPULATIONS
IN AUTONOMOUS REPUBLICS

AUTONOMOUS REPUBLIC	RUSSIAN POPULATION	INDIGENOUS POPULATION
Buryat	74.6	20.2
Kalmyk	55.9	35.1
Udmurt	56.8	35.6
Mordvinian	59.0	35.8
Karelian	63.4	13.1
Bashkir	42.4	22.1
Komi	48.4	30.4
Chechen-Ingush	49.0	41.1
Mari	47.8	43.1
Tatar	43.9	47.2
North Ossetian	40.0	47.8
Yakut	44.2	46.4

TABLE 38

PERCENTAGE OF RUSSIAN AND INDIGENOUS POPULATIONS IN
AUTONOMOUS "OBLASTS"

AUTONOMOUS "OBLAST"	RUSSIAN POPULATION	INDIGENOUS POPULATION
Jewish	78.2	8.8
Adygey	70.4	23.2
Karachay-Cherkess	51.0	33.2
Khakass	76.5	11.8
Gorno-Altai	69.8	24.2

collective and state farms, and even individual brigades, have become genuinely internalized.[38]

Migration is also taking place from the non-Russian republics to other parts of the Soviet Union, mainly Siberia and the far eastern areas, which are sparsely populated and are now being opened up industrially. No precise Soviet data on the numbers affected by this migration are available. The Soviet census of 1959 revealed, however, that 10.7 per cent of the Belorussians live in the R.S.F.S.R., mainly in Siberia, as do 10.4 per cent of the Kazakhs, 9.2 per cent of the Armenians, 9 per cent of the Ukrainians, 2.8 per cent of the Moldavians, 2.4 per cent of the Azerbaidzhanians and 2.1 per cent of the Georgians.

In Lithuania, 92.5 per cent of the indigenous population live in the republic, and 2.2 per cent in Latvia, Belorussia and the Ukraine. There is no indication in the Soviet census data of the whereabouts of the remaining 5.3 per cent, however. Similarly, 6.9 per cent of the Estonian, and 8.6 per cent of the Latvian, populations are unaccounted for. These people are probably in Siberia; they may have been settled there against their will, since the authorities have released no information on them.

Table 39 shows how much progress internationalization had made in the Union and autonomous republics up to 1959.[39]

It can be seen that the Kazakhs, Kirghiz, Bashkirs, Tatars, Mari and Udmurts are already no more than national minorities in their own republics. Among five nationalities—Armenians, Mari, Chuvash, Tatars and Mordvinians—44 per cent or more have migrated to other areas. Between 1939 and 1959 the number of Kazakhs in Kazakhstan dropped from 38 per cent to 30 per cent of the total population; the number of Uzbeks in their native republic, from 65 per cent to 62 per cent of the total; the number of Kirghiz, from 52 per cent to 40 per cent; and the number of Tadzhiks, from 60 per cent to 53 per cent. An official Soviet journal has commented:

Already the national republics are, in essence, multinational republics. In ten out of fifteen Union republics, nonindigenous nationalities comprise more than one-quarter of the entire population. At the same time the percentage of the indigenous nation-

TABLE 39

DISTRIBUTION OF INDIGENOUS POPULATION OF UNION AND
AUTONOMOUS REPUBLICS IN 1959
(in percentages)

POPULATION	RESIDENT IN NATIVE REPUBLIC	RESIDENT ELSEWHERE IN THE SOVIET UNION	PROPORTION OF TOTAL POPULATION OF REPUBLIC
Georgians	97.0	3.0	64.0
Latvians	93.0	7.0	62.0
Lithuanians	92.5	7.5	79.0
Turkmen	92.0	8.0	61.0
Estonians	90.0	10.0	75.0
Russians	86.0	14.0	83.0
Ukrainians	86.0	14.0	77.0
Kirghiz	86.0	14.0	40.5
Azerbaidzhanians	85.0	15.0	67.5
Moldavians	85.0	15.0	65.0
Uzbeks	84.0	16.0	62.0
Belorussians	83.0	17.0	81.0
Kazakhs	77.0	23.0	30.0
Udmurts	76.0	24.0	36.0
Tadzhiks	75.0	25.0	53.0
Bashkirs	75.0	25.0	22.0
Armenians	56.0	44.0	88.0
Mari	55.0	45.0	43.0
Chuvash	52.0	48.0	70.0
Tatars	29.0	71.0	47.0
Mordvinians	28.0	72.0	36.0

ality in the total population of the republics is decreasing. . . .
The percentage of Russians in the national republics is growing
considerably.[40]

This mingling of the population is viewed by the authorities as a
useful spur toward linguistic assimilation. As one author writes:

The following highly significant fact testifies to the importance
of population mobility in this process. Those persons of non-
Russian nationality living more or less scattered outside their own
republics much more often give Russian as their native language.
Whereas in Tadzhikistan 99.3 per cent of all Tadzhiks consider
Tadzhik to be their mother tongue, among Tadzhiks in the
R.S.F.S.R. the figure falls to 86 per cent. The corresponding ratio
in the case of Lithuanians is 99.2 per cent as against 83.8 per
cent, and in the case of Azerbaidzhanians, 98.1 per cent as against
89.7 per cent in the R.S.F.S.R. . . . The growing mobility of the
population is facilitating a gradual linguistic assimilation of nations
and nationalities both in terms of mutual influence and of mutual
enrichment of the national languages, and of the transformation of

one of these languages—Russian—into the common language for all socialist nations.[41]

What has been the manner and scale of linguistic assimilation or "internationalization" of the Soviet nationalities? According to the 1959 Soviet census there are 115 nationalities in the U.S.S.R., of which 80 number over 10,000 each and 35 under 10,000 each. Russians constitute 55 per cent of a total Soviet population of 208,800,000. These peoples may be divided into thirteen linguistic groups: (1) the Slav group, numbering 159,300,000 or 76.3 per cent of the total; (2) the Turkic group, numbering 23,100,000, consisting of Uzbeks, Kazakhs, Azerbaidzhanians, Turkmen, Kirghiz, Tatars, Chuvash, Bashkirs, Yakuts, Karakalpaks, Tuvinians, Karachay, Balkars, Khakass, Altayans, Gagauz, Kalmyks, Nogay, Uygurs, Shors and others; (3) the Finno-Ugrian group, numbering 4,300,000, consisting of Estonians, Mordvinians, Udmurts, Mari, Komi, Karelians, Finns and others; (4) the Latvian-Lithuanian group, numbering 3,700,000; (5) the Armenian group, numbering 2,800,000; (6) the Kartvelian group, numbering 2,700,000, primarily Georgians; (7) the Romance group, numbering 2,300,000, primarily Moldavians; (8) Jews, numbering 2,300,000, including Georgian, Central Asian and Crimean Jews; (9) the Iranian group, numbering 1,900,000, primarily Tadzhiks, Ossetians and Kurds; (10) the German group, numbering 1,600,000; (11) the Chechen-Daghestani group, numbering 1,300,000, comprising Chechen, Ingush, Avars, Lezghians, Darghin, Laks and others; (12) the Abkhaz-Adygey group, numbering 400,000, including also the Kabardians, Abaza and other Cherkess tribes; and (13) other groups, numbering 1,100,000.[42]

Originally, Soviet policy toward these groups was aimed at creating "zonal languages" covering a number of ethnic minorities, as the first stage in transition to a single Soviet language. Now, however, it is held to be possible to proceed directly to the introduction of the common language, although the creation of zonal languages is still held to be valid. As a Soviet ideologist writes:

> Under socialist conditions, partial processes of voluntary assimilation of small ethnic and extraterritorial national groups scattered throughout the large socialist nations by the latter can and do take place. . . . Especially important in this process is adoption by the assimilating ethnic and extraterritorial national groups of the language of the large, advanced socialist nation in which these groups live.[43]

In Georgia, for example, in 1926, 71,400 persons considered themselves Adjars, 243,000 Mingrelians and 13,200 Svans; in the 1959 census, however, only 546 Adjars, 11 Mingrelians and 9 Svans were registered. In 1926, 33,500 persons were registered as Kypchaks and 50,100 as Kurkhs in Uzbekistan, but in 1959, only 105 Kypchaks were counted; all the rest called themselves Uzbeks. In Tadzhikistan the Pamir tribes have been absorbed, and in Azerbaidzhan, the Karapapakhs.

In 1926 in Daghestan, 38,600 persons who considered themselves to be members of various nationalities were counted; in 1959 they all called themselves Avars.

The Soviet authorities are actively promoting this process of assimilation, as is shown by a statement in a leading journal of theory:

> The drawing together and flourishing of nations on the basis of socialist and communist construction is proceeding, not spontaneously, but according to a plan. . . . In our multinational state this is being accomplished through a process of centralized state planning.[44]

Yet even Stalin categorically condemned assimilation in the following terms:

> You know, of course, that a policy of assimilation is absolutely excluded from the arsenal of Marxism-Leninism as being a policy that is against the people, counterrevolutionary and baneful.[45]

It should be stressed that the assimilation taking place in the Soviet Union is linguistic and, to a much lesser extent, the result of mixed marriages, which are comparatively infrequent. It is apparent, too, that there is a long way to go before Russian is regarded by the inhabitants of the non-Russian republics as their mother tongue, the ultimate goal of the party. There is, nevertheless, a trend in this direction: according to the 1926 Soviet census, 6,600,000 non-Russians considered Russian their native tongue; in 1959 the figure was 10,200,000.[46] The degree of linguistic Russification reached in 1959 is shown in Table 40.[47]

Linguistic assimilation through forced Russification was never officially

TABLE 40

LINGUISTIC RUSSIFICATION IN THE SOVIET UNION REPUBLICS

POPULATION	PERCENTAGE OF TOTAL INDIGENOUS POPULATION USING RUSSIAN AS MOTHER TONGUE
Russians	99.8
Belorussians	15.8
Ukrainians	12.3
Armenians	10.1
Latvians	4.9
Moldavians	4.8
Estonians	4.8
Azerbaidzhanians	2.4
Lithuanians	2.2
Tadzhiks	1.9
Uzbeks	1.6
Kazakhs	1.4
Georgians	1.4
Kirghiz	1.3
Turkmen	1.1

a policy of the tsars, and it is not officially sanctioned by the Soviets. The Kremlin today does conduct its cultural policies so that the Russian language is the sole language that can be used for secondary or higher education by the national groups that supposedly have no written language. (The term "nations without a written language" is a pure fabrication by the Soviet power wielders, since all the Moslem peoples of the U.S.S.R., for whom the term was invented, had Arabic script; among these peoples the Tatars, Turkmen and some of the Caucasian groups had this script before the Russians were given the Cyrillic alphabet. The Communists, after coming to power, destroyed this Arabic script.)

Tables 41 and 42 show the percentages of people using Russian, or some other language than their own, as their native language.[48]

TABLE 41

PERCENTAGE OF TOTAL INDIGENOUS POPULATION OF AUTONOMOUS REPUBLICS USING RUSSIAN OR ANOTHER LANGUAGE AS MOTHER TONGUE

PEOPLE	PERCENTAGE
Bashkirs	38 (2.6 use Russian; 35.4 Tatar)
Karelians	29
Mordvinians	22
Komi	11
Udmurts	11
Ossetians	10
Chuvash	9
Kalmyks	9
Tatars	8
Abkhazians	5
Mari	5
Karakalpaks	5
Buryats	5
Daghestani	4
Kabardians	3
Balkars	3
Yakuts	2
Ingush	2
Chechen	1

TABLE 42

PERCENTAGE OF NATIONALITIES HAVING NO SPECIFIC TERRITORY USING RUSSIAN OR ANOTHER LANGUAGE AS MOTHER TONGUE

PEOPLE	PERCENTAGE
Jews	78
Poles	45
Gypsies	40
Germans	25

Tables 40, 41 and 42 show that the Communists have by no means succeeded in internationalizing the non-Russian peoples. In the Union republics only the Belorussians and the Ukrainians, who have lived with the Russians for many generations in the cities and who are themselves Slavs, and the Armenians, of whom some 44 per cent live outside their republic, use Russian to any appreciable degree (10 per cent to 15 per cent) as their mother tongue. Among the Moldavians and the Estonians less than 5 per cent consider Russian their mother tongue, and among the Turkish people and the Georgians the percentage is 2 per cent or less. In the autonomous republics where the people live relatively close together and have not mixed with the Russians, only from 1 per cent to 5 per cent consider Russian their mother tongue. Where the indigenous peoples have mixed, the percentage climbs from 8 per cent (Tatars) to 11 per cent (Komi) and as high as 22 per cent (Mordvinians). The Jews, Poles, Gypsies and Germans who live in the U.S.S.R. do not have their own territories (the Jewish autonomous *oblast,* containing less than 9 per cent of the Jewish population of the U.S.S.R., is an outright fiction), and the party does not recognize them as having a national culture, even "socialist in content." Because of this, these people are more strongly subjected to Russification.

One of the main channels for achieving linguistic Russification is the educational system. Russian is used as the language of instruction in an increasing number of schools. Out of a total of 6,000 national schools in Uzbekistan, for example, 317 teach in Russian; in 1,000 both Russian and the native language are used.[49] In Kirghizia, 317 schools teach in Russian and in 280 schools parallel courses are conducted in both languages.[50] Of the total number of pupils in non-Russian schools in the R.S.F.S.R. in the 1962–63 school year, 27 per cent of the students in the elementary grades, 53 per cent of those in grades five to eight and 66 per cent in grades nine to eleven were taught in Russian. In the Baltic republics, as in the Central Asian republics, a large system of "mixed schools" has been created, with instructions given in both the national language and in Russian. In Latvia alone there were some 240 such schools with 75,000 pupils by the middle of 1963. The official explanation for this development is as follows:

> More and more parents of non-Russian nationality are completely voluntarily sending their children to Russian schools or are requesting that courses in the national schools be given in Russian. . . . Experience shows that by instructing non-Russian children from an early age in the Russian language it is considerably easier for them to grasp the rudiments of science.[51]

Gradual Russification of the educational system goes hand-in-hand with the attempt to replace the non-Russian languages with Russian as a cultural vehicle. This process was begun in 1938 by the abolition of the Latin alphabet, with which the Soviets had earlier replaced the Arabic script traditionally used by the Soviet Moslem peoples, and the imposition of the Cyrillic script. Then followed a systematic Russification of a large part of the vocabularies of the minority languages, in order to create a single philosophical and sociopolitical terminology in all the national minority literatures. The publication of dictionaries was centralized in Moscow, and the native languages were infiltrated by Russian and Western loan words, particularly in the case of technical words, even where equivalents existed in the languages concerned. Words of Arabic, Persian and Turkish origin dealing with science have been systematically weeded out. In a Turkish-Tatar dictionary published in 1958 there were, for example, twice as many Russian loan words as in the previous edition, published in 1929;[52] in an Uzbek dictionary, nearly 18 per cent of the words are of Russian origin, although most of these have Uzbek equivalents.[53] In the literatures of the Turkic nationalities, the admixture of Russian words is so heavy that a novel can hardly be read without a knowledge of both languages.[54] Even translations of Western literature into the national languages are made from the Russian instead of from the original language, despite the fact that there are translators in the national republics who are familiar with Western languages. Sometimes even Russians speak out against this practice: in Kazakhstan the Russian critic V. Lobin made such scathing comments that *Izvestia* rebuked him for delivering an "impertinent affront to the great Russian language";[55] the same paper severely criticized a Georgian "committee for the purification of the national language."[56] In other republics, too, the intelligentsia is disturbed by the Russification of their languages; in Kazakhstan articles of protest have appeared in the local press.[57]

In the case of the very small national minorities, such as the Karelians, Udmurts, Mari, Mordvinians and Ossetians, it has not proved difficult for Russian to oust the native languages as a cultural vehicle. Referring to these peoples, Soviet ideologists put it this way:

> In the U.S.S.R. we have facts showing that many tribes, nationalities and small nations use the Russian language for the development of their national culture, together with their national language.[58]

This is naturally not the case in the major national minority areas, but the communist aim is that all the cultures of the nationalities should eventually be internationalized: Russian will become the sole mother tongue for all the peoples of the U.S.S.R. and ultimately the language of a worldwide communist society. As a leading Soviet philosopher writes:

> It is possible that after the victory of socialism in the majority of countries or throughout the world, one of the existing national languages already fulfilling the function of a means of international communication will be completely voluntarily adopted by all socialist nations as the basis of a future single world language. . . .

> The Russian language, which is the national language for Russians and a common international language for all the peoples of the U.S.S.R. . . . is creating a new linguistic community. . . . This may already be viewed as the prelude to the future merging of the nations into a single communist society.[59]

To the party, creating an international communist culture means the gradual withering away of national differences in the shape of separate languages, ways of life and frontiers. It is claimed that in the Soviet Union a new kind of human being is being created, who will live in a new type of "communist nation" with one language, one culture and a single code of ethics. The nations composing this society will voluntarily give up "bourgeois" concepts of statehood, sovereignty and national culture to merge into the new community. This is the blueprint for the future laid down by the new party program; its formulation explains why the earlier slogan of accelerating the cultural development of each of the Soviet nationalities has given way to a program of denationalization, or internationalism, as it is called. While both the Russian and non-Russian peoples of the U.S.S.R. have made considerable strides forward in education and cultural development over the decades, this development has been highly uneven, as may be clearly seen from Soviet statistics. Whereas 295 out of 1,000 Russians have an elementary, secondary or higher education, the ratios per 1,000 for Ukrainians, Turkmen, Azerbaidzhanians, Uzbeks, Tadzhiks, Kirghiz and Kazakhs are, respectively: 289, 242, 242, 208, 201 and 199.[60] The ratios per 1,000 in the case of the Georgians, Armenians, Latvians and Estonians are higher than for the Russians (375, 323, 369 and 307, respectively), but these peoples possessed a higher cultural level even before their annexation by the Soviet Union.

The ratios of persons with a higher or secondary education per 10,000 of the population are 384 for the entire U.S.S.R., 327 in the Ukraine, 305 in Azerbaidzhan, 300 in Belorussia, 284 in Lithuania, 190 in Kazakhstan, 175 in Kirghizia, 160 in Tadzhikistan, 143 in Uzbekistan and 129 in Moldavia.[61] The Russians, again, have the most scientists per head, with 175 per 100,000. They are followed by the Latvians, with 170; the Azerbaidzhanians, 150; the Lithuanians, 139; the Ukrainians, 82; and the Belorussians, 71. In the Central Asian republics the ratios are as follows: Turkmenistan, 62; Kazakhstan, 56; Tadzhikistan, 53; and Uzbekistan and Kirghizia, 52. The Georgians, Armenians and Estonians again outstrip all other nationalities, with ratios of 269, 260 and 190 per 100,000, respectively.[62] The populations of the autonomous areas are the most backward, as Tables 43 and 44 show.[63]

Tables 43 and 44 not only demonstrate the large gap between the development in the U.S.S.R. as a whole (i.e., primarily Russian) and the majority of the republics, they also show that the gap is in the area of education, especially secondary and higher education and the training of scientific personnel. The republics of Turkestan are three

TABLE 43

NUMBER OF SCIENTISTS IN THE AUTONOMOUS REPUBLICS

NATIONALITY	NUMBER PER 100,000 OF POPULATION
Russians	175
Ossetians	140
Buryats	101
Abkhazians	100
Yakuts	70
Karakalpaks	63
Karelians	63
Komi	63
Tatars	62
Daghestani	49
Kabardians	44
Balkars	37
Kalmyks	37
Bashkirs	35
Chuvash	32
Udmurts	25
Mordvinians	23
Mari	19
Tuvinians	17
Ingush	27
Chechen	9

TABLE 44

NUMBER OF SCIENTISTS IN THE AUTONOMOUS "OBLASTS"

NATIONALITY	NUMBER PER 100,000 OF POPULATION
Cherkess	65
Khakass	50
Adygey	43
Altay	30
Karachay	20

times behind the Russians in training scientists, and even the Ukraine and Belorussia graduate less than one-half the number of scientists per 100,000 the Russians do. The lag of the autonomous republics and *oblasts* in this area is almost catastrophic.

Conflicting views on the way in which the treatment of the nationality question in the new party program should be interpreted exist even among Soviet ideologists, and it is in this discussion that views opposed to denationalization have been voiced. The difference in approach stems from the contradictory and deliberately noncommittal manner in which this whole delicate subject is dealt with in the program. On the one hand it states that the Soviet nationalities will "draw close together" and finally merge, while on the other it claims that they will continue to develop and "flower" as individual entities. This contradiction has given rise to two major questions: Which of the two above processes is the dominating one at the present stage of the Soviet Union's development? Will national statehood, in the shape of the national minority republics, "wither away" before the Soviet state system itself dissolves in the communist society? An attempt to clarify the issue was made in October, 1963, at an All-Union Coordinating Conference attended by specialists in communist ideology and theory from all over the country, whose task it was to resolve these questions. Over 150 papers were read, but no final "coordination" was reached. In fact, the conference became a platform for many representatives' from the non-Russian republics placing the whole emphasis on the "flowering" of the nationalities and preserving of their separate identities. Reporting on the conference in early 1964, a leading party journal of theory wrote:

> Recently, differing interpretations of the relationship between the rapprochement and the fusion of nations have appeared. Broad discussion of this question permits the conclusion to be drawn that rapprochement of the Soviet nationalities at the contemporary stage will undoubtedly contain certain elements of the fusion of nations. . . . But this is no ground for identifying these processes. . . . Obliteration of national differences and certain elements of the merging of nations does not constitute the main and fundamental feature in the development of nations and national relations in the U.S.S.R. at the present stage.[64]

This latter assertion contradicts both the spirit of the new party program and present Soviet policy. It appears to be a concession to the more "nationalist" point of view expressed at the conference, where nearly all the representatives from the non-Russian republics, particularly those from Soviet Central Asia, laid emphasis on the "efflorescence" and not the "fusion" of the Soviet nationalities, interpreting the party program to suit their purpose. The proceedings even gave birth to a new idea: that the Soviet people is a

> new historical community of people of different nationalities. The formation and development of this new international community . . . together with the preservation and development of national communities is one of the most characteristic results of the process of rapprochement among the Soviet nations.[65]

The "Soviet people" thus is not, according to this formula, the organic unity of a single communist community, but merely the sum total of the various "developing" nationalities.

The same clash of views appeared in the discussion at the conference on the fate of the Union and autonomous republics during the construction of communism. In a reference to the periodical *Sovetskoye gosudarstvo i pravo* ("Soviet State and Law"), which had asserted that "denationalization of the autonomous and Union republics is taking place now," *Voprosy filosofii* ("Questions of Philosophy") states that this view, put forward by S. Z. Zimanov and K. N. Nurbekov, did not meet with support from the majority of the participants.[66] The two speakers had declared: "National statehood will wither away earlier than statehood in general," but they were reproved by the main speaker, I. Tsameryan, who said that the Soviet federation would be retained

> right up to the transformation of the Soviet multinational state of the whole people into a communist social self-administration. . . . Nor will national differences disappear immediately after the victory of communism.[67]

These arguments indicate that the advocates within the party apparatus of an accelerated denationalization policy are opposed by those who want to preserve the identity of the nationalities.

A number of speakers at the conference openly proclaimed the need to put an end to cultural and economic discrimination against the national republics, calling for more even cultural development and "fair distribution of the wealth of all the nations and nationalities" of the Soviet Union.[68]

The following general conclusions can be drawn from our analysis of the party and the nationality question:

1. The so-called sovereignty of the Union republics always has been, and remains today, a fiction. There is, however, an unwritten law that allows some republics to exercise a greater degree of self-rule than other republics. On the basis of the ability to select indigenous people for the party, state and economic apparatus and the state language of the republic, there are five non-Russian republics that are self-ruled; the remainder are ruled from the center (*see* Chapter Ten, above).

2. At the beginning of the thirties the party rejected its initial program for liquidating the "actual inequality" among the nationalities of the U.S.S.R. in the areas of economics and culture and subordinated the entire national question to the interests of the new turn in the policies of the party: the abolishment of the NEP, the acceleration of industrialization and all-out collectivization. Whereas all-out collectivization was carried out everywhere in the country, industrialization was effected according to two categories: the economic effectiveness of capital investment and the military-strategic expediency of developing selected regions. This led to the industrialization of the R.S.F.S.R. while the economic and cultural needs of the other national republics were ignored. As a result, the economic and cultural distance between the Russian and the non-Russian peoples not only failed to be reduced, it was actually increased. The present situation can be accurately de-

scribed as the existence of "underdeveloped countries" within the communist empire itself. These underdeveloped countries comprise almost one-half of the Union republics and all of the so-called autonomous republics. These republics are agrarian countries with isolated industrial centers that are populated by Russians.

3. The party has built industrial enterprises in some republics according to the strict principles of "specialization" and "cooperation." This means that these republics have been transformed into appendages of the general economy of the metropolis, either as sources of raw materials or as the delivery points of semifinished goods or machine parts and special equipment. There is no such thing as a "nationality economy" (Soviet economic science does not even know such a term); there are only special branches of the all-Union industrial complex located on the territory of a given republic. All profits from the main industries of the national republics, along with the turnover tax accumulated on the territory of these republics, are forwarded directly to the central state fund in Moscow.

4. The party has embarked on a new course of forced "internationalization" of the national republics, with the result that in a majority of the Union republics and in all the autonomous republics the population is divided between the Russians in the cities and the national peoples in the rural areas. Internationalization has been effected by a highly organized mass migration—not always voluntary—of Russians, Ukrainians and, to a lesser extent, Belorussians, to the regions where new industrial and agricultural enterprises have been founded. The short-range purpose of this internationalization is to bring about a tight encirclement of the indigenous population with a class of imperial colonialists who, because of their superior positions and their national origins, will support the imperial government in the event of any serious Soviet colonial crisis. The long-range political purpose of the internationalization of the republics is to denationalize these republics, turning the national indigenous population from a majority into a minority in order to prepare for a revision, in one form or another, of the statutes of these republics. The party has already succeeded in denationalizing two of the Union republics and twelve of the autonomous republics; these areas now exist as national entities in name only.

5. Internationalization also goes on in the cultural areas of life. The formula of a culture "national in form but socialist in content" has, in actuality, been revised, and the national form (language, customs and traditions) has been doomed to disappear in the interests of internationalization—a synonym for Russification.

6. The "new stage" of the party's nationality policy, as laid down in the 1961 party program with subsequent interpretations by the party ideologists, amounts to the party's more forcefully putting into effect the following predetermined three-stage course during the period of the "construction of communism": (a) the smallest nationalities will be

swallowed up by larger nationalities that are related to them; (*b*) these larger nationalities will be swallowed up by the Russians (in part by language assimilation); and (*c*) the Russsians will be swallowed up by the "new communist man." The final result of the process is to be the formation of a single communist nation, an international communist hybrid with the disappearance of ethnographic entities. The party's advances toward these goals have been rather minor so far, but the measures adopted have been imposing.

7. Many symptoms indicate that the denationalization policy has met with resistance by the Russians in the form of the growth of Russian nationalism. This growth has not yet met with official criticism, but local nationalism has been criticized and its spokesmen have been persecuted. These two tendencies are shown by the constant emphasis in the party program and the party press of the necessity to increase the struggle against all forms of local nationalism, while, at the same time, nothing is said about "great-power chauvinism."

8. The most outstanding characteristic of post-World War II policies toward colonies has been a parallel but contradictory process: Western colonialism has received its death blow, creating scores of young, free and independent states in Asia and Africa; at the same time, communist imperialism has not only held on to previously won territory, it has extended into a colonial empire of a new type. This imperialism is a Eurasian-Soviet empire that has incorporated into its sphere of influence more than a dozen states independent before, during and after World War II. The Soviet leaders are now realizing that it is dangerous to be the only colonial empire in a world without colonies. The idea of national liberation movements, which the Soviet Communists have instigated (in many cases) and supported in the rear of the Western powers, has begun to resound dimly within the Soviet empire. This response to the call for national liberation is transforming the Soviet national question into a serious Soviet *national problem*. The Soviet leadership believes that it can liquidate this problem by denationalizing the nationalities causing the problem.

* CHAPTER XIX *

The Party and Foreign Policy

DURING the almost fifty years of the regime's existence there have been seven different foreign ministers, but basic foreign policy has never varied. Tactics have changed dramatically, as in the case of the Ribbentrop-Molotov pact, but strategy has remained unchanged. Also, while ministers have come and gone, their position in the hierarchy has remained the same. Of the seven foreign ministers only Trotsky had a career in government; the rest were political functionaries of the party Central Committee, of varying abilities, temperament and trustworthiness. Only two, Trotsky and Molotov, were members of the Politburo, and they were already members when appointed to the post; not a single foreign minister from the ranks of professional diplomats has made a career as a member of the Politburo. This is quite understandable, for the Soviet foreign minister is a minister in name only. In practice the first secretary of the party Central Committee is his own foreign minister.

Foreign policy, the secret police and the armed forces are areas of state administration that the first secretary of the party Central Committee does not entrust to the official heads or to the corresponding sections of the Central Committee; these he directs personally. Only the secondary functions of day-to-day control and the selection of secondary cadres in these organs are entrusted to his assistants. Before the formation of the Soviet Union, in 1922, each Soviet republic, the R.S.F.S.R., the Ukrainian S.S.R., the Azerbaidzhan S.S.R., the Armenian S.S.R. and the Georgian S.S.R., had its own diplomatic apparatus in the form of a people's commissar for foreign affairs, who conducted the republic's foreign policy and concluded treaties and agreements on its behalf with other states. Unity with Moscow in foreign policy was achieved by adherence to the party line. In December, 1922, at the First Congress of Soviets of the U.S.S.R., the Soviet republics agreed to the creation of supreme organs responsible for foreign policy, external trade, the armed forces, communications and principles and guidance for general economic, financial and administrative direction.[1] The existing people's commissariats for foreign affairs, foreign trade, communications, mail and telegraph and army and naval affairs were abolished in the constituent republics[2] and combined in Moscow as all-Union people's commissariats. The new U.S.S.R. people's commissariats established branch organs in the governments of the constituent republics.

Until 1944 the People's Commissariat for Foreign Affairs of the U.S.S.R. had representatives in all the constituent republics, as well as agents in those centers in the U.S.S.R. most important from the point of view of international policy.[3] On February 1, 1944, the Supreme Soviet of the U.S.S.R. gave the constituent republics the right to enter into direct diplomatic relations with foreign states, to conclude agreements with them and to exchange diplomatic and consular representatives.[4] This unexpected restoration to the constituent republics of the right to conduct their own foreign policy while leaving internal affairs under immediate direction from Moscow was prompted by the Kremlin's desire to capture votes for each of the sixteen constituent republics in the General Assembly of the projected United Nations organization. In the end it had to be satisfied with three votes—for the U.S.S.R., the Ukrainian S.S.R., and the Belorussia S.S.R.—but it was the only member country to have more than one vote. Ministries of foreign affairs headed by ministers of the local nationality have been established in all the constituent republics, but in practice they have no more authority than the former local representatives of the U.S.S.R. Foreign Ministry. The constitutional right of the constituent republics to conduct an independent foreign policy is, accordingly, a fiction. Official Soviet commentators recognize this fact:

> The diplomatic representative of the U.S.S.R. is the sole representative of the U.S.S.R. in the country in which he is residing. . . . The diplomatic representative carries out in the country of residence general supervision of the activities of all state institutions, enterprises and officials of the U.S.S.R. and of the constituent republics. All these institutions, enterprises and officials must inform the diplomatic representative regarding all important actions they propose to take.[5]

This is a remarkable example, even in the history of Soviet constitutions, of the ascendancy of administrative but effective law over the constitutional but ineffective law of the constituent republics.

The first secretary of the Central Committee of the CPSU, as the immediate supreme head over the Ministry of Foreign Affairs in the party apparatus, receives advice and assistance from the following party organs: (1) the Presidium of the Central Committee, which formally determines the basic principles of foreign policy; (2) the Secretariat of the Central Committee, which assigns and appoints higher diplomatic cadres; (3) the Foreign Department of the Central Committee, which selects international personnel; (4) the Party Organs Department, which approves the appointment of leading cadres to the diplomatic service; (5) the Department of Propaganda and Agitation, which directly operates the press section of the Ministry for Foreign Affairs and the planning of diplomatic propaganda actions; and (6) the

Party Committee of the Ministry of Foreign Affairs, which supervises the work of the party apparatus of the Ministry and informs the Central Committee directly regarding any deficiencies in the work of officials, "irrespective of the positions they occupy," as the party statutes put it.

The secretary of the Party Committee of the Ministry of Foreign Affairs is not appointed by the district committee, as the secretaries of other primary party organizations are; he is appointed directly by the Central Committee of the CPSU itself. The 1952 party statutes specifically stated that

> secretaries of party organizations in ministries must be confirmed by the Central Committee of the party.[6]

The minister of foreign affairs, his deputies and all other high communist officials of the ministry are members of a single party organization for the entire ministry. They must attend local party meetings regularly and pay monthly party dues amounting to 3 per cent of their salaries. Although the minister of foreign affairs, his deputies and his ambassadors form part of the permanent staff of the Secretariat of the Central Committee, they are confirmed in office by the Presidium of the Central Committee. Ministry section heads, embassy counselors, military attachés and consuls general are confirmed by the Secretariat. Secretaries, cultural and trade attachés, leaders of Tass foreign bureaus, special correspondents of national newspapers and secretaries of party organizations in embassies abroad form part of the permanent staff of the corresponding sections of the Central Committee. The minister and ambassadors are appointed by the Presidium of the Supreme Soviet of the U.S.S.R. Deputy ministers and assistants to the ambassador (counselor or head of special section) are appointed by the Council of Ministers of the U.S.S.R. Consuls, secretaries and attachés are appointed by order of the minister of foreign affairs, while military and naval attachés are appointed by order of the minister of defense of the U.S.S.R.[7]

The departments of the Central Committee do not have the right to issue instructions or directives either to the minister of foreign affairs or to his colleagues on matters of foreign policy. However, the Foreign Department and the Department of Propaganda and Agitation and their networks abroad have special responsibility for coordinating Soviet diplomatic actions with the actions of foreign Communist parties and for ensuring that these actions are strongly supported by the party propaganda machine of the Central Committee, both at home and abroad. The Ministry of Foreign Affairs and Soviet embassies are officially dissociated from such actions. But former Soviet diplomats have provided evidence of the active support of these activities by embassies.[8]

In addition, there are a number of state, social and voluntary organizations that either have foreign departments or have been created for the specific purpose of providing propaganda support for Soviet foreign policy. The most important of these is the State Committee for Cultural

Relations with Foreign Countries. In 1960, the U.S.S.R. effected cultural exchanges with 67 countries through this committee. Fifty large Soviet cities maintained close links with 145 cities abroad by exchanging delegations of city councils and municipalities, information, literature, exhibitions and films. In 1960, Soviet films were screened in 96 countries.[9]

Soviet foreign propaganda pays particular attention to Asia, Africa and Latin America. A Soviet handbook states:

> Cultural relations between the U.S.S.R. and the countries of Asia, Africa and Latin America each year increase in scale and importance.[10]

The tentacles of Soviet propaganda not only extend to all areas of cultural life, they reach every corner of the social life of the countries where Soviet ambassadors are accredited. With the object of providing propaganda support for Soviet diplomacy, the U.S.S.R. participates in all international organizations—state, social, cultural and scientific—and even religious organizations; for example, the Russian Orthodox church sent representatives from Moscow to a conference of the World Council of Churches in New Delhi. As of January 1, 1961, the U.S.S.R. was represented in 245 government and non-government international organizations.[11] The Soviet trade unions alone were in contact with the trade unions of more than 80 countries.[12] The Foreign Department of the Central Committee of the CPSU has links with Communist parties in 88 countries, with a total membership of about 40,000,000.[13]

An important aspect of the party's foreign policy is the manner in which it serves as a function of its domestic policy.

Among the elements determining Soviet foreign policy are such primary or substantive factors as the political and ideological, the military and strategic, and the economic. There are also such secondary and shifting factors as peace, the right to national self-determination, "coexistence" and so on. Between these two sets is the national factor, that is, the national interests of the country. The influence of these factors at various stages of Soviet foreign policy varies because of varying conditions. At times they appear to change places, with the primary factors being lost sight of while secondary factors take over. The basic factors of Soviet foreign policy are much older than the Soviet regime, older even than the bolshevism of the RSDRP. They were first formulated in the following statements in *The Communist Manifesto:*

> Communists are accused of wanting to abolish the Fatherland and nationality. Workers do not have a fatherland. You cannot take from them what they do not possess.[14]
>
> . . . .
>
> The most immediate aim of Communists . . . is the conquest of political power by the proletariat.[15]
>
> . . . .
>
> Communists consider it would be despicable to conceal their

views and intentions. They openly proclaim that their aims can only be achieved by the forcible overthrow of the entire existing social order.[16]

The general nature and objectives of Soviet foreign policy are outlined in the following official statements:

> The October Revolution created a state of a new type—a soviet state—and thereby laid the foundation of Soviet foreign policy, which differs in principle from the foreign policy of all other states[17]

and

> Soviet foreign policy is permeated by the spirit of communism, the Leninist party spirit, is carried out in organic unity with internal policy and is its continuation.[18]

Concretely, the basic aim of Soviet foreign policy is the struggle for a "world socialist revolution" finding expression in a new Soviet type of colonialism and imperialism. Soviet imperialism is not a repetition of the familiar variants on classical imperialism; it is supranational and therefore revolutionary and dynamic. It is not economic imperialism, but ideocratic imperialism. It is not primarily interested in raw materials, sales markets, free labor and capital investment—all of which have interested capitalist imperialism; it is interested in *people,* in establishing over them a specific type of political and ideological regime. Soviet imperialism is, accordingly, a new type of imperialism—more elastic, more dynamic and more dangerous. It is a nonracial imperialism aimed at creating new ruling classes to support its policy among the former colonial peoples, while maintaining, of course, a close watch over its own satraps.

Many Western politicians are inclined to regard Soviet imperialism and Soviet foreign policy as continuations of the imperialist policy of Imperial Russia. Others, especially expatriate Russian politicians, are inclined to deny any connection between the two. Both views, psychologically quite explicable, are historically debatable. To identify the foreign policy of Imperial Russia with the foreign policy of Soviet Russia is to overestimate the opportunities, the scale, the character and the intentions of the foreign policy of tsarist Russia and to underestimate the international and intercontinental scale and ideocratic character of Soviet communist imperialism. The foreign policy interests of tsarist Russia were territorial and strategic; they revolved around Eurasia and were thus local. The interests of the U.S.S.R. are ideological and thus global.

Although the Kremlin rulers have developed their foreign policy in a country with definite frontiers, national interests and national goals, they always did and still do regard communist Russia as the material, strategic and human base for the realization of their ultimate aim, the establishment of worldwide communist rule.

Lenin, in whose name the present foreign policy of the U.S.S.R. is conducted, worked out its most important principles, based on the ever-dominant factor of political ideology. Without hesitation, he placed the national interests of Russia at the service of his political and ideological principles. In the "Peace Decree" of October 26, 1917,[19] he appealed to the governments of the warring countries and to their peoples as well, with the obvious aim of converting a national and intergovernmental war into a class and ideological war within the states themselves. To Lenin, peace was only the ending of a war between states and the beginning of wars within states according to his formula: "the conversion of imperialist war into civil war."[20] He was prepared to make any national sacrifices in order to achieve ideological victory, that is, world revolution and world communism. "In questions of foreign policy," he said during the negotiations at Brest-Litovsk on a separate peace in 1918,

> there are before us two basic lines—the proletarian line, which says that socialist revolution is dearer and higher than anything else, and the other, the bourgeois line, which says that national independence is dearer than anything and above everything.[21]

He was, to use his own words, prepared to conclude a "rotten, shameful, annexationist" peace with the Germans, but he was not prepared to abandon his power:

> If the Germans were to say that they demand the overthrow of the bolshevist power then, of course, we should have to fight.[22]

Power was not an end in itself, but the means to an end—the spread of revolution abroad. "We were able," he said, "to sign a peace treaty that did not threaten the revolution."[23]

Lenin's prediction that the October Revolution was only the beginning, the eve of a European and world revolution, was not borne out by the facts; nor was he able to effect the immediate introduction of a fully communist regime within the country, which experienced a neocapitalist stage under the NEP. The foreign policy of this period was at first a policy of maneuvering, of reconnaissance in the enemy rear and of trade relations with the non-Soviet world based on maintenance of the international status quo. The immediate aim of this policy, diplomatic recognition for the October coup and the Soviet regime, was easily achieved. But Lenin retained his Utopian views concerning world revolution, which he continued to think was inevitable, though somewhat delayed. Diplomatic recognition of Soviet Russia by the outside world was important only for legalizing the Soviet illegal apparatus abroad and for facilitating the work of the COMINTERN. Lenin thought that the era of world revolution had begun in the sense that it was possible to organize in the West communist detachments able to carry out their own "October coups" as the Bolsheviks had done in Russia. In a word,

Lenin continued to believe in his theory of organized revolution. Trotsky thought along similar lines, advancing his theory of permanent revolution.

The advent of Stalin brought about a drastic change in communist foreign policy. Stalin considered Lenin's and Trotsky's schemes unrealistic. Just as Lenin did not believe in Marx's automatic revolution, so Stalin did not believe in Lenin's organized revolution, because conditions had changed. Stalin, although he never said so openly, saw that capitalism was modernizing itself and that the economic order of the West was progressing in social matters. Marx's old theory of capitalism and Lenin's newer theory of the "last stage of capitalism" (imperialism as the last stage in the development of capitalism) were refuted by reality and, consequently, the political notions worked out on the basis of these theories were also refuted. Stalin saw the modern state gradually becoming a classless democratic organ of political self-expression and the supreme arbiter of the social world. Instead of the notorious class struggle of the proletariat, an era of civil peace lay ahead, especially in Germany, and the proletariat of Europe was not only opposed to the idea of revolution but was almost entirely in favor of social democracy. This reduced the role of Communist parties to that of exclusive political sects deprived of influence. In the Anglo-Saxon countries the proletariat even favored the bourgeois political parties.

Stalin reviewed Lenin's theory of the organization of revolution in other countries and put forward his own theory, that of the "construction of socialism in one country." Political conclusions of great importance for the outside world emanated from this theory. Soviet foreign policy was made to serve Stalin's internal objectives of industrialization, collectivization and the creation of a gigantic terrorist machine. Soviet diplomacy was also reconstructed, and "coexistence" became the official diplomatic policy. Even small countries immediately bordering on the U.S.S.R. were left in peace. The COMINTERN continued to exist, no longer as the "staff of world revolution," but as the tool of the Soviet foreign policy. The views of Stalin, the "national Communist," prevailed, not only over those of his late master, but also over the views of his living colleagues—Trotsky, Zinoviev and Kamenev. He embarked on the building of "national communism" in one country with some sympathy from those in the outside world who wished to interpret Stalin's victory over Trotsky as the victory of the national form of communism over the more dangerous international communist aspirations of Lenin and Trotsky. Soviet communism was considered tolerable as long as it remained within its own national frontiers.

It soon became clear, however, that Stalin's national communism also served to organize communist revolution in other countries and to create in them communist regimes relying on the U.S.S.R. as their main armed base. He said:

> The victory of communism in one country is not a self-sufficient task. The revolution of a victorious country must not regard itself

> as self-sufficient, but as an assistant, as a means to hasten the
> victory of the proletariat in all countries.[24]
>
> . . . .
>
> The worldwide significance of the October Revolution lies in the
> fact that it is the first stage in world revolution and is a mighty base
> for its further development.[25]

While Russia remained a peasant country it was an ineffective base
against the highly industrialized powers. Industrialization meant preparation of this "mighty base," the creation of a starting point for the
organization of communist regimes relying primarily not on ephemeral
local forces of foreign communists but on the colossal military potential
of the Soviet state. Consequently, the Stalinist theory of the construction
of socialism in one country, the program of industrialization and collectivization and the paramount importance of heavy industry, meant
only one thing as far as foreign policy was concerned—the economic
and technical re-equipping of the country for an active, expansionist,
aggressive policy of world communism. This task was already being
emphasized during the First Five-Year Plan (1928–32):

> The task of the Five-Year Plan consisted of creating in the
> country the necessary technical and economic prerequisites for the
> maximum increase in the defense capacity of the country

said Stalin in his report on "The Results of the First Five-Year Plan."[26]

The Second Five-Year Plan (1933–37) turned the U.S.S.R. into a
first-class military power with an independent technical and economic
base. The Eighteenth Party Congress, in 1939, noted:

> The U.S.S.R. has become an independent economic country that
> satisfies its own economic and defense needs with all the necessary
> technical equipment.[27]

On this basis, at the end of the thirties a review was made of the old
policy of "coexistence," and Soviet foreign policy became more active.
Parts of Poland, Finland, Rumania and the Baltic states were annexed.
At the same time, a "reevaluation of values" in the Soviet ideological
system was announced. A "patriotic revolution" aimed at the exploitation of Russian historical heroes and military leaders. The foreign
policy of old Russia was rehabilitated in certain respects. The conquests of the Caucasus and Turkestan were rewritten as progressive
events. Russian nationalism became a major factor in Soviet foreign
policy.

In the middle of the thirties, Russian nationalism in foreign policy
was a reaction to the triumph of national socialism in Germany; in
internal policy it was Stalin's capitulation before the Russian national
spirit in his attempt to use the dynamism of the Russian national consciousness to further communist aims. During World War II Stalin and
his colleagues never appealed to the communist consciousness of Soviet

citizens and never mentioned Marx and Engels in their propaganda. Standing at Lenin's mausoleum on November 7, 1941, the anniversary of the October Revolution, Stalin said to members of the Red Army:

> May you be inspired in this war by the heroic image of our great predecessors, Alexander Nevsky, Dmitry Donskoy, Kuzma Minin, Dmitry Pozharsky, Alexander Suvorov, Mikhail Kutuzov.[28]

He went on to proclaim the official disbandment of the COMINTERN and an amnesty for religion.

The Soviet authorities adhered to the same line of national propaganda in the constituent republics, calling on their peoples to be worthy heirs of their great forebears, Bogdan Khmelnitsky in the Ukraine, Shamil in the Caucasus, Imanov in Central Asia, etc.

Russia was saved in World War II, not by Soviet communism, but by Russian patriotism, aroused by the crass errors of the German political administration of the day.

The secondary factors influencing Soviet foreign policy include the "struggle for peace," the policy of coexistence, the principle of non-interference in internal affairs and respect for the sovereignty of other states, the recognition of the right to national self-determination, etc. The history of Soviet foreign policy is convincing proof that none of these are primary factors; they are not basic principles determining its interests and direction, but functional and derivative factors, tactical and subject to change. They represent a means and not an end. Were Soviet foreign policy motivated by a genuine recognition of rights to self-determination and to sovereignty, the "people's democracies" in East and Central Europe would not exist, nor would there be three Soviet republics on the shores of the Baltic, not to mention the nations communism subjugated years ago. Even the slogans calling for peace and disarmament, with which the Kremlin has attempted to rally the so-called worldwide movement of supporters of peace and on which Soviet propaganda has expended so much paper and uttered so many speeches, are, according to communist doctrine, Utopian, aimed at deceiving the people. The CPSU program of 1919 declared:

> Slogans of pacifism, international disarmament under capitalism, courts of arbitration, etc. are not only a reactionary Utopia, but directly deceive the workers. . . . Only proletarian communist revolution can lead mankind out of this impasse. . . . This victory of world proletarian revolution requires the greatest possible unity of revolutionary action by the working class in the leading countries.[29]

The same is true of the Leninist legend of coexistence. Although the Communists declare that peaceful coexistence is not just a tactical slogan, their attempted arguments indicate the contrary. As one Soviet commentator on current Soviet foreign policy writes:

> The doctrine of the possibility of peaceful coexistence and peaceful competition of two systems is not a tactical slogan but a

fundamental and organic part of the Leninist theory of the future prospects of a peaceful socialist revolution. This theory is based on the law of the unequal economic and political development of the capitalist countries in the imperialist epoch. From this law stems the proposition that the simultaneous victory of socialist revolution everywhere is impossible. . . . The first development of world socialist revolution after the victory of the October Revolution, Leninism teaches, will take the form of a falling away from the capitalist system by various countries or groups of countries. . . . This means that relations between the states of the two systems will not consist only of clashes and conflicts.[30]

In other words, since communism cannot immediately conquer the whole world, Communists now support Lenin's theory of the "weak link" and choose to conquer one country at a time. Since this process of decay and seizure of free countries from within is, according to this theory, a prolonged one, the communist system in the meantime is prepared for coexistence in the form of competition with the capitalist system. In the words of an official Soviet publication:

The CPSU considers that in the peaceful competition of the two systems—the capitalist and the socialist—victory will certainly fall to the socialist system.[31]

The foreign policy of the U.S.S.R. is similarly conducted, and it "coexists" for the time being: respecting the strong, conquering the weak and sharpening disagreements within the camp of intended victims. Lenin had this in mind when he wrote:

Our foreign policy is that we must exploit disagreements (best of all would be to conquer all imperialist powers, but we shall not be in a position to do that for a long time); our existence depends on the fact that there exist radical divergencies of view among the imperialist powers.[32]

Coexistence, as the Communists understand it, is only a pause, a breathing-space in which to gather strength and lower the political morale of the enemy.

The colonial question is a secondary factor in Soviet foreign policy. In dealing with the colonial question bolshevism starts from the premise that, for the successful realization of a comprehensive plan of world revolution, it is possible and necessary to use colonial and dependent peoples by promising them broad national freedoms, including even the freedom to create independent states. However, in this case also, the nationality question is regarded as a derivative and subordinate part of the general problem of how to achieve world communist revolution. On this Stalin wrote:

The path of victorious revolution in the West lies through the revolution's joining in the colonies' and dependent countries' wars of liberation against imperialism but he went on to point out that it must be remembered that

> the national question is part of the general question of proletarian revolution, part of the question of the dictatorship of the proletariat.[33]

Therefore communism supports only those national movements that weaken the strength of the West and that are prepared directly or indirectly to submit to communist control and leadership.

In this regard, Stalin was following both the spirit and the letter of Leninism. Lenin declared:

> The individual demands of democracy, including self-determination, are not an end in themselves; they are part of the general democratic world movement. It is possible that, in individual concrete instances, individual demands conflict with the general movement—in such a case they must be rejected.[34]

He said elsewhere:

> Not one Marxist, without breaking away from the fundamentals of Marxism and socialism, can deny that the interests of socialism rate higher than the aspirations of nations to self-determination.[35]

Communists must therefore regard the first act—the liberation of colonial and dependent peoples—as an essential step toward the second act—their successful bolshevization. This is the famous Leninist theory of the transition of the bourgeois-democratic revolution (in this instance, a war for national liberation) into a socialist (that is, communist) revolution.

The theory is well illustrated in Khrushchev's attack on the President of the United Arab Republic in 1959. Nasser had divined and exposed Khrushchev's strategy in the Arab world. Khrushchev was forced to reveal his real plans on this matter at the Twenty-first Party Congress, at which he said:

> We must express our views on the fact that a campaign is being conducted in certain countries against progressive forces under the false slogans of anti-communism. In the United Arab Republic an attack has recently been made on communist ideas. . . . I, as a Communist, consider it necessary to say that . . . there are no people more staunch and devoted to the cause of the struggle against the colonialists than Communists.[36]

He revealed the truth that Communists stand for and will continue to stand for the transition from the national type of colonial revolution to the social stage, that is, to the communist stage. As to the final result, he stated:

> After the colonialists have been driven out, when all the national tasks have been solved, the people seek an answer to the social problems life poses. In the ranks of the national liberation movement social processes occur that inevitably give rise to varying opinions concerning the paths for the further development of their states.[37]

A new chapter in the history of Soviet foreign policy has begun. It is not identical with Lenin's and Trotsky's policy of world revolution held in the first years of Soviet power, nor can it be entirely identified with Stalin's and Molotov's postwar course of direct aggression. The new chapter in Soviet foreign policy is linked with the name of Khrushchev, who, while setting himself the same aims as those of the Leninist and Stalinist policies, resorted, in deference to changed circumstances both in the U.S.S.R. and abroad—including the danger of self-destruction in atomic warfare—to other means and other methods: economic expansion, ideological aggression and local revolutionary wars.

The military and political views of the Kremlin are no longer mainly concerned with the problem of its own defense and that of its satellites. At the Twenty-first Party Congress, Khrushchev declared:

> Our country, which has built socialism, was for a long time the only socialist country in the world and was held in hostile capitalist encirclement. It could not consider itself completely secure from military intervention and the danger of the forcible restoration of capitalism. . . . The capitalist states that then surrounded our country were vastly superior in economic and military matters. Now the position is completely changed. Our country is no longer encircled by capitalism. There are two social systems in the world: moribund capitalism and vigorous socialism. . . . The balance of power in the world is now such that we could repel any attack by any enemy. No force in the world can reestablish capitalism in our country and defeat the socialist camp. The danger of the restoration of capitalism in the U.S.S.R. has been excluded.[38]

The victory of socialism in the U.S.S.R. and the creation of a world socialist system, he held, immeasurably strengthened the forces of the international workers' movement, and opened up new prospects for it.[39] The international economic calculations of the Seven-Year Plan were based on these new prospects. They included economic expansion in three forms—economic "self-help and coordination" with the satellites (making the economies of the satellites serve Moscow's foreign policy), "technical and economic aid" to young countries and "peaceful competition between capitalism and socialism in the world arena," meaning fighting for influence over young countries. "Nowadays," said Khrushchev,

> our task consists in achieving the ascendancy of the socialist system over the capitalist system in world production, in outstripping the most highly developed capitalist countries in productivity, in output per head of the population, and in ensuring the highest standard of living in the world.[40]

What are the prospects of realizing this goal? Khrushchev predicted in 1959:

> If one calculates per head of the population, then probably another five years will be necessary after the Seven-Year Plan has

been fulfilled in order to catch up with and overtake the United States in industrial production. In other words, by that time, and perhaps even earlier, the Soviet Union will occupy first place in the world in absolute volume of production and in output per head of the population. This will be the worldwide historic victory of socialism in peaceful competition with capitalism in the international arena. . . . As a result of the fulfillment and overfulfillment of the Seven-Year Plan and also of the high rate of development of the economies of the people's democracies, the socialist countries will produce more than one-half of the industrial output of the entire world.[41]

It is interesting to note that Lenin envisaged this program but was unable to carry it out. He wrote:

We now exert our influence on international revolution mainly by our economic policy. . . . In our lifetime the struggle will be enlarged to a worldwide scale. When we solve this task we shall certainly achieve a conclusive victory on an international scale.[42]

Since the Communists always attach exaggerated importance to economic factors ("Politics is the concentrated expression of economics," wrote Lenin), the Kremlin will regard the capture of key positions in the economy as a necessary prerequisite for the ideological and political capture of a country. This development will prove to be an irreversible process if it is not prevented and paralyzed from without. The fact that the Soviet economy is a state-owned economy, with a monopoly of foreign trade, and that the labor of Soviet citizens has never been regulated by competition, will make the struggle with the Soviet Union on a trading and economic front progressively more onerous and exhausting. The U.S.S.R. will always subordinate its trade and economic war to the interests of policy; if these interests demand the abandonment of economic profits, the Soviet government will abandon them. Stalin underestimated the importance of the economic factor in Soviet foreign policy and refused technical and economic assistance to underdeveloped countries. He believed that in the young states only the form and not the reality of the colonial regime of the Western powers had changed, and that therefore aid to the less developed countries was indirect aid to their former masters. The post-Stalin party leadership has shown considerable flexibility in this matter, and regards Stalin's views as mistaken and harmful for the Soviet Union.

This change of viewpoint laid the foundation for the progress the U.S.S.R. has made in Asia and Africa since Stalin's death. The U.S.S.R. has not only begun to give economic and technical help to developing countries, it has considerably increased trade with some of these countries and has, for the first time, initiated some trade without an economic basis, in the hope of future political justification. Whereas in 1953 the U.S.S.R. had trade agreements with only three Asian countries, by 1958 it had fourteen such agreements.[43]

A similar increase has taken place in the technical and economic aid to Afro-Asian countries. Mukhitdinov, a former member of the Presidium of the party Central Committee, has said that whereas in 1955 the amount of economic and technical aid totalled only tens of millions of rubles, by 1959 the "value of long-term credits amounted to several billion rubles," and that "Soviet credits are very favorable."[44] Between 1954 and the end of 1957, the Soviet bloc concluded agreements with fourteen developing countries promising aid worth $1,900,000,000 in short and long-term credits for goods and assistance. The Soviet Union alone promised $1,300,000,000 of this sum, and its European satellites and Communist China promised about $600,000,000.[45] Although the Free World contributed 76.8 per cent and the Soviet bloc 23.2 per cent of the aid to developing countries, if we exclude the countries linked to the West by defensive alliances (Iran, Pakistan, Indo-China and Turkey), the U.S. contribution to neutral states amounted to 55.4 per cent of the total as against 44.6 per cent for the Soviet bloc.[46] Official Soviet data on economic aid to developing countries at the beginning of 1962 indicate the likelihood of a further increase. The U.S.S.R. was reported to be building in 1965 about 600 industrial enterprises and 100 technical schools in African and Asian countries.[47]

The importance of communist tactics does not lie in their flexibility. Sometimes their inflexibility even leads their government into an impasse—as in the case of war communism under Lenin and the postwar U.S.S.R. under Stalin—particularly when the Communists persist in their errors by flagrantly altering their own tactical doctrine. The effectiveness of communist tactics is a result of their broad compass. This in turn explains their dynamism, which is not a result of the intellectual superiority of the Communist leaders but rather of their plebeian utilitarianism, narrowmindedness and moral unscrupulousness. The reason for the dynamism of communist tactics lies in the Communists' rejection of all moral standards, both religious and traditional. At the Third *Komsomol* Congress, in 1920, Lenin stated:

> We say: morality is that which serves to destroy the old exploiting society. . . . We do not believe in an eternal morality.[48]

Even the system of communist doctrine is subject to this moral or amoral law; if principles that yesterday seemed to be sacrosanct today clash with the interests of the regime, they will immediately be replaced by other principles more in line with the times. The criterion for the replacement of the old principles with new ones is the same power factor: the extent to which an old principle hinders, and a new one consolidates and extends, communist power. Lenin, Stalin and Khrushchev all acted in accordance with this principle. "Dialectics are the soul of Marxism," said Stalin, and the communist leaders have always justified any improbable change in tactics by reference to the laws of dialectics. When the interests of communism require it, even dialectics can prove to be "dialectical." Complete internal freedom to interpret their own teachings as they like, complete lack of any moral restrictions in selection of means, unlimited fanaticism in defense of their own aims and a readiness to sacrifice any ideals—national, social or philosophical —in the name of power—these are the characteristic features of bolshevist tactics. This body of tactical doctrine determines Soviet foreign policy and the selection of the instrument to be used in its accomplishment—the line of Soviet diplomacy and the selection of the Soviet diplomatic apparatus. However, Soviet diplomacy obtains only its moral philosophy from Marxism-Leninism; the means and methods used to carry it out are developed independently. Here it does not ignore what it has inherited from the old classical, or bourgeois, schools of diplomacy, from Machiavelli to Talleyrand and Metternich. The Communists select only those elements that have anticipated the moral system of communism in international relations. Of course, communist teachers disclaim such things as the moral indifference of Talleyrand or the state philosophy of Machiavelli, but in fact they have taken over from them everything that can be fitted into the extremely broad framework of Soviet tactics and strategy.

The common view is that the conservatism found in Marxist orthodoxy to some degree paralyzes communism's tactical flexibility, makes Communists the slaves of their own doctrine, forces them to ram their heads against brick walls for the sake of their principles, to reject opportunistic compromises in the name of the purity of Marxism-Leninism, to sacrifice the advantages to be gained from a given situation if it contradicts official dogma and to cling to prestige when form is preserved, to the detriment of content. Such views of communist tactics in general and communist diplomacy in particular are erroneous. The examination of this question with reference to the tactical teachings of Lenin and the practice of Stalin and the Stalinists is outside the scope of the present work. However, mention can be made of some of the fundamental principles of Leninism on this score. Maneuvering, conciliation, deliberate compromises, skillful use of conflicts in the enemy camp and wooing temporary allies, even among the Communists' enemies, were bequeathed by Lenin to his pupils as the foundation of Soviet diplomacy. Lenin wrote:

> To wage a war for the overthrow of the international bourgeoisie, a war a hundred times more difficult, prolonged and complex than the most stubborn of ordinary wars between states, and in advance to abandon maneuvering, the exploitation, albeit temporary, of the conflicting interests of enemies, to reject conciliation with possible, albeit temporary, insecure, unstable, conditional allies—is this not completely ridiculous?[49]

He also wrote:

> The entire history of bolshevism before and since the October

Revolution is *full* of cases of maneuvering, conciliation, com-promises, even with the bourgeois parties.[50]

The art of maneuvering is the first principle of bolshevist tactics.

Lenin, the greatest of revolutionary aggressors, who always quoted with approval Clausewitz' dictum that even in politics attack is the best form of defense, nonetheless pointed out to his pupils that retreat is also a special art, which must be constantly studied:

> Revolutionary parties must keep on studying. They have learned to advance, now they must show that this science must be supplemented by the science of how best to retreat. They must understand that one cannot conquer without having learned how to advance and retreat correctly.[51]

The second principle in bolshevist tactics is the selection of the best time for an attack, and how to keep the enemy guessing prior to this step. Machiavelli advised the Prince not to let an enemy know that a definite policy prepared in advance is being employed. Lenin adopted the same standpoint. He wrote:

> To tie one's hands in advance, openly to tell an enemy who is presently better armed than we whether we will fight with him and when, is stupidity, and not a revolutionary approach. To engage in a battle when this is known to be favorable to an enemy and not to us is a crime, and such a policy is never of any use for a revolutionary class that is unable to continue "maneuvering, conciliation and compromises" in order to avoid a battle known to be unfavorable.[52]

Until the time is ripe, while one is simply gathering one's own forces and feeling out the strength of the enemy, one must work in the enemy's rear lines, in his camp, even in his home. Hence Lenin formulated the third principle of bolshevist tactics:

> One must learn to work legally in the most reactionary parlia-ments, in the most reactionary trade unions, cooperatives and insurance and other similar organizations.[53]

What if Communists are not admitted to these organizations? Lenin had the answer:

> One must be able to make every type of sacrifice, even in case of need, any tricks, guile, illegal moves, omissions, suppression of the truth. . . . Of course . . . in Western Europe, with its tradi-tion of deep-rooted legalism, constitutional, bourgeois-democratic prejudices, it is more difficult to do such a thing. But it can and must be done systematically.[54]

Admitting that there might be persons in the Bolshevik party who did not agree with such a frank Machiavellian morality in policy, based on the principle that the end justifies the means, Lenin hastily disowned such revolutionaries. He stated at the Seventh Party Congress:

> If you are unable to adjust yourself, are not disposed to crawl on your belly in the dirt, then you are not a revolutionary, but a chatterer, and I do not propose doing this because I like doing so, but because there is no other way, because history has not developed so nicely that revolution matures everywhere simultaneously.[55]

In reply to the question as to why one need enter so reactionary an organization, Lenin answered:

> The revolutionary headquarters of the working class is deeply interested in reconnoitering the bourgeois parliamentary institutions in order to make this work of destruction easier. . . . Communism rejects parliamentarianism; it denies the possibility of a protracted conquest of parliaments; it sets as its aim the destruction of the parliamentary system. *Hence one may only talk of exploiting bourgeois state institutions with the aim of destroying them.* In this sense *only* can the question be posed.[56]

From these general tactical directives comes the fourth principle of communist tactics in regard to international agreements and treaty obligations: the conditional nature of such obligations. One Soviet diplomatic handbook quotes Machiavelli on this question:

> A sensible prince cannot keep his word when this is harmful to him, and when the reasons compelling him to do so no longer exist.[57]

This is the attitude of Leninism-Stalinism toward the importance of agreements and to international law in general. Lenin pointed out to his pupils on many occasions that it was inadmissible to turn agreements into something sacrosanct that must be obeyed whatever the circumstances. After the separate Peace of Brest-Litovsk, Lenin wrote:

> Yes, of course, we are violating the agreement, we have already violated it from thirty to forty times. . . . History shows that peace is a breathing-space for war. . . .[58]

and

> An agreement is a means of collecting one's forces. Some definitely think like children: he has signed an agreement, that means he has sold himself to Satan, gone to Hell.[59]

In spite of any and all treaties, Lenin was ready to begin a war if it was in the interests of communism. He wrote:

> We are not pacifists; we have always declared it would be stupid for the revolutionary proletariat to abandon revolutionary wars, which may prove essential in the interests of socialism.[60]

Elsewhere Lenin expressed his attitude toward international law and the value of international agreements in the eyes of the Bolsheviks more precisely:

As soon as we are strong enough to fight capitalism, we shall immediately seize it by the scruff of the neck.[61]

Such are the foundations of the tactical doctrine of bolshevism; such is the real meaning of communist "coexistence."

What are the general conclusions from the above discussion? Soviet foreign policy is not a national-state policy in the normal meaning of the term, but an international-ideological function of Soviet domestic policy. It is determined, not by the problems and interests of the country, but by those of the ruling segment, the Communist party. The party's interests coincide with the country's national-state interests only when the country is subject to aggression from without. In all other cases they diverge. Soviet foreign policy is based on the same motivating factors as the doctrine of the Communist party itself: the tasks of consolidating the regime and establishing worldwide domination. By its very nature Soviet foreign policy cannot be passive, defensive, conservative. Insofar as it is only one link in the general policy of world revolution and worldwide domination, it is merely a flexible instrument for the achievement of these tasks. Hence it is armed only with offensive weapons; its doctrine is aggressive through and through, even in cases when it is compelled to maneuver or retreat, since it regards such retreats as pauses, as a breathing-space prior to a new advance. Different factors, including the national factor, influence Soviet foreign policy in varying degrees at various stages. Two factors, however, permanently determine Soviet foreign policy: the interests of the authorities inside the U.S.S.R. and the victory of communism outside it. This implies further that the struggle is not for the establishment of abstract communism in the form of a harmonious and social adjustment between peoples, but for the establishment of a single worldwide communist system of government headed by the Soviet Union. These two factors have remained in force in spite of all the actual or apparent zig-zags in Soviet foreign policy from Lenin to Stalin, from the "collective leadership" to Khrushchev, from Khrushchev to Brezhnev.

When peace was concluded with Germany, in 1918, Lenin stated that he was trading space for time; the Kremlin is now trading time for space. The Communists themselves will decide when the time has come to put an end to the period of respite, to "coexistence." This is the greatest danger inherent in any peace with the Communists. All domestic economic plans, the plans for the construction of so-called communism, are, if seen from a foreign political standpoint, merely plans for the preparation of a new combined attack by communism against the Free World, in all sectors—military, political, ideological, economic, scientific and technological.

The economic factor, which to date has not played a great role in determining Soviet foreign policy, is gradually becoming more important. The Kremlin's revival of peaceful competition between communism and capitalism under the slogan "Who will defeat whom?" and the policy of Soviet technical and economic aid to the developing countries are a legalized disguise for communist expansion in the countries concerned. While free capital may be invested in these countries by individuals for purely economic ends, for profit, Soviet investments there will be made by the state only for political ends.

The unrestricted tactical range of Soviet foreign policy, its lack of any moral or ethical considerations and its pragmatic approach to international law, with the resulting freedom of interpretation of any obligations undertaken, make the Soviet government a completely unreliable negotiator in international agreements. Soviet foreign policy regards its rights derived from agreements and treaties as unconditional, but its obligations as conditional. Hence security that is based, not on ability to maintain it, but on agreement and trust in the Soviet government, will be effective only until the Soviets have exhausted the rights granted them by agreement and the advantages connected with them. Thus the Seventh Party Congress, when ratifying the separate peace treaty with Germany in 1918, could grant to the Central Committee the following authority, which exists to this day:

> The Congress especially wants to emphasize that the Central Committee is being given the authority to break at any time all peace treaties with imperialistic and bourgeoisie governments and declare war on them.[62]

In order to understand the foreign policy of the CPSU, it is necessary to examine the nature of the ideological polemics now taking place between Moscow and Peking. Divested of its many insignificant aspects, of the sometimes justified, sometimes simply demagogic mutual accusations, the Sino-Soviet ideological conflict revolves around the following questions. What sort of relationship is there between thermonuclear war and world communist revolution? Have the classic Leninist doctrines on imperialism and world revolution and the tactics and strategy of revolution themselves become outmoded? Has the Leninist doctrine on the "dictatorship of proletariat" become outmoded? What sort of general course is communist diplomacy following? The disagreements between Moscow and Peking on these points are summarized below:

Peking's Position	*Moscow's Position*
1. Imperialist wars are unavoidable even in the nuclear era; they are the source of revolution.	1. Wars are no longer unavoidable; they can and must be prevented, for a nuclear war cannot be the source of revolution.
2. Communists can achieve power by one means alone: violent revolution (in three forms—uprisings, civil wars and conspiracies).	2. Communists can achieve power by two means: (*a*) violence (uprisings, civil wars, conspiracies) or (*b*) peaceful means (parliamentary majority); the selection of one or the other means depends on the circumstances and the state of the opposition by the bourgeois classes.

3. The "dictatorship of the proletariat" and the class struggle will exist in all countries of the socialist camp until the final victory of total communism over the entire world; the "dictatorship of the proletariat" therefore should be preserved and the Communist party should remain a party of the working class.

3. After the victory of socialism and during the period of transition to communism there is no class struggle and therefore the necessity for a "dictatorship of the proletariat" withers away; henceforth there exists an "All-National State," and the Communist party is transformed from a party of the working class into a "party of the whole people."

4. Peaceful coexistence between different social systems is impossible.

4. Peaceful coexistence is not only possible, it has become an "objective necessity" in the age of atomic weapons.

5. The general course of foreign policy of communist states should be the rendering of all possible direct assistance in preparation for world communist revolution.

5. The general course of foreign policy of communist states should be peaceful coexistence as a form of ideological struggle and also as a form of indirect assistance for communist infiltration.

6. The center of the world revolution has shifted to the "weakest link" of the Free World: Asia, Africa and Latin America.

6. The center and motive force for the further unfolding of the world revolution are the socialist countries and also the revolutionary workers' movements in Europe and America.

7. There is only one way to socialism: the Leninist-Stalinist way.

7. There are many ways to socialism, depending on national circumstances.

The positions of Moscow and Peking are also diametrically opposed with respect to many tactical questions of international diplomacy. Although the 1950 military alliance between the U.S.S.R. and China remains in force, Peking never tires of pointing out that Moscow and Washington are now closely collaborating in a conspiracy aimed at establishing their rule over the world; the alleged evidence of this is the 1963 Nuclear Test-Ban Treaty. The Chinese refused to be associated with this "conspiracy" and "treachery," although about one hundred nations subscribed to the treaty. To counterbalance this treaty the Chinese put forward a more radical proposal of their own, calling for total prohibition and destruction of atomic weapons. With the destruction of atomic weapons the Chinese would be spared from the hegemony of either the U.S.S.R. in the communist camp or the U.S. in world politics.

The Soviets support this proposal, not merely for the sake of propaganda. The Kremlin leaders have come to the sober conclusion that the triumph of the world communist revolution according to Lenin's doctrine, i.e., as a result of world war or even as the result of local wars, is possible only if the status quo of Lenin's period can be reestablished in the world political arena: a world without atomic bombs. Only in such a world will the old formulas of Leninism once again assert themselves. Only in such a world is war not connected with the risk of self-destruction; conventional wars with conventional weapons will again become the source of communist revolution and communist conquests. If atomic weapons have made war senseless and impossible, then atomic disarmament will make war not only possible but a real means of settling international disputes in general, and of achieving communist goals in particular. This is why the Kremlin is convinced that the shortest (and the only) road to world communism is through the "humanization of war," i.e., through atomic disarmament.

The Kremlin not only desires atomic disarmament, it also proposes universal disarmament covering all other types of weapons. Without conventional weapons there would no longer be conventional wars. The communist plan of universal disarmament is another precondition for the total victory of the Leninist strategy of world revolution, for universal disarmament by the great democratic powers of the West would make possible *internal revolutionary wars*. All classical revolutions have been accomplished with the help of hand weapons, at times rather primitive—bayonets and sabers, axes and pitchforks. With good organization and the willingness to make sacrifices, a small but dynamic army of revolutionaries can easily overpower a disorganized majority and its police units left unsupported by the forces of a regular army. Of course, the great powers, well organized socially and with democratic traditions of government, would be able to withstand such internal revolutions; but what will happen if the world communist offensive adopts, as is more than likely, the Chinese plan of striking a blow at the "weakest link"—first at Asia, Africa and Latin America, and then at Europe and America alone? When the Communists began to seize, link by link, the entire Afro-Asian and Latin American chain (after the model of Cuba, Viet Nam and the Dominican Republic), the great democratic powers could not come to the aid of these countries nor could they send troops, for they would no longer have such troops under "universal disarmament."

The positions of Moscow and Peking on conventional disarmament do differ significantly. The Chinese Communists consider the slogan of conventional disarmament a temporary one. Peking believes that if the West accepts the Soviet proposal on disarmament the Communists will then be forced to repudiate it. Peking supports the point of view openly expressed in Lenin's program of the CPSU of 1919: "Slogans of pacifism, international disarmament under capitalism, are not only *reactionary utopia* but a *gross betrayal* of the workers aimed at disarming the proletariat." Therefore, Peking believes that to proceed seriously with genuine conventional disarmament is tantamount to disarming the communist revolution in Asia, Africa and Latin America. Against such an argument on the part of Peking, Moscow gave the following rejoinder, in the words of Khrushchev:

> It is absolutely groundless to attempt to represent the struggle for disarmament as an effort to disarm peoples who have risen in a struggle against imperialism. It is clear that disarmament affects in the main the arsenals of the great powers. . . . The peoples of the colonies and the liberated countries only benefit from this "dismantling" of the imperialist military machine from the liquidation of imperialist military bases located on their territories.[63]

In other words, only after such "dismantling" of the military machine of the democratic powers is it possible, in the opinion of the Kremlin, for the communist revolution to succeed, at first in Asia, Africa and Latin America, and then in the West.

It is not our task at this point to analyze the state contradictions between China and the U.S.S.R. These contradictions are so deep, and China's revanchist *Drang nach Norden* for the regain of territories lost by China to Russia in the nineteenth and twentieth centuries (Amur *Oblast,* Ussurijski *Krai,* part of Turkestan and Outer Mongolia) so great, that in perspective they make war between these two communist states, if not unavoidable, at least fully possible.

A careful analysis of the Moscow-Peking disagreements shows that they are not at all disagreements of a competitive nature. They are not even disagreements simply on matters of tactics. Moscow and Peking have the same ultimate goal: the destruction of the democratic world and the establishment of world communist rule. But the methods and the courses of action proposed by each side are so different, or at times so opposite, that they could lead to a final split of world communism into two hostile camps with two opposing ideologies. The present split in communism is closely reminiscent of the split in the Russian Social-Democratic movement in 1903 and the split in world socialism (the Second International) during and after World War I. Indeed, even in the Marxist Social-Democrat movement—in both the Russian and the international movements—the split appeared in the first instance, not over program questions nor over the ultimate goal (socialism), but only over the so-called organizational question, i.e., over questions of tactics, over questions of the methods and means to socialism. In the end, out of Marxist socialism were born two diametrically opposed ideologies and political conceptions—Western democratic socialism and Eastern revolutionary communism.

However, while the split in the old socialism occurred at first as a result of tactical disagreements and later as a result of ideological disagreements, in the present communism the disagreements concern not only tactics and ideology, but also the question of which side should have hegemony—Moscow or Peking— in the "socialist camp," in the world communist movement and in the national-revolutionary movement in Asia, Africa and Latin America. Even since the overthrow of Khrushchev, Peking has continued its attacks on the "Khrushchev revisionists" in the Kremlin. Of the eighty-one Communist parties that signed the 1960 Moscow Declaration on unity on a platform of action, sixty supported Moscow;[64] the rest either supported Peking or remained "neutral." At the same time, in almost all pro-Moscow parties the Chinese created a pro-Peking wing, which in the event of a final split will be formed into a group of independent "Marxist-Leninist Communist parties."

On which side is "Leninist truth" in the ideological conflict between Moscow and Peking? In other words, whose tactics conform to the spirit of Leninism and "guarantee" success for the world communist revolution? Actually, both sides' tactics are "right." Moscow is "right" in its *dualistic* form of tactics (evolution and revolution): seizing power from within in the highly developed industrial nations of the West, while avoiding the unleashing of war (which easily could be transformed into atomic suicide). Peking is "right" in its *single* form of tactics: seizing power by unleashing uprisings and civil wars in the developing nations of Asia, Africa and Latin America, where the risk of an atomic war is minimal and where the social-political conditions are ideal for the application of the Leninist tactic of direct revolutionary actions. Therefore, the "Leninist truth" with respect to communist revolution today may be said to lie in a *harmonious synthesis* of the Moscow-Peking tactics, which is in fact the Kremlin line.

As a well-known Soviet party theoretician, alluding to the Chinese, wrote: "[communism] cannot make absolute any one form of struggle; it must combine them with flexibility, employ skillfully its whole tactical arsenal."[65]

In these differences the Kremlin is guilty least of all. In reply to Moscow's concessions (partial rehabilitation of Stalin), to the ingratiating, even humiliating incantations of its readiness to compromise and come to an agrement, Peking said:

> Between the CPC and CPSU there are only matters that divide and nothing that unites; there are only contrary views and nothing that we might have in common; any unity of action of the CPSU with the CPC is not possible so long as both parties stand on diametrically opposed positions.[66]

Can unity between Moscow and Peking be restored? If so, on what terms? The answer is, yes, it can be restored, but only on the following terms: In the first place, Moscow will have to agree to renew its 1957 nuclear treaty with China, unilaterally abrogated by Moscow in 1959, according to which the Chinese received access to Soviet secrets of thermonuclear weapons production (and the Chinese may in addition demand rockets capable of delivering nuclear warheads). Secondly, Moscow will have to recognize Mao Tse-tung as the lawful teacher and theoretician of the contemporary world communist movement. When the new Kremlin leaders subscribe to these terms, they will cease to be, in the eyes of Peking, "Khrushchev revisionists"—and not a day sooner.

* Chapter XX *

Conclusion: Partocracy

WHAT ARE the characteristic features that distinguish partocracy from the autocratic forms known up to the present time and from the so-called totalitarian states? First of all, grouping the communist, nazi and fascist systems under one general heading, as though in one general *totalitarian* form of government, is a flagrant misunderstanding. Here the temptation to generalize has pushed in the background not only the essence of each of these systems but also the tremendous difference between them. Such an approach loses sight of still another important circumstance: both fascism and naziism were, in the first place, reactions to communist action; secondly, they were imitations of bolshevism, adopting the enemy's weapons and fighting methods for their own arsenals. However, these imitations were and remain a highly imperfect copy of their phenomenal original. This may be illustrated by a comparative analysis of the principal elements in naziism and in communism. Just what is totalitarianism?

This is the Soviet definition:

> A totalitarian state is a variety of bourgeois state with an undisguised terroristic dictatorship of the most reactionary imperialistic elements. Hitler's Germany and fascist Italy were totalitarian states.[1]

This is the English definition:

> *Totalitarian State:* an expression used in reference to the Nazi government of Germany, the fascist of Italy, and the Communistic of Russia in which there is complete centralization of control. In the totalitarian state political parties are suppressed or "co-ordinated" into one party and the conflict of classes is obscured by emphasis on the organic unity of the State.[2]

This is the German definition:

> [Totalitarianism] is the most extreme stage of the tendency toward centralism, uniformity and the one-sided regimentation of all political, social and spiritual life.[3]

The *Fischer Lexicon* also treats nazi Germany, fascist Italy and the U.S.S.R. as totalitarian states. One American researcher, in a special

369

work on this subject, includes the following elements in his concept of totalitarianism: an official ideology, a single mass party, a monopoly of all means of waging effective armed conflict, availability of effective mass communications and a system of terroristic police control.[4] Another researcher adds that totalitarianism has for its goal not the status quo of the old order but a social revolution based on its totalitarian ideology.[5] Thus it turns out that the Soviet and Western sources cited unanimously acknowledge nazi and fascist states as totalitarian states. They agree also that the main content of a totalitarian system is its dictatorial, terroristic nature. But there the similarity of their viewpoints ends. The U.S.S.R. does not acknowledge itself to be a totalitarian state but considers that a totalitarian state is only a "variety" of modern bourgeois, that is, Western, states of law (see the above-quoted Soviet definition). On the contrary, the Western sources quoted find many common features in communism and naziism (fascism) that place them in the rightful relationship as police-totalitarian states.

It must be noted that at the basis of the definition of totalitarianism in Western literature lay not only the practical rule of totalitarian states but the doctrine, and even the terminology, of Mussolini, the founder of fascism. Moreover, what was only an end, an ideal, to Mussolini was considered by researchers as fact; that is, what to Mussolini was to be done was considered by them to exist already. From this arose the blending of communist reality with the fascist dream. This is most clearly evident if we turn to the doctrine of fascism on this question. Thus in his article "Doctrine of Fascism,"[6] Mussolini says that for this doctrine

> everything . . . [is] in the state; nothing human or spiritual exists outside the state. . . . In this sense, the state is totalitarian, and fascist domination synthesizes and unites all values, interprets, develops and personifies the entire life of the people. Outside the state there are no individuals, no groups. . . . Fascism wants to change not the forms of human life but its content, man, his character, his belief.

Here Mussolini is setting off the state against the people, placing the state above the people, as if rephrasing and turning Lincoln's famous formula around, in order to advance a diametrically opposite idea: "people of the state, by the state and for the state." The primacy of the state over law ("The State Theory") was acknowledged as an absolute postulate, while a state of law (the primacy of law over the state) was considered a product of the weakness and decay of democracy. But such an all-powerful, omnipresent state was more an ideal than a reality in an Italy that at that time was strongly Catholic in belief and still officially a monarchy. In this respect Hitler was more successful than Mussolini, but even he was far from achieving the ideal in two important areas—in spiritual life and in the creation of a totalitarian, that is, a nationalized, economic system. The area in which both Hitler (to a larger degree) and Mussolini (to a lesser degree) succeeded was in the establishment of a one-party dictatorship over the state organs—but *without the destruction* of the old state machine. In time, this one-party dictatorship set up its own total control over society; but only the control was total, not the organized direction of society. Only the Communists have attained this total organized direction.

In summarizing the aforementioned definitions of totalitarianism, we see that totalitarianism is comprised of at least the following elements: (1) total state control over society; (2) a system of terroristic police control over citizens; (3) a single ruling party; (4) unification and regulation of all political, social and spiritual life; (5) reliance on the regeneration of society; and (6) reliance on its own race[7] (e.g., the nazi racial theory and practice; genocide of the Chechens, Ingush, Karachay and Balkars, the Crimean Tatars, Volga Germans and the Kalmucks by the Communists during World War II; the doctrine of "Soviet patriotism"; racial factors in the quarrel between Moscow and Peking).

The communist regime has original claim to all these elements except the race theory (Stalin borrowed "naziism" from Hitler). In themselves, however, they still do not make the totalitarian form of rule exceptional, for in one degree or another all the autocratic or tyrannical regimes in history bear or have borne such features. What makes communist power a special new form (or type) of rule lies in the very source and nature of this power: *the will of one party.* As a result, party organs bcome the legislative, controlling and administrative organs of the state. The party's will, "the will to power" and the power of will, almost according to Kant's "categorical imperative" (but without its moral substance!), is declared the absolute law of the state and the regulator of social development.

If Lincoln's government of the people exists "of the people, by the people and for the people" and Mussolini's people of the state exist "of the state, by the state and for the state," then Lenin's *government and people and state exist of the party, by the party and for the party.* Hence there is the ever-present "cult of the party." The party itself is not an ordinary party. It is a "party of a new type," as the Communists themselves have correctly defined it. Its novelty consists in the unique features of its historical mission as a substitute for the state and the state apparatus and in the originality of its internal structure. On one hand it is a closed hierarchical organization with a regular apparatus; on the other, it is an open mass party with a membership of many millions. Therefore the party elite, the *apparatchiks,* virtually represent a "party within a party."

The Communist party is not simply the sole ruling state party; it is not even a state within the state. It is *the* state, but a "new type of state," according to the doctrine of the Communists. Its novelty lies in the fact that the hierarchy of official state legislative organs is only the executive-administrative apparatus for carrying out the decisions and instructions of a parallel hierarchy of formal executive party organs. A modern communist state can exist without its official state apparatus, but it cannot exist without its party apparatus. *Relationships between the party apparatus and the state apparatus are not those of coordination, but of subordination; this in itself eliminates dualism in rule.* Hitler and Mussolini did not smash the old state machine in Germany and Italy, they packed it with their own cadres. Lenin destroyed Russia's old state machine in order to replace it with his new party machine. This machine was the system of partocracy.

The existence of a newly created nominal state machine in the guise of a soviet apparatus served technically to aid the party apparatus in governing the state and politically to give the partocratic regime a "people's" façade.

The police nature of Western totalitarian regimes led mainly to the establishment of general political persecution and the liquidation of all civil freedoms, to the super-state role of the political police and to arbitrary authority on the part of punitive organs against citizens who disagreed with the regime. In short, the political police, as the intelligence and counterintelligence agency, courts and executioners, was detached from the state and existed as a self-contained force. In the partocratic state every part of the entire machine, all of its "transmission belts," its ideology and technology of power, are organically saturated with the all-encompassing, ubiquitous spirit of the secret police: Chekism. Therefore in this state the secret police is only a functional quantity, fulfilling the professional-administrative functions of one of the parts of the partocratic machine. While the Western totalitarian regimes unified, regulated and controlled political, social and spiritual life, in the partocratic state *no* area of life exists without control and regulation, as well as organized direction, by the state. What to Western totalitarians was an ideal of total control became and remains in the hands of the Communists a fact of total organized direction. The two systems even had different starting points. The Western totalitarians retained the old state machine, imposing corresponding fascist methods on it; the Communists destroyed the old state machine and created their own machine. The Western totalitarians preserved the old propertied classes; the Communists completely annihilated them, not only economically, but physically as well. The Western totalitarians banned political parties and dissolved them; the Communists liquidated them both politically and physically.

However, the main feature distinguishing communism from Western totalitarianism was, of course, the radical social revolution—the destruction of the old society with its economic structure and economic principles and the creation of a new social community based on a new economy, a new ruling class and new economic principles. This social revolution, begun by Lenin but interrupted by the period of the NEP forced on him, was continued by Stalin; at the end of the twenties it had made the Communist party the exclusive master of the entire Russian national economy. Nationalization of industry and land, nationalization of urban and rural labor as a consequence of the nationalization of the economy, a monopoly of foreign and domestic trade, nationalization of the means of communication, nationalization of spiritual life and its institutions—all of this was also a "new type" of nationalization. Its novelty lay in the legalization of a party monopoly of ownership of the national economy unprecedented in history. It is not the people nor the state in general, but a small group of people, namely, the party, that plans, controls, manages and distributes the country's wealth. This was to have exceptionally important consequences.

Having based their economic policy on Marx's "being determines consciousness," on Lenin's "politics is concentrated economics" and on Stalin's "whatever the conditions of society's material life—such are its ideas," the Communists began an experiment of worldwide historical significance. The main aim of this experiment was the alteration of man's social, spiritual and moral *nature*. The party monopoly of the country's resources is regarded by the party, not as an end in itself, not as the source of prosperity and enrichment of individual party members, but as the instrument, as the factory, for the voluntary or compulsory alteration of the old and the creation of new *communist people*. The principle of distributing the material wealth of Soviet society, which states that each member of society is rewarded for the labor he expends for the benefit of society, is in practice applied in such a way as to promote the success of this new experiment. Under stable and equal conditions compensation for labor and a position in society's social hierarchy depend upon the individual's attitude toward communist ideology and upon the effectiveness of his personal endeavors in putting this ideology into practice. The main Marxist thesis, that the "base" determines the "superstructure," economics determines politics, "the means of production of material life condition the social, political and spiritual processes of life in general,"[8] was assumed not only as the basis of the techniques of wielding power, but as the foundation of the communist doctrine of the creation of a new, communist man. However, this doctrine not only relies on the party's economic monopoly, but on its monopoly of politics. Lenin even stresses, in contrast to Marx, the predominance of politics over economics, maintaining that politics must be superior to economics.[9] This means, in conformity with the doctrine of the creation of a "new man," that while economics in the hands of the party is a more or less passive factor of indirect influence, politics, that is, power, is the active factor of direct influence. For this reason the Soviet lawyer who writes that in Soviet society party law (politics)

has such a tremendous influence on life, on the process of social

> development, on human relationships that it could not have existed
> in all previous history[10]

and that

> the state under socialism is not restricted to external, formal con-
> trol; it directly organizes the economic and cultural life of society;
> it goes deep into the very heart of life, into its remote processes[11]

is completely right.

As the result of such a role for the political establishment of the party
and its auxiliary state organs, the partocratic regime has achieved more
than simple control—although total control—of political, social and
spiritual life, as did Western totalitarian regimes. It goes further: it
directly rules politics, economics, people's thoughts and feelings. It is
not possible here to consider the interesting problem of just how organically and deeply this new regime is mastering its people in its psychological schemes, but it can be said that it masters them to perfection in its
organizational schemes. And herein lies the secret of the partocracy's
strength and longevity.

We have said that the regime rules not only politics and economics
but the Soviet people's thoughts and feelings. This does not at all mean
that the Communists have mastered the people in a spiritual sense.
They have mastered the *apparatus* of spiritual rule of the people; they
have created a communist elite of spiritual life and they have created
communist works of art, but they have not created a new culture or new
spiritual values. Much is said about the progress of Soviet science and
technology. And this is correct. The exact sciences have performed
miracles in the U.S.S.R. But all of the humanities, without exception,
have remained on the level of 1917. Why haven't the humanities and
social sciences developed, when the exact sciences have had such great
success? The answer is quite simple: mathematicians, physicists, chem-
ists and astronomers have enjoyed freedom of scientific research in the
interests of the *Soviet military machine* (nuclear physics, rocket technology, etc.), while scholars in the humanities can only pursue research
in the interests of consolidating the *Soviet party machine*. A fundamental Leninist principle has been and remains mandatory for the social
sciences: "*Partiinost* (party spirit) in science." This means that in the
U.S.S.R. only those works from the field of the social sciences that are
not only written by the method of historical materialism but are placed
at the service of the party's general line as it is today can be published.
This principle of "party spirit in science" asserts:

> Materialism includes, so to speak, party spirit, [which] makes
> mandatory in any appraisal of an event a direct and frank stand
> on the viewpoint of a definite social group.[12]

This means that the Soviet Union publishes only those works from the
social sciences in which conclusions that benefit communism are predetermined even before the work is written. Instead of painstaking analy-

sis, a prepared Marxist diagram; instead of a working hypothesis, a ready-made truth from Marx, Engels or Lenin; instead of new scientific discoveries or the promulgation of new views, a declaration of the stability of the old Marxist dogma. Therefore it is completely natural that in the U.S.S.R. social sciences exist in name only. There are, of course, talented researchers in these sciences but since Marxism-Leninism is considered the "summit of all sciences," and since a critical approach to it is a crime against the state, all these researchers are engaged only in propagandizing and in popularizing what Marx wrote one hundred years ago or what Lenin said fifty years ago. This explains why Soviet social sciences, in the almost fifty years of the existence of the partocratic regime, have not produced a single outstanding scholar nor a single original book in the fields of philosophy, jurisprudence, history and political economy.

All of this has reference, of course, to the higher spheres of spiritual life, to literature and art. The party not only exercises total control and organized direction over spiritual life, it defines the subject matter and the method of spiritual creativity, the so-called method of socialist realism. The essence of this method is that the past, present and future are visually examined and heard by a Communist in the name of the party and its current policies.

A novel or a opera, a canvas or a sculpture, a movie or a circus must by its specific means and artistic forms propagandize the wisdom of the party and the grandeur of communism. A work outside this assigned party line will not appear or, if it should appear, will be branded "formalistic" and "decadent" and be withdrawn from circulation. It is not surprising, therefore, that all creative unions (writers, composers, artists) are directly subordinate to the Department of Propaganda and Agitation of the Central Committee and to local party committees. Within these departments there are special sections for the direction of each form of art.

This procedure was established in 1923, when the Twelfth Party Congress passed the following resolution:

> In view of the fact that in the past two years artistic literature in Soviet Russia has grown into an important social force, spreading its influence first of all on the masses of youthful workers and peasants, it is essential that the party place on the agenda for its practical work the question of the *organized direction (rukovodstvo)* of this form of social influence.[13]

This was the beginning of the struggle between Russian writers and the Communists; the former sought freedom of artistic creativity, the latter the right to organize direction of artistic creativity on the basis of "social order." This unequal struggle ended in 1934 with the full liquidation of the remnants of creative freedom, the disbandment of various literary creative schools and groups, the creation of a single state Union of Soviet Writers and the proclamation of an identical method for all writers, the method of "socialist realism." Since then Russian literature has produced only one book on the level of world literature, and it was published outside the U.S.S.R.: Pasternak's *Doctor Zhivago*.

From all this it is evident that while Western totalitarianism's control over society was total only in the political arena and was conditionally total in spiritual life, the Soviet system exercises not only absolute total control but absolute and total organized direction of all areas of the political, economic and spiritual life and activity of Soviet man. Communist reality has surpassed Mussolini's dream of the totality of the state's subjugation of man, with only one difference: the state itself has turned out to be totally subjugated by the party. The bolshevist leaders, in setting off their power against not only other totalitarian systems but against democratic systems as well, have every right to declare, as Stalin did:

> The world has never known such a mighty power as our Soviet power; the world has never known such a mighty party as our Communist party[14]

or, as Bukharin did:

> [Communist power is a] gigantic machine, the like of which mankind has not seen in any era of its existence.[15]

The machine's unique features cannot be degraded by placing it in the same class with its weak and far from perfect imitations.

Thus partocracy is a hierarchical system of absolute political, economic and ideological power and the wielding of that power by one party, the Communist Party of the Soviet Union. In this one party legislative, controlling and administrative-proprietary functions are merged and concentrated in a central apparatus, while the organs of government and distribution are dualistic: *the organs of organized direction* in the hierarchy of the party apparatus, *the executive organs* in the hierarchy of the state apparatus. While the Constitution of the U.S.S.R. has only decorative authority for all of these organs, the changing will of the party apparatus has absolute authority.

APPENDIX I

Instructions on the Conduct of Elections of the Leading Party Organs

Confirmed by the Central Committee of the Communist Party of the Soviet Union March 29, 1962

1. In accordance with the statutes of the Communist Party of the Soviet Union, elections of the leading party organs are conducted as follows. In local (factory) shop party organizations and party groups—once a year; in *raion*, city, *okrug*, *oblast* and *krai* party organizations and in the Communist parties of the Union republics—once every two years; in the Communist parties of the Union republics that have *oblast* subdivisions (the Ukraine, Belorussia, Kazakhstan, Uzbekistan), elections of the central party organs may be conducted once every four years.

2. Election meetings of local party organizations, city and *raion* party conferences (*raion* meetings) are held, as a rule, during nonworking times.

3. In local party organizations elections of party committees and bureaus—and in those having no bureau, secretaries and their deputies —are conducted at general party meetings. In individual cases in local party organizations comprising over five hundred Communists, with the permission of either the *oblast* or *krai* committee or the party central committee of the Union republic, elections of party committees may be conducted at party conferences. Representation quotas to the conferences are established by the party committee in agreement with the *raion* or city party committee. Elections of *raion*, city, *okrug*, *oblast*, and *krai* party committees are conducted at the corresponding party conferences, and elections of the party central committees of the Union republics at congresses of the Communist parties of the Union republics. Auditing commissions are elected simultaneously with party committees. Representation quotas to the conferences and congresses are established by the corresponding party committees.

4. Delegates to the *raion*, city and *okrug* party conferences may be elected at *raion* party conferences. In cities with *raion* subdivisions delegates to city party conferences may be elected at *raion* party conferences. Delegates to *oblast* and *krai* party conferences, and to congresses of the Communist parties of the Union republics, are elected at *raion*, city and *okrug* party conferences. Delegates to congresses of the Communist parties of the Union republics may be elected at *oblast* party conferences. In party organizations in cities having *raion* subdivisions, elections of delegates to *oblast* and *krai* party conferences and to congresses of the Communist parties of the Union republics may be con-

ducted directly at *raion* party conferences with the permission of either the *oblast* or *krai* party committees or the party central committees of the Union republics.

5. Reports of the party organs are discussed and approved at plenums of the corresponding committees. In local party organizations this business is conducted at sessions of the party committees and bureaus of the party organizations. Reports of auditing commissions are discussed and approved at commission sessions. Preliminary discussion of reports does not deprive members of the party of the right to criticize the leadership of the party organizations at party meetings, conferences and congresses.

6. Members and candidate members of the party temporarily registered in local party organizations take part in the election meetings of these party organizations on a full basis.

7. The leadership of party meetings, conferences and congresses is elected by open ballot: at election meetings in local, shop party organizations—a presidium or chairman and secretary; at conferences and congresses—a presidium and other leading organs. The numerical composition of the indicated organs is determined by the meeting, conference or congress itself. Delegates with the right of a deliberative vote and representatives of higher party committees may be elected to the leading organs of conferences and congresses.

Personnel Turnover Procedures in Party Organs

8. The principle of systematic renewal of personnel and continuity of leadership is observed in the elections of party organs. In accordance with Paragraph 25 of the statutes of the Communist Party of the Soviet Union, the personnel composition of the central committees of the Communist parties of the Union republics, the *krai* party committees and *oblast* party committees is renewed by not less than one-third at every scheduled election, while the personnel composition of *okrug*, city and *raion* party committees or bureaus of local party organizations is renewed by one-half. Members of local party organizations may be elected to no more than three terms in succession. Secretaries of local party organizations may be elected to no more than two terms in succession. The requirements for personnel turnover in auditing commissions is the same as that for the corresponding party committees. The personnel turnover requirements for party committees must be applied separately to both members and alternate members of these organs.

9. A meeting, conference or congress may elect a particular worker, in view of his political and businesslike qualities, to the leading party organs for a longer term. In such cases a minimum of three-fourths of the votes of the Communists participating in the voting must be cast for the individual concerned. In the election of a Communist to an analogous organ of a different party organization his term of service on this previous committee is not counted.

10. Party members who have been removed from a leading party organ in connection with the expiration of their tenure of office may again be elected at subsequent elections. In the election of a Communist to membership on a committee his tenure as an alternate member of that committee or of an auditing commission is not counted. Members of party committees may not be elected alternate members of those committees or members of auditing commissions immediately upon the expiration of their terms of office in those committees stipulated in Paragraph 25 of the party statutes.

Nomination and Discussion of Candidates for Party Organs

11. Elections of the leading party organs are conducted by meetings, conferences or congresses after they have heard, discussed and reached decisions on the summary report of their corresponding party organ and auditing commission. Prior to the conduct of elections the party meeting, conference or congress first determines, by open vote, the numerical composition of the organ to be elected.

12. Candidates for party organs are nominated by the participants in party meetings, conference delegates or congressional delegates at the party meetings, conference sessions or congressional sessions. Nominations for membership in a party committee, for alternate membership in a party committee and for membership in the auditing commission are made separately. Candidates for the party organs being elected may come from among the delegates to the conference or congress who have the right of a deliberative vote, or from the party membership that is not a part of the delegation to the particular party conference or congress. If a motion is made to close the nominations, the presidium of the meeting, conference or congress will put this motion to a vote of the meeting, conference or congress, which in turn will decide through open ballot to cease or to continue registering new candidates.

13. At *raion, okrug,* city, *oblast* and *krai* party conferences, and at congresses of the Communist parties of the Union republics, consultative meetings of representatives of the delegations may be called by the presidium of the conference or congress in order to conduct the preliminary nominations of candidates for a party organ. Consultative meetings of representatives of party organizations may be conducted for the same purpose at meetings (conferences) of local party organizations if the meeting (conference) so decides. Candidates selected at a consultative meeting of representatives of the delegations are nominated at a session of the party conference or congress in the name of the consultative body. The preliminary nomination of candidates for a party organ at a consultative meeting of reprsentatives of the delegation does not limit the rights of delegates in the nomination and discussion of candidates at the conference or congress itself.

14. At meetings, conferences and congresses prior to the nomination of candidates, those present are informed of the members and alternate

members of party organs whose terms of office in these organizations have expired.

15. Participants in meetings and delegates to conferences and congresses personally discuss at their sessions all nominated candidates in the order in which they have been entered on the list. Every participant in a meeting and delegate to a conference or congress has the unlimited right of rejection and criticism of candidates. If a motion is made to curtail discussion of a particular candidate, the meeting, conference or congress decides to curtail or continue discussion by an open vote on the motion.

16. After the discussion of candidates, separate open votes are taken on all candidates against whom objections are raised, in order to determine if they are to be included or not included on the list for secret balloting. Candidates against whom no objections are raised are not voted on by open ballot but are placed on the list prepared for the elections by closed (secret) ballot.

17. Delegates to party conferences and congresses with a deliberative vote (candidate members of the party at meetings of local party organizations) participate in the discussion of candidates for a party organ with the right of a deliberative vote.

Voting Procedures

18. The following are elected by closed (secret) ballot: (a) members of party committees and bureaus and also secretaries and their deputies (where there are no bureaus) of local and shop party organizations; members and alternate members of *raion* party committees, city party committees, *okrug* party committees, *oblast* party committees, *krai* party committees, the central committees of the Communist parties of the Union republics and members of auditing commissions (*Note:* Elections of party group organizers of party groups may be conducted by open voting if the Communists of the party group do not insist on conducting elections by closed [secret] ballot.); (b) delegates to conferences of local party organizations, to *raion, city, okrug, oblast* and *krai* party conferences, and to congresses of the Communist parties of the Union republics.

19. The following are elected by an open vote: (a) secretaries of party committees, secretaries of bureaus of local and shop party organizations and their deputies—at party committee meetings and at bureau meetings of local and shop department party organizations; (b) secretaries and members (alternate members) of the bureaus of the *raion, city, okrug, oblast* and *krai* party committees, and central committees of the Communist parties of the Union republics—at plenums of the corresponding committees; (c) chairmen of auditing commissions—at meetings of the commissions.

20. For the conduct of closed (secret) balloting and the tallying of the results, the party meeting, conference or congress elects by open

vote an accounting commission, whose size is determined by the meeting, conference or congress. The accounting commission selects a chairman and a secretary. Prior to the voting, the chairman of the accounting commission explains the procedures for conducting the closed (secret) balloting to the participants of the meeting, conference delegates or delegates to the congress. The accounting commission, prior to the secret balloting, prepares the ballots (lists) for the secret balloting and seals the ballot boxes. Accounting commissions are not elected in local party organizations consisting of less than ten party members. The party meeting entrusts the tallying of votes to the chairman of the meeting or to one of the party members of that party organization. The results of the voting are entered in the minutes of the meeting.

21. In enterprises having many work shifts, reports and elections of party committees and bureaus of local party organizations are conducted at party meetings of Communists held by shifts during nonworking time. The discussion of reports and the nomination and discussion of candidates for party organs are conducted at each of the work-shift party meetings. As a result of the discussions of the candidates at all the work-shift party meetings, a common list is drawn up for the conduct of elections by closed (secret) ballot. This voting is carried out at party meetings of Communists by shifts. At the party meeting of each shift an accounting commission is elected and the total tally of votes cast at all shift meetings is computed at a joint meeting of the accounting commissions. The results of the voting are reported to the Communists at shift or shop party meetings.

22. Secret balloting in the election of party organs is carried out at closed meetings or closed sessions of conferences and congresses, at which only members of the Communist Party of the Soviet Union or delegates with the right of a decisive vote are present. Representatives of higher party organs have the right to attend both open and closed sessions.

23. Every participant in a meeting or delegate to a conference or congress who has the right of a decisive vote receives one copy each of the ballot (list) of members nominated by the meeting, conference or congress for election to full membership of the party organ being elected, and one copy of the ballot listing those nominated for election to alternate membership of the party organ being elected. When the ballots are issued a mark is made on the credentials of a delegate to a conference or congress, or on the list of party members attending a meeting, indicating that that particular party member has taken part in the voting.

24. Every participant in a meeting, or delegate to a conference or congress, has the right under closed (secret) balloting to cross out separate candidates or add new ones on the ballot, irrespective of the preliminarily established numerical size of the party organ to be elected.

25. After the voting the accounting commission, without leaving the

building in which the meeting, conference or congress is taking place, unseals the ballot boxes and tallys the votes separately for the candidates for full membership and the candidates for alternate membership in the party organ. Having counted the votes, the accounting commission prepares a record of the proceedings, in which the results of the voting are entered to include the number of "for" and "against" votes received by each candidate. The record of proceedings is signed by all members of the commission.

No one has the right to be in the room in which the votes are counted except members of the accounting commission.

26. The accounting commission reports the results of the voting to the meeting, conference or congress, giving the results for each candidate separately. Those candidates who receive over one-half of the votes of the party members participating in the meeting, or over one-half of the votes of the delegates to a conference or congress who have a decisive vote, are considered elected. Communists nominated for election to party organs for a longer period than defined in Paragraph 25 of the party statutes are considered elected if they receive the votes of not less than three-fourths of those participating in the voting.

27. The report of the accounting commission on the outcome of the elections is confirmed by the meeting, conference or congress. If, as a result of the secret balloting, the number of elected members (alternate members) of a party organ is slightly greater or less than that preliminarily established, the meeting, conference or congress may make the decision to confirm the new numerical composition of the party organ by an open vote—in accordance with the results of the secret balloting. In the case where the majority of the participants in the meeting, conference or congress vote to maintain the preliminarily established numerical composition of a party organ, it is then necessary to discuss the candidates anew and to repeat the closed (secret) balloting.

28. All materials relating to the closed (secret) balloting are kept in the party organs and treated as secret documents until the next elections, after which they are destroyed with official certification.

Notebook of a Party Activist, 1964 (Moscow: 1963).

APPENDIX II

REGULATION ON GROUPS AND POSTS FOR ASSISTING THE COMMITTEES FOR PARTY-STATE CONTROL

Approved by the Committee for Party-State Control* of the Central Committee of the Communist Party of the Soviet Union and the Soviet of Ministers of the U.S.S.R. June 30, 1964

The Central Committee of the Communist Party of the Soviet Union, in fulfilling the directives of the Twenty-second Party Congress, has carried out a basic reorganization of the system of control in the country, basing it on the Leninist idea of unifying party and state control and of creating a system of united, all-embracing, constantly functioning control with the broad masses of workers participating. In accordance with the regulation on the Committee for Party-State Control of the party Central Committee and the Soviet of Ministers of the U.S.S.R., groups and posts for assisting the committees for party-state control have been formed and are functioning in enterprises, at construction sites, in *kolkhozy, sovkhozy,* educational and other institutions and in house-management offices.

1. The groups and posts for assistance are called upon to assist party organizations in the struggle for the greatest possible upsurge of the socialist economy and in the organization of a systematic verification of the actual fulfillment of party and government directives. It is most important in the work of the groups and posts for assistance not only to uncover shortcomings, but to strive to eliminate and foresee them. The groups and posts for assistance work under the guidance of party organizations and corresponding committees for party-state control; they carry out their directives and assigned tasks and systematically report to them on their work. The groups and posts for assistance help the party organizations and organs for party-state control: (*a*) to exercise control over the fulfillment by enterprises, construction sites, *kolkhozy* and *sovkhozy* of plans and tasks in producing industrial and agricultural goods, in increasing the productivity of labor, in lowering costs and improving the quality of goods and in observing the strictest procedures for economizing raw materials and other materials, electric energy and financial means; (*b*) to bring to light internal production reserves and seek their maximum use; to control the installation of scientific and tech-

---

*In 1965 the Committee for Party-State Control was renamed the Committee for Peoples Control, but its organization and character remained the same.

nical achievements and innovations; and actively to clear the way for what is new and progressive; (c) to suppress decisively (the appearance of) lack of discipline in executing decisions of the party and the government and localism and deception toward the state; to seek improvement in the work of the administrative-managing apparatus, its perfection and cost reduction; to eliminate bureaucracy and red tape, slackness and mismanagement; (d) to struggle against the plunder of socialist property, violations of soviet legality, bribery, parasitism and other antisocial offenses; (e) to uncover and eliminate shortcomings in welfare and medical services for the workers and in the way complaints and suggestions of citizens are handled; and to assist in the solution of other tasks placed before the organs for party-state control.

2. Groups for assisting committees for party-state control shall be formed by primary party organizations and corresponding committees for party-state control in enterprises, on construction sites, in *kolkhozy, sovkhozy,* educational and other institutions and in house-management offices by the delegation of representatives of party, trade-union, *Komsomol* and other social organizations chosen at meetings of these organizations (at large enterprises, at conferences) and also at meetings of collective farmers and tenants of house-management boards. In workshops, departments and sectors, districts, brigades of enterprises, construction sites, *kolkhozy* and *sovkhozy,* directorates and departments of institutions, groups or posts for assistance shall be formed from representatives delegated by party, trade-union, *Komsomol* organizations and meetings of collective farmers. The all-factory (all-*kolkhoz,* etc.) group for assistance shall guide the work of all groups and posts formed at a given enterprise, construction site, *kolkhoz, sovkhoz,* educational or other institution. (*Note:* Groups and posts for assistance shall not be formed in the executive committees of workers' soviets, party, trade-union and *Komsomol* organs, editing offices of newspapers and journals, and in general educational schools.)

3. Groups and posts for assistance shall be chosen for a period of two years. The size of the groups and posts shall be determined by the primary party organizations together with the local committees for party-state control, in accordance with the volume of work and the size of the enterprise, construction site, *kolkhoz, sovkhoz* and educational or other institution. The number of members of a group may vary from seven to fifty, and of a post from three to ten. In order to direct current work in large groups, a bureau shall be chosen.

4. The most active, competent and irreproachably honest comrades, who are uncompromising toward shortcomings, Communists as well as non-Communists, the best producers—workers, collective farmers, specialists, office workers, scholars, leaders of culture and the arts, students and also pensioners and housewives—those who are capable of exercising strict control over the fulfillment of party and government decisions, shall be advanced to membership in the groups and posts for assistance.

Members of groups and posts shall function on a social basis. Their work is a basic and honorable social duty.

5. A group for assistance shall be headed by a chairman, and a post for assistance by a leader. They shall be chosen accordingly at meetings of the members of the group or post for assistance by open voting. The chairman of a group shall be simultaneously the deputy secretary of the party organization for control. Groups may also choose one or two deputy chairmen. In enterprises and institutions where there are no party organizations, competent non-party comrades who enjoy the trust and respect of the collective may be chairmen.

6. Organizations that have delegated representatives to groups and posts for assistance, acting either on their own initiative or at the request of the group, may recall their representatives if they have not justified their trust.

7. Groups for assistance to committees for party-state control shall be organizing centers around which the entire social control shall be unified. As the basic form of organization of mass control, they shall conduct their work on the basis of broad initiative and independent action, in close and constant contact with the collectives or workers. Groups shall work in close cooperation with the commissions for the carrying out of the right of control over administrative activities by primary party organizations, with the commissions for social control of the trade unions and with detachments of the *Komsomol* Spotlight. If necessary, they shall carry out joint inspections and draw up proposals and recommendations and strive for their fulfillment. Groups for assistance shall work in accordance with a plan. In order to assure the necessary coordination and to avoid duplication and parallelism in exercising control, the groups shall draw up work plans, taking account of the control measures being taken by social organizations, and present them to party committees (bureaus) or meetings of primary party organizations for examination and approval. The party organizations and committees for party-state control shall acquaint leaders and members of groups and posts for assistance with the most important directives and decisions of the party and the government.

8. Groups and posts for assistance shall, in exercising control, use various forms and methods: inspection, unannounced checks, massive reviews, documentary audits, etc. These shall be conducted on their own initiative as well as at the request of party organizations and committees for party-state control. Workers, collective farmers, office workers, specialists and the *aktiv* of party, trade-union and *Komsomol* organizations, control-auditing personnel of enterprises, construction sites, *kolkhozy, sovkhozy* and institutions shall be broadly drawn on to participate in the control. On the basis of the results of the inspection, the groups shall draw up proposals and recommendations for eliminating the shortcomings revealed. Groups and posts shall periodically verify the implementation of these proposals and recommendations. The

groups and posts for assistance must show integrity and persistence in their work; they must carry what has been started through to the end, strictly observe the objectivity of each inspection, seek to study the material profoundly and thoroughly and strive for exact knowledge of the facts and authenticity of the data.

9. In order to guarantee daily control of more important questions in the activity of an enterprise, construction site, *kolkhoz, sovkhoz,* educational or other institution, permanent and temporary commissions, sectors and temporary posts may be created in groups for assistance. In groups and posts there shall be assignment of duties; as a rule each member of a group and post must have a concrete task.

10. Groups for assistance shall direct the work of detachments, groups and posts of the *Komsomol* Spotlight, which is an important form of mass participation by Soviet youth in the realization of tasks entrusted to the organs for party-state control. They shall assist the *Komsomol* Spotlight and support its initiative in every way possible.

11. Groups for assistance shall be given a wide range of possibilities to place before management, party, trade-union, *Komsomol* organizations and committees for party-state control questions concerning improving a matter, eliminating shortcomings uncovered by them and bringing the guilty to an accounting. Proposals of groups shall be examined by leaders of enterprises, construction sites, *kolkhozy, sovkhozy,* educational and other institutions, primary party, trade-union and *Komsomol* organizations. Leaders of enterprises, construction sites, *kolkhozy, sovkhozy,* educational and other institutions must support in every way possible the groups and posts for assistance in their activity and must create the necessary conditions for the realization by them of their duties.

12. Groups for assistance may acquaint themselves with materials describing the activity of enterprises, construction sites, *kolkhozy, sovkhozy,* educational and other institutions concerning condition of equipment, means of transport and storage of produce, raw materials and other material goods. They may take part in conferences and meetings conducted by economic leaders and party organizations at which questions of production work and welfare services for the workers are examined. They may hear the explanations of persons guilty of not fulfilling decisions of the party and the government on production plans and tasks, and those who have permitted bureaucracy, mismanagement and misuse.

13. In the event of disagreement by the officials of those activities that have been inspected with the proposals and recommendations of groups and posts for assistance, the latter shall submit these questions to party organizations or corresponding committees for party-state control for examination.

14. Groups and posts for assistance shall submit questions to the organs for party-state control all the way up to the Committee for Party-

State Control of the party Central Committee and Soviet of Ministers of the U.S.S.R. They may also submit for their examination proposals that may concern the following: carrying out a more detailed inspection of a given enterprise, construction site, *kolkhoz, sovkhoz,* educational or other institution by the representatives of the corresponding committee; suspending illegal orders and actions of responsible persons that may cause harm to state interests; eliminating shortcomings in the fulfillment by other enterprises of their obligations for cooperative deliveries; and any other questions.

15. Members of groups and posts for assistance shall not be removed from their jobs without the agreement of the organization that delegated them to be members of the groups and posts.

16. Groups and posts for assistance shall widely inform the workers concerning the results of inspections and measures taken to eliminate shortcomings at meetings of collectives and also through the publication of material in wall newspapers, newspapers of wide circulation and other newspapers, and by local radio and television broadcasts. They shall assure that publicity is given only to those verified facts and materials that can aid in eliminating shortcomings and in correctly educating those persons who have committed mistakes and blunders.

17. Groups and posts for assistance shall periodically make reports on their work to party, trade-union and *Komsomol* meetings and meetings of workers. They shall take stock of their work. The basic form for keeping accounts shall be a daily journal.

18. Groups for assistance shall arrange for the regular reception of workers. Boxes shall be placed in prominent places for workers' complaints, statements and proposals, which shall be effectively examined and upon which measures shall be taken.

19. Committees for party-state control and party, soviet and economic organizations shall use existing forms of encouraging the more outstanding members of groups and posts of assistance for good work.

Party Life, No. 14, July, 1964.

APPENDIX III

THE PRINCIPLES OF THE *Komsomol* SPOTLIGHT

In answer to the call of the party for the constant illumination of all segments of the economy with the spotlight of communist control, *Komsomol* organizations are forming detachments of the *Komsomol* Spotlight in factories, plants, mines, at construction sites and on *kolkhozy* and *sovkhozy*. The *Komsomol* Spotlight is an important form of mass participation by the Soviet youth in the realization of the tasks entrusted to the organs for party-state control. Detachments of the *Komsomol* Spotlight organize "raiding" brigades, control posts, staffs for new technology, etc.

The *Komsomol* Spotlight is an active helpmate of party organizations in eliminating deficiencies in the work of enterprises and institutions, in fighting against bureaucracy and red tape, "white-washing," bribery, various types of abuses and infringements on socialist ownership and everything that harms the cause of socialist construction in our country.

Basic in the work of the *Komsomol* Spotlight is the fight for the utilization of all reserves resulting from growth in the productivity of labor. In every place of work, in every sector, enterprise, construction site, on every *kolkhoz, sovkhoz* and institution, the *Komsomol* Spotlight seeks out ways of raising the productivity of labor and of improving quality and lowering costs of production and persistently strives for its full utilization. The motto of the *Komsomol* Spotlight is: "Uncover reserves and exploit them!" The *Komsomol* Spotlight is the champion of all that is new and progressive. The *Komsomol* Spotlight organizes and directs the work of staffs, commissions, groups and detachments for the support of new technology; provides for the active participation of youths and *Komsomol* members in the creation of new machines and in the automation and mechanization of production; and takes under its control the introduction of efficiency suggestions. Young people set a personal example in introducing into production the achievements of science, technology and progressive methods, and they help their co-workers toward this goal. The *Komsomol* Spotlight is an active fighter for economy and thrift; it assists in the maximal utilization of equipment, means of transport and agricultural technology; it fights against mismanagement; it opposes those who do not save the people's kopecks. The *Komsomol* Spotlight is the enemy of indifference, staleness and conventionalism wherever and however they appear. It exposes and submits to universal condemnation those guilty of bureaucracy and red tape and all those who treat the common man, his needs and requests, with scorn.

The *Komsomol* Spotlight works under the leadership of local *Kom-*

somol organs and fulfills the tasks of party organizations, organs for party-state control and *Komsomol* committees. The practical activity of the *Komsomol* Spotlight is directed by groups allied to the organs for party-state control. Detachments of the *Komsomol* Spotlight are created in enterprises, at construction sites, on *sovkhozy* and *kolkhozy* and in institutions, scientific research institutes, drafting bureaus and design organizations. Groups and posts of the *Komsomol* Spotlight are formed in shops, departments and sections.

To the work in detachments and posts of the *Komsomol* Spotlight are attracted the most responsible and energetic young people, *Komsomol* members as well as non-members, who have confidence in the collective and know how to organize and carry out a matter to its conclusion. Soviets (and, in large organizations, staffs) consisting of from nine to fifteen persons and headed by a chairman are elected for the leadership in the everyday work of detachments of the *Komsomol* Spotlight. Spotlight detachment soviets and Spotlight post and group leaders and their deputies are elected at *Komsomol* meetings and conferences for one-year terms. They are accountable in their work to their corresponding *Komsomol* organizations. Staffs of the *Komsomol* Spotlight are created in industrial and agricultural production committees; in *Komsomol* committees at the *raion, oblast, krai* and city levels; and in *Komsomol* central committees at the Union-republic level. These staffs are headed by the secretaries of the corresponding *Komsomol* committees. In the All-Union Leninist *Komsomol* Central Committee, a central staff of the *Komsomol* Spotlight, headed by the secretary of the All-Union Leninist *Komsomol* Central Committee, is formed.

Staffs of the *Komsomol* Spotlight and their leaders are approved for two-year terms by their corresponding *Komsomol* committees and are chosen from the number of leaders of Spotlight detachments, from the number of *Komsomol* activists, foremost production workers, representatives from the intelligentsia and the youth press, radio and television. *Komsomol* committees may, during this two-year term, supplement the members of staffs or remove from them individuals who have not justified the trust placed in them. Staffs, detachments and posts of the *Komsomol* Spotlight systematically give an account of their work to the youth at *Komsomol* meetings, plenums and *aktivs*. With the aim of successfully fulfilling their tasks, the *Komsomol* Spotlight organizes raids, reviews and competitions and forms permanent and provisional committees. The main activity of the projectionists is not only to expose committed violations and deficiencies but most of all to fight for their prevention and elimination. The *Komsomol* Spotlight works in close cooperation with soviets of young specialists, public drafting offices, bureaus of economic analysis and other public organizations.

Detachments and staffs of the *Komsomol* Spotlight take under their control the execution of their operations and, when necessary, inform party organizations and organs for party-state control of the exposure of shortcomings and submit proposals directed toward their elimination. An important precondition for the successful activity of the *Komsomol* Spotlight is wide publicity. The work of staffs and detachments of the *Komsomol* Spotlight, their operations and proposals, are discussed at *Komsomol* and youth meetings and in *Komsomol* committees and are illuminated in the press and on radio and television. The *Komsomol* Spotlight widely uses wall newspapers and extras (flash!), "combat" leaflets, and "windows" of the *Komsomol* Spotlight. At staff and detachment level propaganda-cultural brigades and groups of movie and photography buffs may also be formed.

All activity of the *Komsomol* Spotlight is built on the base of broad initiative and spontaneity of youths and *Komsomol* members. Work in groups, posts, detachments and staffs of the *Komsomol* Spotlight is an honorable and responsible public mission.

Young people who actively participate in the work of the *Komsomol* Spotlight are eligible for such awards as commendation lists, *Komsomol* committees' honor certificates and badges of the Central Committee of the All-Union Leninist *Komsomol* "for active work in the *Komsomol*." The best detachments of the *Komsomol* Spotlight and the most distinguished "projectionists" are noted in "books of honor" of committees at the *oblast* and *krai* levels, in "books of honor" of central committees at the Union republic and all-Union level and in the *Manuscript of* Komsomol *Labor Feats in the Seven-Year Plan.*

Notebook of a Party Activist, 1964 (Moscow: 1963).

NOTES TO CHAPTER ONE*

1. V. I. Lenin, *Works* (3rd ed.; Moscow: 1935), IV, 458.
2. *Ibid.*, II, 184.
3. V. I. Lenin, *On Party Construction* (Moscow: 1956), p. 288.
4. Lenin, *Works, op. cit.*, I, 302.
5. *Ibid.*, IV, 454–56.
6. *Ibid.*, p. 457.
7. *Ibid.*, pp. 468–69.
8. Lenin, *On Party Construction, op. cit.*, p. 168.
9. Lenin, *Works, op. cit.*, XVI, 630.
10. *Ibid.*, p. 147.
11. J. V. Stalin, *Works* (Moscow: 1947), V, 71.
12. Lenin, *Works, op. cit.*, XVI, 633.
13. Lenin, *On Party Construction, op. cit.*, p. 349.
14. Lenin, *Works, op. cit.*, IV, 384.
15. *Ibid.*
16. *The CPSU in Resolutions and Decisions Passed at Congresses, Conferences and Plenums of the Central Committee* (7th ed.; Moscow: 1953), Part I, p. 45.
17. *Ibid.*, p. 43.
18. *Minutes of the Second Congress of the RSDRP* (Moscow: 1959), p. 263.
19. *Ibid.*, p. 265.
20. *Ibid.*, p. 277.
21. Lenin, *On Party Construction, op cit.*, p. 124.
22. *Ibid.*, p. 153.
23. *Minutes of the Second Congress of the RSDRP, op. cit.*, p. 296.
24. *Ibid.*, p. 271.
25. *Ibid.*
26. *Ibid.*, p. 108.
27. *Ibid.*, p. 127.
28. *Ibid.*, p. 279.
29. Lenin, *On Party Construction, op. cit.*, p. 358.
30. *Minutes of the Second Congress of the RSDRP, op. cit.*, p. 375.
31. *Ibid.*, p. 375.
32. *Minutes of the Second Congress of the RSDRP, op. cit.*, p. 375.
33. Lenin, *On Party Construction, op. cit.*, p. 137.
34. *Ibid.*, p. 287.
35. *Ibid.*, p. 124.
36. *Ibid.*, p. 286.
37. *Ibid.*, pp. 273–74.
38. *Ibid.*, p. 161.
39. *Iskra*, June 25, 1904, cited in Lenin, *Works, op. cit.*, VI, 431.
40. Lenin, *On Party Construction, op. cit.*, pp. 155, 245.
41. *Ibid.*, p. 147.
42. *Ibid.*
43. Lenin, *Works, op. cit.*, V, 187.
44. *Ibid.*
45. *Ibid.*, pp. 185–86.
46. *Ibid.*, p. 190.
47. K. Marx and F. Engels, *Works* (Moscow: 1957), XVII, 364.
48. Lenin, *Works, op. cit.*, V, 189.
49. *Ibid.*. p. 187.
50. Lenin, *On Party Construction, op. cit.*, p. 341.
51. *Ibid.*, p. 341.
52. *Ibid.*, p. 339.

*All references to Soviet sources throughout the book are to the Russian editions.

53. *Ibid.*
54. B. Dvinov, *Novy Zhurnal*, No. 59, 1960, p. 216.
55. Lenin, *On Party Construction, op cit.*, p. 367.

NOTES TO CHAPTER TWO

1. V. I. Lenin, *Works* (3rd ed.; Moscow: 1931), XXI, 33.
2. K. Marx and F. Engels, *Communist Manifesto* (Moscow: 1951), pp. 47, 71.
3. K. Marx, *Critique of Political Economy* (Moscow: 1952), p. 7.
4. K. Marx, *Capital* (Moscow: 1931), I, 613.
5. *Ibid.*, p. 603.
6. *Ibid.*, pp. xiv, vx.
7. Marx and Engels, *Communist Manifesto, op. cit.*, p. 8.
8. *Ibid.*, p. 7.
9. J. V. Stalin, *Problems of Leninism* (Moscow: 1947), p. 51.
10. Lenin, *op cit.*, I, 194.
11. *Ibid.*, XVIII, 232.
12. *Ibid.*, XX, 301.
13. *Ibid.*, p. 302.
14. *Ibid.*
15. *Ibid.*, IV, 112–13.
16. *Ibid.*, IX (4th ed.; Moscow: 1952), 8.
17. *Ibid.*, VIII (3rd ed.), 96.
18. *Ibid.*, p. 186.
19. V. I. Lenin, *On Party Construction* (Moscow: 1956), p. 667.
20. Lenin, *Works, op. cit.*, II (3rd ed.), 176–77.
21. *Ibid.*, XXVI, 460.
22. *Ibid.*, IX (4th ed.), 213.
23. *Ibid.*, XXI (3rd ed.), 195.
24. *Ibid.*, XXV, 223.
25. *Ibid.*, p. 176.
26. *Ibid.*, p. 232.
27. *Ibid.*, p. 237.
28. J. V. Stalin, *Works* (Moscow: 1949), X, 73–74.
29. Lenin, *Works, op. cit.*, XXV (3rd ed.), 230–31.
30. *Ibid.*, p. 197.
31. Stalin, *Works, op. cit.*, V, 74–75.
32. *Ibid.*, pp. 75–76.
33. Lenin, *Works, op. cit.*, XXV (3rd ed.), 223.
34. *Ibid.*, p. 196.
35. *Ibid.*, XXI. 54.
36. *Ibid.*, p. 226.
37. *Ibid.*
38. *Ibid.*, p. 194.
39. *Ibid.*, p. 195.
40. K. Marx and F. Engels, *Works* (Moscow: 1957), VIII, 100–101.
41. Lenin, *Works, op. cit.*, XX, 78.
42. *See* Sidney Hook, *Der Held in Der Geschichte* (Stuttgart: 1951), pp. 212–22.
43. L. Schapiro, *The Communist Party of the Soviet Union* (New York: Random House, 1959), apparently does not share this view. Schapiro writes that "Trotsky, no less than Lenin, realized the importance of the seizure of actual power by the party. . . . Trotsky realized more than Lenin the importance of making the actual seizure of power coincide with the symbolic assumption of power by a vote of the Congress of Soviets." (pp. 169–70).
44. S. Possony, *A Century of Conflict* (Chicago: Henry Regnery Co., 1959), p. 65.

45. Stalin, *Works, op. cit.,* V, 79.
46. Lenin, *Works, op. cit.,* XXV (3rd ed.), 205.
47. *The CPSU in Resolutions and Decisions Passed at Congresses, Conferences and Plenums of the Central Committee* (7th ed.; Moscow, 1953), Part I, p. 324.
48. Lenin, *Works, op. cit.,* XIX (3rd ed.), 381.
49. *Ibid.,* XX, 5–6.
50. *Ibid.,* p. 8.
51. *Ibid.,* pp. 600–601.
52. *Ibid.,* pp. 87–88.
53. *Ibid.,* pp. 605–7.
54. *Ibid.,* XXI, 33.
55. *Ibid.*
56. *Ibid.*
57. *Ibid.,* p. 35.
58. *The CPSU in Resolutions, op. cit.,* Part I, p. 376.
59. Lenin, *Works, op. cit.,* XIX (3rd ed.), p 356.
60. *Ibid.,* XXI, 116–19.
61. L. Trotsky, *My Life* (Berlin: 1930), Part II, p. 39.
62. Stalin, *Works, op. cit.,* VI, 342.
63. Lenin, *Works, op. cit.,* XXI (3rd ed.), 198–99.
64. *Ibid.,* p. 330.
65. *Ibid.,* p. 494.
66. *Ibid.,* p. 507.
67. *Ibid.,* pp. 262–63.

NOTES TO CHAPTER THREE

1. V. I. Lenin, *Works* (3rd ed.; Moscow: 1931), XXII, 3.
2. L. Trotsky, *My Life* (Berlin: 1930), Part II, pp. 47–48.
3. Lenin, *op. cit.,* p. 574.
4. *Ibid.,* XXIX (4th ed.), 387.
5. *Pravda,* July 30, 1961, p. 3.
6. *Questions of Labor in the U.S.S.R.* (Moscow: 1958), p. 9.
7. *Ibid.*
8. *Amerika,* No. 55, 1961, p. 12.
9. K. Marx and F. Engels, *Works* (Moscow: 1957), I, 406.
10. *A Short Course in the History of the Communist Party of Bolsheviks* (Moscow: 1945), p. 22.
11. K. Marx and F. Engels, *Selected Letters* (Moscow: 1948), p. 63.
12. Marx and Engels, *Works, op. cit.,* XV, 283.
13. J. V. Stalin, *Problems of Leninism* (Moscow: 1947), p. 35.
14. Lenin, *op. cit.,* XXV (3rd ed.), 441.
15. *Ibid.,* p. 439.
16. *Ibid.,* p. 194.
17. J. V. Stalin, *Works* (Moscow: 1948), VIII, 1.
18. V. I. Lenin, *On Party Construction* (Moscow: 1956), p. 610.
19. *The CPSU in Resolutions and Decisions Passed at Congresses, Conferences and Plenums of the Central Committee* (7th ed.; Moscow: 1953), Part I, p. 683.
20. Lenin, *Works, op. cit.,* XXI (3rd ed.), 261.
21. *Ibid.,* pp. 256–57.
22. *Ibid.,* p. 259.
23. Lenin, *On Party Construction, op. cit.,* pp. 428–29.
24. *Ibid.,* pp. 640–41.
25. Stalin, *Works, op. cit.,* VIII, 34–36.

26. Lenin, *Works, op. cit.* (4th ed.; Moscow: 1952), 30.
27. *The U.S.S.R. As It Is* (Moscow: 1960), pp. 55, 89, 92; *The Worldwide Historical Significance of the Great October Revolution* (Moscow: 1957), p. 69; and *Pravda,* October 18, 1961.
28. Lenin, *Works, op. cit.,* XXV (4th ed.), 191.
29. Stalin, *Works, op. cit.,* V, 5–6.
30. *The CPSU in Resolutions, op. cit.,* p. 414.
31. *Pravda,* July 30, 1961.
32. *The CPSU in Resolutions, op. cit.,* p. 415
33. Lenin, *Works, op. cit.,* XXVI, 208.
34. Lenin, *On Party Construction, op. cit.,* p. 447.
35. *Ibid., pp.* 448–49.
36. *Ibid.,* p. 414.
37. F. Engels, *Anti-Düring* (Moscow: 1951), pp. 264–65.
38. *The CPSU in Resolutions, op. cit.,* p. 416.
39. Stalin, *Problems of Leninism, op. cit.,* p. 429.
40. *Ibid.,* p. 643.
41. *Ibid.,* p. 641.
42. *Ibid.,* p. 646.
43. *Program of the CPSU* (Moscow: 1961), p. 111.
44. *Ibid.,* p. 101.
45. *The CPSU in Resolutions, op. cit.,* p. 414.
46. *Ibid.,* p. 101 (italics in original).
47. *Ibid.,* p. 137 (italics in original).
48. *Questions of the History of the CPSU,* No. 5, 1958, p. 118.
49. Stalin, *Works, op. cit.,* VIII, 1.
50. *Ibid.,* X, 175.
51. Lenin, *A Letter to the Congress* (Moscow: 1956), pp. 10–12.
52. *The CPSU in Resolutions, op. cit.,* p. 499.

NOTES TO CHAPTER FOUR

1. J. V. Stalin, *Problems of Leninism* (Moscow: 1947), p. 595.
2. *Large Soviet Encyclopedia* (2nd ed.; Moscow: 1958), XIX, 293.
3. Lenin, *Works* (3rd ed.; Moscow: 1932), XXIV, 68.
4. *The CPSU in Resolutions and Decisions Passed at Congresses, Conferences and Plenums of the Central Committee* (7th ed.; Moscow: 1953), Part I, p. 444.
5. *Ibid.*
6. *Ibid.,* p. 497.
7. *Ibid.,* p. 498.
8. *Ibid.,* p. 83.
9. *Ibid.,* p. 84.
10. Stalin, *Works* (Moscow: 1949), X, 328.
11. *Ibid.,* p. 400.
12. *Ibid.*
13. *Ibid., pp.* 401–2.
14. *Ibid.,* p. 404.
15. *The CPSU in Resolutions, op. cit.,* Part II, p. 519.
16. Stalin, *Problems of Leninism, op. cit.,* p. 326.
17. *Ibid.,* p. 220.
18. *Ibid.,* p. 340.
19. *Ibid., pp.* 340–41.
20. *Ibid.,* p. 341.
21. *Ibid.,* p. 491.
22. *The CPSU in Resolutions, op. cit.,* Part II (1954), p. 523.

23. Stalin, *Problems of Leninism, op. cit.,* p. 588.
24. *Ibid.,* p. 589.
25. *The CPSU in Resolutions, op. cit.,* Part II, p. 597.
26. See *The Technology of Power,* p. 252.
27. Stalin, *Problems of Leninism, op. cit.,* pp. 395–96.
28. *Large Soviet Encyclopedia, op. cit.,* XIX, 295.
29. *The CPSU in Resolutions, op. cit.,* Part II, p. 427.
30. Stalin, *Problems of Leninism, op. cit.,* p. 598.
31. *Questions of Economics,* No. 1, 1961, p. 67.
32. *Ibid.,* p. 71.
33. *The CPSU in Resolutions, op. cit.,* Part II, p. 1019.
34. *Ibid.,* p. 1020.
35. *Ibid.*
36. *Ibid.,* p. 1024.
37. *Ibid.,* p. 1025.
38. *Large Soviet Encyclopedia, op. cit.,* XXX (1st ed.), 538–39.
39. *The U.S.S.R. As It Is* (Moscow: 1960), p. 74.
40. *The Party of the Bolsheviks in the Period of the Military Intervention and the Civil War* (Moscow: 1949), p. 18.
41. Lenin, *op. cit.* (4th ed.), XXX, 126.
42. D. Voropaev and A. Yovlev, *The Struggle of the CPSU To Create Military Cadres* (Moscow: 1960), p. 106.
43. *Ibid.,* pp. 82–106.
44. *Ibid.,* p. 81.
45. *Ibid.,* pp 112–13.
46. *Ibid.,* p. 126.
47. *Ibid.,* p. 121.
48. *Ibid.,* p. 133.
49. *Ibid.,* pp. 137–39.
50. *Ibid.,* pp. 137, 139, 141, 146.
51. *Ibid.,* p. 171.
52. *Ibid.,* p. 167.
53. N. Khrushchev, *Speech at a Closed Session of the Twentieth Congress of the CPSU* (Munich: 1956), pp. 26–32.
54. A. Uralov (Avtorkhanov), *The Reign of Stalin* (London).
55. *Propagandist and Agitator,* No. 23, 1957, p. 25.
56. Voropaev and Yovlev, *op. cit.,* p. 211.
57. *Shorthand Record of the Extraordinary Twenty-first Congress of the CPSU* (Moscow: 1959) p. 126.
58. *Twenty-second Congress of the CPSU* (Moscow: 1962), Part II, p. 120.
59. *The CPSU in Resolutions, op. cit.,* Part IV (1960), p. 295.
60. Article by Marshal F. Golikov in *Pravda,* October 9, 1961.

NOTES TO CHAPTER FIVE

1. V. I. Lenin, *Works* (4th ed.; Moscow: 1952), VI, 456–59.
2. *Ibid.,* X, 19.
3. *Ibid.,* IX, 214–15.
4. *Ibid.,* XXXIII, 164.
5. *Ibid.,* XXXI, 29.
6. *The CPSU in Resolutions and Decisions Passed at Congresses, Conferences and Plenums of the Central Committee* (7th ed.; Moscow: 1953), Part I, p. 441.
7. *Ibid.,* p. 462.
8. *Ibid.,* p. 521.
9. *Ibid.,* pp. 623–24.

396 THE COMMUNIST PARTY APPARATUS

10. *Ibid.*, p. 783.
11. A. Avtorkhanov, *Stalin and the Communist Party* (New York: 1959), p. 239.
12. *An Account of Party Work in 1922–23* (Moscow: 1923), p. 22.
13. J. V. Stalin, *Works* (Moscow: 1949), XII, 313–14.
14. S. Ivanovich, *V.K.P. (All-Russian Communist Party)* (Paris: 1928), pp. 91–95. Data from an article by G. M. Malenkov in *Bolshevik*, No.s 21–22, 1926, and from *Pravda*, July 14, 1927, and November 2, 1927.
15. *The CPSU in Resolutions, op. cit.*, Part II (1953), p. 778.
16. *Ibid.*, p. 769.
17. See my article in *Herald of the Institute for the Study of the U.S.S.R.* (Munich), No. 1 (18), 1956, pp. 7, 11.
18. *The CPSU in Resolutions, op. cit.*, Part II, p. 917.
19. *Ibid.*, p. 919.
20. *Ibid.*, pp. 924–25.
21. N. I. Bukharin, "Speech at All-Union Young Communist League Congress," *Pravda*, March 21, 1926.
22. J. V. Stalin, *Speech at Plenum of Central Committee, February-March, 1937.*
23. *The CPSU in Resolutions, op. cit.*, Part II, p. 919.
24. *Ibid.*, p. 921.
25. Article by V. S. Nemchinov in *The Worldwide Historical Importance of the Great October Revolution* (Moscow: 1957).
26. *Ibid.*, p. 69.
27. *Statistics of the National Economy of the U.S.S.R.* (Moscow: 1956), p. 19.
28. *The CPSU in Resolutions, op. cit.*, Part I, p. 511.
29. *Ibid.*, p. 521.
30. Stalin, *Works, op. cit.*, XIII, 354.
31. *The CPSU in Resolutions, op. cit.*, Part I, p. 677.
32. *Ibid.*, p. 677.
33. *Ibid.*, p. 678.
34. *Ibid.*, p. 678.
35. *Ibid.*, p. 772.
36. *The Party Worker's Handbook* (Moscow: 1957), p. 412.
37. *The CPSU in Resolutions, op. cit.*, Part II (1953), pp. 923–24.
38. *Ibid.*, Part II (1954), p. 112.
39. *Ibid.*
40. G. Malenkov, "On the Activities of the Central Committee of the CPSU (Bolsheviks)," *An Informative Conference of Certain Party Committees in Warsaw* (Moscow: 1948), p. 144.
41. *Questions of the History of the CPSU*, No. 2, 1958, p. 55.
42. *Ibid.*, pp. 55–56.
43. *Ibid.*, p. 55.
44. Malenkov, *op. cit.*, p. 145.
45. G. Malenkov, "Report on the Nineteenth Congress of the CPSU," *Pravda*, October 6, 1952.
46. *Questions of the History of the CPSU*, No. 2, 1958, p. 63.
47. *Ibid.*, p. 63.
48. *Ibid.*, p. 66.
49. *Soviet Belorussia*, September 22, 1952.
50. *Ibid.*, February 13, 1954.
51. *Dawn of the East*, September 18, 1952.
52. *Pravda*, February 25, 1956.
53. N. Khrushchev, *Report to the Central Committee at the Twentieth Party Congress* (Moscow: 1956), p. 128.
54. *Dawn of the East*, January 28, 1958.
55. *Party Life*, No. 1, 1962, pp. 44–55.
56. *Ibid.*, p. 47.

57. *Ibid.*, pp. 45–47.
58. *Party Life*, No. 1, 1962.
59. *The Size, Composition and Distribution of the Population of the U.S.S.R.* (Moscow: 1961), pp. 50, 51 and 54. *Kommunist* gives the number of workers employed by the state bureaucracy as 1,361,000. (No. 1, 1962, p. 48).
60. *Party Life*, No. 1, 1962, p. 45.
61. *Ibid.*, p. 46.
62. *Ibid.*
63. *Ibid.*, p. 48.
64. *Ibid.*
65. *Ibid.*, pp. 44, 47, 51 and 52.
66. *Ibid.*
67. *Ibid.*, p. 49.
68. *Ibid.*, p. 50.
69. *Ibid.*, p. 49.
70. *Ibid.*, p. 44.
71. *Pravda*, February 22, 1960.
72. *The Statutes of the CPSU* (Moscow: 1952), Articles 40 and 50.
73. *Ibid.*, Article 11.
74. *Party Life*, No. 13, 1960, p. 13.

NOTES TO CHAPTER SIX

1. *Pravda*, October 29, 1961.
2. *The CPSU in Resolutions and Decisions Passed at Congresses, Conferences and Plenums of the Central Committee* (7th ed.; Moscow: 1953), Part I, p. 46.
3. *Ibid.*, p. 116.
4. *Ibid.*, p. 135.
5. V. I. Lenin, *Works* (4th ed.; Moscow: 1952), XXIV, 4.
6. *The CPSU in Resolutions, op. cit.*, Part I, p. 384.
7. *Ibid.*
8. *Ibid.*, p. 384, Article 13.
9. V. I. Lenin, *On Party Construction* (Moscow: 1956), p. 610.
10. *The CPSU in Resolutions, op. cit.*, Part I, p. 443.
11. *Ibid.*, pp. 463, 468.
12. *Ibid.*, pp. 461–62.
13. *Ibid.*, pp. 462, 467, 468.
14. *Ibid.*, p. 660.
15. *Ibid.*, p. 529.
16. *Ibid.*, Part II (1954), p. 371.
17. Lenin, *Works, op. cit.*, XXXIII, 200.
18. *Ibid.*, p. 777.
19. *Ibid.*, pp. 778–79.
20. *The CPSU in Resolutions, op. cit.*, Part II, p. 775.
21. *Ibid.*, p. 782.
22. *Ibid.*, p. 779.
23. *Ibid.*, p. 785.
24. *Ibid.*, p. 927.
25. *Ibid.*, p. 923.
26. *Ibid.*, p. 935.
27. *Ibid.*, p. 927.
28. *Ibid.*, p. 1122.
29. *Ibid.*, p. 1125.
30. N. Khrushchev, *Report to the Nineteenth Congress on Changes in the Statutes of the All-Union Communist Party (Bolsheviks)* (Moscow: 1952), p. 23.

31. N. Khrushchev, *Speech at a Closed Session of the Twentieth Congress of the CPSU* (Munich: 1956), p. 53.
32. *The CPSU in Resolutions, op. cit.,* Part II (7th ed.; 1953), p. 1149.
33. Khrushchev, *Report to the Nineteenth Party Congress on Changes in the Statutes of the All-Union Communist Party (Bolsheviks), loc. cit.*
34. *Kommunist,* No. 16, 1961, p. 102.
35. *Ibid.,* p. 77.
36. *Ibid.,* pp. 113–14.
37. *Ibid.,* p. 104.
38. *Ibid.,* pp. 108–9.
39. *Ibid.,* p. 109.
40. *Ibid.,* p. 108.
41. *The CPSU in Resolutions, op. cit.,* Part II, p. 928.
42. *Kommunist,* No. 16, 1961, p. 108.
43. *The CPSU in Resolutions, op. cit.,* Part II, p. 928.
44. *Pravda,* October 29, 1961, p. 5.
45. *Kommunist,* No. 16, 1961, p. 107
46. *Ibid.*
47. *Ibid.,* p. 78.
48. *Shorthand Record of the Twentieth Congress of the CPSU* (Moscow: 1956), Part II, pp. 500–504; *Party Life,* No. 20, 1957, p. 92 and No. 13, 1960, p. 12; "Kozlov's Speech," *Pravda,* October 29, 1961; and *Pravda,* November 1, 1961.
49. *Pravda,* October 29, 1961, p. 5.
50. *Ibid.*
51. J. V. Stalin, *Problems of Leninism* (11th ed.; Moscow: 1947), p. 606.
52. *Kommunist,* No. 16, 1961, p. 82.
53. J. V. Stalin, *Works* (Moscow: 1949), VI, 181.
54. *Kommunist,* No. 16, 1961, p. 98 (emphasis in original).
55. "Khrushchev's Closing Speech at the Twenty-second Congress," *Pravda,* October 29, 1961.
56. *Kommunist,* No. 16, 1961, p. 102.
57. *The Constitution of the U.S.S.R.* (Moscow: 1960), p. 27.
58. *Pravda,* October 29, 1961.
59. *Ibid.*

NOTES TO CHAPTER SEVEN

1. *Large Soviet Encyclopedia* (1st ed.; Moscow) LXV, 859.
2. *The CPSU in Resolutions and Decisions Passed at Congresses, Conferences and Plenums of the Central Committee* (7th ed.; Moscow: 1953), Part I, pp. 277–78.
3. Article by Ya Berzin, *Large Soviet Encyclopedia, op. cit.,* LXV, 862.
4. L. Kaganovich, *The Party and the Soviets* (Moscow: 1925), p. 11.
5. *The CPSU in Resolutions, op. cit.,* Part I, p. 466.
6. *Ibid.,* p. 467.
7. *Ibid.,* pp. 661–62.
8. *Ibid.,* Part II, p. 131.
9. *Ibid.,* p. 517.
10. *Ibid.,* p. 519.
11. *Ibid.,* pp. 519–20.
12. *Ibid.,* Part I, p. 529.
13. *Ibid.,* p. 869.
14. *Ibid.,* p. 384.
15. *Ibid.,* p. 630.
16. *Ibid.,* pp. 828–29.
17. *Ibid.,* p. 829.

18. *Large Soviet Encyclopedia, op. cit.,* LXV, p. 882.
19. *The CPSU in Resolutions, op. cit.,* Part II, p. 784.
20. *Ibid.,* p. 775.
21. *Ibid.,* p. 935.
22. *Ibid.,* pp. 922–1134.
23. *Statutes of the CPSU* (Moscow: 1961).
24. *Ibid.*
25. *The CPSU in Resolutions, op. cit.,* Part II, pp. 1131–33.
26. "The Cell in the Bolshevik Party," *Large Soviet Encyclopedia, op. cit.,* Vol. LXV.
27. *Statutes of the CPSU, op. cit.,* Article 58.
28. *Ibid.*
29. *Ibid.*
30. *Ibid.,* Article 59.
31. *Questions of Party Work* (Moscow: 1959), pp. 237–38.
32. *Ibid.,* pp. 228–29.
33. *Ibid.,* p. 313.
34. *Statutes of the CPSU, op. cit.,* Article 58.
35. *Questions of Party Work, op. cit.,* p. 264.
36. *Ibid.,* p. 264.
37. *Ibid.,* p. 267.
38. *Ibid.,* p. 253.
39. V. I. Lenin, *A Letter to the Congress* (Moscow: 1956), p. 9.
40. *Questions of Party Work, op. cit.,* p. 256.
41. *Ibid.,* pp. 268–69.
42. *Party Life,* No. 1, 1962, pp. 44–55.
43. *Ibid.,* p. 54.
44. *Ibid.*
45. *Ibid.,* pp. 53–54.
46. *Questions of Party Work,* op. cit., pp. 320–21.

NOTES TO CHAPTER EIGHT

1. *The U.S.S.R.: The Administrative Territorial Divisions of the Constituent Republics* (Moscow: 1960), p. 5, and *Pravda,* November 20, 1962.
2. *Party Life,* No. 6, 1965, p. 3.
3. *Questions of Party Work* (Moscow: 1959), p. 367.
4. *Ibid.*
5. *Statutes of the CPSU* (Moscow: 1961), Article 48.
6. *Questions of Party Work* (Moscow: 1959), p. 355.
7. *Statutes of the CPSU, op. cit.,* Article 51.
8. *Ibid.,* Article 49.
9. *Ibid.* (1952), Article 50.
10. See *Soviet Lithuania,* December 8, 1962, and *Soviet Russia,* December 19, 1962.
11. *Ibid.,* p. 11.
12. *See* F. Kozlov's report in *Pravda,* October 29, 1961.
13. *Questions of Party Work, op. cit.,* p. 370.
14. *Pravda,* October 31, 1961.
15. *Pravda of the Ukraine,* September 29, 1961.
16. *Soviet Belorussia,* September 28, 1961.
17. *The Communist of Tadzhikistan,* September 23, 1961.
18. *The Baku Worker,* September 10, 1961.
19. *Kazakhstan Pravda,* September 29, 1961.
20. *Party Life,* No. 10, 1954, p. 66.
21. *Ibid.,* p. 65.

22. *Statutes of the CPSU, op. cit.* (1961), pp. 27–28.
23. *The U.S.S.R.: The Administrative and Territorial Divisions of the Constituent Republics, loc. cit.*
24. N. Khrushchev, *Report to the Central Committee of the CPSU at the Twenty-second Congress* (Moscow: 1956).
25. *Pravda,* January 9, 1962.
26. *Party Life,* No. 24, 1961, p. 12.
27. *Ibid.,* p. 13.
28. *Ibid.,* p. 14.
29. *Questions of Party Work, op. cit.,* p. 368.
30. *The CPSU in Resolutions and Decisions Passed at Congresses, Conferences and Plenums of the Central Committee* (7th ed.; Moscow: 1953), Part II, p. 1133.
31. *Questions of Party Work, op. cit.,* pp. 373–74.
32. D. Bachshiev, *Party Construction After the Victory of Socialism in the U.S.S.R.* (Moscow: 1954), p. 140.
33. *Questions of Party Work, op. cit.,* p. 374.
34. *Ibid.,* pp. 375–76.
35. *Ibid.,* p. 365.
36. *The CPSU in Resolutions, op. cit.,* Part II, p. 823.
37. *Ibid.,* p. 824.
38. *Ibid.,* pp. 827–28.
39. *Questions of Party Work, op. cit.,* p. 549.
40. *Party Worker's Handbook* (Moscow: 1957), pp. 416–28.
41. *Ibid.,* p. 416.
42. *Ibid.,* p. 420.
43. *Ibid.,* p. 421.
44. *Ibid.,* p. 419.
45. *Ibid.,* p. 423.
46. *Ibid.*
47. *Ibid.,* p. 424.
48. *Ibid.*
49. *Ibid.,* pp. 424–25.
50. *Ibid.,* pp. 426–27.
51. *Ibid.,* p. 427.
52. *Questions of Party Work, op. cit.,* pp. 545–47.
53. *Ibid.,* pp. 546–47.
54. *Ibid.,* p. 547.
55. *Ibid.*

NOTES TO CHAPTER NINE

1. *Questions of Party Work* (Moscow: 1959), p. 372.
2. *Ibid.,* pp. 370–71.
3. *Ibid.,* p. 371.
4. D. Bachshiev, *Party Construction After the Victory of Socialism in the U.S.S.R.* (Moscow: 1954), p. 117.
5. *Ibid.*
6. *The Juridical Dictionary* (Moscow: 1956), I, 523.
7. *Statutes of the CPSU* (Moscow: 1961), Article 21.
8. *Ibid.,* Article 45.
9. *Pravda,* January 27, 1962.
10. *Ibid.*
11. *Questions of the History of the CPSU,* No. 6, 1961, p. 53.
12. *Statutes of the CPSU, op. cit.,* Article 40.
13. *Ibid.,* Article 47.

14. *Party Worker's Handbook* (Moscow: 1957), pp. 432–33.
15. *Ibid.,* pp. 433–34.
16. *Ibid.,* p. 434.
17. *Ibid.,* p. 420.
18. *Ibid.,* pp. 413–18.
19. "Decree of the Plenum of the Central Committee of the CPSU," *Pravda,* November 24, 1962.
20. *Party Life,* November, 1964.

NOTES TO CHAPTER TEN

1. *The Constitution of the U.S.S.R.* (Moscow: 1960), Article 13.
2. *The Size, Composition and Distribution of the Population of the U.S.S.R.* (Moscow: 1959), pp. 28–31.
3. *Ibid.* and "The CPSU in Figures," *Party Life,* No. 1, 1962, p. 49.
4. V. I. Lenin, *Works* (4th ed.; Moscow: 1952), XXII, 135–36.
5. *The Size, Composition and Distribution of the Population of the U.S.S.R.* (Moscow: 1961), p. 25; *Party Life,* No. 1, 1962, p. 49.
6. *Kazakhstanskaya Pravda,* September 30, 1961; *Pravda Vostoka,* September 26, 1961; *Sovetskaya Moldavia,* December 27, 1963; *Sovetskaya Kirghizia,* September 29, 1963; *Sovetskaya Latvia,* December 26, 1963; *Sovetskaya Estonia,* January 9, 1964; *Turkmenskaya Iskra,* December 28, 1964; *Sovetskaya Litva,* January 12, 1964; *Kommunist* (Armenian), January 9, 1964; *Kommunist Tadzhikistana,* December 27, 1963; *Bakinsky Rabochy,* January 11, 1964; and *Zarya Vostoka,* January 31, 1964.
7. *Sowjetstudien* (Munich), No. 11, 1961, pp. 47–65.
8. *Problems of Communism* (Washington, D.C.), XIII, No. 1 (1964), 12; *see* article by M. Rywkin and papers by P. Fedenko, A. Adamovich, and B. Hayit in *Sowjetstudien* (Munich), No. 11, 1961, pp. 1–65; *see also* paper by H. Seton-Watson, *National Policy of the Kremlin* (Munich: Institute for the Study of the Soviet Union, 1954).
9. *Kommunist,* No. 2, 1964, p. 2.
10. *All-Union U.S.S.R. Census Figures* (Moscow: 1962), pp. 206–8. *See also* newspapers cited in (6) above.
11. "The Constitutions of Constituent and Autonomous Republics," *The Constitution of the U.S.S.R., op. cit.,* pp. 803–4.
12. *Ibid.,* p. 802.
13. *Ibid.,* pp. 810–11.
14. *The Statutes of the CPSU* (Moscow: 1961), Article 41.
15. *Ibid.,* Article 47.
16. *Ibid.*
17. *Ibid.,* Article 44.
18. "The Constitutions of Constituent Republics," *The Constitution of the U.S.S.R., op. cit.,* pp. 661–92 and 869–71; *The Baku Worker,* September 10, 1961; *Kommunist* (Armenian), September 24, 1961; and *Soviet Lithuania,* October 1, 1961.
19. *The CPSU in Resolutions and Decisions Passed at Congresses, Conferences and Plenums of the Central Committee* (7th ed.; Moscow: 1953), Part I, p. 443.
20. *Questions of Party Work* (Moscow: 1959), pp. 345–46.
21. *Ibid.,* p. 346.
22. *The Party Worker's Handbook* (Moscow: 1957), pp. 441–42.
23. *Questions of Party Work,* pp. 347–49.
24. *The CPSU in Resolutions, op. cit.,* p. 444.
25. *Pravda,* November 24, 1962.
26. *See* Podgorny's report in *Pravda of the Ukraine,* December 7, 1962.

27. *Soviet Latvia,* December 8, 1962.
28. *Pravda,* November 20, 1962.

NOTES TO CHAPTER ELEVEN

1. *Statutes of the CPSU* (Moscow: 1961), Article 31.
2. *Statutes of the CPSU, op. cit.,* Article 33.
3. *The CPSU in Resolutions and Decisions Passed at Congresses, Conferences and Plenums of the Central Committee* (7th ed.; Moscow: 1953), Part II, p. 371.
4. *Ibid.,* p. 371.
5. *Ibid.,* p. 780.
6. *Ibid.,* Part I, p. 385.
7. *Ibid.,* p. 463.
8. *Ibid.,* p. 657.
9. *Ibid.,* p. 126.
10. *Ibid.,* p. 781.
11. *Ibid.*
12. *Statutes of the CPSU, op. cit.*
13. *The CPSU in Resolutions, op. cit.,* Part II, pp. 968, 1018, 1045, 1094.
14. *Statutes of the CPSU, op. cit.,* Article 39.
15. *The CPSU in Resolutions, op. cit.,* Part I, p. 658.
16. V. I. Lenin, *Works* (3rd ed.; Moscow: 1931), XXV, 604.
17. N. Khrushchev, *Speech at a Closed Session of the Twentieth Congress of the CPSU* (Munich: 1956), p. 53.
18. *Ibid.,* p. 53.
19. *Ibid.,* p. 54.
20. *CPSU in Resolutions, op. cit.,* Part II, p. 1149.
21. R. Conquest, *Power and Policy in the U.S.S.R.* (New York: St. Martin's Press, Inc., 1961), pp. 159–63.
22. *CPSU in Resolutions, op. cit.,* p. 770.
23. *Ibid.,* pp. 770–71.
24. *The CPSU in Resolutions, op. cit.,* p. 914.
25. *Twenty-second Congress of the CPSU: A Verbatim Account* (Moscow: 1962), pp. 363–564; *Party Worker's Handbook* (Moscow: 1957), p. 127; *Pravda,* April 26, 1962 and December 14, 1964; and the current Soviet press. *See also* the supplement to R. Conquest's *Power and Policy in the U.S.S.R., op. cit.,* pp. 464–65.
26. Conquest, *op. cit.,* pp. 464–65.
27. Lenin, *op. cit.,* I, 192.
28. *Ibid.,* IV, 110.
29. *Ibid.*
30. *Ibid.,* p. 111.
31. *Ibid.,* XXV, 592.
32. *1961 Yearbook of the Large Soviet Encyclopedia* (Moscow), p. 63.
33. *Ibid.,* pp. 85, 86.
34. *Ibid.,* p. 85.
35. *The CPSU in Resolutions, op. cit.,* Part IV (1960), p. 590.
36. *Kommunist,* No. 1, 1962, p. 16.
37. *Statutes of the CPSU, op. cit.,* Article 68.
38. V. I. Lenin, *On Party Construction* (Moscow: 1956), p. 491.
39. *Kommunist,* No. 7, 1961, p. 7.
40. *Twenty-second Congress of the CPSU: A Verbatim Account, loc. cit.*
41. *Pravda,* November 24, 1962.
42. *Pravda,* November 20, 1962.
43. *The CPSU in Resolutions, op. cit.,* Part I (1954), pp. 533–34.

44. *The CPSU in Resolutions, op. cit.*, Part I, pp. 719, 725, 726.
45. *Pravda,* November 20, 1962.
46. *Ibid.*
47. *Pravda,* September 14, 1963.
48. *Statutes of the CPSU, op. cit.*, Article 69.
49. *Shorthand Record of the Twentieth Congress of the CPSU* (Moscow: 1956), p. 124.
50. *Ibid.*, and *Pravda,* October 7, 1956.
51. *Pravda,* October 7, 1952.
52. *The All-Union Communist Party of Bolsheviks in Resolutions* (Moscow: 1933), Part II, p. 213.
53. *Pravda,* October 16, 1964.
54. V. I. Lenin, *On Party Construction, op. cit.*, p. 491.
55. J. V. Stalin, *Works* (Moscow: 1948) VII, 390–91.

NOTES TO CHAPTER TWELVE

1. V. I. Lenin, *On Party Construction* (Moscow: 1956), p. 675.
2. *Ibid.*, p. 671.
3. *Ibid.*, p. 574.
4. *Constitution of the U.S.S.R.* (Moscow: 1960).
5. *Ibid.*, Article 134.
6. V. I. Lenin, *Works* (3rd ed.; Moscow: 1931), XXV, 193.
7. *Ibid.*, p. 5.
8. *Constitution of the U.S.S.R., op. cit.*
9. *Verbatim Acount of the Sessions of the Supreme Soviet of the U.S.S.R.* (Moscow: 1946), p. 29.
10. A. Polynov, "The New Structure of the Supreme Soviet of the U.S.S.R.," *Posev,* April 8, 1962.
11. *Pravda,* April 25, 1962.
12. "Constitutions of the Autonomous Soviet Socialist Republics," *Constitution of the R.S.F.S.R.* (Moscow: 1955), pp. 25, 145.
13. V. Vlasov and S. Studenikin, *Soviet Administrative Law* (Moscow: 1959), pp. 36–37.
14. *Ibid.*, p. 112.
15. *Ibid.*, p. 113.
16. *Constitution of the U.S.S.R., op. cit.*, pp. 105–9.
17. *Ibid.*, pp. 114–16.
18. Lenin, *Works, op. cit.* (4th ed.), p. 327.
19. *The CPSU in Resolutions and Decisions Passed at Congresses, Conferences and Plenums of the Central Committee* (7th ed.; Moscow: 1953), p. 499.
20. *Ibid.*, p. 600.
21. *Statutes of the CPSU* (Moscow: 1961), Article 42.
22. *The Soviet State and the Law* (Moscow: 1960), p. 286.
23. Lenin, *Works, op. cit.*, XXI (4th ed.), p. 342.

NOTES TO CHAPTER THIRTEEN

1. *The CPSU on Trade Unions* (Moscow: 1957), pp. 15, 16.
2. *Ibid.*, p. 17.
3. *Ibid.*, p. 20.
4. *Ibid.*, p. 24.
5. *Ibid.*, p. 46.
6. *Ibid.*, p. 490.
7. *Ibid.*
8. *Ibid.*

9. *Ibid.*, p. 530.
10. *Ibid.*, p. 531.
11. *Ibid.*, p. 523.
12. *Ibid.*, p. 532.
13. V. I. Lenin, *Works* (3rd ed.; Moscow: 1931), XXV, 607.
14. *Ibid.*, pp. 607, 608.
15. *The CPSU in Resolutions and Decisions Passed at Congresses, Conferences and Plenums of the Central Committee* (7th ed.; Moscow: 1953), Part 1, p. 468 Articles 60, 61, 63 and 64.
16. *1961 Yearbook of the Large Soviet Encyclopedia* (Moscow), p. 14.
17. *Ibid.*, p. 14.
18. V. I. Lenin, *On Party Construction* (Moscow: 1956), p. 638.
19. *Ibid.*, p. 641.
20. *Ibid.*, pp. 640–41.
21. *Fundamentals of the Soviet State and Law,* ed. M. P. Kareva (Moscow: 1953), p. 445.
22. *The Size, Composition and Distribution of the Population of the U.S.S.R.* (Moscow: 1961), p. 3.
23. *Ibid.*, p. 40.
24. *Ibid.*, p. 37.
25. *Ibid.*, p. 33.
26. *Ibid.*, p. 62.
27. *Ibid.*, pp. 61, 62.
28. *Ibid.*, p. 62.
29. *Ibid.*, pp. 50, 51, 54.
30. Lenin, *Works, op. cit.,* XXIV (4th ed.), 5
31. *Ibid.*, XXV, 391.
32. *See* article by Dr. Sukennitsky in *Contemporary Soviet Society* (Munich: Institute for the Study of the U.S.S.R., 1958), p. 14.
33. *The CPSU in Resolutions, op. cit.,* Part I, p. 902.
34. *Questions of Labor in the U.S.S.R.* (Moscow: 1958), p. 205.
35. *Ibid.*, p. 207.
36. *Party Life,* No. 7, 1962, p. 31.

NOTES TO CHAPTER FOURTEEN

1. *Komsomol Pravda,* April 21, 1962.
2. *Ibid.*
3. *Statutes of the CPSU* (Moscow: 1961), Article 60.
4. *Ibid.*, Article 62.
5. *Young Communist,* No. 11, 1957, p. 73.
6. *Ibid.*
7. *Ibid.*
8. *Ibid.*
9. V. I. Lenin, *Works* (4th ed.; Moscow: 1952), VIII, 124.
10. *The CPSU in Resolutions and Decisions Passed at Congresses, Conferences and Plenums of the Central Committee* (7th ed.; Moscow: 1953), Part I, p. 386.
11. *Large Soviet Encyclopedia* (1st ed.; Moscow), XI, p. 640.
12. *Ibid.*, p. 640–41.
13. *CPSU on the Komsomol and Youth* (Moscow: 1957), p. 36.
14. *Ibid.*, p. 41.
15. *Ibid.*
16. *Large Soviet Encyclopedia, op. cit.,* XI, 647.
17. *Ibid.*, p. 499.
18. *The CPSU in Resolutions, op. cit.,* Part I, p. 783.

19. *Large Soviet Encyclopedia, op. cit.,* XI (1st ed.), p. 643 and IX (2nd ed.; 1958), 337–47; *Komsomol Pravda,* April 21, 1962.
20. *Komsomol Pravda,* April 6, 1958.
21. *Young Communist,* No. 11, 1957, p. 75.
22. *Large Soviet Encyclopedia, op. cit.,* IX (2nd ed.), p. 339.
23. N. Khrushchev, *Speech at a Closed Session of the Twentieth Congress of the CPSU* (Munich: 1956), p. 25.
24. *Komsomol Pravda,* April 16, 1958.
25. *The Komsomol Propagandist's Handbook* (Moscow: 1957), p. 99.
26. *Ibid.,* p. 101.
27. *Ibid.,* p. 102.
28. *Ibid.,* pp. 101, 102.
29. *Questions of Philosophy,* No. 5, 1956, p. 94.
30. *Ibid.,* p. 92.
31. *Komsomol Pravda,* April 12, 1956.
32. *Kommunist,* December, 1956.
33. *Komsomol Pravda,* April 16, 1958.
34. *Ibid.*
35. *The Komsomol Propagandist's Handbook, op. cit.,* p. 88.
36. *Komsomol Pravda,* April 16, 1958.
37. *Komsomol Pravda,* April 14, 1958.
38. V. D. Bonch-Bruevich, *Reminiscences About Lenin* (Moscow: 1965), p. 413.

NOTES TO CHAPTER FIFTEEN

1. *Soviet State Law* (Moscow, 1948), p. 392.
2. *Statutes of the CPSU* (Moscow: 1961), Article 59.
3. *Party Life,* No. 13, 1959, p. 24.
4. *Ibid.,* p. 26.
5. *Ibid.,* p. 24.
6. *Ibid.,* p. 26.
7. *Ibid.*
8. *Pravda,* April 9, 1962.
9. Harry Schwartz, *Russia's Soviet Economy* (New York: Prentice-Hall, 1950), pp. 84–199.
10. J. Stalin, *Economic Problems of Socialism in the U.S.S.R.* (Moscow: 1952), p. 18.
11. *Ibid.,* p. 77.
12. *Ibid.,* p. 92.
13. *Pravda,* September 28, 1965.
14. *Pravda,* October 1, 1965.
15. *Pravda,* September 28, 1965.
16. *Izvestia,* October 14, 1965.
17. *Pravda,* September 28, 1965.
18. *Ibid.*
19. *Pravda,* October 1, 1965.
20. *Pravda,* September 30, 1965.
21. *Pravda,* October 2, 1965.
22. *Ibid.*
23. *Pravda,* September 28, 1965.
24. *Pravda,* September 30, 1965.
25. *Pravda,* October 1, 1965.
26. *Pravda,* September 28, 1965.
27. *Ibid.*
28. *Pravda,* November 16, 1965.
29. *Pravda,* November 21, 1965 (emphasis in the original).

30. *Pravda*, September 28, 1965.
31. *Pravda*, November 21, 1965.
32. *Ibid.*
33. *Party Life*, No. 21, 1965, pp. 8 ff.
34. *Ibid.*
35. V. I. Lenin, *Works* (3rd ed.; Moscow: 1931), XXII, 20.
36. *Ibid.*
37. *Ibid.*, XXVI, 247.
38. *Ibid.*, p. 239.
39. *The CPSU in Resolutions and Decisions Passed at Congresses, Conferences and Plenums of the Central Committee* (7th ed.; Moscow: 1954), Part I, p. 708.
40. *Ibid.*, p. 788.
41. *Ibid.*, Part II (1953), p. 545.
42. J. Stalin, *Problems of Leninism* (11th ed.; Moscow: 1947), p. 297.
43. *The CPSU in Resolutions, op. cit.*, Part II (1954), p. 356.
44. Stalin, *Problems of Leninism, op. cit.*, p. 402.
45. *The CPSU in Resolutions, op. cit.*, Part II, p. 739.
46. *Ibid.*, p. 804.
47. *Ibid.*, p. 807.
48. N. Khrushchev, *Secret Speech at the Twentieth Party Congress* (Munich: 1956), p. 50.
49. *Ibid.*
50. *Ibid.*, p. 6.
51. N. Khrushchev, "Concerning Measures for the Further Development of Agriculture" (Moscow: 1953), p. 17.
52. *Ibid.*, p. 8.
53. V. Vlasov and S. Studenikin, *Soviet Administrative Law* (Moscow: 1959), p. 360.
54. *Ibid.*
55. *Pravda*, March 24, 1962.
56. Khrushchev, *loc. cit.*
57. *Pravda*, November 24, 1962.
58. *Ibid.*
59. *Pravda*, December 14, 1962.
60. *Pravda*, November 24, 1962.
61. *Pravda*, December 26, 1962.
62. *Party Life*, November 22, 1964.
63. *Pravda*, March 27, 1965.

NOTES TO CHAPTER SIXTEEN

1. *The CPSU in Resolutions and Decisions Passed at Congresses, Conferences and Plenums of the Central Committee* (7th ed.; Moscow: 1953), Part I, p. 437.
2. *Ibid.*, p. 439.
3. *Ibid.*, p. 440.
4. *Ibid.*
5. V. I. Lenin, *Works* (4th ed.; Moscow: 1952), XXXI, 154.
6. *Party Political Work in the Soviet Army and Navy* (Moscow: 1960), p. 10.
7. *The CPSU in Resolutions, op. cit.*, Part I, p. 440.
8. *Ibid.*, p. 570.
9. *Ibid.*, p. 569.
10. *Ibid.*, p. 650.
11. *Ibid.*, p. 598.

12. *Large Soviet Encyclopedia* (2nd ed.; Moscow: 1958), VIII, 483.
13. *Party Political Work in the Soviet Army and Navy, op. cit.,* p. 17.
14. *The CPSU in Resolutions, op. cit.,* Part II, p. 134.
15. *Statutes of the CPSU* (Moscow: 1961), Article 65.
16. Article by Marshal F. Golikov in *Pravda,* October 9, 1961.
17. V. P. Artemiev, "The Party and Soviet Forces," *Military Review,* Nos. 2 and 3, February and March, 1964.
18. *Party Political Work in the Soviet Army and Navy, op. cit.,* p. 47.
19. *Ibid.,* p. 49.
20. *Ibid.,* p. 51.
21. *Ibid.,* p. 57.
22. *The CPSU in Resolutions, op. cit.,* Part I, pp. 401–7; *Questions of the History of the CPSU,* No. 2, 1958, pp. 55–56; *Party Political Work in the Soviet Army and Navy, op. cit.,* pp. 10–12.
23. *Party Political Work in the Soviet Army and Navy, op. cit.,* p. 5.
24. V. Voropaev and A. Ivlev, *The Struggle of the CPSU to Create Military Cadres* (Moscow: 1960), p. 227.
25. *Statutes of the CPSU, op. cit.,* Articles 64, 66.
26. *Party Political Work in the Soviet Army and Navy, op. cit.,* pp. 83–84.
27. *Large Soviet Encyclopedia, op. cit.,* XXXII, 173.
28. *The CPSU in Resolutions, op. cit.,* Part I, p. 572.
29. Article by Marshal Golikov in *Pravda,* October 8, 1961.
30. *Large Soviet Encyclopedia, op, cit.,* VIII, 486.
31. *Ibid.,* II, 514.
32. Article by Marshal R. Malinovsky in *Red Star,* May 24, 1962.
33. *Red Star,* August 25 and 28, 1964.
34. *Pravda,* November 7, 1964.
35. *Pravda,* December 10, 1964.
36. *Ibid.*
37. *Red Star,* February 4, 1965.
38. *Ibid.*
39. *Pravda,* June 12, 1965.

NOTES TO CHAPTER SEVENTEEN

1. A. Uralov (Avtorkhanov), *Staline au Pouvoir* (Paris: 1951).
2. V. I. Lenin, *Works* (3rd ed.; Moscow: 1932), XXVII, 140.
3. *Documents of the Great Proletarian Revolution* (Moscow: 1938), I, 112.
4. P. G. Sofinov, *Essays on the History of the All-Russia Extraordinary Commission* (Moscow: 1960), p. 17.
5. *Ibid.,* pp. 19–20.
6. *Ibid.,* p. 40.
7. Lenin, *op. cit.,* XXXIV, 65.
8. Sofinov, *op. cit.,* p. 130.
9. M. Pershin, "The Truth About Bolshevism," *Posev,* No. 11, 1948.
10. Sofinov, *op. cit.,* p. 142.
11. *Izvestia,* No. 29, August 2, 1919.
12. Lenin, *op. cit.* (2nd ed.), XXX, 450.
13. Sofinov, *op. cit.,* p. 215.
14. S. Studenikin, V. Vlasov and I. Evtikhiev, *Soviet Administrative Law* (Moscow: 1950), p. 272.
15. *Ibid.,* p. 274.
16. *Ibid.,* p. 276.
17. V. Vlasov and S. Studenikin, *Soviet Administrative Law* (Moscow: 1959), p. 266.
18. *Statutes of the CPSU* (Moscow: 1961), Article 59.

19. Studenikin, Vlasov and Evtikhiev, *op. cit.,* p. 276.
20. Vlasov and Studenikin, *op. cit.,* p. 266.
21. N. Khrushchev, *Speech at a Closed Session of the Twentieth Congress of the CPSU* (Munich: 1956), p. 20.
22. *Ibid.,* p. 16.
23. *Ibid.,* p. 25.
24. *Party Life,* No. 4, 1957, p. 67.

NOTES TO CHAPTER EIGHTEEN

1. *Pravda,* June 22, 1930.
2. *The CPSU in Resolutions and Decisions Passed at Congresses, Conferences and Plenums of the Central Committee* (7th ed.; Moscow: 1953), Part I, p. 559.
3. *Ibid.,* p. 713.
4. J. V. Stalin, *Problems of Leninism* (Moscow: 1947), p. 51.
5. *Ibid.,* pp. 45–52.
6. R. Pipes, *The Formation of the Soviet Union* (Cambridge, Mass.: Harvard University Press, 1954). *See also* R. Conquest, *The Soviet Deportation of Nationalities* (London: Macmillan Co., Ltd., 1960).
7. *See* papers of P. Fedenko, A. Adamovich and B. Hayit in *Sowjetstudien* (Munich), No. 11, 1961, pp. 1–65. *See also* the paper by H. Seton-Watson, *The National Policy of the Kremlin* (Munich: Institute for the Study of the Soviet Union, 1954), and V. S. Vardys, "Soviet Nationality Policy Since the Twenty-second Congress," in *Russian Review,* No. 4, October, 1965.
8. J. V. Stalin, *The Great Patriotic War of the Soviet Union* (Moscow: 1952), p. 191.
9. *Program of the CPSU* (Moscow: 1961), pp. 112–13.
10. *Ibid.,* p. 113.
11. *Questions of Philosophy,* No. 11, 1962, p. 47.
12. *Program of the CPSU, op. cit.,* pp. 115–16.
13. *Soviet State and Law,* No. 12, 1961, p. 23.
14. *Ibid.,* p. 24.
15. *The CPSU in Resolutions, op. cit.,* Part II, pp. 330–45.
16. *Soviet Socialist Economics* (Moscow: 1957), p. 516.
17. *U.S.S.R. Initial Census Figures, 1959* (Moscow: 1959), p. 7.
18. *Ibid.,* p. 10.
19. *All-Union U.S.S.R. Census Figures, 1959* (Moscow: 1962), pp. 226–27.
20. Ibid., pp. 226–30.
21. *Questions of Philosophy,* No. 11, 1962.
22. *All-Union U.S.S.R. Census Figures, 1959, op. cit.,* p. 31.
23. I. A. Kurganov, *The Nations of the U.S.S.R. and the Russian Question* (Frankfurt: 1961), p. 60.
24. *Pravda,* June 19, 1963.
25. *The Finances of the U.S.S.R.* (Moscow: 1962), pp. 372–73.
26. T. Tulebaev, *Questions of Theory and Practice in the Planning of Budgets in the Union Republics* (Moscow: 1963), pp. 70–89.
27. *Ibid.,* p. 43
28. *Ibid.,* p. 44.
29. *Materials of the Twenty-second Congress of the CPSU* (Moscow: 1962), p. 385
30. *The Finances of the U.S.S.R., op. cit.,* pp. 376–77.
31. Tulebaev, *op. cit.,* p. 45.
32. *Ibid.,* p. 43.
33. *Ibid.,* p. 44.
34. *Kommunist,* No. 2, 1964, pp. 17–18.

35. *Questions of Philosophy*, No. 6, 1963, p. 6.
36. *All-Union U.S.S.R. Census Figures, 1959, op. cit.*, pp. 202, 206–8.
37. *Ibid.*
38. *Questions of Philosophy*, No. 6, 1963, p. 9.
39. P. G. Podyachikh, *The Population of the U.S.S.R.* (Moscow: 1961), p. 110.
40. *Questions of the History of the CPSU*, No. 4, 1964, p. 57, and Podyachikh, *op. cit.*, p. 107.
41. *Questions of Philosophy*, No. 6, 1963, p. 11.
42. Podyachikh, *op. cit.*, pp. 105–6.
43. *Questions of Philosophy*, No. 9, 1961, p. 40.
44. *Ibid.*, p. 31.
45. J. V. Stalin, *The Nationality Question and Leninism* (Moscow: 1950), p. 44.
46. *Questions of Philosophy*, No. 6, 1963, p. 10.
47. *All-Union U.S.S.R. Census Figures, 1959, op. cit.*, pp. 211–25, and Podyachikh, *op. cit.*, p. 107.
48. *Ibid.*
49. *Questions of Philosophy*, No. 6, 1963, p. 11.
50. *Kommunist*, No. 12, 1964, p. 19.
51. *Questions of the History of the CPSU*, No. 4, 1964, p. 59. See also *The Russian Language in the National School*, No. 6, 1963, p. 3; *Political Self-Education*, No. 4, 1960; K. Khanazarov, *The Rapprochement of Nations and National Languages in the U.S.S.R.* (Tashkent: 1963); and V. Kostamarov, *The CPSU Program on the Russian Language* (Moscow: 1963).
52. *See* the article by T. Davletschin in the *East Turkic Review* (Munich), No. 4, 1960, p. 38.
53. *See* the article by B. Hayit in *Sowjetstudien*, No. 11, 1961, pp. 47–65.
54. *See* the article by Andreas Tietz in the *Slavic Review* (Washington), December, 1963, pp. 727–33.
55. *Izvestia*, December 28, 1963.
56. *Izvestia*, September 24, 1963.
57. *Party Life* (Kazakhstan), No. 9, 1959.
58. *Questions of Philosophy*, No. 9, 1961, p. 40.
59. *Ibid.*, pp. 35–36.
60. *All-Union U.S.S.R. Census Figures, 1959, op. cit.*, pp. 234–37.
61. *Ibid.*, p. 47.
62. *The U.S.S.R. National Economy in 1960* (Moscow: 1961), pp. 14–15, 785.
63. *Ibid.*
64. *Questions of Philosophy*, No. 2, 1964, pp. 158–61.
65. *Ibid.*
66. *Ibid.*
67. *Ibid.*
68. *Ibid.*

NOTES TO CHAPTER NINETEEN

1. *History of the Soviet Constitution* (Moscow: 1957), pp. 394–95.
2. *Ibid.*, p. 387.
3. *Soviet Administrative Law* (Moscow: 1950), pp. 250–51.
4. *Constitution of the U.S.S.R.* (Moscow: 1960), Article 18a.
5. *Soviet Administrative Law, op. cit.*, p. 225.
6. *The CPSU in Resolutions and Decisions Passed in Congresses, Conferences and Plenums of the Central Committee* (7th ed.; Moscow: 1953), Part II, p. 1135.
7. *Soviet Administrative Law, op. cit.*, p. 255.
8. *See*, for example, the interesting book by former Soviet diplomat L. Vasiliev, *The Paths of Soviet Imperialism* (New York: 1954), pp. 257–83.
9. *1961 Yearbook of the Large Soviet Encyclopedia* (Moscow), p. 84.

10. *Ibid.*
11. *Ibid.*
12. *Ibid.*, p. 14.
13. *Kommunist,* No. 6, 1962, p. 49.
14. K. Marx and F. Engels, *Communist Manifesto* (Moscow: 1951), p. 53.
15. *Ibid.*, p. 47
16. *Ibid.*, p. 71.
17. "Foreign Policy of the U.S.S.R.," *Large Soviet Encyclopedia* (2nd ed.; Moscow: 1958), VIII, 257.
18. *History of International Relations and Foreign Policy of the U.S.S.R. 1870–1957* (Moscow: 1957), p. 92.
19. V. I. Lenin, *Works* (3rd ed.; Moscow: 1931), XXII, 13–19.
20. *The CPSU in Resolutions, op. cit.,* Part I, pp. 318–24.
21. Lenin, *op. cit.,* XXVII (4th ed.), 261.
22. *Ibid.*, XXII (3rd ed.), 257.
23. *Ibid.*
24. J. V. Stalin, *Problems of Leninism* (Moscow: 1947), p. 102.
25. *Ibid.*, p. 105.
26. *Ibid.*, p. 369.
27. *The CPSU in Resolutions, op. cit.,* Part II (1954), p. 883.
28. J. V. Stalin, *The Great Patriotic War of the Soviet Union* (Moscow: 1952), p. 40.
29. *The CPSU in Resolutions, op. cit.,* Part I, p. 412.
30. I. F. Ivashin, *Studies in the History of the Foreign Policy of the U.S.S.R.* (Moscow: 1958), p. 10.
31. *History of International Relations and Foreign Policy of the U.S.S.R. 1870–1957, op. cit.,* p. 451.
32. Lenin, *op. cit.,* XXXI (4th ed.), p. 444.
33. Stalin, *Problems of Leninism, op. cit.,* p. 47.
34. Lenin, *op. cit.,* XIX, 257–58.
35. Lenin, *op. cit.,* XXII (3rd ed.), 197.
36. N. Khrushchev, "Report to the Twenty-first Party Congress," *Materials of the Extraordinary Twenty-first Congress of the CPSU* (Moscow: 1959), p. 69.
37. *Ibid.*, p. 69.
38. *Ibid.*, pp. 97–98.
39. *Ibid.*, p. 98.
40. *Ibid.*, p. 54
41. *Ibid.*, pp. 56, 59.
42. Lenin, *op. cit.,* XXVI (3rd ed.), pp. 410–11.
43. *Pravda,* January 31, 1959, p. 8.
44. *Ibid.*
45. *The Sino-Soviet Economic Offensive in the Less Developed Countries* (Washington: Department of State, 1959), p. 21.
46. Adolf Weber, *The Soviet Economy and World Economy* (Berlin: 1959), pp. 253–54. For details *see* Joseph S. Berliner, "Soviet Economic Aid," in *The New Aid and Trade Policy in Underdeveloped Countries* (New York: 1958).
47. *Pravda,* January 28, 1966.
48. Lenin, *op. cit.,* XXXI (4th ed.), 266 ff.
49. *Ibid.*, XXV (3rd ed.), 211.
50. *Ibid.*
51. *Ibid.*, p. 177.
52. *Ibid.*, XXXI (4th ed.), 58.
53. *Ibid.*, XXV (3rd ed.), 177.
54. *Ibid.*, p. 199
55. *Ibid.*, XXII (3rd ed.), 324.
56. *Ibid.*, XXV (3rd ed.), 580.

57. *Diplomatic Dictionary* (Moscow: 1948), I, 588.
58. Lenin, *op. cit.*, XXII (3rd ed.), 227–28.
59. *Ibid.*, p. 334.
60. *Ibid.*, XXIII (4th ed.), 360–61.
61. *Ibid.*, XXXI (4th ed.), 413.
62. *The CPSU in Resolutions, op. cit.*, Part I, p. 405.
63. *Pravda*, December 22, 1963.
64. *Pravda*, December 12, 1965.
65. *Pravda*, December 22, 1965, article by L. S. Lepov.
66. *Pravda*, November 16, 1965.

NOTES TO CHAPTER TWENTY

1. *Large Soviet Encyclopedia*, XLIII (2nd ed.; Moscow: 1958), 43.
2. *Encyclopedia Britannica*, XXII (1947 ed.; Chicago), 313.
3. "Staat und Politik," *Das Fischer Lexikon*, p. 294.
4. Carl J. Friedrich, *Totalitarianism* (Cambridge: Harvard University Press, 1959), p. 53.
5. Z. Brzezinski, *Ideology and Power in Soviet Politics* (New York: Praeger, 1962), pp. 15, 19.
6. M. Vishnyak in *Socialist Courier*, No. 9, 1956, p. 169 (a translation from the Italian Encyclopedia).
7. *See* Hannah Arendt, *The Origins of Totalitarianism* (Cleveland: World Publishing Co., 1958).
8. K. Marx, *Critique of Political Economy* (Moscow: 1949), p. 7.
9. Lenin, *Works*, XXXII (4th ed.), 62.
10. M. A. Arzhanov, *The State and the Law in Proportion* (Moscow: 1960), p. 12.
11. *Ibid.*, p. 14.
12. Lenin, *op. cit.*, pp. 380 ff.
13. *The CPSU in Resolutions and Decisions Passed at Congresses, Conferences and Plenums of the Central Committee* (Moscow: 1945), Part I, p. 713.
14. Stalin, *Works*, XIII, 231.
15. *See* the article by N. Bukharin in *Izvestia*, March 30, 1934.

Index

Abaza, 334
Abkhaz-Adygey group, 334
Abkhazians, 325, 334, 336, 340
Academy of Social Sciences, 66, 67
"Activist group," 64
Adjars, 334
Adygey, 334
Adygey *Oblast*, 332
Afro-Asian countries, 355, 357, 358, 365, 366, 367
"Agrarian Question, The" (Lenin), 25
Agriculture, 279–89
Agrogorods (cities in the country), 270
Akhmedov, Mizra, 176
Akimov, 7, 8, 9, 11
Aktiv, 79, 80, 93, 94, 104, 130, 135, 137, 154, 186
Alexander II, 1
All-Russia Congress of Producers, 242
All-Russia Council for Worker Control, 263
All-Russia Extraordinary Commission for Struggle Against Counter-revolution, Sabotage and Speculation; *see* CHEKA
All Russian Bureau of Military Commissars, 291
All-Russian Central Executive Committee, 229
All-Russian Conference (Martov's followers, 1905), 16
All-Russian Conference of Bolsheviks (1917), 35
All-Russian Executive Committee of Soviets, 40, 47
All-Union Central Council of Trade Unions, 61, 84
All-Union Central Executive Committee, 46
All-Union Committee for Agriculture, 285
All-Union party conferences, 110
All-Union Young Communist League; see *Komsomol*
Altay, 340
Altayans, 334
Amnesty for religion, 353
Amur *Oblast*, 366
Andreyev, 107
Angelina, 257
"Anti-party group," 113
Apparatchiks (party bureaucrats), 153, 231, 371

Apparatus, party, legal and illegal, 18, 97
"Appeal to the Citizens of Russia" (Lenin), 42
"April Theses" (Lenin), 34, 35, 83, 247
Arabic, 336, 337, 338
Arakcheyev, 8
Aristov, 224
Armenia, 175, 176, 182, 187, 265, 323, 326, 331, 332, 339, 345
Armenian group, 334
Armenians, 324, 332, 333, 334, 335
Army, 290–306; tasks of bureaus of primary party organizations in, 299
Art, party control of, 375
Artemiev, 302
Artemiev, V. P., 314, note
Article I of party statutes, 7, 8, 12, 16, 75
Artists' Union, 239
Assimilation, policy of, 319, 322
Autonomy of party organizations, 110
Avars, 334, 335
Azerbaidzhan, 174, 176, 182, 265, 318, 319, 320, 323, 326, 331, 332, 333, 339, 345
Adzerbaidzhanians, 332–35

Babeuf, 4, 176
Bagramyan, 71
Balkars, 324, 336, 340
Baltic area, 92, 171, 174, 352
Bashkirs, 324, 325, 332 ff., 336, 340
Belorussia, 112, 175, 176, 180, 324, 330, 336, 340, 346
Belyayev, 224
Beria, 72, 154, 227, 307, 312, 316
Bernstein, 44
Blanqui, 4, 26
Blanquism, 27
Blyukher (Blucher), 72
Bogdanov, 302
Bolsheviks, 7, 12, 17, 22, 46, 62
Bolshevism, 1, 2, 369
Borin, 257
"Bourgeois-democratic revolution," development into "socialist revolution," 24, 355
Brezhnev, 223, 274, 275, 289, 304, 306, 316, 362
Bubnov, 39, 40
Budenny, 69, 71
Budget, Soviet Communist party, centralized, 221
Budgets of Union republics, 328, 329

Bukharin, 80, 99, 376; and "Rightist opposition," 101

Bulganin, 215

Bund (Jewish Social Union), 10

Bureaucrats, 228

Buryats, 324, 325, 331, 336, 340

Cadres, 58–74; of Central Committee Plenum, Secretariat and departments, 211, 212; administration of, 200

Candidates cards, registration and issuance, 149

Capital (Marx), 20, 44, 269, 277

Casus belli, 28, 38

Caucasus, 63, 170, 188, 190, 265, 320, 330, 336

Cell, party, 118 ff.

Central Asia, 171, 174, 176, 265, 330, 334, 336, 339, 341

Central Camp Directorate, 310

Central Committee, 8, 12, 13, 17, 31, 33, 34, 39, 42, 56, 59, 63, 66, 68, 84, 86, 87, 96 ff., 109, 112, 143, 145, 150, 163; administration of, 205; apparatus of, 200, 222; Asian Bureau of, 190, 191; and cadres, 62, 72, 73; commissions of, 217; departments of, 200–206; Inspection Commission of, 104, 222, 223; Inspection Committee of, 219 ff.; instructors and inspectors of, 166; Moslem Bureau of, 190; National Commission of, 188; Party Commission of, 205; Plenum of, 100, 102, 110, 111; Presidium of, 95, 102, 106, 107, 110, 197 ff., 217, 224; relations with party in Union republics, 103; Russian Bureau of, 118; Secretariat of, 101, 106, 107, 110, 199, 210, 214, 217, 224; staff of, 209; Trans-Caucasian Bureau of, 191

Central committees of Union republics, 109, 112, 113, 170–91; departments of, 182 ff.

Central Control Commission, 110

Central Organ, 96 ff.

Central party apparatus, 117

Central party organs, 117

Central Revision Commission, 110

Central Revisory Commission, 214

Central Trade Union Council, 242, 243

Chaplin, 258

Chauvinism, Great Russian, 318, 319

Chechen, 150, 324, 325, 331, 334, 340

Chechen-Daghestani group, 334

"Check on Party Documents, A Review of the" (Central Committee Plenum edict), 147

CHEKA (All-Russian Extraordinary Commission for Struggle Against Counterrevolution, Sabotage and Speculation), 228, 291, 307–10

Chekism, 307 ff.

Chemodanov, 258

Cherednichenko, 303

Cherkess, 332, 334, 336, 340

Chief Political Administration of the Armed Forces, 61

Chief Political Administration of the Soviet Army and Navy, 205

China, 363, 364, 366, 367

Chkheidze, 38, 47

Chuvash, 324, 325, 332 ff., 340

Chuykov, 303

Civil War, 52, 58, 63, 119, 120, 237, 241, 251

Class structure, 81

Coexistence, peaceful, 348, 353, 354, 362, 364

Collective agreements, 249

Collective Farm Center, 283

Collective farm workers in party, 78

Collective leadership, 106, 111, 227

Colleges of advocates, 239

COMINFORM, 86

COMINTERN, 45, 350, 351, 353

Commissars, organization of, 292

Commission for Organizational and Party Questions, 218

Committee for Peoples Control, 263

Committee for State Security; *see* KGB

Communist blocs, 241, 243

Communist Manifesto, The (Marx), 19, 21, 44, 348

"Communist nation," new type of, 339

Communist party, activists, 83, 93; blocs, 241, 243; bureau, 117; bureaucracy, 215, 234; cards, 148, 149; commissions for control in primary party organizations, 266; committees, 117, 121, 134, 186; construction of, 67, 230; enterprises of, 221; grades assigned to party workers, 84; group organizers, 123; groups in non-party organizations, 110, 141, 213, 243; income, 221; informers, 296; maximum salary, 85; membership, 76, 79, 88, 89, 90, 110; organizations in army, 297; personnel turnover, 378; policy discussion, 111, 112; primary organizations, 123, 126, 130; relations with

state apparatus, 372; repopulation of organizations, 112; rights of, 180; in rural areas, 91; social composition of, 76 ff.; specialists in national economy, 90, 91; statutes, 96–116
Communist upbringing, 262
Company political instructor, 292
Composers' Union, 239
Conference, regional, 155, 156
Congress, party, 109, 111, 192 ff., 180; Second (1903), 4, 7, 16, 45, 75, 96, 98; Third (1905), 97; Fourth (1906), 97, 240; Fifth (1907), 98, 240; Sixth (1917), 35, 98, 121, 194, 241, 252; Seventh (1918), 360; Eighth (1919), 57 ff., 76, 99, 194, 290; Ninth (1920), 57, 237, 241; Tenth (1921), 59, 76, 84, 119, 120, 220, 242, 243, 247, 280, 292, 300, 318, 328; Eleventh (1922), 55, 76, 237, 247; Twelfth (1923), 46, 318, 328; Thirteenth (1924), 77, 78, 103, 121; Fourteenth (1925), 60, 102, 119, 195, 256, 282, 293; Fifteenth (1927), 101, 193; Sixteenth (1930), 78; Seventeenth (1934), 78, 102, 193, 220, 248; Eighteenth (1939), 53, 64, 79, 85, 104, 123, 200; Nineteenth (1952), 85, 86, 105, 123, 210; Twentieth (1956), 72, 87, 106, 115, 116, 147, 224, 226, 258, 283, 315; Twenty-first (1959), 355, 356; Twenty-second (1961), 86, 96, 109, 115, 116, 124, 147, 194, 198, 226
Constitution of the U.S.S.R., 230
Constitutional Democrats, 46
"Constitutional Illusions, On" (Lenin), 30
Control of primary party organizations, 105
"Cooperation" between economies of Union republics, 343
Cooperatives, 49, 239
Council of Ministers of the U.S.S.R., 232, 263
Courts, 236
Criticism, 126, 156
Critique of Political Economy (Marx), 19
Cultural bureaucracy, 215
Cultural Workers' Union, 245
Culture, national in form, socialist in content, 179
Cyrillic alphabet, 336

Daghestan, 114, 324, 335, 340
Daghestanis, 325, 334, 336

Danton, 32
Darghin, 334
Daugenov, 176
Decembrists, 4
"Decree on Land," 26
"Decree Concerning the Socialist Enterprise" (Central Committee and Council of Ministers), 273
Demchenko, 257
Democracy in party, 111
Democratic centralism, 15, 97, 100, 102
Democratic revolution, development into socialist revolution, 34
Denationalization, policy of, 322
Denikin, 70, 251, 320
Dialectics, 358
"Dictatorship of the proletariat," 31, 41, 43–45, 320; as Communist party dictatorship, 46–49, 51, 53, 54, 364
Diplomacy, Lenin on, 359
Disarmament, 365
District; see *Raion*
Djilas, 75
"Doctrine of Fascism" (Mussolini), 370
Domestic and foreign policy, decisions on, 216
Donskoy, 353
Driving forces of revolution, 23
Dudintsev, 260
Duma, Fouth State, 14, 33; Petrograd, 40
Dumenko, 306
Dunaevsky, 253, 254
Dzerzhinsky, 40, 309, 310

Economic bureaucracy, 215
Economic factor in foreign policy, 362
Economic Problems of Socialism in the U.S.S.R. (Stalin), 269
Economic strike, development into uprising, 28
Economists, 7
Economy, party's management of, 263–89
Edinstvo (newspaper), 34
Educational statistics, by nationality, 339
"Egalitarian communism," 247
Egorov, 72
Ehrenburg, 259
Elections, Central Committee, 194 ff.; constituent republic central committees, 181 ff.; district and town committees, 138 ff.; *Komsomol,* 250; primary party organizations, 125 ff.; regional committee, 155 ff.; soviets, 232 ff.; trade unions, 245 ff.

Engels, 6, 9, 19, 20, 31, 44, 45, 53, 54, 375
Eremenko, 71
Estonia, 323, 326, 339
Estonians, 324, 331, 333, 335
Evtushenko, 260
Executive power, organs of, 232

Fadeyev, 260
Fascism, 369
Fedko, 251
Feinberg, 258
Finland, 352
Finno-Ugrian group, 334
Finns, 334
First Congress of Soviets of the U.S.S.R. (1922), 345
Five-Year Plan: First (1928–32), 352; Second (1933–37), 352
Forced labor, decree on, 310
Foreign aid, 358
Foreign policy, 345–68
Foreign trade monopoly, 279
Furtseva, 224

Gagauz, 334
Gapon, Father, 15
General Secretary, Stalin's appointment as, 101
Genocide in U.S.S.R., 371
Georgia, 175, 176, 265, 323, 326, 331, 339, 345
Georgians, 324, 332, 333, 334, 337
German group, 334
Germans, 336, 337
Girondism, 12
Golikov, 303
Gorky, 57
Gorno-Altai *Oblast,* 332
Gorshenin, 258
GOSBANK (State Bank), 263
GOSPLAN (State Planning Commission), 173, 248, 263, 264, 265, 270, 274, 285, 286
Gotha program, 44
Govorov, 302
GPU (State Political Administration), 310 ff.
Granin, 260
"Great-power chauvinism," 344
Great Purge, 1936–39, 64, 67, 72, 103, 154, 315
Great Reforms of Alexander II, 1
Grechko, 71
Gridnev, 261
Gromov, 268

Guchkov, 33
Gypsies, 336, 337

"Hegemony of the proletariat," 24
"Hero of Soviet Labor," 68, 69
"Hero of the Soviet Union," 68, 69, 260
Hierarchical principle of party's organizational structure, 5, 13
Higher Party School, 66, 67
Hitler, 259, 371, 372
Horizontal network of supplementary organizations, 3
"How to Organize Competition" (Lenin), 52

Ideocrats, 227
Ideological Commission of Central Committee, 218
Ideology, 6; Marxist, 278
Ignatov, 224
Ilichev, 209, 327
Imanov, 353
"Immanent laws," of capitalism according to Marx, 20; of imperialism according to Lenin, 22
Imperialism, Soviet, 349
Industry, 263–79
Infantile Disease of "Leftism" in Communism, The (Lenin), 27
Ingush, 324, 325, 331, 334, 336
Institute of Red Professors, 222
Insurrection, technique of, 23
Intellectual workers, 247
Intelligentsia, 75, 82, 87
"Internationalists—defeatists," 33
Internationalization, 343; of national republics, 322 ff.
Iranian group, 334
Iskra ("The Spark"), 7, 10, 11, 12
Izvestia, 338

Jewish *Oblast,* 332, 337
Jews, 332–34, 336, 337
"July Events," 35, 36

Kabardinians, 324, 325, 334, 336, 340
Kaganovich, 101, 113, 118
Kalmyks, 324, 331, 336, 340
Kamalov, 176
Kamenev, 32 ff., 39, 46, 99, 256; and "new opposition," 101
Kant's "categorical imperative," 371
Karachay, 334, 340
Karachay-Cherkess *Oblast,* 332
Karakalpaks, 325, 334, 336, 340
Karelians, 325, 331, 334, 338, 340

Kartvelian group, 334
Kautsky, 9, 43, 45
Kazakhs, 324, 332 ff.
Kazakhstan, 112, 176, 177, 180, 235, 264, 323, 327, 328, 331, 339
Kerensky, 33, 36 ff., 99
KGB (Committee for State Security), 312, 314
Khakass, 334, 340
Khakass *Oblast,* 332
Khmelnitsky, 353
Khrushchev, 55, 56, 101, 105 ff., 109, 114, 115, 116, 137, 142, 154, 196, 197, 199, 214, 216, 219, 222, 224, 225, 227, 258, 268, 270 ff., 278, 282, 283, 284, 286, 289, 302 ff., 315, 329, 355 ff., 362, 366; on restricting party membership, 92; "secret report" to Twentieth Party Congress, 72
Khrustalov (Nossar), 47
Kirghiz, 319, 324, 331 ff., 339
Kirghizia, 175 ff., 191, 265, 323, 326 ff., 331, 339
Kirichenko, 206, 224
Kirov, 147, 252, 256, 259
Kolchak, 320
Kolkhoz (collective farm), 56, 279, 289
Kollontay, 242
Komi, 325, 331, 334, 336, 340
Kommunist (periodical), 261
Komsomol (All-Union Young Communist League), 49, 60, 61, 73, 140, 158, 230, 239, 250, 251, 252, 256, 257, 258, 297, 358
Komsomol Pravda (newspaper), 209, 261
Komsomol Spotlight, 388 ff.
Konyov, 71
Kornilov, 37, 38
Kosarev, 258
Kosarev case, 258
Kosygin, 107, 222, 270 ff., 275, 276, 304 ff.
Kozlov, 96, 112, 113, 114
Krai (province), 153 ff., 232
"Kremlin doctors' case," 260, 302
Kronstadt uprising, 255
Kulaks (rich peasantry), 56, 279, 281
Kulatov, 176
Kurds, 334
Kurkhs, 334
Kutuzov, 353
Kypchaks, 334

Labor laws (1940), 271
Laks, 334

Latsis, 309
Latvia, 189 ff., 323, 326, 331, 339
Latvian-Lithuanian group, 334
Latvians, 324, 333
"Laws" of Marxist dialectics, 6
Lazimir, 39
"Leftist opposition," 101, 255
Left Socialist revolutionaries, 39, 40
Lenin, 2, 4, 8–11, 13, 14, 17, 19, 20–32, 117, 120, 129, 192, 207, 208, 214, 219, 226, 230, 238, 242, 244, 248, 257, 276, 280, 283, 284, 306, 308, 314; on dictatorship of the proletariat, 46, 48–53, 57, 58, 67, 70, 75, 76, 78, 84, 98, 99, 108, 109, 111, 350, 351, 354–57; letter to Central Committee of August 30, 1917, 37; of October, 1917, 40; on Hegel's dialectics, 44; on Marx, 44; on origins of Soviet regime, 46; on Soviet diplomacy, 359, 361, 362, 371, 372, 373, 375; on teachings applied in October Revolution, 33–47
"Leningrad case," 260
Leninism, 22
Leont'ev, 276
"Letter to a Comrade About Our Organizational Problems" (Lenin), 13
Lezghians, 334
Liberman, 276, 277
Liebknecht, 207
Lincoln, 371
Lithuania, 323, 326, 331, 339
Lithuanians, 324, 332, 333
Lobin, 338
Local party apparatus, 117
Local party organs, 117
Lominadze, 258
Longo, 206
Lukyanov, 258
Lutovinov, 243

Machiavelli, 27, 59, 69, 188, 359, 360
Machine-tractor stations, political sections in, 282
Main Political Administration, 294–95
Malenkov, 101, 113, 199, 227, 272, 282, 302, 304, 306
Malinovsky, 71, 303
Manifesto of October 17, 1905, 15, 16, 97
Manual workers in party, 78, 234
Mao Tse-tung and Moscow-Peking disagreements, 368
Mari, 324, 325, 331–33, 336, 338, 340
Martov, 7–10, 12, 13, 75

Martynov, 7, 9
Marx, 6, 14, 19, 20, 21, 24, 25, 30, 42, 44, 45, 53, 93, 226, 249, 269, 277, 351, 373, 375
Marxism, 2, 6, 373
"Marxism and Uprising: A Letter to the Central Committee" (Lenin), 31
Mass organizations, present membership, 49
Mazurov, 274
Medvedev, 242
Membership, duties, 108; rights, 109
Mensheviks, 7, 12, 17, 29, 32, 40, 46, 47
Menzhinsky, 309
Mestnichestvo (localism), 265
Metternich, 359
MGB (Ministry for State Security), 311, 312
Migration, 321 ff.
Milchakov, 258
Militarization of party organization, 120
Military, interests of, 374
Military bureaucracy, 215
Military commissar, 291, 292
Military hierarchy, 294
Military-party hierarchy, 292
Military party organizations, growth of, 297
Military political police, 296
"Military Question," resolution of Eighth Party Congress on, 290
Military Revolutionary Committee, 38, 39, 40, 42, 308
Milyukov, 33, 37
Mingrelians, 334
Minin, 353
Ministries, republic, 178; state security, 178; Union-republic, 178
Ministry for Internal Affairs; see MVD
Ministry for the Protection of the Social Order; see MOOP
Ministry for State Security; see MGB
Moldavia, 174, 323, 326, 327, 331, 339
Moldavians, 324, 332, 333, 336, 337
Molotov, 101, 102, 113, 115, 225, 302, 345, 356
Molotov group, 225, 227
MOOP (Ministry for the Protection of the Social Order), 159, 305, 312, 316
"Moral Code for the Builders of Communism," 109
"Moral Code of a Communist," 126
Mordvinians, 325, 326, 331–33, 338, 340
Mukhitdinov, 224, 358
Mussolini, 370–72, 376

Mustafaev, 176
MVD (Ministry for Internal Affairs), 311, 312, 316

Nakachka (pumping), 68
Narodniks, 4, 20
Nasser, 355
National composition of the CPSU, 171
National-revolutionary movement, 367
Nationalism, Russian, 338 ff.
Nationality policy, Soviet, 318–44
Nationalization, 373
"Natural historical" law for the downfall of capitalism according to Marx, 19
Nazarov, 261
Naziism, 369
Nemchinov, 276
NEP (New Economic Policy), 55, 59, 78, 120, 247, 279–81, 284, 342
Nevsky, 353
"New communist man," 339, 344, 373
New Economic Policy; see NEP
"New man," 209
"New opposition," 101, 193, 256
Nietzsche, 6
Nikolaev, 256, 259
Niyazov, 176
NKVD (People's Commissariat for Internal Affairs), 72, 307, 311, 314, 315; troikas, 316
Nogay, 334
Nogin, 38
Non-party organizations, 243
Nossar; see Khrustalov
Novikov, 302
Novy mir ("New World," periodical), 260
Nurbekov, 342

Oblast (region), 153 ff., 172, 173, 232
Obligations of primary party organizations, 125
OGPU (United State Political Administration), 311
One Step Forward—Two Steps Back (Lenin), 4, 12
Onilova, 259
"On the Checking of Party Documents" (Central Committe edict), 147
"On Party Blocs in Institutions and Organizations Outside the Party" (Lenin), 243
"On Party Unity" (Tenth Congress resolution), 120
"On the Rates of Collectivism" (Central Committee decree), 281

"On the Reorganization of the Party" (Lenin), 16
"Organization of professional revolutionaries," 3, 18
Orgburo, 70, 100, 101, 106, 107, 188, 197, 199, 210
Ossetians, 325, 331, 334, 336, 338, 340
Outer Mongolia, 366

Pamir tribes, 334
Partiinost (party spirit), 374
"Partocracy," v, vi, 32, 43, 57, 369–76
Party bureau, 117–32
Party card, 147 ff.
Party committee, 117–32
Pasternak, 376
Pavlyuchenko, 259
Pay of bureaucrats, 83
"Peace Decree" (Lenin), 350
Peking, 276
People's Commissariat for Internal Affairs; see NKVD
Permyaks, 325
Pervukhin, 107
Peters, 309
Petrograd Soviet of Workers' and Soldiers' Deputies, 42
Pilsudski, 251
Pioneer Pravda (newspaper), 209
Plekhanov, 4, 7 ff., 17
Podgorny, 316
Podvoisky, 42
Poland, 352
Poles, 336, 337
Polifem, 253
Politburo, 39–40, 98, 100, 101, 197 ff., 210, 256, 316; becomes Presidium, 106; commissions, 106, 107, 111, 345
Political Administration of the Army; see PUR
Political sections, hierarchy of, 294
Polyansky, 316
Population, in Union and autonomous republics, 331; urban, in autonomous republics, 324, 325; in intellectual occupations, 326, in Union republics, 323
Possony, 9, note
Potresov, 7
Pozharsky, 353
Pravda, 33, 34, 35, 36, 37, 118, 162, 209, 225, 226, 268, 276
Principles of bolshevist tactics, 306 ff.
Procuracy, 236
Production of consumer goods, 304
Production of means of production, 304

Professional revolutionaries, 4, 5
Proletarian (newspaper), 118
Province; see Krai
Provincial committee, 153–69
Provisional Government, 34 ff., 42
PUR (Political Administration of the Army), 61
Purges, of bourgeois specialists (Shakhty Affair), 60; Great, 64, 67, 72, 76; new style, 113; of non-manual workers, 78, 79, 91, 103

Questions of Party Work (anthology), 167
Questions of Philosophy (journal), 261

Rabochee Delo ("Workers' Cause," newspaper), 10
Raion (district), 133–41, 232
Razzakov, 176
Record card, 150 ff.
Red Army, 290–92; foundation on tsarist army, 69–71; purges, 72
Red Navy, 71
Region; see Oblast
Registration card, 151 ff.
"Registration of Members and Candidate Members of CPSU, On the," (Central Committee instructions), 151
Revolution, 1905, 15, 16, 121; February, 1917, 33, 34, 98, 121, 241; October, 1917, 30, 32, 38, 67, 118, 350
Revolution, basic law of, 27; communist, 22
"Revolution and Counterrevolution in Germany" (Engels), 31
Revolution and the State (Lenin), 247
Revolutionary situations, Lenin on, 23, 26, 28
"Revolutionary socialism," 11
Revolutionary War Council, 70; of the Front, 292; of the Republic, 292
Revolutionary wars, internal, 365
"Revolution in World Politics, A" (Lenin), 33
Ribbentrop-Molotov Pact, 345
"Rightist opposition," 101, 193
Rodionov, 316
Romance group, 334
Ruble control, 266
Rumania, 352
Rural executive committee, 232
Rural Regional Committee of the Party, The, 136
Rural soviet, 232
Russia, 235, 331

Russia (White newspaper), 208
Russian language, 321; in autonomous republics, 336
Russian Orthodox Church, 348
Russians, 324, 333; educational statistics, 339; number of scientists, 340
Russification, policy of, 319, 336, 338
Rykov, 34; and "Rightist opposition," 101

Saburov, 107, 353
Scientists, number of in republics, autonomous republics and autonomous *oblasts,* 339, 340
Second Congress of Soviets, 26; composition of, 42
Secretariat, 197
Secret police, 307–17
Secret police bureaucracy, 215
Secret report of Khrushchev to Twentieth Party Congress, 72
Self-criticism, 126, 156
Self-determination, 348, 355
Selkhoztekhnik (agricultural technology department), 285
Semichastny, 305
Separate peace with Germany, 46, 361
Serdyuk, 316
Shamil, 353
Shatskin, 258
Shayakhmetov, 176
Shelepin, 206, 258, 262, 305, 316
Shlyapnikov, 242
Shors, 334
Short Course in the History of the Communist Party of Bolsheviks, 44
Shtemenko, 302
Shvernik, 316
Slav group, 334
Slav representation in central committees of non-slav republics, 175
Slavs, 337
"Slogans, On" (Lenin), 36
SMERSH ("Death to Spies"), 73
Smolny Institute, 41
Smolyakov, 259
Social democracy, Russian, 7, 11, 16
Socialism, victory in one capitalist country, 22
"Socialist camp," 367
"Socialist competition," 69
Social revolutionaries, 32, 46
Sokolnikov, 39
Sokolovsky, 303
Soviet, definition of, 229, note
Soviet of Nationalities, 233–34

Soviet of the Union, 233–34
Soviet of Workers' and Soldiers' Deputies, 34
"Soviet patriotism," doctrine of, 371
Soviets, 47, 49, 58, 229–38
Sovnarkhozy (councils of national economy), 191, 264
Special Council (non-political tribunal of secret police), 316
"Specialization" in economies of republics, 343
Special sections, 296
Special Sector, 205
"Spiritual nourishment," Marxism-Leninism, 65
Sports societies, 239
Staff worker, 139
Stakhanovite movement, 257
Stalin, 5, 116, 120, 161, 191, 192, 196, 197, 214, 219, 220, 224, 227, 248, 255, 256, 269, 274, 281, 283, 303, 305–8, 312, 315, 316, 321; on dictatorship of the proletariat, 46, 49, 53, 55–59, 63–65, 99; on Leninism, 22, 45; on revolution, 28, 29, 32–36, 39, 40, 43; on party, 48, 72, 78, 84, 91, 101, 102, 106, 107, 111, 114, 351, 355–57, 362, 371, 373, 376
State, disappearance of, 53 ff.
State administration, distribution of organs of, 201
State Bank; *see* GOSBANK
State bureaucracy, 215
State Commission for Cultural Relations with Foreign Countries, 347, 348
State Committee for Labor and Wages, 272
State Economic Council, 265
State Planning Commission; *see* GOSPLAN
State Political Administration; *see* GPU
State power, organs of, 232
State Security Committee, Main Administration of Special Sections, 300, 301
"Struggle for peace," 353
Sukhanov, 47
Sukharevski, 272
Supreme Economic Council of the U.S.S.R., 287
Supreme Military Council of the U.S.S.R., 300
Supreme Soviet of the National Economy, 263
Supreme Soviet of the R.S.F.S.R., 235

Supreme Soviet of the U.S.S.R., 229, 230, 232, 233, 268
Suslov, 226
Suvorov, 353
Svans, 334
Sverdlov, 34, 40, 99
System of organizations, 3

Tadzhikistan, 175, 176, 191, 265, 323, 326, 328, 331, 339
Tadzhiks, 324, 333
Talleyrand, 359
Tashenev, 176
"Tasks of the Russian Social Democrats, The" (Lenin), 25
Tataria, 320
Tatars, 324, 325, 331 ff., 336, 340
Technocrats, 228
"Testament" (Lenin), 57, 129
Tomsky, 243; and "Rightist opposition," 101
Totalitarianism, 369 ff.
Town Committee, 133, 141–52
Trade union bureaucracy, 215
Trade unions, 49, 58, 239–49
Trans-Caucasia, 190, 265
Transformation of imperialist war into civil war, 33
"Transmission belts," 372
Trapeznikov, 276
Trotsky, 13, 32, 36, 38 ff., 47, 70, 99, 193, 255, 256, 345, 351, 356; and "Leftist opposition," 101
Trotskyites, 69, 70
Trudoden (work days), 271
Tseretelli, 47
Tukhachevsky, 72, 251
Turkestan, 63, 92, 175, 188, 190, 318, 320, 366
Turkestanis, 175
Turkic group, 334
Turkmen, 324, 333
Turkmenistan, 172, 175, 176, 191, 265, 323, 326, 328, 331, 339
Tuvinians, 334, 340

Udarnichestvo (shock-working) methods, 123
Udmurt, 324, 325, 331, 333, 336
Udmurts, 338, 340
Ukraine, 112, 142, 162, 175, 177, 180, 181, 189, 235, 264, 284, 318, 319, 320, 323, 326, 332, 345, 346
Ukrainians, 324, 333, 337
Uldzhabaev, 176
Union of Soviet Women, 239

Union of War Veterans, 239
Union of Youth, 49
Union of Youth Organizations, 239
Union republics, administration of, 173; composition of party central committees and inspection commissions, 174; population statistics, 170
United Arab Republic, 355
Uritsky, 40
Ussurijski Krai, 366
Ustinov, 305
Uygurs, 334
Uzbekistan, 112, 175–77, 180, 182, 235, 264, 265, 326, 328, 331, 339
Uzbeks, 319, 323, 324, 333

Vanguard, party as, 5
Vasilevsky, 215, 302
Vasilieva, 258
Vershinin, 302
Vershkov, 258
Vertical network of party organizations, 3
Voronov, 302
Voropaev, 72
Voroshilov, 69, 71, 215
Voznesensky, 198
VSNKH (Supreme Soviet of National Economy), 263

Wage scales, workers', engineers' and technicians', 248
War communism, 280
"Weak link" theory, 354, 364
What Is To Be Done? (Lenin), 2, 6, 7
Where to Begin? (Lenin), 23, 207
Who Are the Friends of the People and How Do They Fight the Social Democrats (Lenin), 22, 207
Wiedemeyer, 44
"Will the Bolsheviks Retain State Power?" (Lenin), 47
"Window-dressers," 1961 law of Presidium of Supreme Soviet against, 68
"Withering away of state," 50, 51
Worker and Peasant Youth, First Congress of, 253
Workers' and Peasants' Red Army, Political Administration of, 294
Worker-peasant aristocracy, 234
Worker-peasant group, 215
"Workers at the bench," 78
Workers' democracy, 120
Workers in the party, 78, 103, 121
Workers' Opposition, as "anarchist-syndicalist deviation," 242

Workshop cell, 121
World communist movement, 367
"World mind " (Hegel), 44
"World socialist revolution," 349, 364
Writers' Union, 239

Yakovlev, 206, 253
Yakut, 324, 325, 331, 336
Yakuts, 340
Yepishev, 305
Yesinin, 254
Yesininism, 254
Yezhov, 72, 206, 315
Yezhovshchina; see Great Purge
Young Communist League; see *Komsomol*

Young Pioneers, 239
Youth syndicalism, 254
Yovlev, 72
Yusupov, 176

Zakharov, 71, 303, 305
Zasulich, 7, 13
Zemstvo (local self-government organs), 1
Zhdanov, 154, 321
Zhukov, 71, 73, 74, 215, 295, 300, 302, 303, 306
Zimanov, 342
Zinoviev, 32, 36, 39, 99, 193, 256; and "new opposition," 101
Zonal language, 334